Contents

Constitutional and Administrative Law

Second Edition

S. A. de Smith

Penguin Education

Penguin Education,
A Division of Penguin Books Ltd,
Harmondsworth, Middlesex, England
Penguin Books Inc, 7110 Ambassador Road,
Baltimore, Md 21207, USA
Penguin Books Australia Ltd,
Ringwood, Victoria, Australia
First published 1971
Second edition published 1973
Copyright © S. A. de Smith, 1971, 1973

Made and printed in Great Britain by
Richard Clay (The Chaucer Press) Ltd,
Bungay, Suffolk
Set in Monotype Times

Editorial Foreword

This is the second edition of a first volume of a new series of university texts in law. In the last few years Penguin Books have launched several different series of paperback law books. Many readers are familiar with the series of Pelican Originals such as Wedderburn's *Worker and the Law* and Borrie and Diamond's *Consumer and the Law*. Secondly, there is the series on Law and Society, the function of which is self-evident. Thirdly, the Foundations of Law series has provided short narrative and explanatory texts for students on individual topics such as labour law, monopolies, banking law and practice and sale of goods. The new series, an important extension of Foundations of Law is complementary to these three groups and rounds off the range of Penguin legal publishing.

This series will concentrate on areas of law taught to students working for degrees in the universities and polytechnics. A textbook first written twenty-five or even fifty years ago, however good in its time and however competently amended subsequently by its author and later editors, is not always ideal for the law student of the seventies. I believe that there are areas of law where students and law teachers would agree that their needs are not fully met at present. Many law teachers have developed new approaches in the teaching of their courses. My purpose in this series is to have such lawyers give to all of us the benefits of their experience. The texts will be comprehensive full-length ones, and designed to be self-sufficient for the courses at which they are directed.

Quite the best way to demonstrate these aims is to introduce the first book in the series. Here the Downing Professor of the Laws of England in the University of Cambridge, who has been teaching constitutional law for the last twenty years and more, has been persuaded to publish for the first time his views on the subject at length.

Professor de Smith has asked himself what is important in our constitutional law and how best can it be understood by the student. He has felt free to discard disproportionate emphases suitable only to a bygone age. For instance, he has held in check his massive expertise in Commonwealth constitutional law so as to confine his account to what matters today. Unencumbered by the accumulations of past editions, he is able to describe a living constitution and show us how it works now. Still less is his work Dicey-as-subsequently-amended-or-doubted. His illustrations are, where possible, from recent constitutional experience and often of live topical interest.

Hitherto neglected areas like the Police are given appropriate treatment. The book is entitled *Constitutional and Administrative Law*. This recognizes the increasing tendency to teach some administrative law in first-year public law courses and is consistent with similar requirements in the syllabuses of the revised Bar and Law Society examinations. Those familiar with the author's standard work *Judicial Review of Administrative Action* might have expected him to have concentrated excessively here on judicial review. But this is not so. New developments like the Ombudsman and the role of government in a mixed economic and welfare state are given the attention which they deserve.

Few have mastered (or even tried to master) the vast and disparate sources of constitutional law: Hansard, Blue Books, White Papers, recent political biography, and periodical literature in the political sciences. This author has; he distils the essence of it, and with a sure touch guides the inquisitive reader to those further sources from which he will most benefit.

The subject matter of this book is so important and often so topical that it is constantly changing. It is no surprise that a second edition has been called for so soon. Recent developments have been smoothly worked into the text without making the book much longer and without sacrificing its style as a students' textbook. No doubt the author can look forward to a heavy and persistent revision in the future.

HARRY STREET

12.6.73

Preface

To my astonishment, the first edition of this students' textbook, published in 1971, was nearly sold out within eighteen months. To have it reprinted with corrections was out of the question. Major constitutional developments has taken place or were about to happen – the United Kingdom's accession to the European Communities, the reorganization of local government in England and Wales under the Local Government Act 1972, the recasting of the structure of criminal courts under the Courts Act 1971, the introduction of a horrendous new corpus of immigration law, fresh constitutional initiatives in Northern Ireland, and so on. So a new edition it had to be – and quickly.

Despite the incursion of a spate of new material, particularly on the topics just mentioned, the second edition is barely thirty pages longer than the first. I tried to cover all significant developments down to the end of January 1973, to correct various errors – the worst one eluded the critics – and to clarify and, where necessary, expand the treatment of a number of points. The final draft of the Immigration Rules, and a detailed review of the first edition, fortunately reached me just before I had to deliver the work to the publishers. At proof stage, I incorporated in the main text references to later developments down to the end of May 1973 as far as possible. Certain relevant matters arising since January, notably a White Paper and three constitutional bills for Northern Ireland published in the spring of 1973, and changes in the system of parliamentary committees for scrutinizing delegated legislation, could not be accommodated in this way. I therefore dealt with them briefly in an Addendum.

The known or likely constitutional effects of accession to the European Communities are considered at several points in the book, and a brief note on Community institutions appears as an Appendix. The Report of the Royal Commission on the Constitution had not been published when the book finally left my hands.

If a third edition is ever called for, I propose to rearrange parts of the book more satisfactorily. Perhaps I shall even be able to cause less offence to Scottish readers, though I hope that the present edition is slightly less inadequate than its predecessor on matters north of Berwick-on-Tweed.

But I ought to have made it clear in the first place that my approach would be fundamentally and lamentably Anglocentric.

On one matter I offer no apology. My expressions of personal opinion in this book are selective and fallible; but at least they help to make the book readable in parts, and I can think of no reason at all why any work on constitutional law should be uniformly dull.

I am grateful to the following (as well as reviewers) for volunteering criticisms or responding to my requests for factual information since the publication of the first edition: William Birtles, Kenneth Bradshaw, Richard Buxton, David Foulkes, Professor J. A. G. Griffith, Sir Kenneth Jones, N. E. Leigh, Sir Robert Micklethwait, M. J. Ryle, Professor H. W. R. Wade, A. Wharam, my wife and the late Neil Young. For the defects that remain I must, of course, accept full responsibility. I am also indebted to Derek Barton and Katharine Woodhouse for facilitating publication by their editorial work, and to two expert typists, Mrs J. H. Phillips and Mrs J. Dennett. Charles Clark and Harry Street persuaded me to write this book in the first place. Whether I ought to thank them too I am not quite sure.

Part One
General Foundations

The first chapter asks some elementary questions and indicates answers. What do we mean by a constitution? What matters are dealt with in the constitutions of other countries? Why have we no written constitution in Britain? In what circumstances (if any) might we adopt one? How can constitutions be classified?

Chapter 2 outlines the main features of the British constitution today. It touches very briefly on the theory of the rule of law and the doctrine of separation of powers. It reviews the sources of British constitutional law. And then it goes on to deal at some length with conventions of the constitution, those rules of political practice which have played such an important part in the British system of government. How do they differ from rules of strict law? In what sense are conventions 'rules'? How does one identify conventions? It is easier to ask some of these questions than to answer them. A number of individual conventional rules will be examined in later chapters. In this chapter we give a preliminary indication of the potential impact of European Community law on the constitutional law of this country.

In chapter 3 we ask still more awkward questions. In other countries the constitution is the supreme law. In this country Parliament is traditionally supposed to be entitled to pass any law whatsoever on any subject whatsoever. What makes a constitution valid and supreme? Why is (or was) Parliament sovereign? How do judges behave in other countries when a revolutionary change of government takes place and the new rulers act in ways unauthorized by the constitution? This is a basic question about the foundations of a legal system. Can Parliament's law-making authority ever be restricted? If so, how? Is it really entitled to legislate for any part of the world? Can it effectively limit its own powers in any way? Have its powers been limited by Britain's accession to the European Communities and the enactment of the European Communities Act 1972? Here we take a closer look at Community law doctrine and its possible repercussions on the legal concept of parliamentary sovereignty. Perhaps we are in a transitional phase, where the concept is in the process of being undermined. We do not yet know whether or when United Kingdom courts will change their attitude towards Acts of Parliament.

The suggested answers to quite a lot of the questions posed in this chapter are somewhat speculative. Students may find parts of it difficult. They should not be despondent. The subject-matter of later chapters will be more down-to-earth. Anyone who feels so inclined can read chapter 3 again, and more closely, at a later stage. But what is said about Community law needs to be noted. Problems posed by the new system of which we are now a part will recur at different levels in other chapters where some prior understanding of the relationship between United Kingdom law and Community law will have to be taken for granted. There will be a short statement of the constitutional structure of the Communities in an Appendix.

Chapter 1
Constitutions[1]

What are constitutions?

When de Tocqueville observed that the British constitution did not exist, few people took his remark at its face value. Lawyers have not been deterred from writing books about constitutional law, nor are books by non-lawyers on the British constitution in short supply. Dicey's assertion that we had no administrative law in Britain was a more serious matter; it frightened writers away from the subject for over forty years, and only in the last decade or so has the practising side of the legal profession come to regard administrative law (or the law relating to public administration) as a living reality, wholly worthy of study. But the study of the law of the constitution earned respectability long ago.

In the vast majority of modern states or political societies there exists an identifiable document, or a group of documents, called the constitution, embodying a selection of the most important rules about the government of the country. Books on constitutional law in these countries are usually commentaries on this special document or group of documents – on the historical circumstances in which a constitution came to be adopted, on the political and philosophical assumptions underlying it, on the special position of authority enjoyed by the constitution within the legal order, on the individual provisions of the constitution and their implications, on their amendment, interpretation and practical operation. In so far as these commentaries stray beyond the bare text of the constitution, they show that the terms 'constitution' and 'constitutional law' can be and often are used in a wider sense, to describe matters which are thought to be of 'constitutional' importance – importance, that is to say, in understanding what lies behind and beyond the 'constitution', so that the constitution can be understood as a central feature, but not the sole feature, of the rules regulating the system of government. If the term 'constitution' thus acquires a penumbra of ambiguity, this is not a matter of any great consequence.

1. Several of the points made in this chapter are set out with exemplary lucidity by Sir Kenneth Wheare in his *Modern Constitutions* (2nd edn).

And so studies of constitutional law are likely to range into history, political and legal theory, political science, and legislative and political practice. In those countries where courts have power to inquire into the compatibility of legislative and administrative action with the constitution, books and lecture courses on constitutional law will include a lot of material about judicial review. This is the position in, for example, the United States, Canada, Australia and India. In the United States today it would be absurd to consider the meaning of constitutional expressions such as 'freedom of speech', 'due process of law', and 'the equal protection of the laws', except by scrutinizing recent judicial interpretation, which happens to be far more significant than what the framers of the constitution and its amendments meant or thought they meant by those expressions. Similarly, in Canada the general power of the Federal Parliament to make laws for the 'peace, order and good government of Canada'[2] loses its deceptive simplicity when viewed in the context of restrictive judicial decisions. In Australia the meaning of the important constitutional guarantee of absolute freedom of inter-state trade and commerce has been moulded by the High Court in a series of leading cases by a process of unavowed judicial legislation.

Quite often the text, or much of the text, of a constitution is not intended to be taken literally. It sets out the framework of government, postulates how it ought to operate, and makes declarations about the purposes of the State and society and the rights and duties of citizens; but no real sanction is provided against violation of particular provisions of the constitution. Much of the constitution is 'programmatic', an affirmation of dogma or of objectives to be realized one fine day.[3] In such countries the study of constitutional law may be hardly distinguishable from jurisprudence or political theory; the books on the subject can still be bulky and verbose.

Although written constitutions differ widely in their purposes, form and content, they will normally be found to have two characteristics in common. They will be the fundamental law of the land; and they will be a kind of higher law. They will be fundamental law in so far as they designate the principal organs of government and invest them with authority; thus, they will constitute and define the Legislature, and state what is the scope of its law-making power and the procedure for exercising that power. In other words, they will be the law behind the law – the legal source of legitimate authority. They will also, as a rule, be a higher form of law, in that the law (or some of the law) set out in the constitution will be hierarchically superior to other laws and will not be alterable except by a specially prescribed procedure for amendment. In a number of countries,

2. British North America Act 1867, s. 91.
3. See, for example, Jan F. Triska (ed.), *Constitutions of the Communist Party States.*

courts have jurisdiction to pronounce laws inconsistent with the constitution to be invalid.[4] In order to escape such a fate, a law will have to be properly adopted as a constitutional amendment; and the same procedure will normally apply to a measure designed to 'amend' the constitution by way of addition without subtraction. Procedures for constitutional amendment differ widely from one another, but they usually require the amending measure to be passed by special majorities in the Legislature, or to be submitted to the people voting at a referendum, or both. It is perfectly possible, and is indeed not uncommon nowadays, for various provisions of a constitution to be alterable in different ways; some may be alterable by an ordinary legislative enactment, and others 'entrenched' at various levels against legislative encroachments, depending on the degree of importance originally attached to particular parts of the constitution.[5] In West Germany and Cyprus, certain constitutional provisions were expressed to be unalterable by any means. To this extent the constitutions of those countries were, of course, rigid. But the rigidity or flexibility of written constitutions cannot be ascertained merely by comparing procedures for constitutional amendment. A constitution containing a cumbersome procedure for its own amendment may in fact be very flexible if there is no effective opposition to the party in power; and the majority of modern states have authoritarian regimes. The constitution of Ceylon (now the Republic of Sri Lanka),[6] on the other hand, remained remarkably stable for nearly twenty-five years, although most or all of it could be changed, quite simply, by a bill commanding the support of two-thirds of the members of the House of Representatives. The main reason for its durability was the existence of a volatile multi-party system, in which governments were preoccupied with sustaining their own position in a usually unsuccessful attempt to avoid defeat at the next election.

As every beginner knows, the United Kingdom has no 'constitution' in the narrower sense of the term. There is no document or group of documents called the British constitution. But since Britain has a regular system of government, with a complex of rules defining the composition, functions and interrelationship of the institutions of government, and delineating the rights and duties of the governed, Britain does have a

4. Judicial review of the constitutionality of legislation is not accepted in a number of other countries (for example, France). Unconstitutional legislation may consequently be deemed to be valid for the purposes of application and enforcement in the courts. The only remedy against this usurpation of legislative power will be political.

5. See, for example, Constitution of Jamaica (S.I . 1962, No. 1550, Sched.), s. 49.

6. The republican constitution was adopted in 1972 by a Constituent Assembly, not following the procedure for amendment prescribed by the independence constitution. This was a deliberately contrived 'breach of legal continuity', designed to give Sri Lanka (Ceylon) an 'autochthonous', or home-grown, constitution. See p. 67.

constitution and a body of constitutional law, if these terms are used in a broader sense. Even if Britain did have a formal written constitution, this would not necessarily determine the boundaries of the study of British constitutional law, for many rules of constitutional interest would not be found in the written document itself. In the absence of such a document, an author's selection of topics has to be conditioned by what he personally regards as relevant or instructive.

Why, then, have we no 'constitution'? Why does nearly every other country in the world have one? What topics would probably be dealt with in a constitution for Britain, and why? Before trying to offer answers to these questions, one must touch upon a preliminary problem. Some English lawyers will say that to adopt a written constitution would be pointless. It would be pointless because such a constitution would have no higher sanctity than an ordinary Act of Parliament; it could be amended or repealed the next day by another Act of Parliament, just as if it were an Act for the licensing of rat-catchers. For it is (or has been) a fundamental rule of British constitutional law that the United Kingdom Parliament is incapable of restricting its own omnipotence.

Now, the question of parliamentary sovereignty raises some extremely difficult issues, which we shall examine in chapter 3. For example, how 'fundamental' are the rules about the omnipotence of Parliament? For the moment it is enough to say that an orthodox opinion does not become unassailable merely because it is widely held by distinguished authorities.

What goes into constitutions?

Constitutions are primarily about political authority and power[7] – the location, conferment, distribution, exercise and limitation of authority and power among the organs of a State. They are concerned with matters of procedure as well as substance. More often than not they also include explicit guarantees of the rights and freedoms of individuals. And sometimes, as we have noted, they incorporate ideological pronouncements – principles by which the State ought to be guided or to which it ought to aspire, and statements of the citizens' duties.

There is no pre-ordained stereotype of an ideal constitution. The form and content of a constitution will depend first on the forces at work when the constitution is established and amended, secondly on common-sense considerations of practical convenience, and thirdly on the precedents

7. A club, a trade union and a students' union will also have 'constitutions'. The forms of power with which such constitutions are concerned are not 'political', unless politics are understood in a very wide sense or the organization comes to be dominated in practice by political activity in the normal sense of the term.

available to the politicians and their advisers who draw up the constitution. The first and third points may be particularly important. For instance, there was a very big difference between Ghana's independence constitution of 1957 and its republican constitution of 1960. The 1957 constitution was incorporated in an Order in Council drafted in London after an Independence Conference. The 1960 constitution was drafted in Ghana. The former was a 'Westminster model' type of constitution, an agreed compromise package-deal[8] embodying a parliamentary executive and various safeguards for individual and minority group interests. The latter was made to suit the requirements of Dr Nkrumah alone; it provided for a presidential form of government and included no significant safeguard for the interests of individuals or groups which might have resisted the pretensions of the Convention People's Party. In 1964 the constitution was further amended to make Ghana a single-party state. Clearly the changes made in 1960 and 1964 were strongly influenced by constitutional precedents set in neighbouring French-speaking African states. After the fall of Nkrumah in 1966, local opinion swung away from single-party authoritarianism, and the constitution adopted in 1969 included a wide range of devices designed to prevent serious abuses of legislative and executive power. To put the matter in another way, Ghana had reverted, at least for the time being, to 'constitutionalism' or the idea of limited government. But in less than three years the regime was overturned by a military *coup*. Constitutions in developing countries are apt to prove frail structures, mainly because so much value is attached to the acquisition and retention of political power. Changes of government are likely to be usurpations of power, followed by the suspension or supersession of the constitution.

In order to give an impression of what matters are dealt with in modern written constitutions, we shall glance very briefly at some features of the constitutions of four independent countries – Australia (1900), Mauritius (1968), Cyprus (1960) and Tanzania (1965).

Australia

The Commonwealth of Australia Constitution Act 1900 was passed by the United Kingdom Parliament, acting, in effect, as the agent of constitution-makers in Australia. It provided for the establishment of an 'indissoluble Federal Commonwealth under the Crown', consisting of six states; all of them were formerly self-governing colonies with their own constitutions. Section 9 of the Act of 1900 set out the Constitution of the

8. See generally, Y. P. Ghai and J. P. W. B. McAuslan, *Public Law and Political Change in Kenya*, chs. 5, 13.

Commonwealth of Australia; it had 128 sections; the six states retained their own constitutions, but gave up some of their powers to the new entity. Included in the Commonwealth are certain territories (for example, the Australian Capital Territory) which are not states and are not fully self-governing. Under the constitution, certain powers are given exclusively to the Commonwealth; a number of other powers are allocated concurrently to the Commonwealth and the states, with the proviso that a valid Commonwealth law shall prevail over a state law to the extent that they are inconsistent with one another; the undistributed residuum of power belongs to the states. Law-making powers can be distributed in various ways in a federation – Australia broadly followed the United States pattern; Canada, India and Malaysia all have their different arrangements – but since a federal system is one in which central and regional bodies each have an exclusive area of competence, the 'forbidden zones' must be demarcated in an authoritative document.[9] And since the regions (states, provinces or what you will) are not willing to be totally subordinated to the central (or federal) authorities – otherwise they would have accepted a status akin to local authorities in a *unitary* system – their sphere of autonomy must be protected against encroachments. The constitution therefore provides a special procedure for amending its most important provisions. A proposed constitutional amendment becomes law only if it is approved by a majority of voters at a referendum held throughout the Commonwealth *and* by a majority of voters in a majority (i.e. at least four) of the states; an amendment diminishing certain constitutional rights of a state or altering its boundaries needs the approval of the electors in that state. The general amending procedure is not cumbersome or rigid compared, for example, with the procedure for constitutional amendment in the United States, where an amendment normally has to obtain two-thirds' majorities in both Houses of Congress and then be ratified by three-fourths of the state legislatures. But the Australians tend to be a conservative people, and only five formal constitutional amendments have been approved in over seventy years.

The constitution is divided into chapters. The first deals with the Parliament, the second with the Executive Government, and the third with the Judicature; there are five others, dealing with such questions as new states, financial relations and constitutional amendment. There is no comprehensive bill of rights, though there are a few individual guarantees that could have been put into such a chapter; for instance, the acquisition of property for federal purposes must be 'on just terms' and there is a section on freedom of religion.

9. See generally K. C. Wheare, *Federal Government* (4th edn); G. Sawer, *Modern Federalism*.

A few aspects of the constitution are worth noting:

1. The constitution vests executive power in the Queen and it is exercisable by the Governor-General as her representative. He is to be advised by a Federal Executive Council, comparable to the Privy Council in the United Kingdom. Reference is made to Ministers, but not to the Cabinet or the Prime Minister; as in the United Kingdom, they are creatures of constitutional convention (that is to say, binding constitutional usage), not of strict law. Nothing is said about the responsibility of Ministers to Parliament, though one conventional rule in the United Kingdom is crystallized in constitutional terms: a Minister cannot hold office for more than three months unless he is or becomes a member of one or other House. Certain other conventional rules in the United Kingdom find expression in the text of the Australian constitution – for example, that money bills and resolutions have to be introduced by the Executive – but in general the constitution preserves the quaint dichotomy of strict law and constitutional convention which, as we shall see, is a distinctive feature of British constitutional law.

2. The chapter on Parliament vests the legislative power of the Commonwealth (subject, of course, to the terms of the constitution) in the Queen, the House of Representatives and the Senate. Naturally it deals with such matters as the royal assent, the maximum duration of a House of Representatives, the tenure of office of senators, and what is to happen when the two Houses are in disagreement with one another. These are basic issues. But other matters are dealt with only in certain aspects, or 'until Parliament otherwise provides', or are omitted altogether. Thus, the constitution lays down rules that each original state shall have equal representation in the Senate, but enables Parliament to increase the size of the Senate. It provides that, as nearly as practicable, the House of Representatives shall be twice the size of the Senate. There are entrenched provisions for disqualification for membership of Parliament; presumably these were thought to be particularly important. The basic qualifications of members are laid down, but they may be altered by Parliament; and so on.

3. The chapter on the Judicature vests the 'judicial power of the Commonwealth' in federal courts and 'such other courts as the Parliament vests with federal jurisdiction', and provides for the method of appointment and tenure, and security of remuneration, of federal judges. It goes on to outline the appellate and original jurisdiction of the High Court of Australia. These provisions have been greatly amplified by legislation over the years. But, as they stand in the constitution, they have given rise to some excruciatingly difficult problems of interpretation. And the courts have read into

them implications based on the doctrine of separation of powers,[10] a doctrine which has nothing to do with the distribution of powers between the central and regional authorities in a federation but which has a long and tortuous history behind it.

Mauritius

Mauritius is one of the newest independent members of the Commonwealth – a small, overcrowded, remote, sugar-producing island in the Indian Ocean, with serious communal and demographic problems. It is divided along political lines, and party and communal divisions have tended to coincide. It was therefore important to give minorities some measure of confidence that they would not be subjected to discriminatory treatment at the hands of other groups. The constitution is, therefore, long, fairly complicated, and quite rigid.

1. There is a constitutionally entrenched bill of rights, affording guarantees against unreasonable encroachments upon personal liberty, freedom of expression, conscience, association and assembly, prohibiting unfair discrimination, and laying down minimum safeguards in criminal procedure and for the fair conduct of judicial proceedings. Laws and administrative acts inconsistent with the bill of rights are invalid. Constitutional bills of rights have only become fashionable in the new Commonwealth during the last decade; now they are adopted almost as a matter of course, and the scope of the rights and freedoms, and the circumstances in which they can be restricted, are usually spelt out in great detail.

2. The system of election and the method of legislative representation were highly contentious issues before independence. They are written into the constitution and specially entrenched. Provision is also made for commissions to delimit constituencies and supervise the registration of electors and the conduct of elections; the members of the commissions have security of tenure.

3. The circumstances in which the Governor-General's residual discretionary powers (for example, to remove a Prime Minister, to dissolve Parliament) are exercisable are spelt out in detail instead of being unmentioned as in Australia. The constitution also sets out the main powers of the Prime Minister, the status of the Cabinet and other Ministers, and the principles of ministerial responsibility to Parliament. This is now the usual style of modern Commonwealth constitutions; little room is left for argument as to the content of rules governing delicate political situations.

4. There is fierce competition for white-collar jobs, particularly in the

10. See pp. 38–41.

public service. Powers of appointment, promotion, transfer and dismissal are therefore vested in an independent Public Service Commission. There are also independent Police Service and Judicial and Legal Service Commissions.

5. Mauritius is exceptional in that major discretionary powers to make appointments to politically sensitive posts are vested in the Governor-General instead of the Prime Minister. Thus, the Governor-General personally decides whom to appoint as members of the service commissions, Chief Justice and Ombudsman.

6. The constitution attempts to screen various public functions from political control – for example, by insulating the appointment and removal of judges, the process of prosecution, the audit of public accounts, and the day-to-day control of the police against political dominance.

7. Constitutional amendment is difficult in theory. Whether it is difficult in practice depends on the attitudes of the political parties towards particular proposals. A three-fourths' majority in the Legislative Assembly is needed for the more important parts of the constitution, and a two-thirds' majority for the less important.[11]

Cyprus

The constitution under which Cyprus became independent in 1960 was a most extraordinary document. It was not drafted in London and owed little to British constitutional experience or practice. It was the most rigid, detailed and complicated in the world. Even a brief summary of its characteristics would take us too far afield,[12] for it contained very little of any conceivable relevance for a prospective constitution-maker in the United Kingdom. Whereas the constitution of Mauritius underplays the significance of communal divisions as far as possible, the constitution of Cyprus was dominated by the concept of 'community'. Two separate peoples, the Greek Cypriots (most of whom wanted union with Greece) and the Turkish Cypriots (determined never to submit to Greek Cypriot majority rule and backed in their intransigence by their brethren in nearby Turkey), lived side by side on a strife-ridden island. The constitution was in fact largely dictated by outside forces, and it was so formulated that on no issue of substantial importance to Turkish Cypriots could the views of the Greek Cypriot majority prevail. And the constitution explicitly forbade

11. See further de Smith (1968) 31 *Mod. L. Rev.* 601; Mauritius Independence Order 1968 (S.I. 1968, p. 1871).
12. cf. de Smith, *The New Commonwealth and its Constitutions*, ch. 8; Cmnd 1093 (1960).

both the union of the island with another State and the partitioning of the island.

Two features of the constitution are worth mentioning here. First, governmental authority was divided up in a number of different ways: between the Greek Cypriot President and the Turkish Cypriot Vice-President; between the Council of Ministers and the House of Representatives; between the House of Representatives, on the one hand, and the Greek and Turkish communal chambers, on the other.

Secondly, the matters dealt with in the constitution were in some respects very odd. For instance, the constitution prescribed that for every seven hours of broadcasting time in Greek there were to be three hours in Turkish. It laid down the community from which a coroner was to be drawn for the conduct of an inquest, depending on the community of the deceased. This does at least bring out the point that there is no pre-determined body of subject-matter appropriate for inclusion in a constitution. A written constitution for Britain would surely have nothing to say about coroners; it might, however, include a section about broadcasting services and maintenance of impartiality.

Tanzania

Our last example, the Interim Constitution of Tanzania (1965), belongs to quite a different category. Whereas the constitution of Cyprus was so encumbered with prohibitions as to be almost unworkable – it did break down in December 1963, and probably Humpty Dumpty will never be put together again – the constitution of Tanzania imposed few restraints upon the Government. It is, in fact, a constitution for a one-party State; or, to be more exact, a State monopolized by two single-party systems, one operating exclusively in Tanganyika and the other in Zanzibar. Tanganyika had become independent under a 'Westminster model' type of constitution in 1961, and it adopted a republican constitution, with a President who was both head of State and head of Government, a year later. Early in 1964 Zanzibar's newly independent regime was overthrown by revolution, and union with Tanganyika took place a few months later on a partly federal basis. The 1965 constitution has a number of interesting features in an African context, not the least of them being a procedure for ensuring that elections in Tanganyika to the National Assembly are genuinely contested (though only under the auspices of the single party). There is also a Permanent Commission of Enquiry, a kind of collective Ombudsman, responsible to the President. The constitution of TANU, the single party in Tanganyika, is scheduled to the constitution of the Republic. But built-in constitutional safeguards and guarantees are hard to find. In place of a justiciable bill of rights there is a preambular affirmation of general principle. The tenure of superior judges and the Controller and Auditor-General is protected against arbitrary termination, but there are no corresponding safeguards for the impartiality of the prosecuting process or for the status of civil servants. In Tanzania the constitution is not conceived of as a brake; it is a framework within which the Government and the Party can operate more or less freely in their self-imposed task of national mobilization. There, as in so many new states in Africa and Asia, it is simply not true to say that constitutions spring from a belief in 'constitutionalism' or limited government.

A written constitution for Britain?

We have glanced at four constitutions. We could have made a tour of a hundred and fifty others. Every independent Commonwealth country has a written constitution, with the exception of Britain itself, New Zealand,[13] and a few countries which are in the process of reconstructing new constitutions in place of old ones that have been overturned. Every British colony and protectorate has a written constitution. Indeed, so has nearly every country in the world.[14] Why does Britain stand out as an anomaly?

The answer lies above all in the facts of history. In other countries constitutions have been granted or adopted to mark stages in a progression towards (or a regression from) self-government, to establish the foundations of the machinery of government in a newly independent State (for example, the United States, Cyprus) or a reconstituted State (for example, Malaysia, Tanzania), or to rebuild the machinery of government following the wreckage caused by defeat in war, or to start afresh after a revolutionary upheaval or because of widespread disillusionment with the existing regime, or even to signify a change in ideological attitudes. With very few exceptions, governments in the modern world feel it necessary to point to a constitution as the source of their authority – if only as a badge of legitimacy or respectability.

In Britain none of these factors has been effectively at work. England has not been unambiguously defeated in war, or at least has not been successfully invaded (save by special invitation) since 1066. There were, it is true, two revolutions in England during the seventeenth century. The Civil War of 1642–8 ended with the execution of Charles I in 1649 and the establishment of a republican Commonwealth. From the ferment of political ideas there emerged in 1653 an authentic written constitution,

13. See K. J. Scott, *The New Zealand Constitution*.
14. See A. Peaslee, *Constitutions of Nations*; A. Blaustein and G. Flanz, *Constitutions of the Countries of the World*.

skeletal but readily identifiable, the Instrument of Government. But in the welter of controversy this document (which was to be influential in the North American colonies) was soon reduced to the status of a scrap of paper; the revolution petered out and Charles II was restored in 1660. In 1688 James II was deposed after a reign of three years; the Crown was offered to a usurper, William of Orange, who accepted it jointly with his wife Mary, James II's daughter, and the Glorious Revolution triumphed. The revolutionaries, however, were insistent that they were nothing more than the conservators of the ancient rights and liberties of the people, which James had been seeking to subvert. James, moreover, was deemed to have abdicated. Apart from changing the line of succession to the throne, and enacting, in the Bill of Rights 1689, some fairly important limitations on the royal prerogative, Parliament attempted no fundamental restatement of the constitution. To have made such an attempt would have been politically imprudent,[15] and in any event this was not a time when constitutions had become fashionable. And, indeed, instead of laying the foundations of a written constitution, it formed a base for the concept of untrammelled parliamentary sovereignty. Since then the serenity of historical continuity has survived Jacobite revolts, the French Revolutionary and Napoleonic Wars, riots at home and some bloodied noses in far-away encounters; and the two World Wars of the twentieth century have ended in victory. In modern times Britain has known neither the humiliation of conquest nor the turmoil of full-scale revolution.

Since England was a sovereign State for many centuries, the question of adopting a constitution on the attainment of independence did not arise. But in 1707 England ceased to be an independent State. It entered into union with the independent State of Scotland. This union was founded on Articles of Union negotiated by commissioners representing the two Parliaments, and it was consummated by separate Acts of Union merging the two Parliaments into a new Parliament of the United Kingdom of Great Britain. The Articles of Union, incorporated with the Scottish Act in the English Act of Union, were expressed to be fundamental and unalterable conditions of the Union. They provided a rudimentary framework of a written constitution. Yet south of the border the Act of Union has not been regarded as enjoying any greater binding force in strict law than other statutes of major constitutional importance.[16]

15. Immediately after the Revolution, when the conditions under which the throne should be offered to William and Mary were being discussed, more radical views were canvassed, but they were shelved because an ensuing controversy would have delayed the settlement; see Taswell-Langmead's *English Constitutional History* (11th edn), p. 447; J. R. Western, *Monarchy and Revolution*, ch. 9.

16. See further, p. 74. The legal effect of the Act of Union with Ireland 1800 has also been a matter of controversy.

There are other reasons why the question of adopting a written constitution has seldom been seriously agitated – insularity, a lack of interest in political philosophy, extremist ideology or the constitutional experience of other countries (merging into complacency and convictions of collective superiority), a dearth of enthusiasm among politicians for restraints that might impede their freedom of action when in office, a relatively high degree of homogeneity, a latitudinarian and pragmatic approach to religious and political differences, and a widely diffused acceptance of traditional forms, gradualism and parliamentary methods. Britain's one intractable political (and religious) problem was Ireland; and it is significant that it was in relation to Ireland, in 1885, that fundamental thinking about the restructuring of the British constitution came to the surface. Only after the First World War, with the partitioning of Ireland and the creation of a separate Irish Free State (later Eire, and now the Republic of Ireland), was it possible to sweep this embarrassing problem under the carpet – till 1969.

Has there been any recent development important enough to warrant serious speculation about the prospects of adopting a written constitution for the United Kingdom?[17]

1. A number of factors have tended to undermine social stability or to depress national morale in Britain. There is widespread disillusionment with the main political parties, a 'credibility gap' between promise and achievement; a more sober awareness that any British Government's freedom of action in international and economic affairs is severely circumscribed; a realization that Britain has become less prosperous than several other industrial countries, that the sun is setting on the Empire that was to last a thousand years, that dark strangers are in our midst to stay, that the individual citizen and his parliamentary representative count for little in public affairs, that ancient faiths and habits of deference to authority rest on insecure foundations. But if there are widely diffused feelings of malaise and pessimism, they have yet to crystallize in any clamant demand for basic constitutional change, at least in England. Youthful revolutionaries denounce 'consensus politics' and the institutions of an immoral society, but their protest demonstrations evoke backlash rather than a sympathetic response among the community at large. Cynical apathy is a more pervasive phenomenon, but it is one that militates against constructive, or even destructive, thinking. It has yet to be shown that nationalistic xenophobia, rooted in insecurity and resentment and hitherto directed mainly against Commonwealth immigrants, cannot be accommodated within the main political parties. Even if it cannot be, that would not

17. The Royal Commission on the Constitution had not reported by May 1973.

necessarily portend any constitutional change. There is indeed no sign that a revolutionary situation is about to develop.

2. By acceding to the European Communities on 1 January 1973, the United Kingdom accepted obligations entailing profound changes in our constitutional law. But it is perfectly possible to be a member of the Communities without having a written constitution. If, however, the Communities were to develop into a federal super-State – and that is still a remote prospect – we should probably need to have a written constitution so as to define the limited competence of our domestic organs of government.

3. If separatist sentiment in Scotland and Wales were to assume formidable dimensions, it is conceivable (though unlikely) that a solution to the crisis would lie in the adoption of a partly federal constitution for the United Kingdom. This would involve giving certain exclusive powers to a Scottish Government and Parliament and to a Welsh Government and Parliament, and leaving the United Kingdom Government and Parliament with exclusive but limited powers. Such a scheme could not be effectively implemented except by means of a special constitutional instrument. The scheme would differ from the arrangement under the Government of Ireland Act 1920 under which limited powers were devolved to the Northern Ireland Government and Parliament. The Northern Ireland scheme was devolutionary but not federal. The United Kingdom Parliament retained plenary powers in relation to Northern Ireland.

If, however, it were legally possible – and we shall beg this question for the time being – to create a federal constitution, hierarchically superior to any parliamentary body in the United Kingdom, then the study of constitutional law in this country would attain new dimensions. We should have to consider judicial review of the constitutionality of legislation – a matter which up to now has affected only Northern Ireland. And then there would be other questions to ask. Apart from restrictions on the *territorial* competence of the Legislature, should there not be introduced restrictions on the *type* of legislation it was competent to pass? For instance, might it not be a good thing to have a constitutionally entrenched bill of rights, preventing the Legislature and the Executive from, say, authorizing or taking any retrospective penal measures, or making unreasonable encroachments on freedom of movement or expression, or taking away property rights without compensation? There is a body of opinion favouring such a new departure.[18] To embark upon it would be to

18. See Quintin Hogg, *New Charter* (Conservative Political Centre, 1969), for a personal expression of support for such a concept, though he uses the term 'regionalism' in preference to 'federalism'; cf. Anthony Lester, *Democracy and Individual*

enshrine the principle of limited government in an institutional form, common enough in other lands but novel in Britain. Naturally one would have to work out satisfactory procedures for the amendment of entrenched provisions, and the procedures might differ according to the context.

This having been said, one cannot think that such an idea would be at all attractive to the national parties likely to form a United Kingdom Government. Governing the country would become more difficult. And imagine what the position would have been in 1972 if the United Kingdom Government and Parliament had been *legally debarred* from encroaching on the autonomy of Northern Ireland.[19]

A written constitution for Britain would have to be justified by reference to an overwhelming political need for restricting Parliament's powers. If this justification were established, it would be sensible to include in the constitution a selection of the most important rules about the organs and machinery of government.

Aspects of classification[20]
Written and unwritten

This mode of classifying constitutions has already been discussed. Among liberal democracies in 1972, only the United Kingdom, New Zealand and Israel[21] lacked a written constitution in the narrower sense of the term. But the law of the constitution in those countries can be found in writing – in statutes, law reports, parliamentary standing orders, works of authority, and so on, although an authoritative and reasonably comprehensive document called the 'Constitution' is lacking.

Rights (Fabian Society, 1969), advocating the enactment of a bill of rights which would not, however, be constitutionally entrenched. See also O. Hood Phillips, *Reform of the Constitution* (1970); George W. Keeton, *Government in Action in the United Kingdom* (1970); Sir Cyril Salmon, *The Times*, 4 December 1970.

19. See ch. 30. One should also note the impatience of the United Kingdom Government with inconvenient judicial decisions giving a restrictive interpretation to the Government of Ireland Act 1920. A decision that the Northern Ireland Parliament and Government could not confer powers on British troops for law enforcement was very speedily rectified by the Northern Ireland Act 1972 (passed before Stormont was suspended by the Northern Ireland (Temporary Provisions) Act 1972). For an earlier precedent, removing the constitutional prohibition against taking away property without compensation (Government of Ireland Act 1920, s. 5 (1)), see Northern Ireland Act 1962, s. 14, passed in consequence of the decision in *Belfast Corporation* v. *O.D. Cars Ltd* [1960] A.C. 490.

20. For a more elaborate classification see Leslie Wolf-Phillips, *Comparative Constitutions* (1972). See also Leslie Wolf-Phillips, *Constitutions of Modern States*, Introduction.

21. See E. Likhovski, *Israel's Parliament: The Law of the Knesset* (1971).

Flexible and inflexible

Constitutions for which no special procedure for amendment is prescribed are *prima facie* more flexible than others. But flexibility is a matter of degree, and will not necessarily be predetermined by the formal procedure for constitutional amendment. And some constitutional rules will in practice be more flexible than others. In the United Kingdom the 'constitution' is, in theory, entirely flexible, but legislation to abolish the monarchy or to extend the maximum duration of a Parliament could only be passed in very extraordinary circumstances. In Ghana under Nkrumah the superior judges (other than the Chief Justice) enjoyed security of tenure against the Executive, and their tenure was entrenched by the constitution; but in the political situation existing in 1964 the President had no difficulty in first procuring a constitutional amendment rendering the judges dismissible at his pleasure and then going on to dismiss some of them for incurring his displeasure.

Monarchical and republican

This is no longer a difference of any general importance, because it tells us nothing worth knowing about the form or substance of government. One can have an absolute monarch or one with extensive personal discretionary powers (as in Ethiopia and Nepal), or one with very limited personal powers (as in the United Kingdom and several Commonwealth and Western European countries). One can have a President who is head of State but is not the effective executive head of Government (as in India and West Germany), or one who is both head of State and head of Government (as in the United States and a great many other countries).

Presidential and parliamentary

This method of classification is concerned with the executive branch of government and its relationship with the Legislature. Under a 'presidential' system the head of the executive branch is also head of State, and is not a member of or directly responsible to the Legislature. In a parliamentary system the chief executive is a Prime Minister who is a member of and is responsible to the Legislature. Thus the American system and its imitators are distinguishable from the Westminster model of responsible government. But this kind of classification is not very illuminating, because of the wide variations within each type of system. For example, in Kenya there is an executive President, but he has to be a member of the Legislature; in Tanzania and several of the other presidential regimes in

Africa, the President cannot be a member of the Legislature but (in contrast to the United States) his Ministers must be members of the Legislature, though they are not fully responsible to it. Again, whereas the President of the United States has no power to dissolve Congress, the power of dissolution is vested in Commonwealth executive presidents; and whereas the constitutional powers of the American President are hedged about by checks and balances, presidential heads of government in new states are usually freer from restraints. And the constitution of the fifth French Republic is both presidential and parliamentary.

Single-party and other constitutions

Obviously a constitution under which only one party can legitimately operate tends to differ from one in which, at least ostensibly, freedom of political association is permitted. A constitution for a single-party State is apt to be something of a political manifesto. In such a constitution, lip-service may still be paid to the basic freedoms of the individual. Again, however, constitutional forms may give little indication of what happens in practice. In some states with single-party constitutions there is more freedom of expression than in nearby countries with impeccably liberal constitutions.

Federal and unitary

The difference between a federal and non-federal constitution will often be clear-cut; sometimes it will be only one of degree; sometimes it will be positively misleading. The United States, Australia, Canada, West Germany and Switzerland are manifestly federal States. As we have mentioned, the relationship between the United Kingdom and Northern Ireland under the Act of 1920 was strictly non-federal, since Northern Ireland had no exclusive field of competence, but in practice the degree of regional autonomy till 1970 was substantially greater than that of the republics of the Soviet Union or even the states of Malaysia, both of which countries have nominally federal constitutions. Tanzania is a part-federation, since Zanzibar has exclusive fields of competence both in theory and in practice; but for political reasons the term 'federal' does not appear in the constitution inasmuch as it implies a degree of disunity as well as diversity. The relationship between the United Kingdom and the associated states in the Caribbean, under the West Indies Act 1967,[22] is substantially federal, for the United Kingdom's paramount powers in the states are confined to matters relating to defence and external affairs, and a

22. See p. 662.

short list of other topics; but the United Kingdom and its associated states are not a 'State' for the purposes of constitutional law.

Diarchical and other constitutions

A diarchical constitution can be defined as one in which there is a division of governmental competence between two or more authorities in the State otherwise than on a regional basis. For instance, law-making powers may be divided between the Legislature and the Executive, the former having power to pass laws within a defined field and the latter having an autonomous and exclusive power, derived directly from the constitution, to issue decrees, ordinances or regulations within a defined field; this, broadly speaking, is the position under the French constitution.[23] In Cyprus the constitution provided for elaborate demarcations of competence in the executive functions of government, and also assigned certain legislative functions exclusively to non-territorial Greek and Turkish communal chambers. Such divisions of competence have certain affinities with the separation of powers doctrine, of which more will be said later; they also indicate that the concept of unitary, as distinct from federal, constitutions is not particularly illuminating in some political systems.

23. Barry Nicholas (1970) *Public Law* 251.

Chapter 2
The British Constitution

Characteristics

Here we shall state, or restate, very briefly the main features of the British constitutional system. All the characteristics to be listed differentiate the British constitution from *some* other constitutions.

Unwritten character. The British constitution is not written in a basic document or group of documents.

Continuity of development. It has evolved over the centuries with but few sudden or dramatic changes, and a high degree of historical continuity has been maintained as the constitution has been brought up to date. Of the modern institutions of government, some are still rooted in medieval origins. Among the existing rules of British constitutional law, quite a number were laid down in the seventeenth century or earlier. Our history is still with us. But the constitution is not a museum piece. The greater part of our constitutional law has been made this century.

Parliamentary sovereignty. Parliament as a legislative body can enact any law whatsoever on any subject whatsoever in the eyes of United Kingdom courts, according to the view generally held at the end of 1972.[1] Changes in rules of constitutional law can be effected by ordinary legislation.

Law and convention. Particularly in the working of the executive branch of government and its relationship with the Legislature, the constitution is regulated to a large extent by rules which do not belong to the normal legal categories. These rules are called constitutional conventions. They are rules of political conduct or binding usages, most of which are capable of being varied or of simply disappearing as political conditions and ideas change. If conventions are to be classified as rules of constitutional law, then the term 'law' must be given a very broad meaning. To use the term 'law' in more than one sense is not in itself unusual. Sometimes it is convenient to contrast constitutional convention with 'strict law'. Thus, in strict law (by virtue of the royal prerogative) the Queen can dismiss her

1. For possible exceptions to this basic rule, see ch. 3.

Ministers at pleasure. By convention this legal power is exercisable only in very extraordinary circumstances. And because it is well understood that, save in exceptional situations, the Queen must act in accordance with ministerial advice, Parliament still adopts the form of conferring discretionary powers on Her Majesty. This dichotomy of law and convention pervades much of our constitutional law.

Flexibility. The absence of a cumbersome procedure for altering rules of constitutional importance, the omnicompetence of Parliament and the pliability of many constitutional conventions tend to make the British constitution flexible and easily adaptable. But, as we have pointed out, flexibility is a question of degree. It would be easier in practice to enact legislation to abolish the House of Lords or the hereditary peerage or the Privy Council than, say, to abolish the remedy of habeas corpus. Moreover, not every constitutional convention is flexible in practice; some conventions are very rigid.

Unitary nature. The United Kingdom is a unitary, not a federal, State at the present time. If it were a federal State, Parliament would not be omnicompetent.

Freedom of political activity. The legitimacy of organized dissent and opposition to the Government is recognized by convention; and nowadays there are few oppressive legal restrictions on freedom of expression and association in political controversy. Elections are freely and on the whole fairly conducted.

Limited monarchy. Succession to the throne is hereditary. The functions of the head of State are primarily ceremonial, and despite their amplitude in strict law they are now of little or no political significance in normal times.

Bicameralism. The upper House of Parliament, the House of Lords, still constituted mainly on a hereditary basis, is of minor importance; the lower House, the elected House of Commons, is the focus of political attention.

Parliamentary Executive. The political arm of the executive branch of government is recruited from and located within Parliament, and the Cabinet is collectively 'responsible' to Parliament in general and the House of Commons in particular. A Government would either have to resign or go to the country if it were to forfeit the support of a majority in the Commons.

Executive dominance in the Legislature. Because of the structure of modern British political parties, and the operation of the electoral system and certain constitutional rules, the Government in office is normally able to command parliamentary support for the implementation of almost any policy that it is in practice likely to adopt. The Government has indeed to be *responsive* to parliamentary opinion, as well as to the weight of opinion in the electorate at large, but one must not imagine that it is in any real sense a delegate or agent of Parliament. Parliamentary government is not government by Parliament. The Government governs in and through Parliament. At the same time, it would be erroneous to speak in terms of 'Cabinet dictatorship'. A Government operates within a complex network of constraints, restricting its freedom of manoeuvre.

Impartial public service. The civil service is non-partisan except in so far as it serves the Government in office. Its insulation from political involvement, and the security of tenure enjoyed by its members, have been the product of convention, not of strict law.

Judicial independence. The Judiciary is appointed by the Executive, but it is conspicuously independent both of the Executive and of the Legislature, partly because of rules of strict law but mainly because of extra-legal factors. The prestige of the superior judges in Britain is exceptionally high by any international standard. Whether this fact is related to the self-imposed rule that judges cannot question the constitutionality of duly enacted statutes is a matter for speculation.

Constitutionalism. Despite the absence of constitutionally entrenched guarantees and prohibitions or impregnable institutional bulwarks against the abuse of power, serious encroachments on basic individual freedoms are rare in times of peace, and the protection of dissenting minorities in Britain is more efficacious than in many states which enjoy a superabundance of devices designed to achieve this end. Those rules and practices which do restrain abuses of public power under the British constitutional system are generally observed. The formal restraints are not always as effective as in some other liberal democracies – for instance, Parliament is a less formidable body than the United States Congress; the powers of the courts are significantly narrower than in America; civil liberties are not buttressed by a bill of rights – but there is a widely diffused acceptance of the principle that the restrictive rules of the political game are more important than the retention of power, or the pressing of legal power to the ultimate limit at the expense of individual liberty. In this sense we can say that constitutionalism, or limited government, or the rule of law – the meanings of these expressions overlap – exists in Britain.[2]

2. The readers who feel that these assertions show an establishmentarian bias may wish to consult as correctives Harold Laski, *Parliamentary Government in England*; Ralph Miliband, *The State in Capitalist Society*; Paul O'Higgins, *Censorship in Britain*; D. N. Pritt, *Law, Class and Society*.

The rule of law and the separation of powers

Dicey[3] saw the rule of law as a central feature of the British constitution. He had his own idiosyncratic ideas of what the concept of the rule of law implied. His ideas, rooted in Whiggish libertarianism, were very influential for two generations;[4] today they no longer warrant detailed analysis. Nor would it be justifiable to examine the general concept of the rule of law at length in this book. The concept is one of open texture: it lends itself to an extremely wide range of interpretations. One can at least say that the concept is usually intended to imply (i) that the powers exercised by politicians and officials must have a legitimate foundation; they must be based on authority conferred by law; and (ii) that the law should conform to certain minimum standards of justice, both substantive and procedural. Thus, the law affecting individual liberty ought to be reasonably certain or predictable; where the law confers wide discretionary powers there should be adequate safeguards against their abuse; like should be treated alike, and unfair discrimination must not be sanctioned by law; a person ought not to be deprived of his liberty, status or any other substantial interest unless he is given the opportunity of a fair hearing before an impartial tribunal; and so forth. The concept has an interesting characteristic: everyone who tries to redefine it begins with the assumption that it is a good thing, like justice or courage. When Communist theoreticians extol the merits of 'socialist legality', they could simply substitute the term 'rule of law', though their conceptions of what it connoted would differ from those of liberal democratic ideologists.

The doctrine of the separation of powers, like the rule of law, has usually been discussed as one which *ought* to be embodied in a system of government. But whereas commentators are almost unanimous that the rule of law (whatever it may mean) is splendid, the virtues of the separation of powers do not evoke so enthusiastic a chorus. Perhaps this is partly because the doctrine has acquired a harder core of generally accepted meaning, and because some constitutions survive adequately without relying on it for sustenance.

This is not to say that the quintessence of the separation of powers is easy to distil. The doctrine has emerged in several forms at different periods and in different contexts.[5] It is traceable back to Aristotle; it was

3. A. V. Dicey, *Introduction to the Study of the Law of the Constitution* (10th edn), pt 2, especially ch. 4. The first edition was published in 1885.

4. Sir Ivor Jennings's *The Law and the Constitution* included a sustained critique of Dicey's views, moderated, however, in the later editions. See Appendix 2 to the 5th edn. For more sympathetic assessments, see E. C. S. Wade, Introduction to the 10th edn of Dicey, pp. xcvi–cli; and F. H. Lawson (1959) 7 *Political Studies* 109, 207. cf. Ford (1970) 18 *Political Studies* 220. For further comment see pp. 525–7.

5. For the fullest recent analysis, see M. J. C. Vile, *Constitutionalism and the Separation of Powers*.

developed by Locke; its best-known formulation, by the French political philosopher Montesquieu, was based on an analysis of the English constitution of the early eighteenth century, but an idealized rather than a real English constitution; the disciples of Montesquieu, particularly numerous in the North American colonies, added their own refinements; and today the doctrine survives in a number of curious manifestations. No writer of repute would claim that it is a central feature of the modern British constitution. However, a brief survey of the doctrine brings out more clearly some features of the British system of government.

The doctrine, as propounded by Montesquieu and his followers, may be stated briefly as follows:

1. There are three main classes of governmental functions: the legislative, the executive and the judicial.

2. There are (or should be) three main organs of government in a State: the Legislature, the Executive and the Judiciary.

3. To concentrate more than one *class* of function in any one person or organ of government is a threat to individual liberty. For example, the Executive should not be allowed to make laws or adjudicate on alleged breaches of the law; it should be confined to the executive functions of making and applying policy and general administration.

Even if one accepts the first two propositions, one is not obliged to accept the third. To concentrate a large *quantity* of power in the hands of one person, in the absence of proper safeguards, is surely more dangerous than to combine a few powers analytically different in *quality* in the same hands, if adequate safeguards exist. And a rigorous segregation of functions may be highly inconvenient. In many countries subscribing to versions of the separation of powers doctrine, rule-making powers have been vested in the Executive because it is manifestly impracticable to repose such powers exclusively in the Legislature. The third proposition stated above is therefore both extreme and doctrinaire, and is not taken literally by all proponents of the theory.

One of the implications commonly read into the separation of powers doctrine is that the three branches of government ought to be composed of different *persons*. In the United States for instance, the President and his Cabinet cannot be members of Congress. It does not inevitably follow that the three branches should have no points of contact, though it does follow that the one branch of government should not be in a position to dominate the others. Matters may be so designed that each branch operates as a check on the others. Again we can use the United States as an illustration. The President may veto legislation but has no power to dissolve

Congress; although he holds office for a fixed term and is not dependent on the support of a Congressional majority, he can be impeached by Congress; he appoints federal judges but his appointments need to be confirmed by the Senate;[6] the courts can determine the constitutionality of legislative enactments and administrative action, but judges cannot validly be given powers totally alien to the judicial office; federal judges cannot be removed by the Executive but they can be impeached by Congress. In France, on the other hand, the separation of powers has been understood to preclude the ordinary courts from determining the constitutionality of legislation; yet judicial and administrative functions are commingled in the *Conseil d'État*, and legislative and executive powers in the Presidency.

In Britain[7] we have Cabinet government with a parliamentary Executive; the Law Lords act both as judges and as legislators; the Lord Chancellor is a Minister as well as head of the Judiciary and an active member of the House of Lords in its legislative capacity. Legislative powers are delegated by Parliament to members of the Executive (the Queen in Council, and Ministers); powers to determine justiciable controversies are also confided in Ministers and other non-judicial agencies. Indeed, there never was a time in English constitutional history when the functions of government were neatly compartmentalized. The medieval *Curia Regis*, the King's Council, exercised all three classes of functions. Parliament was a High Court as well as a legislative body. For several centuries the local government authorities in the counties were judicial officers, the justices of the peace. But the modern Judiciary does stand in a special position. Professional full-time judges are disqualified for membership of the House of Commons because any other arrangement would hardly be compatible with the judicial office; the Law Lords generally abstain from politically controversial debate in the upper House, and only the Lord Chancellor and former occupants of that office have a free rein. Moreover, a number of rules and practices insulate judges in office from political pressure.

If we had a written constitution, this insulation of the Judiciary might be more complete. Two examples bring out this point. In the Commonwealth of Australia, as we have seen, the constitution allocates the legislative, executive and judicial powers to the corresponding organs of government. There is a parliamentary Executive, as in Britain, and the Australian courts have declined to hold that parliamentary delegation of legislative powers to the Executive is unconstitutional; but they have held that the judicial power of the Commonwealth can be vested only in

6. Two consecutive nominations made by President Nixon to fill a vacancy on the Supreme Court were rejected by the Senate.

7. See generally, E. C. S. Wade and G. G. Phillips, *Constitutional Law* (8th edn), ch. 3.

'courts' within the meaning of the constitution, and that powers wholly alien to the judicial cannot be vested in those courts.[8] In Ceylon the constitution did not allocate judicial powers in the same form, and it would be reasonable to infer that the separation of powers doctrine had no place in the constitutional jurisprudence of the island. But in a famous case the Judicial Committee of the Privy Council held that implicit in the constitution lay the principle that the province of the Judiciary was immune from the grosser kinds of encroachment by the Executive and the Legislature; hence, retroactive legislation designed to secure the conviction and punishment of particular persons for specified conduct was declared unconstitutional, for it approximated to a non-judicial judgment.[9] One wonders how the War Damage Act 1965, which reversed a judicial decision of the House of Lords[10] with retroactive effect, would have fared if it had been measured against a written British constitution in which judicial review of the constitutionality of legislation was accepted.

It is easy to see, therefore, that the immunity of the Judiciary from interference by the political organs of government could be fortified by a written constitution; and such a constitution would certainly entrench the judges' security of tenure. To that extent the doctrine of the separation of powers, and the climate of thought of which it is a part, has practical value. Whether it would be helpful, as a means of restoring the vitality of Parliament, to separate the Executive from the Legislature in Britain is an interesting but academic speculation. The blending of Executive and Legislature is a fundamental characteristic of the British system of government. To discard it would be a more startling change than the introduction of federalism and entrenched civil liberties in a written constitution.

Sources of British constitutional law

The law of the constitution, though in one sense unwritten, is traceable to written sources, some of which are recognized as authoritative law-making agencies.

Legislation

This is by far the most important single source of constitutional law. In the first place, there are Acts of Parliament such as the Bill of Rights

8. See *Att.-Gen. for Australia* v. *R. and the Boilermakers' Society of Australia* [1957] A.C. 288 (P.C.) affirming the decision of the High Court of Australia *sub nom. R.* v. *Kirby, ex p. Boilermakers' Society* (1956) 94 C.L.R. 254.

9. *Liyanage* v. *R.* [1967] 1 A.C. 259; cf. *Kariapper* v. *Wijesinha* [1968] A.C. 717 (*Liyanage*'s case distinguished).

10. *Burmah Oil Co.* v. *Lord Advocate* [1965] A.C. 75.

1689, the Act of Settlement 1701, the Act of Union with Scotland 1707, and now the European Communities Act 1972, embodying rules of major importance in the history of the constitution. There are numerous Acts dealing with the electoral system and the composition and functioning of Parliament (for example, the Representation of the People Acts, the House of Commons (Redistribution of Seats) Acts, the House of Commons Disqualification Act 1957, the Life Peerages Act 1958, the Peerage Act 1963 (permitting the disclaimer of hereditary peerages), the Parliament Acts of 1911 and 1949 (asserting the primacy of the House of Commons in conflicts between the two Houses), and the Royal Assent Act 1967). There are statutes relating to the monarchy, regulating the succession to the throne, authorizing the adoption of new forms of the royal style and titles, and providing for a regency; but there are not many statutes of general importance defining the authority of the political executive branch. Acts of Parliament have made big changes in the law relating to civil liberties (for example, the Habeas Corpus Act 1679, the Administration of Justice Act 1960, the Public Order Acts, the Defamation Act 1952, the Obscene Publications Acts, the Race Relations Acts 1965 and 1968, the Theatres Act 1968 which abolished theatrical censorship). We have legislation relating to British nationality, the status of aliens, and immigration and deportation; regulating the conditions under which fugitive offenders may be extradited; conferring diplomatic and kindred privileges and immunities. In the general area of administrative law we have major enactments such as the Crown Proceedings Act 1947, the Parliamentary Commissioner Act 1967, and the Tribunals and Inquiries Act 1971, and a host of statutes regulating particular fields of administrative action. And then there are numerous Acts concerning Commonwealth relations, such as the Statute of Westminster 1931 (setting the seal on the concept of Dominion status), the West Indies Act 1967 (introducing the concept of associated statehood), and independence Acts. One has only to glance through the statute book for any year in the late 1960s or early 1970s to appreciate how much legislation of constitutional interest is enacted by Parliament. The overwhelming bulk of this legislation has been introduced by Ministers.

Subordinate legislative instruments are also a source of constitutional law. For example, Orders in Council are made under powers delegated by the self-explanatory Ministers of the Crown (Transfer of Functions) Act 1946; Orders in Council and regulations of constitutional importance can be made under the European Communities Act 1972. Orders in Council (made by the Queen in her Privy Council) and rules and regulations made by Ministers under statutory authority are called statutory instruments within the meaning of the Statutory Instruments Act 1946. In a narrow field, the Crown has an inherent law-making power exercisable by virtue of the royal prerogative; examples of the use of this non-statutory power are Orders regulating the civil service.

Common-law sources

Beneath this general rubric are subsumed rules widely different in character from one another.

(*a*) There is a small group of customary rules, now partly modified by statute, determining what is an Act of Parliament and enunciating the principle of parliamentary sovereignty. Clearly these rules are of fundamental importance in our legal system. Their origins and present status will be examined in the next chapter.

(*b*) The royal prerogative is the gradually diminishing residuum of customary authority, privilege and immunity, recognized at common law as belonging to the Crown, and the Crown alone. In the great *Case of Proclamations* (1611)[11] the judges of the common-law courts emphatically asserted their right to determine the limits of the prerogative; and since the Revolution of 1688 this claim has not been contested by the Crown. Among the prerogatives still exercised by or in the name of the Crown are the appointment of Ministers, the dissolution of Parliament, the power of pardon and the award of honours and dignities; these powers must, as a matter of constitutional convention, normally be exercised on ministerial advice. The immunity of the monarch from prosecution in the courts is another aspect of the royal prerogative.

(*c*) Judicial decisions are also a significant source of constitutional law. Indeed, Dicey went so far as to assert that the British constitution was 'a judge-made constitution'.[12] He was thinking particularly of the rules relating to the liberty of the person, freedom of expression and freedom of association, which had been demarcated largely by binding precedents set by the superior courts. The law of civil liberties is still to a large extent judge-made, though statutory restatement has become increasingly important in recent years. The law relating to judicial review of administrative action is predominantly judge-made, and it has probably developed faster since 1963 than in any comparable period. Again, judicial decisions have set limits not only to the royal prerogative but also to the ambit of parliamentary privilege.

(*d*) Legislation of constitutional importance may be moulded by judicial interpretation; and there are common-law presumptions of legislative intent (for example, that major constitutional innovations cannot

11. 12 Co. Rep. 74.
12. Dicey, op. cit., p. 196.

be introduced,[13] and taxation cannot be imposed,[14] save by virtue of clear and express statutory language) which conserve what are understood to be constitutional principles against casual erosion.

Conventions of the constitution

In order to avoid tedious repetition, and in an attempt to do justice to the complexity of the topic, we shall consign to a separate section the role of conventions as a source of law.[15] Here it is enough to say that if conventions are regarded as a source of law, then it is inappropriate to affirm that the law of the British constitution is part of the ordinary law of the land; for it has at least one source which is extraordinary inasmuch as it begets rules unaccompanied by judicial sanctions or relief.

The law and custom of Parliament (lex et consuetudo parliamenti)

This comprises the rules relating to the functions, procedure, privileges and immunities of each House of Parliament. To a small extent it is statutory, and to a still smaller extent judge-made. For the rest, it is either to be found in resolutions of each House (recorded in the official Journals, in *Hansard*, and on some important matters in standing orders) or not to be found in any authoritative source because it rests on informal understandings or practices. For example, the functions of the Leaders of the two Houses and the party whips, the duty of impartiality cast on the Speaker of the House of Commons, the conventional allocation of time to the Opposition, and the convention that the chairman of the Public Accounts Committee shall be a member of the Opposition, are not formally recorded, though they can be elicited from a reading of parliamentary debates. In any event, the internal proceedings of the two Houses are not cognizable by the courts. For this reason, large tracts of the law relating to parliamentary privilege have never been subject to judicial appraisal. And so a great deal of the law and custom of Parliament lies outside the scope of the *ordinary* law of the land.

13. See, for example, *Nairn* v. *University of St Andrews* [1909] A.C. 147 (votes for women could be conferred only by a direct grant); *Re Parliamentary Privilege Act 1770* [1958] A.C. 331 (important provision of Bill of Rights 1689 not impliedly repealed by generally worded subsequent Act).

14. See, for example, *Att.-Gen.* v. *Wilts United Dairies Ltd* (1921) 37 T.L.R. 884, though see now p. 284. The courts also adopt presumptions against so construing legislation as to oust the supervisory jurisdiction of the superior courts to determine the rights and liabilities of individuals, or to authorize deprivation of private property without compensation; see generally D. L. Keir and F. H. Lawson, *Cases in Constitutional Law* (5th edn), pp. 11–15. The force of the last-mentioned presumption has been weakened: *Westminster Bank Ltd* v. *Beverley B. C.* [1971] A.C. 508.

15. See pp. 47–64.

With the accession of the United Kingdom to membership of the European Communities on 1 January 1973, Community law became a source of the constitutional law of Britain.

Community law[16] is to be found in the Community treaties;[17] in regulations, directives and decisions of Community organs (the Council of Ministers, a political body composed of Foreign Ministers; or the European Commission, a supranational body composed of top Community officials); and in rulings and decisions of the Court of the Communities (the European Court). It is applied *mainly* by courts of the member States, but authoritative rulings are given by the European Court. According to that Court, Community law is distinct from national law but exists alongside it; and where Community law is in conflict with national law, Community law prevails. By section 3 of the European Communities Act 1972, the United Kingdom has accepted the binding authority of the rulings and principles laid down by the European Court. The Court has stated quite clearly several times that no Parliament of a member State can legislate inconsistently with Community law. Hence our acceptance of Community law *seems* to involve a rejection of the doctrine of parliamentary sovereignty. We shall consider this matter more fully in the next chapter. But potentially, at least, the importation of Community law brings with it a constitutional innovation of the highest importance.

A general outline of the structure and functions of the Communities, and of the interrelationship between Community law and national law, will be found in an Appendix. At various points in the book we shall note the actual or likely impact of Community law on the law of this country. In fact the content of Community law has up to now been fairly remote from the subject-matter of constitutional law; for Community law is largely about agriculture, free trade, fair competition, transport regulation, social security and so on. But on certain matters – for example, immigration and aspects of public finance – it bears directly on specific areas of constitutional law.

One very important point needs to be made at this stage. Some rules of Community law are (according to Community doctrine) 'directly applicable' in the sense that they confer rights or impose duties on individuals, rights and duties which are enforceable in national courts without

16. For a good and concise outline, see P.S.R.F. Mathijsen, *A Guide to European Community Law* (1972). See also Appendix.

17. A shorthand expression covering the three original treaties establishing the three Communities (ECSC, EEC and EURATOM), the instruments by which the United Kingdom acceded to the Communities, and various other Community agreements. See the European Communities Act 1972, s. 1.

being re-enacted by the governmental organs of member States. These rules are, in the main, *regulations* made by the Council of Ministers or the Commission. Section 2(1) and part of section 2(4) of the European Communities Act give effect to the concept of 'direct applicability'. The relevant Community rules are to be applied by the courts of this country 'without further enactment' as if they were Acts of Parliament. This is a major constitutional innovation. These regulations will be made in Brussels in consequence of decisions taken in Brussels.[18] And they are *primary* rather than delegated legislation.

Authoritative works

Literature on the constitution has only persuasive authority. Sometimes unusual and abstruse questions of constitutional law arise before a court – for instance, peerage law,[19] or aspects of the royal prerogative,[20] or the law of treason,[21] or the definition of an act of State,[22] or the jurisdiction of the English courts in British protectorates[23] – and reference may then be had to the views of writers of repute for the purposes of guidance. When a particularly awkward question relating to the scope of parliamentary privilege was referred to the Judicial Committee of the Privy Council for an advisory opinion, the opinions of constitutional historians in the eighteenth and nineteenth centuries were copiously cited in order to explain the mischief which an obscure and ambiguous Act of 1770 was designed to cure.[24] In controversies about the existence and scope of individual constitutional conventions – controversies which usually take place outside the courts of law – the views of modern writers such as Jennings, Anson, Dicey, Maitland, Keith, E. C. S. Wade, Hood Phillips, Amery, Mackintosh and others are frequently prayed in aid. On issues of parliamentary privilege, Erskine May[25] is regarded as an exceptionally persuasive authority. It is fair to say that in the diffuse field of constitutional law the opinions of authorities are resorted to more often than in other branches of English law. They are a useful subsidiary source of constitutional law in the broad sense of the term. In administrative law cases the opinions of modern writers have come to be quoted in argument and are occasionally cited in judgments. In cases involving

18. See further Appendix.
19. *Re Parliamentary Election for Bristol South-East* [1964] 2 Q.B. 257.
20. For example, *Burmah Oil Co.* v. *Lord Advocate* [1965] A.C. 75.
21. *Joyce* v. *D.P.P.* [1946] A.C. 347.
22. *Nissan* v. *Att.-Gen.* [1970] A.C. 179.
23. *Ex p. Mwenya* [1960] 1 Q.B. 241.
24. *Re Parliamentary Privilege Act 1770* [1958] A.C. 331.
25. i.e. Sir Thomas Erskine May, *Parliamentary Practice* (18th edn, 1971).

points of Community law, on which few British judges would regard themselves as experts, recourse will surely be made to the opinions of specialist writers.

Conventions of the constitution

There is no rule of statute or common law to the effect that there must be a Prime Minister and a Cabinet, though legislation providing for the payment of ministerial salaries rests on the assumption that these institutions do exist. But clearly the Prime Minister and the Cabinet are cardinal features of the British constitution. They are creatures of convention, not of strict law.

Again, as we have noted, the Queen has enormously wide powers, prerogative and statutory, but she is obliged by convention to exercise these powers on and in accordance with ministerial advice, save in a few very special situations. This is the most important convention of the British constitution. The main exceptions to the general rule will be considered in chapter 4.

There are many other major conventions of the constitution, dealing with relations between the Executive and the Legislature (for example, the rules about ministerial responsibility to Parliament), relations between the two Houses of Parliament (for example, the rule that money bills have to be introduced into the House of Commons), the working of each House (for example, the rule that the Speaker of the House of Commons shall behave impartially), the civil service and the Judiciary.

It is obvious that *some* constitutional conventions are far more important than most of the statutory and common-law rules connected with the British system of government. The convention that the Queen must assent to bills duly passed is overwhelmingly more important than her strictly legal prerogative power to withhold her assent. Since the rules of strict law, in this context and many others, give a grotesquely misleading picture of the rules actually observed, and observed on the assumption that they are binding, constitutional conventions ought to be treated as part of constitutional law.

At once we are in terminological difficulties. In one aspect conventions are law; in other aspects they are not. Dicey was quite clear that they were not ' "laws" in the true sense of that word, for if any or all of them were broken, no court would take notice of their violation'.[26] In other passages he observed that laws were 'rules enforced or recognized by the courts', whereas conventions were 'a body not of laws, but of

26. Dicey, op. cit., p. 27.

constitutional or political ethics', the 'constitutional morality of the day', 'not enforced or recognized by the courts'.[27]

Dicey's distinctions between strict law[28] and constitutional convention were too clear-cut and have been severely criticized;[29] but they have substance.[30] For instance, if the Queen were to refuse her assent to a bill of which she disapproved, no court would deem the bill to be an authentic Act of Parliament. If a Government, defeated on a vote of confidence in the House of Commons, neither resigned nor advised a dissolution of Parliament, no court would take cognizance of this gross breach of convention by granting a declaration that any of the Ministers was not legally entitled to exercise his office. No form of judicial redress is obtainable purely for a breach of convention. And in the eyes of the courts, Parliament is competent to legislate in unequivocal disregard of conventional limitations on the exercise of its powers.[31]

Distinctions of substance between constitutional conventions and rules of strict law are well illustrated by the evolution of Dominion status within the Commonwealth. By 1926 most of the self-governing Dominions were in effect independent States, equal in status, for most purposes, to the United Kingdom. They had achieved this status not by legislation but by the development of conventions, many of which were formally recorded (or created) in resolutions of Imperial Conferences. There remained a few elements of formal inequality. Some of those (for example, the procedure for appointing a Governor-General) could be and were removed by the formulation of new constitutional conventions. Others could not be removed by convention. In strict law the Dominions were still colonies. They were prohibited by section 2 of the Colonial Laws Validity Act 1865 from legislating repugnantly to United Kingdom enactments extending to them as part of their own law. Among these enactments were the Judicial Committee Acts 1833 and 1844, under which the prerogative power of the Crown to grant special leave to appeal from colonial courts to the Privy Council was placed on a statutory footing. This power to give leave to appeal and to hear appeals was not expunged by convention; and in 1926

27. ibid., pp. 417, 422. See also O. Hood Phillips, 'Constitutional conventions: Dicey's predecessors' (1966) 29 *Mod. L. Rev.* 137.

28. The term aptly employed by Sir Kenneth Wheare in *The Statute of Westminster and Dominion Status* (5th edn), ch. 1.

29. Notably by Sir Ivor Jennings, *The Law and the Constitution* (5th edn), ch. 3. See also J. D. B. Mitchell, *Constitutional Law* (2nd edn), pp. 26–39.

30. For a subtle defence of the basis of the distinction, see O. Hood Phillips, 'Constitutional conventions: a conventional reply' (1964) 8 *Journal of the Society of Public Teachers of Law* (N.S.) 60.

31. *Madzimbamuto* v. *Lardner-Burke* [1969] 1 A.C. 645 at 722–3 (legislation dealing with internal affairs of Southern Rhodesia).

the Judicial Committee of the Privy Council held[32] that the Canadian Parliament was incompetent to abolish the appeal by special leave from Canadian courts in criminal matters. The necessary legal authority could be conferred only by United Kingdom legislation. Some of the Dominions pressed for the enactment of enabling legislation, and Parliament passed the Statute of Westminster 1931. This excluded the Dominions from the definition of 'colony', abolished the repugnancy rule and empowered Dominion Parliaments to legislate inconsistently with United Kingdom legislation extending to their countries.[33] Thereafter the Canadian Parliament was able to pass legislation abolishing criminal appeals to the Privy Council.[34]

The distinction blurred

These examples suggest that the distinction between law and convention is reasonably clear. But in a number of contexts the distinction is blurred. In particular, Dicey was exaggerating when he said that conventions were 'not recognized' by the courts. The courts do sometimes take cognizance of conventions and use them as aids to interpretation. Thus, English courts have occasionally supported their refusal to review the grounds on which executive discretionary powers have been exercised by pointing out that a Minister is responsible to Parliament for the exercise of the power.[35] In one Privy Council appeal, Canada's accession to independence, and the convention of equality of status recited in the preamble to the Statute of Westminster, were primary reasons for so interpreting an ambiguous section of the Canadian constitution as to empower the Federal Parliament to abolish appeals to the Privy Council from all Canadian courts in civil cases.[36] In another, more recent, appeal it was contended that appeals from Ceylon courts had been impliedly abrogated by the grant of independence, because the report of the Judicial Committee on such an appeal was issued in the form of an Order in Council affecting the law of Ceylon. The Judicial Committee held[37] that although a

32. *Nadan* v. *R.* [1926] A.C. 482.

33. ss. 1, 2, 11; see generally, Wheare, op cit., and R. McG. Dawson, *The Development of Dominion Status 1900–1936*; and ch. 30.

34. *British Coal Corporation* v. *R.* [1935] A.C. 500. See also *Att.-Gen. for Ontario* v. *Att.-Gen. for Canada* [1947] A.C. 127 (abolition of appeals in civil matters; see below).

35. See, for example, *Liversidge* v. *Anderson* [1942] A.C. 206 (where the Home Secretary was expressly required by regulations to make reports to Parliament); *Carltona Ltd* v. *Commissioners of Works* [1943] 2 All E.R. 560; *Robinson* v. *Minister of Town and Country Planning* [1947] K.B. 702.

36. *Att.-Gen. for Ontario* v. *Att.-Gen. for Canada* [1947] A.C. 127.

37. *Ibralebbe* v. *R.* [1964] A.C. 900. Appeals from Ceylon (Sri Lanka) were terminated in 1972.

legislative Order in Council purporting to alter the law of Ceylon would have been invalidated by the Ceylon Independence Act 1947, a *judicial* Order in Council was, by convention, no more than the formal promulgation of a determination by a court of law which had not yet been deprived of jurisdiction by the Parliament of Ceylon. Again, the High Court of Australia has used constitutional conventions as an aid to statutory interpretation, holding that United Kingdom amendments to copyright legislation in 1928 and 1956 did not alter Australian law in the absence of any indication that they purported to extend to Australia with Australian concurrence; the original legislation passed by the United Kingdom Parliament in 1911 had undoubtedly extended to Australia as part of its law, but conventional limitations on the territorial competence of the United Kingdom Parliament and Government had evolved since that time.[38]

These examples[39] show how constitutional conventions may materially influence judicial decisions. In this sense they may be compared with recitals in the preamble to an Act of Parliament. The terms of preambles are not directly enforceable in a court, but the facts and purposes (and occasionally conventions[40]) there set out may be used as aids to the interpretation of ambiguous provisions in the main body of the Act. Alternatively, conventions may be compared with the Directive Principles of State Policy, which are an integral part of the constitution of India but are expressed not to be 'enforceable by any court';[41] they are nevertheless used as guides to constitutional interpretation.

Some conventions, then, may be indirectly justiciable. And some rules of strict law may be non-justiciable. The latter point can be illustrated in constitutional and administrative law.

1. General duties to provide efficient services are cast by statute on public corporations administering nationalized industries. These duties may be formulated in terms so broad that no person would be able to obtain a

38. *Copyright Owners Reproduction Society Ltd* v. *E.M.I.* (*Australia*) *Pty Ltd* (1958) 100 C.L.R. 597; see Gray (1960) 23 *Mod. L. Rev.* 647; Bennion (1961) 24 *Mod. L. Rev.* 355. The amendment made in 1956, after Australia had adopted the Statute of Westminster, was held moreover to be inoperative in Australia because it was not *expressed* to have been made at the request and with the consent of the Commonwealth of Australia, as was required by section 4 of the Statute. See further pp. 76–7.

39. See further, *Ryder* v. *Foley* (1906) 4 C.L.R. 422; *Commercial Cable Co.* v. *Government of Newfoundland* [1916] 2 A.C. 610.

40. Notably in the preamble to the Statute of Westminster 1931, reciting basic conventions about equality of status in the Commonwealth. A preamble is part of an Act and can be debated and amended during the passage of the bill. Each clause will begin ' Whereas . . .'.

41. Constitution, art. 37.

judicial pronouncement that the corporation had failed to carry out its duty.[42] Sometimes the nationalization Act will state explicitly that these general duties are not enforceable in any court of law.

2. Under the Parliament Act 1911, a money bill passed by the Commons can be presented for the royal assent after one month although it has not been passed by the Lords. The Act defines a money bill and provides that a certificate given by the Speaker of the House of Commons that the bill is a money bill shall not be questioned in any court. If the Speaker's certificate were based on an erroneous interpretation of the statutory definition, no way of raising the issue before a court would be feasible, unless possibly the error was so flagrant as to raise doubts as to the Speaker's good faith.

Examples could be multiplied. It is enough to say that non-compliance with statutory norms is not necessarily coupled with the possibility of judicial sanctions, even the sanction of nullity.

3. There is the curious case of section 1 (2) of the Ireland Act 1949: '. . . it is hereby affirmed that in no event will Northern Ireland . . . cease to be part . . . of the United Kingdom without the consent of the Parliament of Northern Ireland.' This reads like a particularly solemn affirmation of a constitutional convention,[43] binding on the United Kingdom Parliament and Government but placed in the main body of an Act instead of in the preamble. Here the distinction between strict law and convention not only lacks substance but is tenuous in the matter of form.

4. Written constitutions in other countries often embody non-justiciable rules. Some are non-justiciable because the constitution says so. To this category belong those provisions in a number of Commonwealth constitutions requiring the Governor-General to act on ministerial advice.[44] In the constitution of Ceylon, British conventions concerning the exercise of discretionary functions by the Queen's representative were incorporated by general reference; and it was expressly stated that the question whether these conventions had been observed was not to be inquired into by any

42. cf. *Watt* v. *Kesteven C.C.* [1955] 1 Q.B. 408 (duty of local education authorities to have regard to the general principle that as far as possible children are to be educated in accordance with parental wishes (Education Act 1944, s. 76) unenforceable by aggrieved parents in legal proceedings). See also p. 221.

43. See also Cmd 534 (1969 (N.I.), referring to the 'clear pledges made by successive United Kingdom Governments that Northern Ireland should not cease to be a part of the United Kingdom without the consent of the people of Northern Ireland' (§ 56 (1)). See now Addendum. For an argument that section 1 (2) of the 1949 Act was in law a redefinition of the meaning of the United Kingdom Parliament, see Harry Calvert, *Constitutional Law in Northern Ireland*, pp. 23–33.

44. For example, Constitution of Malta (S.I. 1964, No. 1398, Sched.), s. 86(4).

court.[45] Was this constitutional provision not 'law'? Are the Directive Principles of State Policy in the Indian constitution (which are only indirectly justiciable) and the corresponding statements of principle in the constitutions of the Republic of Ireland and Malta not part of the law of the constitution? And what is one to make of those constitutional provisions, common enough in non-Commonwealth countries (for example, France), which impose limitations on legislative competence but cannot be the subject of adjudication because judicial review of the constitutionality of legislation is not an acceptable doctrine?

Why not codify conventions?

One may argue that the illustrations cited above are marginal or anomalous cases which do not significantly weaken the general proposition that conventions are not directly enforceable in courts whereas obedience to rules of strict law is directly enforceable through courts. This is broadly correct. But why is a distinction between strict law and convention maintained at all in the United Kingdom? Why not codify conventions in a strictly legal form? After all, conventions and rules of strict law alike are binding rules.

The answers to these questions are not simple. The reasons for retaining the distinction are various. In the first place, there is the constitutional role of the monarch. Most of the main conventions of the constitution were originally evolved in order to ensure that the monarch exercised his prerogative powers on the advice of Ministers responsible to Parliament. This end could be and was achieved by a gradual process in which royal discretion was quietly eroded. Abrupt changes in the law should, it was felt, be avoided unless the monarch behaved like James II. As long as the monarch played, or thought he was entitled to play, a significant role in the making of policy decisions, it might have been politically imprudent to urge that his dwindling personal influence should be attenuated by statutory restrictions, for example, by requiring him to act on the advice of the Privy Council or the incipient Cabinet or a named Minister. No obvious harm was done by leaving the monarch with wide prerogative powers exercisable in strict law in his personal discretion; and unnecessary friction could have been caused by trying to take them away, particularly as long as a large section of the general public thought of the monarch as the executive head of government. A prerogative power might be converted into a statutory power or duty exercisable under prescribed conditions,

45. Jennings, op. cit., pp. 120–21; see also his *Constitution of Ceylon* (3rd edn). Sir Ivor Jennings was the main architect of the Ceylon constitution. See generally de Smith, *The New Commonwealth and its Constitutions*, ch. 3, on methods of incorporating 'conventional' rules into Commonwealth constitutions.

but these conditions would not include an obligation to act on ministerial advice. *New* statutory powers and duties could be vested in the monarch, the Crown in Council or a named Minister without breaking away too blatantly from historical tradition. And the tradition was not valueless. To involve the monarch personally in the making of important decisions on matters of State lent greater dignity to the business of government; and there were exceptional situations, not easily definable, where the monarch's personal views ought to be taken into account, or even to prevail in a time of constitutional crisis. Even today, time-honoured formal tradition is not easily eradicated unless there are obvious reasons why it should be. If there is urgent pressure for clarification or change (for example, in Commonwealth affairs), conventions may be explicitly set down as conventions in their existing or a modified form, or rules of strict law may replace them.

Secondly, it would be difficult or even harmful to define a number of important conventions. For example, some of the conventions about ministerial responsibility or the working of the Cabinet system are either blurred or experimental. Codification would purchase certainty at the expense of flexibility; informal modifications to keep the constitution in touch with contemporary political thinking or needs would be inhibited. Evolution by conventions is still needed in countries with written constitutions. In some contexts the rules ought *not* to be crystal clear. Clarification would tend to stultify one purpose of conventions – keeping the constitution up to date. Again, a situation may arise in which a convention ought, in the public interest, to be waived; waiver would be more difficult if the convention were set down in unambiguous language. These are, of course, admissions that many conventions are significantly different from typical rules of strict law.

Thirdly, as long as a conventional rule is regularly observed, there is no apparent reason for codifying it.[46] Lay peers regularly comply with their conventional obligation not to present themselves to sit with the Law Lords to hear an appeal in the House of Lords; the Speaker of the House of Commons regularly behaves impartially.[47] If these conventional rules were to be broken, they could simply be restated in formal terms or superseded by statutory rules. In 1909 the House of Lords disregarded its somewhat vague conventional duty to defer in the last resort to the will of the Commons; the sequel was the Parliament Act 1911, redefining relationships between the two Houses on a statutory basis.

46. One could equally say that there is no sound reason for not codifying it. The reasons, sound or unsound, are characteristic inertia masquerading as veneration for unwritten constitutional tradition, and the absence of political pressure for change.
47. There are customary rules of the House of Commons directing the manner in which he is to use his casting vote in the event of a tie.

Nevertheless, it is unsatisfactory that the content, and indeed the very existence, of some of the most important conventions should be indeterminate. There is no consensus of opinion on the *conventional* powers of the Queen to remove a Prime Minister, to require a dissolution of Parliament or to refuse a request for dissolution. Clarification may be brought about by the march of events in a time of political turbulence; but the Queen may then be criticized for having acted 'unconstitutionally' or for having failed to discharge her constitutional duty to act; she will be unable to answer back, and those who will speak for her may have to reply on dubious precedents, debatable opinions of writers, and principles deduced from a concept of the constitutional system with which some are bound to disagree. An authoritative statement, prepared by an expert body, of the conventions regulating the constitutional functions of the monarch might therefore be useful, difficult though it would be to formulate. But if such conventions were to be codified, they ought not to be made directly justiciable,[48] even if they were written into an Act of Parliament or a new British constitution. Experience in new Commonwealth countries has shown that whilst the embodiment of such rules in the texts of constitutions makes for greater certainty, so that people have a clearer idea of what may, must or cannot be done, the burden thrust upon the courts when they are called upon to determine whether prescribed rules have been complied with in a politically sensitive situation is liable to be excessive. Whatever the outcome, the prestige of the Judiciary will probably suffer. If the rules of the game are to be set down, do not require the courts to decide whether, for example, a Prime Minister has been validly dismissed. This is pre-eminently a question about the reins of power. If the constitutionality of such an act is disputed, the controversy is unlikely to be resolved by the pronouncement of a court.[49] However, clarification of the rules by codification may reduce the area of potential conflict.

One point must be made to avoid misunderstandings. Some rules of political behaviour, or standards of conduct in public affairs, have in fact

48. For discussion of this matter, see H. V. Evatt, *The King and his Dominion Governors* (2nd edn), chs. 29–33; Geoffrey Marshall and Graeme C. Moodie, *Some Problems of the Constitution* (5th edn), pp. 34–6; de Smith, op. cit., pp. 86–7; K. J. Keith, 'The Courts and the conventions of the Constitution' (1967) 16 *I.C.L.Q.* 542.

49. Dismissals were held valid in *Adegbenro* v. *Akintola* [1963] A.C. 614 (Western Nigeria) and invalid in *Ningkan's* case [1966] 2 *Malayan L.J.* 187 (Sarawak). See, on the latter case, S. M. Thio (1966) 8 *Malaya L. Rev.* 283; K. J. Keith (1967) 16 *I.C.L.Q.* 542. The decision in the former case was reversed locally by a constitutional amendment having retroactive effect, followed by the abolition of appeals from Nigerian courts to the Judicial Committee. The decision in the latter case was accepted, but a state of emergency was proclaimed, the constitution amended (validity upheld in *Ningkan* v. *Government of Malaysia* [1970] A.C. 379) and the Chief Minister dismissed.

been 'codified', or promulgated in an authoritative form. For instance, the principles governing the private financial interests that a Minister of the Crown can properly retain after appointment can be found in a statement by Sir Winston Churchill published in 1952.[50] These principles embody constitutional conventions because they state rules that ought to be followed by Ministers; and enforced resignation would be the sanction for breaking them. Some other assertions about what is right and proper in public affairs do not enjoy the same degree of importance; or the standards of conduct they lay down may be more elastic; or their original or continuing authority may be disputed; or the consequence of deviating from them may be no more than adverse criticism from political opponents. It may, therefore, be doubtful whether such statements are to be regarded as embodying conventions (or rules) at all. Nearly all discussions about the existence and scope of the *lesser* constitutional conventions include arguments of dubious authenticity.

Interrelationship between law and convention

Law and convention are closely interlocked. To quote Jennings, constitutional conventions 'provide the flesh which clothes the dry bones of the law; they make the legal constitution work; they keep it in touch with the growth of ideas'.[51] Conventions presuppose the existence of a framework of strict law; they do not exist in a legal vacuum. For example, conventional rules about the functions of the Cabinet Office presuppose the existence of a Cabinet, which presupposes the existence of a Privy Council and Ministers appointed by the Crown. In turn, some rules of strict law presuppose conventions. Statutes dealing with ministerial salaries presuppose the existence of a Prime Minister, a Cabinet, Leaders of the Opposition and party whips, though they do not define their functions.[52] And when Parliament gives Her Majesty powers of appointment to offices of State and other statutory discretions, it acts on the tacit assumption that she will use her powers only on ministerial advice.

Again, as we have seen, the line between strict law and convention is sometimes uncertain. Legal duties are not always justiciable, and conventions may be justiciable in so far as the courts use them as aids to construction.

50. 496 H. C. Deb. 701–3 (25 February 1952); reproduced as Appendix 2 to the Report from the Select Committee on Members' Interests (H.C. 57 (1969–70)). See also p. 185.

51. *The Law and the Constitution* (5th edn), pp. 81–2.

52. See especially Ministers of the Crown Act 1964; Ministerial Salaries Consolidation Act 1965; Ministerial and other Salaries Act 1972.

None of these comments is likely to be regarded as controversial. If, however, one asks the question: Are rules of strict law and constitutional conventions obeyed for similar reasons? problems at once arise.

1. Dicey contended that 'the sanction which constrains the boldest political adventurer' to obey a convention he might feel inclined to break was his fear that breach would almost immediately bring him into conflict with the courts and the law of the land.[53] Thus, if the convention that Parliament be summoned each year, or that a Government which has lost the confidence of the House of Commons must resign or go to the country, were to be broken, legal authority for collecting the most productive taxes, for spending money and for maintaining and disciplining a standing army would soon expire, for such authority is granted by Parliament only for a year at a time. Since the Government would have to perform acts devoid of legal authority, Ministers and officials would soon find themselves in the dock or mulcted in damages. Obedience to conventions was therefore buttressed by the sanctions of strict law.

The weaknesses of Dicey's argument are familiar. Some political adventurers may indeed have been deterred from breaking certain conventions for fear of indirectly incurring legal sanctions; but who knows? The boldest adventurer will (as Dicey himself conceded) carry out a *coup d'état* and defy the law. The not so bold is far more likely to be deterred by fear of the *political* consequences – justified charges of unconstitutional conduct, public ridicule or odium, loss of office or even the precipitation of revolution. Moreover, many conventions are not buttressed by the threat of legal sanctions. If the Queen were to refuse her assent to a bill because she disapproved of it, this could not entail breach of any legal rule; but it might lead to *changes* in the law – the abolition of the power to refuse assent, and imposition of statutory duties to exercise other royal discretionary powers on ministerial advice; or enforced abdication, or abolition of the monarchy. If the majority in the House of Commons voted to expel the Opposition, or if a lay peer were to insist on sitting with the Law Lords, or if the Speaker were to make a party political speech in the Commons, conventions would be broken and the consequences might be very unpleasant for those concerned; but obedience to the existing conventions is not explicable in terms of legal sanctions.

2. Conventions are normally observed for a variety of mundane reasons – force of habit, inertia, desire to 'conform', belief that it is 'right' to obey them and wrong to disobey them because they are reasonable rules or because they are part of a reasonable structure of rules which ought to be preserved and upheld. In so far as they are observed by persons

53. Dicey, op. cit., pp. 445–6.

involved in politics who feel inclined to break them, obedience can usually be attributed to fear of disrepute and its political implications. Now, most of us obey the criminal law for much the same set of reasons.[54] If, for example, one finds a purse containing a large sum of money in the street, one is likely to resist any temptation to appropriate and keep it because one feels one *ought* not to behave in such a way. If one's decision to hand it in to the police station is materially influenced by fear of being prosecuted and convicted for theft, the probability is that one will be more concerned with the *social* disgrace involved in a publicized conviction than with the prospect of being fined or sent to prison. The sense of obligation and the fear of disagreeable consequences which tend to induce people to comply with conventions are broadly similar to the corresponding feelings which conduce to observance of the criminal law. There are, of course, many people who will not feel any sense of obligation to return the purse, who will be deterred from dishonesty only by the prospect of detection, and who will fear imprisonment but not loss of social esteem. And some politicians will cheerfully break a hallowed convention (for example, about ministerial responsibility to Parliament) if they think they can carry it off without adverse personal repercussions. Again, some of us will break certain rules of strict law, for example, speed limits on a clear road in a built-up area, without compunction provided that a police patrol car is not in the vicinity, because we do not feel a sense of obligation to obey the rule to the letter. Awareness that a patrol car is close behind us will slow us down, not because we are overcome by a sense of moral obligation but because we do not want to be stopped and perhaps have to pay a fine.

This is not a jurisprudential essay and these points will not be elaborated. It is enough to repeat that the sense of legal obligation is often much the same as the sense of obligation to obey constitutional conventions. One difference between strict law and convention is that legal obligations are on the whole more complex, technical and exactly defined; another is that where there are direct sanctions for breach, strictly legal sanctions tend to be more specific and can be imposed by authoritative tribunals endowed with powers of interpretation. These differences are not trivial. But are they really fundamental?

Identification of constitutional conventions

If one can borrow from the vocabulary of H. L. A. Hart, constitutional conventions, in so far as they impose duties,[55] are primary rules of obligation unaccompanied by an adequate apparatus of secondary rules of

54. cf. Jennings, *The Law and the Constitution* (5th edn), Appendix 4.
55. Some confer powers – for example, the special powers of a Prime Minister.

recognition, interpretation (or adjudication) and change.[56] And the tests for the ascertainment of conventions are neither universally agreed nor, when agreed, easily applied in a large number of marginal cases. Some conventions are clear-cut; some are flexible; some are so elusive that one is left wondering whether in fact the 'convention' is an ethereal will-o'-the-wisp. It is often particularly hard to say whether a political practice has crystallized into a constitutional convention and, if so, what is its scope.[57]

1. Most of the conventions of the constitution are binding usages, understandings or practices.[58] They are forms of political behaviour regarded as obligatory. When or how does a non-binding *usage* become binding? General acceptance by everybody whom the usage affects (the Queen, Ministers, members of Parliament, civil servants or judges) and by authorities on the constitution that there is an *obligation* to continue to behave in that way is, of course, the most satisfactory answer. Such an answer is not always forthcoming. The difficulty can be illustrated by reference to two major conventions. The first is that the Queen is obliged to assent to a bill of which she personally disapproves, unless presumably she is advised by the Cabinet to withhold her assent. The last time the royal assent was refused was in 1708: Queen Anne was not prepared to agree to the creation of a Scottish Militia. But a century later it was still thought imprudent to support bills for the removal of the disabilities attaching to Roman Catholics, on account of George III's personal objections. In 1829 George IV grudgingly gave his assent to such a bill; this can be regarded as an unequivocal normative (or rule-constitutive) precedent, the balance of the constitution having shifted away from independent royal discretion; but in the years between, who can say when usage had hardened into convention? Secondly, it is a convention that the Prime Minister should be chosen from the House of Commons (or from among persons elected to the House if a change of Prime Minister becomes necessary as a result of a General Election). The last Prime Minister to sit in the Lords was Lord Salisbury in 1902. In 1911 the powers of the Lords in money matters were reduced to vanishing point and their right to reject other Commons' bills was confined to a suspensory veto. It was, therefore, arguable that thereafter the Prime Minister had to be chosen from the ranks of the Commons. The question did not arise till 1923, because the most suitable candidates

56. *The Concept of Law*, ch. 5. Hart does not himself characterize conventions in this manner. For him, a system of 'primary rules' unaccompanied by the 'secondary rules' referred to above is exemplified (p. 89) by the customary law of some simple (or primitive) societies.

57. See Sir Kenneth Wheare, *Modern Constitutions* (2nd edn), ch. 8. cf. Marshall and Moodie, op. cit., pp. 26–31.

58. See, for example, the discussion of the conventions on ministerial responsibility (pp. 168–77).

were all members of the Commons. But in that year a vacancy arose because of Bonar Law's resignation on grounds of grave ill-health; the most eligible candidate appeared to be Lord Curzon, but Stanley Baldwin was appointed by the King instead, ostensibly on the ground that since the Labour Party, which was by then the main Opposition party, was almost unrepresented in the Lords, the office ought to go to a commoner.[59] This appeared to be a normative precedent: the King had passed over Curzon because he thought he was *obliged* to do so, and there were good reasons for his choice. If the King had not thought himself obliged so to act – if, for example, he was influenced in his choice of Baldwin by his awareness of Curzon's unpopularity among sections of the Conservative Party,[60] or if a memorandum of advice, heavily emphasizing the unsuitability of Curzon, was thought by the King to be an accurate statement of Bonar Law's views, although the memorandum was in fact composed by another and had put the case far more strongly than Bonar Law would ever have put it[61] – this could still have been cited as a persuasive precedent for the existence of such a convention, given the shift in the balance of the constitution since 1902. But there would have been more room for argument; for the establishment of a new convention would then have to be inferred mainly from propositions about what was necessary for the proper working of the constitution.[62]

2. What if there is substantial disagreement as to the existence or content of a convention? In 1940 both George VI and Neville Chamberlain would

59. See Sir Harold Nicolson, *King George V*, pp. 375–9.

60. As L. S. Amery indicated in his *Thoughts on the Constitution* (2nd edn), pp. 21–2. See also Kenneth Rose, *Superior Person* (1969).

61. See Robert Blake, *The Unknown Prime Minister*, pp. 517–27; Thomas Jones, *Whitehall Diary*, vol. 1, pp. 235–6. See further, on this difficult issue, Robert Rhodes James, *Memoirs of a Conservative* (1969), pp. 150–66; Keith Middlemas and John Barnes, *Baldwin* (1969), pp. 158–69. Probably the truth of the matter will never be known; there are discrepancies in the accounts revealed. Bonar Law did not wish to be and was not consulted. Balfour, whom the King consulted, advised against appointing Curzon. See Kenneth Rose, op. cit., pp. 381–5. J. C. C. Davidson, an influential Conservative backbencher, who wrote, but did not sign, the memorandum, and Colonel Waterhouse, Bonar Law's private secretary, who conveyed it to Lord Stamfordham, the King's private secretary, were markedly hostile to Curzon. Whether a misunderstanding occurred, or whether there was any misrepresentation as to the source of the views expressed in the memorandum, is not entirely clear. Perhaps that incident was unimportant. Lord Salisbury, a Conservative elder statesman, recommended Curzon. Middlemas and Barnes (op. cit., p. 165) assert that Stamfordham himself then 'telephoned to the King and strongly recommended him to send for Curzon'. Possibly Balfour's was the decisive voice. He disliked Curzon but apparently put the case against him to the King solely on the grounds of his peerage. The King made up his mind the same day to send for Baldwin.

62. See further Marshall and Moodie, op. cit., pp. 30–34.

have preferred Lord Halifax to Winston Churchill as Chamberlain's successor. Here it is possible to assert that they were mistaken in thinking that such an appointment would have been constitutionally proper, even if Churchill had been compliant – and fortunately he was not. But if such a view could be seriously entertained on a point which by that time was clearly covered by convention, one must accept that divided counsel may be heard on a great many other, more controversial issues; and that personal inclination and political expediency may well be determining factors. Academic authorities on the constitution enjoy no immunity from partisan sentiment; in the Irish home rule crisis in 1913 both Dicey and Anson, active opponents of the Liberal Government, expressed manifestly unacceptable views on the conventional powers of the King to override his Ministers.[63] And even when an authority on the constitution is able to adopt a more detached attitude, the materials available to him about the precedents may be inadequate – political and royal biographies are the best sources but are not always timely or comprehensive – and opinions on what rules are necessary for the working of the contemporary constitution can reasonably differ. Differences of opinion among practising politicians as to the scope and very existence of the conventions they ought to observe are, of course, both frequent and unreasonable.

3. A convention can be created without any background of pre-existing usage. It can come into being (a) by express agreement, or (b) by a unilateral undertaking, or (c) within a limited field, by a decision imposed by the Prime Minister or adopted by the Cabinet for its own regulation. For example, (a) it was agreed at an Imperial Conference in 1930 that in future the Governor-General of a Dominion should be appointed by the Crown exclusively on the advice of the Dominion Government concerned and that the United Kingdom Government would not even have a formal part to play in such an appointment. (b) In 1949, when Eire left the Commonwealth and became the Republic of Ireland, the United Kingdom Government and Parliament undertook not to exclude Northern Ireland from the United Kingdom without the consent of the Northern Ireland Parliament. (c) In April 1968 Mr Harold Wilson appointed a Parliamentary Committee of the Cabinet, endowing it with very extensive authority, and delegated wider executive powers to existing Cabinet committees. These changes were designed mainly to streamline decision-making by restricting the range of matters which individual Ministers could bring before the full Cabinet. Ministers were obliged to accept the new procedures if they wished to remain in the Government. It seems reasonable to regard them as temporary constitutional conventions.

63. See Jennings, *Cabinet Government* (3rd edn), Appendix 3.

4. Conventions may lose their binding force or change in content. So, of course, may rules of strict law. But conventions tend to change in different, and sometimes mysterious, ways.

A convention established by express agreement may be superseded or modified by agreement. Constitutional conventions share this characteristic with conventional rules of international law. For example, the convention relating to the appointment of Governors-General of Dominions on local advice was understood to extend, by necessary implication, to the removal of Governors-General, and to the appointment and removal of Governors-General of newly independent Commonwealth countries; but at the Mauritius Constitutional Conference in 1965 it was agreed that when Mauritius became independent, the Government of Mauritius would not advise Her Majesty to remove the Governor-General (in whom the constitution would repose a number of unusual and important personal discretionary powers) except on grounds of medical incapacity upon the report of an independent tribunal appointed by the Chief Justice.[64] In this instance the general convention remained, subject to an exception.

Again, decisions by the Prime Minister or the Cabinet about the manner in which the Cabinet is to operate may be superseded by new decisions. But perhaps conventions of this sort ought to be put into a special category in that (like some of the sessional orders of the House of Commons) they are understood to be experimental, though undoubtedly binding until they are altered or discarded in the accepted manner. Judicial precedents are also binding till they are authoritatively reversed, overruled or disapproved. We do not regard them as non-binding merely because their authority may be ephemeral, unless it is clear that they are based on a wrong principle.

A convention may, alternatively, lose binding force because of a major change in circumstances. In 1961 the United Kingdom Government agreed that it would be contrary to convention for Parliament to legislate for Southern Rhodesia on any matter within the competence of the Southern Rhodesian Legislature without the consent of the Southern Rhodesian Government.[65] In 1965 the Government of Southern Rhodesia made a unilateral (and unlawful) declaration of the colony's independence. The United Kingdom Parliament immediately reasserted plenary legislative authority in relation to Southern Rhodesia.[66] This could not reasonably be construed as a breach of convention; the survival of the convention presupposed the continuance of a constitutional relationship which the

64. Cmnd 2797 (1965), p. 8. This convention was not written into the constitution.
65. Cmnd 1399 (1961), p. 3.
66. Southern Rhodesia Act 1965; see also the Southern Rhodesia Constitution Order 1965 (S.I. 1965, No. 1952). For Northern Ireland (p. 60), see Addendum.

Government of Southern Rhodesia had repudiated.[67] Problems of interpretation may arise where changes in circumstances are less dramatic. For example, on Harold Macmillan's resignation from the office of Prime Minister on grounds of ill-health in 1963, the Queen invited Lord Home to form a Government as his successor. Home was known to be the most acceptable candidate to the Conservative Party; but what of the convention that the Prime Minister could not be a member of the Lords?[68] A few months previously, Parliament had passed an Act under which it had become possible for Lord Home to disclaim his hereditary peerage.[69] He promptly disclaimed it, became Sir Alec Douglas-Home, and obtained a seat in the Commons at a by-election shortly afterwards. Presumably this change in the law was understood to have modified the convention to the extent that a peer could become Prime Minister if he agreed to disclaim his title and to try to obtain a seat in the Commons forthwith. If at the time of Home's appointment no such undertaking was offered or extracted, his appointment would probably have been unconstitutional.

Conventions have also disappeared or been varied because they have been disregarded with impunity and with general acquiescence. In this respect they differ from all rules of strict law in this country except local or mercantile customary rules. For example, before 1918 the decision when to advise the monarch to dissolve Parliament had been taken by the Cabinet as a whole. In November 1918 Lloyd George decided to advise a dissolution on his own initiative. Cabinet colleagues not merely acquiesced in this step but erroneously justified it by reference to nonexistent precedents.[70] Thus arose the modern convention that the decision to advise a dissolution was for the Prime Minister alone, though it was still open to the Prime Minister to discuss the matter with his colleagues, privately or in a Cabinet meeting. Doubtless all conventions are binding, but some are more binding than others. (The obvious retort is that the conventions about advice to dissolve Parliament are of major importance.) The disappearance of a convention in these circumstances might alternatively be rationalized on the ground that it had atrophied unobserved, or had dwindled to the status of a non-binding usage, compliance or deviation being equally permissible. Whether a convention retains its binding force, and if so,

67. cf. de Smith, op. cit., p. 42. See also note 31.

68. See pp. 58–60, 155–8.

69. Peerage Act 1963, passed in consequence of the campaign waged by Lord Stansgate (Anthony Wedgwood Benn). All peers by inheritance could disclaim within a year after the Act became law; thereafter only *new* peers by inheritance (or peers who had inherited subject to infancy or another disability) could disclaim (s. 1). See further p. 300.

70. Jennings, *Cabinet Government* (3rd edn), pp. 417–19.

how much, is often demonstrable only by the empirical test of 'break it and see'. The outcome of such an experiment may still be equivocal; breach may be represented, or interpreted after the event, as a mere *ad hoc* waiver;[71] allegations of unconstitutional behaviour are frequently made in the cut and thrust of day-to-day politics and are as often shrugged off, sometimes on the spurious ground that no binding convention on the matter had ever existed;[72] adverse pronouncements by constitutional experts and editorial writers in the better informed daily and weekly journals are not endowed with the aura of prestige that surrounds the judgments of the superior courts.

We arrive at a position where there is a clear case for differentiating some conventions from most rules of strict law. When there are serious doubts as to the scope, even the very existence, of a conventional rule, and no adequate means of allaying those doubts, one cannot expect to find a widespread sense of obligation to obey that rule. Appeals to the voices of authority may evoke a Tower of Babel or the inscrutable muteness of the sphinx. Appeals to precedent may be less convincing than appeals to principle. Perhaps the most persuasive summing up is that 'the crucial questions must always be whether or not a particular class of action is likely to destroy respect for the established distribution of authority and whether or not it is likely to maintain respect for the constitutional system by changing (or sustaining) the distribution of authority'.[73] This distribution of authority implies the maintenance of limited monarchy, representative government, responsible government and efficient government; it implies also that constitutional rules must be compatible with the realities of practical politics. Given the vagueness of these criteria, it is not surprising that no attempt to list the conventions of the constitution in 1973 would command universal assent. If half a dozen constitutional lawyers were separately to set down the conventions governing collective ministerial responsibility, it would be astonishing if six identical sets of answers were to be produced.

71. Thus, the convention of collective ministerial responsibility, in so far as it required Ministers not to disagree with Cabinet decisions in public, was expressly waived by the so-called National Government in 1932 to enable Ministers opposed to the Government's protectionist policies to express their dissent. After a few months the convention was restored, the dissenting Ministers having either resigned or changed their minds. See E. C. S. Wade, Introduction to the 10th edn of Dicey, op. cit., pp. clxxxix–cxc.

72. cf. Dicey, op. cit., p. 441. This is the main single reason why identification of conventions is so difficult. People who ought to be *obeying* conventions deny their existence or unmake them by their disobedience.

73. Marshall and Moodie, op. cit., p. 32. See also Jennings, *Cabinet Government* (3rd edn), ch. 1.

Replacement of conventions by statutory rules: a footnote

We have noted that many conventions could be codified in a statutory or non-statutory form; and that Commonwealth constitutions often include provisions on matters which in this country are regulated solely by convention.[74] We also observed that a loose convention about legislative relations between the Lords and the Commons was replaced in 1911 by a precise set of statutory rules. Writers occasionally mis-state the effect of the Parliament Act by describing it as an enactment of constitutional conventions. On the contrary, it was a partial *supersession* of constitutional conventions by rules of strict law. The other favourite example of the 'enactment' of constitutional conventions is the Statute of Westminster 1931. What this Act did was

1. to recite, in the *preamble*, certain conventions about Dominion status;

2. to relieve the Dominions of legal incapacities attributable to the fact that, before the Statute, they were colonies in strict law; and

3. to provide, in section 4 of the Statute, that no future Act of the United Kingdom Parliament was to extend, or be deemed to extend, to a Dominion as part of its law unless the request and consent of that Dominion were *expressly declared* in such an Act.

The exact legal effect of section 4 is still disputable.[75] But alone among the sections of the Statute of Westminster can it be compared to the enactment of a convention. The corresponding *convention* was set out in the preamble. It records 'the established constitutional position' that no law made by the United Kingdom Parliament 'shall extend to a Dominion as part of its law otherwise than at the request and with the consent of that Dominion'. Even section 4, therefore, does not precisely reproduce constitutional convention; it embodies the substance of the convention but adds something to it.

74. The constitutions of the 'older' Commonwealth countries include rules about financial legislation and parliamentary proceedings which in Britain are regulated by convention or the standing orders of the two Houses of Parliament.
75. See pp. 76–7.

Chapter 3
Ultimate Authority
in Constitutional Law

Parliamentary sovereignty

The Queen in Parliament is competent, according to United Kingdom law, to make or unmake any law whatsoever on any matter whatsoever; and no United Kingdom court is competent to question the validity of an Act of Parliament. Every other law-making body within the realm either derives its authority from Parliament or exercises it at the sufferance of Parliament; it cannot be superior to or even coordinate with, but must be subordinate to Parliament. So has run the most fundamental rule, the 'very keystone', as Dicey put it, of constitutional law in this country.[1] It is usually called the concept of parliamentary sovereignty. In this chapter we shall have to consider how far this doctrine is affected by the United Kingdom's accession to the European Communities. For the moment, let us assume that it remains intact.

Some writers dislike the term parliamentary 'sovereignty', and prefer to use the word 'supremacy'. 'Sovereign' and 'sovereignty' are words of many meanings.[2] We sometimes speak of the Queen as the Sovereign without attributing to her unlimited authority. We speak of sovereignty in international law when we mean independence, or freedom from external control; in this sense Australia is a sovereign State, but it does not have a 'sovereign' Parliament, because the powers of that Parliament are subject to the constitution. Is the constitution, then, 'sovereign' in Australia? To John Austin, the best-known British writer on sovereignty,[3] every developed State had to have a 'sovereign', who made laws in the form of commands which were habitually obeyed, and whose legal authority was absolute, indivisible and illimitable. Obviously the location of sovereignty within a federal constitutional system is, by this token, an unrewarding pursuit.[4] Others have defined the concept of sovereignty in different ways at different periods and in different contexts. Dicey, for instance, referred

---

1. *Introduction to the Study of the Law of the Constitution* (10th edn), p. 70.
2. See F. H. Hinsley, *Sovereignty*.
3. *The Province of Jurisprudence Determined*.
4. For a subtle analysis, see Geoffrey Sawer, *Modern Federalism*, ch. 7.

to the Queen in Parliament as the legal sovereign and the electorate as the political sovereign.[5] Clearly the concepts of national sovereignty, parliamentary sovereignty and popular sovereignty have little in common with one another.[6] Hence there is a case for jettisoning the word 'sovereignty' altogether as being too ambiguous. But to discard the term in favour of the doctrine of 'supremacy' of Parliament is not particularly helpful, if only because the latter term conveys the suggestion that the House of Commons, or the Lords and Commons, as a matter of political or sociological fact, are supreme within the State; and manifestly they are not. And so we shall use the phrase 'parliamentary sovereignty', but to denote a legal concept or group of concepts which do not necessarily carry any implication about the effective seat of political power within the State.

How and when was this principle of the unlimited legislative competence of Parliament established? Was it established by Parliament itself; or by the courts; or by whom? And whence was derived the authority to lay down such a principle? Such questions about the ultimate foundations of constitutional law are not peculiar to the United Kingdom. They arise in countries where the central legislature lacks an unbounded sweep of legislative competence. What are the sources of authority for the validity of the supreme constitutions in those countries?

Foundations of the constitutional order

A written constitution is regarded as the primary source of legal authority within a State. In it lies the explanation of the Legislature's power to make laws, the Executive's power to govern and administer, the Judiciary's power to adjudicate. But if we take one step farther, what is it that confers this legitimating quality on the constitution? This question produces some convoluted answers.

Take the constitution of the Commonwealth of Australia. Here the answer seems fairly simple. The constitution is valid because it was duly enacted by the United Kingdom Parliament, which had power to enact it. Subsequent amendments to the constitution are valid because they have been made in the manner and form prescribed by the constitution. In other words, legal continuity has been preserved.

The case of Australia, however, is exceptional in the modern world. In the large majority of independent states there has been, at one time or another, a breach of legal continuity, and a constitution has been adopted or changed in a manner unauthorized by the pre-existing legal order. This

5. Dicey, op. cit., p. 73.
6. But see p. 82 on the relationship between national sovereignty and parliamentary sovereignty in the EEC context.

is already true of a high proportion of the African states which have become independent during the last decade or so. Since independence they have had revolutions and *coups d'état*; often the constitutional instrument has itself been abrogated and replaced, or suspended and modified, in a manner precluded by the independence constitution. And a few countries have deliberately chosen to adopt a new constitution peacefully but in a manner unauthorized by the pre-existing constitution. This is an assertion of legal nationalism, of what is called 'constitutional autochthony',[7] designed to demonstrate that the authority of the constitution is rooted in native soil, not derived from an imperial predecessor. Such a course has been followed in Eire (the Republic of Ireland), India and now Sri Lanka (Ceylon). A constitution is adopted by a Constituent Assembly in the name of the people, or presented to the people for their approval; it will not receive the royal assent like normal constitutional amendments.

Take again the constitution of the United States of America. Since its adoption in 1787 it has remained intact, apart from amendments duly made in terms of the constitution. But was the constitution valid in the first place, and if so, why? In 1776 the Thirteen Colonies had unlawfully declared their independence of Britain, and had repudiated the sovereignty of the United Kingdom Parliament.[8] 'We, the People of the United States', proceeded to 'ordain and establish a constitution'. In fact it was formulated at a convention consisting of delegates from the several states and then ratified by the Congress. The name of the 'sovereign' People was invoked to confer upon the constitution moral authority and binding force.

The vague concept that ultimate 'sovereignty' resides in the 'people' is widely acceptable because of its political overtones. Even where a constitution has been overturned from above or below by manifestly illegitimate means, it is commonplace for the *de facto* holders of power to assert that they derive their mandate from the people, because it is awkward to be stigmatized as an undemocratic usurper. And by producing a constitution approved by or on behalf of the people, the accolade of legitimacy is achieved. Or is it?

It is one thing to say that government should rest on the consent of the governed; it is another thing to proclaim that a constitution has acquired the force of supreme law merely because it has obtained the approval of an irregularly convened Constituent Assembly or of a majority of the electorate or both. Yet to assert that all constitutions (or constitutional

7. Wheare, *Constitutional Structure of the Commonwealth*, ch. 4.
8. The United Kingdom Government recognized the independence of the United States in 1783 , but the American Colonies Act 1766 (the Declaratory Act), reiterating the paramount sovereignty of the United Kingdom Parliament, remained on our statute book till 1964.

amendments) procured in a manner inconsistent with the pre-existing legal order are legally invalid will land one in a morass of absurd and insoluble difficulties. If the constitution of the United States is a nullity, then presumably only the United Kingdom can validate (with retroactive effect) the millions of governmental measures and judicial decisions taken in that country since independence. This is plainly ridiculous, for nobody doubts that the United States became an independent State in international law before the end of the eighteenth century. In any case, whence did the United Kingdom Parliament derive its omnicompetence? In July 1688 James II dissolved his Parliament. In December he fled the country, having dropped the Great Seal of the Realm in the Thames a few days earlier. William of Orange, having reached London, met groups of peers, former members of Parliament and other notables; they advised him that elections should be held in the boroughs and counties. The Convention of Lords and 'Commons' met in January 1689, and next month offered the Crown to William and Mary jointly, subject to conditions set out in a Declaration of Right. The offer having been accepted, the Convention passed an Act asserting that it *was* Parliament,[9] and then enacted the Bill of Rights, incorporating the Declaration of Right. Clearly the Convention 'Parliament' had been irregularly summoned; its affirmation of its own legal authority carried the matter no farther; there had been no King from December 1688 (assuming that James II was deemed to have abdicated or to have forfeited the Crown) till February 1689; William III had no hereditary legal title to the throne and therefore had no authority to assent to bills.[10] Has every purported Act of Parliament since 1688 been a nullity? Is a Stuart still the rightful King?

Once questions such as these are asked,[11] one must acknowledge that in certain circumstances a breach of legal continuity, be it peaceful or accompanied by coercion and violence, may have to be treated as superseding the constitutional and legal order and replacing it by a new one. Legal theorists have no option but to accommodate their concepts to the facts of political life. Successful revolution sooner or later begets its own legality. If, as Hans Kelsen has postulated, the basic norm or ultimate principle underlying a constitutional order is that the constitution ought to be

9. Crown and Parliament Act 1689.

10. cf. F. W. Maitland, *Constitutional History of England*, pp. 283–5; Taswell-Langmead's *English Constitutional History* (11th edn), pp. 445–59.

11. One possible answer, deducible from rationalizations of late medieval practice when usurpations of the throne were not uncommon, is that William became King *de jure* after he had dissolved the Convention 'Parliament' and the *new* Parliament of 1690 had validated the legislation passed by the Convention. As a matter of State necessity (see p. 70) a *de facto* King had been regarded as competent to summon a lawful Parliament. I am indebted to Dr F. M. Brookfield for this suggestion.

obeyed,[12] then the disappearance of that order, followed by acquiescence on the part of officials, judges and the general public in laws, rules and orders issued by the new holders of power, will displace the old basic norm or ultimate principle and give rise to a new one.[13] Thus, might becomes right in the eye of the law.

This is a persuasive rationalization of the legal consequences of a successful revolution, like the rebellion of the American colonists or the English Revolution of 1688. It does not, however, answer all questions. It offers a description, not a prescription. It does not dictate what attitude judges and officials *ought* to adopt when the purported breach of legal continuity takes place. However, in recent years judges in Pakistan,[14] Uganda[15] and Rhodesia[16] seem to have proceeded on the assumption that they have to accept a successful revolution as a law-constitutive fact if they remain in office.[17]

Here we are beginning to stray far afield. The argument can be summarized in this way: sooner or later a breach of legal continuity will be treated as laying down legitimate foundations for a new constitutional order, provided that the 'revolution' is successful; there is, however, no neat rule of thumb available to judges during or immediately after the 'revolution' for the purpose of determining whether the old order survives wholly, in part or not at all. It so happened that the Revolution of 1688 gave a clear pointer to the Judiciary. There was a suspension of business in the courts, and after the throne had become vacant new judges had to be appointed because of a 'demise of the Crown'. These appointees were not at all likely to call the validity of the regime in question.[18] After a while (at the latest, after the failure of the Jacobite revolt in 1715) it would have been merely silly for a judge or commentator to deny that the Bill of Rights 1689 and other legislation passed after the Revolution were valid. Efficacy

12. *Pure Theory of Law* (2nd edn, transl.), p. 201; *General Theory of Law and State*, p. 115.

13. *General Theory of Law and State*, p. 118. See also H. L. A. Hart, *The Concept of Law*, pp. 114–16, 118–19, for a similar but not identical formulation.

14. *The State* v. *Dosso* P.L.D. 1958 S.C. 533. But in 1972 the court held that the case had been wrongly decided: *Jilani* v. *State of Punjab* P.L.D. 1972 S.C. 139.

15. *Uganda* v. *Prison Commissioner, ex p. Matovu* [1966] E.A. 514.

16. *R.* v. *Ndhlovu* 1968 (4) S.A. 515.

17. There is now a substantial body of legal literature on the problems arising from these and similar cases. Most of the articles are referred to in Dennis Lloyd, *Introduction to Jurisprudence* (3rd edn), ch. 7; A. W. B. Simpson (ed.), *Oxford Essays in Jurisprudence* (1973), chs. 2 (Eekelaar), 3 (Finnis).

18. And in 1689 the Commons committed two former King's Bench judges, Pemberton and Jones JJ., to prison for a decision prior to the Revolution (see *Jay* v. *Topham* (1689) 12 St. Tr. 821), in which they had overruled a plea to the jurisdiction and given judgment against the Serjeant at Arms for an arrest carried out on the orders of the House. This was held to be a breach of the House's privileges.

and acquiescence had established a new basis for legality. The particular circumstances in which the Revolution of 1688 took place, and its immediate practical consequences, laid a secure foundation, moreover, for judicial acceptance of the doctrine of absolute parliamentary sovereignty. The doctrine grew out of a particular state of affairs. A fundamental change of a political nature may bring about a fundamental change in legal doctrine.

The concept of necessity

One other comment must be made. In some situations where unconstitutional action has been taken by persons wielding effective political power, it is open to a judge to steer a middle course. He may find it possible to assert that the framework of the pre-existing order still survives, but that deviations from its norms can be justified on grounds of *necessity*. The principle of necessity, rendering lawful what would otherwise be unlawful,[19] is not unknown to English law; there is a defence of necessity (albeit of uncertain scope) in criminal law,[20] and in constitutional law the application of martial law is but an extended application of this concept. But the necessity must be proportionate to the evil to be averted, and acceptance of the principle does not normally imply total abdication from judicial review or acquiescence in the supersession of the legal order; it is essentially a transient phenomenon. State necessity has been judicially accepted in recent years as a legal justification for ostensibly unconstitutional action to fill a vacuum arising within the constitutional order in Pakistan,[21] Cyprus,[22] Rhodesia[23] and Nigeria.[24] To this extent it has been

19. See generally Glanville Williams (1953) 6 *Current Legal Problems* 216.

20. cf. J. C. Smith and Brian Hogan, *Criminal Law* (3rd edn), pp. 157–64; P. R. Glazebrook [1972 A] *Camb. L.J.* 87.

21. *Special Reference No. 1 of 1955* [1955] 1 F.C.R. 439; Sir Ivor Jennings, *Constitutional Problems in Pakistan*. For a somewhat different approach to this principle, see *Jilani's* case (note 14, above).

22. *Att.-Gen. of the Republic* v. *Mustafa Ibrahim* (1964) Cyprus Law Reports 195; de Smith in *Annual Survey of Commonwealth Law 1965* (ed. Wade), pp. 3, 76–8.

23. *Madzimbamuto* v. *Lardner-Burke* 1968 (2) S.A. 284, a decision of the Rhodesian Appellate Division given before the court was prepared to recognize the success of the rebellion as fully legitimating the *de facto* Government; cf. note 16 above. On appeal the Privy Council (Lord Pearce dissenting) rejected the principle of necessity as applied by the Rhodesian judges [1969] 1 A.C. 645. However, it should not be inferred that the principle has no application at all in constitutional jurisprudence. Notwithstanding Lord Camden C.J.'s famous dictum in *Entick* v. *Carrington* (1765) 19 St. Tr. 1030 at 1073, that 'with respect to the argument of State necessity . . . the common law does not understand that kind of reasoning', such a principle was applied a few years later by Lord Mansfield in *R.* v. *Stratton* (1779) 21 St. Tr. 1045 at 1224; see also *Sabally and N'Jie* v. *Att.-Gen.* [1965] 1 Q.B. 273 at 293, *per* Lord Denning M.R.

24. *Lakanmi and Ola* v. *Att.-Gen.* (*West*), 24 April 1970, where the Supreme Court of

recognized as an implied exception to the letter of the constitution. And perhaps it can be stretched far enough to bridge the gap between the old legal order and its successor.[25]

Parliamentary sovereignty surveyed

In its early days Parliament was a judicial as well as a law-making body. It was the High Court of Parliament, supreme over other courts. But it did not follow that its law-making competence was unlimited or unrivalled.

In the first place, the supremacy of the Crown in Parliament was rivalled by the Crown acting outside Parliament. The Crown claimed and exercised an autonomous prerogative power to make laws by ordinance or proclamation. Not until James I's time do we find an unequivocal pronouncement by the courts that the King could not change the general law of the land by virtue of the prerogative.[26] The King, moreover, claimed power to impose taxation incidentally to the exercise of prerogative powers (such as the power to regulate foreign affairs including external trade, and the power to take emergency measures for the defence of the realm) recognized as being vested in him; and in two great constitutional cases of the seventeenth century, the *Case of Impositions* (1606)[27] and the *Case of Ship Money* (1637)[28] – the latter decided after the *Case of Proclamations* – the courts upheld the validity of this ancillary taxing power. But the Bill of Rights 1689 laid it down that the raising of money for the use of the Crown by pretence of prerogative was unlawful. Again, the Crown had claimed – and the courts upheld the claim within certain limits in cases decided in 1674[29] and 1686[30] – a prerogative power to dispense with the operation of a statute for the benefit of an individual; but the Bill of Rights declared that in future dispensations would be invalid. The Bill of Rights also declared that the 'pretended power of suspending of laws' by prerogative was unlawful; this was a reference to James II's disastrous attempt to

---

Nigeria, rejecting the Government's arguments, held that the military take-over in January 1966 had been a manifestation of necessity, not a revolutionary breach of legal continuity; and that fundamental rights under the pre-existing constitution were still in force save in so far as they were modified by the operation of necessity. This analysis of the facts may be regarded as courageous but far-fetched.

25. See, for example, note 11. Necessity here becomes a 'supra-constitutional' principle.

26. *Case of Proclamations* (1611) 12 Co. Rep. 74. This is perhaps the leading case in English constitutional law.

27. *Bate's Case* (1606) 2 St. Tr. 371.

28. *R.* v. *Hampden* (1637) 3 St. Tr. 825.

29. *Thomas* v. *Sorrell* (1674) Vaughan 330.

30. *Godden* v. *Hales* (1686) 11 St. Tr. 1165.

enforce the suspension of the statutes which discriminated against Dissenters and Roman Catholics[31] – a premature experiment in religious toleration, albeit toleration with an ulterior motive, which precipitated a Glorious Revolution against royal tyranny. Thus did Parliament effectively dispose of the pretensions of the Crown to rival or subordinate its authority.

Since the Bill of Rights also changed the succession to the throne, so that title to the Crown was itself dependent on parliamentary authority, it would have been very difficult thereafter to contend that there were legal bounds to the powers of Parliament. Earlier in the seventeenth century there had been no dearth of juristic pronouncements on the limitations on Parliament's competence, though they jostled with others proclaiming the transcendent and absolute authority of Parliament.[32] In James I's time there were dicta to the effect that Acts of Parliament contrary to common right and reason,[33] or making a man a judge in his own cause,[34] were void. That there were prerogatives inseparable from the King's person, so that no Act of Parliament could deprive him of them, was generally conceded;[35] but one of those 'inseparable' prerogatives was the dispensing power. After the Revolution of 1688 and the Bill of Rights – the product of an alliance between parliamentarians and common lawyers – these were but empty phrases. Faintly re-echoed by the words of Blackstone in 1765, paying lip-service to the primacy of natural law,[36] they had long since ceased to have legal significance; for the judges had tacitly accepted a rule of obligation to give effect to every Act of Parliament, no matter how preposterous its content.

The omnicompetence of Parliament, at least in respect of persons, matters and territory under the jurisdiction of the Crown, in the eyes of the courts can be supported by numerous dicta and some decisions squarely in point, and is illustrated by legislative practice. Attempts to impugn the validity of Acts of Parliament because of inconsistency with rules of inter-

31. See *Trial of the Seven Bishops* (1688) 12 St. Tr. 183.

32. Dicta, extra-judicial and other, are collected together and discussed in Geoffrey Marshall's *Parliamentary Sovereignty and the Commonwealth*, ch. 5.

33. *Dr Bonham*'s case (1610) 8 Co. Rep. 114 at 118, *per* Coke C. J. Contrast Coke's extra-judicial comment in vol. 4 of his *Institutes*, p. 36: 'of the power and jurisdiction of Parliament, for making of laws in proceedings by Bill, it is so transcendent and absolute, as it cannot be confined either for causes or persons within any bounds.'

34. *Day* v. *Savadge* (1614) Hob. 85 at 86, 87, *per* Hobart C. J.; see also the surprising dicta by Holt C. J., in *City of London* v. *Wood* (1701) 12 Mod. 669 at 686–8. The modern view of Parliament's authority to make a man a judge in his own cause is stated by Willes J., in *Lee* v. *Bude and Torrington Junction Rly* (1871) L.R. 6 C.P. 576 at 582.

35. D. L. Keir and F. H. Lawson, *Cases in Constitutional Law* (5th edn), pp. 77, 78, 87, 93, 96.

36. *Commentaries*, i, p. 41 (laws are invalid if contrary to the law of nature). Blackstone's words were taken seriously in the North American colonies.

national law have been rejected.[37] When a taxpayer challenged the validity of assessments made under a Finance Act on the ground that they were directed partly to an unlawful purpose (the manufacture of nuclear weapons with a view to their possible use) it was held that even if such a purpose were contrary to international law:

What the statute itself enacts cannot be unlawful, because (it) is the highest form of law that is known to this country. It is the law which prevails over every other form of law, and it is not for the court to say that a parliamentary enactment . . . is illegal.[38]

Parliament has in fact passed retroactive penal legislation,[39] prolonged its own existence, transformed itself into a new body by the Acts of Union with Scotland and Ireland, repealed and amended provisions of those Acts which were to have permanent effect,[40] altered the procedure for making laws (under the Parliament Acts) and followed the new procedure, and changed the succession to the throne (by the Bill of Rights, the Act of Settlement 1701, and His Majesty's Declaration of Abdication Act 1936). The courts will endeavour to construe Acts of Parliament so as to avoid a preposterous result, but if a statute clearly evinces an intention to achieve the preposterous, the courts are under an obligation to give effect to its plain words.[41] The safeguards against the enactment of such legislation are political and conventional, not strictly legal.

37. See, for example, *Mortensen v. Peters* 1906 14 S.L.T. 227; *Cheney* v. *Conn* [1968] 1 W.L.R. 242. Similarly, the Crown in the exercise of its prerogative power to delimit the extent of territorial waters is not bound by international law: *Post Office* v. *Estuary Radio Ltd* [1968] 2 Q.B. 740 at 757. But there is a rebuttable presumption that neither Parliament nor the Crown intended to violate a treaty or other rule of international law (ibid.). See also p. 134.

38. *Cheney* v. *Conn* [1968] 1 W.L.R. 242 at 247, *per* Ungoed-Thomas J. See also *R.* v. *Jordan* [1967] *Crim. L. Rev.* 483 (an unsuccessful attack by Colin Jordan on the constitutional validity of the Race Relations Act 1965); *Madzimbamuto* v. *Lardner-Burke* [1969] 1 A.C. 645 at 723; *Blackburn* v. *Att.-Gen.* [1971] 1 W.L.R. 1037 at 1041, *per* Salmon L.J.

39. An Act of 1541 enabled Lady Rocheford, an accessory to Catherine Howard's adultery, to be tried and executed for treason although she had become insane after arrest: Nigel Walker, *Crime and Insanity in England*, pp. 183–4.

40. An attempt to impugn the Irish Church Act 1869, which had changed an unalterable provision of the Act of Union with Ireland by disestablishing the Church of Ireland, failed in *Ex p. Canon Selwyn* (1872) 36 J.P. 54. This decision is criticized, on the ground that the Act of Union with Ireland was a constituent Act, limiting the competence of the United Kingdom Parliament, by Harry Calvert, *Constitutional Law in Northern Ireland*, pp. 27–33. cf. J. D. B. Mitchell, *Constitutional Law* (2nd edn), pp. 69–74.

41. See, however, the anomalous decision in *Green* v. *Mortimer* (1861) 3 L.T. 642 (private Act of Parliament treated as void because the court thought its provisions were absurd).

Possible legal limitations on parliamentary sovereignty
Acts of Union

It can reasonably be argued that the Acts of Union with Scotland and Ireland were constituent Acts, establishing a new United Kingdom Parliament and setting limits to its powers.[42] The case for still regarding the Act of Union with Ireland 1800 in this light has been undermined by a series of basic legislative changes.[43] The case for so regarding the Acts of Union with Scotland 1707 is not so weak. Much water has indeed flowed under the bridges since that time, but the position of the Established Church in Scotland and the Scottish system of judicature, entrenched as fundamental and unalterable in the Articles of Union, remains largely intact.[44] Although the immunity of the surviving fundamental principles of the Union from legislative encroachment by the United Kingdom Parliament without Scottish consent[45] is probably to be regarded now as a matter of convention rather than of strict law, one cannot be certain that Scottish courts would take this view. In *MacCormick* v. *Lord Advocate* (1953) Lord Cooper was of the opinion that violation of fundamental terms of the Union would be unlawful, but non-justiciable in a United Kingdom court.[46] No Scottish court has held a public Act of Parliament to be void since the Union. But if the Court of Appeal in England can suggest in 1972 that a court *may* have jurisdiction to hold a private Act of Parliament void for fraudulent misrepresentations to Parliament[47] – a jurisdiction not exercised in England since 1790[48] – can one say with complete assurance that it is too late for Scottish courts to take a bold and unprecedented initiative?[49]

Substantive content of legislation: the general rule

Parliament can undoubtedly delegate its powers, setting limits to the authority of the delegate and retaining power to revoke the grant and a

42. See p. 28, above.

43. cf. note 40; the biggest changes up to 1973 were the establishment of the Irish Free State (now the Republic of Ireland) and a subordinate Northern Ireland Parliament (prorogued and suspended by the United Kingdom Parliament in 1972). Moreover, at the time of the Union, Ireland was not unambiguously an independent State.

44. Subject to minor but significant exceptions. See the Universities (Scotland) Acts 1853 and 1932.

45. But how is Scottish consent to be signified? Through the M.P.s for Scottish constituencies and the Scottish peers at Westminster? Through an *ad hoc* constituent body?

46. 1963 S.C. 396 at 411–13. See also D. N. MacCormick [1972] *Public Law* 176–9; T. B. Smith [1957] *Public Law* 99.

47. *Pickin* v. *British Railways Board* [1972] 3 W.L.R. 824.

48. *Biddulph* v. *Biddulph*, cited in *Pickin's* case at 832.

49. See generally Mitchell, op. cit., pp. 69–74.

concurrent power to legislate. But can it effectively *deprive* itself of power to legislate on any matter or otherwise predetermine the future content of its own legislation? There is authority for the proposition that it cannot. An Act of 1919 laid down a scale of compensation for owners of compulsorily acquired slum property, and it stated that 'so far as inconsistent with that Act [other statutory] . . . provisions shall not have effect'. These provisions were held to have been impliedly repealed to the extent that they were inconsistent with other provisions in an Act of 1925, even if they were intended (which was doubtful) to have permanent effect.[50]

If there is a general rule that Parliament can do anything except bind its own future action, this may be regarded either as a limitation of parliamentary sovereignty or as a necessary characteristic of that sovereignty, since sovereignty inheres in Parliament as a continuing representative institution and not in one Parliament at a given moment of time. There is another, more mundane, explanation of the rule, divorced from ideas about sovereignty: public policy requires that no legislative body be competent to frustrate its primary purpose by creating a vacuum save where expressly authorized to do so – for example, by a written constitution. Put in this form, the principle applies to non-sovereign legislatures. Local authorities are incompetent to disable themselves from making a by-law on any matter within their allotted field.[51] And if this is an important factor sustaining the rule, then there remains the possibility that parliamentary omnicompetence can be restricted where the imposition of a fetter is consonant with the proper functions of Parliament.

Territorial competence

The orthodox view is that Parliament is competent to make any law whatsoever for any part of the world whatsoever, and that United Kingdom courts are under an obligation to give effect to any such law. Courts in territories subordinate to the United Kingdom are under a like obligation, but not courts in foreign countries.[52] The obligation of courts in independent Commonwealth countries is debatable.[53]

Now, it is quite clear that Parliament can attribute legal consequences

50. *Vauxhall Estates Ltd* v. *Liverpool Corporation* [1932] 1 K.B. 733; *Ellen Street Estates Ltd* [1934] 1 K.B. 590.

51. See, for example, *Cory (William) & Son Ltd* v. *City of London Corporation* [1951] 2 K.B. 475.

52. Or, possibly, a court in a British protected state (which is not part of Her Majesty's dominions) where the Crown has only limited jurisdiction, in respect of an Act of Parliament going beyond the Crown's jurisdiction: Sir Kenneth Roberts-Wray, *Commonwealth and Colonial Law*, 139–41.

53. See pp. 76–8.

in United Kingdom law to acts done by aliens in foreign countries. It did so recently by the Hijacking Act 1971.[54] And it could presumably make it an offence in United Kingdom law for a Frenchman to smoke in the streets of Paris.[55] But it is at least doubtful whether, even in terms of United Kingdom law, it has an unlimited competence to change the laws of independent countries. Since it would not, in practice, assert such authority,[56] the question is unlikely to arise before a United Kingdom court. However, untested assertions about Parliament's omnicompetence are an inadequate basis for ascribing to Parliament powers inconsistent with international comity and common sense.

Total or partial abdication by Parliament

If the United Kingdom Parliament were to proceed to liquidate itself by passing an Act transferring its functions to a new supranational European body or distributing those functions among (say) new Parliaments for England, Scotland, Wales and Northern Ireland, it would be absurd to suggest that a notional United Kingdom Parliament still existed and that it could resume its identity at any time and continue to exercise sovereign authority. Because this would be absurd, Parliament must be accepted as having the power to abdicate by extinguishing itself, thus 'committing suicide'. But what if Parliament continued to exist but purported to give away *part* of its sovereignty to another country or to new legislatures within the United Kingdom or to a supranational body?[57] Would this not be as ineffectual as an attempt by Parliament to preclude itself from repealing or amending a Licensing Act? We shall consider this in three contexts: (1) Commonwealth affairs; (2) adoption of a written constitution; and (3) accession to the European Communities.

1–Independence in the Commonwealth

The most familiar, but not the most illuminating, questions turn on the legal effect of section 4 of the Statute of Westminster 1931,[58] ostensibly

54. See also *Joyce* v. *D.P.P.* [1946] A.C. 337; Statute of Treasons 1351 (treason can be committed by alien in foreign country).

55. Jennings, *The Law and the Constitution* (5th edn), pp. 170–71.

56. Unless one takes the view that on or soon after UDI, Southern Rhodesia acquired the attributes of independent statehood; cf. Southern Rhodesia Act 1965; Southern Rhodesia Constitution Order 1965 (S.I. 1965, No. 1952); *Madzimbamuto* v. *Lardner-Burke* [1969] 1 A.C. 645; cf. *R.* v. *Ndhlovu* 1968 (4) S.A. 515. For the peculiar position of the Australian states, see ch. 30.

57. cf. the controversy over the Irish Home Rule Bill in 1886: Marshall, op. cit., pp. 63–7; Anson (1886) 2 L.Q.R. 427,

58. See p. 64, and see also ch. 30 with particular reference to the states of Australia.

precluding Parliament from legislating for a Dominion unless the Act in question recited the Dominion's request and consent. Section 4 might be interpreted as (a) laying down a rule for the construction of statutes but (b) not imposing a fetter on the omnicompetence of Parliament because (i) it merely prescribed the insertion of a particular form of words in an Act, and Parliament could not effectively bind itself in this way[59] and (ii) in any event the power of Parliament to make any law whatsoever for any place whatsoever could not be surrendered. On this last point, we have a Privy Council dictum in a Canadian appeal supporting the view stated above;[60] an equivocal decision of the High Court of Australia;[61] and dicta in a Privy Council appeal from Ceylon,[62] and in South African cases decided while that country was still in the Commonwealth,[63] supporting a more radical interpretation – that such a provision was a renunciation of Parliament's plenary authority to make laws for those countries otherwise than in accordance with the requirement laid down by Parliament. ('Freedom once conferred cannot be revoked.')[64] There is also an intermediate position: that United Kingdom courts would be obliged to give effect to Acts plainly intended to alter the law in Commonwealth countries despite non-compliance with the statutory conditions, but that the *local* courts, and on appeal the Privy Council (applying local law), would be entitled, or even obliged, *not* to apply such an Act.

59. cf. Maugham L.J. in *Ellen Street Estates Ltd* v. *Minister of Health* [1934] 1 K.B. at 597: Parliament 'cannot bind itself as to the form of subsequent legislation'. It is hard to know how much should be read into this dictum, since the question was whether Parliament could effectively prescribe that a statute should be repealable or alterable only by *express* words; held, it could not, even if had purported to do so, which was doubtful,

60. *British Coal Corporation* v. *R.* [1935] A.C. 500 at 520 ('the Imperial Parliament could, as a matter of abstract law, repeal or disregard s. 4 of the Statute').

61. *Copyright Owners Reproduction Society* v. *E.M.I.* (*Australia*) *Pty Ltd* (1958) 100 C.L.R. 597. The decision (see p. 50, note 38) did not give a clear indication of what the attitude of Australian courts should be if a United Kingdom statute were now unambiguously to purport to change the law of Australia without reciting the necessary request and consent of the Commonwealth of Australia. cf. Peter J. Hanks in (1968) 42 A.L.J. 286. In a limited range of situations Parliament may legislate for the Australian states without the concurrence of the Commonwealth Government. See pp. 659–60.

62. *Ibralebbe* v. *R.* [1964] A.C. 900 at 918 (on the irrevocable 'surrender' of Parliament's power by the Ceylon Independence Act 1947) and 924 (on the surrender of the Crown's prerogative legislative power).

63. *Ndlwana* v. *Hofmeyr* [1937] A.D. 229 at 237; *Harris* v. *Donges* [1952] 1 T.L.R. 1245 at 1261, *sub nom. Harris* v. *Minister of the Interior* 1952 (2) S.A. 428.

64. *Ndlwana* v. *Hofmeyr*, above. See, to like effect, Ivan C. Rand (1960) 38 *Can. Bar Rev.* 135 at 149; *Blackburn* v. *Att.-Gen.* [1971] 1 W.L.R. 1037 at 1040, *per* Lord Denning M.R. (though his Lordship also cited, without disapproval, the dictum in the *British Coal Corporation* case, note 60).

If one looks at independence Acts since 1960, the case for a traditionally conservative construction becomes weaker; for the United Kingdom Parliament has purported to renounce its power to legislate for those countries altogether. For example, section 1 (2) of the Mauritius Independence Act 1968 provides: 'No Act of the Parliament of the United Kingdom passed on or after the appointed day [i.e., independence day] shall extend, or be deemed to extend, to Mauritius as part of its law; . . .' Is Parliament competent simply to resume its legislative sovereignty over Mauritius tomorrow?

From the point of view of the Mauritian courts, the answer is clearly not. The words of the Independence Act are unambiguous. Moreover the achievement of independence should in itself be understood as having liberated the legal order of Mauritius from its hierarchical subordination to that of the United Kingdom, so that the omnicompetence of the United Kingdom Parliament ceased to prevail in the local legal system.[65] And, looking at the matter from a common-sense point of view, one must suggest that English courts should adopt the same attitude. The United Kingdom Government and Parliament have renounced their authority over Mauritius, surrendering it to the competent authorities in Mauritius. One must also recognize that common sense does not always prevail in legal theory.[66]

2–A written constitution

If the rule of judicial obedience to Acts of Parliament can be reformulated so that Parliament can effectively deprive itself of part of its sovereignty by surrendering it or transferring it to authorities *outside* the territorial limits of the United Kingdom, why can it not be reformulated by accepting that Parliament can do exactly the same thing *within* the territorial limits of the United Kingdom? Suppose, for example, that a federal constitution were enacted, retaining a United Kingdom Parliament but purporting to restrict its legislative powers. For the courts dogmatically to insist that, so long as the United Kingdom Parliament existed, there was a mysterious rule, both fundamental and unalterable, precluding them from recognizing the efficacy of a transfer of part of its absolute sovereignty to Welsh and Scottish Parliaments, would be extremely odd, if the new federal constitution restricting parliamentary competence was known to have general public support as well as a parliamentary majority behind it. One's guess

65. See Kenneth Robinson in *Essays in Imperial Government* (ed. Robinson and A. F. Madden), p. 249. The case would be even clearer if Mauritius had become a republic.
66. cf. pp. 75–7.

is that rather than make themselves ridiculous, the courts would fall into line and vary the 'fundamental' rule. They could vary it *ad hoc* (by declaring in a concrete case that an enactment of the reconstituted United Kingdom Parliament was inoperative) or by a general pronouncement (as when the House of Lords, acting extra-judicially, announced the abandonment of the self-imposed basic rule that it was bound by its own earlier decisions).[67] Law in the courts ought not to rest on assumptions that blithely ignore fundamental changes in constitutional structure.

One can carry this argument still farther. At present Parliament, as we have noted, is incapacitated from binding its own future action as to the substantive content of legislation where this would leave a legislative vacuum. But if Parliament adopted a written constitution under which no legislature in the United Kingdom was competent to violate certain rights and freedoms (for example, by enacting *ex post facto* penal legislation), it would be sensible for the judges to uphold the constitution against future legislative encroachments, provided at least there was a prescribed procedure for constitutional amendment. In other words, the fundamental rule of judicial obligation ought to be regarded as flexible, not immutable; as being susceptible to reformulation in the light of drastic innovations in legislative practice and corresponding changes in the climate of informed opinion about the limits of legislative authority.[68]

3–Effect of accession to the European Communities[69]

As was pointed out in an earlier chapter, our constitutional law must now take into account Community legislation made by organs not subordinate

67. [1966] 1 W.L.R. 1234 (Practice Statement). Rupert Cross, *Precedent in English Law* (2nd edn), 206–7, takes the view that a similar Practice Statement modifying the rule of absolute judicial obedience to Acts of Parliament would be strictly *ultra vires*, though if it were acquiesced in and acted upon it would effect a legal revolution. See also H. W. R. Wade, 'The basis of legal sovereignty' [1955] *Camb. L.J.* 172 (an important and influential article), arguing that this basic rule or ultimate legal principle is alterable by judicial decision but not by statute. I have difficulty in understanding why a purported statutory modification of the present customary common-law rule should be treated either as nugatory or as less 'binding' than other statutory enactments merely because the present rule (i) is extremely important and (ii) was established neither by statute nor by judicial decision but by judicial accommodation to political facts. Nevertheless, the argument in the text above is confined to expressions of opinion as to what the judges ought to do or are likely to do if a fundamental structural change in the British constitutional system were to be adopted, and as to the present territorial scope of the rule of judicial obedience to statutes.

68. The duty of the courts would probably be indicated expressly or by necessary implication by the text of such a constitution. The constitution itself might be adopted by a Constituent Assembly set up by parliamentary authority, and then be submitted for the approval of the electorate at a referendum.

69. For a useful outline of Community law, see P.S.R.F. Mathijsen, *A Guide to*

to Parliament. In particular, the Council of Ministers and the Commission are empowered by the treaties to make regulations having direct effect in member States and creating individual rights and duties enforceable in national courts. The concept of 'directly applicable' Community rules is recognized and implemented by section 2 (1) of the European Communities Act 1972. Certain provisions of the treaties themselves are 'directly applicable' in the sense described.[70] Directives and decisions issued by the Council or the Commission normally require further implementation by the Governments or other parties to whom they are addressed, but exceptionally they too may be directly applicable in national courts.[71]

Questions of the highest constitutional importance have now arisen. At this stage we can only guess how they will be resolved. What if a directly applicable rule of Community law (say, a regulation) conflicts with an Act of Parliament? According to section 2 (4), 'any enactment passed *or to be passed* [subject to certain exceptions] shall have effect subject to' the provisions of section 2 (1). Surely this is not a mere rule of construction, to be displaced if the Act and the regulation cannot be harmonized? It states that Acts of Parliament shall *have effect subject to* directly applicable rules of Community law. We can assume that legislation already in existence on 1 January 1973 or (after that date) when the Community regulation is made will be impliedly repealed by the latter to the extent that the two sets of rules are irreconcilably in conflict. But what of post-accession United Kingdom legislation that is plainly inconsistent with a *prior* Community regulation? One can assume that our courts will do their utmost so to construe legislation as to avoid such a collision. However, according to prevailing British doctrine, primacy should be accorded in the last resort to the subsequent United Kingdom statute, unless perhaps this doctrine has been undermined by the combined effect of the wording of section 2 (4) and the political fact of Britain's accession to the Communities. Now, according to well-settled Community doctrine, Community law (and not merely 'directly applicable' Community law) ought to prevail over *all* inconsistent national law, antecedent and subsequent. As the European Court of Justice (the Court of the Communities)

European Community Law (1972). See also Gerhard Bebr (1971) 34 *Mod. L. Rev.* 481. On the issues relating to Britain's accession, esp. F. A. Trindade (1972) 35 *Mod. L. Rev.* 375 and references there cited; Mitchell, Kuypers and Gall (1972) 9 *Common Market L. Rev.* 134. See also Appendix to this book.

70. For example, art. 16 of the EEC Treaty: see *Re Export Tax on Art Treasures (No. 1)* [1969] C.M.L. Rep. 1; ibid. (No. 2) [1972] C.M.L. Rep. 699. See also pp. 45–6.

71. *Grad* v. *Finanzamt Traunstein* [1971] C.M.L. Rep. 41; *S.A.C.E.* v. *Italian Ministry of Finance* [1971] C.M.L.Rep. 123.

has said, 'the member States, albeit within limited spheres, have restricted their sovereign rights,'[72] and 'no appeal to provisions of internal law of any kind whatever can prevail' over this cession of authority.[73] By section 3 (1) of the European Communities Act 1972, questions of Community law 'shall be determined' by our courts 'in accordance with the principles laid down by and any relevant decision of the European Court'.

The European Court gives primacy to Community law even where there is no *direct* conflict with national law. If Community rules have been promulgated to 'occupy the field' in a matter within Community competence, national Parliaments cannot pass *any* law on such a matter, except possibly for the ancillary purpose of implementing those rules locally on points of detail.[74] It seems, moreover, that if a competent Community organ has made a treaty on a matter within its competence, member States cannot legislate (or even enter into executive agreements with non-member States) so as to detract from the operation of the Community policy, at least if that policy has been embodied in Community rules.[75]

If these pronouncements are to be taken at their face value, parliamentary sovereignty is dead. However, things are not always as they seem in the Communities. For instance, in 1972 West German courts had yet to accept the Court's ruling that Community law prevails over inconsistent provisions of national constitutions.[76] Italy was dragging its feet in implementing Community policies.[77] French courts were reluctant to refer questions of Community law to the European Court. And most of the pronouncements by the Court on the primacy of Community law were made on preliminary rulings under Article 177 of the EEC Treaty, under which the Court does not interpret national law but merely delivers a general interpretation of Community law in a case referred by a national court. If the national court can then apply the Community doctrine as declared by the European Court to the case before it, it should do so. If it cannot (for example, because of national constitutional doctrine) the expectation is that the national authorities will pass amending legislation

72. *Costa* v. *ENEL* [1964] C.M.L. Rep. 425 at 455.
73. *Re Export Tax on Art Treasures (No. 2)* [1972] C.M.L. Rep. 699 at 708.
74. See, for example, the *Hauptzollamt Hamburg* case [1970] C.M.L. Rep. 141 at 153; the *Norddeutsches Vieh* case [1971] C.M.L.Rep. 281 at 293; *Re Imported Thai Sand Flour*, ibid. 521.
75. *Re European Road Transport Agreement* [1971] C.M.L.Rep. 335 (dicta) – a difficult case.
76. See the *Internationale Handelsgesellschaft* case [1972] C.M.L. Rep. 258, 330.
77. A point well illustrated by the *Export Tax* cases (above). Again, value added tax was introduced in the Communities in 1971, but Italy did not adopt it till two years later.

(or adopt a constitutional amendment) as soon as possible. If this action is not taken, the national authorities can be brought before the Court by the Commission as defaulters (Articles 169–71).[78] But the most that the Court can do (for special powers of the Commission, see p. 675) is to make an unenforceable declaratory judgment against the Government in question. *It cannot hold national legislation to be void* for inconsistency with Community law. The Court is not at all like the Supreme Court of the United States.

Given that the Communities are not and do not purport to be a true federation, that national independence and 'sovereignty' are preserved in form, that the effective policy-making organ is not the supranational Commission but the Council of Ministers, which will not override the vital interests of a member State,[79] that the Communities are as yet primarily concerned with economic and social rather than political matters, and that the United Kingdom's membership may, for all one knows, not be permanent,[80] it is quite possible that British courts will, *for the time being*, still give primacy to subsequent United Kingdom legislation in direct conflict with Community law, notwithstanding the wording of the European Communities Act. Government spokesmen in Parliament were certainly mindful of this possibility, indeed probability. As good Europeans they were carrying out Community obligations, but they were aware that United Kingdom judges were quite likely not to accept that the doctrine of parliamentary sovereignty had been demolished by statute.[81] And so this unique Act is a fascinating exercise in equivocation, a wilful manifestation of legislative schizophrenia. Or, to vary the metaphor, the United Kingdom Government has seated Parliament on two horses, one straining towards the preservation of parliamentary sovereignty, the other galloping in the general direction of Community law supremacy.

78. This was the procedure adopted in the second *Export Tax* case, after the Italian Government and Parliament had failed to give effect to the Court's ruling under art. 177 implying that this long-standing tax was incompatible with the EEC Treaty,

79. The 'right of veto' is not embodied in the treaties but is implicit in the informal Luxemburg Agreement of 1966, made to meet President de Gaulle's objection to decisions reached in accordance with the treaties by majority vote.

80. The EEC Treaty is expressed to be permanent. But nobody doubts that Parliament under a Labour Government could effectively take the United Kingdom out of the Communities, although this would be the most serious of all violations of Treaty obligations.

81. cf. Professor H. W. R. Wade's article (note 67). See also Sir Geoffrey Howe, the then Solicitor-General, 838 H.C. Deb. 1311–22 (13 June 1972), for a careful analysis of section 2 (4) in this context.

A possible intermediate position is that the doctrine of parliamentary sovereignty has been changed but would revive if Parliament took the 'revolutionary' step of excluding the United Kingdom from the Communities.

What is an Act of Parliament?

Let us now disregard the major issues just considered. How far, if at all, do the courts at the present time have jurisdiction to determine whether what purports to be an Act of Parliament is, as a matter of law, an authentic statute which they are bound to apply?

The rule that judges ought to apply Acts of Parliament can be classified as a common-law rule, albeit a rule of outstanding importance. The meaning of the Queen in Parliament, and of an Act of Parliament, are governed partly by customary common law and partly by statute. The jurisdiction of the courts to examine the authenticity of purported Acts of Parliament can be considered by using inferences (in which considerations of public policy are of some consequence) drawn from common-law and statutory rules.

1. At common law, Parliament as a legislative body consists of the House of Commons, the House of Lords and the Queen. Each House must record its assent to a bill separately and the Queen has at least a formal discretion whether to assent to bills passed by them. The methods of giving and communicating the royal assent are regulated or prescribed by statute.[82] When Parliament is dissolved, its sovereignty is temporarily in abeyance since it is unable to legislate; there is a House of Commons, but it has no members because their seats have become vacant; there is a House of Lords, but it is incapacitated from sitting (except as a court of law) during a dissolution.

2. The customary common-law rule that each House has to pass a bill before it can be presented for the royal assent has been modified by statute. The Parliament Acts 1911 and 1949 authorize the presentation of a bill for the royal assent if certain conditions have been complied with, although the House of Lords has not passed the bill.

3. In order to express its sovereign will, Parliament must be constituted as Parliament and must function as Parliament within the meaning of existing common law and statute law. Unless these antecedent conditions for law-making have been fulfilled, the product should not be regarded as an authentic Act of Parliament.[83]

82. Royal Assent Act 1967. An Act of Parliament is now duly enacted if the royal assent is signified (i) by Letters Patent signed by Her Majesty under the Great Seal and pronounced in the customary manner (i.e. by Royal Commissioners in the House of Lords, the Commons also being present), or (ii) as above but announced to each House separately by the Speaker of that House (so as to avoid interruptions of the proceedings of the Commons because of the arrival of Commissioners in the Lords), or (iii) by Her Majesty in person, in the presence of both Houses. For forms of the assent, see Crown Office Rules Order 1967 (S.I. 1967, No. 802).

83. This proposition is stated dogmatically and cannot be demonstrated to be

4. Nevertheless, if an official copy of what purports to be an Act of Parliament, bearing the appropriate customary words of enactment (normally[84] 'Be it enacted by the Queen's most excellent Majesty, by and with the advice and consent of the Lords Spiritual and Temporal, and Commons, in this present Parliament assembled, and by the authority of the same, as follows') is produced, the courts *may* well accept this as conclusive evidence that the measure is authentic and has been duly passed. The words of enactment have been varied by statute for measures passed under the Parliament Acts without the consent of the Lords.

In other words, the courts may take the view that they *lack jurisdiction* to pronounce an ostensibly authentic Act of Parliament to be a nullity even though in fact Parliament has not functioned according to existing law. But we need to explore this point farther, because the position is by no means clearly settled.

The enrolled bill rule

The idea that an ostensibly authentic Act of Parliament is incontrovertible in a British court is supported by opinions of writers and judicial decisions and dicta. The main decisions involve unsuccessful attacks in the nineteenth century on the validity of private Acts of Parliament on the ground that they have been passed in disregard of parliamentary standing orders[85] or procured by fraudulent misrepresentation[86] (though the Court of Appeal has recently indicated that a private but not a public Act might be impugned on the latter ground).[87] In one of these cases it was affirmed[88] that:

---

correct, but is founded on logic. It enjoys widespread support among modern writers (for example, R. T. E. Latham, *The Law and the Commonwealth*, pp. 523–4, Sir Ivor Jennings, *The Law and the Constitution* (5th edn), ch. 4, J.D.B. Mitchell, *Constitutional Law* (2nd edn) ch. 4, R. F. V. Heuston, Geoffrey Marshall, Hamish Gray, D. V. Cowen, B. Beinart, note 110 below). Keir and Lawson, *Cases in Constitutional Law* (5th edn), pp. 7–9, adopt a non-committal position. Hood Phillips, *Constitutional and Administrative Law* (4th edn), p. 71, accepts the general logical proposition but is reluctant to draw inferences from it as to the permissible scope of judicial inquiry.

84.   Extra words are added for money bills. The usual enacting formula was evolved in the fifteenth century. By virtue of the Statute Law Revision Act 1948, s. 3(1) (*a*), it can be omitted altogether in a revised edition of the Statutes of the Realm. *Semble* omission of a recital that the House of Commons or (unless otherwise provided by statute) the House of Lords had consented to an Act, would render the measure nugatory: *The Prince's Case* (1606) 8 Co. Rep. 1a at 20a.

85.   *Edinburgh and Dalkeith Rly* v. *Wauchope* (1842) 8 Cl. & F. 710 (H.L.).

86.   *Lee* v. *Bude and Torrington Junction Rly* (1871) L.R. 6 C.P. 576; *Tukino* v. *Aotea District Maori Land Board* [1941] A.C. 308 at 322–3.

87.   *Pickin* v. *British Railways Board* [1972] 3 W.L.R. 824. For public Acts see *Labrador Co.* v. *R.* [1893] A.C. 104 at 123; *Tukino* v. *Aotea District Maori Land Board* [1941] A.C. 308 at 322–3.

88.   *Wauchope's* case at 725, *per* Lord Campbell.

All that a Court of Justice can do is to look to the Parliament Roll: if from that it should appear that a bill has passed both Houses and received the Royal Assent, no Court of Justice can inquire into the mode in which it was introduced into Parliament, nor into what was done previous to its introduction, or what passed in Parliament during its progress in its various stages through Parliament.

Several comments can be made on this much-quoted passage.

1. A peculiar sacrosanctity used to be attributed to the Parliament roll, the formal record of the High Court of Parliament,[89] upon which the originals of all Acts were engrossed in manuscript. Practice changed over the years.[90] From 1497 the original text was retained in the House of Lords and a *copy*, made on a Parliament roll, was sent to the Chancery. Since the middle of the nineteenth century, two copies of a bill as assented to have been printed on vellum, and the Clerk of the Parliaments then adds his signature for the purpose of authentication; the 'original' is kept in the House of Lords, and the duplicate 'Parliament roll' copy now goes to the Public Record Office.[91] There seems to be no reason of basic principle why these two official texts should preclude all further judicial inquiry whatsoever into the procedure followed prior to enactment.

2. Copies of the Act are also printed by the Queen's Printer at Her Majesty's Stationery Office and sold to the public. Under section 9 of the Interpretation Act 1889, judicial notice must be taken of all public Acts of Parliament passed since 1850; this states a rule of evidence[92] and does not specify what is an authentic Act of Parliament.

3. The courts will not encroach upon the exclusive preserves of the two Houses. Article 9 of the Bill of Rights 1689, provides that 'proceedings in Parliament ought not to be impeached or questioned in any court or place out of Parliament'. They fall within the province of parliamentary privilege. Hence the courts will refuse to inquire into such questions as whether either House was mistaken as to the facts, whether a bill had two, three or thirty-three readings, whether a quorum was present, and so on. Perhaps they would even disclaim jurisdiction to inquire whether a

89. See Jennings, *The Law and the Constitution* (5th edn), p. 139 and Appendix 3. But cf. R. F. V. Heuston, *Essays in Constitutional Law* (2nd edn), pp. 16–20.

90. For a historical survey, see Maurice F. Bond, 'Acts of Parliament' (1958) 3 *Archives* 201.

91. Erskine May, op. cit., p. 557. I am indebted to the Clerk of the Parliaments and the Clerk of the Records in the House of Lords for verification of the information set out above. It must be obvious that the modern 'Parliament roll' copy of a statute need not enjoy the unique status of an original engrossed on the ancient Parliament roll, irrespective of judicial dicta suggesting that it does.

92. For the various rules of evidence relating to proof of Acts of Parliament, see *Halsbury's Laws of England* (3rd edn), vol. 15, pp. 365–7.

bill was in fact passed in the same form by both Houses.[93] If, however, it were to be asserted that a bill had not obtained a majority at the final reading in the House of Commons, they might well be prepared to go behind the official text of the Act and examine the Journal of the House and the notes of the official shorthand writers,[94] on the grounds that the alleged defect was peculiarly gross and that 'a court must not decline to open its eyes to the truth'.[95] Even so, it is doubtful whether a court would be prepared to conduct such an inspection without leave of the House, because the House has asserted the privilege not to have its internal proceedings investigated.[96]

4. What if it is alleged that procedural or formal requirements laid down by *statute* have not been complied with during the passage of a bill? Some modern statutes[97] have laid down procedural rules to be observed *before* a particular class of bill is introduced in Parliament. These rules are probably no more than directory; that is to say, non-compliance will not vitiate the end-product. One can arrive at this conclusion by two alternative assertions. The first is that the giving of the royal assent and publication with the appropriate words of enactment cure *all* prior defects. The second is that the rules in question are not of such fundamental importance to be regarded as conditions precedent to the validity of subsequent legislation.[98] Clearly these are different approaches, the second implying that com-

93. Doubts on this point are expressed by Maitland, *Constitutional History of England*, pp. 381–2. See also *Craies on Statute Law* (7th edn), pp. 37–40; the point is unsettled. Examples of such errors, and other irregularities in the enactment of bills, being followed by validating or amending legislation, are given by Erskine May, op. cit., pp. 597–9. The question whether the discrepancy between a bill as passed by the Commons and the bill as passed by the Lords rendered the Act invalid was actually argued before a court in *Pylkington's* case (1455; discussed by D. V. Cowen in 16 *Mod. L. Rev.* at 275–7) but no final decision was recorded.

94. cf. *Halsbury's Laws of England* (3rd edn), vol. 15, p. 367. See also B. Beinart, 'Parliament and the Courts' [1954] *Butterworth's South African Law Review* 135.

95. cf. *Bribery Commissioner* v. *Ranasinghe* [1965] A.C. 172 at 194 (dealing with the jurisdiction of the courts, at least in Ceylon, to inquire whether a prescribed Speaker's certificate had been given in the due form on a bill before enactment). The comment in the text above is necessarily speculative. See further Beinart, loc. cit., for a very full review of these questions.

96. Erskine May, op. cit., pp. 85–6. See also pp. 318, 320.

97. For example, Consolidation of Enactments (Procedure) Act 1949.

98. cf. *Clayton* v. *Heffron* (1961) 105 C.L.R. 214, where part of the procedure prescribed for the resolution of a disagreement between the two Houses of Parliament in Victoria had not been observed in the passage of a bill; held, the requirements were only directory. Contrast *Bribery Commissioner* v. *Ranasinghe* [1965] A.C. at 200 (held that the giving of a Speaker's certificate was a necessary part of the legislative process, and its omission was not cured by royal assent to a bill).

pliance with statutory procedural rules of fundamental importance might be regarded as a condition precedent. One is not obliged to assume that fundamental rules of such a character lie within the exclusive cognizance of Parliament itself.

5. It is unlikely that a court would be prepared to issue an injunction to restrain the submission of a bill for the royal assent or otherwise intervene while a bill was before Parliament.[99] Judicial redress could be sought after the royal assent. A person having a direct interest might obtain a declaration that the measure was a nullity.[100] Alternatively, its validity might be challenged indirectly by way of defence to a prosecution under the 'Act'. The Attorney-General could probably obtain an injunction to prevent a public body from exceeding its statutory powers by promoting a private bill before the matter came before Parliament.[101]

6. One can nevertheless imagine situations in which a measure purporting to be an Act of Parliament might be treated as nugatory by a court. For example, the Parliament Acts enable certain bills to be presented for the royal assent without the consent of the Lords, and provide that a certificate given by the Speaker of the Commons before a bill is presented for assent, and endorsed on the bill that the requirements of the Acts have been complied with, shall be conclusive for all purposes and shall not be questioned in any court.[102] But bills to prolong the duration of a Parliament beyond five years are explicitly excluded from the Parliament Act procedure.[103] If such a bill were to be passed by the Commons alone, certified by the

99. The main reason being that this would be a breach of parliamentary privilege – an objection that would not apply to proceedings before a colonial legislature: *Rediffusion (Hong Kong) Ltd* v. *Att.-Gen. of Hong Kong* [1970] A.C. 1136. Injunctions have been awarded in Australia, but are unlikely to granted in future. See G. Sawer (1944) 60 *L.Q.R.* 83; Z. Cowen (1955) 71 *L.Q.R.* 336; D. G. Benjafield and H. Whitmore, *Principles of Australian Administrative Law* (4th edn), pp. 228–31; R. D. Lumb, *Constitutions of the Australian States* (3rd edn), ch. 5; J. I. Fajgenbaum and Peter J. Hanks, *Australian Constitutional Law* (1972), ch. 12; Enid Campbell, *Parliamentary Privilege in Australia*, pp. 85–9.

100. cf. *Pickin* v. *British Railways Board* [1972] 3 W.L.R. 824.

101. *Att.-Gen.* v. *London and Home Counties Joint Electricity Authority* [1929] 1 Ch. 513 (unlawful expenditure of funds for the purpose). But the jurisdiction to award an injunction will be sparingly exercised and is unlikely to be exercised at all in proceedings between parties. See *Bilston Corpn* v. *Wolverhampton Corpn* [1942] Ch. 391 (no injunction to restrain breach of undertaking, confirmed by statute, not to oppose introduction of bill); Holdsworth (1943) 59 *L.Q.R.* 2. cf. p. 396.

102. Parliament Act 1911, ss. 2(2), 3; Parliament Act 1949. For the Speaker's certificate that a bill is a money bill within the meaning of the 1911 Act, see s. 1(3) of that Act.

103. 1911 Act, s. 2(1).

Speaker and assented to by the Queen with words of enactment stating that it had been passed in accordance with the Parliament Acts,[104] a court should surely treat that 'Act' as a nullity, because it was 'bad on its face'; the body purporting to enact it would not be 'Parliament' within the meaning of existing law. The fatal defect[105] would be apparent without any judicial intrusion into the proceedings of either House; the purported Act would be no more efficacious than a resolution of the House of Commons.[106] A broadly similar analysis might be applicable to a situation in which a Regent assented to a bill to alter the succession to the throne or the establishment of the Church in Scotland, in disregard of the prohibitions contained in the Regency Act 1937.[107] These are no doubt somewhat fanciful hypotheses, but by putting extreme examples, the limitations of an apparently rigid rule can be exposed.

Redefinition of the meaning of Parliament

Parliament is capable of redefining itself for particular purposes. It did so by the Parliament Acts, which provided a simpler, optional procedure for legislation on most topics.[108] It could make the procedure simpler still by abolishing the House of Lords. What if it were to lay down a more cumbersome procedure for legislating and prescribe it as the only procedure to be followed? Suppose, for example, that Parliament were to pass an Act stating that changes in parliamentary constituencies made by independent boundary commissions were to have direct legal force, that

104. As we have already indicated (see p. 51), an erroneous certificate that a bill was a money bill would be probably accepted as conclusive unless the error was so gross as to be indicative of bad faith. This is because the practical consequences of holding a money bill to be a nullity might be extremely grave.

105. Or to use the colourful phrase used in *R*. v. *Arundel* (*Countess*) (1617) Hobart 109 at 111, the 'death wound'.

106. Which has no legal effect outside the walls of Parliament (*Stockdale* v. *Hansard* (1839) 9 Ad. & E. 1; *Bowles* v. *Bank of England* [1913] 1 Ch. 57), unless given such an effect by Act of Parliament: see Provisional Collection of Taxes Act 1968; and ch. 14.

107. Regency Act 1937, s. 4(2). This provision might, of course, be held to be merely directory, though such an analysis seems implausible.

108. Professor H. W. R. Wade ([1955] *Camb. L.J.* 172) regards measures passed under this procedure as a special form of delegated legislation. I respectfully prefer Dr Geoffrey Marshall's view (*Parliamentary Sovereignty and the Commonwealth*, pp. 42–6) that such legislation is primary and not delegated. Professor Hood Phillips (*Constitutional and Administrative Law* (4th edn), p. 76) goes so far as to characterize legislation passed with a Regent's assent 'as a kind of delegated legislation', and on this ground would justify a judicial decision to the effect that an 'Act' assented to by a Regent in contravention of s. 4(2) of the 1937 Act was invalid. He has also suggested (*Reform of the Constitution*, pp. 18–19, 91–2) that the Parliament Act 1949 is a nullity because the 'delegate' created in 1911 enlarged its own limited powers in passing it.

no bill to vary these changes was to be presented for the royal assent unless it had first obtained the support of a majority of the voters at a referendum, or had been passed at its final reading with the support of two-thirds of the full membership of the House of Commons; and that no bill to amend or repeal that Act was to be presented for the royal assent unless that same procedure had been followed.[109] Could Parliament nevertheless amend or repeal the Act by ordinary legislative procedure?[110]

1. It is not enough to incant the phrase: 'A sovereign Parliament cannot bind its own future action.'[111] One of the questions to be asked is: 'What is meant by "Parliament"?' Another – essentially the same question expressed in a different way – is whether there cannot be new mandatory legal rules as to the manner and form of law-making which Parliament must observe if its enactments are to be recognized as authentic. The

109. Unless this last entrenching provision was present – it is absent from section 1(2) of the Ireland Act 1949 – it could easily be argued that the Act imposing the special requirement could itself be amended or repealed by ordinary legislative procedure.

110. Among the main recent contributions are those by D. V. Cowen (1952) 15 *Mod. L. Rev.* 282, (1953) 16 *Mod. L. Rev.* 273; B. Beinart [1954] *Butterworth's South African Law Rev.* 135; Geoffrey Marshall, *Parliamentary Sovereignty and the Commonwealth* and *Constitutional Theory*, ch. 3; R. F. V. Heuston, *Essays in Constitutional Law* (2nd edn.), ch. 1; H. W. R. Wade [1955] *Camb. L.J.* 172; Sir Ivor Jennings, *The Law and the Constitution* (5th edn), ch. 4; J. D. B. Mitchell, *Constitutional Law* (2nd edn), ch. 4; Hamish R. Gray (1953) 10 *U. of Toronto L.J.* 54; W. Friedmann (1950) 24 *Australian L.J.* 103; O. Hood Phillips, *Constitutional and Administrative Law* (4th edn), pp. 60–76; Harry Calvert, *Constitutional Law in Northern Ireland*, ch. 1.

111. In this context the implications of *Att.-Gen. for N.S.W.* v. *Trethowan* (1931) 44 C.L.R. 394; [1932] A.C. 526 are often misunderstood by students. Under the constitution of New South Wales as amended by local legislation passed in 1929, a bill to abolish the upper House could not be presented for the royal assent unless it had first been approved by the electorate at a referendum, and a like requirement extended to any bill to amend or repeal this procedure. Following a change of government in 1931, bills were passed by both Houses of the New South Wales Parliament to remove the referendum rule and to abolish the upper House; neither bill was submitted to a referendum. Injunctions were obtained to restrain submission of the bills for the royal assent. This may have been an inappropriate remedy (see *Hughes and Vale Pty Ltd* v. *Gair* (1954) 90 C.L.R. 203 at 204–5), but the decision on the point of substantive law was clearly correct. Confusion has been caused by the fact that New South Wales had a non-sovereign legislature; and section 5 of the Colonial Laws Validity Act 1865, which applied to New South Wales, provided that a 'colonial' legislature could make laws relating to its constitution, powers and procedure 'in such manner and form as may . . . be required' by existing law. The applicability of section 5 furnished one reason for holding the improper procedure to be unlawful; the decision should have been the same, however, even if New South Wales had had a 'sovereign' legislature: see cases cited in notes 114 and 115 below. There is a common but wholly unfounded misconception that *because* New South Wales had a non-sovereign legislature and was held to be competent to 'bind its own future action', *it therefore follows* that a sovereign legislature like the United Kingdom Parliament is incompetent to do so.

much-quoted dictum that 'Parliament cannot bind itself as to the form of subsequent legislation'[112] carries us nowhere, for it was uttered merely to rebut the optimistic argument that Parliament had protected an ordinary enactment against implied repeal.[113] Another question, as we have already seen, is the extent to which the courts have jurisdiction to determine whether 'Parliament' has acted in conformity with the law behind Parliament.

2. Modern decisions in constitutional cases arising in South Africa[114] and Ceylon[115] show that a sovereign (i.e. omnicompetent) Parliament must function in the manner prescribed by existing law in order validly to express its legislative will. In each of the cases the constitution had laid down a special procedure (a two-thirds' majority of the two Houses in joint session, or a two-thirds' majority in the lower House, at final reading) to be followed for the enactment of legislation on certain important matters. In each of them the courts held that where bills dealing with these 'entrenched' matters had been passed by *ordinary* legislative majorities and had been duly assented to and printed, they could not be accepted as authentic Acts of Parliament. There was to be read into the constitution a necessary implication that 'Parliament' bore different meanings for different purposes.

3. These decisions, extremely interesting though they are as illustrations of basic principle, are of doubtful persuasive authority when we try to answer our hypothetical problem set in a British constitutional context.

112. Note 59.

113. cf. *R.* v. *Drybones* [1970] S.C.R. 282 (Can.) for the position of an extraordinary enactment (the Canadian Bill of Rights 1960) which the majority of the Supreme Court held would prevail over inconsistent legislation not expressed to be made 'notwithstanding' the Bill of Rights. See also F. M. Auburn (1972) 35 *Mod. L. Rev.* 129; E. Likhovski, *Israel's Parliament: The Law of the Knesset*.

114. *Harris* v. *Donges* [1952] 1 T.L.R. 1245, *sub nom. Harris* v. *Minister of the Interior* 1952 (2) S.A. 428 (two-thirds' majority of both Houses of the South African Parliament required by the South Africa Act 1909 for removal of Cape coloured voters from the common voters' roll; held, a measure passed by both Houses sitting separately by simple majorities was not an authentic Act of Parliament, although it had been assented to); see also *Minister of the Interior* v. *Harris* 1952 (4) S.A. 769 (an 'Act' constituting the two Houses as the 'High Court of Parliament' with power to override the previous decision by a simple majority, also held to be a nullity). See, however, *Collins* v. *Minister of the Interior* 1957 (1) S.A. 552, where the desired result was achieved by a sufficiently circuitous route. For the literature on this series of legal battles, see Marshall, *Parliamentary Sovereignty and the Commonwealth*.

115. *Bribery Commissioner* v. *Ranasinghe* [1965] A.C. 172 (royal assent did not cure failure to obtain a two-thirds' majority in the lower House for a measure inconsistent with the constitution). See further *R. (O' Brien)* v. *Military Governor, N.D.U. Internment Camp* [1924] I.R. 32 (failure to submit a bill to a referendum held fatal to the validity of an ostensibly authentic Act; see Heuston, op. cit., pp. 11–14).

In the first place, in each of them the wording of a Speaker's certificate on the face of the Act or bill in question (or the absence of such a certificate) indicated that the specially prescribed procedure had not in fact been followed. Although the decisions suggest that the courts can look at the original of the bill as presented for assent (and are not confined to the bare text of the published Act), they do not offer clear guidance on the proper limits of a court's scope of inquiry if there is no requirement of a Speaker's certificate, or if a Speaker's certificate or the words of enactment are notoriously false or are alleged to be false. As far as British courts are concerned, these questions remain open. In the second place, none of them deals with the legal effects of *self-imposed* procedural requirements by the Parliaments of those countries; the requirements had been imposed by the constitutional instruments from which the Parliaments derived their authority to make law.

4. None the less, there is no *logical* reason why the United Kingdom Parliament should be incompetent so to redefine itself (or redefine the procedure for enacting legislation on any given matter) as to preclude Parliament *as ordinarily constituted* from passing a law on a matter. (There are, of course, doubts as to the jurisdiction or willingness of the courts to intervene.) If Parliament can make it easier to legislate, as by passing the Parliament Acts or abolishing the House of Lords, it can also make it harder to legislate.

5. Hence a two-thirds' majority rule might be analysed either as a re-definition of the meaning of 'Parliament' or a prescription of essential procedural conditions before Parliament could speak with an authentic voice; a rule imposing a duty to hold a referendum could quite persuasively be analysed as the addition of a fourth element to 'Parliament', in much the same way as the Parliament Act procedure can be analysed as involving the conditional subtraction of one of the three elements from Parliament.

6. Such an analysis can be attacked on the ground that once it is conceded that Parliament can make legislation on any topic more difficult, one must then concede that it can make legislation impossible. If it can lay down a two-thirds' majority rule it can lay down a nine-tenths' majority rule, and a similar rule for the majority to be obtained at a referendum. In this way it could, by imposing requirements as to the manner of legislating, in practice bind itself not to change the substantive content of future legislation, and this would be contrary to both established principle and public policy; a legislative vacuum must not be created; consequently the courts ought not to recognize the legal efficacy of *any* such restrictive rule. The only ways of answering this point are that there exist *political* safeguards against the adoption of such restrictive rules, just as there are

political safeguards against the enactment of preposterous laws by ordinary legislative procedure; and that a court could draw a common-sense line between binding rules regulating the manner of legislating and ineffectual rules which if accepted as binding would, in substance, stop Parliament from legislating at all.[116] One must, however, recognize the distinct possibility that a court might decide not to engage in such a delicate exercise.

To devote more space to this conundrum would hardly be worth while. We are in the realm of speculative conjecture. To dwell there longer would be justified only if there were a substantial likelihood that our hypothetical situation would assume practical importance.

Practical limitations on the legislative power of Parliament

Some of these limitations are considered more fully in chapters 7, 10 and 12. We have already considered the possible legal effect of entry to the European Communities. Even if membership does not curb the formal legal sovereignty of Parliament, the obligations entailed by membership mean that in practice Parliament will have to abstain from legislating, or legislating in particular ways, on a number of important topics; and that legislation (mainly under delegated authority conferred by section 2 (2) of the European Communities Act 1972[117]) will have to be passed in conformity with Community requirements.

When one asks what are the practical limitations on the exercise of parliamentary supremacy, one is also asking what are the effective restraints operating on the Government; for the legislative programme is largely dominated by the Government. In the first place, a Government's freedom of action is inhibited by its international position, and in particular by international obligations which it has undertaken. Quite apart from the pervasive influence of Community law, a Government would need to have very strong reasons for introducing legislation inconsistent with its obligations under the European Convention on Human Rights, GATT, or other multilateral conventions to which this country had acceded. Again, when the Government is obliged to seek a very large loan from external sources, it may be compelled to introduce restrictive fiscal and economic measures by legislation as a condition of receiving the money.

Secondly, the Government would not sponsor legislation which flagrantly violated a constitutional convention restricting the territorial ambit or subject-matter of legislative competence. It would not initiate legislation

116. See W. Friedmann (1950) 24 *Australian L.J.* at 105–6.
117. See ch. 15.

intended to encroach on the autonomy of an independent Commonwealth country or, for example, to impose changes in the laws of the Channel Islands on purely domestic matters. It has often been stated that the Government must not 'exceed its electoral mandate' by introducing major constitutional changes which have not been foreshadowed by its election manifesto. One may accept that there exists a loose convention to this effect,[118] but one must recognize that unforeseen contingencies always arise during the life of a Parliament, that the country cannot exist on a diet of dissolutions, that a party's election manifesto does not have to be comprehensive and that a vote cast at a General Election does not imply conscious support for every aspect of a party's programme. The concept of the electoral mandate is too often a thin veil for political cant.

Thirdly, the Government will not introduce legislation which it believes to be incapable of enforcement. Occasionally an Act proves subsequently to be unenforceable (for example, the Southern Rhodesia Act 1965, asserting Parliament's paramount authority over the breakaway colony), but that is another matter. Nor will an Act be passed which requires the cooperation of the general public but which flies in the face of strong public opposition. It was one thing to pass legislation suspending capital punishment for murder or abolishing corporal punishment for criminal offences – legislation to which a majority of the electorate was opposed, but which could be implemented by judicial and administrative action or inaction affecting a small number of persons. It would be another thing to make it an offence to manufacture or sell all alcoholic liquor.

Fourthly, although unpopular legislation may be passed, the Government would not introduce and its normally obedient supporters in Parliament might refuse to support legislation which would court inevitable electoral disaster in the later stages of the life of a Parliament. Repeal of all restrictions on Commonwealth immigration would fall into this category.

Fifthly, a Government's freedom of legislative initiative is circumscribed to some extent in so far as it is customary or expedient (or both) to consult in advance and pay some regard to the views of powerful organized interest groups, which are also able to exert pressure through their spokesmen in Parliament.

Three other points must be made. First, there are still those who will

118. A distortion of this doctrine – that it would be wrong for a Government to go to the country till it had carried out its entire electoral mandate – cannot stand up to examination.

Much of the discussion about the refusal of the Heath Government to go to the country or hold a referendum on the question of accepting and implementing the terms agreed for Britain's entry into the Communities presupposed that a convention to the effect stated in the text above did exist. The Government claimed that it had an implied electoral mandate for entry. But the outcome illustrated how loose was the convention.

solemnly affirm that Parliament ought not to legislate against the weight of public opinion; and even that the purpose of constitutional conventions is to ensure that government is conducted in accordance with public opinion. Stated in these general terms, such propositions are unacceptable. The British system of parliamentary government is above all a system of *government*. It is not a system geared to a series of opinion polls or referenda in which the garbled voice of the people is equated with deity.[119] Among the factors which the Government and members of Parliament have to take into account is the strength of public sentiment on particular issues. But this is one factor among many. Members of Parliament are representatives but not delegates of their constituents; nor is the Cabinet a committee of the House of Commons or of Parliament. A Government and its parliamentary supporters ought to act in the way they think best in the general interests of the country. It is open to the electorate to use criticism and ridicule, to exert pressure on their representatives by legitimate means, to voice their displeasure at by-elections and to turn the Government out at the next General Election. But there is no constitutional convention to the effect that a Government which loses the confidence of the country must resign or advise a dissolution of Parliament, so long as it commands a majority in the House of Commons.

The second point should be stated in order to balance this account, though its connection with the idea of the supremacy or sovereignty of Parliament is only marginal. Although Parliament, for political purposes, is not to be thought of as a collective entity, and although in the last resort a Government will normally be able to bring its supporters in the House of Commons (and its supporters and opponents in the House of Lords) reluctantly to heel, the last resort is seldom reached. Because Parliament exists, because the Opposition in the House of Commons is always probing for opportunities to discredit the Government, and because Governments prefer convincing their backbenchers to bullying them, and are anxious to avoid public recriminations within the party in front of the Opposition, a Government needs to explain and justify its position to Parliament, and through Parliament to the public at large, as persuasively as possible and with an outward show of unity. Moreover, parliamentary time is not unlimited; and draconian action to curtail debate when obstructive tactics are used in the House of Commons can prove counter-productive. These factors undoubtedly influence the content of legislation, as well as curbing a Government's general freedom of action. Prudence often dictates caution and compromise.

Finally, there is a temptation to overstate the virtues of the Westminster system of responsible and representative government. Such a tendency

119. Though cf. p. 95.

was apparent in 1971 and 1972, when there was a genuine case for submitting the question of British entry to the EEC to a referendum of the electorate. Referenda were held in the other three applicant States. There are many cogent arguments against having recourse to referenda.[120] But when one was confronted with a single, albeit complex, issue of extraordinary constitutional importance, it was not at all congenial to listen to the blandly repetitive assertion that we do not conduct our affairs that way in this country.

120. Arguments for and against the use of referenda, with comparative material, are considered by Philip Goodhart, *Referendum* (1971). See also Cecil S. Emden, *The People and the Constitution* (2nd edn), ch. 12.

Part Two
The Executive

In this Part are collected the more important or interesting rules about central government. As far as is practicable they have been set against their political background. But this is not a textbook on politics or public administration, and it does not purport to give a full account of how Britain is governed.

Textbooks on constitutional law usually deal with Parliament first and the Government afterwards. Here the order is reversed (apart from the earlier treatment of parliamentary sovereignty), mainly because the author regards the Government as being more important than Parliament. But Government and Parliament (Executive and Legislature) are closely interlocked, and some matters discussed in this Part of the book will reappear in Part Three.

Chapter 4 covers a wide range of topics – the rules of law about the monarchy; residual matters on which the Queen may still be entitled by constitutional convention to act in her personal discretion; the scope of the royal prerogative, a bundle of rights, privileges and immunities belonging to the Crown and to the Crown alone; the law relating to the activities of the executive branch of government and its officers in foreign affairs. The common thread running through this chapter is the Queen, or the Crown. In British constitutional law we do not recognize 'the State' as a legal concept.

Chapter 5 deals with the Privy Council, now only a 'dignified' organ of government, and with its active committees, including the Judicial Committee. In chapter 6 we consider the roles of the Prime Minister and his Cabinet colleagues in the scheme of government, and we stray beyond constitutional law into a controversial area of politics. We also examine the various meanings of the doctrine of ministerial responsibility. Chapter 7 goes on to outline the structure of central government, including an account of bodies ancillary to Departments, and some of the rules about the organization of the civil service and the legal and constitutional position of its members. Here we have to record a number of changes.

Chapter 8 deals with some aspects of the constitutional position of the armed forces of the Crown and their members. In chapter 9 we consider topics of more obvious contemporary importance – in particular, the legal and constitutional status of the bodies operating nationalized industries, and the machinery by which they are scrutinized or controlled. These industries are not run by government Departments, but it is convenient to discuss them alongside chapters dealing with the central government. In this area, too, changes are taking place.

Chapter 4
The Crown and the Royal Prerogative

Constitutional monarchy[1]

The Queen today remains a symbol of national identity, a focal point of national loyalty, transcending partisan rivalry and strengthening social cohesion. The national anthem is 'God Save the Queen'; British coins and postage stamps bear her image; the Queen personifies the State and the nation, their history and continuity. The Government is Her Majesty's Government; government is carried on in the Queen's name; sovereignty is attributed to the Queen in Parliament; wide legal powers are vested in Her Majesty or in Her Majesty in Council; the courts are the Queen's courts. Coronations, royal weddings and funerals, and an investiture of a Prince of Wales,[2] are great national occasions, bringing the past into the present amid splendid pageantry and ancient ritual. The Queen is pre-eminently a 'dignified'[3] element in the British constitution. She is also a pillar of the Established Church, an exemplar of family virtue, a personage to whom deference is paid by all in public life in a society where habits of deference are diminishing. She embodies the hereditary principle at a time when entitlement to the exercise of authority or the enjoyment of a preferred status by reason of birth is increasingly questioned. She has the misfortune to be required to live in a glare of publicity and to have reposed in her expectations which no ordinary mortal can hope to fulfil. The smallest indiscretion or verbal lapse may be the subject of adverse comment to which she will be unable to reply on her own behalf. She must,

1. By far the best modern account is to be found in Sir Ivor Jennings's *Cabinet Government* (3rd edn), especially chs. 12–14. The most recent royal biographies, the Duke of Windsor's *A King's Story*, Sir Harold Nicolson's *King George V* and Sir John Wheeler-Bennett's *King George VI*, are also instructive. For more popular accounts of the role of the monarchy, see Jeremy Murray-Brown (ed.), *The Monarchy and its Future* (1969); Andrew Duncan, *The Reality of Monarchy* (1970). Detailed factual information is to be found in the Report of the Select Committee on the Civil List, 1971 (H.C. 29 (1971–72)).

2. On which see Blumler, Brown, Ewbank and Nossiter (1971) 19 *Political Studies* 149.

3. The term used by Walter Bagehot in his classic study, *The English Constitution* (Fontana edn), p. 61.

therefore, endeavour so to comport herself as to give offence to nobody; not only must she never do or say the wrong thing, but she must always do and say the right thing, irrespective of her private inclinations. Although, in England at least, republican sentiment is very weak, the strength of positive enthusiasm for the monarchy may have diminished in recent years; some of the magic and mystery of monarchy have (almost inevitably) rubbed off, but a revival of stronger monarchical sentiment, perhaps based on more modern foundations, is always possible.[4]

From the late Victorian era till the middle years of the present century, the monarchy was an important factor cementing the unity of the British Empire. Local nationalist sentiment in the colonies was subdued by the well-inculcated loyalty of simple peoples to the occupant of the throne. In those self-governing Dominions which were populated mainly by settlers of British stock, the growth of national self-assertion could be accommodated with the fundamental concept of common allegiance to a common and indivisible Crown. This concept broke down in the Irish Free State (Eire), and then in South Africa. In 1949 the Commonwealth Prime Ministers agreed to accept the continuance of India's membership of the Commonwealth as a republic on the understanding that India would recognize the King as Head of the Commonwealth. By the end of 1972, when there were thirty-one full and independent members of the Commonwealth, the Queen was head of State in only ten of them and was represented (except in the United Kingdom) by a Governor-General; sixteen were republics and five[5] had indigenous monarchs. She remains Head of the Commonwealth, but in this symbolical capacity she exercises no constitutional function. For each of those Commonwealth countries of which she is still head of State she has a separate title.

It was assumed that a convention recited in the preamble to the Statute of Westminster 1931 – that the assent of the Parliaments of the Dominions was required for any change in the law touching the succession to the throne or the royal style and titles – applied to all independent Commonwealth countries of which she was head of State. The Dominion Prime Ministers were consulted in 1936 by Baldwin, the United Kingdom Prime Minister, to ascertain whether they would approve of Edward VIII's proposed marriage to Mrs Simpson; a majority of them emphatically agreed with the British Government's opposition to the idea, and Edward VIII abdicated. Appropriate legislation was then passed by the United

4. cf. the favourable impact made by the recent television film, *Royal Family*, and the personal popularity of the present Prince of Wales (note 2).
5. Malaysia, Lesotho (formerly Basutoland), Swaziland, Tonga and Western Samoa. The Republic of Nauru was a 'special member'. See ch. 30.

Kingdom Parliament to give effect to the King's decision and to exclude him and his descendants from the line of succession.[6] The conventional procedures were also followed in 1948 when George VI ceased to be Emperor of India, and 1953 when Elizabeth II adopted separate titles for her several realms.[7]

Today the personal characteristics of a monarch's proposed consort would be unlikely to arouse strong emotions outside the United Kingdom. Since, moreover, the number of independent Commonwealth countries continuing to owe allegiance to Her Majesty will diminish as a result of republican trends, the constitutional niceties relating to the law touching the succession to the throne and the royal style and titles will probably be reduced to matters of small practical consequence.[8]

The principal convention of the British constitution is that the Queen shall exercise her formal legal powers only upon and in accordance with the advice of her Ministers, save in a few exceptional situations. In independent Commonwealth countries the powers of the Governor-General, her personal representative, are similarly restricted, except in so far as they may have been enlarged or attenuated by the text of the constitution.[9]

This is not to say that the monarch must be a mere cypher. As Bagehot wrote,[10] she has 'the right to be consulted, the right to encourage, the right to warn'. He could have added that she also has the right to offer, on her own initiative, suggestions and advice to her Ministers even where she is obliged in the last resort to accept the formal advice tendered to her.

To be more explicit, she has the conventional rights to receive Cabinet papers and minutes, to be kept adequately informed by the Prime Minister (with whom she has regular weekly audiences) on matters of national

6. His Majesty's Declaration of Abdication Act 1936.

7. The Royal Titles Act 1953 recognized the authority of the Queen to adopt a new title for the United Kingdom and for the other territories for whose foreign relations the United Kingdom Government was responsible. The style and title proclaimed for the United Kingdom and its dependencies was 'Elizabeth II, by the Grace of God of the United Kingdom of Great Britain and Northern Ireland and of her other Realms and Territories Queen, Head of the Commonwealth, Defender of the Faith.' See further de Smith (1953) 2 *I.C.L.Q.* 263. The validity of this measure in relation to Scotland (she was the first Elizabeth to be Queen of Scotland) was unsuccessfully challenged in *MacCormick* v. *Lord Advocate* 1953 S.C. 396, partly on the grounds of lack of *locus standi*.

8. The adoption of a separate royal title for a newly independent Commonwealth country of which Her Majesty remains Queen has not recently been accompanied by the assent of the Parliaments of other independent Commonwealth countries. To this extent the convention recited in 1931 has partly lapsed.

9. See generally de Smith, *The New Commonwealth and its Constitutions*, ch. 3. See also pp. 25, 51–2, 658.

10. Bagehot, op. cit., p. 111.

policy, to receive Foreign Office dispatches and telegrams and other State papers,[11] and to be notified of proposed appointments and awards to be made in her name so that she can express her views informally. She can make such private comments as she thinks fit; she can remonstrate and offer strong objections to a proposed course of action. How much attention is paid to her views will depend upon the context and her personal experience and stature. Any objection that she may raise to the introduction of politically controversial legislation to which the Cabinet is committed is unlikely to be pressed or taken seriously, particularly if the Government is not of a conservative complexion; the monarch, aware of the monarchy's conservative image,[12] is obliged to use extreme tact. On the other hand, the advice that is tendered to her as to non-political appointments (for example, to archbishoprics) may well be coloured by the monarch's private views, especially if she is as familiar with the possible candidates as is the Prime Minister and if she will subsequently have personal contacts with the holder of the office. At this level the monarch's influence may be considerable. More generally, the length and range of her experience of public affairs, and her personal acquaintance with a large number of overseas dignitaries, may lend weight to suggestions she chooses to offer. George VI was never a political sage; but there are some grounds for believing that his comments in 1945 may have been instrumental in persuading Attlee to reconsider and then change his original intention of placing Bevin in the Treasury and Dalton in the Foreign Office;[13] and we know that in 1944 he took it upon himself in effect to direct Churchill not to accompany the invasion force to Normandy.[14] George V had a mind of his own, as well as a high place in popular esteem, and his habits of gruff and forthright expression doubtless influenced not

11. Which take her two or three hours a day to read. Memorandum of the Queen's Private Secretary to the Select Committee on the Civil List (H.C. 29 (1971–72)), Minutes of Evidence, App. 13, § 3.

12. Victoria, after 1868, was an unabashed Conservative partisan, and not infrequently exceeded the limits of constitutional propriety in expressing her views. Edward VII, neither as partisan nor as diligent, got on well with both Conservative and Liberal Governments. George V and George VI, profoundly conservative in temperament and sympathies, had a clear grasp of the implications of limited monarchy, behaved almost invariably with scrupulous constitutional decorum, and had friendly personal relations with non-Conservative Prime Ministers. Edward VIII, less conventional in temperament and given to serious lapses of discretion (see especially Keith Middlemas and John Barnes, *Baldwin* (1969), pp. 978–80), fell foul of his Conservative Ministers, but there was no foundation for the belief that his political sympathies lay with the Left; see, for example, his own admission in *A King's Story* (note 1), pp. 276–7.

13. Wheeler-Bennett, op. cit. This supposition was, however, discounted in 1959 by Earl Attlee. The accuracy of Attlee's recollection of the matter is not beyond question; see Tom Driberg (1969) 50 *The Parliamentarian* at 165.

14. W. S. Churchill, *The Second World War*, vol. 5, *Closing the Ring*, pp. 547–50.

only the manner in which advice was presented to him but also, on occasion, the substance of that advice. He appears to have exercised some influence over senior military appointments; his expostulations addressed to the Prime Minister over the forcible feeding of militant suffragettes probably conduced to a change of policy; he did his best, though with scant success, to lower the political temperature during the recurrent Irish troubles in the first half of his reign.[15]

In times of national crisis the role of a non-partisan head of State as a bridge-builder is potentially significant. When the possibility of civil war in Ireland over the home-rule issue became imminent in 1914, George V took the initiative in convening an inter-party conference, with the Prime Minister's agreement, and addressed its opening session. In 1931, after the collapse of Ramsay MacDonald's Labour Government, he encouraged the formation of a National Government under MacDonald's leadership, but did not exert any improper pressure. If the normal machinery of democratic government breaks down, the monarch's ill-defined residuary discretionary powers may have to be exercised in novel or highly unusual circumstances. Obviously personal interventions of this kind may imperil the status of the monarchy; they are therefore justifiable only as the least of evils. If only because one cannot readily envisage all these hypothetical situations, it is impracticable to state exhaustively the scope of the residual powers. However, the main situations in which the Queen has, or may possibly have, a conventional right to exercise her prerogative powers[16] without or against ministerial advice can be briefly listed:

Appointment of a Prime Minister

On several occasions during the past fifty years the choice of a new Prime Minister upon the resignation of the incumbent has not been pre-determined by constitutional rules, and the monarch has had to exercise a judicious discretion. For reasons to be explained in a later chapter,[17] the Queen has now been relieved of this responsibility save where no party leader commands a majority in the House of Commons.

Dismissal of a Government

If a Government, having lost its majority in the House of Commons, were to insist on remaining in office instead of offering its resignation or advising a dissolution, the Queen would be justified, after the lapse of a reasonable

15. Nicolson, op. cit., *passim*.
16. For the definition of prerogative, see pp. 114–16.
17. See pp. 156–8.

period of time, in requesting the Prime Minister to advise her to dissolve Parliament and, if he were to refuse, in dismissing him and his Ministers. She would also, it is submitted, be justified in dismissing her Ministers if they were purporting to subvert the democratic basis of the constitution – for example, by prolonging the life of a Parliament in order to avoid defeat at a General Election, or by obtaining an electoral majority through duress or fraudulent manipulation of the poll. Expediency would be the only factor restricting her discretion. Since such an intervention on her part would tend, in Asquith's phrase,[18] to make the Crown 'the football of contending factions' at an ensuing General Election, and since no Government has been unambiguously dismissed since 1783,[19] this, the most drastic form of royal initiative, must be a recourse of last resort, an ultimate weapon which is liable to destroy its user.

Insistence on a dissolution

Much the same considerations apply as those applicable to the dismissal of a Government. It is true that the Queen might urge upon the Prime Minister that a dissolution would be in the best interests of the country, and he might reluctantly agree to advise her to dissolve. But if he did not agree, and the Queen were to insist on a dissolution, then she would have to remove the Prime Minister and find a new one; the procedure upon a dissolution of Parliament entails the making of an Order in Council and the issue of a royal proclamation under the Great Seal, and this requires the cooperation of Ministers. Unless, therefore, the Prime Minister's own colleagues were prepared to form a new Government, the Queen would have to send for the Leader of the Opposition and ask him to form a Government for the purpose of an immediate dissolution. She would then become a 'football of contending factions'.

To this general analysis, one qualification must be added; she may *possibly* have a right to insist on a dissolution before agreeing to exercise her prerogative to create new peers in order to swamp opposition to the Government in the House of Lords.[20]

Refusal of a dissolution

If a Prime Minister were improperly to request a dissolution, the Queen would at least be entitled, and might perhaps be obliged, to reject it. For example, if a Prime Minister whose party had been defeated by the

18. Quoted in Jennings, op. cit., p. 408.
19. For the equivocal precedent of 1834, see Jennings, op. cit., pp. 403–5.
20. See pp. 107–8.

Opposition party at a General Election were to request an immediate second dissolution on the ground that the victory of his opponents had been obtained by misrepresentations to the electorate, or if Neville Chamberlain in 1940 had, instead of resigning, requested a dissolution at a time when the country was threatened with military defeat, the monarch could justifiably refuse, since resignation would be the only proper course for the Prime Minister to adopt. Undoubtedly there are other situations in which a request for a dissolution could be refused; cogent arguments to this effect have been advanced over the years by monarchs, their advisers, and writers of authority. Confident identification of those situations is not easy. In the first place, in the United Kingdom there has been no unequivocal instance of an absolute rejection of a request for a dissolution in modern times,[21] though on several occasions requests have been granted with reluctance. Secondly, the absence of precedents for a refusal means that the scope of the power to refuse has to be inferred from general constitutional principles; and opinions will differ both on the definition of those principles and the inferences to be drawn from them. Thirdly, some modern writers have argued that the usage of acceding to requests has mysteriously hardened into a binding convention never to refuse a request, or that the power to refuse exists 'in theory but not in practice', or that the monarch is too remote from political realities or too likely to be swayed by conservative influence or prejudice or too vulnerable to criticism to exercise an independent discretion. Hence, such a refusal would now be highly controversial, unless the request itself was manifestly improper; and this fact alone must make any attempt at definition highly tentative.

Perhaps the following proposition would command a wide measure of support: the Queen may properly refuse a Prime Minister's request for a dissolution if she has substantial grounds for believing (i) that an alternative Government, enjoying the confidence of a majority of the House of Commons, can be formed without a General Election, and (ii) that a General Election held at that time would be clearly prejudicial to the national interest.

21. In November 1910 George V was thought to have refused a request for dissolution but to have changed his mind after discussing the matter with senior Ministers: Jennings, op. cit., p. 424. See, however, the more equivocal account of this episode given by Sir Harold Nicolson in his official biography, *King George V*, pp. 125–39 and 150.

For extensive examinations of refusals of requests for dissolution by Governors-General and Governors in self-governing Commonwealth countries, see Eugene Forsey, *The Royal Power of Dissolution of Parliament in the British Commonwealth*; H. V. Evatt, *The King and his Dominion Governors* (2nd edn). See also B. S. Markesinis, *The Theory and Practice of Dissolution of Parliament* (1972).

As thus formulated, her power could seldom be appropriately exercised except where no party leader in the House of Commons enjoyed an overall majority.[22] Even then it might prove impolitic for her to exercise the power. The minority Prime Minister might resign at once, protesting volubly, instead of acquiescing quietly in her decision; and she might be mistaken in her belief that a stable alternative Government could be formed without an election, in which case she would be obliged to grant the new Prime Minister what she had refused to his predecessor, thus conveying in some quarters an impression of partisanship.[23] Protests notwithstanding, a refusal would probably be justified and broadly acceptable if a Prime Minister, placed in a minority within his own Cabinet and threatened with repudiation by his parliamentary party, suddenly asked for a dissolution in order to forestall the prospect of his imminent supersession.[24] Refusal might be still more readily justifiable if the rebels were known to be prepared to form a coalition Government with an opposition party, or if the country were in the throes of a serious economic crisis or widespread civil strife. *A fortiori*, a Prime Minister who has actually been repudiated by his own parliamentary party in favour of one of his colleagues can claim no constitutional right at all to demand a dissolution. It is also possible to imagine a marginal situation in which the fact that a General Election had been held only a short while previously might tip the balance against granting a request for a dissolution.

22. Though Neville Chamberlain (in the hypothetical case mentioned above) still enjoyed the support of his Cabinet and a majority of the House. Refusal of a request for a dissolution in these circumstances would have been justified, however, by reason of extreme national danger.

23. This was the embarrassing situation in which Lord Byng, the Governor-General of Canada, found himself in 1926. It does not follow that in refusing a dissolution to Mackenzie King and then granting one to Meighen, the former Opposition leader (who lost the ensuing General Election), Lord Byng had acted unconstitutionally; but Mackenzie King insisted that he had in fact so acted. See Forsey, op. cit.

In 1924, George V granted a dissolution to Ramsay MacDonald when the first Labour Government was defeated on a matter of confidence in the House. He did not, however, consider himself constitutionally obliged to grant the request.

24. This was broadly the position in South Africa in September 1939, when the Governor-General, Sir Patrick Duncan, refused a dissolution to General Hertzog, who favoured a policy of neutrality against the views of a majority of his colleagues and his party, and had been placed in a minority on this issue in the House. Hertzog resigned and Smuts, having accepted office as Prime Minister, was able to form a Government with a stable majority. cf. Markesinis, op. cit., chs. 5, 7, arguing that royal discretion is narrower than is suggested in the main text above, and rejecting the still broader view adopted by Forsey. It would not have been justifiable for the Governor of Northern Ireland to refuse a dissolution to Captain O'Neill in 1969; the Prime Minister was seeking, albeit unsuccessfully, to subdue rebellion within the ranks of the Unionist Party by appealing to the electorate, but he was known to have the backing of a majority in his Cabinet and retained a majority in the House.

Coercion of the Lords[25]

In 1712, Queen Anne created twelve new hereditary peers in order to secure the approval of the House of Lords for a peace policy. In 1832, William IV reluctantly accepted (after having initially rejected) his Government's advice to create a sufficient number of Whig peers to carry the Reform Bill (substantially enlarging the franchise and reforming the electoral constituencies) through the House of Lords, which had rejected three similar bills in rapid succession. The creation of the new peerages became unnecessary because some Tory peers, apprised of the threat, abstained from voting against the bill, which duly passed. A broadly similar situation arose in 1910–11. The Lords had rejected the Liberal Finance Bill in 1909. They agreed to pass it only after the Government had gone to the country and had been returned to power (though the Liberal Party lost its absolute majority in the House of Commons) in January 1910.[26] The Government had decided to introduce legislation to reduce to a suspensory veto the power of the Lords to reject a bill outright. Edward VII expressed the view that it would not be justifiable to ask him to exercise his prerogative to swamp the Lords with new hereditary peers in order to pass such legislation unless the electorate had shown themselves to be in favour of it. In May 1910 he died, shortly after the introduction of the Parliament Bill. Asquith, the Prime Minister, agreed to advise the new King, George V, to dissolve Parliament so that the electorate could pronounce its verdict on the bill. The King reluctantly agreed to the creation of the requisite number of peers if the Government were returned and the Lords refused to pass the bill. This contingent promise was not disclosed till after the Government had been returned to power at the second General Election of 1910 – the results were almost identical to those in the January election – and the Lords, in July 1911, had passed wrecking amendments to the bill. In August 1911 the Lords accepted the rejection of most of their amendments by the Commons, and passed the bill by a small majority.

Neither in 1831–2 nor in 1910–11 was it accepted that the Government had an absolute right to require the monarch to exercise his prerogative for such a purpose. Jennings, commenting on the present conventional rules, wrote that it was 'clear that the power to refuse is extant'.[27] However, an outright refusal might compromise the political neutrality of the

25. See Jennings, op. cit., pp. 428–48, for an analysis of the precedents.

26. The balance between the Liberals and the Conservatives was held by the Irish Nationalists and the Labour Party, who generally supported the Liberal Government. See Roy Jenkins, *Mr Balfour's Poodle*, and ch. 13.

27. Jennings, op. cit., p. 447. Any reasoned opinion expressed by Sir Ivor Jennings is entitled to the greatest respect.

monarchy. The imposition of a requirement that approval of the electorate for the measure for which the exercise of the prerogative[28] was so sought should first be obtained might well be justifiable.[29] In practice the situation is unlikely to arise, now that the Parliament Acts have reduced the suspensory veto of the Lords to one month for money bills and just over a year for other public bills.

Refusal of the royal assent

In 1913 and 1914, George V appears to have thought that he retained a residual power to refuse his assent to the Irish Home Rule Bill,[30] though he did in fact assent to it. Refusal of the royal assent on the ground that the monarch strongly disapproved of a bill or that it was intensely controversial would nevertheless be unconstitutional. The only circumstances in which the withholding of the royal assent might be justifiable would be if the Government itself were to advise such a course – a highly improbable contingency[31] – or possibly if it was notorious that a bill had been passed in disregard of mandatory procedural requirements; but since the Government in the latter situation would be of the opinion that the deviation would not affect the validity of the measure once it had been assented to, prudence would suggest the giving of assent.

Appointments and honours[32]

The Queen personally appoints members of her own private household; by far the most important member of her staff is her Private Secretary, who maintains contact with the Prime Minister and overseas dignitaries on her behalf, offers her and others informal counsel on matters of constitutional propriety and ceremonial decorum, and has been known to occupy a key position, as a liaison officer, in delicate constitutional situations.

When other appointments are made in her name, and when titles, honours and dignities are bestowed, she must act on the Prime Minister's advice (or, in the case of Commonwealth countries of which she is Queen, on the advice of the relevant Prime Minister) except on the appointment of a new Prime Minister and in the award of certain honours. Membership of the Royal Victorian Order is granted for personal services to the monarchy; normally no political implication is to be read into such an

28. On the statutory power to create life peerages, see pp. 298, 299, 309.

29. See p. 104, on insistence upon a dissolution.

30. Jennings, op. cit., pp. 395–400.

31. It could hardly arise unless a change of Government occurred without a General Election within the brief interval between the passage of the bill and its presentation for assent.

32. See generally Peter G. Richards, *Patronage in British Government*; Jennings op. cit., ch. 14.

award, but in November 1965, after the unlawful unilateral declaration of independence by the Ministers in Southern Rhodesia, she created Sir Humphrey Gibbs, the loyalist Governor, a K.C.V.O., acting in her personal discretion. When he retired in July 1969 she awarded him the G.C.V.O. She is also entitled to make appointments to the Order of Merit and the Orders of the Garter and the Thistle in her discretion. Suggestions may, of course, emanate from the Prime Minister, just as she may herself initiate suggestions for the bestowal of titles, honours and dignities in respect of which she must act on the Prime Minister's advice.

The Queen also has numerous social and ceremonial functions to perform in her capacity as head of State.[33] Among them are State visits to foreign and Commonwealth countries and the reception of heads of State from overseas. In the constitutional law of the United Kingdom a great many formal acts have to be done by her in the traditional manner, and require her personal signature or approval. She also presides in person at meetings of the Privy Council, and reads the Queen's speech at the opening of a new Parliament or a parliamentary session. She receives letters of credence from newly appointed foreign ambassadors, receives homage from new bishops, and holds some two hundred formal audiences of one sort or another in the course of a year, apart from dispensing a great deal of informal entertainment.

Legal rules affecting the monarchy

Title to the Crown is hereditary; the line of succession depends partly on statute and partly on customary common-law rules. Upon the death or abdication of a monarch, the throne and the prerogatives of the Crown pass at once – there is no interregnum:[34] 'the king never dies' – to the person next in succession. Lineal Protestant descendants of Sophia, Electress of Hanover, are alone eligible to succeed.[35] If the reigning monarch has children, sons succeed before daughters, and in accordance with primogeniture. When George VI died leaving two daughters and no son, it was assumed that the elder daughter was entitled to succeed as Elizabeth II, and did not inherit the throne jointly with her sister as a coparcener in accordance with the feudal law of succession to real property.

Roman Catholics and persons marrying Roman Catholics are excluded

33. H.C. 29 (1970–71), § 17, and note 11.

34. The last interregnum in British history occurred in 1688–9. James II was deemed to have abdicated on 11 December 1688 (the day he first tried to flee the country and dropped the Great Seal into the Thames). 'From that day until the day when William and Mary accepted the crown, 13 February 1689, there was no king of England' (Maitland, *Constitutional History of England*, p. 284).

35. Act of Settlement 1701. Edward VIII and his issue were excluded by His Majesty's Declaration of Abdication Act 1936.

by statute from the throne; and the monarch must be in communion with the Church of England, declare himself to be a Protestant, swear to maintain the Established Churches in England and Scotland, and take the Coronation Oath.[36] Until the attitude of the Church of England towards divorce is changed, it can be assumed that the monarch will be advised not to take a divorced person as consort.[37]

The law relating to the succession to the throne is uniform throughout Her Majesty's dominions. The diversification of the royal titles in 1953 implied that the Crown was no longer indivisible or undivided;[38] but although the Queen of Malta, for example, is probably to be regarded as a different legal person from (though the same natural person as) the Queen of the United Kingdom and its dependent territories, the Queen of some of the older Commonwealth countries is perhaps still regarded as the same legal person as the Queen in the United Kingdom even though she bears a different title. However, in so far as the Crown is still undivided, it may be unwise to read implications into the concept. There is no doubt that legal proceedings can be brought by one of Her Majesty's realms against another, or by one Australian state against another, or that the prerogatives of the Crown in right of Canada may be at variance with her corresponding prerogatives in right of a province of Canada.

Immediately upon a demise of the Crown, it is customary to convene an Accession Council, composed of Privy Councillors and other leading citizens – in 1952, Commonwealth High Commissioners in London were also present – by whom the Queen is formally proclaimed. The Coronation Service will take place some months later; it is attended by picturesque ceremonial, but has no significance in relation to the legal attributes or powers of the monarch. Edward VIII was never crowned.

For most legal purposes no distinction is drawn between the Crown and the monarch; and references to the Sovereign for the time being are to be construed as references to the Crown.[39] In some contexts a distinction must necessarily be drawn. Thus, a conspiracy to cause the death, or an

36. Provisions to this effect are contained *inter alia* in the Bill of Rights 1689, the Act of Settlement 1701 and the Succession to the Crown Act 1707. The Coronation Oath, prescribed by statute immediately after the Revolution of 1688, and subsequently modified by statute, has since been modified without statutory authority. Elizabeth II swore to govern the peoples of her realms and territories according to their respective laws and customs, and to maintain the established Protestant religion in the United Kingdom.

37. This is to be inferred from the circumstances surrounding Edward VIII's decision in 1936 to abdicate, the King having been advised by the Cabinet that they and the Dominion Governments could not approve of his proposed marriage to Mrs Simpson.

38. See p. 101. Contrast *Williams* v. *Howarth* [1905] A.C. 551. See further de Smith, *The Vocabulary of Commonwealth Relations* (1954).

39. Interpretation Act 1889, s. 30. See further, p. 114.

attempt on the life, of the Queen Regnant is treason, which is still punishable by death.[40] A conspiracy or attempt to depose the Queen is treason felony.[41] Ordinary civil proceedings can be brought against the Crown but not against the Queen.[42] The general concept of allegiance, however, imports duties owed to the Queen which can equally be expressed in the form of duties owed to the Crown.

The royal family

Miscellaneous rules of law and custom affect members of the royal family. Under the archaic Royal Marriages Act 1772, the marriage of a descendant of George II (other than the issue of princesses who have married into foreign families) is void unless the Queen has signified her formal consent.[43] Such a person may marry without her consent if he is over twenty-five, provided that he gives twelve months' notice to the Privy Council and the two Houses of Parliament do not register objection during that period. The monarch's consort does not in general occupy a special position in the eyes of the law, though violation of the chastity of a female consort is treason.[44] Prince Albert was designated as Prince Consort, and he exercised a substantial and beneficent influence over Queen Victoria in constitutional matters till his death in 1861. Prince Philip has not been so designated, but has been accorded official precedence immediately after the Queen; and if a regency were to become necessary in certain circumstances during Her Majesty's reign, he would become Regent.[45] The monarch's eldest son becomes Duke of Cornwall on birth; he will later be created Prince of Wales. His life, the life and chastity of the Princess of Wales during marriage, and the chastity of the monarch's eldest daughter being unmarried are protected by the law of treason.[46] The title of 'Royal Highness' is conferred upon the sons and daughters of the monarch and on the sons' wives, and on the children of the monarch's sons. The social impact, both at home and abroad, of the royal family and its individual members is an interesting psychological phenomenon which cannot be pursued within the compass of this book.

40. Statute of Treasons 1351. It is also treason to commit these offences in respect of the King's consort, but not in respect of the consort of a Queen Regnant.

41. Treason Felony Act 1848.

42. See further, ch. 28.

43. For a persuasive argument to the effect that the Act of 1772 does not apply to any of Queen Victoria's descendants, see C. d'Olivier Farran (1951) 14 *Mod. L. Rev.* 53.

44. Statute of Treasons 1351. See also note 40.

45. Regency Act 1953, s. 1. The circumstances would be (i) if a child of Her Majesty succeeded to the throne while under eighteen years of age; or (ii) if Her Majesty became incapacitated and no other person was eligible to be Regent.

46. Statute of Treasons 1351.

No general statutory provision existed until 1937 for the exercise of the royal functions if the monarch were an infant, or were incapacitated or absent from the realm. The Regency Act 1937 dealt with these matters; it was amended by Acts of 1943 and 1953. Under the present law:

(i) There is to be a regency if the Sovereign is under eighteen years of age, or if the Sovereign is incapacitated by infirmity of mind or body or is 'for some definite cause not available' (for example through being a prisoner of war) for performing the royal functions. A declaration as to the Sovereign's incapacity or unavailability is to be made by the Sovereign's spouse, the Lord Chancellor, the Speaker of the House of Commons, the Lord Chief Justice and the Master of the Rolls, or any three or more of them; and a regency will continue till a declaration as to the removal of the incapacity is similarly made. The Regent is to be that person of full age who is next in the line of succession to the throne,[47] provided that he is a British subject resident in the United Kingdom and is not disqualified on religious grounds. He may exercise all royal functions except that he is precluded from assenting to a bill to alter the succession to the throne or to repeal the Acts securing the Scottish religion and Church.[48]

(ii) If the Sovereign is suffering from a lesser degree of incapacity than would justify the establishment of a regency, or if she is or intends to be temporarily absent from the realm, she may appoint Counsellors of State (not a Council of State) by letters patent and delegate to them such royal functions as may be specified. They may not, however, dissolve Parliament except on her express instructions, or grant any title or dignity of the peerage. The Counsellors of State are to be the spouse of the Sovereign, the four persons next in succession to the throne (unless disqualified for being Regent or absent from the realm), and Queen Elizabeth the Queen Mother.

Crown revenues[49]

For many centuries no distinction was drawn in financial matters between the King in his public capacity (the Crown) and the King in his private capacity. The King was expected to live of his own, through feudal dues,

47. Subject to the proviso summarized in note 45.

48. For the possible effect of disregard of this prohibition (Regency Act 1937, s. 4(2), see p. 88.

49. For the substantial body of law on this matter, see *Halsbury's Laws of England*, title 'Constitutional Law'. For a brief historical survey see Maitland, *Constitutional History of England*, pp. 430–38. For the present position, see Report of the Select Committee on the Civil List, 1971 (note 1).

income from Crown lands (including the Duchies of Cornwall and Lancaster) and sundry prerogative fiscal rights, such as treasure trove and the forfeited property of outlaws and convicted felons; and to provide for the ordinary expenses of government out of his privy purse. Only for special purposes was he to have recourse to Parliament in order to obtain extra money by the levying of taxation. When he did come to Parliament, the Commons (especially under the early Stuarts) were apt to demand redress of grievances before agreeing to grant taxes or to appropriate supplies. Gradually this system broke down and parliamentary grants were made to the Sovereign for the time being for his private purposes during his lifetime. In exchange the Sovereign surrendered to the Exchequer most of the time-honoured hereditary revenues of the Crown.

In 1800 the Sovereign was enabled by statute to hold land in a *private* capacity; this is alienable and is rateable. But the Queen is personally exempt from most forms of taxation.[50] Today the Queen's private estates are managed separately from the Crown lands, which are exempt from fiscal burdens and are administered by Crown Estate Commissioners.

A Civil List Act is passed at the beginning of each reign, providing for annual sums of money[51] for Her Majesty's privy purse, salaries and expenses of her household, and miscellaneous matters including annuities and expenses of some other members of the royal family. When an increase in the Civil List is sought, there will be private consultations between party leaders and the matter will be referred to a Select Committee of the House of Commons for inquiry and report before legislation is introduced. The Act now regulating the royal grant from Parliament is the Civil List Act 1972, amending the Civil List Act 1952.[52]

Signification of the royal pleasure

Fortunately, not every act of government done in the Queen's name requires her personal participation. Nevertheless, either by custom or by statute, she has to take part in a great number of such acts. For example, when an Order in Council has to be made, or when any other transaction has to take place in Council, she must preside at a formal meeting of the Privy Council. About ten meetings are held annually. Some royal appoint-

50. For the complex rules and practices in these matters, see the 1971 Report, especially Appendices 1 and 12.

51. The Civil List is charged on the Consolidated Fund and does not, therefore, require annual authorization by Parliament.

52. The Civil List was thereby increased from £475,000 to £980,000 a year. Some royal expenses are borne on departmental votes. The Queen has not drawn the sums allocated to her privy purse.

ments (for example, ambassadors) are made under the royal sign manual[53] (the Queen's personal signature); some (for example, appointments of most Cabinet Ministers) are made by personal delivery of the seal of office. Many classes of acts (for example, the issue of royal proclamations, writs for the holding of elections, letters patent for the conferment of peerages, the appointment of royal commissions, and charters of incorporation for boroughs and universities, and the ratification of certain treaties) involve the affixing of the Great Seal of the Realm, of which the Lord Chancellor is custodian; this can normally be brought into use only by virtue of a warrant under the royal sign manual.

The royal prerogative

The royal prerogative, 'in its nature singular and eccentrical',[54] can be roughly described as those inherent legal attributes which are unique to the Crown. For 'the Crown' we can substitute 'the Queen'. Prerogative powers belong to the Queen as a person as well as to the institution called the Crown; in law the Queen is the Crown, or Her Majesty's Government,[55] or the State, except where an Act of Parliament or common sense differentiates them expressly or by necessary implication.[56] Powers and duties are often vested by statute directly in named Ministers. But prerogatives are non-statutory attributes of the Crown, not statutory attributes of its servants.

Prerogatives are *inherent* in so far as they are derived from customary common law. They are *legal* in so far as they are recognized and enforced by courts; and, as the *Case of Proclamations* (1611)[57] made abundantly plain, their ambit is determinable by the courts. When Blackstone described the prerogative as 'that special pre-eminence which the King hath, over and above all other persons, and *out of the ordinary course of the common law*, in right of his regal dignity',[58] he was not asserting that the Crown could conclusively determine the limits of its own prerogative; he

53. Among other acts done under the royal sign manual is the granting of a royal pardon. See also Criminal Law Act 1967, s. 9.

54. Blackstone, *Commentaries*, vol. 1, p. 238.

55. Or 'Her Majesty's Government in the United Kingdom'. See, for example, Jamaica Independence Act 1962, s. 1(1), and other statutes dealing with external relations.

56. See pp. 110, 112–13. For a skilful critique, see Geoffrey Marshall, *Constitutional Theory*, pp. 17–34.

57. 12 Co. Rep. 74. A proclamation forbidding under penalty new building in and around London was held to be unlawful. Similar proclamations had been issued and enforced under Elizabeth I – for example, a proclamation of 7 July 1580 made at Nonsuch.

58. loc. cit. (italics supplied).

was merely emphasizing the *uniqueness* of the prerogative. Prerogative attributes are not shared with subjects, though there may be close similarities; the royal prerogative in time of real or apprehended war differs in degree rather than kind from the general common-law doctrine of necessity. Recently the courts have stopped using the term 'Crown privilege' to describe the power to procure the exclusion of evidence from judicial proceedings on grounds of public interest, and it must be doubted whether this is to be regarded as a prerogative at all, because it is not a power peculiar to the Crown.[59]

The prerogative consists mainly of executive governmental powers – powers to conduct foreign relations, to make war and peace, to regulate the disposition of the armed forces, to appoint and dismiss Ministers, to dissolve Parliament, to assent to bills, and so on. The exercise of these powers is controlled by constitutional convention. It also includes immunities (for example, the Queen's personal immunity from suit or prosecution, and from liability to income tax), privileges (for example, proprietary rights over royal fish, the status of the Crown as a preferred creditor) and miscellaneous attributes, such as the prerogative of protection which is in some aspects a legal duty.

Other definitions can be considered. To Dicey,[60] the royal prerogative was 'the residue of discretionary or arbitrary authority, which at any given time is legally left in the hands of the Crown'. This definition is incomplete because it is restricted to powers. However, it includes some important features. It stresses the *residual* features of the prerogative within the realm. The prerogative is traceable to the days before Parliament ever existed, but cannot be enlarged by the Crown except in certain dependent territories. 'It is 350 years and a civil war too late for the Queen's courts to broaden the prerogative.'[61] Prerogatives can be and have been abrogated or diminished by statute; the Crown Proceedings Act 1947 deprived the Crown (but not the monarch in her private capacity) of various immunities in civil litigation. They have also been lost by other means. For certain colonies the Crown could lose its plenary legislative powers under the prerogative by granting a representative legislature.[62] Prerogative powers in the administration of justice passed into the hands

59. See especially *R.* v. *Lewes JJ., ex p. Home Secretary* [1972] 3 W.L.R. 279 (H.L.). Another reason may be that such claims, even if made by Ministers, are reviewable by the courts: see *Conway* v. *Rimmer* [1968] A.C. 910. and ch. 28.

60. *Introduction to the Study of the Law of the Constitution* (10th edn), p. 434. His definition has been cited in a number of judgments.

61. *British Broadcasting Corporation* v. *Johns* [1965] Ch. 32 at 79, *per* Diplock L.J. See also *The Zamora* [1916] 2 A.C. 77 (the Crown may mitigate but not extend its own prerogative in prize law).

62. *Campbell* v. *Hall* (1774) 1 Cowp. 204 and ch. 30.

of Her Majesty's judges.[63] Other prerogatives came to be shared by subjects and lost their original character and function.[64] Some appear to have quietly withered away.[65] Yet a vanishing prerogative is a strange creature, for there is no generally accepted principle of law that a prerogative may be lost merely by desuetude.[66]

Prerogative discretionary powers are also *absolute* (which is what Dicey meant by 'arbitrary') in the eyes of the courts, in the sense that once the existence, scope and form of a prerogative power are established to their satisfaction, the courts have disclaimed jurisdiction to review the propriety or adequacy of the grounds upon which it has been exercised.[67] The principle has been reiterated in recent cases where attempts have been made to impugn the exercise of prerogative powers to conclude treaties,[68] disseminate information,[69] and to refuse to commute a sentence.[70] In this respect prerogative powers must be differentiated from statutory discretionary powers. With but few exceptions, an exercise of a statutory discretion can be challenged in the courts by a person aggrieved on the grounds that it has been directed to a purpose outside the contemplation of the parent Act.[71] But it would seem that no court would be prepared to review the grounds for refusal or revocation of a passport, because this is a royal prerogative,[72] though a court might arrive at the conclusion that a power claimed by the Crown (for example, to take property for defence purposes) existed in law but imported a duty to pay compensation to the person whose interests were encroached upon.[73]

63. See especially *Prohibitions del Roy* (1607) 12 Co. Rep. 63 (King could not administer justice in person). For criticisms of the casuistic reasoning adopted by the judges, see Dicey, op. cit., p. 18.

64. For example, the prerogative writ *ne exeat regno* by which the monarch could (and possibly still can (see J. W. Bridge (1972) 88 *L.Q.R.* 83) command a subject not to leave the realm, at least in time of emergency; cf. *Felton* v. *Callis* [1969] 1 Q.B. 200, showing the strict limitations of the scope of the writ in proceedings between subjects.

65. For example, the power to impress men into the navy.

66. F. W. Maitland, *Constitutional History of England*, p. 418. See also pp. 118, 126.

67. See, for example, *R.* v. *Allen* (1862) 1 B. & S. 850 (grounds for entering a *nolle prosequi*); *Engelke* v. *Musmann* [1928] A.C. 433 (recognition of diplomatic representative for purpose of according diplomatic immunity – a matter now regulated by statute); *Chandler* v. *D.P.P.* [1964] A.C. 763 (disposition of armed forces; though cf. the reservation entered by Lord Devlin at 809–10) and see p. 133.

68. *Blackburn* v. *Att.-Gen.* [1971] 1 W.L.R. 1037; *McWhirter* v. *Att.-Gen.* [1972] C.M.L. Rep. 882.

69. *Jenkins* v. *Att.-Gen.*, The Times, 13 August 1971.

70. *Hanratty* v. *Lord Butler*, The Times, 12 May 1971.

71. See, for example, *Padfield* v. *Minister of Agriculture* [1968] A.C. 997.

72. *Secretary of State for Home Department* v. *Lakdawalla* [1972] Imm. App. Rep. 26.

73. For example, *Burmah Oil Co.* v. *Lord Advocate* [1965] A.C. 75. In practice the distinction between jurisdiction to determine the ambit of a prerogative and lack of

After the Norman Conquest the King enjoyed proprietary and other rights, privileges and immunities in his capacity as the highest feudal lord in the realm. He also enjoyed governmental powers, shifting and ill-defined. King John was forcefully reminded by his barons at Runnymede that his governmental authority was not absolute; and a generation later Bracton, the great jurist, was to proclaim that the King was *sub Deo et lege*, beneath God and the law. But in a large area of government the King remained *legibus solutus*, free from legal restraints, in providing for the public weal; and he could sit as a judge in his own courts but could not be judged by them. By the end of the Middle Ages his field of absolute discretion had contracted; his judicial power was exercisable through his judges, his legislative power, including his power to impose taxation, was normally exercisable only through Parliament; yet there were exceptions to the general rule, and the boundaries between what were soon to be called the absolute prerogative (exercisable as the King thought fit) and the ordinary prerogative (exercisable only through Parliament and the courts) still lacked clear definition.

After the turmoil of the Wars of the Roses, in which tyranny jostled with anarchy, came the long period of strong monarchical government under the Tudors. The King's Council was revivified, in the form of a Privy Council with subordinate regional councils, as a prime instrument for expressing and imposing the royal will; the new conciliar courts of Star Chamber and High Commission also served as organs for the enforcement of royal proclamations and the administration of matters of public law. Under Henry VIII the status both of Parliament and of the courts of common law diminished; only in Elizabeth I's later years, when the threat to national survival had receded, did they show a revival. By this time a fairly coherent theory of the royal prerogative, detached from its feudal roots, had been developed. Matters of private right were for the courts of common law and equity; matters of State, or public right, were for the King and his extraordinary tribunals, and the King could withdraw such questions from the cognizance of the courts.[75] But where lay

---

jurisdiction to determine the grounds on which it may properly be exercised is not clear-cut, and in some cases it is so indistinct that judicial review of prerogative powers is assimilated to judicial review of statutory powers. See D. G. T. Williams, [1971] *Camb. L.J.* 178. See also Addendum.

74. For an excellent survey, see D. L. Keir and F. H. Lawson, *Cases in Constitutional Law* (5th edn), ch. 2. See further W. S. Holdsworth, *History of English Law*, vol. 4, pp. 201 ff; vol. 6, pp. 20 ff; vol. 10, pp. 140–425.

75. By issuing the prerogative writ *de non procedendo rege inconsulto*. The writ fell into desuetude after James I's use of the writ in *Brownlow's* case (1615) 3 Bulst. 32 had been successfully resisted by Coke C.J. and his brethren.

the boundary between the two? In what circumstances could the monarch make penal laws without parliamentary sanction, tax without Parliament, commit to prison otherwise than through the ordinary courts? Answers which could be glossed over under Elizabeth could no longer be avoided when James I, the first of the hapless Stuart line, innocent of tact and beset with ineluctable economic and religious problems, ascended the throne to face his unruly Parliament and contumacious Judiciary.

We have already touched on the history of the contests that followed.[76] The judges of the common-law courts, sometimes remoulding the law under the guise of declaring it, insisted that they were the proper persons to determine the limits of the King's powers; that the King 'hath no prerogative but that which the law of the land allows him'; that he could not create new offences by proclamation under the prerogative;[77] that he could not sit as a judge in his own courts,[78] or withdraw matters of State from their cognizance.[79] Some of these rulings were disregarded by the King, and he dismissed Coke and other obstinate men from the bench. Charles I followed his father's example but with even less guile; and his struggles with the men of Parliament (among whom the common lawyers were prominent) were to be resolved only on the field of battle. With him perished the concept of the divine right of kingship, and the maxim that the King could do no wrong could no longer be equated with the assertion that everything a King did was right in the eyes of the law.

Under the early Stuarts some of the more extravagant contentions of the Crown were supportable by reference to common-law doctrine. When the courts held that he could levy taxes under his prerogative for the regulation of external trade,[80] and that 'the special command of the King' was a valid return to a writ of habeas corpus brought to secure release from imprisonment without trial for refusal to pay royal fiscal exactions,[81] their decisions were founded on precedent. The decision in *Hampden's* case,[82] that unparliamentary charges could be levied on the subject incidentally to the prerogative to deal with national emergencies, of which the King was the sole judge, is questionable, and flamboyant assertions of the scope of the prerogative appeared in the judgments; but the majority decision was not manifestly erroneous in law, biased though some of the judges may have been in favour of untrammelled royal discretion in matters touching the public good. And, as we pointed out

76. See p. 71.
77. *Case of Proclamations* (1611) 12 Co. Rep. 74.
78. *Prohibitions del Roy* (1607) 12 Co. Rep. 63.
79. *Brownlow's* case (see note 75).
80. *Bate's* case (1606), 2 St. Tr. 371.
81. *Darnel's* case (1627) 3 St. Tr. 1.
82. *Case of Ship Money* (1637) 3 St. Tr. 825.

earlier,[83] it was generally accepted by seventeenth-century lawyers that some of the absolute prerogatives were inseparable from the person of the King, who could not be deprived of them even by Act of Parliament.

Charles I's Parliaments nevertheless abrogated some of the prerogatives upheld by the courts. The Petition of Right 1628 purported to prohibit unparliamentary taxation[84] and imprisonment without trial by special command of the King.[85] More important, the Long Parliament in 1641 abolished not only ship-money[86] but also the conciliar courts which the King had continued to use as his instrument to by-pass the restraints upon his prerogative imposed the courts of common law. With the death of the Star Chamber and the removal of criminal jurisdiction from the Privy Council, the distinction between matters of public law and matters of private law began to dissolve, for the ordinary courts of common law and equity acquired an all-embracing jurisdiction.

There followed the Civil War, the execution of Charles I, the Cromwellian Commonwealth and protectorate, and the restoration of Charles II in 1660. But any attempt by Charles to reassert his father's sweeping pretensions would have been foredoomed to failure; and Charles was astute enough to appreciate this fact. His brother, James II, was not, and his brief reign (1685–8) ended in disaster and precipitate flight. The Bill of Rights 1689 placed the succession to the throne on a statutory basis, declared that the pretended prerogative of suspending the operation of laws was illegal and that no prerogative dispensation from an obligation to comply with a statute was to be valid in future[87] (though the prerogative of pardon was preserved), and made all unparliamentary taxation by pretence of prerogative illegal.[88] The Act of Settlement 1701 again altered the succession, provided that no royal pardon could be pleaded in bar of an impeachment, and gave the judges security of tenure against the Crown; they were to hold office during good behaviour, but were to be removable on the address of both Houses of Parliament.

The Revolution Settlement still left the King with wide prerogative

83. p. 72.

84. The formulation was not unequivocal, but was clear enough to reverse the effect of the decision in *Bate's* case (1606) 2 St. Tr. 371.

85. cf. *Darnel's* case (1627) 3 St. Tr. 1. The Petition of Right was couched in language appropriate for a request to redress grievances, but it was passed by both Houses as if it were a bill and was assented to (with great reluctance) by Charles I and enrolled with the Acts of Parliament.

86. cf. *Hampden's* case (see note 82).

87. cf. *R.* v. *Customs and Excise Commissioners, ex p. Cook* [1970] 1 W.L.R. 450 at 454–5 (invalidity of extra-statutory tax concessions offered by authority of the Treasury).

88. Taxation by Community regulation will be a constitutional innovation. See p. 284.

powers – powers actively exercised by William, Mary and Anne – but the extent of power had become less significant than the safeguards against its abuse. After the Hanoverian succession in 1714, the prerogative came increasingly to be used on ministerial advice, though there was a temporary reversal of the trend in the early years of George III's reign. The impeachment of royal advisers of whom Parliament disapproved was gradually replaced by the political sanctions implicit in the principle of ministerial responsibility to Parliament. Following the expansion of the franchise in 1832, the House of Commons became a more formidable body than the Lords; members and Ministers had to be more responsive to the opinion of the electorate; the political influence of the monarch in the constitutional system dwindled, and by the end of Victoria's reign the range of prerogative powers exercisable by convention in the monarch's personal discretion was but little wider than it is today. The area of prerogative has also been gradually eroded by statute, but in strict law it still encompasses most of the attributes inherent in the Crown in 1690.

Some general problems

If one were to devote a whole book to examining the scope of the royal prerogative today,[89] one would still leave a number of questions unanswered. Writing in 1888, Maitland observed that there was 'often great uncertainty as to the exact limits' of the prerogative; and he concluded his short but masterly survey with these words: 'Thus our course is set about with difficulties, with prerogatives disused, with prerogatives of doubtful existence, with prerogatives which exist by sufferance, merely because no one has thought it worth while to abolish them.'[90] The problem of identification, then, is very real. No comprehensive authoritative statement was offered in medieval times; and in the seventeenth century the scope of the prerogative was hotly disputed. We can identify, as a matter of historical interest, some of the disputed and undisputed prerogatives of which the Crown has been explicitly deprived by statute. But the concept of the prerogative as a bundle of inherent and residuary attributes is intrinsically vague. In 1957 a Committee of Privy Councillors thought that telephone-tapping authorized by a Minister might possibly be justified as a manifestation of an ancient prerogative power to intercept communications between subjects;[91] yet it is more than doubtful whether such a

89. cf. Joseph Chitty, *The Prerogatives of the Crown* (the best-known monograph, written in the early nineteenth century); A. B. Keith, *The King and the Imperial Crown*; G. S. Robertson, *Civil Proceedings by and against the Crown*.

90. *Constitutional History of England*, pp. 418, 421.

91. Cmnd 283 (1957), pt 1. cf. R. F. V. Heuston, *Essays in Constitutional Law* (2nd edn), pp. 50–52.

prerogative ever existed. That the Crown still has certain prerogative powers in time of grave national emergency to enter upon, take and destroy private property seems clear. The conditions under which these powers are exercisable are far from clear, partly because the powers were never precisely defined, partly because the scope of the war prerogative was not considered in general terms by the courts for nearly three hundred years, and partly because in modern times various statutory provisions have been made for these matters.[92] Again, it is not clear how far the royal prerogative in foreign affairs and the concept of an 'act of State' are coterminous.[93]

Archaic prerogatives: a suggestion

In a recent Scottish appeal to the House of Lords, Lord Simon of Glaisdale said that 'a rule of the English common law, once clearly established, does not become extinct merely by disuse'; it may 'go into a cataleptic trance', but, like Sleeping Beauty, it can be revived 'in propitious circumstances'. It cannot, however, revive if it is 'grossly anomalous and anachronistic'.[94] Probably this proposition offers the best available explanation of the fate of obsolescent prerogatives like the powers to forbid a subject to leave the realm, and to impress him into naval service.[95] Conceivably the former power might revive in circumstances which are, admittedly, hard to envisage;[96] but the latter power must surely be unresponsive to any Prince Charming.

Statute and prerogative powers

The relationship between statute and prerogative remains strangely abstruse. Statutes can bind the Crown;[97] and a prerogative can be abolished by express words. Alternatively the wording of a statute may leave no room for doubt that Parliament, when conferring powers on the Crown, intended to leave the prerogative intact;[98] or to maintain the

92. See *Att.-Gen.* v. *De Keyser's Royal Hotel Ltd* [1920] A.C. 508; *Burmah Oil Co.* v. *Lord Advocate* [1965] A.C. 75; *Nissan* v. *Att.-Gen.* [1970] A.C. 179.

93. *Nissan*'s case (see note 92 and pp. 135–6).

94. *McKendrick* v. *Sinclair* 1972 S.L.T. (H.L.) 110 at 116, 117.

95. See p. 116, notes 64, 65.

96. Particularly in view of provisions of Community law relating to freedom of movement, and the development of international law doctrine on the matter.

97. See generally, pp. 124–6.

98. For example, Emergency Powers (Defence) Act 1939, s. 9; Crown Proceedings Act 1947, ss. 11(1), 40(1).

prerogative but regulate the way in which it can be exercised.[99] Puzzles arise where Parliament neither extinguishes nor saves a prerogative but simply confers powers on the Crown in an area hitherto occupied only by prerogative. In such a situation, the Crown must indeed abide by any statutory restrictions imposed on the exercise of its powers (for example, procedural requirements, or a duty to pay compensation) and cannot fall back on its original absolute prerogative. To the extent of *this* inconsistency the prerogative is abrogated.[100] But suppose a statute merely covers the same ground as prerogative without expressly restricting the Crown's competence. Do statute and prerogative then co-exist, or is the prerogative swallowed up and superseded?[101] If superseded, does it revive when the statute is repealed?

Answers to these questions must be tentative. Because the prerogative is tenacious and the Crown is not readily held to be bound by mere implication,[102] the courts are unlikely to hold that a prerogative (for example, to declare the extent of territorial waters[103]) has been excluded by implication unless legislation evinces a very clear intention to cover the field in question exhaustively.[104]

Assuming that a prerogative is superseded by a statute and the statute is later repealed, it is submitted that the prerogative ought not to be held to revive unless it is a major governmental attribute[105] or is otherwise consonant with contemporary conditions.[106] Hence archaic Crown privileges or immunities expressly abolished by the Crown Proceedings Act

99. See Royal Assent Act 1967.

100. *Att.-Gen.* v. *De Keyser's Royal Hotel Ltd* [1920] A.C. 508 (requisitioning).

101. See the differences of opinion on this point expressed by Lord Denning M.R. and Russell L.J. in *Sabally and N'Jie* v. *Att.-Gen.* [1965] 1 Q.B. 273. See also K. O. Roberts-Wray, *Commonwealth and Colonial Law*, pp. 164–6, 169–72, 190–7.

102. See p. 124.

103. *R.* v. *Kent JJ., ex p. Lye* [1967] 2 Q.B. 173; *Post Office* v. *Estuary Radio Ltd* [1968] 2 Q.B. 740; *The Fagernes* [1927] P. 311; Territorial Waters Order in Council 1964 (S.I. 1965, p. 6452A); Territorial Waters Jurisdiction Act 1878.

104. See the cases in which prerogative wardship jurisdiction, exercisable through the High Court, has been invoked in areas covered by legislation dealing with the care and education of children. The courts have asserted the continued existence of the prerogative but are reluctant to invoke it (see, for example, *Re M* (an Infant) [1961] Ch. 328; *Re Mohamed Arif* [1968] Ch. 643 (a Commonwealth immigrant case)). See also note 125.

105. As in the *De Keyser* case (see above; power to requisition for defence purposes in wartime), in which event the prerogative may reasonably be held to lie in suspense; see [1920] A.C. at 539–540. See also ibid., 554, 561.

106. cf. *New Windsor Corporation* v. *Taylor* [1899] A.C. 41 (local customary franchise of tollage superseded by statutory right; statute later repealed; held, old franchise was not thereby revived). The terms of sections 11(1) and 38(2) (*a*) of the Interpretation Act 1889 may not be irrelevant in this general context. See also p. 121.

1947 should not be construed as having been restored merely by a repeal of the relevant parts of the Act.

The prerogative today: domestic affairs

Prerogative powers in an emergency will be considered in a later chapter.[107] The other surviving prerogatives in domestic affairs are a mixed bag of residual loose ends; some linger on as reminders of feudal days, some are of major importance in the conduct of public affairs. Most of the prerogatives are rights and powers, but it may be convenient to touch first on the main prerogative attributes which are in the nature of privileges, immunities and duties.

The King (or Queen Regnant) can do no wrong. Over the years the prerogative of perfection has borne a variety of meanings, ranging from the total unaccountability of the monarch to any human agency, to the simple rule that the monarch in person cannot be prosecuted or sued for a wrongful act in the courts. The latter rule still prevails, though it is possible to bring a petition of right against the monarch in the High Court for alleged breaches of contract and a few other legal wrongs, thus obtaining a judicial remedy unaccompanied by coercive relief. Before the Crown Proceedings Act 1947 the King in his natural capacity was undifferentiated from the King in his public capacity; it was therefore impossible (subject to a small number of exceptions) to sue the Crown as a matter of strict law for tortious acts or omissions; the Crown could not even be made vicariously liable for the torts of its servants committed in the course of their employment, for this would be to impute wrongdoing to the monarch. Fortunately this absurd anachronism has been substantially removed from our law.[108]

Since the days of Elizabeth I it has been acknowledged that acts done by the Crown purportedly under the prerogative may be held by the courts to be *ultra vires*[109] – a proposition challenged only by the most extreme Stuart theoreticians.

Because it may be unseemly to hold the monarch personally to account for an invalid or potentially controversial act performed by her in her public capacity, custom requires the participation of Ministers in most of such acts – for example, by countersignature, or by presence at a Privy Council meeting where formal business is transacted. Thus, it is the Ministers who attract responsibility.

107. See ch. 23.
108. See ch. 28, where the state of the law is considered in more detail.
109. See, for example, *Willion* v. *Berkley* (1561) Plow. 223; *Case of Monopolies* (1602) 11 Co. Rep. 84b.

The King is a preferred creditor. If a debtor is insolvent, the Crown has priority as a creditor at common law. This matter is now largely regulated by statute. But in the levying of execution or distress against the property of a subject, the Crown still enjoys priority under the prerogative.

Time does not run against the King (Nullum temporis occurrit regi). The normal periods of limitation did not apply to the Crown in criminal proceedings and as a plaintiff in civil litigation. In most forms of civil proceedings, and to a lesser extent in criminal proceedings, this immunity has been abrogated by statute.

The Crown is not bound by statute save by express words or necessary implication. In its origin a prerogative immunity, this proposition can also be formulated as a particular rule of statutory interpretation. It covers the imposition of obligations, restraints and other burdens. General words directed to such ends will normally be construed as excluding the Crown unless the purpose of the Act would be frustrated were the Crown held to be exempt from their operation.[110] To apply this principle rigidly today would be unreasonable. Although in some contexts it would be incongruous or contrary to public policy to hold the Crown impliedly subject to the same liabilities as the public at large, in others it would be unjust to hold the Crown exempt merely because an Act would be still workable despite the exemption of the Crown from its ambit. But the principle has, on the whole, been rigidly applied; and Crown immunity has been understood to mean that Crown tenants, and tenants of a body ancillary to the regular armed forces, do not enjoy the protection of the Rent Acts,[111] that government Departments do not have to obtain planning permission in order to effect a material change in the use of land occupied by them,[112] that land occupied for Crown purposes (for example, for use as county courts[113]) is immune from local rates,[114] that a court cannot make an order for the abatement of a nuisance committed in a hospital

110. *Bombay Province* v. *Bombay Municipal Council* [1947] A.C. 88; though cf. *Madras Electric Supply Corpn Ltd* v. *Boarland* [1955] A.C. 667 (where the word 'person' in a special rule in an Income Tax Act was held to include the Crown). The prerogative immunity in Scots law is possibly less far-reaching: J. D. B. Mitchell [1957] *Public Law* 304. And for the earlier English rule that the Crown was impliedly bound by statutes passed for the public good, see *Chitty on Prerogative* (1820), p. 382.
111. *Territorial Forces Association* v. *Nichols* [1949] 1 K.B. 35; *Tamlin* v. *Hannaford* [1950] 1 K.B. 18 (dicta). This rule has since been modified by statute.
112. *Ministry of Agriculture* v. *Jenkins* [1963] 2 Q.B. 317.
113. *R.* v. *Manchester Overseers* (1854) 3 E. & B. 336.
114. See generally *Mersey Docks and Harbour Board Trustees* v. *Cameron* (1864) 11 H.L.C. at 464–5. See now General Rate Act 1967. In any event, the Crown does in practice pay contributions in lieu of rates in respect of exempt hereditaments.

administered under the National Health Service,[115] and even (till the Road Traffic Acts were expressed to bind the Crown) that a Crown servant on duty driving a vehicle for Crown purposes and under superior orders to deliver a load quickly, could not be convicted of exceeding a statutory speed limit.[116]

The narrower principle, also founded on the prerogative, that the Crown is immune from central government taxation in the absence of express words or necessary intendment, has a more secure and rational basis. Why should an intention be imputed to Parliament to raise money *from* the Government? Government Departments are exempt from income tax; so is the Queen in her personal capacity;[117] civil servants in their private capacities are not, of course, exempt. However, difficult marginal cases arise. Public bodies which are servants or agents of the Crown, or which act as instruments of the Crown, are exempt. But how and where is a court to draw the line? The general functions of local authorities, and public corporations conducting the affairs of nationalized industries, are not performed as servants or agents of the Crown; they enjoy a substantial degree of independence from the Crown, and their functions are not unambiguously within the province of central government;[118] they do not, therefore, attract the immunities and privileges of the Crown.[119] For similar reasons the BBC has been held to be subject to income tax.[120] The Custodian of Enemy Property was held to be a Crown servant, mainly because of the degree of control that Ministers were entitled to exercise over him, and tax was therefore not payable on the income from property disposed of by him while acting in that capacity.[121] Hair-splitting distinctions may still have to be drawn where

115. *Nottingham Area No. 1 Hospital Management Committee* v. *Owen* [1958] 1 Q.B 50. For another aspect of Crown immunity (in respect of patented drugs) in connection with the National Health Service, see *Pfizer Corporation Ltd* v. *Ministry of Health* [1965] A.C. 512.

116. *Cooper* v. *Hawkins* [1904] 2 K.B. 164. See now Road Traffic Regulation Act 1967, s. 97, binding the Crown. For a critique of *Cooper* v. *Hawkins* (questioning the idea of 'superior orders' in this context) see Glanville Williams, *Crown Proceedings*, pp. 49–52.

117. See p. 113, above.

118. See *Mersey Docks and Harbour Board Trustees* v. *Gibbs* (1866) L.R. 1 H.L. 93 on the separate legal status of autonomous and semi-autonomous public authorities.

119. See *Tamlin* v. *Hannaford* (note 111), on nationalized industries; and generally J. A. G. Griffith, 'Public Corporations as Crown Servants' (1952) 9 *U. of Toronto L.J.* 169. The now defunct Central Land Board was held to be a Crown servant; *Glasgow Corporation* v. *Central Land Board* 1956 S.C. (H.L.) 1. That nationalized industries do not enjoy Crown immunities is now usually made clear by statute. See, for example, Post Office Act 1969, s. 6(5); p. 220.

120. *British Broadcasting Corporation* v. *Johns* [1965] A.C. 32.

121. *Bank voor Handel en Scheepvaart* v. *Administrator of Hungarian Property* [1954] A.C. 584.

it is doubtful whether a body is a Crown agent, or where a body is clearly not a Crown agent but performs functions associated with the business of central government.

The prerogative of protection. This prerogative does not fit neatly into any analytical category. In some aspects it is a duty, in others a power.[122] The Crown has a duty to 'protect' its own subjects by granting them diplomatic protection in foreign countries; but this duty is not directly enforceable in a court of law, and in any event the 'duty' is now probably limited to citizens of the United Kingdom and Colonies and British protected persons. It is under no legal duty to grant them passports. Nor is it under any legal duty to offer armed protection to such of its intrepid subjects as engage in hazardous ventures on the high seas or in foreign countries; if it decides in its discretion to offer this form of protection, it can impose a condition that the subject shall pay for the protection offered.[123] The Crown does owe limited duties of protection to persons owing allegiance, including aliens owing local allegiance; the extent and implications of these duties will be considered later.[124]

The capacity of the Crown as *parens patriae* implied a prerogative to protect the welfare of infants. This power or duty has long been exercised only through the Queen's courts by judges; in other words, it has become an 'ordinary' prerogative as distinct from an 'absolute' prerogative. But an alien infant owing local allegiance is within the scope of the prerogative of protection, so that the Chancery Division has jurisdiction to exercise its discretion whether to make him a ward of court.[125] In so far as the prerogative of protection encompasses the superintendence of charities and the welfare of persons of unsound mind, it appears to have been almost entirely engulfed by statute.

Miscellaneous domestic prerogatives

Power to appoint and dismiss Ministers, to dissolve and prorogue Parliament, and to assent to legislation is derived from the prerogative. As the fountain of honour the Queen creates hereditary peerages and confers

122. See two thought-provoking articles by H. Lauterpacht (1947) 9 *Camb.L.J.* 330, and Glanville Williams (1948) 10 *Camb.L.J.* 54. See also Clive Parry (ed.), *A British Digest of International Law*, vol. 5, s. 3; and pp. 437–40.

123. *China Navigation Co.* v. *Att.-Gen.* [1932] 2 K.B. 197. See also *Glasbrook Bros.* v. *Glamorgan C.C.* [1925] A.C. 270 (no charge can be required for supplying reasonable police protection, since there is a pre-existing legal duty to afford such protection; a charge can, however, be imposed for providing protection going beyond what is reasonably necessary); see now Police Act 1964, s. 15, and p. 381, note 6.

124. See pp. 437–40.

125. *Re P.* (*G.E.*) (*an Infant*) [1965] Ch. 568. See also note 104.

other titles and dignities. As head of the Established Church, she appoints archbishops and diocesan bishops, and assents to measures of the General Synod approved by both Houses of Parliament. As head of the armed forces, she directs their disposition and commissions officers. War is declared and a state of war terminated by virtue of the prerogative.

The diffusion of government information,[126] the determination of the extent of territorial waters[127] and the regulation of the civil service[128] fall partly or wholly within the scope of the prerogative. Whether the exclusion and expulsion of friendly aliens was permissible under the prerogative is doubtful;[129] these matters are in any event regulated exclusively by statutory authority today.[130] Enemy aliens can be interned or expelled. The issue and revocation of a United Kingdom passport fall within the prerogative.

The Queen is the fountain of justice, and in relation to the administration of justice, several prerogatives remain vested in the Crown. There is a prerogative power to create new courts, but only courts to administer the common law.[131] Prosecutions for indictable offences are conducted in her name. The power to enter a *nolle prosequi*, to stop or discontinue a prosecution on indictment, is exercised by the Attorney-General[132] on behalf of Her Majesty; this power is occasionally used to secure the discontinuance of a private prosecution. The prerogative of pardon (exercisable in England only on the advice of the Home Secretary) is used to grant absolute or conditional pardons to persons convicted of criminal offences,[133] or to remit part of the sentence of imprisonment or the fine imposed. A conditional pardon substitutes, by commutation, a different penalty for that imposed by the court; whether the person convicted could reject the condition is a nice question;[134] in the last resort the Crown could,

126. See note 69.
127. See p. 122.
128. See ch. 7.
129. Cedric Thornberry (1963) 12 *I.C.L.Q.* at 422–8; Parry (ed.), *A British Digest of International Law*, vol. 6, pp. 83–105. Dicta in modern cases support the idea of a prerogative to refuse admission (see *Musgrove* v. *Chun Teeong Toy* [1891] A.C. 272; *Poll* v. *Lord Advocate* (1899) 1 F. (Ct. of Sess.) 823; *Schmidt* v. *Home Secretary* [1969] 2 Ch. 149) and to deport (*Att.-Gen. for Canada* v. *Cain* [1906] A.C. 542), but their authority is questionable.
130. See ch. 16.
131. *Re Lord Bishop of Natal* (1864) 3 Moo. P.C.C. (N.S.) 115.
132. See J. Ll. J. Edwards, *The Law Officers of the Crown*, pp. 227–37.
133. It would seem that a pardon may be granted *before* conviction; but this power is not exercised. The line between pardon before conviction and the unlawful exercise of dispensing power is thin. For surviving restrictions on the power of pardon, see Wade and Phillips, *Constitutional Law* (8th edn), pp. 321–3.
134. See Peter Brett (1957) 20 *Mod. L. Rev.* 131.

if it saw fit, grant a free pardon. In 1967 statutory provision was made for the release of prisoners on parole.[135]

The Crown also has prerogative rights and powers in respect of *bona vacantia*, sturgeon and certain swans and whales,[136] coinage, the granting of charters of incorporation, the award of franchises (including the right to hold markets and fairs, and to collect tolls[137] from bridges or ferries), the construction and supervision of harbours, and the printing and publication of statutes and other legislative instruments, the authorized version of the Bible and the Book of Common Prayer.[138]

The prerogative today: external affairs
General

External relations are conducted pre-eminently under prerogative powers. Not only the declaration of war, the dispatch of armed forces and the annexation of territory, but also the conclusion of treaties, the accrediting and reception of diplomats, the recognition of new states and revolutionary governments fall within the scope of the prerogative. Such acts are sometimes called acts of State – assertions of State sovereignty in international relations. The term 'acts of State' is also used in other specialized senses; and it does not invariably connote an act done in pursuance of the royal prerogative.[139]

The Crown had a prerogative power to legislate for the Channel Islands (which are not part of the United Kingdom), but the power has not been exercised in respect of Jersey for many years, and if it has indeed survived the introduction of representative legislatures in Jersey and Guernsey it probably does not extend to the imposition of taxation without the consent of the Insular Authorities, or to the abrogation of other ancient privileges guaranteed to the Islands.[140]

As we have already indicated, prerogative powers in relation to dependent territories are not merely a residue.[141] For colonies acquired by conquest or cession they are plenary in the absence of special circum-

135. Criminal Justice Act 1967, ss. 59–62.

136. Other archaic prerogative proprietary rights were abolished by the Wild Creatures and Forest Laws Act 1971.

137. See *Nyali Ltd* v. *Att.-Gen.* [1956] 1 Q.B. 1.

138. And may license their printing and publication by others, but not so as to authorize a breach of copyright: *Oxford and Cambridge Universities* v. *Eyre and Spottiswoode Ltd* [1964] Ch. 736.

139. See pp. 135–6.

140. See ch. 30.

141. p. 115.

stances; and they may be lost but later resumed.[142] For colonies acquired by settlement, its prerogative legislative power is more limited and has been largely superseded by statute. In those dependent territories which are not British possessions the prerogative is again more than a residue. In colonial-type protectorates (of which the only surviving specimen in 1973 was the British Solomon Islands Protectorate) the legislative powers of the Crown, though regulated by the Foreign Jurisdiction Acts, were derived from the prerogative; and the Crown can extend its own jurisdiction even though it may have originally been limited.[143] In British protected states (the sole survivor in 1973 being Brunei) which had indigenous rulers and enjoyed a degree of autonomy, the Crown did not claim unlimited jurisdiction; but it acquired such jurisdiction as it possessed by virtue of the prerogative,[144] and we must assume that in terms of British constitutional law the Crown was competent to enlarge as well as diminish it by prerogative.

Treaties and treaty implementation

By 'treaties' we mean international agreements. They may be called treaties, conventions, covenants, pacts, charters, agreements, protocols, even statutes, declarations or exchanges of notes. They may be bilateral or multilateral; they may be concluded between heads of State, or between governments, or between governments and international organizations. They may deal with political, defence, economic, legal, social or cultural matters. Any such international instrument to which the United Kingdom is a party binds the United Kingdom in international law. Normally it becomes binding only when ratified by the Executive, though some agreements have effect upon signature, and a few have effect only when approved by Act of Parliament. The treaty itself may specify when and in what circumstances it shall come into effect. It is a constitutional usage, and possibly a binding convention, to lay the texts of international agreements before both Houses of Parliament for twenty-one days before ratification, if ratification is required.[145]

The conclusion of a treaty is an act of State and an exercise of the royal prerogative, even though the Queen has not played a formal role in the matter (for example, by granting full powers to plenipotentiaries to

142. *Campbell* v. *Hall* (1774) 1 Cowp. 204; *Sammut* v. *Strickland* [1938] A.C. 678.
143. *Sobhuza II* v. *Miller* [1926] A.C. 518; *Nyali* v. *Att.-Gen.* [1956] 1 Q.B.1 (affd. [1957] A.C. 253); Roberts-Wray, *Commonwealth and Colonial Law*, pp. 187–97; H. F. Morris and James S. Read, *Indirect Rule and the Search for Justice* (1972), ch. 2.
144. Roberts-Wray, op. cit., p. 116.
145. Geoffrey Wilson, *Cases and Materials*, pp. 453–4. This is commonly called the 'Ponsonby' rule.

negotiate and sign on her behalf, and by ratifying the treaty under the Great Seal); the prerogative, or part of it, may be exercised by the Secretary of State for Foreign and Commonwealth Affairs as her delegate. We need not go into the details of this complex branch of the law. But one point stands out. Whereas in a number of legal systems (for example, the United States of America, West Germany), a treaty is self-executing – i.e. it becomes part of the municipal law, the law of the land, as soon as it is finally concluded[146] – this is not the rule in United Kingdom law. With few exceptions, internationally binding obligations still need to be given legislative effect if they are to be enforced as law by the courts of this country.[147] They may be given such effect if their provisions (or some of them) are incorporated in or scheduled to an Act of Parliament, or in a statutory instrument (for example, an Order in Council) made under the authority of an Act of Parliament,[148] or in a prerogative instrument in the case of territorial waters.[149]

There is at least one clear exception to the rule that the Executive cannot alter the law applied in United Kingdom courts merely by incurring international obligations. The Crown can by agreement abridge its own prerogative powers in relation to a protected state, or indeed abrogate them altogether and recognize the independence of the state (for example, the Maldive Islands, Kuwait or Tonga[150]); but these questions are unlikely to come before a United Kingdom court. European Community treaties are a second potential exception, for according to Community law certain provisions of such treaties may be 'directly applicable' in the laws of member States.[151] There may be another exception. In a flight of fancy,

146. In the United States, however, treaties require the sanction of a two-thirds' majority in the Senate; instruments known as executive agreements do not.

147. This rule is clearly settled; the leading authority is *The Parlement Belge* (1879) 4 P.D. 129 at 154.

148. For example, extradition treaties, under the Extradition Acts. If a treaty needs legislative implementation, it is unlikely to be ratified by the Crown until the necessary legislation is passed.

149. Note 103.

150. For Tonga, see Cmnd 4490 (1970). Consequential legislation was passed in respect of Tonga, which remained within the Commonwealth (Tonga Act 1970), but not for the others.

151. This is a complex point. Article 95(1) of the EEC Treaty (prohibiting various discriminatory trade practices) is directly applicable, without further enactment, in the laws of member States. But the United Kingdom has incorporated this rule into municipal law by implication in enacting the European Communities Act 1972; see ss. 1, 2(1), 3, Sched. 1. Under the Act, future Community treaties (which *may* contain directly applicable provisions) are to be authenticated by Order in Council (s. 1(3) – will this be *giving statutory effect* to such a treaty?), and the Order in Council will have to be approved in draft by resolutions of both Houses if the United Kingdom is itself a party to it (ibid.).

Walter Bagehot asserted that the Crown had a prerogative power to cede Cornwall.[152] It is very doubtful whether the Crown has a prerogative to cede any part of the United Kingdom. But there have been past examples of the cession of parts of Her Majesty's dominions beyond the seas by prerogative acts[153] (for example, the recognition of American independence in 1783), especially in treaties of peace. If this prerogative has disappeared, it is not clear how, though in modern practice the transfer of British territory and the implementation of a peace treaty are always effected by statute.

If the United Kingdom had a federal constitution, a situation might arise (as it has arisen in Canada) whereby the Executive had an unfettered power to enter into international obligations, binding on the State in international law, but Parliament lacked full power to give effect to its undertakings because the subject-matter of the agreement fell within an exclusive domain of regional competence.

The general rule is that a treaty is not a source of legal rights directly enforceable against the Crown in United Kingdom courts, even though it may be intended to benefit particular individuals (for example, where the Crown receives money from a foreign government by way of compensation for injuries done to them);[154] it is an act of State, not a transaction in the nature of a contract or a declaration of trust.[155] Under the Foreign Compensation Acts 1950 and 1969, the allocation of sums received from foreign governments under treaty as compensation for the confiscation or destruction of British-owned property is made on a discretionary basis by an independent statutory body, the Foreign Compensation Commission. A claimant before the Commission may impugn in the courts a determination that he did not comply with the *statutory* conditions necessary to establish a claim, or a determination reached in disregard of minimum procedural standards,[156] but he cannot obtain a judicial declaration that he is entitled to any particular sum. Community treaties stand in a special

152. *The English Constitution*, Introduction to the 2nd edn (Fontana edn), p. 287.

153. See generally Roberts-Wray, op. cit., ch. 4. See also *Damodhar Gordhan* v. *Deoram Kanji* (1876) 1 App. Cas. 332.

154. *Rustomjee* v. *R.* (1876) 2 Q.B.D.69. The position is the same where the provisions of the treaty have been implemented by statute: *Civilian War Claimants' Association Ltd* v. *R.* [1932] A.C. 14. But see below on Community treaties.

155. Though in the *Civilian War Claimants' Association* case, Lord Atkin indicated (at 26–7) that the position might be different if the Crown purported expressly to act as trustee or agent for a subject.

156. *Anisminic Ltd* v. *Foreign Compensation Commission* [1969] 2 A.C. 147; cf. Foreign Compensation Act 1950, s. 4(4); Tribunals and Inquiries Act 1958, s. 11. See now Foreign Compensation Act 1969, s. 3, superseding s. 4(4) of the 1950 Act, and providing for an appeal on points of law from determinations of the Commission to the Court of Appeal. See pp. 571–2, below.

position; they are capable in Community law (adopted in this country by the European Communities Act 1972) of conferring or imposing judicially enforceable legal rights and obligations on individuals.

Conclusive declarations by the Crown on matters of State

In the late Victorian era a Miss Mighell issued a writ for breach of promise of marriage against a Mr Albert Baker; whereupon Mr Baker revealed to the court that he was none other than the Sultan of Johore (who had been living for a time in England under a pseudonym), and pleaded sovereign immunity from the jurisdiction of the court. On behalf of the Crown, the Colonial Office obligingly certified that he was the sovereign ruler of an independent State. The court accepted this certificate as conclusive evidence of the facts stated (although the claim of Johore, a British protected state in Malaya, to be an independent international person was tenuous in the extreme), and the defendant having thus established his immunity from suit, Miss Mighell's action could proceed no further.

This somewhat bizarre case[157] illustrates the disinclination of the courts to make an independent determination of certain questions of law and fact in politically sensitive areas; they have indeed abdicated in favour of the Executive. Some of these questions concern jurisdictional immunity: a head of State enjoys sovereign immunity; a government of an independent State and the public property of that State[158] enjoy state immunity; and persons having diplomatic or consular status enjoy immunities of various kinds, depending on their position in the diplomatic mission or consulate.[159] Diplomatic and consular immunities have recently been restated by statutes giving effect to the terms of multilateral international conventions.[160] Whether a person is entitled to diplomatic or consular status and if so, to what category he belongs, is conclusively determined by a certificate entered by a Secretary of State;[161] these certificates are now

157. *Mighell* v. *Sultan of Johore* [1894] 1 Q.B. 149.

158. Difficult questions may arise as to the immunity from suit of publicly owned vessels belonging to independent states.

159. For the application of these principles to situations arising in the Commonwealth, see Roberts-Wray, *Commonwealth and Colonial Law*, pp. 585–95.

160. Diplomatic Privileges Act 1964; Consular Relations Act 1968. See also the International Organizations Act 1968; Diplomatic and other Privileges Act 1971.

161. Broadly speaking, under the 1964 Act (i) the head of the mission and the principal members of the staff and their families are immune not only from criminal liability but also from most forms of civil liability; (ii) members of the administrative and technical staff are immune from criminal liability but not from civil liability save in respect of acts performed in the course of their official duties; (iii) members of the domestic staff are immune neither from criminal nor from civil liability for acts outside

given under statutory authority, but the conclusiveness of certificates on questions of sovereign and state immunity entails an exercise of the prerogative. Immunities from suit may be waived in the appropriate form. Members of many diplomatic missions in London have taken full advantage of their immunity by refusing to pay penalties for car parking offences.

By virtue of the prerogative, the Crown is also entitled to determine conclusively a range of other matters:

1. Whether a state of war exists between Her Majesty and a foreign country. Thus, in one case, soon after the end of armed hostilities in the Second World War, the Crown was still detaining and wished to deport a German national as an enemy alien; he brought an application for a writ of habeas corpus, contending that the state of war was at an end and that in any case Germany no longer existed as a State; the court accepted as conclusive a certificate entered by a Secretary of State contradicting these contentions.[162]

2. Whether a State is recognized by Her Majesty as an independent State.

3. Whether the government of another country is recognized by Her Majesty as the *de jure* or *de facto* government, or as neither.

These issues usually arise in connection with claims to jurisdictional immunity, but they may also arise in other context – for example, what effect, if any, is to be accorded in English law to the enactments, orders, or judgments of organs of such a political body.[163]

---

the course of their duties. Although a certificate tendered by the Secretary of State is conclusive as to the matters specified in the text above, the courts retain jurisdiction to ascertain whether, for categories (ii) and (iii), the conduct in question took place in the course of official duties: see *Empson* v. *Smith* [1966] 1 Q.B. 426. They are also entitled to decide questions of waiver and submission to the jurisdiction. See also *Agbor* v. *Metropolitan Police Commissioner* [1969] 1 W.L.R. 703 for independent judicial determination of a question (whether premises were the 'private residence of a diplomatic agent') arising under the 1964 Act.

162. *R.* v. *Bottrill, ex p. Kuechenmeister* [1947] K.B. 41.

163. See, for example, *Carl Zeiss Stiftung* v. *Rayner and Keeler Ltd* (No. 2) [1967] 1 A.C. 853 (Foreign Secretary certified that Her Majesty's Government did not recognize the German Democratic Republic (East Germany) *de facto* or *de jure*, but that the USSR was recognized as being entitled to exercise *de jure* authority there; House of Lords accepted this declaration as conclusive, but nevertheless attributed legal effect to a decree of the unrecognized government since it was to be regarded as a subordinate organ of a recognized government). *Semble*, such a certificate is not absolutely conclusive where the question is one of usurpation of sovereignty in a British dependency: *Adams* v. *Adams* [1971] P. 188 (Rhodesia).

On determination of the limits of United Kingdom territorial waters, see p. 122, note 103.

Under the Foreign Jurisdiction Acts, a certificate submitted to the court by a Secretary of State as to the extent of the jurisdiction of the Crown in a protected state or a protectorate is conclusive, but the court is not under an obligation to request such a certificate.[164]

We must not suppose that rules such as these are eccentricities peculiar to British constitutional law. In a number of legal systems the courts look to the Executive for authoritative guidance on matters lying especially within the domain of external affairs; and some systems have developed a coherent concept of non-justiciable 'political questions'. In this country there is no coherent concept; moreover, some questions with marked political overtones are decided by the courts on the basis of the evidence and legal submissions where there is no provision for a conclusive executive certificate or where no such certificate is tendered.[165]

It is also true that in some systems the rules of international law form part of municipal (or domestic) law, and the courts will make an independent determination of the content and applicability of those rules. In Britain the courts adopt a rebuttable presumption that Parliament has not intended to legislate inconsistently with rules of public international law, and common-law rules will, as far as practicable, be so stated as to conform with corresponding international rules[166]; but if there is a plain inconsistency, the international law rules will have to give way.[167] Only the Prize Court in wartime purports to apply international law as such, and even this court must, of course, enforce statutes conflicting with international law. Rules of Community law again stand in a special position; for United Kingdom law is to have effect *subject* to any relevant Community law rules.[168]

164. Foreign Jurisdiction Act 1890, s. 4.

165. See, for example, *Adegbenro* v. *Akintola* [1963] A.C. 614, a Privy Council appeal (who was the lawful Premier of Western Nigeria?); *Agbor's* case (note 161 above; question of entitlement to occupation of diplomatic premises in London arising out of the civil war in Nigeria); *Re Al-Fin Corporation's Patent* [1970] Ch. 160 (whether North Korea was a 'foreign state' within the meaning of s. 24 of the Patents Act 1949; the Foreign Office explicitly refrained from expressing a view on the matter). Contrast *Buck* v. *Att.-Gen.* [1965] Ch. 745, where the English Court of Appeal would have disclaimed jurisdiction, as a matter of comity, to declare the constitution of a former colony (Sierra Leone) invalid following the grant of independence; and cases where ulterior motives are attributed by prisoners to governments seeking their surrender as fugitive offenders; p. 442 below.

166. See, for example, *Salomon* v. *Customs and Excise Commissioners* [1967] 2 Q.B. 116. If the United Kingdom legislation purports to give effect to an international convention, the wording of the convention can be considered as an aid to interpretation: *Post Office* v. *Estuary Radio Ltd* [1968] 2 Q.B. 740. See also pp. 72–3.

167. See, for example, *Cheney* v. *Conn* [1968] 1 W.L.R. 242.

168. European Communities Act 1972, ss. 2(4), 3(1). See further pp. 79–82.

Acts of State and legal proceedings[169]

Acts of State are primarily prerogative acts of policy in the field of external affairs – for example, the declaration of war, the conclusion of a treaty, an annexation of territory, the recognition of a foreign sovereign, state or government. However, there can be no all-inclusive short definition, covering the different senses in which the term 'act of State' has been used. In one aspect an act of State is a manifestation of national sovereignty by the executive branch of government. When the courts say that an act of State is not cognizable by municipal courts (i.e. United Kingdom courts, and, for most purposes, the Judicial Committee of the Privy Council), they usually mean that once it is established to their satisfaction that an act performed by or with the authority of the Crown or a foreign government falls within the legal concept of an act of State, they are not concerned with the propriety of the grounds on which it has been exercised; they do not mean that the Crown can remove a matter from their jurisdiction by the bare assertion that it is an act of State.[170] In this sense judicial attitudes towards pleas of prerogative and acts of State are identical.

There are, however, certain differences of substance or terminology between some acts of State and some prerogative acts:

1. Not every prerogative act is called an act of State; the latter term is reserved for executive acts having effect in external affairs or performed in relation to persons not fully within the protection of the Crown. The granting of a new charter to an English university is a prerogative act but is not called an act of State.

2. A cause of action against the Crown can seldom be founded on a valid act of State (for example, the conclusion of a treaty).[171] On the other hand, a lawful exercise of the prerogative (for example, the taking of property for defence purposes) may give rise to a justiciable claim against the Crown for compensation.[172]

---

169. For a typically illuminating short survey, see D. L. Keir and F. H. Lawson, *Cases in Constitutional Law* (5th edn), pp. 155–63. For full studies, see W. Harrison Moore, *Act of State in English Law*; E. C. S. Wade (1934) 15 *B.Y.I.L.*98; W. S. Holdsworth (1941) 41 *Columbia L. Rev.* 1313; J. G. Collier [1968] *Camb. L.J.* 102. See further pp. 437–40.

170. *Entick* v. *Carrington* (1765) 19 St. Tr. 1030; *Musgrave* v. *Pulido* (1879) 5 App. Cas. 102.

171. See p. 131; or on an annexation (*Secretary of State for India* v. *Kamachee Boye Sahaba* (1859) 12 Moo. P.C.C. 22); Collier, loc. cit., at 105–9.

172. See *Nissan* v. *Att.-Gen.* [1968] 1 Q.B. 286 (C.A.); *Att.-Gen.* v. *De Keyser's Royal Hotel Ltd* [1920] A.C. 508. Note also the distinction between prerogative powers and acts of State drawn in *Commercial and Estates Co. of Egypt* v. *Board of Trade* [1925]

3. It is sometimes said that the term act of State refers only to acts performed outside Her Majesty's dominions. This cannot be correct. Although acts of State can be performed outside her dominions, certain acts of State (for example, the making of a treaty) may also be performed inside them. The detention of an enemy alien in wartime[173] or the deportation of such a person[174] can be classified either as a prerogative act or as an act of State; this is merely a matter of terminology.

4. It is also sometimes said that act of State cannot, whereas the royal prerogative can, be pleaded by way of justification in proceedings instituted by a British subject. This suggestion will be considered below.

5. In certain situations a British subject may successfully plead that an ostensibly unlawful act is lawful because it was carried out in pursuance of an act of State of a foreign government, the validity of which will be recognized by an English court.[175] Such acts would not generally be called prerogative acts.

6. There are doubts as to the operation of the royal prerogative outside Her Majesty's dominions,[176] doubts which do not apply with equal force to acts of State. That certain prerogative powers (for example, in relation to the disposition of the armed forces, and in relation to protected states) are exercisable on foreign soil is reasonably clear; what is not clear is where the line is to be drawn.

7. The term 'act of State' is sometimes loosely used to include acts done in pursuance of statutory authority which has superseded prerogative (for example, the conclusiveness of a certificate as to diplomatic immunity).

Acts of State encroaching on individual rights

An act of State has been described as 'an act of the executive as a matter of policy',[177] and as 'an exercise of sovereign power'.[178] Those descriptions

1 K.B. 271 (prerogative power of angary; wartime requisitioning of goods within the realm belonging to absent neutral; compensation payable). In that case Scrutton L.J. (at 290) and Bankes L.J. (at 297) said *obiter* that act of State could never be pleaded as a defence to an action in tort arising out of an act done in the realm. But the plaintiff was non-resident and apparently did not owe local allegiance. On principle, therefore, it is arguable that act of State could have been successfully pleaded, but for the fact that the situation fell within the rules governing angary.

173. *R.* v. *Vine Street Police Station Superintendent, ex p. Liebmann* [1916] 1 K.B. 268.

174. *Netz* v. *Chuter Ede* [1946] Ch. 224; *R.* v. *Bottrill, ex p. Kuechenmeister* [1947] K.B. 41.

175. *Dobree* v. *Napier* (1836) 2 Bing N.C. 781; *Carr* v. *Fracis Times and Co.* [1902] A.C. 176; F. A. Mann (1943) 59 *L.Q.R.* 42, 155; Michael Zander (1959) 53 *Am. J.I.L.* 826. The act must be within the foreign government's own jurisdiction.

176. See *Nissan* v. *Att.-Gen.* [1970] A.C. 179; note 181, below.

177. E. C. S. Wade (1934) 15 *B.Y.I.L.* at 103.

178. *Salaman* v. *Secretary of State for India* [1906] 1 K.B. 613 at 639.

fit most of the situations in which conduct has been held in judicial proceedings to constitute an act of State. But there have been cases in which the quality of an act of State has been attributed to the individual initiative of a not very senior Crown servant ratified by the Crown.[179] On the other hand, the requisitioning and use of a hotel in Cyprus by British troops engaged in a peace-keeping operation was recently held not to fall within the description of an act of State.[180] Since the Law Lords gave a number of different reasons for their conclusion on this point, the case is not helpful except in so far as it suggests that nowadays only acts which are part of or necessarily incidental to a high-level policy decision (and possibly other acts expressly ratified by the Crown) will be treated as acts of State.

Many of the decisions on act of State have an archaic flavour. They deal with the annexation of territory in India and Southern Africa in the heyday of imperial expansion, when judges often seemed to be as executive-minded as the Executive. It is not certain how much weight should be attached to some of these decisions; sometimes it is not even clear what were the material facts. But the principles laid down in them may still have to be taken into account in connection with claims arising from acts done by British peace-keeping forces overseas; the age of military intervention is not over, though one can optimistically assume that nowadays intervention will seldom take place except at the request or with the concurrence of the government of the territory or country concerned or as part of a United Nations force. Unfortunately the only modern case in which the Crown pleaded act of State as a defence in legal proceedings (*Nissan* v. *Att.-Gen.*) was a disaster for students of the law. The decision of the House of Lords lacks any clear *ratio decidendi* on any point now under consideration. Important questions of law were raised but left half-answered or unanswered, and points that once seemed clear were left shrouded in obscurity.[181]

179. For example, *Buron* v. *Denman* (1848) 2 Ex. 167 (see below).
180. *Nissan* v. *Att.-Gen.* [1970] A.C. 179.
181. [1970] A.C. 179. For critiques, see D. R. Gilmour [1970] *Public Law* 120; J. W. Bridge, (1971) 34 *Mod. L. Rev.* 121; Collier [1969] *Camb. L.J.* 166; see also H. W. R. Wade, *Administrative Law* (3rd edn), pp. 293–6; de Smith (1969) 32 *Mod. L. Rev.* 427. N, a British subject in Cyprus, was claiming that he was entitled to (i) *compensation* for the requisitioning of his hotel, and the use of the contents, under the royal prerogative; or (ii) declarations as to a breach of contract; or (iii) a declaration that he was entitled to damages in tort for trespass to his chattels. The Crown denied the allegations and also pleaded act of State; it then withdrew the defence of act of State in respect of claim (iii). The case was not finally disposed of but determined on preliminary points of law. No majority view emerged in the Lords as to the definition of an act of State; the scope of the *defence* of act of State (for instance, when, if at all, it was available against British subjects; whether it was available against claims not sounding in tort); or whether acts of State and prerogative acts were materially

The following observations about the state of the law must therefore be regarded as very tentative:

1. Act of State can successfully be pleaded by way of defence to an action in tort brought by an alien in respect of an ostensibly wrongful act committed against him outside Her Majesty's dominions by the Crown or with the authority, antecedent or subsequent, of the Crown: *Buron* v. *Denman* (1848), an action for trespass.[182] The rationale of this rule is twofold: an alien in a foreign country or on the high seas does not ordinarily owe allegiance to the Crown[183] and is therefore not entitled to the protection of the Crown or indeed protection against the Crown; and he can look to his own government for diplomatic redress and, if any appropriate forum exists, the institution of proceedings for a breach of international law. Whether these are adequate reasons for treating a deliberate wrong perpetrated at the instance of the Crown as being a non-justiciable matter is questionable.

2. It has been said that in this respect British protected persons in British protectorates or protected states (which are not technically parts of Her Majesty's dominions) are in no better position than aliens in foreign countries.[184] This proposition has no adequate basis today.[185] For other legal purposes, British protected persons have much the same status as citizens of colonies;[186] they probably owe allegiance, at least in a protectorate; they cannot enjoy the same diplomatic protection against the Crown as citizens of independent States; surely, then, they ought to be regarded as enjoying a minimal degree of legal protection against arbitrary action by the Crown? Even if the Crown has unlimited, or potentially

---

distinguishable; or whether the royal prerogative to take or destroy property subject to compensation applied outside Her Majesty's dominions.

182 (1848) 2 Ex. 167. A British naval officer, with general instructions to suppress the slave trade, exceeded them by landing in West Africa, destroying a barracoon (shed) and liberating slaves belonging to a Spaniard; his conduct was ratified by the Crown and he was awarded a large gratuity. The Spaniard's action for trespass failed. Today no action for trespass to land (as distinct from goods) situate abroad would be entertained by the High Court. This point was relevant to the statement of claim in *Nissan's* case.

183. Unless he is an alien who has left family, goods or effects here, evincing an intention to return, or possibly if he holds a British passport. See p. 438.

184. *R.* v. *Crewe (Earl), ex p. Sekgome* [1910] 2 K.B. 576 at 606; decisions in some Commonwealth jurisdictions; and statements in various textbooks. For the background, see Morris and Read, note 143, above. An exception is sometimes made for colonial-type protectorates. See *Ex p. Mwenya* [1960] 1 Q.B.241.

185. See especially Kenneth Polack (1963) 26 *Mod. L. Rev.* 138.

186. For example, since 1948 they have not been included within the definition of aliens. See further p. 422.

unlimited, *legislative* jurisdiction in such a territory,[187] it does not follow that the Crown has an inherent coextensive *executive* authority to ride roughshod over individual rights.[188]

3. A person who is a friendly alien (even though he is engaging in unfriendly conduct) within Her Majesty's dominions owes local allegiance and is therefore entitled to protection, so that act of State cannot be pleaded in respect of a tortious act done to him with the authority of the Crown: *Johnstone* v. *Pedlar*.[189]

4. *A fortiori*, act of State is not a defence to an action arising out of such an act done to a British subject within Her Majesty's dominions: *Walker* v. *Baird* (1892).[190]

5. Nor, so it would seem, is act of State available as a defence to a tort committed against a British subject outside Her Majesty's dominions (for example, Cyprus).[191]

6. Possibly, however, propositions 4 and 5 ought to be qualified so that immunity from the plea of act of State is confined to those British subjects who are citizens of the United Kingdom and Colonies, the residual category of British subjects without citizenship, and British protected persons, since citizens of independent Commonwealth countries, who are British subjects in United Kingdom law only by virtue of their citizenship of those countries,[192] owe allegiance primarily or solely to their own states or governments,[193] and are entitled to international protection by them.

7. It is doubtful how far, if at all, aliens owing local allegiance to the Crown but temporarily absent from the realm are entitled to immunity from a plea of act of State.[194]

187. *Sobhuza II* v. *Miller* [1926] A.C. 518.
188. In conquered or ceded colonies it will usually have unrestricted prerogative legislative power, but its executive power to invade the rights of their inhabitants is limited by the confines set by law.
189. [1921] 2 A.C. 262 (seizure of money belonging to American arrested for subversive activities in Dublin, then a part of Her Majesty's dominions, not defensible as act of State). Possibly the decision would now be different if the act complained of were done in an independent Commonwealth country. See the points made at p. 439 below.
190. [1892] A.C. 491 (seizure of lobster factory in Newfoundland, in purported implementation of a treaty with France).
191. This defence having been abandoned in *Nissan's* case (note 181, above). Cyprus, although within the Commonwealth, is a republic and therefore not within Her Majesty's dominions.
192. British Nationality Act 1948, s. 1(3) as amended.
193. For example, they cannot be convicted of treason in United Kingdom law unless the conduct in question was treasonable if done by an alien in a foreign country (ibid., s. 3(1)). See further p. 439.
194. See pp. 437–8 below. *Semble* in any event act of State is pleadable in respect

8. All persons, including citizens of the United Kingdom and Colonies, may become the *indirect* victims of an act of State by the Crown. Act of State in this context does mean an act of high policy. Thus, a declaration of war may frustrate contracts. Upon the acquisition of territory the Crown does not succeed to the obligations of the predecessor government, but has a free discretion whether or not to accept them: *Cook* v. *Sprigg* (1899);[195] *West Rand Central Gold Mining Co.* v. *R* (1905).[196]

9. There is also some authority for the proposition that in certain ill-defined circumstances direct injury inflicted on citizens of the United Kingdom and Colonies may be justified under the plea of act of State. For example, it has been suggested that damage done by the armed forces in the course of a military operation falling short of war to the property of citizens on foreign soil may be an act of State and therefore non-compensable.[197] (If it were attributed to an exercise of the royal prerogative, compensation might be payable by the Crown as a matter of obligation.)[198] In this sense the defence of act of State would be a by-product of an 'act of policy'. Again, the seizure of British-owned property on behalf of the Crown may possibly be so connected, causally and in point of time, with an act of State (for example, a treaty or an annexation) as to be regarded as part of it or necessarily incidental to it;[199] but it is very doubtful whether a court ought ever to accept such an argument today.

The accidents of litigation will doubtless resolve some of these problems, and throw up new ones, before the century is out.

---

of seizure of property within the realm belonging to a non-resident alien who does *not* owe local allegiance; though cf. note 172 above.

195. [1899] A.C. 572 (refusal to recognize railway concession granted by former government to one who was apparently a British subject).

196. [1905] 2 K.B. 391 (refusal to accept responsibility for allegedly wrongful seizure of gold bars by former South African Republic).

197. There are dicta to this effect in *Nissan's* case [1970] A.C. 179 at 221 (Lord Morris), 235 (Lord Wilberforce) and 240 (Lord Pearson); Lord Pearce (at 227) left the point open and only Lord Reid (at 213) rejected this view.

198. *Burmah Oil Co.* v. *Lord Advocate* [1965] A.C. 75; but no compensation would be claimable as of right during a state of war or apprehended war for battle damage or denial damage, even in Her Majesty's dominions: War Damage Act 1965. In *Nissan's* case Lord Reid (at 213) and Lord Wilberforce (at 236) doubted whether the *Burmah Oil* rule about the prerogative applied to foreign soil. (The *Burmah Oil* case arose within Her Majesty's dominions.) Lord Denning M.R. in the Court of Appeal ([1968] 1 Q.B. 286 at 340) and Lord Pearce ([1970] A.C. at 229) took the broader view of the applicability of the prerogative.

199. See, for example, *Secretary of State for India* v. *Kamachee Boye Sahaba* (1859) 12 Moo. P.C.C. 22; *Salaman* v. *Secretary of State for India* [1906] 1 K.B. 613 (seizures of property of former rulers upon annexation of their territory; presumably they became British subjects on annexation). In *Cook* v. *Sprigg* [1899] A.C. 572, see note 195 above – 'a case of doubtful authority' (*per* Lord Wilberforce in *Nissan's* case [1970] A.C. at 232) – it is not clear whether the plaintiff's property was in fact seized.

Chapter 5
The Privy Council

I

The Privy Council, like the monarchy, is an ancient and dignified institution of government. Unlike the monarchy, it is not an important feature of the British constitutional system. If the monarchy were to be abolished, a new personage or institution would have to be endowed with the functions which only a head of State can exercise. The functions now performed by the Privy Council and its committees could be distributed tomorrow among other existing organs of government, and few people in the United Kingdom would notice any difference. Only the Judicial Committee of the Privy Council, which is in fact a court, almost entirely concerned with the hearing of appeals from Commonwealth countries overseas, would obviously need to be replaced by a separate new institution.

The role of the Privy Council in English constitutional history has often been exaggerated. Some have seen the Privy Council as the direct lineal descendant of the medieval King's Council; others regard it as the direct progenitor of the modern Cabinet. The truth of the matter is more complex. It is complex for various reasons: because the royal advisory, consultative and decision-making bodies seldom had their composition or functions neatly defined; because development was discontinuous; because terminology often failed to keep pace with, or to reflect, major constitutional changes; and because historians still disagree with one another about material facts. Whom the King had about him, and what those persons did, might be determined by the will of a strong-headed King, the pressure exerted upon a weak one, or the exigencies of the time.

The early Norman *Curia Regis*, or King's court, knew nothing of the separation of powers. A body of royal officials and advisers, augmented from time to time by the King's tenants in chief, it was a court, a council, a judicial, executive, deliberative and law-making body. Under the Plantagenets the need for specialization brought partial fission. The Exchequer, a court of law and a department of State, was the first to establish a distinct identity. There followed the Court of Common Pleas, and in the thirteenth century emerged a Court of King's Bench. But the King's

Bench was intimately connected with the King's Council, and not until the reign of Edward I (1272–1307) was it finally established as a separate court with professional judges – a court, however, which, like the Council, was very much an emanation of the Crown. And the *Curia Regis* also threw off the Chancery, at first an administrative office for the issue of writs and other royal instruments, but soon to become the court of equity too.

Meanwhile, a new institution, Parliament, had slowly taken shape. Originally Parliament meant not 'an institution but an event';[1] it was the King's Council of household officials and other officers of State, enlarged by often reluctant magnates, in Parliament, in deliberation as the Great Council of the Realm. Other kinds of meetings – talking-shops – were sometimes called parliaments. Late in the thirteenth century, representatives of local communities and the lower clergy would also be summoned from time to time. From the representative element evolved a House of Commons, sitting separately from the enlarged Council which was the immediate progenitor of the House of Lords. Parliament in its early years was a judicial forum to which petitions for redress could be addressed, as well as a deliberative and legislative assembly; it became known as the High Court of Parliament. And the residual jurisdiction of the Council overlapped with the jurisdiction of Parliament. The late medieval legal and constitutional system was singularly fluid.

The history of the Council, after the splitting up of the *Curia Regis* and the rise of Parliament, is confused and obscure. A King would choose his counsellors or they would be thrust upon him. Under the Lancastrians, attempts to conduct government through a baronial council of over-mighty subjects, feuding with one another and dominating a King such as Henry VI, foundered in the Wars of the Roses. Later in the fifteenth century the Council began to re-emerge as the King's effective instrument; and under the first two Tudors a new model of conciliar government was evolved. As we have noted, there was an ill-defined residuum of conciliar judicial power. By the accession of Henry VII the Council had come to sit more or less regularly in the Star Chamber. Under Henry it exercised a very wide range of judicial and administrative functions.[2] It was not the obsolescent Great Council, or the Lancastrian Council, nor was it yet the Court of Star Chamber,[3] at least in name; nor was it the Privy Council,

1. T. F. T. Plucknett, *A Concise History of the Common Law* (5th edn), p. 151. See also p. 229.

2. The leading account is C. G. Bayne, *Select Cases in the Council of Henry VII* (Selden Society, vol. 75, 1956), especially the editor's long introduction.

3. An Act of 1487, *Pro Camera Stellata*, used to be thought of as having created the Court of Star Chamber. In fact it delegated to a group of members of the Council jurisdiction to try a limited range of offences.

though Henry VII had his own inner group of advisers, courtiers and officials. In Henry VIII's time we can identify a body of councillors sitting in public as the Court of Star Chamber, exercising a penal jurisdiction narrower than the jurisdiction of Henry VII's Council, meting out speedy, often rough, justice, following inquisitorial procedures, bringing to book rebellious or defiant subjects, slothful or perverse magistrates and corrupt jurors and officials, enforcing its judgments efficiently, developing new branches of public law (for example, riot, sedition, libel), and generally making amends for the deficiencies of the common law and the cumbersome procedure of the common-law courts. This was indeed the King's Council, but clearly a different kind of council from its precursors. And other new conciliar, prerogative courts were established – for example, the Court of Requests, mainly for the hearing of poor men's causes, and the Court of High Commission, mainly for the punishment of ecclesiastical offences after the Reformation.

Henry VIII's Council was not, of course, primarily a judicial body. It was pre-eminently a powerful instrument of government. There were councillors learned in the law, who sat as judges or gave the King legal advice; there were ordinary councillors or councillors at large, officials and dignitaries who took little part in the main work of the Council; above all, there emerged in the 1530s a small group, expert in politics and administration, belonging to the King's Privy Council, the heart of the governmental machine.[4] The functions of this Privy Council were not formally differentiated from those of the Council at large; it could exercise judicial and legislative functions as well as advise and administer.

As the popularity of the monarchy waned under the early Stuarts, so were its instruments resented. The common lawyers viewed the conciliar courts with misgivings or jealousy, and found them encroaching upon their own jurisdiction. The Star Chamber and the Court of High Commission came to be regarded by the King's opponents as engines of oppression. After eleven years of non-parliamentary government under Charles I, the common lawyers and the men of Parliament had their revenge. In 1641 all the conciliar courts except the Court of Chancery were abolished, never to be revived, and the Privy Council's pretensions to determine the rights of subjects were abrogated. But the Council retained appellate jurisdiction in causes arising outside the United Kingdom; and this power is today exercised by the Judicial Committee of the Privy Council, a modern court of law.

Charles II, after the Restoration in 1660, showed little enthusiasm for governing through the full Privy Council, a heterogeneous and unwieldy body. In so far as he was prepared to impart his confidences to anybody,

4. G. R. Elton, *The Tudor Revolution in Government*, ch. 5.

he preferred to deal directly with individual Ministers or with small committees of the Council, such as the committee for foreign affairs;[5] or better still, with an informal Cabal, meeting him privately in his Cabinet or closet. The furtive way in which matters of high policy were discussed and determined evoked some resentment; a scheme was devised in 1679 for reducing the Privy Council to thirty members and restoring its authority as an advisory body, but Charles, having agreed to be guided by the re-modelled Council, went blithely along his own devious road. Indeed, never again did the Privy Council resume its place as a primary instrument of government. After the Revolution of 1688 policy was shaped by the monarch in conclave with selected groups of Ministers, or by Ministers in conclave with one another. True, the Act of Settlement 1701 provided that 'all matters and things relating to the well-governing of this kingdom which are properly cognizable in the Privy Council shall be transacted there', and that all resolutions of the Council be signed by those assenting to them; but this provision was repealed before it came into effect. In 1714 came the Privy Council's dramatic swansong. As Anne lay dying, a meeting of the Privy Council was convened, and the weight of opinion was enough to stifle Bolingbroke's plans for instating the son of James II. Instead, George I, the first of the Hanoverian line, succeeded in accordance with the Act of Settlement. The Council then subsided into political quiescence, active only through the work of its functional committees. As the eighteenth century advanced, the Cabinet (which had never been a formal committee of the Privy Council) crystallized as the effective executive organ of government.[6]

II

The Privy Council today[7] has more than three hundred members. All are entitled to be addressed as 'The Right Honourable . . .'. Members must be British subjects in United Kingdom law, or citizens of the Republic of Ireland. Appointments are made by letters patent on the Prime Minister's advice, and are for life, though a Privy Councillor (or Counsellor) may be removed on advice or at his own request.[8] By convention, all Cabinet

5. Specialized committees of the Privy Council, including a Foreign Committee, existed under the early Stuarts: D. L. Keir, *Constitutional History of Modern Britain since 1485* (9th edn), p. 164.

6. See p. 151.

7. The Scottish Privy Council was merged with the English Privy Council in 1708, after the Act of Union. There is a separate Privy Council for Northern Ireland but no new appointment to membership of that body is to be made in future. See Addendum.

8. Sir Edgar Speyer was removed for his pro-German sympathies after the First World War, and Mr John Profumo was removed at his own request in 1963.

Ministers must be sworn as Privy Councillors. It is also conventional or customary to appoint the Archbishops of Canterbury and York, the Speaker of the House of Commons, the Lords of Appeal in Ordinary (the Law Lords), the Master of the Rolls, the Lords Justices of Appeal, the Lord Chief Justice and the President of the Family Division. Senior non-Cabinet Ministers, dignitaries and eminent judges from Commonwealth countries and a small number of other persons upon whom it is appropriate to confer a special honour for public service or political eminence (for example, leadership of the Liberal Party) may also be appointed.

Upon admission, a new Privy Councillor must swear an oath or make an affirmation not to divulge any matter disclosed to him confidentially in the Council. The general understanding has been and still is that the secrecy of Cabinet proceedings is preserved by the undertaking thus given; yet this view cannot be sustained by a literal interpretation of the oath, because the Cabinet is neither the Privy Council nor a committee of the Privy Council.

Meetings of the Privy Council are held in the presence of the Queen (or Counsellors of State if she is absent from the realm or indisposed), normally at Buckingham Palace. The business transacted is purely formal, approving and recording decisions already taken elsewhere. The Lord President of the Council, a senior Minister (who need not be a peer), is responsible for the summoning of members and the preparation of the list of business; usually only three or four members are called, and they will be Ministers concerned with the matters to be transacted; meetings of the Council are very brief; indeed, the members remain standing. On rare ceremonial occasions a larger meeting, including persons other than Ministers, is convened – for example, to proclaim a new monarch, or to hear the monarch give consent to a royal marriage.

The dissolution, summoning and prorogation[9] of Parliament are effected by royal proclamations in Council; so are the declaration and termination of a state of war, and the declaration of a statutory state of emergency. *Projets de loi* (bills) passed by the States of Jersey and Guernsey are assented to by Order in Council; and it is by Order in Council that the Royal Courts of the islands are directed to register Acts of the United Kingdom Parliament having effect in the islands.

Some Orders in Council are of a judicial character, formally promulgating the report (or judgment) of the Judicial Committee.[10] The great majority are legislative Orders in Council. Apart from those few Orders

9. See ch. 10.
10. The distinction between a judicial and a legislative Order in Council was clearly emphasized in *Ibralebbe* v. *R.* [1964] A.C. 900. See pp. 49–50.

in Council which are still made under prerogative powers (for example, for altering the constitutions of a now diminishing group of colonies,[11] for altering rates of pensions for the armed services, for dealing with recruitment to the civil service, coinage, or the delimitation of territorial waters),[12] legislative Orders in Council are made in pursuance of powers delegated to Her Majesty in Council by statute. These have exactly the same status as regulations made by individual Ministers under delegated legislative powers; they fall within the definition of 'statutory instruments',[13] are numbered and published in the annual volumes of Statutory Instruments, and differ from departmental regulations only in their formal source. Unless they are of exceptional importance (in which case parliamentary draftsmen may be enlisted) they are drafted by the legal advisers to the Department with whose business they deal. The reasons for giving Her Majesty power to make Orders in Council on certain matters instead of vesting a Minister with power to make regulations are partly traditional and partly psychological. It is more dignified and impressive for an independence constitution, or an instrument giving effect to an extradition treaty or creating new parliamentary constituencies or altering electoral boundaries, to be made by Her Majesty in Council. Or so it seems to some people; and appearance is occasionally more important than reality, even if hardly anyone is misled by the ceremonial trappings. The draft Orders are not discussed at the meeting of the Council; the Lord President reads out their titles,[14] the Queen (who has been fully informed in advance of the business to be transacted) approves them orally, and they are then authenticated by the signature of the Clerk of the Council and the affixing of the seal of the Council.

III

We have already referred to functional committees of the Privy Council. The oldest of the supervisory committees – it was established in 1660 – was the Committee for Trade and Plantations. This was to beget two separate departments of State, the Board of Trade and the Colonial Office. Several of the committees set up in the nineteenth century (for

11. For example, colonies originally acquired by conquest or cession, such as Gibraltar and the Seychelles.

12. Prerogative Orders in Council of a legislative character are published as an Appendix to the annual volumes of Statutory Instruments. They are not, of course, *statutory* instruments.

13. Statutory Instruments Act 1946, s. 1, and the regulations made thereunder. See ch. 15.

14. The titles of Orders in Council have recently been abbreviated. Instead of a Fiji (Constitution) Order in Council we had simply a Fiji (Constitution) Order 1966.

example, for education, agriculture and health) ended by parting with their functions to public boards, autonomous, semi-autonomous or under the aegis of a Minister, which subsequently became fully-fledged government Departments headed by a Minister. A few years ago there were still Privy Council committees on scientific and industrial research, agricultural research, medical research, atomic energy and nature conservancy; these functions, coordinated by the Lord President of the Council, have been transferred to Departments old and new.

In 1972 the Privy Council had a miscellany of standing committees, none of recent origin, and most resting on a statutory basis – the Universities Committee, reporting on petitions concerning Statutes of the Universities of Oxford and Cambridge and their colleges; a somewhat similar Scottish Universities Committee; a Baronetage Committee to report on claims to baronetcies; the Political Honours Scrutiny Committee (a committee of three persons, not being members of the Government, reporting in the first instance to the Prime Minister on the suitability of persons to be recommended by him for the award of titles and dignities for political services);[15] and committees on the Channel Islands and the Isle of Man, to which bills passed locally are referred for report. The Honours Committee (composed of elder statesmen, one from each of the main parties) and the Universities Committees are fairly active, non-political, advisory bodies. The Committees on the Channel Islands and the Isle of Man are composed of the Lord President, the Home Secretary and other Ministers; they are political organs of the United Kingdom Government, but seldom do they meet and deliberate as committees. There are *ad hoc* committees – for example, to consider applications by other institutions for charters and Statutes; and committees of the Council, or consisting of Privy Councillors, to consider special problems appropriate for investigation by an eminent non-partisan body, for instance the interception of communications by executive order or the use of questionable interrogation techniques by security forces. And then there is the Judicial Committee. Hence the Privy Council is not entirely superfluous. Although all its non-judicial functions could be transferred to the Cabinet or departments of State, and its committees could be detached as autonomous statutory bodies or as advisory bodies to Departments, such a redistribution would not in every instance be as convenient as the present arrangements, and in some cases the retention of ancient forms is of political value. But the Lord President of the Council has almost become a Minister without portfolio, so light are his 'departmental' duties; in recent years he has been made

15. For the origin of this committee, see Jennings, *Cabinet Government* (3rd edn), pp. 469–71. If the committee reports adversely and the Prime Minister nevertheless proceeds with his recommendation, the Queen is to be informed.

Leader of the House of Commons, the Minister in charge of government business in the House. The official staff of the Privy Council Office is now extremely small.

IV

The Judicial Committee of the Privy Council[16] can be mentioned at this point. After the abolition of the conciliar courts, the Council was still able to entertain appeals from the overseas dominions of the Crown. With the expansion of the colonial empire, it became essential to make adequate provision for the determination of appeals, and in 1833 Parliament constituted a Judicial Committee of the Privy Council; its composition and jurisdiction have been modified many times since.

In 1972 the Judicial Committee consisted of the Lord President (who never sits), persons who hold or have held high judicial office in the United Kingdom and are Privy Councillors, and leading members of the Judiciary from certain Commonwealth countries (notably Australia and New Zealand) from which appeals still lie to the Privy Council. The quorum of the Judicial Committee is three; normally five members sit to hear an appeal;[17] more often than not, they are the Law Lords. The Judicial Committee is sometimes referred to as the Board; its reports are in the form of advice and are promulgated, as we have seen, by Order in Council. It is not strictly bound by its own decisions. Before 1966 no dissenting opinion could be delivered, because advice to the Crown should not be divided, but this anachronistic rule has now been abandoned.[18]

The Judicial Committee's jurisdiction is regulated by statute, subordinate legislative instruments, and local constitutions and legislation. It hears appeals from the superior courts of the Channel Islands, the Isle of Man, colonies, protectorates, associated states, and such independent Commonwealth countries as have retained the appeal from their own courts. In 1971 eighty-two appeals were pending or had been received from courts overseas. Of these cases, seventeen came from Malaysia, fifteen from Ceylon, seventeen from various Caribbean and Atlantic territories and eleven from Australia; the sources of the others were far-flung. Appeals may lie as of right, with leave of the court below, or by special leave of the Judicial Committee. The power to grant special leave to appeal is a prerogative power placed on a statutory basis, and cannot be

16. K. O. Roberts-Wray, *Commonwealth and Colonial Law*, pp. 433–63.
17. In the *Australian Banks Nationalisation* case (*Commonwealth of Australia* v. *Bank of N.S.W.* [1950] A.C. 235), a Board of seven members was convened. Two members died during the hearing, which was of unprecedented length.
18. Judicial Committee (Dissenting Opinions) Order 1966 (S.I. 1966, No. 1100).

abrogated by a colony.[19] Appeals in criminal matters lie only by special leave, save in matters concerning the guarantees of fundamental rights and freedoms embodied in constitutions since 1959; generally the appeal will lie as of right in the latter class of case. Petitions for special leave to appeal are granted sparingly; and the Judicial Committee declines to act as a general Court of Criminal Appeal.

By virtue of the Statute of Westminster 1931, and subsequent independence Acts, independent Commonwealth countries have acquired power (subject to any restriction imposed by their own constitutions) to terminate the appeal, and a number have done so. Among Commonwealth countries which achieved independence before 1950, Canada, India and now Ceylon (Sri Lanka)[20] have abolished all appeals; the Commonwealth of Australia has in effect excluded appeals in federal constitutional cases;[21] appeals still lie on a wide range of matters from New Zealand but are infrequent. If a Commonwealth country which becomes a republic or comes under a separate monarchy on or after the attainment of independence still wishes to retain the appeal, this may be done by one of two methods: by providing either (i) that appeals shall be referred by the local head of State to the Judicial Committee, which will submit its report to him (as in Malaysia), or (ii) that appeal shall lie not to 'Her Majesty in Council' – the form used in the constitutions of those countries of which the Queen is still head of State – but simply to the 'Judicial Committee'.

Under the constitutions of some Commonwealth countries, a superior judge cannot be removed except for inability or misbehaviour established to the satisfaction of the Judicial Committee following an adverse report by a local judicial tribunal of inquiry.

The Judicial Committee of the Privy Council is essentially a Commonwealth court, but it also has a place in the legal system of the United Kingdom. Here its jurisdiction is exclusively statutory and, like the powers of the Privy Council itself, comprises a mixed assortment.

1. It hears appeals from the decisions of certain professional disciplinary bodies, medical, dental, optical and in respect of professions ancillary to

19. Southern Rhodesia remained a colony despite the unilateral declaration of independence (UDI) by its government in November 1965, and the purported abolition of the appeal to the Privy Council by the Smith Constitution was therefore ineffective in law; see *Madzimbamuto* v. *Lardner-Burke* [1969] 1 A.C. 645. The Appellate Division of the High Court of Southern Rhodesia refused to follow this Privy Council decision and accepted the Smith Constitution as binding: *R.* v. *Ndhlovu* 1968 (4) S.A. 515.

20. Shortly before the adoption of a republican constitution in 1972.

21. Privy Council (Limitation of Appeals) Act 1968 (No. 30). Total abrogation of appeals would require a constitutional amendment. In matters arising under the laws of the Australian states, appeals still lie direct from the State Supreme Courts to the Privy Council.

medicine. It also has a limited appellate jurisdiction from higher ecclesiastical courts, and in wartime it hears appeals from the Prize Court. In 1971 it heard four appeals in professional disciplinary cases and four ecclesiastical appeals.

2. Under section 7 of the House of Commons Disqualification Act 1957, a member of the public may apply to the Judicial Committee for a declaration that a member of the House is subject to a statutory disqualification under that Act. This replaces the old common informer procedure.[22]

3. The Crown may, under section 4 of the Judicial Committee Act 1833, refer any matter to it for an advisory opinion. Unlike its appellate determinations, which are advisory only in form, such opinions are truly advisory, though they will almost invariably be treated as authoritative. It would be possible so to refer a matter that was not characteristically justiciable, though in practice its advice has been sought only on legal questions.[23] The last special reference was made in 1957, at the request of the House of Commons and upon the initiative of the Committee of Privileges, in order to obtain an authoritative interpretation of the effect of an obscure eighteenth-century statute on the article of the Bill of Rights which guarantees freedom of speech and proceedings in Parliament.[24] Under the Government of Ireland Act 1920, constitutional questions arising in Northern Ireland may also be specially referred to the Judicial Committee for an opinion; the opinion delivered will, however, have the effect of a judgment and will not be merely advisory.[25]

22. See further ch. 11.
23. See Roberts-Wray, op. cit., p. 449, for a synopsis of the matters specially referred. In 1966 and again in 1968 the British Government in its negotiations with Mr Ian Smith about the conditions under which it might grant independence to Rhodesia, proposed that there should be specially entrenched constitutional provisions for an *appeal* to lie to the Judicial Committee in respect of unfairly discriminatory *constitutional amendments* made in Rhodesia. See Cmnd 3159 (1966), p. 10 (the *Tiger* proposals); Cmnd 3793 (1968), p. 9 (the *Fearless* proposals). In the past, mixed questions of law and policy were occasionally referred for an advisory opinion to a mixed *ad hoc* committee of the Privy Council, composed of judicial and other members of the Council: see, for example, *Re States of Jersey* (1853) 9 Moo. P.C.C. 185.
24. *Re Parliamentary Privilege Act 1770* [1958] A.C. 331. This was one stage in the controversy in the *Strauss* case; see pp. 317–18 below.
25. ss. 51–3. Appeals lie from the Court of Appeal in Northern Ireland to the House of Lords. Special references to the Judicial Committee of the Privy Council for advisory opinions in matters concerning Northern Ireland may also be made under section 4 of the 1833 Act. See further Harry Calvert, *Constitutional Law in Northern Ireland*, chs. 7, 15. And now see Addendum.

Chapter 6
Cabinet and Prime Minister

Background

As we noted in the last chapter, Charles II preferred to consult a small group of confidential advisers instead of the full Privy Council on matters of State, and the Privy Council never regained the status it had enjoyed from the reigns of Henry VIII to Charles I. From this inchoate group of advisers there emerged the modern Cabinet. Evolution of Cabinet government was facilitated by the fact that two political parties or factions, the Whigs and the Tories, had formed in the latter years of Charles II's reign; the Whigs had sought to exclude Charles's Roman Catholic brother, James, Duke of York, from the line of succession, and the Tories, defenders of the Duke, afterwards James II, were not men upon whom it was prudent for William of Orange to rely when he accepted the invitation to the throne. Moreover, there was a Whig majority in Parliament after 1688; the King needed to carry Parliament with him, and for this purpose it was necessary to give ministerial posts to Whigs. The Lords of the Committee, the Cabinet, the Junto – the designations varied – were nevertheless viewed with suspicion by those Privy Councillors who were excluded from the inner conclave and also by parliamentarians who objected to the growth of royal influence in the Commons. The Act of Settlement purported not only to restore the authority of the Privy Council but also to exclude from membership of the House of Commons 'any person who has an office or place of profit under the King, or receives a pension from the Crown'. These provisions, however, were repealed before they took effect. If they had survived, English constitutional history might have been a different tale.

We shall not attempt to give a detailed summary of eighteenth-century developments.[1] The principle that the Cabinet was to be a politically homogeneous body, presided over and led by a Prime Minister, who had full authority over the appointment and removal of his colleagues and who owed his position not to the favour of the Crown but to the support

1. There is a good short account, with references to further reading, in John P. Mackintosh, *The British Cabinet* (2nd edn), ch. 2.

of a majority in the House of Commons, developed fitfully rather than gradually. One could hardly say that it was securely established till the accession of Sir Robert Peel to office in 1841; and this was after the broad extension of the franchise and the reform of the distribution of seats and constituencies brought about by the Representation of the People Act 1832.

In a confused story it is easy to be beguiled into seizing upon a striking event and magnifying its importance. The abstention of George I, a Hanoverian who did not speak English, from attendance at Cabinet meetings after 1717[2] may seem to have been the crucial factor in shifting the balance of power away from the Crown and towards the Cabinet, but even this is by no means clear. The absence of the King possibly made the Cabinet itself less important and some individual Ministers more important. What is reasonably clear is that Sir Robert Walpole, who normally presided in Cabinet meetings from 1721 to 1742, can post-humously lay claim to having been the first Prime Minister, albeit the King's Prime Minister: he was the King's principal and trusted adviser and a supreme manipulator of the House of Commons, using patronage and bribery in the Whig and royal interests, and he was able to procure the removal of some of his discordant or uncongenial colleagues. Yet there remained in his time two Cabinets, an inner group and an outer or nominal Cabinet (which included household officers, non-political officers of State and the Archbishop of Canterbury, and which did not fade away till George III's reign). The influence of the King in matters of government was still potentially strong, and included the determination of what matters should be referred to the Cabinet and full power to reject ministerial advice. Walpole did not have a free hand in his selection of colleagues; as a collective entity even the Inner Cabinet still lacked authority and cohesion; when Walpole finally fell from office, most of his fellow-Ministers stayed doggedly at their posts. The very existence of the office of Prime Minister as a regular feature of the constitution was not recognized in the middle of the eighteenth century, though by then the Cabinet had at least established its respectability. Not till the formation of the first Ministry headed by William Pitt the Younger in 1783 did Britain have an undoubtedly dominant Prime Minister, dominant not only over his colleagues and the House of Commons but also, to a substantial extent, over the will of the King; and Pitt's dominance was not inevitable but was explicable by reason of

2. George I would converse with his Ministers in French and Latin; his retirement from Cabinet meetings may have been due not so much to problems of communication as to his lack of grasp of English politics and his loss of interest in Cabinet proceedings. He continued to see Ministers privately, but tended to lean on German advisers. His successor, George II, was closer to Walpole. George III was very much the King of England in the early years of his reign.

his personal talents, George III's loss of prestige because of his partial failure (dramatized by Britain's defeat in the American War of Independence, followed by the fall of his instrument, Lord North) to reassert royal authority over the main direction of national policy, and the onset of the King's first spell of mental illness in 1788. In the years between Walpole and Pitt there had been phases of mixed Ministries, sporadic and often decisive royal intervention and amorphous constitutional fluidity. And the King forced Pitt himself to resign. But the Cabinet had grown in stature as an autonomous institution under Pitt as royal influence had declined, and those matters discussed and decided by the Cabinet were seldom referred to it by the King. Although it was not until after 1832 that the effective choice of a Ministry and Ministers passed from the monarch's hands, the central role in the formation as well as the execution of policy had moved irrevocably into the hands of the King's Ministers. George III's incapacity, the unpopularity of his son, first as Prince Regent and then as George IV (1820–30), and the mediocre ability of William IV (1830–37), ensured that the trend towards the eclipse of the King as the effective head of the Executive would be maintained. For practical purposes the Prime Minister and the Cabinet became the principal organs of executive government, dependent no longer on royal favour but on the confidence of a majority in the House of Commons, which rested on a more representative basis after 1832.

Executive power: a conventional approach

No series of terse comments on existing practice can be free from dogmatic assertion, or be based on sufficient or reliable information on matters which are still to a large extent confidential; nor can a brief description pay proper regard to the work of constitutional and political historians or students of politics and political sociology. Recent investigations into the processes by which major policy decisions have been made, the nature and influence of pressure groups, the organization and behaviour of the two main political parties in and out of Parliament, the selection of parliamentary candidates by constituency parties, the impact of the media of information on the vicissitudes of public opinion, the realities behind voting behaviour, and so on, have contributed much to an understanding of how the British constitutional and political system works in practice. This book is concerned less with evaluation than with rules and institutions.

The rules about the principal institutions of executive government are not, of course, mainly rules of strict law. The monarchy and the Privy Council are encrusted with rules of strict law in abundance; but they are not principal institutions of executive government. The Cabinet and the Prime Minister, on the other hand, are hardly recognized in the statute book and they are almost invisible in the law reports. The Prime Minister is the keystone of the Cabinet arch, a sun around which planets revolve, an elected monarch, a President, or what you will; yet he was not mentioned in an Act of Parliament till 1917,[3] and the main statutes relating to his office are those providing for his salary and pension.[4] His powers and duties are determined almost exclusively by convention and usage. The Cabinet has been virtually ostracized by the parliamentary draftsman. It appeared in 1937 (also in the context of ministerial salaries) but has made little further progress towards statutory recognition.[5] Its composition, mode of selection, powers and procedures have to be elicited from political announcements, inference, breaches of confidence, and optimistic speculation. The strict law of the constitution tells us as much and as little about political parties and the Leader of the Opposition.[6]

It is nevertheless possible to list a number of conventional rules about the Prime Minister and the Cabinet. The authenticity of some of the rules is dubious, since their binding force is sometimes questionable and they are apt to change with a disconcerting frequency; moreover attempts to ascertain them are bedevilled by a paucity of reliable up-to-date information. Again, it is possible to place a variety of reasonable interpretations on the relationship between the Prime Minister and his Cabinet at any given moment of time; and students of politics have of late disagreed with

3. Chequers Estate Act 1917, providing him with an official residence.

4. Now Ministerial and other Salaries Act 1972, replacing the Ministers of the Crown Act 1937. His salary is £20,000 a year – he also receives £3000 as a MP – and his pension (see also Parliamentary and other Pensions Act 1972, s. 26) is £7500 a year. Of his salary, the sum of £5000 is allowed as non-taxable expenses. See further note 5. There are one or two other random statutory references to the Prime Minister: see, for example, Chevening Estate Act 1959, Schedule; Parliamentary Commissioner Act 1967, s. 8(4) (below).

5. Under the First Schedule to the Ministerial and other Salaries Act 1972 the salaries of specified Ministers are reduced if they are not members of the Cabinet, in which case the 'First Lord of the Treasury' (see below) is to determine their exact salaries, as well as the salaries of certain other Ministers. Cabinet papers and proceedings (certified as such by the Secretary of the Cabinet with the approval of the Prime Minister) are not to be divulged to the Parliamentary Commissioner for Administration (the 'Ombudsman') in the course of his investigations: Parliamentary Commissioner Act 1967, s. 8(4). The Cabinet Office lies outside the Commissioner's field of inquiry: ibid., Sched. 2, note 6.

6. See Ministerial and other Salaries Act 1972, Sched. 3 (definition of the meaning of Leader of the Opposition by reference to the largest opposition party); Companies Act 1967, s. 19 (directors' reports to disclose contributions by companies to political parties). See also *John* v. *Rees* [1970] Ch. 345 (natural justice to be observed by party's national executive before disaffiliating or suspending activities of a constituency party).

one another sharply on the relative standing of the Prime Minister and his Cabinet. But the most significant fact is that nearly all commentators regard the Cabinet as being in some degree subordinate to the Prime Minister. Hardly anyone today will make out a case for the proposition that the Prime Minister is merely *primus inter pares*, the first among equals, except in the formal sense that all are servants of the Crown. The central feature of recent controversies is the question how far it is justifiable to speak of Prime Ministerial government rather than Cabinet government.[7] For two centuries the Cabinet has been regarded as the primary executive organ of government, discussing and deciding the main issues of national policy and coordinating the work of the Departments. Is this still true?

The principal modern conventions concerning the Prime Minister and the Cabinet are:

1. The Prime Minister is invariably designated First Lord of the Treasury. The legislation providing for his salary and pension presupposes that he will fulfil this dual role.

2. Although his Treasury duties may be nominal – the Minister effectively in charge of the Treasury is the Chancellor of the Exchequer – it seems to follow that the Prime Minister must be (or must become immediately after his appointment) a member of the House of Commons, if only because the House of Lords no longer has any control over finance. There are other, more obvious reasons why he must be in the Commons: the unrepresentative character of the Lords, its diminished status in the constitution since 1911, the role of the House of Commons as the political cockpit and the fact that a Government has to retain a majority in the Commons to remain in office but can flout a hostile House of Lords.

7. Among writings on this subject in the last decade, the prime ministerial thesis has been argued with particular force by R. H. S. Crossman, Introduction to Walter Bagehot, *The English Constitution* (1963 edn); John P. Mackintosh in *The British Cabinet* (though in a more guarded form in the 2nd edn); and Humphry Berkeley, *The Power of the Prime Minister*. It has been opposed no less vigorously by Herbert Morrison, *Government and Parliament* (3rd edn); D. N. Chester in (1962) 15 *Parliamentary Affairs* 519; George W. Jones in (1965) *Parliamentary Affairs* 167 (reprinted in *Policy Making in Britain* (ed. Richard Rose), p. 307); and Patrick Gordon Walker, *The Cabinet* (revised edn, 1972). See also Ronald Butt, *The Power of Parliament* (2nd edn); Ian Gilmour, *The Body Politic*; Sir Ivor Jennings, *Cabinet Government* (3rd edn). For a particularly well-argued appraisal, see A. H. Brown 'Prime Ministerial power' [1968] *Public Law* 28, 96. See also Anthony King (ed.), *The British Prime Minister*. Gordon Walker's evaluation is particularly important, the author having had considerable experience as a Cabinet Minister. Crossman's essay was written before he became a Minister, but he has substantially reiterated his views in *Inside View* (1972). See further John P. Mackintosh, *The Government and Politics of Britain* (1971).

Apart from Lord Home, who swiftly transmuted himself into a member of the Commons,[8] no Prime Minister has been a member of the Lords since 1902.

3. As First Lord of the Treasury he had responsibility for civil service affairs and his approval was required for proposals for the appointment of permanent heads of departments. In 1968 a new Civil Service Department was constituted, but the Prime Minister also became the Minister for the Civil Service, retaining his main responsibilities. The Head of the Home Civil Service is the Permanent Secretary to the Civil Service Department and is directly responsible to the Prime Minister.

4. The general rule is that in appointing a Prime Minister, the Queen should commission that person who appears best able to command the support of a stable majority in the House of Commons.

A change of Prime Minister may be necessary because of the resignation, death or dismissal of the incumbent. The last possibility, dismissal, would arise only in highly exceptional circumstances and, one would suppose, in a near-revolutionary situation;[9] in such a context the Queen would have to find somebody to form an emergency Government, perhaps without a majority in the House but prepared to advise a dissolution of Parliament at the earliest practicable moment. All vacancies in the office since Victoria came to the throne have arisen through resignation or death. Resignation may occur because the Government has been defeated at a General Election (as in 1945, 1951, 1964 and 1970) or has collapsed through internal dissension (as in 1931) or has been defeated on a matter of confidence in the House of Commons (as in 1895[10] and 1923[11]). In such cases it is the duty of the Government as a whole to resign (unless, in the event of a defeat in the House, the Prime Minister elects to advise a dissolution[12]) and of the Queen to send for the Leader of the Opposition or, when a Government resigns as soon as the results of a General Election are known and Parliament still stands dissolved, the person who was Leader of the Opposition in the House of Commons before the dissolution;[13] he will normally accept office as Prime Minister, but in an excep-

8. See p. 62. See also pp. 58–60 and 157–8 for further reasons why the Prime Minister must be in the Commons.

9. See pp. 103–4.

10. When Lord Rosebery's Government was defeated on the 'cordite vote'.

11. When Baldwin's Conservative Government was defeated on an amendment to the address in reply to the King's speech. See also the 1924 case (below).

12. Ramsay MacDonald so advised in 1924, and George V accepted his advice though he was not obliged to do so. *No* Government has been defeated in the House on a clear issue of confidence since that time.

13. Assuming, of course, that his party has won a majority at the General Election

tional situation may prefer to advise (as Baldwin advised in 1931) that a coalition Government under another person[14] be formed. The resignation of a Prime Minister may take place for other reasons – because of ill health or old age, or because he feels or is persuaded to feel that he has become a liability to his party or an obstacle to the formation of a coalition in wartime. In these situations, which have often arisen in the last fifty years – in 1923 (Bonar Law), 1935 (MacDonald), 1937 (Baldwin), 1940 (Neville Chamberlain), 1955 (Churchill), 1957 (Eden) and 1963 (Macmillan) – the party in office still retains a majority in the House and the Prime Minister's resignation is personal, almost as if he had died in office; the Ministers place their offices at his successor's disposal, but the Government as a whole does not vacate office. His successor may decide to make few changes, and those Ministers who continue in their posts do not have to be reappointed. But how is his successor chosen? If Labour is in office, the Queen should wait until the Parliamentary Labour Party has chosen its new leader, and then send for him. With a change of Conservative Prime Minister, the monarch had a personal discretion till February 1965, when the Conservative and Unionist Party adopted a new procedure for electing a party leader by ballot among Conservative M.P.s.[15] It can, therefore, be assumed that the Queen will not now have to exercise personal discretion on a change of Conservative Prime Minister, as she had to exercise a discretion in 1955, 1957 and 1963. In 1955, however, Sir Anthony Eden (now the Earl of Avon) was the obvious successor to Churchill. On the resignations of Eden in 1957 and Macmillan in 1963 the successor was not obvious. In 1957 she consulted Sir Winston Churchill and Lord Salisbury, two elder statesmen of the party; neither of them was any longer a candidate for the office; both recommended Harold Macmillan in preference to R. A. Butler, the alternative choice, and she commissioned Macmillan to form a Government. In 1963 the position was more difficult. Macmillan, having decided to resign on grounds of

---

and he has himself been re-elected in a constituency. When an Opposition party has won an overall majority in the House at the General Election, it is conventional for the Government to resign before the new Parliament meets.

14. In this instance, MacDonald, the outgoing Prime Minister, who cut himself adrift of the majority of his Labour colleagues. In a multi-party situation, where the Government has lost its majority but the Opposition cannot command one, the Leader of the Opposition may alternatively agree to form a minority Government. If he will not take office at all, the Queen may be placed in serious difficulty in her quest for a successor.

15. In July 1965 Mr Edward Heath was elected leader by this new procedure in succession to Sir Alec Douglas-Home (formerly Lord Home) who resigned the leadership; the party was then in opposition. Labour party leaders are elected annually when the party is in opposition; Conservative leaders do not have to be re-elected.

health, arranged for soundings to be taken among the Cabinet, the Parliamentary Party, the Conservative peers and the constituency parties; the collective weight of opinion appeared to favour Lord Home, and Macmillan advised the Queen accordingly. Although the monarch was not obliged to seek or follow the outgoing Prime Minister's advice, she could hardly have acted otherwise in those circumstances. The procedure and its outcome gave rise to some dissatisfaction within the party, which decided to alter its practice soon afterwards.

Hence the Queen is unlikely to have to exercise such a discretion again unless no party has an overall majority in the House, or the formation of a coalition is advised, or a coalition, having been formed, disintegrates. In such situations her duty will be to take such counsel as is proper and expedient to assist her in deciding who is the most appropriate person to invite to form a Government with a reasonable prospect of maintaining itself in office. That person will normally, but not invariably, be the leader of the largest party in the House of Commons.[16] In any event, the procedures now adopted by all the major parties (including the Liberals) for electing their own leaders seem to carry a necessary implication that the Prime Minister, when appointed, shall be a member of, or shall be about to occupy his seat[17] in, the House of Commons.

5. The Prime Minister presents a list of his proposed ministerial colleagues for the Queen's approval. She may make observations, suggestions and objections, but the Prime Minister is entitled to insist on his own choice. Junior Ministers are appointed by the Prime Minister without prior reference to the Queen.

6. The Prime Minister decides which Ministers are to be members of the Cabinet. His selection will be determined mainly by personal inclination and political expediency. By convention or custom, certain Ministers – the Chancellor of the Exchequer, the Secretary of State for Foreign and Commonwealth Affairs, the Home Secretary, the Lord Chancellor, the Secretary of State for Scotland, the Secretary of State for Defence, and that Minister whom the Prime Minister designates as Leader of the House

16. For a fuller and authoritative discussion of the conventions, prior to the change in Conservative Party practice, see Jennings, *Cabinet Government* (3rd edn), ch. 2. Mackintosh's *The British Cabinet* (2nd edn) is a highly informative work on political practice and relationships but is not primarily concerned with the identification of conventions.

From 1931 to 1935 MacDonald held office as Prime Minister of the 'National' Government although he was the leader of a small minority party. He was dependent on the favour of the Conservatives, the majority party and the dominant partner in the coalition; his personal position was conspicuously weak.

17. Where a change of Prime Minister is necessary after an election while Parliament stands dissolved.

of Commons – must always be in a peacetime Cabinet; and it would be odd if Ministers in charge of certain other main Departments (for example, education, social services, agriculture) were to be excluded. All Cabinet Ministers must be sworn as members of the Privy Council.

7. In assigning Ministers to Departments the Prime Minister must have regard to certain well-established conventions. All Ministers[18] must be or become members of one or other House of Parliament; if a Minister is not a member of either House at the time of his appointment, he must obtain a seat at the earliest opportunity or resign. Hence although it was proper to appoint Mr Patrick Gordon Walker as Foreign Secretary in 1964 in spite of his defeat in his constituency at the General Election, it was necessary for him to resign from office when he failed to win a seat at a by-election shortly afterwards. Each Department must have a ministerial spokesman in the House of Commons; no corresponding rule applies to the Lords. The Chancellor of the Exchequer must be a member of the House of Commons.

8. The Prime Minister may require a Minister to resign at any time and for any reason he thinks fit. If the Minister refuses to comply, the Prime Minister may in the last resort advise the Queen to dismiss him. In July 1962, Mr Macmillan in effect dismissed seven of his Cabinet colleagues, including the Chancellor of the Exchequer and the Lord Chancellor, in a drastic purge. Whether there are any circumstances in which the Queen could properly refuse a Prime Minister's advice to dismiss his colleagues is debatable.[19]

9. The Prime Minister may decide to advise a dissolution without prior reference to the Cabinet. In some situations, as we have already noted,[20] it would be constitutionally proper for the Queen to refuse such a request, absolutely, temporarily or conditionally, and one of those situations may be the case of a Prime Minister, placed in a minority in his own Cabinet, seeking to appeal to the electorate against his colleagues instead of following the more appropriate course of resigning. Nevertheless, the widespread assumption that it is within the Prime Minister's sole authority to

18. Except the Lord Advocate and the Solicitor-General for Scotland, one or both of whom have not infrequently been outside Parliament under Labour Governments.

19. Sir Ivor Jennings has asserted (*Cabinet Government* (3rd edn), p. 86) that: 'The Queen must not intervene in party politics. She must not, *therefore* [my italics], support a Prime Minister against his colleagues. Accordingly, it would be unconstitutional for the Queen to agree with the Prime Minister for the dissolution of a Government in order to allow the Prime Minister to override his colleagues.' This view is sustainable if the Prime Minister is known to have been placed, or is believed to be on the point of being placed, in a minority in his own Cabinet, but not otherwise.

20. See pp. 104–8.

fix the date of the next General Election enhances his personal power in relation to his ministerial colleagues and his party, and in the country as a whole.

10. When Parliament is dissolved the Government continues in office; it vacates office only if the election results show that it has lost its majority in the House, in which case it must resign.

11. The Prime Minister has substantial control over the organization as well as the personnel of central government. Not only does he choose, switch, promote, demote and discard his colleagues; he places them in an informal order of seniority;[21] he can take the initiative in creating a new Department or ministerial office, winding up a Department, and transferring functions from one Minister to another (though in some instances the change can only be effected by legislation); he can decide to create a new committee of the Cabinet, prescribe its terms of reference and give it decision-making powers; he can determine when the Cabinet shall meet; and in the last resort he can decide what shall or shall not be discussed at Cabinet meetings. He can thus control the allocation of functions between Cabinet, Cabinet committees and individual Departments. He can also decide which non-Cabinet Ministers shall be appointed to membership of Cabinet committees. Through his control over the Cabinet Office – a Cabinet Secretariat was created by Lloyd George in 1916 – he is in a position to see that the decisions of the Cabinet and its committees are implemented.[22]

12. He is entitled to say what issues shall be referred to him personally for decision outside the Cabinet. Inter-departmental disputes or deadlocks in Cabinet committees may be resolved by his informal rulings. And he may simply, by an uninvited personal initiative or pronouncement, confront his colleagues with a *fait accompli*.

13. The Prime Minister personally presides not only in the Cabinet but also in some of the more important standing committees of the Cabinet – for example, the Defence and Oversea Policy Committee. In the not so distant past, Prime Ministers also saddled themselves with heavy departmental responsibilities, as Foreign Secretary or Minister of Defence. This is likely to be a disadvantage nowadays, but the Prime Minister, as the country's principal spokesman on the international scene, must inevitably

21. A 'pecking order' emerges in the list of Ministers and Heads of Public Departments, at present published by Her Majesty's Stationery Office five times a year. The order in which the names of Cabinet Ministers appear is generally attributed to the Prime Minister's personal decision. It does not follow, however, that the Prime Minister is impliedly indicating that the second name in the list is that of his most appropriate successor.

22. On the Cabinet Office, see pp. 163, 164–5.

concern himself closely with foreign and Commonwealth affairs, matters of defence and security, and economic policy. For a short period in 1967–8 Mr Wilson was effectively in charge of his own creation, the Department of Economic Affairs. Mr Heath was the driving force behind Britain's decision to join the European Communities.

14. Since the Prime Minister is an international figure and a national leader, he is potentially capable of dominating his colleagues. His visits overseas to discuss matters of high policy, his speeches, answers to questions and interventions in the House of Commons, his performances on television and his other public addresses attract a degree of attention which no other politician in the country is likely to emulate. Moreover, he controls the Government's information services. As leader of his party he has another powerful organization behind him to project his image in its most favourable light; for if the public reputation of the Prime Minister sags, the prospects of the party remaining in office after the next General Election will dwindle; and it is not easy to remove a party leader tenacious of office and of the authority and deference that go with it.

15. At a General Election, the voters know that they are choosing a Government. To many of them, the choice is not so much between party programmes or party images as between the personal qualities of the Prime Minister and the Leader of the Opposition. If a Prime Minister and his advisers on public relations see this as the dominant factor in voting behaviour, the consequence will be the devotion of a disproportionate amount of publicity to the Prime Minister at the expense of his colleagues.

16. The Prime Minister enjoys, by convention, substantial powers of patronage. Some of these powers are apt to be a nuisance – 'Damn! another bishop dead', as Lord Melbourne remarked – and others, such as the power to advise on appointments to the highest judicial and military offices, are of no political advantage to him because of expectations that appointments shall be non-partisan. But there are others which enhance his personal authority, if only because the hope of preferment tends to muffle the voices of carping critics. One who attracts the favourable notice of the Prime Minister or those closest to him may cherish the prospect, if not of political office, at least of a place in the honours list, even a peerage, or perhaps the chairmanship of one of the multifarious statutory corporations, advisory and consultative bodies, royal commissions or committees of inquiry by virtue of the Prime Minister's nomination. The increase in the peripheral adjuncts of government, as the reach of central government has expanded and its workings have become more complex, has undoubtedly enlarged the area of ministerial patronage.

17. The Prime Minister is the channel of communication between the Cabinet and the Queen. It is his duty to keep her adequately informed on matters of State, and she holds a private audience with him weekly. These contacts tend to enhance the prestige of his office.

Executive power: some correctives

We have said a good deal about the Prime Minister but precious little about the Cabinet. Because the Prime Minister's conventional powers and general authority in the scheme of the constitution are very great, and because one can point to examples of dramatic Prime Ministerial decisions (such as Eden's decision to engage in the Suez venture, or Macmillan's decision to dismiss a third of his Cabinet) taken outside the Cabinet, one can easily be led to the conclusion that the Cabinet is no more than a Prime Minister's instrument at any given time. For reasons which must already be fairly obvious, it is too early to draw such a conclusion.

Disquisitions on the sovereignty of the Prime Minister bear some resemblance to discussions of the sovereignty of Parliament. Parliament in its wisdom might pass any number of appalling Acts without stepping beyond the limits of its constitutional authority, but somehow it does not regularly perpetrate gross abuses of its formal omnipotence. If a Prime Minister were to behave in a preposterous manner he would lose credit among his senior colleagues (who would resign if he had not already dismissed them), in the country and in his party; such a combination will be fatal to anyone but the most reckless autocrat, and a reckless autocrat who will neither resign nor mend his ways may have to be dealt with by unconventional and even extra-legal means. No modern Prime Minister has been a reckless autocrat. Illustrations of high-handed behaviour indicate not so much what a Prime Minister can do as the extent to which he may place his own position at risk. The misfortunes of Suez undermined Eden's health and personal prestige, and his resignation soon followed; Macmillan's standing in the Conservative Party and among the electorate, so strong in 1960, was not restored and may have suffered irretrievable damage by the dismissals of 1962.

The personification of a Government by the Prime Minister is also an uncertain asset. In March 1966 the size of the Labour Party's electoral victory could be attributed mainly to admiration of Harold Wilson's capacity to inspire confidence in his ability. The financial and economic crisis in the autumn of 1967 impaired the Prime Minister's personal credibility as an astute leader; his Government and his party might have suffered less in popular support if they had not been so closely identified with the qualities of their leader.

And so one soon arrives at the conclusion that few conclusions except the banal and platitudinous can be drawn from recent experience. The authority of a Prime Minister will depend mainly on such variables as the confidence and popularity he commands as a leader, his intellectual grasp of the problems of government, his tactical acumen, his performances as an orator and on the floor of the House of Commons,[22] his ability to make quick and acceptable decisions and to carry his senior colleagues and his party with him, the stature of those colleagues (particularly as potential alternative Prime Ministers), the international climate, the state of the country's economy, sheer luck, and the often fickle moods of public opinion[23] ('It's time for a change'). In wartime the personal authority of a Prime Minister may be overwhelming, as it was under Lloyd George from 1916 to 1918 and under Churchill from 1940 to 1945; it was by no means overwhelming under Asquith from 1914 to 1916 or under Chamberlain from 1939 to 1940. One is tempted to assert that all generalizations are false, including, of course, the one just offered.

It is at least questionable whether the effective power of the Prime Minister in relation to that of his ministerial colleagues has been greater in the period since 1945 than during the inter-war years. Certainly the powers of the Executive have grown as the reach of the central government into the nation's economy has extended and the welfare State has been nurtured. But most of these powers (including powers of appointment) are vested in named Ministers. No matter how versatile, energetic and able a Prime Minister may be, he can never be in a position to exercise close supervision over all the increasingly complex activities of the Departments, or indeed keep fully abreast of the technological and scientific developments with which their expert officials and advisers must be familiar. Coordination, supervision and the resolution of disagreements are achieved through inter-departmental committees, Cabinet committees and the Cabinet as a whole, as well as by the Prime Minister's informal rulings and by the machinery of the Cabinet Office. The chairmen of the more important committees may thus acquire a largely independent base of influence, even though they hold their places by the grace of the Prime Minister.

22. The resignation of Sir Alec Douglas-Home from the leadership of the Conservative Party in July 1965, some months after the party had suffered defeat at a General Election, is attributable first to a general awareness (not least among his own colleagues) that in some of these qualities he compared unfavourably with Mr Harold Wilson, and secondly to a capacity for self-effacement rare among politicians.
23. Yet Mr Richard Crossman, having conceded points such as these at the beginning of the Introduction to *Inside View*, goes on to restate his concept of Prime Ministerial government.

Some of the propositions set out in the preceding section must also be amplified or qualified. The Prime Minister does indeed control the Cabinet's agenda, but in practice he will often find it imprudent and will sometimes find it impracticable to exclude discussion of a question which other Ministers regard as important. He decides when the Cabinet is to meet; he presides at meetings; he is not bound to defer to the opinion of a majority of the Cabinet on any given issue, but if he persists in by-passing or attempting to override a majority of his colleagues the Government will soon disintegrate through resignations,[24] and it is therefore in his interest to attempt by persuasion to establish a consensus in favour of his own views (if he has already formed a firm view) but not to press his colleagues too hard. The fact that by the act of resignation an individual Minister may consign himself to years in the political wilderness is not enough to encourage a Prime Minister to court mass resignations or a major revolt.

Again, it is sometimes said that the power of the Prime Minister (acquired since the First World War) to advise a dissolution of Parliament without the prior concurrence of his colleagues places in his hands an enormously potent weapon to subdue restiveness or crush rebellion within the ranks. Here analogies with nuclear weapons are relevant. They can be used, but the result is likely to be suicidal; hence threats to use them may not always be taken seriously. For a Prime Minister overtly to remind fractious or openly rebellious colleagues or party backbenchers that he might feel obliged to request a dissolution, the disloyal being denied official party support at the ensuing General Election, is seldom a wise move. If the threat is carried out, the electorate may well turn away from a party in disarray and put the Opposition in office; a penal dissolution is apt to prove a boomerang and everybody knows this. This is not to say that an open threat by the Prime Minister to advise a dissolution will have no positive political impact whatsoever; but it does imply that the fairest comparison is with a threat by the Prime Minister to tender his Government's resignation. Dissent is better dealt with by bold leadership, or by accommodation and compromise, or, if necessary, by the dismissal of malcontents from the Government, or withdrawal of the party whip from backbench rebels, or simply by non-endorsement of a candidate at a General Election to be held at an indeterminate date; again, everybody knows this, and facts which everybody knows tend to condition political behaviour.

When one says that the Prime Minister controls the Cabinet Office, one is not asserting that this Office is merely his pliant instrument. The

24. On ministerial threats of resignation as a tactical weapon to influence government policy, see R. K. Alderman and J. A. Cross, *The Tactics of Resignation*, ch. 2.

main constitutional function of the Office[25] is to provide a Secretariat for the Cabinet and its committees, distributing memoranda and agenda papers, recording proceedings and compiling and circulating minutes. Documents issued by the Secretariat go to departmental Ministers who are not members of the Cabinet. The work of the Secretariat therefore enables all Ministers to become better informed about major decisions and their factual background. This makes a Government more efficient, and incidentally justifies a reduction in the size of a Cabinet; it does not necessarily elevate the Prime Minister still higher above his colleagues, though it provides special briefs for the Prime Minister and helps him to follow up action taken in pursuance of decisions. The Cabinet Office, moreover, is not the Prime Minister's private office. It is staffed mainly by permanent civil servants, of whom a substantial proportion are officers of high seniority and standing; and the Secretary to the Cabinet, the head of this Office and just as independent as his colleagues, is possibly the most important member of the public service. Nevertheless, a Prime Minister's close personal relations with the Secretary to the Cabinet[26] will place him at an advantage in controlling the machinery of central government. He will also have close relations with the Director-General of the new Central Policy Review Staff.[27]

The Prime Minister also has a small separate Private Office: this is also composed mainly of established civil servants,[28] but it will naturally include persons whom the Prime Minister finds particularly congenial. It is still far too minute to rival the influence of the Cabinet Office in the general working of the machinery of central government. Any comparison with the White House staff of an American President would be derisory.

Some of the many internal restraints that are potentially capable of curbing a Prime Minister's freedom of action are illustrated by the fate of the proposal to introduce an Industrial Relations Bill in 1969.[29] Clauses

25. See generally, R. K. Mosley, *The Story of the Cabinet Office* (1969). In 1971 and 1972 the administrative coordination of negotiations and arrangements for Britain's entry into Europe was a matter for the Cabinet Office. Following Britain's entry, the Office has remained the clearing-house for Community affairs.

26. Patrick Gordon Walker (*The Cabinet*, p. 55) comments that 'the Cabinet Secretary has become something like a Permanent Secretary to the Prime Minister'.

27. See p. 194.

28. In late 1972 it comprised a principal private secretary to the Prime Minister, four private secretaries (two for home affairs, one for overseas affairs and one for parliamentary affairs), the influential but strictly apolitical confidential secretary for appointments, a political secretary, three press secretaries, three information officers, and three assistant private secretaries. The Prime Minister's parliamentary private secretary (an M.P.) was also included in the list. The personnel of the Cabinet Secretariat numbered at least a hundred.

29. The incoming Conservative Government procured the enactment of the Industrial Relations Act 1971.

of the bill providing for the imposition of judicially enforceable sanctions against participants in 'wildcat' strikes were strenuously advocated by the Prime Minister, the Secretary of State for Employment and Productivity and other senior members of the Government. They were also, so it appeared from opinion polls, generally favoured by a large majority of the public. The Conservative Party thought that the penal clauses were, if anything, too weak. The introduction of legal sanctions was implacably opposed by the Trades Union Congress. The trade union view was buttressed by a majority of the National Executive Committee of the Labour Party; Mr James Callaghan, the Home Secretary and a member of the reconstituted Parliamentary Committee of the Cabinet (the new 'inner Cabinet') cast his vote with the majority of the National Executive, and was promptly dropped for the time being by the Prime Minister from the Parliamentary Committee, though he remained a member of the Cabinet. In the course of the lengthy negotiations with the Council of the Trades Union Congress it became clear that the Government would have great difficulty in carrying its own backbenchers with it, and the Labour movement in the country would be deeply riven and that the party was in danger of losing its financial backing from the trades unions. Opinion within the Cabinet appears to have gradually moved against its original policy. In June it was announced that the bill would not be proceeded with during that session, and that in any event the penal clauses would be dropped altogether in return for a solemn declaration of intent by the Council of the Trades Union Congress that it would take action to prevent 'unconstitutional' work stoppages and, if necessary, apply its own internal sanctions against violators. Mr Wilson hailed the extraction of this declaration of intent as a famous victory; the party took pleasure in the outcome; nobody resigned. Others, less sympathetic, spoke of capitulation to a powerful pressure group, and pointed out that the Government had already decided to abandon part of its restrictive incomes policy and to withdraw the bill for the reform of the Lords in order to facilitate the introduction and passage of its Industrial Relations Bill.

Cabinet committees: a note

The Cabinet committee system is clearly of first-class importance in the machinery of central government. But the secrecy enveloping this system is even harder to penetrate than the working of the Cabinet itself. In no official publication is there so much as a full list of these committees, let alone the names of their chairmen and members, a statement of their functions, or their relationships with the Cabinet as a whole.[30] When a

30. The need for complete secrecy was justified by Sir Burke Trend, the Secretary

Government has departed from the political scene, a fuller account of its committee system may become available:[31] contemporary details are rarely divulged.

Disclosures made in 1968, however, made it possible to glean impressions of the system then in being.[32] There were standing committees and *ad hoc* committees. The principal standing committee, created in that year, was the Parliamentary Committee, composed of the Prime Minister and nine senior Ministers; it met twice a week and made decisions on a wide range of policy issues; its decisions were reported to the Cabinet, which was reduced to meeting once a fortnight. Issues decided by the Committee could be reopened by any Minister in the full Cabinet, but seldom with any prospect of success.

There were other standing committees with executive powers as well as powers to make recommendations. The Prime Minister presided over the Defence and Oversea Policy Committee[33] and the Economic Policy Committee; the Chancellor of the Exchequer over the Public Expenditure Scrutiny Committee; the Leader of the House of Commons over the Future Legislation Committee (which considered projected bills) and the Legislation Committee (which considered the current legislative programme and the details of bills and major statutory instruments); there was a Social Services Committee, a Home Affairs Committee, and so on. Ministers dissatisfied with a committee decision could appeal to the Prime Minister but no longer to the Cabinet as a whole unless the chairman agreed. Chairmen of committees could also bring potentially contentious matters to the attention of the Prime Minister or the Parliamentary Committee. Some of these procedural arrangements signified a temporary diminution in the status of the Cabinet. But the system in being at any time reflects both the idiosyncratic style of an individual Prime Minister and the

---

of the Cabinet, giving evidence before the *Franks Committee on Section 2 of the Official Secrets Act 1911* (Cmnd 5104 (1972), Minutes of Evidence, vol. 3, pp. 324–6) as being essential for the maintenance of collective responsibility for Cabinet decisions – a most unconvincing reason – and the prevention of leakages. cf. 'Whitehall's Needless Secrecy', *The Times*, 3 May 1973, naming sixteen committees.

31. See Herbert Morrison, *Government and Parliament* (3rd edn), ch. 2.

32. John P. Mackintosh, 'Mr Wilson's Revised Cabinet System', *The Times*, 21 June 1968. For a general description of recent Cabinet committee systems, see Mackintosh, *The British Cabinet* (2nd edn), pp. 510–18. See also Patrick Gordon Walker, *The Cabinet*, Appendix, for a list of the standing committees of the Cabinet in 1964.

33. The composition of this committee had been announced in 1963 (Cmnd 2097) – a curious phenomenon, since this committee deals with the most highly confidential matters, and a primary reason for preserving secrecy about the composition of committees is to prevent journalists from guessing accurately what topics are under discussion.

constraints, both extrinsic to and within the Government, to which he feels himself subject.

Many of the Cabinet committees are supported by a parallel committee of senior officials belonging to the Departments whose political heads are members of the principal committee. Some of the committees have begotten specialized sub-committees. It should be re-emphasized that Ministers not of the Cabinet may be and are appointed to Cabinet committees. Senior officials (and in the case of the Defence and Oversea Policy Committee, the Chief of the Defence Staff and the chiefs of staff of the three armed services) may also be invited to attend while a particular issue is under consideration. An official may even represent his Department on a Cabinet Committee. The head of the Central Policy Review Staff[34] was present at Cabinet meetings under Mr Heath's Government.

Ministerial responsibility

That the Cabinet and its members are 'collectively responsible' is an undoubted constitutional convention. But what does collective responsibility signify? In many of the newly independent Commonwealth countries British conventions have been spelt out in some detail, often with modifications, in the texts of the constitutions. On Cabinet responsibility, Barbados is nevertheless laconic. 'The Cabinet shall be the principal instrument of policy and shall be charged with the general direction and control of the government of Barbados and shall be collectively responsible therefor to Parliament'.[35] It is wise not to attempt to define in a constitutional document what exactly collective responsibility means, because the outlines of the concept are so vague and blurred. It can be described at a high level of generality; it can be illustrated by specific examples; a neat but comprehensive set of propositions cannot be devised, if only because the gulf between traditional constitutional theory (to which lip-service may still be paid) and political practice yawns so widely.

Responsible for what and to whom? And what exactly do we mean by 'responsible'? Does the substitution of words like 'accountable' or 'answerable' clarify the issues at all?[36] Perhaps it is more helpful to begin with the concept of the *individual* responsibility of Ministers, which raises some of the questions in a still more difficult way. Historically,

34. See p. 194.

35. Barbados Independence Order 1966 (S.I. 1966, No. 1455), Schedule, s. 64(2).

36. cf. Geoffrey Marshall and Graeme C. Moodie, *Some Problems of the Constitution* (5th edn); A. H. Birch, *Representative and Responsible Government*; John P. Mackintosh, *The British Cabinet* (2nd edn); Andrew Shonfield, *Modern Capitalism*, Part 4; D. N. Chester and Nona Bowring, *Questions in Parliament*, Appendix 2; Henry Parris, *Constitutional Bureaucracy*, chs. 3, 4, 10.

moreover, the principle of individual ministerial responsibility preceded the doctrine of collective responsibility.

All Ministers, whether they be in or outside the Cabinet, are responsible for their personal acts, the general conduct of their Departments and acts done (or left undone) in their name by their departmental officials. Responsibility may be political, legal, or both political and legal; and the meaning of responsibility, and the persons or bodies to whom it is owed, will vary according to the context.

Ministers are legally responsible in their private capacities for acts which they order or authorize to be done, or in which they actively participate. If, for example, such an act proves to be a trespass, the Minister can be sued personally for damages as a tortfeasor. To Dicey, the personal liability of Ministers and officials for civil wrongs before the ordinary courts applying the ordinary law of the land, subject to any special statutory powers that might be vested in them to encroach on private rights, was a cardinal feature of the rule of law in Britain. Today this aspect of ministerial responsibility is of little practical importance, for since 1947 it has been possible to sue the Crown as the Minister's employer for torts committed in the purported exercise of legal powers and duties.

Ministers are legally and politically responsible for formal acts done by the monarch, under prerogative or statutory powers, in which they have participated by virtue of their attendance at a meeting of the Privy Council, or their countersignature of the royal sign manual or their custody of a royal seal. The strictly legal rationale of these customary procedures has now disappeared.

Parliament used to bring Ministers to account by a semi-judicial process. The King could do no wrong in the eyes of the law (unless he was Charles I or James II) and it was more satisfactory and expedient to attack his advisers for their evil counsel by charging them with high crimes and misdemeanours. The Commons were the accusers; the Lords were the judges; the process was called impeachment. Not only Ministers, but officials and judges accused of corruption, were impeached; the verdicts were not necessarily a foregone conclusion. During the course of the eighteenth century votes of censure against Ministers and Governments gradually replaced the cumbersome machinery of impeachment; political accountability was better achieved without a heavy-handed political trial. The last impeachment was brought in 1805;[37] the procedure has never been abolished but is in practice obsolete.

37. The defendant (who was acquitted) was Lord Melville, formerly Treasurer to the Admiralty. The last impeachment before that was the case of Warren Hastings, Governor-General of India; the proceedings, instituted in the 1780s, dragged on for years. The first impeachment took place in 1376.

As long as Ministers were men appointed and dismissed by the King in his personal discretion, men with whom he would confer individually or in small groups, their first loyalty was to the monarch. Individual ministerial responsibility to the Crown remained a reality for more than a century after the existence of a Cabinet was publicly acknowledged. Responsibility in this form was superseded by the development of collective Cabinet responsibility, a responsibility owed simultaneously to the Crown and Parliament, then (after the effective withdrawal of George III from political leadership) to Parliament rather than to the Crown,[38] and then, after the enlargement of the franchise in 1832, to the House of Commons rather than to Parliament as a whole. The implications of collective responsibility were not fully worked out till the years after 1867, when a further and more substantial extension of the franchise led to the evolution of mass political parties. To these implications we shall return. They are not identical with the implications of individual responsibility, but the two concepts are intertwined and co-exist.

Ministers are politically answerable in respect of matters lying within their statutory or conventional fields of responsibility. They are responsible not only for their personal acts but for the conduct of their Departments. The area of statutory responsibility is determined by the legislation (if any) establishing their offices and particular Acts and subordinate legislative instruments endowing them with powers and duties. If a Minister has no power or duty to take any action with regard to a matter, he cannot properly be held accountable to Parliament for what is done or left undone; hence, a Minister is not expected to answer parliamentary questions about the day-to-day administration of nationalized industries[39] and many other public corporations, or most of the activities of local government authorities or the police.[40] To some Ministers powers and duties are assigned by convention – for example, to the Secretary of State for Foreign and Commonwealth Affairs, most of whose functions are non-statutory; to the Home Secretary in respect of advice on the exercise of the prerogative of pardon; to the Attorney-General in respect of decisions whether to enter a *nolle prosequi* to stop a trial on indictment. The conventions may, like those just referred to, be well-established, surviving changes of government; or they may be the product of an informal re-allocation by the Prime Minister of responsibilities among his Ministers, especially Ministers such as the Lord President of the Council,

38. For the modification by Parliament of its first decision early in the eighteenth century to keep Ministers and royal placemen out of the House of Commons altogether, see p. 151.

39. But see p. 222.

40. See ch. 17.

the Lord Privy Seal, the Chancellor of the Duchy of Lancaster and the Paymaster-General, whose formal departmental functions are small or nominal.

The meaning of political responsibility cannot be precisely defined. If a Minister is personally blameworthy, he ought to make a public admission of his responsibility. Personal culpability may be attributable to private or public conduct unbecoming to a Minister of the Crown, in which case there will be an expectation that he will resign;[41] or to bad judgment or departmental maladministration, in which case there cannot be said to be any clear-cut convention about a duty to offer resignation.[42] Unless the Prime Minister is unwilling to stand by the Minister under attack – and in this context the personal authority of a Prime Minister is of great importance – a Minister may choose, and has not infrequently chosen in recent years, to brazen out appalling indiscretions, gross errors and omissions, plans gone awry and revelations of disastrous mismanagement within his Department. If the Opposition is allowed time to move a vote of censure, or if a supply day is selected for the purpose of moving a motion to reduce the Minister's salary, the Minister can confidently expect to emerge triumphant in the division lobbies, with members voting strictly along party lines. Yet his victory may prove to be pyrrhic and ephemeral. The Prime Minister may shift him to another office carrying less prestige in the next ministerial reshuffle; he may 'kick him upstairs' to the Lords; he may quietly call for the Minister's resignation at a moment less embarrassing for the Government, or gratefully accept a half-hearted offer of resignation if it comes. A Minister who is incapable of explaining and justifying his conduct of affairs persuasively in the face of a hostile Opposition, or to the satisfaction of independent political commentators, is a liability to the Government and the party.

Given that the idea of ministerial culpability for personal failings is so shapeless, a detailed analysis of *degrees* of ministerial responsibility for the conduct of departmental affairs and officials would not be very helpful. A Minister is expected to answer questions about these matters in Parliament unless the question must be disallowed by parliamentary practice (for example, because it deals with an issue *sub judice*) or unless the

41. Mr John Profumo resigned in 1963 after it was revealed that he had made a false statement to the House of Commons in rebuttal of allegations about his private life. Mr J. H. Thomas in 1936 and Dr Hugh Dalton in 1947 resigned after it became known that they had perpetrated premature disclosures of provisions of the Budget, though in Dr Dalton's case there was not the slightest suggestion of any improper personal motive and his indiscretion had no adverse effect on the country's finances.

42. See S. E. Finer (1956) 34 *Public Administration* 377; P. J. Madgwick (1966–7) 20 *Parliamentary Affairs* 59; R. K. Alderman and J. A. Cross, *The Tactics of Resignation*.

Minister feels bound to refuse an answer or a full answer on grounds of national security, in which case he will have to face the prospect of personal criticism.[43] In answering questions, or in replying to a debate, he cannot be expected to accept that he is himself culpable whenever a departmental official has committed a dishonest act or has disobeyed instructions or exceeded his authority. He is entitled to explain in public what has occurred; but he cannot totally absolve himself of responsibility. To use a colloquialism which, eluding exact definition, is still well understood, he must, in the last resort, 'carry the can'.[44] If maladministration within his Department is attributable to bad organization or procedures or defective supervision, or exists on such a large scale or at so high a level that he ought to have been able to prevent it, then he is in some degree blameworthy.[45] But Sir Thomas Dugdale's personal decision to resign as Minister of Agriculture in 1954 because of the exposure of maladministration by senior officials (of which he had had no personal knowledge) in the over-celebrated Crichel Down affair[46] was not demanded by convention; certainly other Ministers have not sought to emulate him by exacting the supreme political penalty on themselves, and it would be unrealistic to expect them to do so, particularly if wide decision-making powers have been delegated to the official concerned.[47] Even Mr James Callaghan's resignation from the office of Chancellor of the Exchequer in November 1967, after he had long striven but finally failed to save the pound from devaluation, was considered to be commendable rather than

43. For a list of matters on which successive Ministers have refused to answer questions, either for reasons of public interest or because they lie outside the field of ministerial responsibility, see *Report of the Select Committee on Parliamentary Questions* (H.C. 393 (1971–2), pp. 114–17). In 1956 Eden, as Prime Minister, refused to disclose the circumstances in which Commander Crabb, a naval security officer, lost his life in Portsmouth Harbour – in fact he was drowned while investigating Soviet warships at anchor – but stated that what was done was not authorized or approved by a Minister and that disciplinary action would be taken.

44. Cf. the Report of the Parker Committee on the Use of Authorized Procedures for Interrogation of Persons Suspected of Terrorism in Northern Ireland (Cmnd 4901 (1972)), indicating that the unlawful practices adopted had never in fact been authorized by a Minister and may not have even been known to Ministers. They were nevertheless politically answerable for the conduct of the security forces.

45. cf. the slightly different formulation by the then Home Secretary, Sir David Maxwell Fyfe, in 530 H.C. Deb. 1285–8 (20 July 1954), quoted in Geoffrey Wilson, *Cases and Materials on Constitutional and Administrative Law*, pp. 69–70.

46. Cmd 9176 (1953); Cmd 9220 (1954); Wilson, op. cit., pp. 64–9; J. A. G. Griffith (1955) 18 *Mod. L. Rev.* 557; D. N. Chester (1954) 32 *Public Administration* 389. Dugdale was later elevated to the peerage as Lord Crathorne. In 1972 he was chairman of the Political Honours Scrutiny Committee (see p. 147 above).

47. As in the Vehicle and General affair; note 52.

obligatory. His immediate translation to the Home Office was not out of keeping with the spirit of the contemporary constitution.

The political answerability of Ministers has helped to preserve the impartiality and anonymity of civil servants; they have been reasonably secure from public censure and, therefore, find it easier to give unstinted loyalty to a succession of political masters. But official anonymity has not been an unmixed blessing; and, as the Fulton Committee on the civil service pointed out,[48] it is gradually being eroded. It is being eroded, in particular, by the activities of specialized select committees of the House of Commons[49] and the Parliamentary Commissioner for Administration[50] (the Ombudsman). The Parliamentary Commissioner not only scrutinizes departmental procedures but has, on rare occasions, singled out identifiable civil servants for criticism.[51] He has yet to go as far as the judicial tribunal of inquiry on the collapse of the Vehicle and General Insurance Co. (1972), which affixed blame on a named senior civil servant in the Department of Trade and Industry for failing to set in motion an investigation of the Company's affairs, but exonerated the responsible Ministers.[52] If this type of inquisition were to become frequent, it would be impossible to expect civil servants not to answer back. Nevertheless, ministerial responsibility remains as a protective, if slightly tattered, cloak for the civil service, and at least no serious complaint of political partisanship against senior civil servants has yet been substantiated.

The *collective responsibility* of the Cabinet to the House of Commons is still sometimes spoken of as a democratic bulwark of the British constitution. After all, did not five Governments resign between the years 1852 and 1859 as a result of being defeated on votes of confidence in the House?[53] (True, democracy was then a pejorative term, but who cares?) Rather more to the point is that no Government has forfeited the confidence of the House since 1924, when Ramsay MacDonald's first Labour Government, which never had an overall majority in the House, found itself deserted by its Liberal allies. On several occasions since 1945, Governments have been defeated in the House on particular issues because their whips have been outmanoeuvred by the Opposition or because of

48. Cmnd 3638 (1968), vol. 1, p. 93.

49. See ch. 12.

50. See ch. 29.

51. See, for example, H.C. 316 (1968–9) (*Third Report of the Parliamentary Commissioner for the Session 1968–9*).

52. H.C. 133 (1971–2); the report was debated in 835 H.C. Deb. 33–161 (1 May 1972). There was much criticism that the civil servant concerned had not been granted adequate facilities to defend himself before the tribunal of inquiry. See Addendum.

53. Particulars are supplied by Jennings, *Cabinet Government* (3rd edn), pp. 512–15.

absenteeism. The Government has then usually mustered its full resources and procured a reversal of the vote. There has been no defeat on an unequivocal issue of confidence,[54] such as the budget resolutions or the address in reply to the Queen's speech at the opening of a session. Mr Harold Wilson was able to sustain himself in office from 1964 to 1966 with a majority of less than six; and he then won a handsome victory at a General Election held at the most advantageous moment for his party. Neville Chamberlain, on the other hand, decided to resign after a vote in the House on a motion of censure in May 1940; but the motion was defeated by eighty-one votes. It is a nice question which was the more significant fact – that he retained a substantial parliamentary majority after having forfeited the confidence of the general public, or that thirty-three Conservatives voted against their own leader and eighty others abstained.

Because a Government must maintain a majority in the House of Commons as a condition of survival – it can ignore defeats in the Lords – it has to ensure party solidarity. Doubtless this reduces the results of most of the contentious debates in the House to foregone conclusions; but a Government which is driven to rely on disciplinary sanctions and threats of sanctions, and an autocratic disregard of the interests of the Opposition and private members generally in the allocation of parliamentary time, is not going to endear itself to the electorate. The fact that the executive branch is parliamentary has an influence, which cannot be quantified, on the style of British politics.

Collective responsibility also implies that all Cabinet Ministers assume responsibility for Cabinet decisions and action taken to implement those decisions. A Minister may disagree with a decision[55] or with the manner of its implementation, but if he wishes to express dissent in public he should first resign.

These two propositions need to be explained and qualified.

1. The convention of public unanimity is settled, at least to the extent that it will be regarded as constitutionally improper for a Minister to remain in office if he has overtly dissociated himself from Cabinet policy. It is open to the Prime Minister to condone a verbal indiscretion by a colleague, and even to overlook a studied refusal by a colleague to offer positive commendation of a policy which he dislikes, though the line between half-hearted formal acquiescence and hints of real disagreement may wear

54. There is no formal definition of a matter of confidence. If a Government explicitly states that it regards a vote as one of confidence, or if the Opposition has moved a motion of no confidence, the Government must, of course, stand or fall by the result.

55. And ask to have his dissent recorded in the Cabinet minutes: John P. Mackintosh, *The British Cabinet* (2nd edn), p. 523.

thin. But in this century only for a few months in 1932 has the convention been expressly waived, on the issue of tariff protection under a coalition Government; this experiment was not a success, and despite occasional deviations from the norm since that time, the general principle is clear.

2. Public unanimity conforms to expectations of the electorate (which frowns upon a Government in disarray) and strengthens the hands of a Government in relation to its own backbench dissenters, the Opposition and political commentators, all of whom are alert to any suspicion of discord within the Cabinet. But from time to time, when a Minister finds the strain of maintaining a tight-lipped silence insupportable, he will deliberately 'leak' his 'unattributable' private views to a journalist. This practice[56] has been defended[57] as being necessary for the preservation of the basic convention – in much the same way as discreet adultery might be justified as the only means of safeguarding the state of holy matrimony. Leaking (as distinct from 'briefing', which involves the authorized disclosure of information[58]) may be resorted to by Ministers, including the Prime Minister, to fortify or explain their position when there is a split in the Cabinet. A notable example was the disclosure to backbenchers and journalists of divisions in 1967 over the question whether to resume arms sales to South Africa.[59] The convention can be interpreted and applied very flexibly.

3. The obligation to preserve an outward show of unanimity about past decisions is supposed to continue after the Government, or the Minister who had been placed in a minority, has left office. But the force of this obligation is weak.

(a) If a Minister has decided to resign because of disagreement on a policy issue[60] he is customarily allowed to publish the nature of the disagreement in his letter of resignation and to make a resignation speech in Parliament if he so wishes.

The general principle is that disclosures of Cabinet discussions or decisions by former Ministers are permissible only with the Sovereign's

56. Now well documented. See Colin Seymour-Ure, *The Press, Politics and the Public*, ch. 6; Jeremy Tunstall, *The Westminster Lobby Correspondents*; Patrick Gordon Walker, *The Cabinet* (1972 edn), pp. 26–33.

57. Gordon Walker, pp. 27–8, 32.

58. cf. Mr James Callaghan, giving evidence to the Franks Committee on Official Secrecy: 'You know the difference between leaking and briefing. Briefing is what I do and leaking is what you do' (Cmnd 5104 (1972), vol. 4, p. 187).

59. Gordon Walker, pp. 29–30; Harold Wilson, *The Labour Government 1964–1970*, pp. 470–76; George Brown, *In My Way*, pp. 163–7.

60. See Alderman and Cross, op. cit., Appendix. In 1968, Mr George Brown, Foreign Secretary and Deputy Leader of the Labour Party, resigned on a procedural issue about the method of taking major policy decisions.

consent, communicated by the Prime Minister of the day through the medium of the Cabinet Office. The formal basis of the procedure is said to be the Privy Councillor's oath of secrecy, broadly interpreted. It is also buttressed by the Official Secrets Acts, which prohibit the unauthorized disclosure of information acquired in confidence in one's capacity as a Crown servant. Moreover, the national interest, and the interest in encouraging the utmost frankness in Cabinet discussions leading up to a policy decision, will sometimes be prejudiced if it is thought that Ministers will be at liberty to rush into print or be propelled on to the television screen with their memoirs and reminiscences as soon as they leave office. Yet over the years, and particularly since 1970, ex-Ministers have disclosed with impunity Cabinet discussions and disagreements. If they submit their memoirs to the Cabinet Office, it seems that they are merely given a selective vetting to eliminate references damaging to security or external relations, and apparently there is no formal grant of authorization to publish. What is the basis of this remarkable divergence of political practice from constitutional theory? According to the Secretary of the Cabinet, there is a 'long and honourable convention in our public life, that anybody who has held a public office which makes him accountable to public opinion . . . is entitled before he dies to put on record his own version of the events in which he has played a part'.[61] This is an interesting rationalization of the facts of life. But where does it leave the 'convention' of collective responsibility?

(b) The convention (such as it is) extends to decisions of which a Minister was not aware at the time but to which he subsequently gave his tacit approval by continuing in office with full knowledge of the facts. But here the force of the convention is even weaker. One can hardly expect a Minister to accept the same degree of responsibility for a decision in which he had no opportunity to participate as for a decision where he had such an opportunity.

(c) For this reason the *ex post facto* responsibility of non-Cabinet Ministers for Cabinet decisions is not at all clear-cut, unless the Minister concerned was a member of a Cabinet committee which took or recommended the actual decision. Criticism of a Cabinet decision by the Minister after his departure from office may be condoned, if he learned of it only when Cabinet minutes were circulated to him; it ought to be excused if the decision was never brought to his notice at all.

4. Nevertheless, a non-Cabinet Minister will not be allowed to express public disagreement with government policy and remain in office, unless it is expedient for the Prime Minister to overlook the transgression; for a

61. Cmnd 5104 (1972), vol. 3, pp. 330–32.

transgression it is, notwithstanding the too often repeated, and too little analysed, assertion that collective responsibility applies only to members of the Cabinet. The practice followed in Attlee's Government after 1945 was instructive. The Government Chief Whip in the House of Lords described the Government handling of a dock labour dispute as 'absolutely crazy'; out he went. The Parliamentary Secretary to the Ministry of Agriculture did not survive his public criticism of the Government's 'feather-bedding' of farmers. And out went a group of parliamentary private secretaries (not even Ministers, but unpaid aides to individual Ministers) who failed to support the Government in an important division on the Ireland Bill which recognized (*inter alia*) the continued partition of Ireland. Here again the importance of an individual Prime Minister's style of governing is the most material fact.[62]

5. Just as Ministers are expected to be loyal to their colleagues, so they can reasonably claim to be entitled to the loyalty of their colleagues if they run into public criticism in implementing agreed Cabinet policies. If they implement them badly, or if they incur criticism as a result of purely departmental failings or indications of personal ineptitude, they will not have any corresponding claim to corporate solidarity. In 1935, the Foreign Secretary, Sir Samuel Hoare, exceeded his mandate by concurring in an agreement that would have given the Italian invaders of Abyssinia a slice of that country. The Cabinet could have repudiated Hoare but decided to stand by him. When the terms of the agreement were published, a national outcry arose. In an attempt to retrieve its reputation, the Cabinet then insisted on Hoare's resignation.[63] In the circumstances this was a clear breach of convention. Hoare was duly rewarded for allowing himself to be sacrified for the national good; he was given another, not quite so exalted, Cabinet post a few months later.

62. In 1969 Dr Jeremy Bray, a junior Minister, wished to publish a critical study of the use of technology in government, drawing on his experience in office. The Prime Minister refused to permit him to continue in office if he published. Dr Bray resigned. His book (*Decision in Government*) was published in 1970.

63. See Middlemas and Barnes, *Baldwin*, ch. 31 ('The Hoare–Laval Pact'). On almost every other matter the authors show great sympathy with Baldwin.

Chapter 7
Ministers, Departments and Civil Servants

Central government
Ministers and Departments

In December 1972 there were nineteen Cabinet Ministers; and twenty-four full Ministers, as well as the four Law Officers of the Crown, who were not members of the Cabinet. In addition, there were over fifty junior Ministers – parliamentary under-secretaries of state,[1] parliamentary secretaries, financial secretaries, Government whips,[2] and the like. In short, the Ministry numbered about one hundred. A large majority of those full Ministers who sat in the Commons had unpaid backbench M.P.s as their parliamentary private secretaries. All but nine of the senior Ministers were members of the Commons. About a fifth of the membership of the House of Commons consisted of members of the Government or M.P.s closely associated with the work of Ministers, though the maximum number of holders of paid ministerial offices, who may sit and vote in the House, is fixed by statute at ninety-one.[3]

Yet in 1914, when the Government had already begun to assume responsibility for providing minimum standards of social welfare, the number of senior ministerial offices, excluding the Law Officers, was only twenty-one. The big increase since that time is attributable to a large expansion in the functions and activity of central government.

Of the ministerial offices at the outbreak of the First World War, some had disappeared well before 1972. Gone were the Secretaries of State for India, for the Colonies, and for War, and the First Lord of the Admiralty. There was no longer any call for a separate Department to deal with Indian affairs; the Colonial Office had been merged with the Common-

1. If the Minister in charge of a Department is a Secretary of State.
2. Government whips have various designations. The Government Chief Whip in the House of Commons is the Parliamentary Secretary to the Treasury. Other Government whips in the Commons hold nominal offices in the Royal Household or are styled Junior Lords of the Treasury or merely Assistant Whips. In the Lords all Government whips hold nominal offices connected with the Royal Household.
3. Ministers of the Crown Act 1964, s. 3(2). The maximum numbers of holders of various classes of political offices to whom salaries may be paid are also fixed by statute: Ministerial and other Salaries Act 1972.

wealth Office (the successor in title to the Dominions Office, 1924–47) in 1966, and the latter with the Foreign Office, under a single Secretary of State, in 1968; the War Office, the Admiralty and the Air Ministry disappeared in 1964, and instead there was an integrated Ministry of Defence under a Secretary of State supported by Ministers of State and parliamentary under-secretaries. Some ministerial offices in 1914 had survived under their then existing designations (Prime Minister, Lord Chancellor, Chancellor of the Exchequer, Secretary of State for the Home Department, Lord President of the Council, Lord Privy Seal, Chancellor of the Duchy of Lancaster, Paymaster General) and some had been renamed. Thus, the Secretary for Scotland had become a Secretary of State, the Secretary of State for Foreign Affairs was Secretary of State for Foreign and Commonwealth Affairs, the President of the Local Government Board had become the Secretary of State for the Environment,[4] the President of the Board of Education was the Secretary of State for Education and Science, the President of the Board of Agriculture and Fisheries was the Minister of Agriculture, Fisheries and Food and the Postmaster General was the Minister of Posts and Telecommunications. The office of Chief Secretary to the Lord Lieutenants of Ireland had lapsed long before, but in 1972 the office of Secretary of State for Northern Ireland was created.

The Cabinet at the end of 1972 consisted of the following Ministers: Prime Minister and First Lord of the Treasury; Secretary of State for the Home Department; Secretary of State for Foreign and Commonwealth Affairs; Chancellor of the Exchequer; Lord Chancellor; Lord President of the Council (Leader of the House of Commons); Secretary of State for Defence; Secretary of State for Northern Ireland; Secretary of State for Social Services; Chancellor of the Duchy of Lancaster (Common Market affairs); Secretary of State for Trade and Industry; Secretary of State for the Environment; Secretary of State for Employment; Secretary of State for Education and Science; Secretary of State for Scotland; Lord Privy Seal (Civil Service Department); Secretary of State for Wales;

4. In the years between, most of the functions of the Local Government Board had been transferred to the Ministry of Health; the Ministry of Town and Country Planning took over most of the functions of this Ministry during the Second World War, and in 1951 became first the Ministry of Local Government and Planning and then the Ministry of Housing and Local Government. The Ministry of Health was later merged into the Department of Health and Social Security under a Secretary of State for Social Services. In October 1969, the Minister of Housing and Local Government ceased to be a member of the Cabinet and, with the Minister of Transport, was subordinated to a new Secretary of State for Local Government and Regional Planning, but the Ministry retained its identity. In 1970 the Department of the Environment was created and the pattern of Ministers was recast: see note 5.

Minister of Agriculture, Fisheries and Food; Minister of Trade and Consumer Affairs.

It cannot be said that there have been changes of high constitutional importance in the machinery of central government during the last few years. The most interesting development has probably been the evolution of five very large Departments – the Ministry of Defence; the Foreign and Commonwealth Office; the Department of Health and Social Security; the Department of the Environment; the Department of Trade and Industry. In 1970 the powers formerly exercised by three separate Ministers (Housing and Local Government; Transport; Public Building and Works) were vested in a Secretary of State for the Environment.[5] He was assisted by three new non-Cabinet Ministers (Local Government and Development; Transport Industries; Housing and Reconstruction) who had no Departments of legislative powers of their own. The Ministry of Technology and the Board of Trade were absorbed by a Department of Trade and Industry. By the end of 1972 the new Secretary of State was being assisted by four full Ministers – for Trade and Consumer Affairs; for Industrial Development; for Industry; and for Aerospace and Shipping – and by four junior Ministers; and he had general responsibility for most of the nationalized industries.

A second feature, of longer standing, is the large number of full Ministers not in charge of Departments. This is attributable partly to the extensive involvement of central government in economic and social affairs, and partly to the need for having full Ministers available for the conduct of discussions and negotiations outside England or with national interest groups. In December 1972 thirteen of these 'deputy' Ministers were styled Ministers of State.

Departments and other agencies

Under the British system of government it is expected that there shall be a Minister politically accountable for the more controversial acts of central government agencies. Political accountability cannot readily be achieved unless the activity is carried on by a Department or Office directly headed by a Minister.[6]

This general proposition needs to be qualified. Although the prospects for taking major government activities 'out of politics' are limited, the

5. S.I. 1970, No. 1681.

6. Contrast the position in Sweden, where major central administrative functions are vested in independent boards without a political head. See Report of the Fulton Committee on the Civil Service (Cmnd 3638 (1968), vol. 1, pp. 138–40); Nils Herlitz, *Elements of Nordic Public Law*, and p. 211.

allocation of governmental functions to largely autonomous bodies has become an important feature of public administration in Britain today. None of the nationalized industries is now run by a government Department, though Ministers retain a restricted range of powers and duties in relation to them.[7] Then there are miscellaneous other bodies performing what can broadly be described as functions of central government but lying outside the reach of detailed ministerial control. Most of them are statutory creations, but a few are non-statutory; some are incorporated, some are not; their sources of revenue are various; none is headed by civil servants, but some are staffed by them; some have executive powers, some are merely advisory, some are both; there is no common pattern. Their powers may involve the provision of a public service (for example, the British Broadcasting Corporation, the Commonwealth War Graves Commission, the Forestry Commission, the National Museums and Art Galleries), the regulation or management of a public service (for example, the Independent Broadcasting Authority, the Countryside Commission), or the regulation or promotion of private and public activity (for example, the Civil Aviation Authority, the Race Relations Board, the Development Commission, the Arts Council, the various agricultural and horticultural marketing boards, the Commission on Industrial Relations, the National Research Development Corporation, the British Tourist Authority). The functions of the British Council, which is not a government Department – its officers and servants are not civil servants – range over all these fields and are also advisory.

Then there is an assortment of bodies staffed mainly or entirely by civil servants but without any ministerial head, though a Minister is answerable in Parliament for some or all of their activities.[8] They have been kept at arm's length from the principal Departments for a variety of reasons: because they perform specialized functions which are not likely to be politically controversial; because some of these functions ought not to be the subject of political controversy (for example, because they are judicial or analogous to the judicial); or because the organ was originally created outside the framework of a political Department and there has never been a sufficiently strong reason for bringing it within one. Some are so closely

7. See ch. 9.

8. Thus, the Chancellor of the Exchequer answers a question in the House of Commons in connection with Her Majesty's Stationery Office, the Central Office of Information, the Treasury Solicitor, the Department of the Government Actuary, the Royal Mint and the National Debt Office; the Meteorological Office is answered for by the Secretary of State for Defence, the General Register Office by the Secretary of State for Social Services; the Secretary of State for the Environment answers for the Ordnance Survey. The Lord Chancellor answers in the Lords for the Land Registry and the Public Record Office.

associated with a political Department that they are in effect sub-departments, for example, the Board of Inland Revenue, the Board of Customs and Excise, the Export Credits Guarantee Department, and perhaps the Intervention Board for Agricultural Produce;[9] the Government Actuary's Department, the Royal Mint, the National Debt Office, and the Treasury Solicitor's Office. Others, to which a separate vote may be allocated in the Civil Estimates,[10] are more loosely associated with political Departments – for example, the Central Office of Information, Her Majesty's Stationery Office, the Charity Commission, the Crown Estate Office, the Registry of Friendly Societies, the Public Works Loan Board, the Land Registry, the Ordnance Survey, the Meteorological Office, the Public Record Office, the Registrar General's Office.

Whether every one of the bodies listed in the latter group is properly to be described as a government Department is questionable. There is no recognized definition of a government Department; normally it is understood to mean a central government body staffed by civil servants and receiving its funds directly out of moneys provided by Parliament,[11] but anomalies abound; the 'rich Byzantine structure'[12] of British central government is nowhere more apparent than in these twilight zones. For instance, the Exchequer and Audit Department is headed by the conspicuously independent Comptroller and Auditor-General; perhaps this Department, like the Office of the Parliamentary Commissioner for Administration, ought not to be regarded as a government Department at all but should be placed in a spacious compound reserved for watchdogs. Is the Supplementary Benefits Commission (formally the National Assistance Board) a government Department or sub-department? It is a body corporate staffed by civil servants and is very closely linked with the Department of Health and Social Security,[13] but its *members* are not civil

9. Established to operate the EEC's common agricultural policy in the United Kingdom (European Communities Act 1972, s. 6).

10. This feature is, however, inconclusive of status. For example, there is a separate vote for the British Council.

11. W. J. M. Mackenzie and J. W. Grove, *Central Administration in Britain*, pp. 183–4; see also Sir Ivor Jennings, *Cabinet Government* (3rd edn), ch. 4. Schedule 2 to the Parliamentary Commissioner Act 1967 lists government Departments and other authorities subject to investigation, without distinguishing the one group from the other.

12. Brian Chapman, *British Government Observed*, p. 18.

13. See Ministry of Social Security Act 1966, ss. 2, 3 and First Schedule; National Assistance Act 1948 (repd); D. N. Chester and F. M. G. Willson, *The Organisation of British Central Government, 1914–1964*, pp. 16–17, 173–4; Jennings, *Cabinet Government* (3rd edn), pp. 92, 102–3. The constitutional position of the Development Commission, a promotional body created in 1909 to assist in rural development, is not altogether dissimilar, and it has a separate vote in the Civil Estimates; but its functions

servants, and the Secretary of State has no power to control and is not responsible to Parliament for its decisions in individual cases. Probably, therefore, the Commission should be classified as a semi-autonomous public corporation.

The Metrication Board, the Community Relations Commission, the National Economic Development Council and the Development Commission are undoubtedly instruments of central government policy, but their functions are advisory, their membership is partly or wholly non-official and they would not ordinarily be thought of as government Departments. The University Grants Committee, though sometimes described as a government Department, is an advisory and allocative body, enjoying a very substantial degree of independence as a buffer between the Department of Education and Science and the Treasury, on the one side, and the universities on the other; it exists because of government policy, but is not a formal instrument of government. The Law Commissions also owe their existence to an act of policy; but their chairmen are superior judges and their members, though salaried, are entirely independent of the Government, and their functions are also advisory; probably they should no more be regarded as government Departments than the Council on Tribunals.

Government Departments dealing with domestic affairs make use of a great number of standing advisory committees and councils composed of outside experts or representatives of interest groups. (The 'corporatist' principle, under which positive government is qualified by the deference paid to powerful organized private bodies, is apparent in many areas of public activity[14] – for example, in the composition of the economic development councils, other promotional bodies, and above all in the agricultural marketing boards and central regulatory bodies controlling the professions.) Occasionally, the functions of such a committee (for example, the National Insurance Advisory Committee) are prescribed by statute; usually the committee rests on a less formal basis. At a more exalted level, there are the advisory councils concerned with government-sponsored research.[15] In 1972 there were a General Advisory Council for Science and Technology, and Medical, Agricultural, Science, Social Science and Natural Environment Research Councils. A full description of the machinery of central government would require an account of the functions exercised by these multifarious ancillary bodies.

---

are to *advise* the Treasury in making grants; though the officers of the Commission are civil servants, its members are unpaid non-officials; clearly this is not a government Department.

14. cf. Andrew Shonfield, *Modern Capitalism*, ch. 6 and pp. 160–63, 231–3.

15. cf. Science and Technology Act 1965.

Matters historical and legal

Of the modern ministerial offices, a few are traceable to the Tudor period and even earlier. The office of Lord Chancellor was primarily judicial in its origins; Wolsey was probably the last Lord Chancellor to be the highest officer of State, but today the Lord Chancellor remains a prominent member of the Cabinet as well as head of the Judiciary. The Lord President of the Council has survived the atrophy of the Privy Council as a political institution and is now invariably one of the senior members of the Cabinet. The modest status of the Chancellor of the Duchy of Lancaster has been enhanced; latterly he has been the Minister for European Community affairs. The Lord Privy Seal, originally the custodian of a seal which had to be produced before the Great Seal of the Realm, in the custody of the Lord Chancellor, could be issued, is a Minister without a Department. Recently he has had responsibility subject to the Prime Minister for the Civil Service Department. A more interesting phenomenon is the office of Secretary of State, which developed from a secretarial office in the royal household and became, in the seventeenth century, an important ministerial post. In Charles II's time there were two Secretaries of State; by 1784 there were three; the numbers increased as the functions of government extended and became more complex, and in 1972 there were eleven.[16] Their individual responsibilities are seldom prescribed by statute, and indeed where powers and duties are conferred by legislation on 'a' or 'the' Secretary of State, the function could, as a matter of strict law, be exercised by any of the Secretaries of State unless one is specifically designated by the Act or Order.

The office of Chancellor of the Exchequer is less ancient; the Lord High Treasurer[17] was a high officer of State in Tudor times and before, but the office was put into commission and discharged by a board composed of Lords Commissioners of the Treasury in 1714. The Board never meets, but the First Lord of the Treasury is now invariably the Prime Minister, and the Second Lord, in charge of the Treasury, the principal Department of State, is the Chancellor of the Exchequer; the Junior Lords sign formal Treasury warrants, but their main function is to act as Government whips in the Commons. Several of the surviving medieval offices of the Royal Household are occupied by Government whips in the Lords.

The existence of some ministerial offices (for example, Lord Chancellor, Secretary of State) is derived from the prerogative, but statutory functions can be assigned to a prerogative office-holder. The majority of ministerial

16. The maximum number cannot, in practice, exceed thirteen. cf. Ministerial and other Salaries Act 1972, Sched. 1, Parts I, V.
17. Mackenzie and Grove, op. cit., pp. 167–70.

offices have been established by legislation. The Minister is created a corporation sole, given a seal of office and entrusted with a loosely defined range of functions which can be supplemented by other statutes and statutory instruments. In general, legislation recognizes the Minister, not his Department; and acts done by departmental officials will be performed in the Minister's name. Under the Ministers of the Crown (Transfer of Functions) Act 1946, as amended, functions may be transferred by Order in Council from one Minister to another, the designations of Ministers may be altered, and Ministers and their Departments may be similarly wound up. In order to create a ministerial office with entirely new executive functions, an Act of Parliament is required unless the office is that of a Secretary of State. All Ministers hold office during Her Majesty's pleasure and are removable, by convention, on the advice of the Prime Minister.

Within the general framework of the principle that a Minister must not allow a conflict to develop between his public responsibilities and his private interests, detailed rules and criteria had been laid down by Prime Ministers limiting the permissible range of private activities of members of a Government.[18] For example, Ministers must not hold directorships in public companies or engage in speculative investments in respect of which information acquired in their official capacities might be beneficial; though they are not required to dispose of all private shareholdings. Association with non-profit-making organizations may also be incompatible with the discharge of ministerial duties. The principles are flexible enough to accommodate special cases when it appears to the Prime Minister expedient to do so. When Mr Frank Cousins became Minister of Technology in 1964 he was allowed to retain the office of General Secretary of the Transport and General Workers' Union on indefinite leave; on his resignation from ministerial office in 1966 he resumed his activities as union secretary.

The civil service

A civil servant is a Crown servant (other than the holder of a political or judicial office or a member of the armed forces) appointed directly or indirectly by the Crown, and paid wholly out of funds provided by Parliament and employed in a Department of government. The definition of a civil servant has not yet given rise to serious legal problems; the meaning of the term 'Crown servant' (which may include bodies corporate) has posed bigger difficulties.[19]

18. Jennings, *Cabinet Government* (3rd edn), pp. 106–110; Geoffrey Wilson, *Cases and Materials on Constitutional and Administrative Law*, pp. 73–5. See also p. 55.

19. See pp. 125–6, 220, 613.

It is not, of course, realistic to think of the civil service only as a body of advisers to Ministers. First, a great number of decisions, the responsibility for taking which is committed by law to Ministers, are in fact taken by civil servants in the Minister's name without reference to the Minister personally.[20] Unless the class of decision is so important that nothing less than the Minister's personal attention is appropriate, the courts will accept the propriety of such a procedure even though the Minister has not explicitly authorized the civil servant to make the decisions.[21] However, in immigration law special legal consequences are attached to decisions taken by the Secretary of State in person.[22] Secondly, some statutes vest powers of decision directly in named classes of civil servants (for example, customs and excise officers, inspectors at town planning inquiries). Thirdly, in some Departments large questions of policy will in practice be decided by civil servants with the Minister's formal concurrence. A combination of thrustful and strong-minded senior civil servants, complex issues demanding both a substantial body of factual knowledge and an appreciation of the personal qualities of persons with whom the Department has to deal, and an inexperienced, indolent, ill-endowed or indecisive Minister, will sometimes lead to a situation in which a Minister dwindles to a political mouthpiece of his civil servants. A limited range of personal experience suggests that such a situation is less common than is often supposed. Civil servants may seek to influence a ministerial decision in a particular direction by their methods of selecting and summarizing facts, stating the problems and presenting alternative courses of action to the Minister, and they are usually expert in putting to a Minister the objections against a decision that he may wish to take; but they are aware of the need for preserving political neutrality by conscious self-restraint, and the constitutional importance of having an effective political head of their Department.[23] Ministers, if only for reasons of self-respect and personal ambition, know that they must be able to present departmental decisions persuasively to their colleagues, to Parliament, to the public at large and to any groups with whom they have been negotiating. To observe the treatment meted out by a not especially assertive Minister to a semi-political speech drafted for him by one of his senior policy advisers can be a most instructive experience.

20. A point made spectacularly but perhaps over-emphatically by the judicial tribunal of inquiry into the *Vehicle & General Insurance Co.* affair: H.C. 133 (1971–2); see p. 173.

21. *Carltona Ltd* v. *Commissioners of Works* [1943] 2 All E.R. 560; *Lewisham Borough* v. *Roberts* [1949] 2 K.B.608 at 629; *R.* v. *Skinner* [1968] 2 Q.B. 700.

22. Immigration Act 1971, ss. 13(5), 14(3), 15(4); see ch. 19.

23. See also Crossman, *Inside View*, pp. 70–71.

Political activities of civil servants

Overt political partisanship cannot be reconciled with the principle of official impartiality. Civil servants are disqualified by statute for membership of the House of Commons; and a civil servant who wishes to stand at a parliamentary election is obliged by regulations of the service to resign his post before announcing himself as a candidate or prospective candidate, though in certain cases[24] he will be entitled to reinstatement if he is not elected or after he has ceased to be a member of the House. By pursuing logic to a facile conclusion, one will rapidly decide that all civil servants ought to be denied every form of political activity except that of casting a vote at an election. But the reasons of public policy that impose the utmost discretion on civil servants closely associated with the work of their Minister are largely irrelevant to the van driver, the worker in a Royal Ordnance Factory, the porter and the junior clerk. In order to allow civil servants a reasonable measure of freedom of political expression, they were divided by a Treasury circular into three main groups.[25] The 'politically restricted' were senior members of the service; they were debarred from national political activities (including the public expression of views on matters of national political policy), but were entitled to take part, with the permission of their Department, in local political activities, provided that they acted 'with moderation and discretion, particularly in matters affecting their own Department'. Secondly, there was a large 'intermediate' group, consisting of clerical officers, typists, and persons charged with technical and specialized responsibilities not involving questions of political policy. Members of this group could be given permission by their Department to take part in both national and local political activities; permission was likely to be refused, however, to officers who came into direct contact with members of the public in the course of participating in discretionary decisions (for example, at employment exchanges or tax offices) or who were closely associated, though in a subordinate capacity, with Ministers and senior policy-makers. The remainder of the civil service, and much the largest group, was politically unrestricted,[26] except in so far as they had to observe the Official Secrets Acts, could not engage in

24. Those civil servants who are not in the 'restricted' or 'intermediate' groups: see below.

25. The rules are stated in *The Civil Service*, vol. 4, pp. 402–5 (Evidence submitted to the Fulton Committee on the Civil Service: Report, Cmnd 3638 (1968)). See also Wilson, op. cit., pp. 87–96. They followed broadly the guidelines indicated by the Report of the Masterman Committee (Cmnd 7718 (1949)) which was appointed following representations from the staff side of the civil service that a wider measure of freedom of political activity ought to be allowed.

26. Subject to the rules about parliamentary candidature.

political activity while on duty or in uniform or on official premises, and had to observe a due measure of restraint so as to avoid embarrassing their Ministers and Departments.

Private interests of civil servants[27]

There is no precisely formulated code of conduct governing the private economic activities of civil servants, but they must not allow a conflict to develop between their public responsibilities and their private interests as shareholders and investors. Fortunately, cases of corruption among senior civil servants are exceedingly rare. A certain amount of disquiet has been caused by the frequency with which senior officers, upon their retirement, are appointed to executive or advisory posts in commercial and industrial firms with which they have conducted direct negotiations while they were officials; but under rules of the service such offers of appointment cannot be accepted within two years of retirement except with the consent of the Government.[28]

Anonymity and secrecy

Government Departments have often been criticized for their disinclination to divulge interesting and useful information to members of the public.[29] The fiction that all departmental decisions were taken by the Minister (who is alone politically answerable for them), coupled with a deep-seated belief that any exposure of the processes of departmental decision-making would tend to cause trouble and reduce administrative efficiency, brought about a state of affairs in which secretiveness was sometimes carried to absurd lengths. Twenty years ago the present writer was precluded from publishing certain entirely innocuous material about the manner in which a Department disposed of appeals affecting individual interests; the information was divulged to the Franks Committee on Administrative Tribunals and Enquiries[30] a few years later. Inspectors' reports to Ministers on housing and town planning inquiries were not disclosed – and the courts upheld the departmental view that natural

27. See Chester and Wilson, op. cit., pp. 117–19.
28. *The Civil Service*, vol. 4, pp. 393–6.
29. For recent measured criticisms, see David Williams, *Not in the Public Interest* (1965); Report of the Fulton Committee on the Civil Service, Cmnd 3638 (1968), ch. 8. For the Labour Government's response to the Fulton Committee's criticisms, see *Information and the Public Interest* (Cmnd 4089 (1969)). For review of section 2 of the Official Secrets Act 1911, see ch. 21.
30. Cmnd 218 (1957).

justice did not require their disclosure[31] – till 1958.[32] The Franks Committee's emphasis on the need for openness in the procedures for taking decisions on matters directly impinging on individual rights led to a healthy ventilation of the corridors of Whitehall which has enhanced public confidence in the processes followed. The prevailing image of central administration is less monolithic. And it is fair to say that, for many years past, senior civil servants have been more accessible for informal interviews than their bureaucratic counterparts in a number of other countries (provided, at least, that the interviewer was not proposing to publish 'confidential' information); and that formal and informal consultations between officials and representatives of organized interest groups has long been a feature of central administration in Britain.

Criticism of departmental secrecy has recently been concentrated on nine main issues:

1. If a Minister did not personally participate in a decision, which civil servant made it in his name? It may be important to know this, because of the possibility of making informal representations with a view to securing review of a decision within the Department. Sometimes the official identifies himself; sometimes he does not, either because he attributes the decision to the Minister or because a decision made by an unnamed official is communicated in a letter signed by another. Seldom will the national interest be prejudiced by more exact identification. Recently the Parliamentary Commissioner for Administration, who has access to departmental files and can interrogate civil servants, has revealed some of the carnal facts that lie beneath the veil.

2. What criteria does a Department adopt in exercising discretionary powers affecting individual interests? Departmental practice in disclosing the principles applied has varied; the Inland Revenue has been particularly helpful to prospective taxpayers, while lips in the Home Office were firmly sealed even on general considerations affecting the immigration and deportation of aliens. But the Home Office now publishes not only the immigration rules but also instructions to immigration officers. The Department of the Environment issues Development Control Policy Notes; and so on. There is still a great deal of room for improvement.[33]

3. What were the reasons for the decisions? It is often difficult and usually inconvenient to give adequate reasons for one's decisions. It is particularly difficult to do so if the decision was not purely personal but was in effect

31. *Local Government Board* v. *Arlidge* [1915] A.C. 120.
32. See further, ch. 25.
33. For a penetrating analysis of this type of problem in the United States, see Kenneth Culp Davis, *Discretionary Justice*.

a collective decision resulting from discussions among colleagues. Courts can nevertheless be required to give reasons for judicial decisions and Ministers reasons for political decisions. Civil servants still tend to put up a stiff resistance to the idea that they ought to give reasons for their decisions, even when those decisions have a direct impact on individual rights; and they justify their inhibitions all the more readily to themselves inasmuch as the decisions are usually made in the Minister's name and may indeed be collegiate decisions. But reluctance is slowly being overcome by statutes imposing on Ministers a duty to give reasons for certain types of decisions, usually those made after a formal hearing or inquiry.[34]

4. By what procedure was a decision reached? Rarely can it be justifiable to withhold general information about settled departmental procedures from the public, except on grounds of national security. But this type of information is not made systematically available: unless the procedure is prescribed by legislation, it emerges through disclosures to interested parties, evidence given to parliamentary scrutinizing committees and other committees of inquiry, and investigations and reports by the Parliamentary Commissioner for Administration. Only occasionally does a Department proffer information about its internal procedures on its own initiative.

5. What are the facts on the basis of which departmental decisions are taken? Of late there has been a great improvement in the dissemination of statistical and general factual information by Departments and other organs of the central government.[35] But Departments still tend to be unduly reticent about the disclosure of the nature and contents (and even sometimes the very existence) of particular items of information, particularly before a decision has been taken; and premature and unauthorized disclosure is apt to evoke over-reaction.[36]

6. What are the Government's plans and forecasts? Here again there has been a marked improvement in the supply of published information, especially in economic affairs; and the Government publishes occasional Green Papers[37] putting forward tentative proposals for public discussion before they have finally crystallized. Clearly Departments cannot be expected to disclose all their provisional plans in advance, any more than

34. See, for example, Tribunals and Inquiries Act 1971, s. 12.

35. See the interim progress report, *Developments on Fulton*, issued by the Civil Service Department early in 1969. cf. the strictures of the Fulton Committee on excessive secrecy in the administrative process (Cmnd 3638 (1968), pp. 91–2).

36. cf. the initial Government reaction late in 1972 to a disclosure in the *Sunday Times* of a long-term plan for reducing railway passenger services.

37. For example, on value added tax, local government finance, constitutional reform in Northern Ireland.

they can be expected to reveal all their sources of confidential information. But complaints about the slowness of progress towards a system of more 'open government' persist.

7. Should not civil servants be readier to explain departmental policies? Once again it is possible to say that the sphinx now gives tongue more freely, though utterances tend to be guarded, not least because of a civil servant's apprehension of committing himself in a way that would embarrass his Minister. The Fulton Committee has urged that this development should be carried farther, and that Ministers (who frequently lack detailed knowledge of what is going on in their Departments) should not be regarded as the only proper departmental spokesmen.[38] Yet there are big risks involved in individualizing a government Department in this way.[39]

8. Should not civil servants be prepared to justify in public the merits of departmental policies? The lines between explanation and justification, between departmental and political policies, may be thin; and the Fulton Committee was aware of the danger of erasing them. Governments come and go. To encourage permanent civil servants to play the political partisan would damage both service morale and public confidence in the service. Moreover, it would be hard to impose upon a civil servant a duty to justify (as distinct from explain) his Minister's policy in public controversy[40] while denying him any right to express his personal misgivings; yet the open expression of doubt and dissent would undermine relations between Ministers and their permanent advisers. It is surely right that the rules governing the conduct of statutory inquiries in respect of planning appeals and compulsory purchase orders should preclude questions being put to civil servants with a view to eliciting their opinions on the merits of Government policies.

9. Is not the public entitled to know what advice was given to a Minister by his civil servants on matters of policy, and who gave particular advice? In general, the answer to this question must be in the negative. Regular public exposure of advice and opinions tendered by civil servants at the

38. Cmnd 3638 (1968), pp. 93–4.

39. cf. Henry Parris, *Constitutional Bureaucracy* (1969), ch. 10.

40. Senior civil servants are in fact sometimes called upon to explain (and defend) *departmental* policies before parliamentary and departmental select committees, royal commissions and so on, and to submit to close interrogation. Recent examples are the proceedings of the House of Commons Select Committee on the Parliamentary Commissioner for Administration, and the two Franks Committees. One gleans a lot of interesting information from reading the Minutes of the Evidence, and no harm is done provided that the questioner and the questioned show due discretion and that the departmental policy is not one that is the Minister's idiosyncratic policy or one dictated by party politics.

formative stages of policy would detract from the efficiency of the service by restraining frank and forthright expressions of points of view. The loyalty of civil servants in implementing departmental decisions, once a decision has been taken, is well known. What is not well known is the vigour with which senior civil servants contest one another's views, and indeed the views of the Minister, before the decision has been finally arrived at.

Regulation, organization and structure

The civil service is regulated primarily under the royal prerogative. Formal prerogative Orders in Council relating to the civil service are, however, few. Regulations, minutes and circulars issued formerly by the Treasury, and since 1968 by the Civil Service Department,[41] have been the main substance of the law and custom of the civil service; they are supplemented by a few statutes (for example, the Superannuation Acts) and judicial decisions (for example, on civil liability, tenure of office). The Permanent Secretary of the Civil Service Department is also Head of the Home Civil Service. There are separate Heads of the Diplomatic Service (the Permanent Under-Secretary of State to the Foreign and Common-wealth Office) and of the Scientific Civil Service (the Government's Chief Scientific Adviser, a member of the Cabinet Office). The Civil Service Commissioners have been placed within the Civil Service Department; they are mainly responsible for the recruitment and selection of civil servants by competitive examination and interview. Departments also recruit their own specialist and temporary staff by other methods; promotions within the service, except at the very highest levels, are matters reserved for individual Departments. Top appointments are made by the Prime Minister on the recommendation of the Head of the Home Civil Service, who is assisted by a senior appointments committee composed of permanent secretaries and senior professional officers.[42]

The elaborate procedural and substantive rules relating to conditions of service, promotions and tenure have been evolved to a large extent by means of collective agreements reached by the system of National and Departmental Whitley Councils, at which representatives of the 'official' side of the civil service (senior officials) negotiate and consult with representatives of the 'staff' side. If agreement cannot be reached, the matter may be committed to an arbitral body or the Government may take a unilateral decision. In any event, the Whitley system is technically only

41. The Minister for the Civil Service Order 1968 (S.I. 1968, No. 1656) made under the Ministers of the Crown (Transfer of Functions) Act 1946. This was a statutory transfer of powers derived mainly from the prerogative.

42. *Developments on Fulton* (Civil Service National Whitley Council, 1969), para. 74.

advisory.[43] The rules governing 'established' (or permanent) civil servants are promulgated by the Civil Service Department and are assembled in an official (but inaccessible) publication, *Estacode*.

Since the Report of the Fulton Committee, the structure and organization of the service have been under detailed internal scrutiny, and a full survey would be beyond the bounds of the present book. Briefly, in 1970 a Department of State had a permanent secretary (or permanent under-secretary of state) who was the Minister's principal official adviser, deputy secretaries, under-secretaries, assistant secretaries, principals and assistant principals. These were the members of the administrative class, the gifted generalists or all-rounders, recruited in the main by competitive examination and interview from young Oxbridge arts graduates.[44] Some Ministers also introduced a small number of temporary senior advisers from outside the service on a short-term basis. There were other schemes for the recruitment of older candidates at a senior level.

Beneath the administrative class there were a larger number of officers in the executive class and a considerably larger number of clerical officers. A Department would also have its specialists – legal advisers, scientists, accountants, perhaps surveyors, engineers, architects and doctors, and supporting ancillary personnel. There were, in addition, various special classes – for example, inspectors of taxes.

The civil service was thus divided both horizontally and vertically. The Fulton Committee proposed reconstruction and simplification. In particular, the Committee severely criticized the cult of the amateur generalist in the administrative class, called for a higher degree of 'professionalism' in technical expertise and competence in business management and in social administration at the highest level, and urged that closer attention be paid to organization and methods, forward planning and research, advanced training of entrants, mobility between grades and secondment to and from the service, and a diminution of the security of tenure enjoyed at present by the less efficient members of the service.

Despite the intemperate wording of some of the Committee's comments, its recommendations gave impetus to change.[45] The Civil Service Department was created soon afterwards. In 1970 a Civil Service College

43. See evidence submitted to the Fulton Committee, vol. 4, pp. 500–510. Some matters are dealt with by direct negotiation with the various staff associations. See further, B. A. Hepple and Paul O'Higgins, *Public Employee Trade Unionism in the United Kingdom: The Legal Framework* (1971); this was written before the Industrial Relations Act 1971.

44. Before the Northcote-Trevelyan Reforms in the second half of the nineteenth century (see Fulton Report, ch. 1 and Appendix 3), recruitment was mainly by patronage.

45. See, for example, John Garrett, *The Management of Government*; D. Keeling, *Management in Government*; Sir William Armstrong, *Professionals and Professionalism*

for advanced training was opened. Within the service, separate grades have been merged or grouped together; stratification has diminished, promotions and transfers have been facilitated. Special arrangements have been made for the compulsory retirement of the inefficient. Modern methods of job analysis, personnel management, planning and budgetary accounting, bandied around by their abstruse initials, are all the rage.[46]

The Heath Government also introduced a small top-level Central Policy Review Staff, headed by a Labour peer and industrialist, to advise Ministers on forward planning, the allocation of priorities and issues cutting across departmental boundaries, such as the Concorde project, sponsored research, the role of the City of London, and policy on energy, population and the regions.

The remarkably high degree of security enjoyed by established civil servants, surpassed only by the Judiciary, was not recognized by rules applied in the courts. In the eyes of the common law, civil servants held their offices at the pleasure of the Crown. Their offices could be vacated summarily at any time for any reason that Her Majesty thought fit.

The common-law rule that a civil servant has no right of recourse to the courts for wrongful dismissal is reasonably clear.[47] But what is the basis of the rule; and are there any exceptions to it? It has sometimes been said that a civil servant enjoys a legal status but is not employed under a contract.[48] Even if this is so, it would not preclude the officer from recovering damages for wrongful dismissal, or, indeed, a declaration that he was entitled to reinstatement.[49] And at least one decision of the House of Lords has rested unambiguously on the presupposition that the relationship between civil servants and the Crown is contractual.[50]

Again, the fact that the power to appoint and regulate the conduct of civil servants is derived from the royal prerogative is not inconsistent with

in the Civil Service; R. G. S. Brown, *The Administrative Process in Britain*; the following publications by the Civil Service National Whitley Council: *Developments on Fulton*; *Fulton: A Framework for the Future; Fulton: The Reshaping of the Civil Service; The Shape of the Post-Fulton Civil Service*; G. W. Jones, 'The eclipse of Fulton', *New Society*, 17 August 1972.

46. See, for example, Peter Jay, 'PESC, PAR and politics', *The Times*, 3 January 1972. PPBS is the other favourite.

47. See, for example, *Shenton* v. *Smith* [1895] A.C. 229 (P.C.); *Terrell* v. *Secretary of State for the Colonies* [1953] 2 Q.B. 482.

48. See Leo Blair (1958) 21 *Mod. L. Rev.* 265, [1958] *Public Law* 32.

49. cf. *Vine* v. *National Dock Labour Board* [1957] A.C. 488 (dock labourers); *Ridge* v. *Baldwin* [1964] A.C. 40 (chief constables).

50. *Sutton* v. *Att.-Gen.* (1923) 39 T.L.R. 294. The point was not argued and the precedent is therefore *sub silentio*; but all the Law Lords assumed that the engagement in question was contractual. See now *Kodeeswaran* v. *Att.-Gen. of Ceylon* [1970] A.C. 1111 (P.C.), supporting this view.

the existence of a contract of employment. The Crown can enter into binding contracts (for example, for the supply of food) in the exercise of its prerogative functions.

Yet, assuming that the relationship is contractual, it appears that the right to dismiss at pleasure cannot be displaced by engagement for a fixed period,[51] or by official circulars[52] or non-statutory regulations[53] laying down a regular procedure to be followed before dismissal. It is indeed doubtful whether any ostensibly contractual term inconsistent with the power of the Crown to dismiss at pleasure (for example, a statement that a Crown servant would be dismissible only 'for cause',[54] or for inability or misbehaviour) would be endorsed by a court, unless, of course, the restriction on the Crown's freedom to dispense with a servant at will had been imposed by statute.[55] Now, if the power to dismiss at pleasure were to be construed as an ordinary implied term of a contract, it could be displaced by an express term of a contractual engagement incompatible with it.[56] If it cannot be so displaced, this must be either because the Crown is incapacitated from fettering its future executive discretion in this way[57] (so that an incompatible undertaking would simply be *ultra vires* and void[58]) or because it is a special kind of implied term, imported by precedent and for reasons of public policy into all engagements with the Crown irrespective of their wording. These rationalizations of the rule are unconvincing and cast doubt on the content of the rule. Public policy may indeed suggest that an unsuitable or redundant civil servant should be dispensible at any time when the interests of the State so demand; but this merely means that a court of law ought not to award a declaration that a dismissed civil servant is entitled to reinstatement; it does not imply that he should be denied monetary compensation for wrongful dismissal.

The Industrial Relations Act 1971 has made an important addition to the law. If a civil servant is unfairly dismissed, he may now be awarded statutory *compensation* up to a maximum of £4160 by an industrial tribunal, which may also recommend that he be re-engaged.[59] An appeal on a point of law lies to the National Industrial Relations Court.

51. *Dunn* v. *R.* [1896] 1 Q.B. 116.

52. *Rodwell* v. *Thomas* [1944] K.B. 596. But see *Sutton* v. *Att.-Gen.* (note 50); and Blair [1958] *Public Law* at 43–6.

53. *Riordan* v. *War Office* [1959] 1 W.L.R. 1046.

54. Though cf. *Reilly* v. *R.* [1934] A.C. 176 at 179–80 (dicta): *Robertson* v. *Minister of Pensions* [1949] 1 K.B. 227 at 231 (dictum).

55. As in *Gould* v. *Stuart* [1896] A.C. 575 (P.C.). See also below.

56. See dicta cited in note 54 above; and see *Sutton* v. *Att.-Gen.* (1923) 39 T.L.R. 294.

57. cf. *Rederiaktiebolaget Amphitrite* v. *R.* [1921] 3 K.B. 500; pp. 611–12 below.

58. See *Riordan's* case [1959] 1 W.L.R. at 1053; *Rodwell* v. *Thomas* [1944] K.B. at 602.

59. Industrial Relations Act 1971, ss. 22–4, 106, 116–19, 162. The concept of

The salaries of civil servants are determined by standing references to arbitral bodies. There have been judicial dicta to the effect that a civil servant has no legally enforceable right to his pay.[60] Even if this is a correct statement of the common-law rule regarding future payments, it is now clear that at common law a civil servant is entitled to recover any part of his salary withheld from him in respect of the work he has already done.[61]

The superannuation of civil servants is regulated by statute, but before 1972 the wording of the legislation presupposed a lack of judicially enforceable entitlement to the rates of superannuation prescribed or indeed to any pension at all.[62] Questions of law arising out of civil service superannuation schemes are now potentially justiciable.[63]

Security procedures[64]

The growth of peacetime espionage, particularly in connection with nuclear research and technology, led to the adoption of special security measures within the civil service in 1948. Following the defection of two senior Foreign Service officials, Burgess and Maclean, to the Soviet Union, and the conviction of some Crown servants, including George Blake, an important controller of British agents,[65] for espionage, committees were appointed to investigate and report on security procedures. Their recommendations[66] resulted in the introduction of new procedures. Typically, all the new rules rest on a non-statutory basis.

'unfair' dismissal is related to non-observance of the principles laid down in the Code of Practice prepared by the Secretary of State for Employment (ss. 2–4). A Minister may exclude a Crown employee from the protection of the Act on grounds of national security (s. 162(7)).

60. *Mulvenna* v. *Admiralty* 1926 S.C. 842 at 859; *Lucas* v. *Lucas* [1943] P. 68 at 78 (criticized by D. W. Logan (1945) *L.Q.R.* 240).

61. *Kodeeswaran* v. *Att.-Gen. of Ceylon* [1970] A.C. 1111, disapproving dicta to the contrary effect and applying general principles.

62. Superannuation Act 1965, s. 79. See *Nixon* v. *Att.-Gen.* [1931] A.C. 184.

63. Superannuation Act 1972, s. 2(6).

64. Harry Street, *Freedom, the Individual and the Law* (3rd edn), pp. 228–37; David Williams, *Not in the Public Interest*, chs. 3, 7–9; Wade and Phillips, *Constitutional Law* (8th edn), ch. 40; Geoffrey Wilson, *Cases and Materials on Constitutional and Administrative Law*, pp. 108–16; and two comparative studies, David C. Jackson (1957) 20 *Mod. L. Rev.* 364, Mark R. Joelson [1963] *Public Law* 51.

65. *R.* v. *Blake* [1962] 2 Q.B. 377. For his activities he was sentenced to three consecutive terms of imprisonment of fourteen years each. He escaped from prison to Eastern Europe in 1967, and was subsequently awarded the Order of Lenin.

66. Cmd 9715 (1955) (the Privy Councillors' Report); Cmnd 1681 (1962) (the Radcliffe Report).

The procedures have been applied to only a small proportion of civil servants, holding positions where personal unreliability might give rise to serious risks to national security. They have been more selective (though not necessarily more efficacious) than those adopted in the United States; and British civil servants have not had to endure the solemn silliness of indiscriminate loyalty oaths.

In 1948 it was decided that civil servants with Communist or Fascist affiliations should not be employed in work vital to the security of the State. Where practicable they would be transferred to non-secret work. From a provisional decision by a Minister that an official ought to be transferred or removed on security grounds, an appeal would lie to an advisory tribunal, the 'Three Advisers', who would meet in private. In 1952 civil servants employed on top secret work became subject to a more rigorous form of scrutiny, known as 'positive vetting', extending to general character defects; no reference to the Three Advisers would lie from an executive decision in this context. High-level reports on security measures, published in 1955 and 1962,[67] emphasized that personality or behavioural defects or disorders, such as homosexual conduct, alcoholism and drug addiction (which might render an official vulnerable to blackmail or subject to financial temptation), as well as known political affiliations or sympathies, were indicators of security risks; but precautionary measures in such cases were left to departmental action. Security procedures were modified in 1957; and in 1964 a new, and almost inevitably non-statutory, organ, the Security Commission, under the chairmanship of a superior judge, was set up to investigate, at the Prime Minister's request, breaches of security in the public service, and to report and advise generally on security arrangements.[68]

Proceedings before the Three Advisers (who are normally retired civil servants and whose findings are not binding on the Minister) do not conform to the standards of natural justice imposed on a judicial tribunal. After the Minister has decided that a *prima facie* case has been made out – there is no preliminary hearing[69] – particulars of the allegations are disclosed to the Advisers, but the civil servant will not be supplied with details which would reveal the sources of the information against him. The civil servant may appear in person, but he cannot be represented by a lawyer or anybody else; he is merely entitled to be accompanied by a friend when he is presenting his opening statement. He may call witnesses to testify to his character and record, but he is unable to cross-examine the

67. See above.
68. The other members of this standing commission are judges and very senior ex-members of the civil service and the armed forces. See Addendum.
69. Though the civil servant may make written representations to the Minister.

anonymous and invisible informants. The advice tendered by the tribunal to the Minister is not revealed.

This procedure may well be 'a travesty of justice as Englishmen are accustomed to it'.[70] The Franks Committee had insisted[71] that the proceedings of statutory administrative tribunals should be characterized by 'openness, fairness and impartiality'; it is questionable whether any of these criteria is met by the machinery outlined above, though it can be assumed that Ministers and the Advisers do their best to act fairly. But to speak of a travesty belittles the fact that even the most lenient security programme must rest on a harsh assumption: that measures injurious to possibly innocent persons will have to be taken on the basis of reasonable suspicions, suspicions insufficient to justify a prosecution. The balance will inevitably be delicate. We have no means of evaluating the soundness of the decisions that have in fact been taken, or how much harm might be done if the 'defendant' or the representative he would prefer to choose were to be supplied with full particulars of the case against him and were to be given the right to confront informants. It is worth mentioning that in the first thirteen years of the special security programme, only twenty-four civil servants were dismissed and twenty-four others were induced to resign on security grounds, and eighty-three were transferred to non-secret work.[72] During the two World Wars, thousands of innocent and innocuous persons were placed in preventive detention as a result of policy decisions and excesses of executive zeal.

Security precautions extend beyond the civil service and the Atomic Energy Authority.[73] Government contracts placed with private firms for secret work include terms which have the effect of barring any employee of the firm who is designated by the Minister as a security risk from having access to secret matters. In 1956 ICI dismissed their assistant solicitor because the Government, on ostensibly flimsy grounds, refused to place with them any further secret contract to which he would have access. Such an employee is now able to have his case referred to the Three Advisers.[74]

70. Street, op. cit., p. 235.
71. Cmnd 218 (1957), p. 5.
72. Joelson [1963] *Public Law* at 56–7.
73. Under the First Schedule to the Atomic Energy Authority Act 1954, the Authority may not terminate the employment of any of its employees on security grounds without the consent of the Minister (now the Secretary of State for Trade and Industry).
74. For non-statutory references of politically sensitive immigration 'appeals' to the Three Advisers, see ch. 19.

Chapter 8
Constitutional Position of the Armed Forces

Structure and status[1]

The armed forces are instruments of the central government, equipped, disciplined and trained for the exercise of physical force in the interests of the State. In a large number of new states, and in a few that are not so new, the military servants of the State have recently become masters. No constitutional or legal device can afford a guarantee against a military take-over when the political structure is in a condition of decadence or collapse. The British rules relating to the status of the armed forces presuppose a set of public attitudes and assumptions towards the roles of the civil and military powers within the State. The primacy of the civil power is a sociological as well as a constitutional fact. No British Government has been overthrown by military force since 1688. No senior officer of the regular armed forces has ever been Prime Minister except the Duke of Wellington (1828–30, 1834), and he had long since retired from active service.

The feudal levy, supplied by military tenants of the Crown, was abolished in 1660. The pre-Norman *fyrd*, a national levy, had been transformed into the militia, and it was regulated by statute in 1661. But such was the rancour aroused by James II's use of troops that the Bill of Rights 1689 prohibited the raising or maintenance of a standing army within the realm in time of peace without the consent of Parliament. Since a regular armed force was necessary at that time, a Mutiny Act, giving the requisite parliamentary authority, was passed but was limited to a year's duration. Annual Mutiny Acts were passed for nearly two hundred years. In 1881 an Army Act was passed, embodying rules of military law which had previously been embodied in the Mutiny Acts and articles of war.[2] When a separate air force was created in 1917, a similar Act was passed. These were kept alive for periods of twelve months by Army and Air Force (Annual) Acts. In 1955 the Army and Air Force Acts were revised and consolidated, and

---

1. This chapter will not deal with the reserve forces (see Reserve Forces Act 1966) or the auxiliary, territorial or women's services.
2. Till the eighteenth century, articles of war for the governance of soldiers had been issued only in time of war.

the system of annual renewal was modified; instead of an annual Act of Parliament (the debates on which provided the Opposition with a useful opportunity for consuming legislative time) they would be renewed from year to year by Orders in Council, which would be subject to approval in draft by both Houses of Parliament. After five years of renewal, however, an enabling Act of Parliament would be required. The last enabling Act was the Armed Forces Act 1971.

The maintenance of a navy, which was seldom, if ever, regarded as an instrument of royal oppression, has never needed parliamentary approval. The navy exists by virtue of the royal prerogative; indeed, the prerogative power to impress seafaring men into the navy has never been expressly abrogated. But naval discipline is dependent on an Act of Parliament (the Naval Discipline Act 1957, as amended), and the money needed for the navy, as for the other armed services, has to be determined by the Government and authorized by Parliament. Parliamentary debate on any of the armed services may take place on the presentation of the annual estimates, the introduction of supply legislation, and any other legislative measures relating to them. Since 1971 the Naval Discipline Act has been renewable annually and quinquennially like the Army and Air Force Acts.

How far the army and the air force are regulated by prerogative is an interesting but obscure question. The disposition of the forces[3] and the commissioning of officers certainly fall within the scope of the prerogative. The enforcement of military discipline and the trial of offences under military law are regulated by statute; and statutory regulations made by the Defence Council may prescribe terms and conditions of service.[4] Pay and pensions are determined by royal warrants under the prerogative. Although the relationship between a member of the forces and his employer, the Crown, has a distinct statutory flavour, there is ample judicial authority for the proposition that, save where a sentence has been imposed by a court-martial or other statutory disciplinary authority, the relations between the soldier and the Crown are not cognizable by the courts. Not only is he disabled from suing for wrongful reduction of pay[5] or arrears of pay,[6] but he cannot sue for wrongful dismissal[7] even, it seems, in the face of inconsistent statutory or contractual provisions; nor can an officer

3. *Chandler* v. *D.P.P.* [1964] A.C. 763.

4. Armed Forces Act 1966, s. 2.

5. *Worthington* v. *Robinson* (1897) 75 L.T. (N.S.) 446 (an action against a superior officer); *Leaman* v. *R.* [1920] 3 K.B. 663; cf. Logan (1945) 61 *L.Q.R.* at 260.

6. *Ex p. Napier* (1852) 21 L.J.Q.B. 332; cf. Glanville Williams, *Crown Proceedings*, 69.

7. *Re Poe* (1833) 5 B. & Ad. 681; *Grant* v. *Secretary of State for India* (1877) 2 C.P.D. 445; *De Dohsé* v. *R.* (1886) 3 T.L.R. 114. The Industrial Relations Act 1971 does not affect the position; it does not apply to military servants of the Crown.

resign his commission without leave.[8] An ex-member of the forces cannot sue for his pension. These rules are based partly on the prerogative and partly on an overriding judge-made concept of public policy which frowns upon litigation between the soldier and his employer. On the other hand, the Crown can hold the soldier to the terms of his enlistment to serve for a term of years unless he purchases his discharge, and it exercises this power.

Central government organization for defence is now based partly on prerogative but mainly on statute.[9] In 1972 there were a Secretary of State, a Minister of State for Defence and three parliamentary under-secretaries of state, one for the royal navy, one for the army and one for the air force. Within the Ministry of Defence there is located a Procurement Executive, using up-to-date managerial and accounting techniques.[10]

There is a chiefs of staff committee, composed of the Chief of Defence Staff and the chiefs of staff of the three services; they have a right of direct access to the Prime Minister and are occasionally asked to attend Cabinet meetings. The detailed regulation of the services is entrusted to a statutory Defence Council consisting of the Secretary of State and the Minister of State, the chiefs of staff, the Permanent Under-Secretary of State to the Ministry of Defence, the Chief Scientific Adviser to the Government and the Chief Executive for Procurement. For each of the three services there is a separate Defence Board. At Cabinet level there is a Defence and Oversea Policy Committee, presided over by the Prime Minister; the Secretary of State for Foreign and Commonwealth Affairs, the Chancellor of the Exchequer and the Home Secretary are among its members; the service chiefs of staff are frequently invited to attend. The Security Service, which is responsible for counter-intelligence, has intimate links with the Prime Minister, the Secretary to the Cabinet, the Ministry of Defence, the Foreign Office, the Home Office and the Special Branch of the Metropolitan Police.[11]

In Britain, as in a large number of other countries, there is a tendency for regular officers in the armed services to show a profound distaste for party politics or to hold views sympathetic to the far right wing in politics; or to entertain both attitudes simultaneously, if sometimes unwittingly. But it is part of the service tradition to accept a position of subordination

8. *Marks* v. *Commonwealth of Australia* (1964) 111 C.L.R. 549; *O' Day* v. *Commonwealth*, ibid., 599.

9. See Cmnd 2097 (1963); Defence (Transfer of Functions) Act 1964 and statutory Orders in Council made thereunder.

10. Cmnd 4641 (1971); Colin Turpin, *Government Contracts*, pp. 122–3.

11. cf. David Williams, *Not in the Public Interest*, chs. 7, 8; Cmnd 2152 (1963) (the Denning Report). The Head of this Service is directly answerable to the Home Secretary.

to the civil power – a tradition rudely interrupted by the Curragh incident in Ireland early in 1914,[12] but unbroken since then[13] – and although the British public has often been disenchanted with its political leaders, it is averse from turning to the regular armed forces for salvation. Even in times of civil disorder within the realm, the forces must normally (as we shall see in a later chapter)[14] act only under the direction of the civil authorities.

Military law and the civil law

As Dicey emphasized, a soldier[15] is, for most purposes, a civilian in uniform. Although he is subject to certain special rules of law, he is not exempt from the general law of the land.[16]

Those rules which differentiate soldiers from other sections of the community are a consequence of their special responsibilities. Regular soldiers, like civil servants, are disqualified for membership of the House of Commons.[17] The regulations of the service restricting the political activities of members of the forces are stricter than the corresponding rules for civil servants. A regular soldier is absolutely prohibited from standing as a parliamentary candidate. In practice a serviceman who applied for nomination papers as a parliamentary candidate would be given his discharge by the service authorities. This practice became too well known in 1962. A gallant 600 – and more – put in requests for nomination papers as candidates at two impending by-elections. The liberal practice of the service in granting discharges was peremptorily suspended. A select committee of the House of Commons was hastily appointed to examine the problem; upon this committee's recommendation, a special advisory committee (appointed by the Home Secretary) was set up to scrutinize the bona fides of would-be candidates seeking their discharge from the services. Only one of the prospective candidates for one of the seats was

12. cf. Sir Harold Nicolson, *King George V*, pp. 237–40 (when fifty-eight officers in Dublin, including a General, purported to resign their commissions rather than take part in coercing Ulster into an undivided self-governing Ireland).

13. It is possible, however, that the Wilson Government's decision not to attempt to crush by force the rebellion in Southern Rhodesia in or after November 1965 was partly influenced by doubts as to the morale of the troops.

14. See ch. 23.

15. 'Soldier' is here used to include members of the navy, the air force and the marines, as well as the army, subject to verbal modifications.

16. *Introduction to the Study of the Law of the Constitution* (10th edn), ch. 9. See also *Lynch* v. *Fitzgerald* [1938] I.R. 382; Keir and Lawson, *Cases in Constitutional Law* (5th edn), p. 212.

17. House of Commons Disqualification Act 1957, s. 1(1).

recommended for discharge. Having been demobilized, he announced that he had decided, after all, not to stand.[18]

Serving members of the forces are entitled to vote by post or proxy at elections; they are exempt from jury service; they may make informal wills while on actual military service. They are immune from personal liability in tort for death or injury inflicted on another member of the armed forces on duty or on land, premises or transport being used for the purposes of the forces, and are unable to recover damages against the Crown (or individual members of the forces) in respect of death or injury in such circumstances, if the responsible Minister certifies that the death or injury was attributable to military service for the purposes of a pension;[19] no corresponding rules extend to civil servants. We have already referred to the non-justiciability of claims against the Crown relating to wrongful discharge, pay and pensions.

Serving members of the armed forces are subject to military law as well as the ordinary law of the land. Military law is a readily ascertainable body of rules, collected in the official *Manual of Military Law*.[20] It is primarily a body of criminal law, contained in statutes and subordinate legislative instruments. It must be sharply distinguished from martial law, which is not a crystallized code of rules at all but a state of affairs in which there has been a complete breakdown of civil authority and the governance of the populace is handed over to or assumed by a military commander.[21]

In the United Kingdom, certain very serious criminal offences committed by members of the forces are triable only by the civil (i.e. ordinary criminal) courts. Other offences are triable by court-martial. A court-martial is composed of military officers sitting without a jury; they are assisted by a judge advocate, a barrister who sums up the evidence and advises the court on questions of law. Minor offences are triable summarily by commanding officers. A number of offences under military law have no equivalent in the ordinary criminal law – for example, conduct to the prejudice of good order and military discipline.

Till 1951 the enforcement of military discipline and the criminal law by courts-martial was largely a self-contained system; only superior officers and, in the last resort, the Army Council (as it then was) could review a conviction of a person subject to military law or the sentence imposed on him, with an ultimate right of recourse to the royal prerogative of mercy. True, the High Court would issue habeas corpus to direct the release of a person detained by the military authorities if he was not subject to military

18. R. L. Leonard, *Elections in Britain*, pp. 64–5. The advisory committee still exists.
19. Crown Proceedings Act 1947, s. 10. See further ch. 28.
20. See also James Stuart-Smith (1969) 85 *L.Q.R.* 478.
21. See ch. 23.

law, or certiorari to quash a decision if jurisdiction had been manifestly exceeded.[22] But although the High Court was capable of exercising the same supervisory jurisdiction (by orders of certiorari, prohibition and mandamus) over courts-martial as over other inferior statutory tribunals, in practice it was extremely reluctant to intervene even when grave procedural irregularities had been established;[23] the judges affirmed that they would interfere if the 'civil rights' of an individual had been infringed, but were conspicuously vague in explaining what they meant by the civil rights of a soldier.[24] A similar reluctance to appear to prejudice the administration of military discipline in any way whatsoever was exhibited by the courts in other contexts: in the decisions on dismissal and pay; in decisions that no action would lie against members of a court-martial or a commanding officer for false imprisonment or malicious prosecution while acting within their jurisdiction even if actuated by improper motives and lacking reasonable cause,[25] and that reports written by a superior officer upon another officer in the course of duty[26] and the proceedings of a military court of inquiry enjoyed absolute privilege in the law of defamation.[27] Military discipline and justice in the courts seemed to be uneasy bedfellows.

Some of the older decisions on immunity from civil liability may still be good law. But the administration of military discipline is no longer a self-contained system. In 1951 a Courts-Martial Appeal Court, composed of High Court judges and Scottish and Northern Ireland judges of like status, was constituted and given jurisdiction to hear appeals from courts-martial after internal review procedures had been exhausted. Thus was reasserted the primacy of the civil power. Recourse to the common-law supervisory remedies (other than habeas corpus) became largely superfluous; in any event these remedies have territorial limitations, whereas the jurisdiction of the new court extends to courts-martial held in any part of the world.

Under the present law[28] appeal will lie to the court, after military remedies have been exhausted, against a conviction by a court-martial. Leave of the Appeal Court must be obtained, and the court has no juris-

22. As in *R. v. Wormwood Scrubs Prison Governor, ex p. Boydell* [1948] 2 K.B. 193.
23. As in *R. v. Army Council, ex p. Ravenscroft* [1917] 2 K.B. 504; *R. v. Secretary of State for War, ex p. Martyn* [1949] 2 All E.R. 242; *R. v. O.C. Depot Battalion, R.A.S.C. Colchester, ex p. Elliott*, ibid. 373.
24. See *Re Mansergh* (1861) 1 B. & S. 400, and *Martyn*'s and *Elliott*'s cases, above.
25. *Heddon v. Evans* (1919) 35 T.L.R. 642. See also *Johnstone v. Sutton* (1786 1 T.R. 493, 510, 784; *Fraser v. Balfour* (1918) 34 T.L.R. 502.
26. *Dawkins v. Paulet* (1869) L.R. 5 Q.B. 94.
27. *Dawkins v. Rokeby* (1875) L.R. 7 H.L. 744.
28. Consolidated in the Courts-Martial (Appeals) Act 1968.

diction to entertain an appeal against sentence alone. A further appeal will lie to the House of Lords at the instance of the accused or the Defence Council (the respondent) if the Appeal Court or the Lords give leave and the Appeal Court certifies that a point of law of general public importance is involved. The royal prerogative of mercy is preserved.

Superior orders

Before 1966 a member of the forces might incur double jeopardy. If he were convicted of an offence under military law, he could still be charged with and convicted of the same offence in a civil court, though the latter was to take into account any sentence imposed by the military authorities. (Conviction by a civil court precluded trial for the same offence by court-martial, though the facts constituting the civil offence might give rise to a separate *disciplinary* charge under military law.) Since 1966 the anomaly has been largely removed. Conviction by a court-martial precludes trial by a civil court for any offence that is substantially the same.[29]

A member of the forces may nevertheless stand in double jeopardy in a different context. If, in obedience to superior orders, he commits a criminal offence or a civil wrong (for example, wounding a rioter in circumstances where this is not reasonably justifiable) he may incur legal liability before the ordinary courts. If, on the other hand, he refuses to obey an order because he believes it to be unlawful, he may be court-martialled. It may be said that the dilemma is unreal because it is not an offence under military law to disobey an unlawful command; a soldier cannot be convicted for disobedience unless the command was lawful. But since a soldier is a member of a disciplined force conditioned to the habit of obedience, and since, moreover, a court-martial may well hold the command to be lawful, the dilemma and the risk can be very real. Is it reasonable, then, to assert that obedience to superior orders can never be a defence to an unlawful act in proceedings before the courts? The Nuremberg War Crimes trials proceeded on the footing that superior orders were no defence, though they might be pleaded in mitigation of punishment. This general proposition is adopted in modern editions of the *Manual of Military Law*, though it is conceded that obedience to superior orders may afford a defence to particular offences by, for instance, negativing the existence of criminal intent where this is relevant. Doubts as to the content of the rule still persist. In a much-quoted South African case, decided during the Boer War,[30] it was held that an honest belief in

29. See Armed Forces Act 1966, ss. 25, 26, 35.

30. *R.* v. *Smith* (1900) Cape of Good Hope S.C. 561; Geoffrey Wilson, *Cases and Materials*, p. 435. See also *Keighley* v. *Bell* (1866) 4 F. & F. 763 at 790, *per* Willes J.

the lawfulness of an order to shoot an African civilian was a good defence to a charge of murder, the order not being manifestly illegal. The dangers of such a principle are illustrated by the facts of the case; and there is no general rule of criminal law that a reasonable mistake of law is a defence.[31] Yet a reasonable mistake induced by an order given by a military superior to do an act which, in the circumstances, is not manifestly illegal may in some situations be akin to the operation of duress on a soldier, and can fairly be analysed in that fashion. The civil liability of the soldier will not necessarily be governed by the same considerations, particularly where vicarious liability can be affixed to the Crown.

Civilians and courts-martial

Courts-martial outside the United Kingdom have jurisdiction over a wide range of civilian dependants and employees of the forces. Twenty-seven trials of civilians by court-martial took place in 1967.[32] Their jurisdiction extends not only to all criminal offences under English law but also to certain offences of a disciplinary nature (for example, breach of a local curfew). The jurisdiction embraces criminal offences in respect of which United Kingdom courts have no extraterritorial jurisdiction, and others which, if committed in the United Kingdom, would be triable only in a civil court.

This is not an entirely satisfactory state of affairs: pre-trial safeguards are not as efficacious as in a civil court;[33] guilt and sentence are determined by a simple majority of a panel of military officers who will hardly ever have legal qualifications; the accused will often lack the services of a lawyer to defend him.[34] The existence of the Courts-Martial Appeal Court is an ameliorating factor but cannot cure every defect. The main approaches to reform are (i) exclusion or attenuation of the jurisdiction of courts-martial over civilians,[35] coupled with an extension of the extra-territorial jurisdiction of United Kingdom courts; (ii) a general assimilation of the proceedings before a court-martial to those before an ordinary

31. See J. C. Smith and Brian Hogan, *Criminal Law* (3rd edn), p. 148.

32. Gordon Borrie, 'Courts-martial, civilians and civil liberties' (1969) 32 *Mod. L. Rev.* 35.

33. For example, the Judges' Rules (see p. 464) need not be applied (*R. v. Harris-Rivett* [1956] 1 Q.B. 220) and there is nothing exactly equivalent to a preliminary hearing before an ordinary criminal court.

34. The accused is, however, entitled to be represented by a defending officer. On the quality of judge advocates, see Borrie, loc. cit., pp. 47–8.

35. cf. the position under American constitutional law as interpreted by the Supreme Court of the United States: *Reid v. Covert* 354 U.S. 1 (1957), and subsequent cases holding that trial of civilian dependants and employees by court-martial was unconstitutional.

criminal court; (iii) a differentiation between the procedure observed by courts-martial in hearing charges against civilians and charges against members of the forces. The third possibility would be resented by members of the forces. An alternative possibility – vesting all criminal jurisdiction in the local courts – could not be generally acceptable to opinion in this country.

Under the Visiting Forces Act 1952, members of visiting Commonwealth forces, and of such other countries as may be designated by Order in Council (in pursuance of an international agreement for common defence), stationed in the United Kingdom, and their civilian components, are exempt from the jurisdiction of the ordinary criminal courts in respect of offences[36] committed on duty or against the persons of forces personnel or the property of the forces and their personnel; the operation of the Act has been extended to certain British dependencies. In addition, tort claims are settled by special arrangements and are not determinable by the ordinary courts unless the claimant is denied satisfaction through administrative channels.

36. See note 35 on constitutional limitation of the jurisdiction of American courts-martial over civilians – a point not yet established in 1952, when the agreement was made and the Act was passed. American courts-martial try American servicemen for those criminal offences excluded from the jurisdiction of the local courts.

Chapter 9
Public Boards and
Nationalized Industries

Government and quasi-government bodies[1]

Britain is governed primarily by central government Departments and
elected local authorities. We have seen that, apart from Departments
directly headed by Ministers, there are also subordinate central Departments or sub-departments which are not Ministries; they are not directly
headed by a Minister, but they consist of civil servants and a Minister
usually has substantial or full control over them.[2] Subordinate Departments shade off into bodies auxiliary to but not integral parts of the
executive branch of government, bodies managerial, regulatory, promotional, investigatory and advisory, bodies that defy orderly classification
by reference to any meaningful criteria, if only because they have been set
up by Government and Parliament *ad hoc* to discharge a variety of
specialized tasks best performed by institutions partly autonomous and
free from comprehensive political control. The least incoherent group of
these 'quasi-governmental' bodies are the corporations administering
nationalized industries.

Central government in the narrower sense is not conducted exclusively
in Whitehall and its environs. Quite apart from the substantial devolution
of responsibility for Scottish affairs to sub-departments of the Scottish
Office located in Edinburgh, and the lesser measure of devolution for
Welsh affairs to the Welsh Office,[3] several of the United Kingdom Departments maintain regional and local organizations and offices.[4] Among the
Departments with regional offices are the Department of the Environment,
the Ministry of Agriculture and Fisheries, the Department of Trade and
Industry and the Department of Health and Social Security. Still better

1. cf. Sir Arthur Street, 'Quasi-Government Bodies since 1918', in *British Government since 1918* (Institute of Public Administration, 1950).
2. pp. 181–3.
3. See ch. 30.
4. See Brian C. Smith, *Regionalism in England*, vols. 1 and 2 (Acton Society Trust,
1964–5); Gavin McCrone, *Regional Policy in Britain*; A. H. Hanson and Malcolm
Walles, *Governing Britain*, ch. 10. For the DTI, see Cmnd 4942 (1972).

known are the local employment exchanges of the Department of Employment, social security offices and inland revenue offices. Immigration officers of the Home Office, and customs officers of the Board of Customs and Excise, are stationed at seaports and airports. And various public corporations, particularly those managing nationalized industries, are organized partly on a regional basis.

In 1972 there was no pattern of regional government in England. Instead, there was a patchwork quilt of overlapping *ad hoc* regions for the provision, regulation or coordination of particular services. Functional regionalism would move a stage further in 1973 with the reorganization of the National Health Service and water authorities on a regional basis. The Government had not accepted the Redcliffe–Maud Commission's recommendations for establishing provincial councils in England as indirectly elected regional planning authorities,[5] but the Report of the Royal Commission on the Constitution was still awaited.

Devolution of central decision-making powers to provincial and local authorities has a long history. In England the Plantagenet kings had their sheriffs, and they and the local populace were subject to the septennial inquisitions of the king's justices in eyre. The Tudors had not only a Star Chamber but also Councils of the North and of Wales and the Marches. Later the relationship between the Crown and colonial Governors entailed a delegation of the royal prerogative. In a number of continental countries local government was, for centuries, government by individual agents of the central administration. In some African and Asian political societies the first European explorers found a devolutionary system of government already well established; in East Africa, for example, the will of the Kabaka of Buganda was executed locally by a hierarchy of royal officials – *saza*, *gombolola* and *muluka* chiefs. But in England, at least after 1688, any such system would have been incompatible with the facts of life. There was a deeply ingrained hostility to the assertion of royal authority within the realm. The functions of central government were grudgingly conceded to comprise the defence of the realm, the conduct of foreign affairs, the governance (at one remove) of the plantations and colonies, the regulation of external trade, aspects of the administration of justice and the levying (within narrow limits) of taxation. The authority of the Privy Council as an instrument of positive government had been undermined and nothing had taken its place save the intermittent supervisory jurisdiction exercised by the Court of King's Bench. Local government in the boroughs lay in the hands of merchants, tradesmen, craftsmen, professional men and professional gentlemen; the governing bodies or

5. Report of the Royal Commission on Local Government in England (Cmnd 4040 (1969)), ch. 10.

councils were self-perpetuating oligarchies; corruption and maladministration were rife; public utility, sanitation and welfare services were often negligible. In the counties the unit of local administration was the parish; each parish had its unpaid conscripts to serve as constable, surveyor and overseer of the poor; their activities were supervised, and the transgressions of the parishioners were punished, by a justice of the peace, a centrally appointed, unpaid and frequently unjudicial member of the squirearchy;[6] the justices also exercised a miscellany of judicial, legislative and administrative functions (for example, levying rates, securing the upkeep of bridges, highways and gaols) at county quarter sessions, mainly in accordance with judicial forms, again subject only to the judicial superintendence of the King's Bench. It is particularly interesting that the maintenance of law and order within the realm, pre-eminently, one would expect, a function of central government, was instead committed to unpaid and untrained local citizens. Even today the police are partly a local responsibility.

By the end of the eighteenth century the state of local administration was becoming catastrophic. There were no adequate local government organs or services in the new industrial towns, and the social cohesion of rural areas was being disturbed by the agricultural revolution, the growth of a landless proletariat, unemployment and migration to the factory areas.

The best-known milestone on the long road to reform was the Municipal Corporations Act 1835, under which provision was made for elected town councils in boroughs; elected county councils were not constituted till 1888. For our present purposes, a more important development was the creation of *ad hoc* authorities to deal with the problem of providing particular services.

The *ad hoc* public authority was not a nineteenth-century invention. The unhappily named Commissioners of Sewers had been responsible for land drainage and coast protection, particularly in East Anglia, since the fifteenth century; like the county justices they mocked theories of the separation of powers by commingling judicial with administrative and ancillary legislative functions.[7] In the latter part of the eighteenth century many *ad hoc* local bodies were established under private Acts of Parliament – partly elective improvement commissioners, to regulate the paving, lighting and sanitation of urban areas; corporations to build workhouses for the relief of the poor; turnpike trustees to construct and maintain main roads for the use of stagecoaches by levying tolls. These local palliatives

6. Squire Western in Henry Fielding's *Tom Jones* was not a mere caricature.
7. See Edith G. Henderson, *Foundations of English Administrative Law*, pp. 28–34. The commissioners observed judicial forms and were a court of record.

had no connection with the central government. But the age of reform, ushered in by the Representation of the People Act 1832, soon threw up a new highly centralized *ad hoc* authority, the Poor Law Commissioners.[8] The inspiration of this experiment lay in the utilitarian philosophy of Jeremy Bentham; the immediate progenitor, and the first secretary to the Commissioners, was Bentham's disciple, Edwin Chadwick.[9]

The three Commissioners, though appointed by the Crown, were free from effective ministerial or parliamentary control. Their powers were so widely drawn as to be virtually all-embracing within their field. Regulations made by them were subject to disallowance by the Privy Council, and they had to make an annual report to the Secretary of State which had to be laid before Parliament; but in matters of policy as well as day-to-day administration the 'three tyrants of Somerset House', and their zealous secretary, had in effect a free hand. With bureaucratic efficiency and insensitivity they rode roughshod over local vested interests and reorganized workhouses with little regard to human problems, reconstituting parish vestries under guardians of the poor and subjecting them to detailed direction and superintendence. Their practice consorted ill with the philosophy of *laissez faire*, and their efforts to promote the greatest happiness of the greatest number were not conspicuously successful. Perhaps the Commissioners would have been spared if they had had a ministerial spokesman in Parliament, or even if they had had the benefit of a modern public relations organization. But they fell a victim to hostile criticism and in 1847 a new Poor Law Board, with a parliamentary president, was constituted. Curiously, in 1848 an autonomous General Board of Health, responsible for public sanitation, was established by statute according to the pattern of the defunct Poor Law Commission. This Board was wound up after a few years, and for much the same reasons; its functions were redistributed between the Privy Council and the Home Office. In 1871 the Local Government Board with a parliamentary head was established; this was a board in name only, for in substance it was a government Department. Gradually rational schemes for distributing functions between the central government and elected local authorities emerged.

The failure of the Poor Law Commission and the General Board of Health to command public support did not spell the doom of the *ad hoc* quasi-governmental authority. In the second half of the nineteenth century

8. Poor Law Amendment Act 1834. But the idea of carrying on an aspect of central administration through a board rather than a Ministry was not novel. See Henry Parris, *Constitutional Bureaucracy*, p. 82ff.

9. Sir Cecil Carr, *Concerning English Administrative Law*, ch. 1.

new non-departmental bodies, set up to supply specialized public services, began to spring up. They were less rigorously screened from political authority; they were subject to financial controls and a measure of general ministerial regulation, though they were free from detailed central control. Usually the governing body included elected representatives of the operators, and sometimes elected representatives of the 'consumers', of the service provided. In some respects they resembled the late eighteenth-century local *ad hoc* authorities[10] and their random latter-day successors.[11] The prototype, constituted under a private Act of Parliament, was the Mersey Docks and Harbour Board (1857). The Port of London Authority (1908) was cast in a similar mould.

Between 1909 and 1939 new *ad hoc* authorities were set up: the Development Commission (1909) (to promote rural development), the Road Board (1909) (to improve the system of main roads), the Forestry Commission (1919), the British Broadcasting Corporation (by royal charter in 1926), the Central Electricity Board (1927) (to control the generation and transmission though not the distribution of electricity), the Racecourse Betting Control Board, the Unemployment Assistance Board and the British Overseas Airways Corporation were the best-known bodies operating at a national level. The London Passenger Transport Board (1933) provided a public service in the metropolitan region. These bodies shared two characteristics in common: none was exempt from every form of ministerial control, but each enjoyed a substantial measure of autonomy. Most of the governing bodies were appointed by the Government and were not elected. Attempts to classify them more exactly or to explain the reasons why they were constituted in a particular form would be even less rewarding than a general analysis of 'administrative' tribunals. Some were managerial, some promotional, some regulatory, some advisory. Most, but not all, were bodies corporate. None was part of a government Department.[12]

Since 1945 the process of 'adhockery' has continued. In particular, semi-autonomous public corporations, in their various manifestations, have been entrusted with an increasing range of functions in relation to the national economy. Each of the nationalized industries has been constituted as a separate public corporation. To this extent public corporations have become less amorphous. At least the reasons why they have been established are becoming more apparent. But although the nationalization of industry may be a political and economic innovation, it has afforded little that is of special interest to a student of constitutional law.

10. J. D. B. Mitchell, *Constitutional Law* (2nd edn), p. 216.
11. J. F. Garner, *Administrative Law* (3rd edn), pp. 319–20.
12. See further pp. 180–81.

The role of government in the mixed economy and the welfare State: a brief sketch[13]

1. A number of public services are provided by elected local authorities.[14] These services include schools, sanitation, street lighting, traffic control, housing, environmental planning and certain welfare services (for example, child care). Before the introduction of the National Health Service many local authorities provided hospitals. Till the post-war nationalization measures of the Labour Government, a majority of gas undertakings and a substantial number of electricity undertakings were operated by local authorities. Municipal enterprise has suffered as a result of pressure to achieve uniform standards by centralization, though there still exist local transport undertakings, even municipal banks and airfields. In one important area, the regulation of public passenger transport, decentralization of responsibility from the Secretary of State to metropolitan counties is taking place.[15]

2. A few local public services are provided or regulated by *ad hoc* authorities composed wholly or mainly of members of the local authorities in the area.[16]

3. A large proportion of social services are provided directly or indirectly by the central government. Social security benefits are dispensed by the Department of Health and Social Security, which also organizes and controls the National Health Service; hospitals are managed out of central government funds by appointed Regional Hospital Boards and Hospital Management Committees; financial assistance to the destitute is supplied by the appointed Supplementary Benefits Commission, again out of central funds.

4. Land use is closely regulated by the Department of the Environment and local planning authorities. Governmental action to create new towns administered by development corporations has checked the concentration of industry and population in big conurbations.

5. A public service may be operated directly by a government Department. The one conspicuous example was the Post Office, which became a semi-

---

13. Books and articles about these matters date rapidly. For a valuable review of recent history, see Samuel Brittan, *Steering the Economy: The Role of the Treasury* (1969). See also Henry Roseveare, *The Treasury* (1969); Frank Broadway, *State Intervention in British Industry, 1964–1968* (1969); Joan Mitchell, *The National Board for Prices and Incomes* (1972). For a more general analysis, see W. Friedmann, *The State and the Rule of Law in a Mixed Economy* (1971).

14. See ch. 18.

15. Local Government Act 1972, s. 202; see also Transport (London) Act 1969.

16. Garner, op. cit., pp. 319–20.

autonomous public corporation in 1969 after more than a century of departmental operation.

6. Governments may participate in or regulate the economy in a variety of ways. They make take over the assets of a privately owned company and appoint its directors without destroying its legal capacity as a company; thus Cable and Wireless Ltd, a company responsible for international telecommunications, became government-owned in 1947.[17] They may acquire a majority or minority shareholding in a privately owned company in return for the right to appoint directors.[18] They may and do grant subsidies and loans, and offer tax incentives, to commercial and industrial firms for research and development or to prevent large-scale unemployment by salvaging an ailing firm or industry or to promote development in a needy region.[19] They may influence the location of industry and office development by systems of licensing. They may set up a semi-autonomous public corporation like the Highlands and Islands Development Board and supply it with public funds. They may constitute a semi-autonomous body like the Civil Aviation Authority to regulate public and private enterprise[20]; or a Monopolies Commission and a Restrictive Practices Court to regulate aspects of private enterprise. If fiscal controls and tax policies are incapable of restraining inflation or deflation or maintaining a satisfactory balance of payments or keeping unemployment down to an acceptable level or encouraging economic development, growth or productivity, then a compulsory restriction of prices, charges and incomes may have to be imposed, monitored by semi-autonomous boards.

It is questionable whether, at the present time, a book on constitutional law should proceed far beyond these generalities. When the Conservative Government came to office in 1970 it intended to restrict the role of Government and public enterprise in the national economy. State-owned

17. Under section 130 of the Post Office Act 1969 the Treasury was empowered to dispose of these assets to the Post Office, but no immediate steps were taken for that purpose.

18. See T. C. Daintith in W. Friedmann and J. F. Garner (eds.), *Government Enterprise*, ch. 3. cf. Industry Act 1972, s. 7(3) (*a*), (4), (5), imposing restrictions on this kind of government intervention.

19. The principal legislative instruments for achieving these purposes in 1972 were the Industry Act 1972 and the Local Employment Act 1972. See also Cmnd 4942 (1972); Mineral Exploitation and Investment Grants Act 1972. Regional development might subsequently be promoted by European Community policies.

Agricultural subsidies are to be replaced by agricultural import levies with a view to adoption of the Communities' common agricultural policy; a new government Department, the Intervention Board for Agricultural Produce, was set up to implement that policy (European Communities Act 1972, s. 6).

20. Civil Aviation Act 1971.

public houses were sold off;[21] the Land Commission was dissolved;[22] so was the Industrial Reorganization Corporation, which had succoured lame ducks;[23] powers were assumed to enable the fringe activities of nationalized activities to be reduced;[24] the advisory National Board for Prices and Incomes and the Consumer Council were wound up; and so on. But in 1971 the insolvent Rolls-Royce company was nationalized;[25] Government aid rescued the Clydeside shipbuilding industry from disaster; soon a Minister for Industrial Development and an Industrial Development Executive were created to provide selective financial assistance for industry.[26] Late in 1972 a temporary standstill in price, rent and wage increases was imposed;[27] and in January 1973 a longer-term compulsory policy to combat inflation, at least as rigorous as the Labour Government's,[28] was announced.[29] A Cabinet Minister for Trade and Consumer Affairs was appointed; in 1973 there would be a Director-General of Fair Trading, a Consumer Protection Advisory Committee, and a new Monopolies and Mergers Commission with wider powers than the existing Monopolies Commission; the Restrictive Practices Court would have a broader jurisdiction.[30]

Potentially some of these developments were of considerable constitutional interest; but so many of them were influenced by economic and political vicissitudes that the most appropriate commentator was the journalist.

Nationalization of industry through the vesting of privately or locally owned assets in a (usually monopolistic) public corporation, subject to the payment of compensation, has been the most characteristic feature of public enterprise since 1945. As we have noted, nationalization can assume more than one form; Cable and Wireless Ltd did not become a public corporation, and the assets of the Bank of England were transferred to the Treasury. But there is a broad general pattern: a new body corporate is constituted; its governing body is appointed by a Minister and is then given a substantial degree of freedom to conduct the enterprise in day-to-day matters in its own discretion; the Minister retains powers to give it

21. Licensing (Abolition of State Management) Act 1971.
22. Land Commission (Dissolution) Act 1971.
23. Industry Act 1971.
24. See, for example, Coal Industry Act 1971; Transport Holding Company Act 1971; Iron and Steel Act 1972; Civil Aviation Act 1971, s. 40(1)(c).
25. Rolls-Royce (Purchase) Act 1971.
26. Industry Act 1972. The Minister was subordinate to the Secretary of State for Trade and Industry.
27. Counter-Inflation (Temporary Provisions) Act 1972.
28. cf. Prices and Incomes Acts 1966, 1967 and 1968.
29. Cmnd 5205 (1973); Counter-Inflation Act 1973.
30. Fair Trading Bill 1972–3.

directions of a general character and certain specific powers; Treasury sanction is required for ventures with large financial implications; the corporation has its own assets and is expected broadly to pay its own way; its employees are not civil servants. The form of nationalization was suggested partly by the British Broadcasting Corporation, partly by the experience of the London Passenger Transport Board. Nationalization as an instrument of political and economic policy was conceived by the Labour Party and implemented when the first Labour Government with an overall majority in the House of Commons came to power in 1945.[31] Private ownership of the principal means of production and distribution was regarded as morally wrong and detrimental to the public interest; it was necessary to supplant the profit motive with a zeal for public service, to revivify declining industries, to achieve levels of efficiency which private enterprise was incapable of reaching, and to install the Government on the commanding heights of the economy. Coal, electricity, gas, inland transport, airways, and the iron and steel industry were nationalized between 1946 and 1951. Iron and steel were denationalized under a Conservative Government in 1953, and renationalized under a Labour Government in 1967. That nationalization had ceased to be regarded pre-eminently as a political creed was, however, illustrated by the nationalization of atomic energy under the Conservatives in 1954. Developments since the return of the Conservative Party to office in 1970 have already been outlined. Perhaps one day we shall see the semi-autonomous agency or commission, regulating the conduct of private enterprise, installed as a characteristic feature of the British administrative system.[32] But as yet they still order things differently in the United States.[33]

Nationalized industries: legal and constitutional issues

Detailed examination of the structure, organization and functions of individual nationalized industries falls outside the scope of this book.[34]

31. See generally W. A. Robson, *Nationalised Industry and Public Ownership* (2nd edn); A. H. Hanson, *Parliament and Public Ownership*; *Nationalisation – a Book of Readings*; R. Kelf-Cohen, *Twenty Years of Nationalisation*; Leonard Tivey, *Nationalisation in British Industry*; W. Friedmann and J. F. Garner (eds.), *Government Enterprise*; David Coombes, *State Enterprise: Business or Politics?* (1971); C. D. Foster, *Politics, Finance and the Role of Economics* (1971); Richard Pryke, *Public Enterprise in Practice* (1971).

32. The Civil Aviation Authority has certain features of an American-type agency, but it is under fairly close Government control; see G. Ganz [1972] *Public Law* 215 at 224–30. The Fair Trading Bill may possibly evoke close analogies.

33. See, for example, Bernard Schwartz and H. W. R. Wade, *Legal Control of Government* (1972), ch. 2.

34. See further Robson, op. cit.; J. A. G. Griffith and H. Street, *Principles of*

The main bodies conducting the affairs of the industries are the National Coal Board (which has divisional executives); the Central Electricity Generating Board and area electricity boards (responsible for generation, transmission and distribution) and the Electricity Council (a coordinating body which advises the Secretary of State); the South of Scotland Electricity Board and the North of Scotland Hydro-electricity Board; the British Overseas Airways Corporation, British European Airways (controlled by the British Airways Board;[35] they are not monopolistic bodies, and they are to be merged by 1974) and the British Airports Authority[36] (which controls the four principal airports in Britain); the British Gas Corporation with a regional organization,[37] replacing the Gas Council and its area boards; the Atomic Energy Authority; the British Steel Corporation;[38] the Post Office;[39] a complex network of inland transport authorities,[40] including the British Railways Board, the British Docks Board, the British Waterways Board, the National Freight Corporation (which is to provide a publicly owned freight transport service and to promote the provision of integrated freight services), the Scottish Transport Group, the London Transport Executive and other regional transport authorities designated by the Secretary of State, and the National Bus Company; and the British Broadcasting Corporation, which operates under a royal charter and a quinquennial licence.[41]

The responsible Minister (the Secretary of State for Trade and Industry, or for the Environment, or for Scotland; or the Minister of Posts and Telecommunications[42]) appoints (or advises the appointment of) members of the governing boards; the members will hold office for fixed periods;

Administrative Law (4th edn), ch. 7; J. F. Garner, *Administrative Law* (3rd edn), ch. 10; J. D. B. Mitchell, *Constitutional Law* (2nd edn), ch. 12; Friedmann and Garner, op. cit., chs. 1, 2.

35. Civil Aviation Act 1971, Part 3.

36. Constituted under the Airports Authority Act 1965.

37. Gas Act 1972.

38. Constituted under the Iron and Steel Act 1967.

39. Post Office Act 1969.

40. See the Transport Act 1968, amending the Transport Act 1962. The original nationalization Act was the Transport Act 1947; none of the nationalized industries has undergone so much structural change as the transport services.

41. The Independent Broadcasting Authority (Television Act 1964; Sound Broadcasting Act 1972) is a regulatory rather than an operational body; commercial television and radio programmes are provided through regional programme companies to which it allocates contracts.

42. Who is generally responsible for the Post Office and has what is in practice a lesser responsibility for the BBC; the Governors of the BBC are formally appointed by Her Majesty in Council. The BBC is *sui generis*; Ministers' powers are very wide, but politicians have observed a self-denying ordinance.

the Minister has powers of dismissal (which have seldom been exercised[43]) and a power not to re-appoint them. Broad policy control rests in the hands of the Minister; day-to-day administrative control lies in the hands of the governing bodies; an indeterminate zone where policy merges with day-to-day administration lies between. A typical statutory provision is that the Minister shall have power to give the board directions of a general character as to the exercise of its functions on matters appearing to him to affect the national interest.[44] In some instances – for example, the Atomic Energy Authority,[45] the British Steel Corporation[46] – he will have a general power to give specific directions, subject to qualifications.[47] Powers to give specific directions to the aviation authorities are wider.[48] The nationalization Acts also confer upon the Ministers particular powers. Thus, the Minister is empowered to prescribe the form of the corporation's accounts and appoint auditors, except where (as with the Atomic Energy Authority) the accounts are audited by the Comptroller and Auditor-General; his sanction is required for large schemes of capital investment or reconstruction or public borrowing; in some instances he may advance sums (for example, for maintaining uneconomic railway services).[49] Ministerial and Treasury approval is also needed for money advanced out of the National Loans Fund for any large-scale scheme of public investment or borrowing. The Minister will be entitled to call for information from the board regarding its activities. The board must present its accounts and an annual report to the Minister. He is usually empowered to prescribe schemes for training and research; or his approval of such schemes will be necessary. There is no set pattern of ministerial authority.

In most cases the corporations have been expected and required to conduct their affairs as commercial undertakings operating in the public interest and to be financially self-supporting over a period of years; the BBC and the Atomic Energy Authority, which are financed primarily out of licence fees prescribed by the Government and direct government grants respectively, have always been exceptions. Solvency has not, however, always proved to be an attainable objective and financial obligations have had to be modified. The maintenance of an arm's length

43. But in 1970 the Minister terminated the appointment of the then chairman of the Post Office.

44. For example, Coal Industry Nationalisation Act 1946, s. 3(1); Post Office Act 1969, s. 11.

45. Atomic Energy Authority Act 1954, s. 3.

46. Iron and Steel Act 1967, ss. 7(2), 8.

47. See also Transport Act 1968, s. 6(1) (power to give specific directions to transport authorities upon the recommendation of the National Freight Integration Council).

48. Civil Aviation Act 1971, ss. 4, 40.

49. Transport Act 1968, s. 39. See also Transport Grants Act 1972.

relationship between Ministers and boards has also been impracticable in some instances, because of (1) the political repercussions of many day-to-day decisions, or errors or misfortunes in management – for example, public reaction to power cuts, or increases in fares or charges, or closures of uneconomic pits or transport services, or the dislocation caused by strikes in major industries providing public services; and the political and economic implications of a nationalized airline buying foreign aircraft in preference to more expensive British-manufactured aircraft; (2) pressure by individual M.P.s to secure ministerial intervention in various matters of detailed management, and party political criticism of the performance of industries that were nationalized as an act of political conviction; (3) the need for coordinated national economic planning, which may be inimical to the pursuit of efficiency by individual industries in isolation from other aspects of the economy; and (4) the unforeseen dependence of some nationalized industries on government financial aid and therefore more detailed government control. In the early 1970s the Government was impelled to intervene in serious labour disputes involving the industries; to supplement the boards' resources in order to enable them to arrive at wage settlements; to write off massive deficits; to finance programmes for expansion or rationalization; and to bring the industries within the ambit of its mandatory counter-inflationary policies.[50]

Again, the formal lines of demarcation between ministerial authority and the board's autonomy are often unclear. The role of determining policy guidelines must inevitably be shared between the Minister and the board; precisely how the policy-making function is in fact to be distributed is not and cannot realistically be defined. In any event, where does *national* policy begin and end? That all uneconomic pits or that no uneconomic pit should be closed would surely be a national policy decision. A decision that some uneconomic pits should be closed might be regarded either as a matter of national policy or as a matter of industrial management, according to the particular political, social and economic context. Decisions which uneconomic pits should be closed, when, and in what circumstances, would be primarily matters of industrial management, but they could assume national dimensions. Practice has varied; in some industries the Minister has offered little policy guidance; in others he has frequently intervened in matters of detail but without giving formal directions. Indeed, up to 1968 only two *general* statutory directions on matters of national policy had been given by Ministers to boards.[51] Ministers prefer

50. It appeared that aspects of the Fair Trading Bill would also apply to the industries.

51. First Report from Select Committee on Nationalized Industries, Session 1967–68 (Ministerial Control of the Nationalized Industries) (H.C. 371–1 of 1967–68), para. 649.

to exert informal pressure on boards; this has been facilitated by regular personal contacts with their chairmen. Constitutionally this may be an unsatisfactory anomaly. More clearly demarcated powers and prohibitions can be enshrined in legislation; the outcome will not necessarily be conducive to efficiency or harmony.

Legal status

The corporations can sue and be sued in their own names. Their employees are their own officers and servants. It is doubtful whether any of the corporations is an agent or servant of the Crown enjoying Crown immunities and privileges;[52] some of the recent Acts have placed these questions beyond doubt.[53] The National Health Service authorities on the other hand exercise their functions on behalf of the Crown.[54] The Atomic Energy Authority is a marginal case, for it is closely controlled by the Secretary of State and derives its revenue mainly from the central government; still, for most legal purposes other than liability to rates and taxes it is treated as an autonomous body corporate, not as a Crown servant.[55]

The legal powers vested in the corporations are extensive, and although a person having a sufficient legal interest can impugn the validity of their acts and decisions, successful challenges will be rare, first because of the breadth of their powers[56] and, secondly, because of the disinclination of the courts to afford *locus standi* to members of the general public,[57] though it is open to the Attorney-General to sue for an injunction or a declaration.[58]

For the functions of the Committee, see p. 223. For the Government's reactions to the report, see Cmnd 4027 (1969).

In 1972 the Secretary of State for Trade and Industry was responsible for the fuel, power, energy and airways corporations, the Secretary of State for the Environment for the other transport corporations, the Secretary of State for Scotland for the Scottish corporations and the Minister of Posts and Telecommunications for the Post Office and the broadcasting corporations.

52. *Tamlin* v. *Hannaford* [1950] 1 K.B. 18 (former British Transport Commission); *BBC* v. *Johns* [1965] Ch. 32; p. 125.

53. For example, Transport Act 1968, ss. 52(5), 160–162; Post Office Act 1969, s. 6(5).

54. *Nottingham No. 1 Area Hospital Management Committee* v. *Owen* [1958] 1 Q.B. 50. See also *Pfizer Ltd* v. *Ministry of Health* [1965] A.C. 512. But the hospital boards and management committees can sue and be sued in their own names.

55. Atomic Energy Authority Act 1954, s. 6.

56. See, for example, *Roberts (Charles) & Co.* v. *British Railways Board* [1965] 1 W.L.R. 396; though cf. *South of Scotland Electricity Board* v. *British Oxygen Co.* [1956] 1 W.L.R. 1069; [1959] 1 W.L.R. 587.

57. See, for example, *McWhirter*'s case (note 60) and Addendum.

58. See pp. 377–8, 603–4 and Addendum.

The primary legal duties of the corporations are so broadly drawn (for example, 'to provide an efficient service . . .') that they must be regarded as non-justiciable; indeed, the general duties of the British Railways Board and the National Freight Corporation are expressly declared to be unenforceable in a court,[59] though section 106(1) of the Transport Act 1968 goes to the other extreme by providing that the maintenance duties of the British Waterways Board may be enforced in judicial proceedings by any person. Whether a duty is potentially susceptible of judicial enforcement must depend mainly on the degree of precision with which it is formulated.[60] If a board were to refuse to comply with its duty to act in conformity with a direction properly issued to it by a Minister, the latter could presumably compel performance of the duty by obtaining an order of mandamus, or alternatively be awarded a judicial declaration that the board was in breach of its duty; but matters have yet to be brought to this pass, and in such a situation a Minister might prefer to exercise his powers of dismissal.[61]

Public accountability and extra-judicial safeguards

The main reason for vesting the ownership of nationalized industries in semi-autonomous public corporations, instead of bringing them within the framework of normal departmental administration, was to encourage a competitive spirit of initiative and enterprise. The civil service ethos would, it was thought, inhibit the managerial staff of the industries from making untried experiments in new fields; it would induce an excess of caution and addiction to precedent; officials would always be looking over their shoulders, apprehensive of the parliamentary inquisitor. Hence an attempt was made to insulate the industries from the rigours of question time by restricting ministerial responsibility for the conduct of their affairs. Against this background, the scope of parliamentary scrutiny is inevitably more limited than it was in relation to the Post Office before it ceased to be a government Department.

Parliamentary questions. In the early phase of nationalization, the Minister of Fuel and Power and other superintending Ministers refused to answer

59. Transport Act 1962, s. 3(4); Transport Act 1968, s. 1(3). See also Iron and Steel Act 1967, s. 3(4); Post Office Act 1969, s. 9(4).

60. Hence it appears that the duty of the IBA to satisfy themselves that as far as possible programmes do not include matter offensive to public feeling (Television Act 1964, s. 3(1)(a)) falls narrowly within the area of duties enforceable at the suit of the Attorney-General; *Att.-Gen., ex rel. McWhirter* v. *IBA* [1973] 2 W.L.R. 344.

61. As the members of the governing body of RTE (the Irish equivalent of the BBC) were dismissed in November 1972. As a matter of strict law, it would be possible for the BBC's licence to be revoked.

questions about matters concerning the industries which in their opinion related to day-to-day administration and were therefore outside their responsibility. In accordance with the rules of the House of Commons, all questions of a like nature to those to which answers had been refused were simply disallowed. This gave rise to a good deal of dissatisfaction, and in 1948 the Speaker announced a modified ruling: if it appeared to him that such a question raised a matter of urgent public importance, he would allow the question to be put; it would be up to the Minister to decide whether to answer it. When in doubt, the clerks at the table (who in the first instance receive notice of questions to be put in the House) have generally taken a broad view of the latitude thus granted in accepting questions;[62] and Ministers have not often refused to answer a question on the ground that it related to day-to-day management or administration, though some of the questions tabled and answered might well have been rejected on that ground.[63]

Clearly a Minister can properly be asked to answer a question within the field of his statutory responsibility – for example, a question about appointments he has made and has power to terminate or has terminated or why he has or has not given an approval or a specific direction which he is required or empowered by statute to give. A Minister can also be asked questions about his extra-statutory official activities (for example, informal consultations with board chairmen) if they come to the notice of M.P.s. The more difficult cases – and the pegs on which the majority of questions about nationalized industries are hung – are questions about whether the Minister proposes to give (or why the Minister has not given) certain directions of a general character to a board in the national interest, and questions asking the Minister to obtain statistical information from a board. The former type of question often relates to a matter of marginal generality; the latter may be strictly admissible but tends to involve the staff of the boards in a large amount of work. (Members can and do address still more questions direct to the chairmen of the boards.[64]) The insulation of the boards from political accountability through questions to Ministers is therefore far from complete. And question time in the House of Commons is the cockpit of party conflict.

62. See generally D. N. Chester and Nona Bowring, *Questions in Parliament*, pp. 301–5.

63. First Report of the Select Committee on Nationalized Industries for 1967–8 (H.C. 371–1 of 1967–8), paras. 852–3. Out of sixty-four questions in 1966–7, asking for Ministers to give 'general directions' to boards, forty-six were answered though some of them trespassed on matters of day-to-day management.

64. In 1966, 550 questions were tabled on British Railways alone in the two Houses; the Board had to reply to 246 of them. M.P.s also sent over 1100 letters to the chairman of the Board: loc. cit., para. 856.

Parliamentary debate. Debate on the conduct of a nationalized industry may take place on public bills (especially bills increasing a corporation's borrowing powers or reconstructing the organization of the industry), on private bills promoted by one of the corporations[65] and on subordinate legislation concerning the industries; on substantive motions to discuss a particular matter, or on a supply day (where the topics for debate are chosen by the Opposition), or on the annual reports and accounts of the corporations after they have been laid before Parliament, or on the reports of the Select Committee on Nationalized Industries; or a private member may lead a brief debate on the affairs of a public corporation on the daily motion for the adjournment of the House of Commons. The rules of procedure governing debate are generally less restrictive than those governing the scope of parliamentary questions, and the issues raised may range beyond the area of ministerial responsibility.

Select committee on nationalized industries.[66] This investigatory committee of the House of Commons was first set up in 1951. In 1955 it was reconstituted with terms of reference so absurdly narrow that the committee reported that there was nothing that it could usefully do. In 1956 it was given new terms of reference, empowering it to examine the reports and accounts of nationalized industries whose boards were appointed by Ministers. By 1972, Cable and Wireless Ltd, the Independent Broadcasting Authority, the Horserace Totalisator Board and certain functions of the Bank of England had been brought within its terms of reference, but its general remit is confined to statutory bodies whose annual receipts are not wholly or mainly derived from Parliament or the Government. The Atomic Energy Authority and the British Broadcasting Corporation remain outside its field of inquiry. The Committee is appointed each session, and has some eighteen members, selected in accordance with party strengths in the House. The chairman is a backbencher on the Government side of the House. Most of its members have had specialized knowledge of industry or management. Like other select committees of the House, it has power to take evidence and compel the production of witnesses and documents. It has no regular research staff, but is advised by senior Treasury officers and has engaged special consultants to assist in some of its inquiries.

During the course of a session it will examine and report on the work of one or two of the boards. From 1966 to 1968 it conducted an exhaustive inquiry into ministerial control and published a lengthy report with

65. Though cf. *Pickin* v. *British Railways Board* [1972] 3 W.L.R. 824 (p. 74).
66. See David Coombes, *The Member of Parliament and the Administration*; A. H. Hanson in *The Commons in Transition* (ed. Hanson and Bernard Crick), ch. 4.

detailed recommendations, not all of which were acceptable to the Government.[67] It hears evidence from the chairmen and other members of the governing boards, senior officials from the sponsoring Departments, and occasionally from Ministers and outside experts. Despite a measure of discontinuity in its membership, the Committee has itself acquired a good deal of collective expertise, and it is an essentially non-partisan body. It has performed useful services in familiarizing M.P.s and interested members of the public with what goes on within the industries, making those who run the industries more conversant with and responsive to informed outside opinion, and from time to time offering constructive criticisms and recommendations for reform. It has also helped to lower the political temperature of the discussions about the nationalized industries; and it has provided a model for new specialized scrutinizing committees of the House dealing with aspects of governmental activity. Despite the increased burden that its work has cast upon the senior staff of the industries, it has justified its existence in a properly unspectacular way.

Other controls. The Government has appointed, over the years, *ad hoc* inquiries, headed by independent experts, to examine and report on aspects of the nationalized coal, gas and electricity industries and the nationalized airlines. Some of these reports have been followed by statutory reorganization.

The accounts of the nationalized industries (apart from atomic energy) are not audited by the Comptroller and Auditor-General, but they can be examined by him in conjunction with the Public Accounts Committee of the House of Commons, since they are required to be laid before Parliament. The expenditure and administration of those public corporations (such as the BBC) which are subsidized out of moneys provided by Parliament are also subject to scrutiny by the Expenditure Committee of the House.[68] In practice these committees, which have had more than enough work to do, have paid little attention to those nationalized industries within the jurisdiction of the special Select Committee.

The nationalized electricity, gas and inland transport bodies have national and area consultative committees or councils; the Post Office has users' national councils. These associated bodies, mainly appointed by the superintending Minister, have no executive powers; in general – there is no fixed pattern – their functions are to represent the consumer interest, to receive and consider complaints by members of the public, and to advise the Minister or the relevant board on matters referred to them or in some cases on their own initiative. The membership of area electricity and gas consumers' councils has to include representatives nominated by

67. See note 51 above.
68. For these committees, see pp. 288–90.

local authority associations. Under the Gas Act 1972 local authority representation on regional consumers' councils is substantial, and the national consumers' council includes the chairmen of regional councils.[69] The councils and committees make annual reports which are published. The general consensus of opinion is that as guardians of the interests of consumers these bodies have not fulfilled a conspicuously significant function;[70] in a large report in 1971, the Select Committee on Nationalized Industries put the point more forcefully.[71] Nevertheless, in September 1970 objections by the Post Office Users' National Council to certain proposed increases in postal charges were followed by a formal ministerial directive to the Post Office not to impose them. The Iron and Steel and Industrial Coal Consumers' Councils have been wound up in compliance with Community obligations.[72]

Yet there is a real dilemma: watchdogs whose bark is feeble and whose bite is imperceptible are hardly worth keeping; but the nationalized industries, already subjected to a depth and range of public scrutiny to which no privately owned industrial undertaking has to submit, are understandably reluctant to encourage the development of more effective oversight of their operations.[73]

The position of the broadcasting authorities is different. The BBC has an appointed but independent General Advisory Council; the IBA also has a number of specialized advisory committees on such matters as religious and educational broadcasting, the maintenance of advertising standards and local commercial radio broadcasting. Complaints are dealt with primarily by internal procedures, but the BBC has constituted a high-powered independent Programmes Complaints Commission to consider representations by dissatisfied complainants and the IBA has set up a small Complaints Review Board.[74]

69. ss. 8–13, Sched. 3.

70. J. A. G. Griffith and H. Street, *Principles of Administrative Law* (4th edn), pp. 322–7; J. F. Garner, *Administrative Law* (3rd edn), pp. 316–9.

71. H.C. 514 (1970–71) (*Relations with the Public*). The Government accepted some of the committee's recommendations designed to give the councils more autonomy, but rejected the suggestion that transport users' consultative committees should have power to consider railway fare increases and closures as being inimical to efficiency (Cmnd 5067) (1972).

72. European Communities Act 1972, Sched. 3, Part IV. The Domestic Coal Consumers' Council is to continue, but in accordance with the recommendations of the Select Committee (above) the National Coal Board will cease to be represented on it.

73. Representative expert bodies may, however, perform valuable advisory functions. cf. the advisory Freight Integration Council established under Part I of the Transport Act 1968. See also *Consumer Consultative Machinery in the Nationalized Industries* (HMSO, 1968).

74. See Report of the Committee on Privacy (Cmnd 5102) (1972), 219–49; Television Act 1964, s. 9; Sound Broadcasting Act 1972, s. 2.

Part Three
Parliament and Legislation

Chapter 10 deals first with the historical evolution of Parliament, then
with some of the basic rules about the working of Parliament (for
example, adjournment, prorogation and dissolution), and finally with the
general functions of parliamentary institutions within the scheme of the
British constitution. Once again we observe the close interrelationship of
the Executive and the Legislature. But although the Government is the
dominant force in Parliament and although legislation is primarily a
function of the Government in office, it is an oversimplification to speak
of Cabinet or Prime Ministerial dictatorship.

The next two chapters are about the House of Commons. First there
are the rules relating to the right to vote, the delimitation of
constituencies (a controversial topic), the conduct of electoral campaigns
and the system of voting (with a comment on some alternative systems),
legal disqualifications for membership, the selection of candidates, and
ways of disputing the validity of elections. Second, we shall consider the
functions and procedure of the House of Commons, including the
process of legislation, discussion of financial matters, scrutiny of policy
and administration, and the roles of backbenchers. In these two chapters
we do not ignore the roles of national political parties. Nor can we possibly
ignore the constitutional implications of accession to the Communities.
Chapter 12 includes comments on Community legislation, the effects of
Community membership on financial legislation, and the importance of
improving our rudimentary techniques of scrutinizing the work of
Government (and now the work of the Communities) by specialized
committees.

There follows a chapter on the House of Lords and the means of
resolving conflicts between the two Houses; this includes a review of
recent changes in the membership and functions of the upper House, and
comments on the imaginative but abortive reform scheme of 1968–9.

In chapter 14 we are on well-trodden ground – the privileges and
immunities of the Houses of Parliament and of their members acting in
their capacity as members. Two select committees of the House of
Commons have recently recommended some modest reforms in the law

of parliamentary privilege, but the House is very slow to act in these matters.

Part Three concludes with a chapter on subordinate legislation (mainly legislation by Ministers under powers delegated by Act of Parliament). Delegated legislation could alternatively have been discussed in Part Six of the book ('Administrative Law'), but it has been placed here because it *is* legislation and, like most of Parliament's own general legislative output, it is initiated by Ministers. We shall be particularly concerned with the special safeguards against the abuse of delegated powers. Attitudes towards the dangers inherent in delegated legislation have often been excessively alarmist – a point underlined in the course of this chapter. But some recent developments, and in particular accession to the Communities, have brought the need for adequate safeguards into the foreground once again.

Chapter 10
Parliament:
Background and Framework

Evolution

British institutions are typified by continuity. The hereditary monarchy and many of its trappings belong to the Middle Ages[1] as well as to the present. In the administration of justice, the House of Lords as an appellate body, the Queen's Bench and the Chancery Divisions of the High Court, the justices of the peace and the jury are all clearly traceable to medieval institutions. The lineage of the Privy Council and its successor, the Cabinet, is more obscure, but at least an interrupted chain linking them with the medieval King's Council is discernible. And the history of Parliament goes back to the thirteenth century.

Today the word Parliament is still ambiguous. As a legislative body, Parliament is the Queen in Parliament – the Queen assenting to a bill passed by the House of Lords and the House of Commons, or by the Commons alone under the Parliament Acts procedure. But the word 'Parliament' is often used to mean simply the two Houses. And the term 'member of Parliament' normally means a member of the House of Commons. This element of ambiguity is less conspicuous than in the Middle Ages. At least Parliament is recognized as a political institution regulated by detailed rules governing its structure, membership and functions. As we have noted, in its earliest days Parliament was not an institution but a colloquy[2] – the King and his Council in Parliament – with a fluctuating membership and an inchoate structure, meeting irregularly and for a variety of reasons.

The medieval Parliament was, in a sense, a national assembly, in which the several estates of the realm, the nobles, the prelates and the commonalty, were present in person or through their representatives. But there were early national assemblies which were not called Parliaments; and at least till the early years of the fourteenth century there were national

1. Though the early English monarchs were elected from within the hereditary royal house.
2. See p. 142. See generally, S. B. Chrimes, *English Constitutional Ideas in the Fifteenth Century*, ch. 2; Helen Cam, *Law-Finders and Law-Makers in Medieval England*, ch. 7; Taswell-Langmead's *English Constitutional History* (11th edn), ch. 6.

assemblies called Parliaments to which representatives of the Commons were not summoned. Such an assembly might be convened because the King needed to consult a wider gathering of notables on a matter of State than would be present in his Great Council or Inner Council; or because the King had to raise money and found it expedient to rest his exactions on a broad-based body of consent; or because he wanted to promulgate new laws (though there was at first no necessary connection between legislation and Parliament); or because he wanted to fortify his own position against over-mighty subjects; or because other notables wished to fortify their own position against their rivals and the King. The Model Parliament of 1265 was summoned by Simon de Montfort in the name of the captive Henry III.

To 1265 can be traced the origin of a House of Commons; though more than a century was to pass before the Commons were accepted as being effectively equal to the Lords as a constituent element in Parliament, and not until early Tudor times was there a clearly defined and funda-mental structure of two separate Houses, forming an institution quite distinct from the King's Council. Montfort's Parliament included the noblemen, the bishops and abbots (the Lords Temporal and Spiritual), and the Commons – two knights from each shire, elected by the ancient county courts, and two citizens or burgesses elected by each city or borough. Thus the Commons represented territorial communities; and the 'knight of the shire was the connecting link between the baron and the shopkeeper'.[3] The Commons would attend upon their betters in a humble capacity; but before the end of the reign of Edward III (1327–77) they had asserted themselves, claiming rights to consent to taxation, to concur in new legislation, even to impeach the King's Ministers; and in 1376 they elected their first Speaker. In the reign of Richard II they became still more aggressive, attacking Ministers and claiming privileges of freedom of speech[4] and freedom from arrest. But not until the accession of James I (1603) were they again to play so pugnacious a role in the constitution.

In the fifteenth century the authority of Parliament and its constituent elements fluctuated amidst the turmoil of baronial revolt and civil war. But it must be understood that throughout the medieval period Parliament was as much a court as a deliberative or legislative body. The House of Commons itself was never a court; but the Lords in Parliament, as lineal successors to the Great Council, were a superior court of record, enter-

3. T. B. Macaulay, *History of England*, vol. 1, p. 32. Ecclesiastical proctors, elected representatives of the lower clergy, also sat with the Commons for about a hundred years but withdrew into convocation before 1400.

4. The first such claim was made in respect of Richard Haxey, who was not an elected member. See p. 314.

taining bills, petitions and appeals, and acting as judges in cases of impeachment by the Commons. The House of Lords today is the highest appellate court in the country, as the High Court of Parliament was in the past.

If we view Parliament at the accession of Elizabeth I, we shall find two distinct Houses. The Lords now consisted of hereditary peers and bishops; royal advisers who were not noblemen had been excluded, and the abbots had been ousted when Henry VIII dissolved the monasteries. The membership of the Lords was only about a hundred. The Commons was a larger body; it had been inflated by the creation of new boroughs by the Crown and the integration of Wales within the realm. There were still two knights for each shire, but since 1430 they had been elected by 40s. freeholders. Each borough had two members; the franchise varied according to local charters and customs. There was a residential qualification for members of the Commons, but it was frequently ignored. Property qualifications for members were low; they were to be raised to an inordinately high figure in 1710. Formal Commons Journals were started in 1547.

We have already touched upon the struggles between King and Parliament under the early Stuarts, the Revolution Settlement following the deposition of James II, and the gradual ascendancy of the Cabinet after the Hanoverian succession. This is not a study in constitutional history, and so we shall pass to a statement of some of the basic rules concerning Parliament. Of the detailed rules relating to the franchise, elections, and membership of the two Houses, and the law and practice regulating their functions, interrelationship and privileges, we shall have more to say in later chapters.

Some basic rules
Frequency of Parliaments

Even after Parliament had become established as an institution of government, meetings of Parliament were irregular and the duration of meetings was apt to be short. Elizabeth I (1558–1603) maintained good relations with her Parliaments, but they were sitting for less than six months of her entire reign. James I did without a Parliament from 1614 to 1621. He was surpassed by his son, Charles I, who ruled without Parliament from 1629 to 1640. James II prorogued Parliament a few months after his accession in 1685, and never summoned it to meet again.

The Bill of Rights 1689 provided that Parliament 'ought to be held frequently'. By virtue of the Meeting of Parliament Act 1694 (which is still in force) not more than three years must elapse between the dissolution of one Parliament and the meeting of its successor. In practice, and by convention, Parliament must be summoned to meet each year. The most remunerative taxes and grants of supply to the Crown are provided by Act of Parliament annually; and authority for the maintenance of the army and its discipline requires annual renewal by the authority of both Houses.

The two Houses. The House of Commons is a wholly elected body; the House of Lords is wholly non-elected. Since the late Middle Ages it has been an accepted rule that the two Houses meet, deliberate and vote separately. There is no statutory or other provision for joint sessions, though for certain purposes there can be joint select committees. A bill may be introduced in either House unless it is a Finance Bill (authorizing taxation) or a Consolidated Fund or Appropriation Bill (authorizing national expenditure), in which case convention and the privileges of the Commons require that it be introduced in that House and by a Minister. Other money bills may now be introduced in the Lords (H.C.S.O. No. 58A). But it is a constitutional convention, and one of fundamental importance, that every amendment or motion to authorize central government expenditure, or to increase or impose a tax, must have the Queen's recommendation[5] – that is to say, it must be introduced or moved by a Minister. This necessarily implies that the power of the purse belongs to the Government and not to private members. Hence, if a bill introduced by a private member requires the expenditure of public money for the fulfilment of its purposes – and it does so require more often than not – the member must be able to persuade a Minister to move a financial resolution in the House; otherwise the bill cannot be passed. No such restriction applies in the United States Congress or in a number of other foreign legislatures.

The customary common law rule is that a bill cannot become law unless it has been passed by both Houses and assented to by the Queen. Under the Parliament Acts 1911 and 1949 most classes of bills may, after a period of delay, be presented for the royal assent, although they have not been passed by the Lords.[6]

Duration of a Parliament

In 1694 it was enacted that no Parliament was to last more than three years. This provision was repealed by the Septennial Act 1715 (passed in the state of alarm engendered by the first Jacobite revolt) which extended

5. These rules are partly embodied in standing orders of the House (S.O. Nos. 58, 58A (August 1971), 89–91).

6. See pp. 304–6.

the maximum duration of a Parliament to seven years. The Parliament Act 1911 reduced this period to five years (s. 7), and laid it down that the new procedure whereby a bill could be presented for assent without the Lords' consent was not to apply to bills to prolong the life of Parliament (s. 2(1)); these rules are still in force. Parliament may, however, prolong its own life by an Act passed in the normal manner. Thus, the Parliament elected in 1910 was prolonged by annual Acts during the First World War, and was not dissolved till November 1918; the Parliament elected in 1935 was similarly prolonged during the Second World War and was dissolved in June 1945. An attempt by a Government to procure the deferment of a General Election in any situation other than one of armed conflict would provoke a serious constitutional crisis.

Parliament may be, and nearly always is, dissolved by the exercise of the royal prerogative before its five-year term comes to an end. We have already considered the constitutional conventions regulating the exercise of this prerogative.[7] The main practical effect of these conventions (save in those circumstances in which the Queen is entitled to refuse a request for dissolution) is to enable the Prime Minister to choose the most advantageous, or least disadvantageous, date for a General Election. The fact that this power lies in his hands tends both to enhance his stature within the Government and to rally the ranks of party waverers once it is suspected that a dissolution may be imminent. If the power to dissolve were to be eliminated (so that we had Parliaments of fixed duration) or narrowly restricted, one could expect party discipline within the House of Commons to be more difficult to enforce.

The modern practice is for the Prime Minister to announce the date of the dissolution and election (after he has tendered the necessary advice to Her Majesty) about ten days before the actual dissolution. Dissolution is effected by a royal proclamation in Council, which also names the date for the summoning of the new Parliament; under electoral rules, this must be not less than twenty week-days after the dissolution. In practice polling day will be about a month after the announcement of the intended dissolution,[8] and a couple of weeks will elapse thereafter before the new Parliament meets.

The proclamation is followed immediately by an Order in Council, directing the Lord Chancellor to issue writs to the returning officer (who will be the mayor or chairman of a local authority or the sheriff of a county) in each constituency to cause an election to be held on the day named, and writs of summons to individual peeers and bishops to attend the meeting of the new Parliament.

7. See pp. 104–8.
8. See R. L. Leonard, *Elections in Britain*, pp. 7–8.

The commencement of a Parliament is accompanied by picturesque ceremonial. Parliament is formally opened by Lords Commissioners in the House of Lords. The Commons repair to their own chamber to elect a Speaker and swear in members. The following day or shortly afterwards, Her Majesty attends in person to read the Queen's speech in the House of Lords;[9] this speech is prepared for her under the direction of the Prime Minister, and outlines the Government's legislative programme for the session and its broad policies. The Commons are present at the bar of the House of Lords. The main substantive business of the new Parliament begins with a general debate in each House on the address in reply to the Queen's speech.

At common law, Parliament was dissolved automatically by a demise of the Crown (the death or abdication of the monarch). This rule was abrogated by statute in 1707. Under the present law[10] the effects of a demise of the Crown are: (i) the two Houses are to meet immediately if prorogued or adjourned; and (ii) if the demise of the Crown occurs while Parliament is dissolved, the *old* Parliament is to meet and, subject to a further dissolution, may continue in being for six months. This could still lead to a ridiculous anomaly, if a new House of Commons had already been elected but had not yet met.

Sessions: prorogation and adjournment. It is the invariable custom for the life of a Parliament to be divided up into a number of sessions. These are usually of about one year's duration, though there is no fixed practice. If Parliament were not to sit at all for a full year, some vital Acts which have to be renewed or passed annually would lapse. A speech from the throne is read by the Queen in the Lords, with the Commons in attendance, at the opening of each session. Typically, a session will begin and end in October and will be interspersed with adjournments each night, at weekends, at Christmas, Easter and Whitsun, and during the long summer recess beginning late in July. It is possible for the Commons to be sitting while the Lords are adjourned. Nowadays the Commons sit for about 160 days altogether during a calendar year. Each House determines, on the Government's initiative, on which dates it will adjourn and re-assemble.

A session of Parliament is terminated by prorogation, a prerogative act; a short formal speech is made on behalf of the Queen, summarizing the work done during the session, and then Parliament stands prorogued till a named date, which (unless prorogation precedes a dissolution) will be

9. If she is unable to attend personally, the Lord Chancellor reads it on her behalf.
10. Succession to the Crown Act 1707; Meeting of Parliament Act 1797; Representation of the People Act 1867.

only a few days later, when a new session will be opened by the reading of the Queen's speech. These dates are decided on the Government's advice. Prorogation has the effect of causing all public bills that have not yet passed into law to lapse; if they are to be reintroduced in the new session they must go through all their stages again. Private bills (i.e. bills of a local or personal character) are carried forward into the new session by resolution of each House, so that they can be continued at the stage they have already reached. The main casualties of a prorogation will be public bills introduced by private members (private members' bills) but occasionally bills introduced by Ministers (Government bills) will lapse too. Prorogation therefore serves two purposes: to induce the Government to manage its legislative programme efficiently, and to discourage back-benchers from getting above themselves.

The reason why Parliament is adjourned, instead of standing prorogued, in midsummer is strictly practical. In the first place, if it becomes necessary to recall a prorogued Parliament to deal with a matter of unexpected urgency, a royal proclamation has to be issued. It is simpler and may be more expeditious to reassemble an adjourned Parliament; this can be done by the Speaker and the Lord Chancellor acting on the Prime Minister's request.[11] Secondly, at the end of a summer recess it is often desirable to spend a few days dealing with unfinished legislative business (for example, considering late Lords' amendments to Government bills), debating an important issue that has arisen during the recess or making policy announcements before the session terminates.

The role of Parliament

It has often been said that Parliament has three main constitutional functions: making laws; controlling national expenditure and taxation; and a third class of function, comprising criticism of national policy, scrutiny of central administration, and procuring the redress of individual grievances.

A preliminary difficulty with this classification is that the word 'Parliament' is being used in different senses.[12] There are more serious difficulties

11. This practice is provided for in standing orders of the House of Commons (S.O. No. 122) and sessional orders of the House of Lords. The Speaker and the Lord Chancellor are not obliged to comply with the Prime Minister's request, but it would be remarkable if they were to refuse unless no substantial reason for the request was supplied.

Parliament must also be summoned to meet within five days if a royal proclamation of a state of emergency is made under the Emergency Powers Acts 1920 and 1964. See ch. 23.

12. See p. 229.

inherent in any classification by reference to function when expressed in legal or institutional terms. The familiar classification is too much at variance with the facts. Legislation is primarily a function of Government. Even if one ignores the mass of non-parliamentary or subordinate legislation made by the Queen in Council or Ministers, a very large majority of Government bills, introduced into Parliament by Ministers, are passed into law substantially in their original form. In 1948–9, 102 Government bills were introduced and 101 were passed. In 1970–71, seventy-seven Government bills were introduced and all but one were passed. The year 1969 happened to be a particularly bad one for the Government's legislative programme; exceptions do not prove rules, but the general rule stands out plainly enough. In the three sessions from 1968 to 1971, forty out of 293 private members' bills actually introduced became law.[13] Again, Parliament 'controls' national finance in the formal sense that its sanction is needed for the imposition of taxation and the authorization of expenditure; but bills authorizing public expenditure are dominated even more than the content of ordinary legislation by the will of the Government, and in particular the views of the Treasury. A lot of time in the House of Commons is spent on debating what are in form financial matters; but the House has largely given up the pretence that it has real authority over these measures, and most debates on public expenditure concentrate on aspects of policy and administration to which questions of expenditure may be only peripheral.

The deeper one digs, the bigger yawns the gulf between appearance and reality. Neither Parliament nor the House of Commons acts as a collective entity save on special and rare occasions. In recent years political scientists, though prone to disparage or be ignorant of legal rules, have rightly concentrated their attention on party organization and activity in and out of Parliament;[14] the role of pressure groups operating on Ministers, civil servants, parties and M.P.s; the potential expansion of select scrutinizing committees; the meaning of public opinion;[15] and the nature of General Elections to the House of Commons. In other words, parliamentary institutions cannot meaningfully be considered in isolation from the forces which influence decisions; and some of those decisions may not even require to be formally registered by Parliament. Having made this point, we must reiterate that this is a book about constitutional law and not a general work on British government. Our main emphasis must, therefore,

13. Corrected figures, taken from Burton and Drewry (1972) 25 *Parliamentary Affairs* 123 at 126.

14. The last major work written by Sir Ivor Jennings, the most eminent of modern British constitutional lawyers, was a three-volume treatise on *Party Politics*.

15. See especially David Butler and Donald Stokes, *Political Change in Britain*.

be placed on aspects of parliamentary institutions which are not necessarily the most important.

Against this complex background, the question: What is the constitutional role (or what are the functions) of Parliament? becomes altogether too ambiguous. Answers will depend on whether one is thinking of the Queen in Parliament, the two Houses, or the House of Commons alone; on whether one is thinking of all the members on the Government side, or of those members on the Government side who are not Ministers, or of members on the Opposition side; on whether one is thinking of the political activities of members outside as well as inside Parliament. One can set out the following general propositions:

1. The House of Commons gives the Government a legitimate foundation. The Prime Minister must be that person who is best able to command the support of a majority of members of the House; he is normally the leader of the majority party; the majority party in the House is identified by the party affiliations of the successful candidates in individual constituencies at a General Election. The Prime Minister forms a Government;[16] the members of the Government must be or become members of one or other House. Thereafter supporters of the Government in the House of Commons sustain it in office by thwarting the Opposition's motions of censure and enabling the Government to enact its legislative programme.

2. The role of the Opposition in the House of Commons must be conditioned by the constant need to present itself to the electorate as the alternative Government. This objective can be frustrating when the next General Election may be four years distant. But it will not be thought of as unattainable, for the main political parties are broadly based; they are not reflections of a permanent majority or minority group (the situation in Northern Ireland was essentially different); there is a sizeable floating vote; we have free elections; only twice this century has the same party won three consecutive General Elections.[17] To say that the function of the Opposition is to oppose would be an over-simplification; a substantial majority of Government bills are passed without any move to reject them, and there is a large area of common ground between the two main parties on matters of national policy. The Prime Minister often gives the Leader of the Opposition confidential information and consults with him privately on non-party matters of national concern. But in fulfilling its role the

16. The Government, when formed, does not (as in some countries) have to obtain a formal parliamentary vote of confidence.

17. The Liberals in 1906 and 1910 (twice), though in the 1910 elections they failed to obtain an overall majority of seats in the Commons and retained office only with the support of minority parties; and the Conservatives in 1951, 1955 and 1959.

Opposition will frequently attack the Government in debate and at question time on issues of principle and detail. Parliament is the only public forum in which Ministers are obliged to present reasoned (and sometimes unprepared) answers to these criticisms. And indirectly the Opposition may influence major policy decisions. A Government will sometimes adopt or adapt, without acknowledgement, popular Opposition policies (for example, on immigration) in order to improve or retrieve its own standing in the eyes of the electorate.

3. Irrespective of the political complexion of the Government in office, the Conservative Party has maintained a large permanent majority in the House of Lords. But because of the peculiar composition and limited powers of the upper House, the roles of Government and Opposition in the Lords cannot be considered in the same terms as in the Commons. Perhaps incongruously, it is possible to review the constitutional functions of the House of Lords more coherently than those of the House of Commons.[18]

4. In both Houses, and particularly in the Commons, the Government's policies and its conduct of administration are subjected to open scrutiny; and adverse criticism does not come only from members on the Opposition side. To this extent Parliament is a 'grand inquest of the nation'. Voting figures in the division lobbies tell only part of the story. Criticism often takes the form of putting down detailed amendments to Government bills; these amendments are not necessarily, or indeed usually, prompted by considerations of party politics and Ministers will seldom be able to afford merely to brush them aside. Fuller investigation of aspects of policy and administration will be a matter for select scrutinizing committees.

5. The House of Commons provides a forum for ventilating the grievances of individuals, localities and organized groups. An M.P. may raise such an issue by asking a parliamentary question, raising the matter in debate (especially the debate on the daily adjournment of the House), putting down amendments to bills, or seeking to introduce a private member's bill himself. However, effective *redress* for injustices suffered by individuals at the hands of the Administration is more likely to be achieved outside Parliament, by members' letters and other representations to Ministers, or through an inquiry by the Parliamentary Commissioner for Administration into a complaint of maladministration referred to him by an M.P., through a more formal committee or tribunal of inquiry or by statutory machinery for appeal or by judicial review.

6. The House of Commons links the general public, local and national political parties, organized interest groups, private members and Ministers

18. See ch. 13.

in a network of relationships. The House is a centre for intercommunication. So important is this role that if a House of Commons did not exist, one would have to be invented.

7. The publicity given to its proceedings, moreover, tends to enhance public interest in public affairs, and to educate and inform by the wider diffusion of facts, arguments and statements of policy. This tendency must not be exaggerated. Few people read *Hansard*; in England only three daily newspapers, with a total circulation of barely two millions, offer even a moderately adequate coverage of parliamentary proceedings; most of the electorate now obtains its information about current affairs mainly from television programmes, and party political broadcasts are not popular with viewers except during an election campaign; professions of intent by politicians are regarded with widespread scepticism; because the outcome of divisions in the House of Commons is normally a foregone conclusion, parliamentary debates fail to attract the attention given to contests where the result is in doubt.

8. The promotion of private bills in Parliament is still the principal means whereby local authorities and other public bodies obtain special legal powers beyond those granted by the general law of the land. In the eighteenth century, and for a large part of the nineteenth, the private Act was the most common form of legislation. For the past hundred years or so, the public general Act has taken over the leading role, but private legislation is still important. Some of these themes will be developed in the course of the next three chapters.[19]

19. For a helpful comparative study, see K. Bradshaw and D. Pring, *Parliament and Congress* (1972).

Chapter 11
The House of Commons:
Elections and Members

Background

Till 1832 the later medieval basis of representation in the House of Commons was almost unchanged. Each county returned two members, elected by 40s. freeholders; each borough returned two members, elected on franchises broad and narrow. Upon community representation there had been superimposed in 1603 a special form of corporate representation – a handful of members elected for university constituencies by graduates of those universities. Since the close of the Middle Ages the balance of representation had been tilted in favour of the towns by the granting of charters of incorporation to new boroughs. But some of the ancient boroughs had become depopulated; still they returned their two members. Several of the biggest new industrial towns in the North and the Midlands had no separate representation at all. Where the electorates were tiny, seats would be in the pockets of wealthy noblemen, who bought votes and installed their own nominees in the Commons. Boroughs were sold or sold themselves. Bribery of voters by candidates and their patrons was also rampant at elections in those constituencies where the electorate was not too large to be unmanageable. Nepotism, bribery and corruption were similarly the dominant elements in party management in the House, particularly from the ascendancy of Walpole till the emergence of Pitt the Younger. Government was by the propertied classes, and almost inevitably for the propertied classes; and despite the preponderance of borough seats in the Commons, the landed interest was dominant, and overwhelmingly dominant in the Lords and in the Ministry.

The movement for parliamentary reform, checked in its early stages by reaction against the excesses of the French Revolution, and the fear of change inspired first by the Revolutionary and Napoleonic wars and then by signs of ferment among the exploited urban masses at home, gathered momentum in the late 1820s. Religious disqualifications for membership of the House of Commons were modified; the disabilities of nonconformists were removed in 1828 and those of Roman Catholics in 1829. (Jews had to wait for this privilege till 1858, Quakers till 1868 and non-believers till 1888). But only 5 per cent of the adult population were enfranchised by 1831. Votes and seats for women lay nearly a century away.

The immediate effects of the intensely controversial Representation of the People Act 1832 (the Great Reform Act) were hardly dramatic. The electorate was increased to 7 per cent; the county franchise was extended beyond freeholders to include holders of other substantial interests in land, and a uniform franchise comprising all male householders of dwellings worth £10 a year was established for the towns. More important were the abolition of the separate representation of depopulated boroughs and the creation of new constituencies in the industrial areas. Patronage and corrupt practices in Government and Parliament substantially diminished. Bribery and corrupt practices at elections had passed their heyday, though they continued to flourish for another half century.[1] Universal suffrage and democracy were concepts still abhorred by all but a few radical visionaries; but the urban middle classes were now more than fairly represented in the Commons; the political influence of the landed gentry was on the wane; the Commons became the dominant House, and modern principles of ministerial responsibility took root; and if *laissez faire* was the dominant economic philosophy, political liberalism was not totally unresponsive to heretical opinions about social justice.

The property qualification for membership of the House was abolished in 1858. In 1867 came the second major instalment of electoral reform. The electorate was doubled: in the counties property qualifications for the franchise were retained but in a relaxed form; in the boroughs all householders and men occupying £10 a year lodgings were given the vote. With the enfranchisement of the urban artisan class, Parliament discovered a new concern for public education, public health and other rudimentary social services, and trade unionism received the full accolade of legitimacy. The age of collectivism began to flourish. The passage of the Second Reform Act, moreover, gave impetus to a new development, of the greatest constitutional importance – the organization of mass political parties on a national scale.

The secret ballot was introduced in 1872. In 1883 the law relating to corrupt and illegal practices at elections was redefined in strict terms. The Representation of the People Act 1884 introduced a common franchise for town and country; this enfranchised a large proportion of agricultural workers, and about two-thirds of the adult male population now had the right to vote. By virtue of the Redistribution of Seats Act 1885, the single-member constituency became the general rule, and inequalities between constituency electorates were reduced.

1. cf. Cornelius O'Leary, *The Elimination of Corrupt Practices in British Elections, 1868–1911*.

The following have been the main twentieth century reforms.[2] In 1918 universal manhood suffrage was introduced, and women over thirty were given the vote for the first time and on the same basis. In 1928 the voting age for women was reduced to twenty-one. In 1944 standing non-political machinery was established for the delimitation of parliamentary constituencies; changes in the machinery were made in 1949 and 1958. By the Representation of the People Act 1948, plural voting was ended; the university seats were abolished, and so was the extra vote accorded to occupiers of business premises in a constituency and their spouses; the surviving two-member constituencies were split up into single-member constituencies, and the electoral system was based roughly on the principle of one man (or woman), one vote, one value.[3] By the Representation of the People Act 1969 the minimum voting age was reduced from twenty-one to eighteen. The House of Commons Disqualification Act 1957 rationalized the law relating to disqualifications for membership of the House.

The modern electoral system
The franchise

In order to exercise the franchise in a parliamentary constituency, a person must be included in the electoral register for that constituency. The register is compiled annually, on the basis of information provided by householders, by the registration officer, who will be the clerk to a local authority. A person, though legally qualified to vote in every other respect, will not be permitted to vote if his name is not on the register.

To be included in the register, a person must[4]

1. be eighteen years of age, or be due to attain his eighteenth birthday within twelve months of the publication of the register, thus becoming eligible to vote in an election held after his birthday;

2. be a British subject or a citizen of the Republic of Ireland;

3. not be subject to any legal incapacity;[5]

and

4. be resident in the constituency on the qualifying date (10 October in Great Britain)[6] for compiling the register.

2. See further David Butler, *The British Electoral System since 1918* (2nd edn).
3. Electoral law was then consolidated by the Representation of the People Act 1949 which, subject to various amendments, remains the basis of the present law. The law relating to delimitation of constituencies is based on the House of Commons (Redistribution of Seats) Acts 1949 and 1958; see p. 245.
4. Representation of the People Act 1949, s. 1, as amended by s. 1 of the Representation of the People Act 1969.
5. See p. 244.
6. Electoral Registers Act 1953.

The following points should be noted:

(a) It is a criminal offence for a person to vote in more than one constituency even though his name appears on the electoral register for each constituency. Again, it is an offence to vote if one knows or has reasonable grounds for believing that, notwithstanding one's appearance on the electoral register, one is subject to a legal disqualification. Hence although absence from the register is conclusive of inability to vote, presence on the register is not conclusive of entitlement to vote.

(b) British subjects include not only persons 'belonging' to the United Kingdom itself but all citizens of the United Kingdom and Colonies, and all persons who are citizens of independent Commonwealth countries in terms of their own laws.[7] The fact that the laws of many independent Commonwealth countries do not designate their own citizens as British subjects is immaterial; what matters is the definition of British subject in United Kingdom law. Citizens of the Republic of Ireland (which is not a Commonwealth country) are not British subjects in United Kingdom law, but they are excluded from the definition of aliens[8] and are accorded much the same rights and privileges in the United Kingdom as citizens of Commonwealth countries.[9]

(c) To be included in the register, a person who is otherwise qualified needs to be 'resident' at an address in the constituency only on the qualifying date. No *period* of residence is necessary, except in Northern Ireland where three months' continuous residence is required. A person ought not to be put on the register unless his *ordinary* place of residence[10] is in the constituency. However, according to a recent decision of the Court of Appeal, university students pursuing their courses of study are entitled to be registered in the constituency where they are residing for that purpose.[11]

7. British Nationality Act 1948, s. 1(3) as amended. See pp. 420–21. Temporary anomalies can arise. At the end of 1972 Pakistan (which had left the Commonwealth) was still listed in the British Nationality Act 1948, but Bangladesh (which had joined the Commonwealth) was not. Presumably citizens of Bangladesh qualified for inclusion on the register as if they were still citizens of Pakistan; but it was arguable that citizens of Pakistan ceased to be British subjects in United Kingdom law when Pakistan left the Commonwealth.

8. ibid., s. 32(1).

9. See generally British Nationality Act 1948, s. 3(2); Ireland Act 1949, s. 2; and more specifically, section 1 of the Representation of the People Act 1949.

10. A prison will not be accepted as an address for the registration of a person incarcerated there; nor is a mental hospital a place of residence for registration purposes.

11. *Fox* v. *Stirk* [1970] 2 Q.B. 463. If they have a home in another constituency, they can be registered there as well. They must not, of course, vote in more than one constituency. See also Susan Maidment [1971] *Public Law* 25.

(d) Persons with service qualifications (members of the armed forces, Crown servants and British Council officials overseas, and their spouses living overseas with them), and merchant seamen, are entitled to be treated as if they were resident in a constituency on the qualifying date, provided that they would have been so resident but for their assignment elsewhere.[12]

Disqualification. The following classes of persons are not entitled to exercise the franchise, even if their names appear on the electoral register.

(i) Aliens.[13]

(ii) Infants (persons under eighteen years of age).

(iii) Peers, other than peers of Ireland. Abolition of this disqualification was envisaged by the Parliament Bill withdrawn in 1969.

(iv) Persons serving sentences of imprisonment.[14]

(v) Persons convicted of corrupt practices at elections (who are disfranchised for five years); and persons convicted of illegal practices at elections (election offences of a lesser order), who are also disfranchised for five years but only in respect of the constituency in question. The line drawn between corrupt and illegal practices is not altogether logical. To incur unauthorized expenditure to promote the election of a candidate is a corrupt practice; to publish a false statement that a candidate has withdrawn from the contest is an illegal practice.

The register

The registration officer must issue a provisional electoral register for the constituency on 28 November; this is to be exhibited in public libraries and other public buildings. Any person may object to the inclusion or exclusion of any name by 16 December; the registration officer must hear and determine any objection and may rectify the register accordingly. An appeal lies from his determinations to the county court and thence, on a point of law, to the Court of Appeal; alternatively his determination, or that of the county court judge, may be impeached before a Divisional Court of the Queen's Bench Division.[15] The register for the constituency

12. See pp. 242, 249.

13. This term excludes citizens of the Republic of Ireland (see above). British protected persons are not British subjects and are not, it seems, entitled to be registered or to vote, or (probably) to be elected to Parliament.

14. Representation of the People Act 1969, s. 4. Such a person may, of course, have been correctly included in the electoral register before his term of detention began.

15. By an application, made by a party aggrieved, for an order of certiorari to quash the determination (for example, for excess of jurisdiction) or for an order of mandamus to compel him to perform his public duty.

comes into force on 16 February and is operative for any election held there during the following twelve months.

Delimitation of constituencies

In the American Constitution it is laid down[16] that no state shall deny any person within its jurisdiction 'the equal protection of the laws'. In *Baker* v. *Carr* (1962),[17] one of the most remarkable and influential decisions ever given by the United States Supreme Court, it was held that the equal protection clause implied the doctrine of 'one man, one vote, one value', so that electoral districts (constituencies) established under state law for the federal House of Representatives had to have approximately equal numbers of electors. This decision, and others that followed,[18] led to a massive legislative reapportionment of electoral districts not only for congressional elections but also at the state and local levels so as to modify the prevailing over-representation of sparsely populated rural areas.

No decision of a United Kingdom court could propel Parliament willy-nilly into radical reform. The present machinery for constituency delimitation, based on a scheme introduced in 1944,[19] is designed to work impartially and to promote approximately equal electorates; but the last word rests with Parliament, and politics tends to keep creeping in.

Under the House of Commons (Redistribution of Seats) Acts 1949 and 1958, four Boundary Commissions, one each for England, Scotland, Wales and Northern Ireland, are charged with the duties of reviewing representation in the House of Commons, and submitting to the Secretary of State reports recommending such redistribution of seats as may be necessary at intervals of not less than ten or more than fifteen years. As soon as may be after they have reported, the Home Secretary must lay their reports before Parliament, *together with* drafts of Orders in Council giving effect, with or without modifications, to their recommendations for boundary changes. The Acts thus permit the Home Secretary to vary but

16. Fourteenth Amendment, s. 1.
17. 369 U.S. 186 (1962).
18. See, for example, *Reynolds* v. *Sims* 377 U.S. 533 (1964) (principle of broadly equal electoral districts held to govern representation in *both* houses of a state legislature; contrast the position in the United States Senate).
19. See generally David Butler, *The British Electoral System since 1918* (2nd edn). The original Act was the House of Commons (Redistribution of Seats) Act 1944. There had been no general redistribution since 1918 despite the movement of population from city centres to suburbs. The movement was accelerated during and after the Second World War; and new towns to syphon off population from the big cities were deliberately created and expanded as an act of policy.

not to ignore or reject the recommendations. If the draft Orders are approved by resolutions of each House, Orders in Council will then be made, and will have effect at the next General Election.

The chairman of each Commission is the Speaker of the House of Commons; the deputy chairman must be a superior judge; each Commission has two other members who are not to be M.P.s, and is advised by senior public officials – in England, the Registrar-General and the Director-General of Ordnance Survey. The Commissions are guided by a number of rules laid down in the Acts. When a Commission has provisionally decided to recommend changes, it must give public notice of its proposals in the constituencies concerned and invite representations to be made to it; it may conduct local inquiries. The total number of constituencies (all of which are to be represented by a single member) for Great Britain is not to be substantially greater or less than 613; this number is to include at least seventy-one Scottish and thirty-five Welsh constituencies; there are also to be twelve constituencies in Northern Ireland. The electorate of a constituency is to be as near as practicable to a quota ascertained by dividing the total electorate within the region covered by a Commission by the number of constituencies in that region; deviations from the quota are permissible in order to respect local government boundaries or for reasons of geographical dispersal. Scotland and Wales are over-represented in strictly mathematical terms, but most of their constituencies with small electorates are large in area, sparsely populated and with mediocre internal communications. Northern Ireland was under-represented at Westminster because it had its own Parliament at Stormont. The total number of United Kingdom constituencies is not fixed by Act of Parliament; since 1955, however, it has been 630.[20] At the next General Election after 1970 it is likely to be 635.

Each set of proposals by the Commissions has proved controversial. The first reports of the Commissioners, in 1948, recommended very extensive boundary changes in the light of shifts in the distribution of population since 1918; the Commission for England also deviated from the rules to give an advantageous weightage to rural areas, which happened to be mainly Conservative; the Labour Government redressed the balance by introducing amending legislation to add seventeen urban seats, eight of which were in fact won in 1950 by Conservative candidates. The 1954 reports of the Commissions were implemented in full but aroused a good deal of local resentment. Two unsuccessful attempts were made to impugn the validity of recommendations or draft Orders in Council in the courts.[21]

20. By virtue of Orders in Council made under the House of Commons (Redistribution of Seats) Acts.

21. *Hammersmith B.C.* v. *Boundary Commission for England, The Times,* 15 December

For technical reasons it was not easy to see how in practice the courts could be persuaded to go into the question of *vires*.[22] The 1969 recommendations[23] precipitated a crisis. If they had been fully implemented, the Labour Party might possibly have lost about ten seats at the next election, mainly through the disappearance of depopulated urban constituencies. Some weeks after they had been received, the Home Secretary presented them to Parliament[24] but did not produce draft Orders in Council to give effect to them, either with or without amendment. Instead, the Government decided to implement them only in part, explaining that local government areas were being subjected to a comprehensive review, that there ought not to be too big a discrepancy between local government and parliamentary constituency boundaries, and that it would be undesirable to have two major delimitations within the course of a few years. The Home Secretary introduced a new House of Commons (Redistribution of Seats) Bill, implementing the recommendations for Greater London and a few very large constituencies but absolving him from performance of his

---

1954 (attempt to obtain mandatory injunction to direct the Commission to withdraw its recommendations *after* it had reported; held, the Commission had no power to do this); *Harper* v. *Home Secretary* [1955] Ch. 238 (attempt to prevent draft Order in Council, already approved by both Houses, from being presented to Her Majesty in Council). See generally James T. Craig [1959] *Public Law* 23.

22. Among the difficulties are the unavailability of injunctions against Crown servants acting as such (Crown Proceedings Act 1947, s. 21), the fact that the courts are fearful of encroaching on parliamentary privilege by interfering with a 'proceeding in Parliament' (though this objection would not arise if there were a reasonable interval between publication of the report and laying before Parliament) and the provision of the 1949 Act (unaffected by the 1958 Act) that the validity of an Order in Council thus made cannot be called in question in any legal proceedings whatsoever (s. 3(7)). In an extreme case a court might nevertheless be persuaded to intervene; and in any event it might be possible to obtain an order of mandamus to compel the Home Secretary to comply with his express statutory duties (see text).

23. The period between reviews had been extended to a maximum of fifteen years by the 1958 Act.

24. The reports were published as Command Papers, and presented to the House of Commons (see S.O. No. 119) by being placed in the Votes and Proceedings Office. It was at first claimed on behalf of the Home Secretary that they had not been 'laid' before Parliament within the meaning of the parent Act; hence the duty to lay draft Orders in Council at the same time did not arise. When the reports were presented to the House a second time, accompanied by draft Orders (see below), they were expressed to have been laid in pursuance of the Act; again they were deposited in the Votes and Proceedings Office. It seems artificial in the extreme to contend that the first laying was not a performance of a statutory duty but an act of obedience to Her Majesty's command. cf. *Att.-Gen.* v. *De Keyser's Royal Hotel Ltd* [1920] A.C. 508; pp. 121–3 above. And see *R.* v. *Immigration Appeal Tribunal, ex p. Joyles* [1972] 1 W.L.R. 1390, showing that presenting a Command Paper to the House *is* laying within the meaning of the Act.

existing statutory duty to give effect to the Commissions' recommendations. The Opposition and some independent critics maintained that the bill involved gerrymandering.[25] The Conservative majority in the Lords passed the bill but only subject to wrecking amendments. The two Houses adjourned for the summer recess in a state of deadlock, with the Home Secretary facing the prospect of an application to the High Court for an order of mandamus to compel him to carry out his legal duties. When Parliament reassembled, the Home Secretary moved compromise amendments, and warned that if the Lords rejected them, he would lay all the recommendations for constituency changes together with draft Orders giving effect to them, but would ask Government supporters not to approve any of them. The Lords rejected the Commons' amendments to the bill. The application for mandamus was withdrawn,[26] the Home Secretary having declared that he would comply with his statutory duty. The bill lapsed on prorogation, and no attempt was made the following session to override the Lords under the Parliament Acts procedure. Instead, the reports and draft Orders giving effect to them were laid before the Commons by the Home Secretary; and the draft Orders were duly voted down by the House.[27] The subsequent General Election in 1970 was therefore conducted on the basis of the 1954 delimitation.

In November 1970 the new Conservative Home Secretary reintroduced the draft Orders and they were given parliamentary approval.[28]

Method of voting

The general rule is that on election day voters must go in person to the appropriate polling station in their constituency, where they will be handed a ballot paper listing the names of the candidates. The voter enters a polling booth and makes a cross in a space alongside the name of one candidate; the voter folds the ballot paper and drops it into a sealed ballot box. The fiction that a voter chooses the most suitable candidate irre-

25. See also George Brown, *In My Way*, pp. 255–6. But Lord George-Brown had already resigned from the Government at the relevant time.

26. *R.* v. *Home Secretary, ex p. McWhirter, The Times*, 21 October 1969. No order was made as to costs and the Home Secretary agreed to make an *ex gratia* payment to the costs of the applicant, a voter in one of the constituencies affected by the English Commission's recommendations. The several interesting issues raised by the application (for example, whether it constituted an impeachment of 'proceedings in Parliament'; see ch. 14) were not determined.

27. 791 H.C. Deb. 428–571 (12 November 1969). The Attorney-General, winding up the debate for the Government, declared (col. 550) that the Home Secretary's actions had been 'lawful . . . sensible and wise', and that only 'the malicious and the misinformed could be capable of taking any other view'.

28. S.I. 1970, Nos. 1674, 1675, 1678, 1680.

spective of his party affiliations was maintained by a rule precluding the incorporation in the ballot paper of words indicating the political attitudes of candidates – a rule which caused some difficulty not long ago in a Welsh constituency where there were three candidates named Jones – till section 2 of the Representation of the People Act 1969 permitted the insertion of up to six words descriptive of the candidate's political associations.

In the celebrated case of *Ashby* v. *White* (1703)[29] it was held that the right to vote was in the nature of a proprietary right, and that a returning officer refusing for improper motives to allow a qualified elector to cast his vote was liable in damages. Under section 50 of the Representation of the People Act 1949, no civil liability is incurred by an election officer in respect of a breach of his official duties, though he may be criminally liable. No election officer may refuse to give a ballot paper to a person whose name appears on the register. If he has grounds for believing that any such person is legally disqualified (for example, by reason of infancy, or because he has already voted) it is his duty so to warn him; if that person nevertheless proceeds to vote though disqualified, he may be prosecuted for an election offence.

Special arrangements are made for casting of votes by persons with service qualifications and by persons who have applied to be registered as absent voters. As a general rule, a service voter may vote by post or by proxy; an absent voter (for example, one who is unlikely to be able to vote in person by reason of the nature of his employment which often takes him outside the constituency, or because of physical infirmity or religious observance) may vote by post.

At the close of the polls (9 or 10 p.m.) the ballot boxes are transported to a central counting station in the constituency and emptied, and the ballot papers are counted together with postal and proxy votes. The candidate with the largest number of votes is declared by the returning officer to be elected. There is no requirement that a candidate obtain a minimum percentage of the total vote to be elected.

By-elections to fill vacancies caused by death, resignation or other cause are conducted in essentially the same manner.

The British system of election is often called 'first past the post'. It has been criticized as unfair to small parties. For example, at the General Election of 1964, Liberal candidates obtained 11·2 per cent of the national vote but only nine (i.e. 1·4 per cent) of the seats in the House; in those constituencies where they had put up candidates, the Liberals obtained an average of 18·5 per cent of the vote. The figures above speak of injustice. But the figures tell only part of the story. A General Election is, in effect, the choice of a Government. A party winning 48 per cent of the national

29. 2 Ld. Raym. 938.

vote is almost certain to have an overall majority of seats in the House.[30] Many people who might otherwise be inclined to vote for Liberal candidates either abstain from voting or vote for a candidate of one of the two major parties in order not to 'waste' their vote; they will believe (probably rightly) that the election of a few more Liberal members will not affect the formation of the next Government. If potential Liberal voters were made to feel that their votes would really count, the fortunes of the party might revive dramatically,[31] at least in the short term.

There is obviously a case for reforming the electoral system with a view to reducing the discrepancy between votes cast for and seats won by a party campaigning on a national scale. The most favoured systems[32] are the alternative vote and proportional representation. The *alternative vote* is used in single-member constituencies at elections to the Australian House of Representatives when there are more than two candidates. The voter must place the candidates in order of preference by marking his ballot-paper 1, 2, 3. . . . If no candidate obtains an absolute majority by counting first preferences, the candidate at the bottom of the poll is eliminated, and his second preference votes are distributed among the other candidates, and so on (if necessary) till one candidate has more than 50 per cent of the vote. The result may be that the candidate placed second on the first count wins the seat. A closer correspondence between votes cast and seats won can be achieved by a system of *proportional representation*. The best-known proportional systems are the single transferable vote (STV) and the party list system; there are numerous variants, including mixed systems. Proportional systems require multi-member constituencies. Under STV (which is used in elections in the Republic of Ireland and Malta and for the Australian Senate) the voter marks his preferences numerically against the names of candidates; where a candi-

30. In 1966 Labour, with 48 per cent of the national vote, won 363 seats; the Conservatives, with 42 per cent, won 253. In 1951, however, Labour won more votes (48·8 per cent to 48 per cent) but the Conservatives won 321 seats to 295 and formed a Government. The main reason for the discrepancy in 1951 was that Labour piled up very big majorities in a number of safe seats but lost several marginal seats by very small majorities.

31. The factors operating on voters at a General Election do not usually have the same force at a by-election, and some spectacular Liberal victories at by-elections have been recorded in recent years. An avowedly regional party, campaigning only in a few constituencies (for example, the Welsh Nationalist and Scottish National Parties and the sundry anti-Unionist parties in Northern Ireland), may win a number of seats corresponding more closely to its share of the United Kingdom vote and can even be over-represented in strictly mathematical terms.

32. For fuller details see, for example, Enid Lakeman, *How Democracies Vote*; W. J. M. Mackenzie, *Free Elections*; J. F. S. Ross, *Elections and Electors*; Institute of Electoral Research, *Parliaments and Electoral Systems*. For a useful short critique, see Peter G. J. Pulzer, *Political Representation and Elections in Britain* (2nd edn), ch. 2.

date has obtained a large enough percentage of the total poll to ensure that he must be elected,[33] his second preferences are redistributed among the other candidates, and so on till all the seats are filled. The larger the number of seats to be filled in a constituency, the more closely will their allocation reflect the electoral support enjoyed by the various candidates. Under the party list system in its simplest form, each party puts up a national list of candidates in ranking order; each voter casts a single vote for one party list; a party obtaining 40 per cent of the national vote will fill 40 per cent of the seats with the candidates ranked highest in its list.

Various Western European countries use proportional electoral systems. More often than not they bring about coalition or minority governments because no party wins an overall majority. This is not necessarily an unmitigated disaster, though in the United Kingdom coalition and minority governments have tended to be unstable or indecisive or both. But plans for basic changes in the electoral system[33a] founder on the combined hostility of the two main parties. Each party believes that under the first-past-the-post system it has a good chance of winning the next (or next but one) General Election with an outright majority; and to win an election is to win power for four or five years. Why, then, meddle with our ancient institutions which have served us so well for so long? At least in this context, 'consensus politics' are not a figment of the imagination.

Members

Before touching upon the conduct of an election campaign, we need to say something of the qualifications for membership of the House of Commons and the ways in which a candidate may be selected.

Disqualification for membership of the House

There are three preliminary points. First, there is no list of basic qualifications; there is simply a list of disqualifications. The former property and residential qualifications for candidates were abolished long ago; it is indeed fairly unusual for a candidate from one of the two main national parties to be a local man, though he is often expected by his constituency party to take up local residence when he becomes their prospective candidate. Secondly, some disqualifications, significant in their day, have been removed by statute as being obnoxious or unnecessary. All religious dis-

33. If, for example, four seats are to be filled in a constituency where 100,000 persons vote, a candidate obtaining $[100,000/(4 + 1)] + 1$ (i.e. 20,001) votes from first preferences will be declared elected, because it is impossible for any four other candidates to beat him.

33a. Outside Northern Ireland; see Addendum.

qualifications had been removed by 1888; the disqualification (or lack of qualification) of women was removed in 1918; the remaining disqualifications attached to Government contractors and Crown pensioners were abolished in 1957. Thirdly, if a candidate is subject to a legal disqualification, the returning officer is not allowed to reject his nomination papers if they are otherwise in order; his rights to be elected and to sit in the Commons are determinable (as we shall see[34]) by other means if he is elected to the seat.

The following are disqualified:[35]

1. Aliens. For this purpose, citizens of the Republic of Ireland are not aliens.

2. Persons under twenty-one years of age.[36]

3. Persons suffering from severe mental illness. They were disqualified at common law; the non-statutory disqualification has been supplemented by section 137 of the Mental Health Act 1959 under which the Speaker must be notified if a member is detained as a mental patient; if the member is still detained as a mental patient six months later, his seat will be vacated.

4. Peers and peeresses in their own right,[37] other than peers of Ireland (who are not qualified to sit in the House of Lords[38]).

5. Persons serving sentences for treason. A member who is sent to prison for any other offence is now merely prevented from sitting and voting while still serving his sentence;[39] but the House may resolve to expel him. One serving a sentence of imprisonment for a non-treasonable offence is not disqualified for election now.[40]

6. Bankrupts. A debtor who is an undischarged bankrupt is disqualified

34. See pp. 255–6, 261–2.

35. See Sir Thomas Erskine May, *Parliamentary Practice* (18th edn), ch. 3; *Halsbury's Laws of England* (3rd edn), vol. 28, *Parliament*, with Cumulative Supplement. Some disqualifications do not automatically cause vacation of the seat but debar a member from sitting and voting while subject to the disability. In practice it is impossible to *sit* without participating in a vote; the recurrent formal resolutions passed every day without a division will entail a unanimous vote.

36. This provision was preserved by the Family Law Reform Act 1969 which for most legal purposes reduced the age of majority to eighteen; see s. 1(4) of that Act and para. 2 of Schedule 2. Before 1832 several infants (including Charles James Fox) nevertheless sat as members.

37. For the meaning of this concept, see p. 298.

38. See *Re Earl of Antrim's Petition* [1967] 1 A.C. 691.

39. This appears to be the result of the amendment of s. 2 of the Forfeiture Act 1870 by s. 10 of and Part III of the Third Schedule to the Criminal Law Act 1967.

40. Whether this result of the enactment of the Criminal Law Act 1967 was intended is questionable; cf. ss. 1, 10(2) of that Act.

for election, and a member of the House thus adjudged is disqualified from sitting and voting when the House takes notice of the court order, and remains disqualified for five years after his discharge, unless the court annuls its order or, in discharging him, certifies that his bankruptcy was not attributable to his own fault. A member who becomes bankrupt does not automatically vacate his seat at once; the court is not obliged to notify the Speaker of its order for six months.

7. Persons convicted of corrupt and illegal practices at elections. These disqualifications are rather more extensive than those affecting the exercise of the franchise by persons so convicted.[41]

8. Clergy: a motley collection of statutory provisions, enacted at different times to meet particular problems, disqualify some ministers of religion but not others. Ministers of the Church of England, the Episcopalian Church of Scotland and all other Protestant clergymen (including ministers of the Church of Ireland)[42] ordained by bishops, except ministers of the disestablished Church of Wales, are disqualified; so are Roman Catholic priests, and ministers of the Established (Presbyterian) Church of Scotland; but nonconformist ministers, and ministers of non-Christian denominations, are not disqualified. To say that the law is a mass of archaic anomalies is one thing; to rationalize it, given the discordant sentiments expressed by the religious bodies themselves, is another. A select committee of the House which investigated the whole matter in the early 1950s recommended[43] that no change be then made, and the same view was taken by another select committee a few years later.[44] This strange tangle is likely to be with us for some time.[45]

9. Ministers of the Crown: not more than ninety-one holders of specified ministerial offices may sit and vote at any one time in the House of Commons (Ministers of the Crown Act 1964, s. 3(2) and Schedule). Since by convention a Minister must have or obtain a seat in one or other House, the appointment of a person to ministerial office when the maximum number has already been reached implies that he must be a peer or be granted a peerage; or that a sitting member be granted a peerage to make room for him; or that legislation be passed rapidly to regularize the position; or (possibly) that the new Minister be given an office not hitherto

41. Representation of the People Act 1949, ss. 139, 140, 151, 152; see also p. 244.
42. *Re MacManaway* [1951] A.C. 161.
43. H.C. 200 (1952–53).
44. Select Committee on the House of Commons Disqualification Bill (H.C. 349 (1955–56)).
45. Though informed opinion in the Church of England now seems to favour repeal of the disqualifications: see *Church and State* (1970), pp. 57–8 (The Report of the Archbishops' Commission).

recognized by statute; though amending legislation would again be needed to provide him with a salary and legal powers.[46] The maximum number of persons to whom salaries may be paid as holders of certain ministerial offices is prescribed by statute.[47]

The history of the statutory limitation of numbers of Ministers in the Commons is linked with restrictions on the holders of non-political offices. In the sixteenth century the House of Commons asserted, as a matter of privilege, a right to exclude from membership the holders of certain public offices, the tenure of which was incompatible with attendance in the House. In Charles II's time the Commons became uneasy at attempts by the Crown to manage and control it by patronage, and a movement developed to exclude all holders of offices and places of profit under the Crown from membership of the House. This movement succeeded under William III. But the separation of the Executive from the elected legislative House never became operative; the relevant provisions of the Act of Settlement 1701 were amended in 1705 and 1707, and a broad distinction was drawn between old offices of profit, which did not disqualify,[48] and new offices, which did disqualify, subject to various exceptions interpreted as authorizing members appointed to subsequently created *political* offices to sit, provided that they resigned their seats and were then successful in a by-election; this inconvenient requirement was finally abolished in 1926. Many new non-political offices disqualified absolutely. In 1937 the Ministers of the Crown Act rationalized the law by grouping ministerial offices and specifying how many holders of offices in each group could sit and vote in (i.e., be members of) the House of Commons at any one time. The permissible number was enlarged by individual Acts creating new Ministers, and again, in more general terms, by the House of Commons Disqualification Act 1957 and the Ministers of the Crown Act 1964. The modern policy is to strike a balance between the principle that every major Department ought to have a ministerial spokesman in the Commons and the undesirability of having the Government side of the House overweighted by Ministers at the expense of backbenchers.

10. Holders of public offices. The meaning of an office or place of profit which disqualified or rendered its holder liable to vacate his seat and stand for re-election remained obscure, and also highly inconvenient, for till 1951 a common informer could sue a disqualified member for a

46. The last two expedients were resorted to in 1964 when Mr Wilson appointed a number of Ministers in excess of the maximum then authorized: see A. E. W. Park (1965) 28 *Mod. L. Rev.* 338.

47. Ministerial and other Salaries Act 1972.

48. Except that the holder had to resign and then submit himself to re-election at a by-election. He could then retain his 'office of profit' and sit in the House.

penalty of £500 for each day on which he had sat and voted; frequently Parliament would be asked to pass an Act indemnifying an individual member against the legal consequences of having accepted in good faith a position (for example, unpaid membership of a special tribunal) which might still be construed as an office or place of 'profit' in the gift of the Crown. The only remedy was to replace the general phrase by an explicit list of offices, tenure of which ought to disqualify because they required a degree of political impartiality or a burden of continuing responsibility incompatible with membership of the House of Commons. A bill to this effect was introduced in 1955, amended after detailed examination by a select committee of the House,[49] and passed into law as the House of Commons Disqualification Act 1957.

The main classes of persons thus disqualified for membership are:

(a) Professional full-time judges.

(b) Civil servants.

(c) Members of the regular armed forces.

(d) Full-time members of a police force.

(e) Members of the legislatures of non-Commonwealth countries.[50]

(f) Members of independent public boards and commissions, the chairmen and sometimes the members of 'administrative' tribunals, and other persons occupying offices requiring political neutrality, judicial detachment or other characteristics inconsistent with membership of the House. These disqualifying posts were listed in full in the First Schedule to the Act; the list may be varied by statute, or by Order in Council made in pursuance of a resolution of the House. The Act is often reprinted in an amended and up-to-date form so that candidates and members may know how they stand.

11. Acceptance of the offices of bailiff or steward of the Chiltern Hundreds or the Manor of Northstead. This is the traditional manner of resigning membership; these offices are nominal offices of profit under the Crown, and acceptance of any of them was expressly preserved as a ground of disqualification by section 4 of the 1957 Act.

12. Expulsion by resolution of the House. The House may declare a

49. For the report of the Select Committee, see H.C. 349 (1965–66). For the report of an earlier committee, reviewing more fully the history of the problem, see H.C. 120 (1940–41).

50. This excludes members of the Parliament of the Republic of Ireland. Dual membership for persons residing outside the British Isles is hardly feasible, though Westminster M.P.s who are members of the European Parliament will perhaps contrive to achieve the impossible. Commonwealth peers occasionally sit in the House of Lords, but until winds of change began to blow through the corridors of Westminster, absentee membership of the Lords was quite acceptable.

member's seat vacant, either because he has incurred a legal disqualification or for any other reason whatsoever; this is one of its privileges. It cannot, however, prevent that person from standing as a candidate at a by-election.[51]

Effect of disqualification. 1. If a person already subject to a legal incapacity (for example, peerage) is elected to membership, (a) the House may declare his seat vacant or (b) a petition may be lodged to have him unseated in pursuance of the finding by an election court that his election was void.[52]

2. If a sitting member incurs a disqualification, then (a) the House may declare his seat vacant, if it is not automatically vacated by the nature of the disqualification; or (b) any member of the public may apply to the Privy Council for a declaration that a member is disqualified under the 1957 Act; the matter is to be referred to the Judicial Committee;[53] or (c) the House itself may petition the Crown to have the matter referred to the Judicial Committee for an advisory opinion;[54] or (d) the House may, if it thinks fit, waive the effect of a disqualification under the 1957 Act if it has already been removed;[55] or (e) a common informer may still pursue his action for penalties against an episcopally ordained clergyman who sits and votes while subject to the disqualification.[56]

Selection of candidates

Under our present system of two alternately dominant parties, a large majority of seats will be 'safe' for either the Conservative or the Labour candidate at a General Election,[57] unless there is a substantial swing in

51. See pp. 321–2.

52. For election petitions, see pp. 261–2. When Mr Anthony Wedgwood Benn succeeded to his father's peerage as Viscount Stansgate, he argued that he was entitled to retain his seat in the Commons because he had not applied for a writ of summons to the Lords. The House referred the matter to the Committee of Privileges; the Committee found against Mr Wedgwood Benn and the House adopted its report and declared his seat vacant. He stood as a candidate at the ensuing by-election, which he won, but was unseated on an election petition by his defeated opponent: *Re Parliamentary Election for Bristol South-East* (1961), reported [1964] 2 Q.B. 257. When the Peerage Act 1963 was passed he immediately disclaimed his peerage and was able to regain his seat.

53. House of Commons Disqualification Act 1957, s. 7. The applicant must furnish security for costs. No such proceeding has been brought; this is hardly surprising.

54. Under section 4 of the Judicial Committee Act 1833. This procedure was adopted in *Re MacManaway* [1951] A.C. 161.

55. As by resignation from the disqualifying office: 1957 Act, s. 6.

56. Under the House of Commons (Clergy Disqualification) Act 1801.

57. The position may be more fluid at a by-election, where candidates from smaller

public support away from one of the parties, in which case safe seats may become marginal. Hence the selection of the official candidate for the Conservative or Labour Party, as the case may be, will as a rule effectively determine who will win the seat. For most of those who vote, a General Election is a ritualistic affirmation of support for (or hostility to) one of the two main national parties and a means of choosing a Government; and an unattractive candidate will seldom cause his party to lose the seat. In England, no Independent M.P. other than the Speaker of the previous Parliament was elected even at a by-election between the 1950 General Election and 1973.[58] In Scotland, Wales and Northern Ireland the pattern is not identical; Liberals (outside Northern Ireland) and Nationalists may win a fair proportion of the seats, and the personal attributes of candidates will sometimes count for more than the blessing of a mass party organization. Even an Independent may have a chance in the Celtic fringes.

The role of political parties in the British system of government is too big a topic to be considered adequately in a primarily legal work.[59] We shall touch briefly upon the part played by the parties in the House of Commons in the next chapter. In the selection of candidates, party choice is wholly unregulated by rules of strict law, and depends on extra-legal[60] party rules and practices. In many states in the United States of America, and in a few other countries, statutory provision is made for primary elections to select official party candidates. This democratic safeguard is absent in Britain (though recently some Conservative constituency associations have conducted informal polls to select prospective party candidates), and party choice is normally determined by an inner group of party activists and national office-holders.

Selection[61] is mainly a matter for local constituency parties. In the Labour Party, nominations of prospective candidates come from ward branches and affiliated organizations (normally trades unions). Transport House (the Labour headquarters) has lists of officially approved candidates. The executive committee of the constituency party draws up a

---

national or regional parties, or even independents, may benefit from a big 'protest' vote or large-scale abstentions. At by-elections the voters know that they are not participating in the choice of a Government.

58. For the figures from 1900 to 1945, see David Butler and Jennie Freeman, *British Political Facts and Figures 1900–1968* (3rd edn), p. 121. cf. p. 258 below.

59. The leading modern work is R. T. McKenzie, *British Political Parties* (2nd edn).

60. Though cf. *John* v. *Rees* [1970] Ch. 345 (natural justice to be observed in disaffiliation or suspension of local party organization).

61. See R. L. Leonard, *Elections in Britain*, pp. 65–81 for a good short account, and Michael Rush, *The Selection of Parliamentary Candidates* (1969) for a very full study.

short list, and the candidate is then chosen, subject to the approval of the National Executive Committee of the party, by a selection conference of the constituency party's general management committee. Occasionally a prospective candidate, or a sitting member, is vetoed as an official candidate by the National Executive Committee; this will lead to the nomination of another candidate with official backing at the national level, and may entail disaffiliation of the constituency party. A Labour candidate lacking official backing will normally have no chance at all of being elected. The General Election of 1970, however, furnished a spectacular exception to the rule: the octogenarian member for Merthyr Tydfil in South Wales was not readopted by his constituency party as the official candidate, but he stood as an Independent and won the seat, handsomely defeating the official candidate. In 1973 this feat was emulated at Lincoln.

At the General Election of 1970, 129 Labour M.P.s (not all of them in working-class occupations) were 'sponsored' by trades unions, in that the union made a contribution to the expenses of their constituency organizations and election campaigns;[62] and all but seventeen were elected. But over a half of all Labour M.P.s were university educated and only a quarter were in working-class occupations.

Selection procedure among the Conservatives is broadly similar to that of the Labour Party, though ratification of the final choice is made by a general meeting of the whole constituency association[63] (and occasionally by postal ballot of members). The Conservative Central Office also has its approved list, but it hardly ever refuses to endorse a local choice. Conservative candidates and M.P.s are not allowed to make more than a nominal contribution to their constituency association's funds. In practice Conservative M.P.s come from a smaller range of social groups than Labour M.P.s. Of those elected in 1970, 77 per cent had been to public schools and over a half to Oxbridge; the corresponding figures for Labour M.P.s were 20 per cent and 24 per cent.[64] Although about a third of the working-class votes Conservative in an average election year, only one or

62. See also Mr Douglas Houghton's Memorandum to the Select Committee on Members' Interests (Declaration) (H.C. 57 (1969–70), pp. 120–25). Companies contributing to national party funds must now disclose the fact in their accounts: Companies Act 1967, s. 19. As was to be expected, the contributions go overwhelmingly to the Conservative Party. A large part of the Labour Party's income is derived from trades unions and the political levy imposed on their members.

63. Liberal candidates are selected at a meeting of all paid-up members of the constituency party.

64. See Peter G. Richards, *The Backbenchers* (1972), pp. 21–2. The school-teaching profession was far more strongly represented on the Labour benches. Company directors (see Andrew Roth, *The Business Background of M.P.s*) and farmers are numerous on the Conservative side. See further Butler and Pinto-Duschinsky, *The British General Election of 1970*.

two manual workers will occupy Conservative seats. Nevertheless, the differences between the social complexions of the front benches of the two parliamentary parties are now less striking than their similarities.

There is no constitutional procedure whereby an M.P. can be compelled by his constituents to vacate his seat, but it is open to the constituency party or association to adopt a different candidate at the next General Election if they are dissatisfied with their member's conduct or political stance. This can be a very real threat to a member's independence. A member may, of course, be refused official backing by party headquarters at an election. It is also open to the national party headquarters to seek to protect the member; but their practical freedom of action is restricted, especially in the Conservative Party.[65]

Electoral campaigns

Following a dissolution, candidates wishing to stand for election must submit nomination papers (signed by a proposer, a seconder and eight other voters) to the returning officer within eight clear days; polling day will be nine clear days afterwards – in practice on a Thursday. The rules governing by-elections are basically the same except that the issue of the writ for holding an election will be made by the Speaker on the resolution of the House of Commons. By custom the necessary motion is moved by a whip from the party which held the seat before the vacancy arose. A party fearing loss of such a seat sometimes refrains from moving the motion for months, leaving the constituency unrepresented.[66] There are various statutory provisions[67] enabling writs for by-elections to be issued by the Speaker at the request of any two members during a parliamentary recess; it would be interesting to see this procedure invoked against the wishes of the party that held the seat.

Before party candidates are nominated, it is usual for them to be formally adopted at a special constituency members' meeting, though that is not required by law. But every candidate must appoint an election agent (who may be himself), and the agent will be accountable to the returning officer after the polls for election expenditure. Some frivolous candidatures may still be discouraged by the rule that upon nomination a candidate must deposit the sum of £150, which will be forfeited if he fails to obtain more than one-eighth of the votes cast.

65. Peter G. J. Pulzer, *Political Representation and Elections in Britain* (2nd edn), pp. 77–81.
66. Swindon was without a member for seven months in 1969.
67. For example, Election of Members in Recess Act 1858; Election in Recess Act 1863.

Attempts have been made by legal regulation to ensure as far as possible that election campaigns are fairly conducted.[68] Bribery, treating and undue influence in the nature of duress are corrupt practices. Candidates are allowed to send an election address to each voter free of postage, and are not to be refused permission to hire schools maintained by the local education authority for election meetings. Under non-statutory agreements between the main parties, the broadcasting authorities allocate time for party political programmes in a reasonably equitable manner on a national basis. And expenditure on elections is limited by law so that not too much weight shall be given to the power of the purse. The law relating to election expenses is in some respects intricate, obscure and unsatisfactory – characteristics reflecting not merely the intrinsic difficulty of detailed regulation but also the influence of vested interests in the main parties which would prefer the law to be vague on certain points. The main general rules are:

1. That no expenditure may be incurred with a view to promoting or procuring the election of a candidate at an election by any person other than the candidate himself or his agent or a person authorized by the agent.[69]

2. That the maximum expenditure to be incurred at an election shall be restricted to £450 for a constituency, plus 5p for six registered voters in a county constituency, and 5p for eight registered voters in an urban constituency.[70]

3. That certain kinds of expenditure (notably on broadcasting from outside the United Kingdom except by arrangement with the BBC and the IBA[71] which might give a wealthy party an unfair advantage shall be absolutely prohibited.[72]

The difficulties are mostly concerned with the first of these rules, taken in conjunction with the second. What is the relevant period for the purpose of election expenditure? Does it begin with the announcement of a forthcoming dissolution, the proclamation of dissolution, the adoption of

68. Probably the best account of the details of electoral law is in Halsbury's *Laws of England* (3rd edn), vol. 14, *Elections*, with Cumulative Supplement.
69. Representation of the People Act 1949, s. 63 (as amended).
70. ibid., s. 64, as amended by s. 8 of the Representation of the People Act 1969.
71. 1949 Act, s. 80(1), as amended by s. 9(5) of the 1969 Act. Broadcasts within this country about a constituency during an election period cannot include a candidate without that candidate's consent (1969 Act, s. 9).
72. But the prohibition on the use of bands, torches, flags and banners (1949 Act, s. 97) has been removed (1969 Act, s. 10). Restrictions on the use of motor cars for conveying voters to and from the polls were abolished in 1958.

candidates, the presentation of nomination papers?[73] Probably the earliest of these dates is the relevant one,[74] though in a sense the party organizations are waging a continuous electoral campaign throughout the life of a Parliament. Again, does expenditure at the national level during the election period have to be apportioned between all constituencies in which the party's candidates are standing, or is it only relevant to consider propaganda distributed or otherwise used in the particular constituency? British electoral law places its emphasis, with a disarming lack of conviction, on the individual constituency and the individual candidate; and the general interpretation, supported directly or indirectly by two modern judicial decisions, is that only expenditure for the purpose of promoting the election of an individual candidate in his constituency (as distinct from expenditure directed to procuring the election or defeat of candidates of a particular party in general) has to be counted as an election expense.[75] Neither of the main parties is likely to challenge this benevolent interpretation. In any event, newspaper articles and comments and political broadcasting programmes (as distinct from advertisements) are expressly excluded from the definition of election expenses, even if the money is spent with a view to promoting the election of a particular candidate.[76]

References in this chapter to the role of the returning officer must not obscure the fact that the burden of organizing the machinery of an election, and particularly the poll and the count, rests mainly on the registration officer.

Election petitions

A voter or a defeated candidate may lodge a petition against the validity of an election.[77] Since 1868 petitions have been heard by an election court, now consisting in England of two judges of the Queen's Bench Division, who may sit in the constituency in question. From the early

73. Authorities are considered in *H.L.E.* (3rd edn), vol. 14, pp. 176–9.

74. See sections 9(2), (3), of the 1969 Act, adopting the early date for the purpose of Part II of the 1969 Act.

75. See *R.* v. *Tronoh Mines Ltd* [1952] 1 All E.R. 697 (newspaper advertisement by company advocating defeat of the Labour Government at the impending General Election of 1951, held not an election expense within the meaning of s. 63 of the 1949 Act); see also *Grieve* v. *Douglas-Home* 1965 S.C. 313 (Wilson, *Cases and Materials*, p. 152; party political broadcast featuring the then Prime Minister held not to be expenditure 'with a view to' procuring his election in his constituency).

76. 1949 Act, s. 63(1), proviso, as amended by s. 9(4) of the 1969 Act; this amendment resolved any doubt that survived the decision in *Grieve* v. *Douglas-Home* (see above) on party political broadcasts.

77. The law is now governed by Part III of the Representation of the People Act 1949.

seventeenth century till 1868 disputed elections had been determined as a matter of privilege by the House of Commons itself, many of whose members had been elected by means of what would now be regarded as corrupt and illegal practices, and voting in the House, not unexpectedly, tended to run along party lines.

Petitions based on illegal or corrupt practices or other irregularities at parliamentary elections are now extremely rare; this is partly because very close contests are uncommon and even if the court finds that irregularities were present it may determine that the result ought to stand since they were unlikely to have affected the result.[78] A petition may also be lodged on the ground that the successful candidate was subject to a legal incapacity – for example, peerage.[79] In such a case the court may, if satisfied that the incapacity existed, either declare the election void (so that a by-election has to be held) or, if satisfied that the voters for the successful candidate had had his incapacity sufficiently brought to their notice so that they must be deemed deliberately to have thrown their votes away, award the seat to the runner-up.[80] Normally the petition has to be lodged within three weeks of the date of the election.

In form the judgment of an election court is a report to the Speaker, which the House is directed by statute to accept. By the act of resolving that the report be recorded in the Journals of the House, the empty shell of the ancient privilege of the House is preserved.

We have already taken note of other methods by which the qualification of an elected member to sit in the House may be challenged and determined.[81]

78. There are other reasons, including the maxim that dog does not bite dog: see Wilson, *Cases and Materials*, p. 159.

79. See *Re Parliamentary Election for Bristol South-East* [1964] 2 Q.B. 257 (the Stansgate Peerage case). See also the Northern Ireland cases of *Mitchell* and *Clarke* [1958] N.I. 143, 151 (successful candidates serving long sentences for felony, then a disqualification for election).

80. Thus, the Bristol South-East seat was awarded to Viscount Stansgate's (Mr Anthony Wedgwood Benn's) defeated opponent after the by-election caused by the resolution of the House declaring the seat to be vacant.

81. See pp. 255–6.

Chapter 12
The House of Commons: Functions and Procedure

Introduction
Officers

In 1972 the House of Commons had 630 members, including the Speaker. The first business of the House at the opening of a new Parliament is to elect a Speaker from among its members; the Queen formally signifies her approval of the Commons' choice. The Speaker is expected to be an absolutely impartial chairman of debate; in no sense is he a spokesman for the Government. In early days he was the spokesman for the Commons in relation to the Crown and the Lords. His function of presenting the views of the Commons to the monarch made his position fraught with hazard, and the show of reluctance that he puts up today as he is propelled gently to the Speaker's chair after his election is a reminder of things past.

His election is normally unopposed in the House, and he is not always a member on the Government side. He can be removed by a simple resolution of the House, but this state of affairs will arise only if he has comported himself with serious impropriety. The usual practice is to re-elect the Speaker of the preceding Parliament if he has been returned at the General Election and is willing to stand for office again. As Speaker he detaches himself from his former party affiliations,[1] and if he contests his seat at a General Election it will be as an Independent.

The Speaker does not participate in debate, even when the House is sitting in committee. Nor does he vote on a motion, unless a casting vote from the chair is required; the manner in which he is to cast such a vote is circumscribed by precedent. His main functions in the House are to maintain decorum in debate, to call upon members to speak, to give rulings on points of order and on a question whether a *prima facie* case of breach of privilege has been established, and to act as the servant of the House (for example, in directing the issue of writs for filling vacancies) or as its spokesman (for example, in delivering a reprimand or admon-

1. Suggestions that the Speaker's constituents are in effect unrepresented in the House because of his non-political role overlook the fact that he will take up their problems with Ministers and in that capacity may carry greater weight than an ordinary back-bencher.

ition to one found guilty of contempt of the House; or in communications with legislatures overseas or on ceremonial occasions). As the incarnation of the ancient dignity of the House, he is habitually treated with great respect, indeed deference. Important discretionary functions fall to be discharged by him from time to time – for example, certifying whether a bill is a money bill within the meaning of the Parliament Act 1911; suspending a member for a day for disorderly conduct, or naming a member (who may then incur a period of suspension) for persistent disregard of the authority of the chair;[2] appointing members of the panel of chairmen of committees at the beginning of each session;[3] deciding whether to accept a motion for the closure of debate, and whether to put to the House for debate a question raised as an urgent matter of public importance. He has a salary similar to that of a High Court judge, charged on the Consolidated Fund so that it does not require annual renewal, and a house within the Palace of Westminster; when he retires he will be offered a peerage.

The office of Deputy Speaker is filled by three members elected by the House – the Chairman and Deputy Chairmen of Ways and Means. At least two belong to the party in office, but when in the chair, they are expected to observe the same impartiality as the Speaker. Most of the Speaker's powers are exercisable by them.

The Speaker is assisted by the Clerk of the House of Commons, the other clerks at the table (whose functions are by no means merely clerical) and a personal legal adviser and administrative officer, Speaker's Counsel. The Serjeant at Arms attends upon the Speaker; he executes orders of the House (for example, to clear the public galleries; to take a person into custody), and is generally responsible for the domestic staff arrangements of the House.

Records

The formal record of the transactions of the House is the Journal of the House, published annually. The Journals do not purport to summarize all that has occurred in debate. They are admissible in evidence in court. Each day the votes and proceedings of the House are recorded and circulated to members; they will record the decisions of the House and its committees, and in due course their substance will be entered in the Journals. The official report (*Hansard*) is a daily verbatim transcript of all that was said and done in the House in the course of parliamentary

2. See p. 325, note 51.
3. For the functions of the Business Committee of the House (consisting of the chairmen, and other members nominated by the Speaker), see p. 272.

business; it includes, in what is in effect an appendix, written answers to questions. This is published by Her Majesty's Stationery Office with the authority of the House. It does not include reports of the proceedings of standing committees or select committees, which are published separately. Reports ordered to be laid before the House of Commons and published otherwise than in pursuance of royal or ministerial authority are called House of Commons papers, as distinct from Command papers. The Lords have their own Journals, minutes of proceedings, official reports, and series of papers.

The law and custom of Parliament (lex et consuetudo parliamenti)

The main essentials of parliamentary procedure are contained in the standing orders[4] of the House, which are published by the Stationery Office from time to time and may be varied by a simple majority of the House, and in sessional orders which, for example, authorize the appointment of select committees which the House has not yet decided to establish on a permanent basis. Changes in these orders frequently emanate from recommendations of the Select Committee on Procedure. Separate standing orders for private bills are issued.

In addition, the conduct of parliamentary proceedings is regulated to a small extent by statute (for example, the procedure on consolidation bills) and common law; and to a large extent by resolutions of the House, Speakers' rulings and unwritten customs or conventions. Some of the most important practices governing the allocation of parliamentary time are not enshrined in any formal authoritative document.

Parliamentary privilege[5] stands in a slightly different category, though it is clearly part of the law and custom of Parliament. It is to be found partly in legislation and case-law, mainly in resolutions of each House, and hardly at all in standing or sessional orders or in unwritten conventions.

The debating chamber

In many legislatures the chamber is in the shape of a horseshoe, and members are able to signify their ideological position by placing themselves on the far left, the far right, or at a suitable intermediate point; speeches are normally delivered from a rostrum. The chamber of the

4. The standing orders referred to in this edition are those adopted in 1971 (and published as an Appendix to the eighteenth edition of Erskine May, *Parliamentary Practice*), subject to amendments down to the end of 1972.

5. See ch. 14.

House of Commons is rectangular; the Government benches are on the right of the elevated Speaker's chair, the Opposition are to his left. Today this division symbolizes the character of parliamentary government. Ministers sit on the Government front bench and their supporters behind them; the Opposition front bench faces them. On each side of the House the undemarcated line between frontbenchers and backbenchers will be significant. Members speak from their places and do not declaim from a rostrum; this conduces to an informal style of debate, discouraging the rhetorical flourish.[6] However, informality has its limits. Members must address themselves to the chair; when referring to other members they are to mention them not by name but by description ('the honourable member for Stretchford East'); pejorative epithets are out of order; smoking, and reading newspapers, are unfortunately not permitted.

Facilities for members

The number of seats in the House is insufficient to accommodate all members at any one time. This dearth of space (which seldom gives rise to problems except immediately before an important division on a motion) is deliberately designed to foster the atmosphere of an intimate club; it also harks back to the days when for most members politics were far from being a full-time occupation. (Salaries were not paid to members till shortly before the First World War.) In 1973 a member's salary was £4500;[7] £1000 a year was allowed as secretarial expenses; there were various other allowances for research assistance and travel, and free telephone calls and postage from the House. The facilities provided for members outside the chamber are on the whole unimpressive,[8] though there is a good library with a useful reference service.[9] The House frequently sits late into the night. Since members normally have a multiplicity of responsibilities besides attendance in the House, it is perhaps surprising that the quality of backbenchers is good and has almost certainly improved since the 1950s; this is hardly attributable to financial rewards,[10]

6. One of the arguments adduced against permitting television broadcasting o debates is that this would encourage members to 'play to the gallery'.

7. Raised in accordance with recommendations by the Review Body on Top Salaries. See further 828 H.C.Deb. 1248–52 (20 December 1971).

8. See generally Bernard Crick, *The Reform of Parliament* (2nd edn).

9. See further A. Barker and M. Rush, *The Member of Parliament and his Information*.

10. Bribery of members is almost unknown. On sponsorship and retainers by pressure groups, see pp. 258, 273 and 319–20. Fringe benefits, such as invitations to appear on television and write articles for the press, are, of course, a not unattractive by-product of political fame and acumen for some members.

a sense of security[11] or leisured ease, or a feeling that a backbencher is likely to set the course of the ship of state, but rather to such factors as the hope of ministerial office one fine day, a sense of excitement at being 'in the know' and close to the hub of political activity, or a desire to attract public attention to one's causes, opinions or oneself. M.P.s are on the whole a good deal more articulate than the average member of the community, and it is unkind to criticize them for having sought a place in that forum which offers the most dignified platform for eloquence and enshrines their public utterances in imperishable prose.

Parties in the House[12]

In 1937 the Ministers of the Crown Act formally recognized the status of the Leader of the Opposition, providing for a salary, charged on the Consolidated Fund, to be paid to him. This was right and proper, for he is the alternative Prime Minister, and a fundamental feature of the British parliamentary system is that the leadership of the largest opposition party really is an alternative Government and should therefore be encouraged to behave like one; in short, being Leader of the Opposition[13] is a full-time job. Under the Ministerial and other Salaries Act 1972, his salary is £9500, and the Chief Opposition Whip in the Commons gets a salary of £7500; salaries are also paid to two Assistant Opposition Whips, and to the Leader of the Opposition and the Chief Opposition Whip in the Lords.

When Labour is in opposition, the Leader of the Party, the Deputy Leader and the Chief Whip are elected annually by the Parliamentary Labour Party. So are the Chairman of the Parliamentary Party (a backbencher) and twelve M.P.s and three peers; collectively they form the Parliamentary Committee or Shadow Cabinet. Decisions of the Shadow Cabinet – the allocation of subject responsibilities to its members is a matter for the Party Leader – are reported weekly to the Parliamentary Party. Lurking in the background lie the National Executive Committee of the Party (elected by the party's annual national conference and including prominent trade unionists and other non-parliamentary figures) and

11. But pension rights for ex-members have recently been extended: Parliamentary and other Pensions Act 1972.
12. See especially Peter G. Richards, *The Backbenchers* (1972), chs. 3, 11. This book is a valuable and concise work of reference. See also Dick Leonard and Valentine Herman (eds.), *The Backbencher and Parliament* (1972).
13. Defined (Ministerial and other Salaries Act 1972, Sched. 3, para. 1) as that member 'who is for the time being the Leader of the party in that House in opposition to Her Majesty's Government having the greatest numerical strength in the House . . .'. Any dispute as to who is the occupant of this post is to be determined conclusively by the Speaker.

the resolutions passed by the annual conference itself. The relationship between the party leadership and those elected bodies is fluid and intriguing,[14] but a strong party leader such as Gaitskell has contrived to impose his own policies in the face of an unacceptable majority vote at the party conference. Within the House of Commons, the Parliamentary Party elects M.P.s to serve with shadow Ministers on specialized party committees relating to defined areas of government. When Labour is in office, the leadership is not elected annually. Rapport with the Wilson Government was maintained[15] by a liaison committee of the Parliamentary Party, comprising the Chairman of the Parliamentary Party, elected vice-chairmen, the Leader of the House of Commons and the Government Chief Whip, and by contacts between specialized subject groups (and particularly their chairmen) and the relevant Ministers. There are also regional groups. In 1969 subject group chairmen were holding monthly meetings with the Prime Minister and the Chairman of the Parliamentary Party had a weekly discussion with the Prime Minister.

The pattern in the Conservative Party is broadly similar, though the ostensibly democratic elective principle is less prominent even when the party is in opposition. The Party Leader is elected by the Parliamentary Party and is then presented to the National Conference, but he does not need to be re-elected annually. It is he who appoints the Deputy Leader, the Chief Whip, the Party Chairman and the Shadow Cabinet; he also has ultimate control of the party bureaucracy,[16] a function vested, within the Labour Party, in the National Executive Committee. The Party's annual conference[17] has tended to be more deferential than the corresponding Labour Party conference, but signs of animated controversy are now perceptible. Within the Parliamentary Party there are elected specialized and regional committees – twenty-five in 1973.[18] All backbench members belong to the 1922 committee, a body to which the leadership must pay careful attention despite the fact that in form this committee is only a discussion group.[19]

Party organization within the House is therefore far from being a

14. See generally R. T. McKenzie, *British Political Parties* (2nd edn). For a less detailed review see Jean Blondel, *Voters, Parties and Leaders* (2nd edn).

15. Douglas Houghton, *The Times*, 28 August 1969, and (1969) 40 *Political Quarterly* 454.

16. But see Michael Pinto-Duschinsky (1972) 20 *Political Studies* 1, for practical limits to this control.

17. The conference is called the Annual Conference of the National Union of Conservative and Unionist Associations.

18. *The Times*, 27 December 1972.

19. John P. Mackintosh, *The British Cabinet* (2nd edn), pp. 580–81, mentions some of the decisions influenced by the committee.

haphazard affair. Whether a party is in office or in opposition, the role of the whips is of crucial importance in conveying the views of the rank and file to the leadership and vice versa; in keeping members informed by circular of forthcoming parliamentary business; in giving the expected times of divisions in order to secure a high attendance – by underlining the matter once, twice, or thrice; failure to comply with a three-line whip without a very good excuse is often to be construed as an act of rebellion against the leadership – in arranging, in consultation with whips on the other side, for an indisposed member, or one with an urgent outside commitment, to absent himself by 'pairing' him with another member who also wishes to be absent from the division, so that neither party will obtain an advantage; in making informal recommendations to the leadership about the suitability of backbenchers for preferment; in supplying names of members to serve on committees of the House and in helping to impose party discipline by suasion, admonition and, if necessary, threats that the party whip may be withdrawn or that the ultimate sanction of expulsion from the Parliamentary Party may be imposed. However, disciplinary penalties on Labour members may be imposed only by the Parliamentary Party itself and the Conservative whip is hardly ever withdrawn. Those Labour M.P.s who, by defying a three-line whip, enabled the European Communities Bill to pass, were not disciplined. All Government whips are now salaried and the Chief Whip attends Cabinet meetings. The senior whips also have an important part to play in organizing the distribution of parliamentary time.

Business of the House[20]

The House normally sits from 2.30 p.m. till about 10.30 p.m. from Monday to Thursday and from 11 a.m. till 4.30 p.m. on Friday. Standing orders recognize that priority shall be given to Government business,[21] but allocate twenty Fridays during a session to private members' bills and motions.[22] In practice private members are allowed to determine the course of business on other occasions – for example, in debates on the daily adjournment or the recess and Consolidated Fund Bills, and at question time. An approximately equal amount of time to that allocated to private members is placed at the disposal of the official Opposition, which dominates the twenty-nine supply days. If, moreover, the Opposition

20. On this topic and many other aspects of parliamentary institutions, Sir Ivor Jennings's *Parliament* (2nd edn, 1957) is still of great value, though it needs to be supplemented by more recent studies.
21. See S.O. Nos. 6(1), 15.
22. S.O. No. 6(2), (5).

wishes to put down a motion of censure on the Government it is incumbent on the Government to give up a day for such a debate unless the request is part of a campaign of obstruction.

Government business includes not only bills but also motions to debate reports of committees and royal commissions (on which the Government will express its views and submit to comment and criticism), motions to approve certain subordinate legislative instruments, formal Government statements, procedural motions (for example, to curtail debate on a bill), and more general motions which serve as a peg on which a debate may hang.

This picture hardly corresponds with the image of a legislative body dominated by the Executive, particularly when one recalls that the Executive has to pay regard to the views of powerful pressure groups, to stirrings among its backbenchers and party loyalists outside Parliament, and in some contexts to the voice of public opinion – not to speak of international pressures, and political popularity polls and by-election results in so far as they may influence political morale. Furthermore, a good deal of the time spent on Government bills is absorbed by critical speeches and debates on amendments. On the other hand, not all parliamentary business is transacted on the floor of the House. And a Government with an overall majority in the House is almost certain to succeed, by marshalling support in the division lobbies and if necessary using its majority to alter the parliamentary timetable, in securing the enactment of the great bulk of its legislative programme.

Form and substance are therefore intertwined but in convoluted shapes. The main responsibility for the business of the House is vested in the Leader of the House of Commons (usually the Lord President of the Council), assisted by the Government Chief Whip. They are expected to consult their opposite numbers 'behind the Speaker's chair'; parliamentary time is allocated 'through the usual channels' on a basis of bargain and compromise, on the understanding that, subject to standing orders and convention, the Government has the biggest claim and may be able to impose its own priorities by resolutions suspending standing orders or otherwise adjusting the normal timetable. Each Thursday in the House the Leader of the Opposition asks the Leader of the House to announce the business of the House for the forthcoming week. This is a question to which he may know the answer already; if he or any other member is dissatisfied, there is then an opportunity for public protest, and the Government, anxious not to leave itself open to justifiable criticism, will have already taken this possibility into account.

The following devices are available to enlarge the amount of time available to the Government – and, indeed, the House generally – for debate on the floor of the House:

1. Bills may be debated in standing committee (and now second reading committee), so that other proceedings can take place simultaneously on the floor of the House. The use of these small committees, sitting 'upstairs', has now become a very important feature of contemporary parliamentary procedure.

2. Standing orders relating to times of sitting may be suspended to postpone the time of the daily adjournment (a device frequently resorted to) or provide for special sittings on Fridays or weekends (a device unpopular in nearly all quarters). Again, the provisional date of adjournment for a recess may be postponed if urgent business is incomplete; a motion for this purpose may be resisted by the Opposition.

3. Standing orders may be suspended so as to enable the Government to annex private members' time. Any proposal to this effect would be deeply resented today.[23]

4. Procedural devices are available for shortening debate, and are sometimes used to prevent protraction of the proceedings by the official Opposition or backbenchers. The first is the *closure*.[24] In its simplest form, this involves a member (usually a Government whip, rising at a prearranged time) purporting to move, in the course of debate, that 'the question be now put'. Unless the Speaker (or Deputy Speaker) regards such a motion as an abuse of the rules of the House or an infringement of the rights of the minority, he must put this question forthwith without further discussion; if the motion is passed, with at least 100 members voting in favour, then the question then under debate (for example, that the bill be read a second time, or that the House do now adjourn) is put to the House and voted on immediately. The closure was first introduced into the House on the Speaker's responsibility in 1881 after a continuous filibuster of forty-one hours by Irish home rulers who had decided that if Britain would not let Ireland govern herself, the Irish would do their best to prevent Britain governing herself; standing orders were adopted in 1882 to regularize the situation. The *guillotine* is a form of closure by compartments. If debate on a bill, particularly in committee, is likely to be, or is being, unduly protracted, the Leader of the House introduces a resolution under which a prescribed maximum number of days will be allocated to each stage of the bill. Unless prior agreement between the two sides of the House has been reached, debate on such a motion is likely to be acrimonious, and the Government will be well advised to adopt such a

23. Private members' time was suspended during the Second World War and was only restored in the 1948–9 session.

24. See S.O. Nos. 30, 31. See also S.O. No. 2, which enables a Minister to move suspension of a late sitting till the following day.

procedure only in case of dire necessity. When the resolution has been passed, detailed compartmentalization of the bill will be effected by the Business Committee of the House, and in standing committee by a sub-committee.[25] When the appointed hour is reached the guillotine falls; the chairman must interrupt debate and the committee (or the House) must pass on to the next phase even though many amendments have not yet been reached. One should also mention in this context a separate matter – the power (formerly called the *kangaroo*) vested in the Speaker at report stage and the chairman in committee to select for discussion some amendments to a bill and not to call (thus jumping over) others covering substantially the same ground. This power, unlike the closure and guillotine, is conferred not by resolution of the House but by standing orders,[26] is frequently exercised, and rarely evokes serious controversy.

Legislation

Most of us want to see some parts of English law changed, so as to rectify an injustice or an anomaly, or to prohibit conduct of which we strongly disapprove, or to enable something to be done in the interests of the general public or a section of it or merely ourselves. But if we are to transform our prescriptions into remedial medicine, we need power, influence or persistence, or a combination of all three. If the general law of the land is to be altered, Parliament must pass an Act, or Ministers must be persuaded to make new regulations under powers already vested in them by statute. Most of the public bills introduced into Parliament emanate from government Departments; nearly all of them will be passed. A fair number of bills are introduced by private members; not many of them will reach the statute book. The vast bulk of rules and regulations made under statutory authority are departmental, apart from local by-laws. If, then, one cannot be a Minister or a senior civil servant, one ought to start a campaign, or better still, form or join an organization likely to influence the lawmakers. One can hope to exercise some influence within a major political party, particularly if one is elected to the House of Commons; though party discipline will impose its constraints. Or one can join what is usually called a pressure group. And perhaps one will be moved to form or join such a group in order to prevent the law being changed for the worse.

Pressure groups[27] fall into two main classes, the sectional or interest

25. S.O. Nos. 43, 44, 74.

26. S.O. Nos. 33, 65(3).

27. Political scientists are responsible for a rapidly growing body of literature on this important subject. See generally S. E. Finer, *Anonymous Empire* (2nd edn); J. D. Stewart,

groups and the promotional or 'cause' groups. To the former class belong such powerful groups as the Trades Union Congress, the Confederation of British Industry, the National Farmers' Union, the British Medical Association, and associations representing different categories of local authorities. The degree of influence wielded by some of these bodies may vary according as the Government is Labour or Conservative. The power of the General Council of the TUC was demonstrated in 1969 when the Labour Government found it expedient to abandon legislative proposals for industrial relations. In 1971 and 1972 individual unions demonstrated their power in resisting implementation of the Conservative Government's industrial relations and wages policies. The influence of the Confederation of British Industry,[28] less obtrusive but more pervasive, resting on technical expertise, ample funds, representation on numerous official, advisory and consultative bodies, familiarity with the corridors of power and contacts with Ministers, civil servants, M.P.s and peers, must obviously be greater under a Conservative Government. The major sectional pressure groups are always significant, because a Government needs their cooperation and sometimes cannot withstand their opposition; because they represent large organized elements of the community; because they are wealthy, and can use their funds to employ research staff and to mount extensive publicity campaigns if necessary; because they have, or may be able to obtain, active members and sympathizers in Parliament;[29] because they are represented on advisory bodies connected with Departments; because their office-holders will have direct

---

British Pressure Groups; A. Potter, *Organised Groups in British Politics*; S. H. Beer, *Modern British Politics*. There are numerous case studies of the activities of individual pressure groups. See, for example, H. Eckstein, *Pressure Group Politics* (on the British Medical Association).

28. See W. P. Grant and D. Marsh (1971) 19 *Political Studies* 403.

29. The activities of parliamentary lobbyists are not regulated by law in this country. In the United States, where the influence of individual members of Congress may be considerably greater than that exercised by any M.P. in this country, and standards of financial probity in public life are less exacting, they are subject to detailed regulation. In 1969 a Select Committee of the House of Commons rejected proposals that a register of members' private interests be maintained (H.C. 59 (1969–70)). On the relation between outside organizations and parliamentary privilege, see pp. 319–20. It is a custom of Parliament that an M.P. having a private financial interest in a matter on which he speaks in debate shall declare his interest. But the rule that he is not allowed to cast a vote on such a question has only been enforced once in the last hundred years on a public matter (H.C. 57 (1969–70), xii) and in practice the scope of the rule seems to be confined to private bills. The Select Committee of 1969 recommended a not very exacting code of conduct for members, defining rules for *disclosure* of interests and stressing the impropriety of *advocating* an issue in respect of which a member is being or expects to be financially rewarded by an outside body. No action had been taken by the House by the end of 1972.

access to Ministers and senior civil servants. For a Department to introduce a bill directly affecting the interests of such an organization without
prior consultation with its representatives is exceptional; it is still more
exceptional for regulations to be made without such consultation. Consultation does not presuppose concurrence, but the content of the bill or
the regulations will frequently be influenced by these discussions. In the
case of bills, moreover, detailed amendments put down in Parliament
often originate from a pressure group. And a few bills passed, and a larger
number of regulations made, during the course of a year will be traceable
to the initiative of pressure groups, operating on Departments and private
members.

The pressure group which exists to promote a cause (for example, the
RSPCA, the Howard League for Penal Reform, Justice, the Lord's Day
Observance Society) rather than a sectional interest is far less likely to be
consulted at the formative stage of legislation, but it may help to procure
the enactment of legislation (usually introduced as a private member's
bill) or the amendment of bills. Relatively small but energetic and well-
organized pressure groups, using special reports or adept propaganda
directed towards influential persons rather than the general public, have
been largely instrumental in converting parliamentary majorities to such
causes as the abolition of capital punishment for murder, reform of the
criminal law relating to abortion and homosexual acts, the abolition of
theatre censorship, and the importation of the Ombudsman under the
name of the Parliamentary Commissioner for Administration. The
European Movement played a part in converting sceptics into supporters
of British accession to the EEC.

The end-product of legislation is an interplay of departmental initiative,
party political policies, pressure group activities and initiative of individual
M.P.s or groups of M.P.s. A glance through the Public General Acts for,
say, 1968, shows that the majority of the seventy-seven measures passed
into law were not inspired by political ideology or the pressure groups
just described, though some of their detailed provisions were influenced
by party political or pressure group views. A number were fundamentally
non-controversial, dealing with the machinery of financial administration,
technical law reform (for example, implementing reports of the Law
Reform Committee or the Law Commission) or the consolidation of
scattered enactments. Some were traceable to internal departmental
initiative, some to reports of independent bodies, some to international
agreements. On the whole an unexciting lot, no doubt, though of more
than usual interest to constitutional and administrative lawyers; and the
Commonwealth Immigrants Act, the Race Relations Act and the Theatres
Act were controversial in ways cutting across the usual party lines and

were by no means routine departmental measures. The first was a major policy decision conceived in haste, with eyes firmly fixed on domestic political repercussions, the second a policy decision taken after careful consideration of independent expert reports, and the third a private member's bill viewed benevolently by the Government. No Act uncongenial to the Government was passed, though a number of amendments to Government bills were accepted with reluctance. This evidence suggests that the picture of parliamentary legislation as a function of government is slightly over-coloured but by no means a caricature; and that it is easy to over-emphasize the parts played by party political programmes (except during the first year of a new Parliament) and pressure group activities in determining the content of the statute book.

Legislative procedure[30]

The Future Legislation Committee of the Cabinet considers departmental and inter-departmental proposals for new Government bills in principle, and arranges provisional priorities. The Legislation Committee of the Cabinet considers approved bills in detail, allocates firm priorities and keeps the parliamentary timetable under close review. The Leader of the House of Commons is chairman of both committees.

Consultation with interest groups is likely to be most active when a bill has been approved in principle, though it may take place before any firm decision has been made (for example, after publication of the report of an independent committee or royal commission) to which the group will almost certainly have submitted evidence. Recently Governments have taken to issuing Green Papers, setting out tentative legislative proposals for public discussion.[31]

A memorandum of instructions will be prepared by the sponsoring Department, or possibly an inter-departmental committee, for submission to parliamentary counsel, who will prepare a first draft of the bill. The bill may undergo several drafts before it is introduced into Parlia-

30. The principal source of information is *The Process of Legislation*, Second Report of the Select Committee on Procedure, July 1971 (H.C. 538 (1970–71)). See also Ivor F. Burton and Gavin Drewry (1972) 25 *Parliamentary Affairs* 123–62 for a detailed analysis of public legislation in 1970–71.

31. See, for example, Cmnd 4621 (1971) on value added tax, introduced by the Finance Act 1972. White Papers, stating firm or provisional decisions prior to publication of a bill, are more common. Shortly before the Industrial Relations Bill was published, a detailed 'Consultative Document' was issued. The publicity and opportunity for parliamentary debate afforded prior to the European Communities Bill were, however, quite exceptional.

ment. The final draft will be scrutinized by a Law Officer of the Crown as well as the Legislation Committee. Responsibility for the European Communities Bill was generally ascribed to the Solicitor-General, Sir Geoffrey Howe.

Introduction and first reading

Bills may be introduced in the Commons or the Lords. In the interests of good tactical management, a number of Government bills which are not likely to arouse party political opposition begin their career in the Lords. The existence of the upper House makes it possible to have more adequate parliamentary debates on legislation than would be the case if we had a unicameral Legislature. Money bills, however, must normally be introduced in the Commons (but cf. p. 232), and a tax bill must be preceded by a resolution of the Commons approving its introduction.

The normal method of introducing a public bill into the Commons is by its ministerial sponsors presenting a dummy print of the bill at the table; one of the clerks then reads out the title of the bill, which is thus deemed to have been read a first time; the bill is ordered to be printed and published, and a date fixed for the second reading.

Public bills introduced by private members can obtain a first reading in one of three ways. The first is by obtaining a high place in the ballot for the right to introduce private members' bills. In practice a member needs a high place to have any real prospect of seeing his bill pass through all its stages into law. Promotional pressure groups and sometimes the Government whips will seek to induce a well-placed private member to introduce a bill of their own devising. Several Law Commission bills have been enacted in this way. If the Government is particularly well disposed to a bill, a Minister will move any necessary money resolution, and the assistance of parliamentary counsel may be made available to its sponsor. Sometimes a Government may give up part of its own time to enable the bill to pass its final stages in the House. Secondly, a private member's bill may be introduced without leave of the House under S.O. No. 37. If such a bill is unopposed and skilfully managed, it has a chance of becoming law. Thirdly, any member may get up in his place at the beginning of public business on Tuesdays or Wednesdays and ask leave of the House to introduce a bill. The Speaker may allow him a few minutes to explain the nature and objects of the bill and also another member a similar opportunity to speak in opposition; the House then divides on the question whether to give leave.[32] Even if this preliminary hurdle is cleared, bills introduced under the 'ten-minute rule' seldom pass into law because they

32. S.O. No. 13.

cannot even be debated unless the Government is prepared to surrender some of its own time.[33]

Before a private bill – a bill of a local or personal character – can be introduced and read a first time, elaborate statutory provisions and standing orders have to be complied with. Private bills of a personal character are now almost obsolete; they were used extensively in the nineteenth century to provide for the naturalization of aliens and for divorces entitling the parties to remarry, until these changes in status could be effected by administrative action or judicial decrees under general enabling legislation. The nineteenth-century flurry of railway private bills is now part of economic history. Yet private legislation is not dying out. In 1971 eighty-one Public General Acts were passed, but there were also seventy-three 'Local and Personal' Acts.[34] Private bills are promoted mainly by local authorities seeking to acquire special powers; some are promoted by other public corporations, and a few by large public companies.

A local authority cannot promote a private bill to alter a local government area or to alter its status or electoral arrangements.[35] If a county or district authority wishes to promote a bill, it must give public notice, pass the necessary resolutions by an absolute majority, and confirm the resolution after the bill has been deposited in Parliament.[36] Within the House, the bill must pass the close scrutiny of the Examiners of private bills, who have to be satisfied that all the preliminary formalities, including the giving of notice to persons directly affected,[37] have been complied with. If these obstacles are successfully overcome, the bill is given a first reading.

Second reading

The occasion provided for parliamentary debate on the principles of a bill is the second reading stage. No amendment to individual clauses is

33. The Heath Government after 1970 proved less accommodating than the Wilson Government towards surrender of Government time for private members' bills. In the three sessions from 1968 to 1971, eighteen balloted private members' bills, seven under S.O. No. 37 and five under the ten-minute rule became law. Surprisingly, ten private peers' bills also became law during this period. See Burton and Drewry, loc. cit., p. 126. See also p. 236 for the failure rate. For the social influence of private members' legislation, see Peter G. Richards, *Parliament and Conscience* (1970).

34. The number included one Provisional Order Confirmation Act (see note 39) and a few Scottish private measures.

35. Local Government Act 1972, s. 70 (in force by April 1974).

36. ibid., s. 239. For the more elaborate procedure in force at the end of 1972 see W. O. Hart, *Introduction to the Law of Local Government and Administration* (8th edn), ch. 13.

37. cf. *Pickin* v. *British Railways Board* [1972] 3 W.L.R. 824, p. 74.

permissible. Rejection of a bill at second reading may be moved either by a reasoned amendment explaining why the bill should not be read a second time or by an amendment to postpone second reading. A private member's bill may be simply 'talked out' because the allotted time has expired. Private bills are normally unopposed at second reading.

Historically the second reading stage has always taken place in the House itself. Under recent amendments to standing orders, the second reading debate on a bill may be conducted in committee in two sets of circumstances:

1. On the motion of a Minister, a bill certified by the Speaker as relating exclusively to Scotland may be referred to the Scottish Grand Committee (consisting of all members for Scottish seats, with a sprinkling of Sassenachs to redress the political balance) for this purpose (S.O. Nos. 67, 68), provided that fewer than ten members object.

2. Any other public bill may now similarly be referred to a special second reading committee, consisting of between sixteen and fifty members, provided that ten days' notice of the motion is given and fewer than twenty members object (S.O. No. 66). From 1965 to 1971 only thirty-three bills had been so referred.

The committee reports to the House, which formally resolves that the bill be read a second time.

Money resolution

Till 1967 financial clauses in a bill had to be considered in Committee of the Whole House, with the Speaker out of the chair;[38] the Speaker then reoccupied the chair and the financial resolution was formally reported to the House. To save time, the financial resolution has now been telescoped into a single stage, the Speaker remaining in the chair. The necessary motion must still be moved by a Minister.

Committee stage

The committee stage of a bill follows second reading. It is the stage most likely to be guillotined if the two sides of the House are unable to agree on a timetable. There has been a big increase in the use of standing committees since the Second World War. Now all public bills other than the annual bills providing for public expenditure and bills for the confirmation

38. The need for the Speaker to leave the chair on such occasions was explicable on the grounds that the power of the Commons to withhold taxes and supplies from the Crown was historically of paramount importance, and the Speaker had at times been under the monarch's influence.

of provisional orders[39] go to standing committees unless the House otherwise resolves; since 1968 the annual Finance Bill (providing for taxation) has been taken wholly or partly in standing committee. The alternative is for a bill to be taken in Committee of the Whole House, which means that the House cannot proceed with any other business while the committee is sitting. Bills that are thought by the Government to be straightforward and not seriously controversial, and bills of major constitutional importance (such as the European Communities Bill or a bill to reform the Lords or alter the distribution of seats in the Commons) will be debated in Committee of the Whole House. The prospect of massive expenditure of time on the Parliament (No. 2) Bill in Committee of the Whole House induced the Government to withdraw it in April 1969; if the bill had been sent upstairs to a standing committee in the first place, the Government might perhaps have maintained patience.[40]

Standing committees consist of between sixteen and fifty members, chosen by the Committee of Selection in accordance with party strengths,[41] and having regard to their special qualifications. They usually sit in the mornings. Scottish bills may be committeed to a Scottish standing committee unless the second reading has been opposed by more than five members,[42] and bills dealing purely with Wales and Monmouthshire to a standing committee including all M.P.s from that area.[43]

In committee amendments to individual clauses of the bill are debated;[44] if no amendment to a clause is put down, that clause cannot be discussed except on the motion that the clause stand part of the bill. Proceedings are rather less formal than in the House; members may speak more than once to the same question. The Law Officers of the Crown have the right

39. Certain public general Acts empower Ministers to make provisional orders conferring special powers on public authorities. These orders are provisional in that they do not have effect till confirmed by a Provisional Order Confirmation Act. A provisional order usually entails a local inquiry at which objectors may be heard; the provisional order confirmation bill is technically a public bill, but its committee stage is similar to the committee stage of a private bill (see below).

40. See p. 296. But if a guillotine motion had become necessary at any stage, the Government would have been apprehensive about the outcome, given the opposition of many of their backbenchers to the bill.

41. A primary reason why the Labour Government, returned to office in February 1950 but with a tiny majority, had to go to the country again the following year, was that it could not risk sending any important bill to standing committee, since the absence of two of its supporters from a division could lead to a defeat. Its legislative programme was therefore badly impeded.

42. S.O. Nos. 67(4), 69.

43. S.O. No. 73(2); such a committee is seldom constituted. There is also a deliberative Welsh Grand Committee, composed of all those M.P.s and up to five others (S.O. No. 72).

44. Subject to the chairman's power to select amendments: see p. 272.

to attend standing committees and take part in their deliberations, but they are not entitled to vote unless they are members of the committee; their presence is often important, for obscurities in drafting need to be clarified and the implications of proposed amendments made clear. The Minister in charge of a bill (who can speak on a Finance Bill even if he is not a member of the committee) will frequently put down amendments to his own bill in committee in the light of afterthoughts by members of the Government or officials or parliamentary draftsmen, or other representations made from inside or outside the House following second reading. Amendments put down by backbenchers or the Opposition front bench will sometimes be accepted, or withdrawn on the understanding that the Minister will reconsider the matter in an attempt to meet the point in an alternative formulation. Hundreds of amendments were made to the Local Government Bill 1972 during its passage through Parliament. The European Communities Bill, on the other hand, though intensely controversial and a prodigious consumer of parliamentary time, was not amended at all.

To anyone at all familiar with American legislative bodies, it will be apparent that proceedings in committee on a bill are fundamentally different in the two countries. In the United States an enormous number of bills will be introduced; for practical purposes they will begin their careers in committee and will often fail to re-emerge; if they are 'reported out', they will still have to compete with a great many others to complete their remaining stages; the personal influence of the committee chairman may be decisive. The committee stage is inquisitorial and the committee will be small; oral and written testimony will be taken from members of the executive branch, outside experts, and representatives of interest groups. The only British analogy with the congressional legislative committee is the select committee. But only in exceptional circumstances will a bill be committed to a select committee;[45] in Britain such a committee is used predominantly as a device for parliamentary scrutiny of administration. However, statute law revision bills (to clear away dead wood from the statute book)[46] and consolidation bills (to bring together all the existing statute law on a matter in one Act, subject to minor modifications)[47] go to a joint select committee of the two Houses. Such bills now emanate from the Law Commissions.

Proceedings in committee on an unopposed private bill and also on a hybrid bill, and to a large extent on a provisional order confirmation bill,

45. Bills on the Queen's Civil List and on the discipline of the armed forces have gone to select committees. They also have to go through a normal committee stage.

46. See, for example, the Statute Law Revision Act 1948.

47. Some interesting variations from ordinary legislative procedure are prescribed by the Consolidation of Enactments (Procedure) Act 1949. *Quaere* whether observance of the special procedure laid down is mandatory. See Erskine May, op. cit., pp. 512–3.

are quite different from those on public bills. A private bill will be considered by a small committee, of four in the Commons or five in the Lords. The bill will have been drafted by parliamentary agents. The promoters must prove the preamble, stating the facts accounting for the bill and its objects, to the satisfaction of the committee; petitioners against the bill, having established their *locus standi*, may argue against the preamble and put down amendments to clauses; the parties may be represented by counsel, call evidence and make submissions. The proceedings of the committee have the outward trappings of a quasi-judicial contest between parties, though the committees may give paramountcy to extraneous factors directed to the furtherance of the public interest.

Report stage

The bill, as amended, is reported to the House. The Speaker takes the chair. If it is a private bill, the report stage may be a formality. If a public bill considered in Committee of the Whole House emerges unamended, there is no report stage. If a bill has been considered in standing committee, other members may wish to put down their amendments on report, subject again to the Speaker's power of selection. Again, if the Government has afterthoughts it may decide to put down amendments or new clauses or schedules on report. It is possible for a bill to be sent back to committee at report stage. Bills considered at second reading in standing committee or by the Scottish Grand Committee may have their report stage taken before such a committee if a Minister so moves and fewer than twenty members object.[48]

Third reading

More often than not, a bill is read a third time immediately the report stage is concluded. The third reading will not now be debated at all unless six or more members give notice that they wish for a debate or a postponement.[49] If there is a debate, it will be brief and general in its terms. Only minor verbal amendments may be made; the bill may, theoretically at least, nevertheless be rejected at the end of the debate.

Lords' bills and amendments

The procedure on bills in the Lords is similar to that in the Commons, but there is no money resolution stage and the committee stage is taken

48. S.O. No. 73. A standing committee (other than the Scottish Grand Committee) so constituted must have between twenty and eighty members.
49. S.O. No. 56.

in the whole House, with the Lord Chairman of Committees in the chair, and there is no provision in standing orders for the closure or guillotining of debate. A public bill passed by the Lords cannot become law unless the Commons also pass it. A public bill passed by the Commons can become law under the Parliament Acts procedure although the Lords fail to pass it without amendment or reject it. Disagreements between the two Houses on clauses of a bill may be resolved in this manner, but it is more usual for one House (normally the Lords) to give way or for a compromise to be reached; a small committee is appointed by one House to give reasons why it disagrees with the other's amendments.

Quorum in the Commons

The general rule (subject to exceptions for certain hours and days and certain types of business) is that the quorum of the House and in Committee of the Whole House is forty.[50] This means not that forty members have in fact to be present in the chamber at all relevant times, but that if the House divides on a motion, the business under discussion stands over till the next sitting unless forty or more members have taken part in the division. It is the responsibility of the Government whips to ensure that a sufficient number of their backbenchers are in the vicinity of the chamber to scurry in when a vote is called for. In standing committee the quorum is one-third of its members or seventeen, whichever is the less.[51]

Royal assent

Under the new procedure introduced by the Royal Assent Act 1967, the House can simply be notified that the royal assent to a bill has been granted, and it does not have to interrupt its proceedings and adjourn to the Lords' chamber to hear the royal assent signified orally.

Community legislation

Community legislation directly applicable without further enactment in this country[52] does not pass through any of these stages. Such legislation consists mainly of regulations made by the Council of Ministers or the Commission. In Community law, regulations are secondary legislation. In

50. S.O. No. 29, as amended in November 1971.
51. S.O. No. 65(1). Private members' bills are no longer 'counted out'
52. European Communities Act 1972, s. 2(1).

United Kingdom law they must rank as primary and not delegated legislation. New parliamentary machinery will be needed to keep members informed of Community legislative proposals in their formative stages; to enable effective representations to be made to the Community authorities; and to give proper consideration to the implications of the regulations once they have been made. It will also be necessary to scrutinize Community *directives* and *decisions*, which do not normally have *direct* effect in the laws of member States but which oblige them to implement the Community rules and policies there embodied by appropriate domestic procedures. Those procedures may entail legislation.

Financial procedure

The main departmental responsibility for the management of the national economy rests with the Treasury, under the Chancellor of the Exchequer.[53] A Department bearing the main brunt of decisions affecting national income and expenditure, the value of the pound, the country's international balance of payments and the cost of living is necessarily of crucial importance.

The initiative in tax policy is vested in the Treasury alone.[54] The details of the Chancellor of the Exchequer's budget speech are revealed to his Cabinet colleagues only the day before it is delivered in the House. In matters of public expenditure, Treasury approval is required for all large-scale items, not only at the central departmental level but also by public corporations and, directly or indirectly, by local authorities. The hand of the Treasury extends to approval of the standard terms of Government contracts and pricing policies. The influence of the Treasury at any given time is, of course, partly dependent on the personal stature of the Chancellor, and his ability to carry the Prime Minister and the Cabinet along with him. That influence has traditionally been exercised in the interests of economy and caution. In 1958 Mr Peter Thorneycroft, unable to convince the Cabinet of the need for scaling down the annual estimates, resigned with his two junior Ministers; the Macmillan Government survived his departure.

No attempt will be made here to present a general review of public finance. Instead, the raising of taxes and expenditure of public money will be viewed in a parliamentary context.

53. See generally Samuel Brittan, *Steering the Economy: The Role of the Treasury*; Lord Bridges, *The Treasury*; Henry Roseveare, *The Treasury*. From 1964 to 1969 there was a separate Department of Economic Affairs.
54. Subject to Community rules: see below.

Taxation

Taxes are collected by or under the Board of Inland Revenue, the Board of Customs and Excise and the Estate Duty Office. Some taxes – for example, stamp duties, death duties – imposed by statute have effect till the statute is amended. Others – notably income tax, surtax, customs and excise duties – have effect only till the end of the tax year and require renewal by Parliament in the annual Finance Act. No charge may lawfully be levied on the subject by the Crown except under authority conferred by express statutory language; the fact that an Act may be unworkable unless charges are imposed in the course of its administration is irrelevant.[55]

However, membership of the Communities will have major constitutional effects. First, the United Kingdom has agreed to adopt the Communities' common external tariff and its agricultural policy (involving the imposition of import levies) over a five-year transitional period.[56] Secondly, the rates of customs duties and agricultural levies *can be varied* by *directly applicable* Community regulations.[57] Thirdly, the Communities are to be progressively financed out of their '*own resources*', which will comprise the proceeds of customs duties (less 10 per cent for the cost of administration), agricultural levies, and eventually up to 1 per cent of a harmonized value added tax, all collected by member States for Community purposes.[58] *United Kingdom authorities will be levying and collecting money under Community law as agents for the Communities. Moreover, payments required to meet Britain's Community obligations will be charged on the Consolidated Fund.*[59]

55. The leading case is *Att.-Gen.* v. *Wilts United Dairies Ltd* (1921) 37 T.L.R. 884. See also *Liverpool Corporation* v. *Maiden (Arthur) Ltd* [1938] 4 All E.R. 200 (local authorities). The Bill of Rights provides that no charge on the subject should be levied by pretence of prerogative without the consent of Parliament, but the principle stated in the text above ranges beyond prerogative exactions and, indeed, beyond central government. However, charges may be imposed by the Crown on the subject without express statutory authority for providing services (*China Navigation Co.* v. *Att.-Gen.* [1932] 2 K.B. 197) which it is under no prior legal obligation to furnish.

56. See *The United Kingdom and the European Communities* (Cmnd 4715 (1971)). An Intervention Board for Agricultural Produce has been set up to implement the agricultural policy (European Communities Act 1972, s. 6).

57. European Communities Act 1972, ss. 2(1), 5, 6.

58. This was agreed by the Communities in 1970 (Cmnd 4867 (1972)), and promulgated by a Community regulation in 1971, subject to modifications agreed in the instruments of accession (Cmnd 4862 – 1 (1972), pp. 51–3). See also European Communities Act, s. 1, Sched. 1, para. 6. Till 1980 payments by this country will be lump sums fixed as percentages of the Community budget.

59. European Communities Act 1972, s. 2(3). See for Consolidated Fund Services, p. 287. The purpose of charging these monies on the Consolidated Fund is to reduce parliamentary scrutiny over them. See further 831 H.C.Deb. 1137–1242 (22 February 1972).

Before 1968 the budget was introduced in the Committee of Ways and Means, a Committee of the Whole House, with the Speaker out of the chair. This committee has now been abolished and the budget statement is made by the Chancellor in the House itself. At the same time, a White Paper is published containing a financial statement and commentary on the budget; this now includes economic data for the recent past and predictions for the immediate future, indicative both of the broader range of the Treasury's functions and of pressure to give the public fuller information.

The budget will be introduced in late March or early April. For tax purposes the financial year runs from 6 April to 5 April in the following year. The Finance Bill, incorporating tax legislation, is unlikely to receive the royal assent till late July. But authority to collect the most remunerative taxes will have expired on 5 April. In order to bridge this gap, statutory authority exists[60] to enable essential taxes to be levied immediately after the budget. As soon as the Chancellor sits down, resolutions approving these tax proposals are passed and have statutory effect forthwith by virtue of the Provisional Collection of Taxes Act 1968. Under section 5 of this Act (as amended), resolutions can be (and are) passed, giving provisional statutory effect, for ten days,[61] to the proposed new rates of income tax, value added tax, corporation tax and customs and excise duties for the financial year; they must be confirmed by the House within ten days; the Finance Bill must be read a second time within twenty-five days and passed into law by 5 August, if the resolutions were passed in March or April, or within four months in other circumstances; otherwise the collection of taxes on the basis of the resolutions becomes retroactively invalid. This tends, of course, to restrict the period in which it is practicable to dissolve Parliament.

Debate on the budget will continue for several days on a general resolution which does not have to be passed forthwith. The Finance Bill is then published and read a second time. At the committee stage – if taken in standing committee, many additional days become available for the business of the House – a very large number of amendments will be put down and some will be accepted or compromise amendments put down by the Government. The Government cannot be too amenable, because the sum to be raised by taxation is geared both to its general economic

60. It was needed because such taxes could not lawfully be imposed merely on the strength of budget resolutions: *Bowles* v. *Bank of England* [1913] 1 Ch. 57. The position was regulated for the future by the Provisional Collection of Taxes Act 1913.

61. See also s. 1 of the 1968 Act, under which the resolutions can be given firm statutory effect (subject to the provisos mentioned in the text above) without a confirming resolution.

policy and its commitments as to the quantum of expenditure, but minor concessions are possible. Since there will not have been a full range of prior consultations with interest groups or expert committees before the budget is introduced, the practical implications of the proposed changes in tax law will not always have been appreciated by the Treasury, and it may welcome suggestions – for example, that a particular tax will cause undue hardship or be too difficult or costly to enforce. The bill will usually also modify aspects of tax law which do not need annual enactment.

Amendments will again be put down when the bill is reported to the House. After third reading, proceedings in the Lords will be a formality.

The passage of a Finance Bill is not invariably smooth, but there can be no comparison with the course of events in the United States Congress. In 1968 the Committee of Ways and Means of the House of Representatives successfully insisted on a reduction of $6,000,000,000 in the Administration's 'budget' (i.e. proposals for expenditure) before consenting to a 10 per cent tax surcharge.

Supplementary budgets and other legislation to levy money (for example, to introduce higher National Health Service charges) may be introduced during a parliamentary session. In the autumn 'budget' of 1970, the Chancellor of the Exchequer took the extraordinary step of announcing that there would be a reduction in the standard rate of income tax in the next annual budget.

National expenditure

Public expenditure also requires statutory authority. About two-thirds of central government expenditure is customarily authorized on an annual basis.

As expenditure in the public sector of the national economy has grown, new machinery for coordinating departmental programmes has had to be constructed. An inter-departmental Public Expenditure Survey Committee (PESC) was set up early in the 1960s to consider the medium-term implications of existing policies.[62] In December 1969 the Treasury published the first of its annual projections of public expenditure extending over a five-year period.[63] Within this general framework, detailed annual spending programmes are evolved. During the summer decisions are taken on the aggregate of public expenditure for the next financial year

62. See H.C. 410 (1968–69), pp. 19–22, for its place in the modern scheme. For the earlier system and recommendations for change, see the Plowden Report on the Control of National Expenditure (Cmnd 1432 (1961)).

63. Cmnd 4234 (1969). This was foreshadowed by proposals advanced in Cmnd 4017 (1969).

and functional priorities are determined. Towards the end of the same calendar year, the departmental estimates are prepared and discussed with the Treasury. Departmental freedom of action will have been curbed by the decisions taken in the summer. The Treasury's own freedom of manoeuvre in effecting economies will also have been fettered by those decisions, by international commitments and by legislation providing for social security benefits, as well as a variety of domestic political considerations influencing the direction and amount of government spending.

Bulky volumes of the estimates are published in February and March. They are divided into classes, 'votes' (for individual Departments, sub-Departments, and certain other bodies financed out of central funds), sub-heads and further details; the corresponding figures for the current year are set out. For the purpose of national expenditure, the financial year extends from 1 April to 31 March. Parliament has to debate the estimates – redress of grievances precedes supply – and the result of its deliberations (or rather, the deliberations of the House of Commons) will be embodied in the Appropriation Act, which is usually passed in July. The Act authorizes the withdrawal from the Bank of England, and the expenditure, of the sum total of the estimates, and appropriates in its schedules money for prescribed votes. But the Government needs drawing and borrowing powers before this. To bridge the gap, a sum (called the vote on account) authorizing the prospective expenditure of 35 to 40 per cent of the total sought will be granted by one or more Consolidated Fund Acts passed before the beginning of the financial year. These Acts will also authorize expenditure on supplementary estimates for the year just ending, and may ratify an excess vote to a Department which overspent its allotted sum in the previous year.[64]

Those items of expenditure for which annual authority is needed are called Supply Services; the others (comprising interest on the national debt, the Civil List, and the salaries of judges, the Speaker, the Leader of the Opposition and other persons whose conduct in office ought not to be the subject of annual debate, and now sums required for the discharge of Community obligations) are Consolidated Fund Services. The Consolidated Fund is a notional account kept at the Bank of England. In 1968 many of its functions and revenues were allotted to a new account, the National Loans Fund.[65]

An annual two-day debate now takes place in the House of Commons

64. Unappropriated sums can be made available in an emergency out of the Civil Contingencies Fund. Such grants are scrutinized by the Comptroller and Auditor-General and the Public Accounts Committee (see below) and are often the subject of a critical report.

65. See National Loans Act 1968.

on the Government's general projections of public expenditure. Debates on the estimates used to be conducted mainly in Committee of Supply, another Committee of the Whole House; this too has been abolished, and since 1967 supply business has been conducted in the House as normally constituted, or in the Scottish Grand Committee. Twenty-nine (not necessarily consecutive) parliamentary days are devoted to supply; this includes debates on the main estimates, supplementary estimates, excess votes and reports from the select committees of the House dealing with expenditure. These debates are no longer seriously regarded as if they were a form of detailed scrutiny of expenditure; in any event the estimates are treated by the Government as matters of confidence and are always approved by the House. No member (not even a Minister) can move a motion to increase an estimate or to spend money on another object. The choice of topics to be debated is, by convention, left to the Opposition. Traditionally the peg on which debate is hung has been a motion to reduce the Minister's (or the Department's) vote by a nominal sum; now a more widely or narrowly framed motion – even a motion to annul a statutory instrument – can be put down on a supply day. The Opposition uses its time to criticize aspects of Government policy; the gist of its criticisms may well be that too little money is being spent or that money is being spent on the wrong objects. The content of a debate may bear no direct relationship to expenditure at all – for example, policy towards Rhodesia. Debates on the Consolidated Fund and Appropriation Bills are occasions for motions by private members successful in a ballot; thus, one finds that the honourable member for Orpington addressed the House on the second reading of the Appropriation Bill from 5.19 a.m. to 5.43 a.m. one July morning in 1969 on the tribulations of gypsies, and elicited a ministerial reply.[66]

The task of scrutinizing government spending is entrusted to two select committees of the House, which have attained the dignity of a place in standing orders. In 1971 the Estimates Committee[67] was replaced by an Expenditure Committee, consisting of forty-nine members.[68] Its terms of references are to consider papers on public expenditure (including the estimates) presented to the House and to consider in particular how the policies implicit in them can be carried out more economically. Like all select committees it has power to send for persons, papers and records;

66. Expenditure for the fulfilment of Britain's Community obligations, being a Consolidated Fund Service, probably cannot be debated on a supply day except perhaps in the context of a report by the Expenditure Committee. It could be debated in connection with a Consolidated Fund Bill.

67. See Nevil Johnson, *Parliament and Administration*.

68. S.O. No. 87.

it can examine Ministers and civil servants; the Government does not, however, make the contents of departmental files freely available on request.[69] It works mainly through sub-committees, and it has power to engage expert assistance for particular inquiries. The Estimates Committee was the only select committee empowered to maintain a general oversight over efficiency in central administration, and it had scrutinized matters as diverse as penal institutions, the legal aid scheme, the BBC and expenditure on British bases overseas. But it was understaffed and overstretched, and its searching reports were not always taken seriously by Departments. The Expenditure Committee, a higher-powered body with slightly broader terms of reference, was soon experiencing one of its predecessor's problems. After eighteen months it had published ten reports, covering topics such as the British Council, government expenditure on education and the arts, the probation and after-care service, and National Health Service facilities for private patients, but only three had been debated in Parliament and Departments were being characteristically dilatory in commenting on its recommendations.[70]

The Public Accounts Committee[71] was established in 1861 and is composed of fifteen members. Although, as in all select and standing committees, they are selected according to party strengths, the committee is scrupulously non-partisan – so much so that there is a well-settled convention that its chairman shall be a member of the Opposition; he is usually a former junior Minister at the Treasury. It scrutinizes the public accounts (appropriation accounts) which have been drawn up by the Comptroller and Auditor-General and his Exchequer and Audit Department, and may recommend changes in the form of the accounts. In addition, it is entitled to examine the expenditure of other sums voted by Parliament, and those accounts of public bodies which have been laid before Parliament, even though the Comptroller and Auditor-General has not audited them.

The Exchequer and Audit Department has a staff of some five hundred. It conducts a continuous audit within the Departments and carries out special test audits; it works closely with the departmental accounting officers, who are normally the permanent secretaries. The Comptroller and Auditor-General also has the responsibility for checking the legality of withdrawals from the Consolidated Fund and the National Loans

<hr />

69. See Cmnd 3479 (1968) for a refusal by the Foreign Office to supply confidential information sought by the Select Committee on Agriculture.

70. See its special report, H.C. 476 (1971–72).

71. See Basil Chubb, *The Control of Public Expenditure*; Gordon Reid, *The Politics of Financial Control*; E. L. Normanton, *The Accountability and Audit of Governments*; H.C. 410 (1968–69).

Fund. He is an independent public officer, not a civil servant; he is appointed by the Crown on the Prime Minister's advice but is removable only for misbehaviour in pursuance of an address from both houses of Parliament, and his salary is charged on the Consolidated Fund. The Public Accounts Committee has before it his report on the accounts, and he sits with the Committee; this strengthens its position greatly when it interrogates the departmental accounting officers. Its reports draw attention not only to financial irregularities but also to wasteful and extravagant expenditure and imprudent contractual transactions. They are treated with the greatest respect in Whitehall. Its weakness is that the malpractices or blunders to which it refers will have occurred not less than a year beforehand and sometimes a good deal farther back, and the money may have been squandered beyond recall, as when financial irregularities perpetrated by members of a body to which the author had the honour to belong at the end of the Second World War were responsible for the loss of well over £50 millions to the Exchequer.[72] But the report of an inquest may not be unproductive as a spur to remedial action; for instance, the adverse report of the Public Accounts Committee on excess profits made by an armaments firm under a contract for the supply of a guided missile led to a repayment by the firm and tighter contracting procedures.

This committee, then, is an indispensable watchdog, highly effective in its own limited area; its bark causes quicker reactions than the bites of others. The Comptroller and Auditor-General and the Public Accounts Committee have now been given access to the accounts of university institutions in receipt of central government funds. Whether this will prove to be a form of parliamentary scrutiny encroaching but mildly upon traditional academic autonomy is still a matter for conjecture.

Scrutiny of policy and administration

Under Standing Order No. 22, the Speaker or chairman may direct a member who persists in tedious repetition to discontinue his speech. This is a useful working rule; and this important section will therefore be abbreviated.

The general role of the official Opposition has already been considered. Its main procedural opportunities for criticizing the Government or individual members arise in the debate on the address in reply to the Queen's speech at the beginning of a session, debates on the budget and on supply days, debates on motions of censure or other substantive motions (for example, on a formal motion for the adjournment) for which the Government gives up part of its own time, second reading debates,

72. For the doleful tale see H.C. 115 (1946–47).

and at question time. But the time saved by recent procedural changes enabling more legislation to be considered in standing committees has been filled by Government legislation rather than general debate.[73] Back-benchers have their opportunities on the occasions set aside for private members' motions,[74] on the motion for the adjournment each day and before a recess, at question time and, if any succeed in catching the Speaker's eye, in the course of general debate. They can also put their names to 'early day motions', which are in the nature of demonstrations of protest, concern or occasionally loyalty; these motions are tabled but are hardly ever debated in the House.

Ordinary business may be interrupted to debate a matter of urgency under Standing Order No. 9. A motion to adjourn to discuss 'a specific and important matter that should have urgent consideration' can be moved by any member, at short notice, immediately after question time. It lies within the Speaker's discretion whether to allow the motion to be put; leave is not readily granted. If this obstacle is overcome, and if the motion is approved by the House or supported by forty members rising in their places, the motion will be debated either that evening or the following day.

Members and question time[75]

Members of Parliament receive some 250,000 letters from members of the public each year, making complaints (often about their local authorities or the conduct of a nationalized undertaking) which usually call for some kind of remedial action or request for information. In addition, most members now hold local 'surgeries' to deal with the personal problems of their constituents. If a matter calling for further action falls within the area of ministerial responsibility, the member will usually write to the Minister about it and perhaps talk to him personally; if no satisfactory answer is received, the member may well decide to raise the issue at question time, or pass a complaint alleging injustice caused by mal-administration to the Parliamentary Commissioner for Administration to investigate. If a grave public scandal is suspected, and pressure is exerted on the Government, a special independent inquiry or a formal judicial tribunal of inquiry may be set up.[76]

73. H.C. 538 (1970–71), para. 4.

74. Under the Heath Government twelve Fridays a session were devoted to private members' bills and eight to private members' motions. See also p. 288 above.

75. See D. N. Chester and Nona Bowring, *Questions in Parliament*; Patrick Howarth, *Questions in the House.*

76. See chs. 25 and 29 for the investigation of alleged abuses under the Parliamentary Commissioner Act 1967 and the Tribunals of Inquiry (Evidence) Act 1921.

Tabling questions in the House is one form of obtaining publicity for individual grievances; redress may be forthcoming because a parliamentary question is threatened, or because it has been put down, or because the answer given to the question is manifestly unsatisfactory and the Minister feels that he is appearing in a bad light, or because the member presses home his point by giving notice that he will raise the issue again on a half-hourly debate on the daily adjournment; but if no redress has been granted by question time, the likelihood is that no redress will be offered at all. A question to a Minister is rather a method of ventilating a grievance than of securing a remedy.

Questions to Ministers may serve other purposes. They may even be put for the purpose of eliciting factual information, in which case an oral answer will seldom be requested; the answer will then be given in writing, and circulated together with answers to oral questions which there was no time to reach. (Question time lasts for some forty-five minutes, on Mondays to Thursdays.) They may be inspired questions; a member is asked to put down a question so that the responsible Minister can make a public statement.[77] They may be, and often are, carefully designed to cause a Minister the maximum amount of embarrassment. Although a question for which an oral answer is requested must normally be tabled two days in advance, the question may be an opening gambit, to be followed by a supplementary question of which no prior notice is given. Parliamentary reputations have been made and ruined in the rapid cut and thrust of question time. For a few minutes the House comes to life audibly and visibly: wit,[78] feigned or genuine outrage, cheers and jeers intrude upon the solemnity of the proceedings; Government and Opposition are briefly locked in fascinating verbal combat; the Prime Minister and the Leader of the Opposition may gain or lose a point or two in the public opinion polls; a backbencher shows his ministerial potential, and the House wonders how much longer the Minister of Cosmology can last.

Whatever may be the intrinsic value of parliamentary questions, their popularity with the M.P.s is increasing. In the 1970–71 session there were 33,946 questions on the order paper, more than half requesting written answers.[79]

77. But a Minister should not carry this practice to a point where opposition questions cannot be put; nor should departmental civil servants be induced to take part in such a game. See Report of the Select Committee on Parliamentary Questions (H.C. 393 (1971–72)).

78. Winston Churchill, still Prime Minister at seventy-nine, was asked to constitute a Ministry of Fisheries separate from the Ministry of Agriculture. Explaining his refusal, he observed that 'there are many ancient links between fish and chips' (528 H.C.Deb. 2274).

79. H.C. 393 (1971–72), Minutes of Evidence, p. 58.

As has already been pointed out,[80] questions may and normally will be refused if they relate to matters lying outside the field of ministerial responsibility. Among inadmissible questions[81] are those on matters *sub judice*, but the scope of this exclusionary rule has now been narrowed so as to enable the Speaker to admit questions in his discretion though they relate to matters pending adjudication in a civil court, if the issue raised concerns a matter of national importance or the exercise of a Minister's discretion challengeable only on narrow grounds before the court.[82]

Specialized select committees of the House

A serious weakness of the House of Commons is the ineffectual role of so many backbenchers – no less ineffectual because it cannot be quantified. Able men and women discover that their opportunities to contribute significantly to debate are few, that their influence on Government policy from the back benches or in opposition seems negligible, that even in the privacy of parliamentary party meetings the leadership is rarely moved by their arguments and that the conduct of public administration cannot be effectively scrutinized by the House. If Parliament is the grand inquest of the nation, the roles of coroner and corpse are apt to be confused.

Any effective participation of backbench M.P.s in decision-making will continue to present very great difficulties as long as Governments maintain majorities in the House with the aid of an electoral system under which the winner can expect to take almost all, and as long as constitutional rules leave the spending power entirely in the hands of the Executive. But, as the experience of the Public Accounts Committee and the Committee on Nationalized Industries has shown, it is possible, within the existing British parliamentary system, for members to *influence* the conduct of administration and to modify aspects of policy by their scrutiny of administrative activity as members of select committees.

In 1966 there existed the two select committees mentioned above, the Estimates Committee and the Select Committee on Statutory Instruments. Other select committees, not directly concerned with central administration, were also appointed sessionally – for example, the Committee of Privileges, a House of Commons Services Committee, an almost dormant Committee on Public Petitions – and a Select Committee on Procedure was regularly constituted. But in 1967 a new and potentially fruitful

80. See pp. 171–2, 221–2.
81. See Erskine May, op. cit., pp. 324–9.
82. 839 H.C.Deb. 1589–1627 (28 June 1972), a relaxation directly related to controversial proceedings before the National Industrial Relations Court; see H.C. 298 (1971–72). This rule has been applied to contempt of court [1973] 2 W.L.R. 452; p. 371.

experiment was begun. Two specialized select committees on agriculture and on science and technology were appointed. Their terms of reference were general, but it was understood that they would keep under review and report to the House on the conduct of departmental administration in the areas concerned. The experiment was not an unqualified success. Some members proved wayward in their attendance; the committee on agriculture became self-assertive and showed more interest than the Minister in the agricultural policy of the Common Market; the relationship between the committees, the civil servants whom they interrogated, the responsible Ministers and the House as a whole was inevitably experimental, but proved more abrasive in its early stages than optimists had hoped. The Select Committee on Agriculture was discontinued early in 1969 by a decision made by the Government and ratified by the House. But it was succeeded by new specialized select committees – a committee on education and science (which distinguished itself by sending a sub-committee to visit centres of student unrest, thus evoking a sufficient degree of disturbance for its own proceedings to be disrupted on two occasions[83]), a committee on race relations and immigration, a committee on overseas aid, a committee on Scottish affairs and a small committee on the Parliamentary Commissioner for Administration (which rapidly justified its existence).[84] In 1970 the incoming Conservative Government decided to continue with the experiment on a more limited scale, but to sponsor the establishment of a stronger Expenditure Committee.[85] The committee on race relations and immigration continued to publish useful reports.[86] In 1972 the committee on science and technology, having publicly disagreed with Ministers and the head of the Central Policy Review Staff about the role of research councils and departmental organization for research, went on to publish a suppressed departmental report on the role of Government in developing and exploiting inventions.

The committees have offered some detailed and imaginative suggestions for administrative reorganization, and have made themselves, the House in general, and interested members of the public, better informed about central administration and the views of the administered. This has at least diminished the excessive concentration of inaccessible facts and in-

83. One of which (in the spring of 1969) was directly observed by the author. For the committee's consequential report, including recommendations for closer central Government control over aspects of higher education, see H.C. 449–1 (1968–69). Most of its recommendations were disregarded.

84. See further ch. 29.

85. Cmnd 4507 (1970); 806 H.C. Deb. 618–735 (12 November 1970). See also pp. 288–9 on the Expenditure Committee. In December 1972 an *ad hoc* select committee was appointed to consider the Government's proposed tax credit scheme.

86. See, for example, p. 386, note 38.

scrutable motives secreted within the ample bosom of the Executive. To put the case for specialized committees in its most conservative form, they will give some M.P.s something useful to do, and an awareness that they are doing something useful. It is not difficult to criticize the committees for being superficial, over-ambitious, tactless, ineffectual or even too deferential.[87] Far more difficult will be the task of maintaining and strengthening a system of scrutinizing committees. For there must now be created machinery capable of effectively scrutinizing the work and output of European Community organs as well as departmental policies and administration in this country. This is a task for which inquisitorial committees of the Legislature should be pre-eminently suited. As the Select Committee on Procedure observed in July 1972,[88] 'the entry of Britain into the Communities presents a profound challenge to many of the established procedures of Parliament which, if not adequately dealt with, could leave Parliament substantially weaker *vis-à-vis* the Executive'.

87. Deference has been attributed by the originator of the experiment to the fact that members are chosen by the whips and tend to pull their punches for fear of impairing their hopes of preferment: Richard Crossman, *Inside View*, pp. 103–4. It must not, of course, be assumed that because the committees have been criticized for incompatible reasons none of the charges is to be taken seriously. For preliminary assessments, see Alfred Morris (ed.), *The Growth of Parliamentary Scrutiny by Committee*; A. H. Hanson and Bernard Crick (eds.), *The Commons in Transition*; John P. Mackintosh, *The Government and Politics of Britain*, ch. 10; Richards, *The Backbenchers*, ch. 6. Most are pessimistic.

88. H.C. 448 (1971–72), para. 9. See also pp. 282–3, 284.

Chapter 13
The House of Lords

Prologue

In November 1967 the Labour Government initiated formal discussions with representatives of the two main opposition parties with a view to arriving at an agreed scheme for the reform of the composition and functions of the House of Lords. By June 1968 a large measure of agreement had been reached. Then the Government, irritated by the refusal of the Lords to approve (at the first time of asking) an Order in Council imposing mandatory UN sanctions against Rhodesia, broke off the talks and produced its own scheme, closely based on what had already been agreed. A White Paper embodying the Government's proposals[1] was debated in November 1968. It was approved in principle by the Commons by 270 votes to 159. The breakdown of the voting figures is remarkable; although the Government had put on a three-line whip, and although the Opposition front benches were in general sympathy with the proposals, forty-five Labour backbenchers, 104 Conservatives, eight Liberals and two other members voted in the Noes lobby. The Lords agreed to the proposals by 251 votes to 56.

Nevertheless (or perhaps consequently) trouble lay ahead for the Government. A bill to implement the proposals[2] was read a second time in the Commons. But when it went to Committee of the Whole House, a multitude of amendments were put down by backbenchers. Many members objected to the excessive patronage that the scheme would have placed in the Prime Minister's hands; some Conservatives objected to the erosion of the hereditary principle or the weakening of the party's strength in the upper House; some Labour members saw the proposals as a means of shoring up a crumbling citadel of aristocratic privilege and wealth which ought to be demolished altogether or left alone to crumble away. In the end the Government gave up. In April 1969 it withdrew the bill, to make room for a still more controversial Industrial Relations Bill which was never introduced at all during that Parliament.

1. *House of Lords Reform* (Cmnd 3799 (1968)).
2. It was generally known as the Parliament (No. 2) Bill.

To the 1968–9 proposals for reform of the Lords we shall return. Perhaps proposals like them will be revived. Yet prediction would be unwise. More than sixty years ago a General Election was fought on the slogan 'end or mend' the Lords. Since then, four quite substantial measures have been passed, bringing the House into closer rapport with modern views about British governmental institutions. But the House still remains to outward appearances a preposterous anachronism, to be derided rather than admired. Strange to say, it is the best second chamber in the Commonwealth and one which stands comparison with its counterparts in almost any developed country one cares to mention.

Composition
Introduction

Some legislatures are born bicameral, some achieve bicameralism, some have bicameralism thrust upon them. Many have sustained themselves unendowed with this benefit; some – New Zealand, for example – have shed or been bereft of their second chamber, reverting to unicameralism without disastrous consequences. The English Parliament was not exactly born; somehow it grew up, but as a bicameral institution. From the Great Council of the Realm in Parliament two Houses emerged. The evolution of the House of Lords, the direct lineal descendant of the Great Council, was none the less halting and irregular. At first the King's tenants in chief and great officers of State and the prelates attended the Great Council; soon the lesser tenants in chief came to be represented by the knights of the shires. A concept of baronage and hereditary peerage was already developing by the end of the thirteenth century; the onerous duty of attendance became a right to attend by virtue of inheritance of a peerage. With the disappearance of the abbots and those officers who were not ennobled, the modern House of Lords had taken shape by the middle of the Tudor period.[3] The Commons clearly had the dominant voice in taxation, but the Lords indirectly maintained ascendancy in Parliament by virtue of their social status (which brought some of them close to the monarch), the deference paid to the landed gentry and the episcopacy, and the influence of wealthy individual peers over elections to and allegiance within the lower House. The Reform Act of 1832 sounded the knell; the political influence of the Lords was undermined by further extensions of the franchise and the growth of mass parties; the Parliament Act of 1911 definitively emphasized the primacy of the Commons, and the upper House was shorn of all pretensions to a prominent place in the nation's affairs.

3. Separate Lords' Journals go back to 1521.

Membership

The superior judges and the Law Officers of the Crown still receive writs of summons to attend with the Lords at the opening of a new Parliament, but they never take part in the proceedings of the House unless they are peers. The following are entitled to membership:

1. The Lords Spiritual. These are the Archbishops of Canterbury and York, the Bishops of London, Durham and Winchester, and the next twenty-one senior diocesan bishops of the Church of England, seniority being determined by the date of appointment to a see; they cease to be eligible to sit as Lords Spiritual after retirement. Other ecclesiastics may sit only if granted peerages. The 1968 proposals for Lords' reform envisaged a reduction in the number of bishops to sixteen. In early Tudor times the Lords Spiritual had constituted half the membership of the House.

2. Hereditary peers of England (before 1707), Great Britain (1707–1800) and the United Kingdom (1801–   ): they are dukes, marquesses, earls, viscounts or barons.[4] In 1972 they were over eight hundred in number; more than half of the hereditary peerages of the United Kingdom had been created (on the advice of the Prime Minister) since 1900, though none was conferred in the years 1965–72. Some of the surviving ancient hereditary peerages were created by the issue of a royal writ of summons followed by the actual taking of the seat; such peerages descended to heirs general, including women. All modern hereditary peerages have been created by letters patent; they do not descend to women unless there is an express provision in the letters patent for inheritance by heirs female. But although a woman might be a peeress in her own right, she had no right at common law to take a seat in the Lords; and this disability was not removed by the general words of the Sex Disqualification (Removal) Act 1919: see *Viscountess Rhondda's* case (1922).[5] Under the Life Peerages Act 1958 a life peerage conferring the right to sit can be bestowed upon a woman; and the Peerage Act 1963 enabled all peeresses in their own right to sit in the Lords.[6]

4. The holder of a peerage may simply be known as 'Lord' X. A baron is almost invariably so styled. Some confusion can be caused by 'courtesy titles'; thus, the eldest son of the Duke of Marlborough has the courtesy title of the Marquess of (or Lord) Blandford, but he is not a peer.

5. [1922] 2 A.C. 339 – an unconvincing report by a majority of the Committee of Privileges of the House of Lords, praying in aid the presumption of statutory intent against the indirect introduction of major constitutional change.

6. The wife of a peer is not, as such, a peeress in her own right. She may be elected to a seat in the Commons.

3. Peers of Scotland, who have inherited peerages created before the Act of Union.[7] Till the Peerage Act 1963 they elected sixteen of their own number to represent them for the duration of a Parliament; now they have an unrestricted right to take their seats. Peers of Ireland no longer have any right to sit in the Lords[8] but may be elected to the Commons.

4. Life peers, created under the 1958 Act; they number about two hundred. Non-hereditary peerages had been created under the prerogative, but it was held in the nineteenth century that conferment of such a peerage bestowed no right to sit in the Lords; such a right could only be given by statute.[9] It was thought that a number of persons with radical sympathies who were prominent in public life would be willing to accept life peerages but not hereditary peerages; the Life Peerages Act was passed mainly in the hope of strengthening and broadening the composition of the House of Lords. A number of the baronies conferred under the 1958 Act have been created after consultation between the Prime Minister and the leaders of the opposition parties.

5. Lords of Appeal in Ordinary, appointed for life under the Appellate Jurisdiction Acts. They are appointed as judges but are not precluded from taking part in general debate,[10] and they are indeed still entitled to sit in the House after they have retired from judicial office. The maximum number entitled to be paid as Lords of Appeal at any one time is now eleven.

It will be seen that some members of the House of Lords (the Lords Spiritual) are not peers, and that not all peers (for example, peers of Ireland) are entitled to sit. Alienage, infancy, bankruptcy and imprisonment for treason are also disqualifications for sitting. There is no provision for expulsion of a peer by resolution of the House in its legislative capacity.

The potential membership of the House is over one thousand. Some peers who have succeeded to hereditary peerages have never applied for writs of summons;[11] other peers have been granted, or have been deemed to obtain, leave of absence[12] under a standing order designed to discourage

7. Any Scotsman on whom a peerage has been bestowed since the Act of Union has been a peer of the United Kingdom.

8. *Re Earl of Antrim's Petition* [1967] 1 A.C. 691. Before 1922, when the Irish Free State was constituted, peers of Ireland elected twenty-eight representative peers for life. The machinery for filling vacancies caused by death then lapsed.

9. *Wensleydale Peerage Case* (1856) 5 H.L.C. 958; see p. 309 below.

10. See generally Gavin Drewry and Jenny Morgan (1969) 22 *Parliamentary Affairs* 226; Louis Blom-Cooper and Gavin Drewry, *Final Appeal*, ch. 10.

11. The number in 1968 was eighty-one (Cmnd 3799 (1968), p. 5).

12. Erskine May, op. cit., p. 215. In 1968, 192 members of the Lords had leave of absence. At the beginning of each Parliament the Lord Chancellor sends a letter to

habitual absentees ('backwoodsmen') from descending on Westminster in strength to vote down a controversial reform measure emanating from the Commons – a practice which had become an embarrassment to the more cautious Conservatives. The average daily attendance is below three hundred,[13] but the number can still rise sharply on an important occasion. On 28 October 1971 the House voted 451 to 58 in favour of the principle of entry into the Common Market.

A peerage may fall into abeyance or become extinct, but cannot be alienated; nor could it be renounced at common law. Mr Anthony Wedgwood Benn's persistent campaign to disclaim the Stansgate peerage to which he had succeeded came to fruition in the Peerage Act 1963. Under this Act a peer may disclaim for his own lifetime a hereditary peerage to which he has succeeded, provided that he makes the disclaimer within twelve months of succession or coming of age. If he is an M.P., or a parliamentary candidate who is then elected to the Commons, he has only a month in which to make up his mind. After disclaimer, he becomes a commoner; he may subsequently be granted a life peerage but not a hereditary peerage. One upon whom a peerage has been personally conferred cannot disclaim it. Fewer than a dozen peers by inheritance had in fact disclaimed their peerages by 1973; not surprisingly, Mr Wedgwood Benn was the first of the few. The Earl of Home soon disclaimed his peerage in 1963 and became an M.P. after having been appointed Prime Minister; Viscount Hailsham (Mr Quintin Hogg) also rejoined Mr Wedgwood Benn in the Commons but returned to the Lords as a life peer on being appointed Lord Chancellor in 1970. The effect of the Act has not seriously affected the balance between the two Houses, but it has belatedly removed a source of injustice to reluctant peers.

Peers are not paid a salary for attendance, but they may claim travelling expenses to and from their homes and also reimbursement of up to £8.50 daily for expenses incurred in attending.

---

each member asking if he wishes to apply for leave of absence; and at the beginning of each session he puts the same question to members who have neither applied for leave of absence nor attended, or who have been granted leave of absence for the previous session. One who has obtained leave of absence for that Parliament or that session, or who has not replied to the letter, is expected not to attend the House during the relevant period unless he gives a month's notice of his desire to attend, though he cannot apparently be prevented from speaking or voting if he nevertheless presents himself.

13. In the 1967–8 session it was 230: Cmnd 3799 (1968), p. 4. In 1955 (before the Life Peerages Act 1958) it was only ninety-two. The attendance record of peers of first creation was, not surprisingly, better than that of peers by inheritance.

Functions and work of the House

The Lord Chancellor, sitting on the woolsack, presides in the House,[14] but he lacks the coercive disciplinary powers of the Speaker of the Commons. Proceedings in the Lords sometimes resemble a game of cricket without an umpire; probably no other legislative body maintains so high a degree of gentle decorum. Another engaging eccentricity is that the Lord Chancellor often leaves the impartial (and extremely comfortable) cushion of the woolsack to speak for the Government.[15] When the House is in committee the chair is taken by the Lord Chairman of Committees. The House has a Gentleman Usher of the Black Rod to attend on the Lord Chancellor and execute the orders of the House. The clerk of the House is styled Clerk of the Parliaments; he prepares and presents bills for the royal assent; he is removable only on an address by the Lords.

The White Paper of 1968 referred[16] to seven functions of the House: (i) its appellate role; (ii) the provision of a forum for debate on matters of public interest; (iii) the revision of Commons' bills; (iv) the initiation of less controversial public bills; (v) the consideration of subordinate legislation; (vi) scrutiny of the activities of the Executive; and (vii) scrutiny of private legislation.

The judicial functions of the House (i) will be considered separately[17]; so will function (v).[18] Function (vi) is not performed adequately; a stronger, reformed second chamber could do better. Reference has already been made to function (vii). The second, third and fourth functions are of some consequence.

Several factors impair the efficiency of the Lords. The House is aristocratic and non-elective; its members do not represent any body of constituents and are thought of as speaking for a small section of the community. Moreover, as is well known, a peerage is often granted as a reward to party loyalists or as a consolation for Ministers who, no longer measuring up to their jobs, are 'kicked upstairs'. The House has a permanent Conservative majority, more conservative on the whole than any Conservative Government that is likely to emerge from the Commons. Governments do not depend on the favour of the Lords for their continuance in office. The House has no power over money matters; it

14. That part of his salary which he receives as Speaker of the House of Lords is not charged on the Consolidated Fund, though the salary of the Speaker of the House of Commons is so charged. See Ministerial and other Salaries Act 1972, s. 1.
15. Another Minister is now Leader of the House of Lords.
16. Cmnd 3799, pp. 2–3.
17. See pp. 307–10.
18. See p. 345. See now Addendum.

cannot impose its will on the Commons in legislation but can be overridden by the Commons; it is vulnerable to a hostile Labour Government because of lack of a firm basis of public support, and, conscious of this fact, is very reluctant to exercise the suspensory powers over legislation which it retains; the Government can brush aside opposition in the Lords more readily than in the Commons, mainly because a high-handed attitude on its part is less likely to have adverse electoral repercussions;[19] the Government front bench in the Lords is seldom strong and much of the excitement aroused by questions and debates in the Commons is therefore lacking in the Lords.

On the other hand, the quality of members and speeches is often high. Those upon whom peerages are conferred are usually persons of considerable experience of politics, the public service or industry or who have otherwise made their mark in public or intellectual life. They bring to the House a wide range of expertise. They tend to be elderly, but there is a leavening of young peers by succession. In recent years the House has become markedly more liberal in its outlook towards matters of social and penal reform; the effect of the Life Peerages Act has been conspicuously beneficial. For example, the original initiative in relaxing the law relating to homosexual conduct (the Sexual Offences Act 1967) came from the Lords, not the Commons; a big majority in the Lords against the abolition of capital punishment for murder in the early post-war period was converted to an abolitionist majority in the mid-1960s.[20] The leisurely timetable of the Lords gives the backbencher more opportunities to speak than in the Commons; and debates on matters which cut across party lines, raising controversial moral issues out of which the Government is more likely to incur odium than attract credit by adopting a positive position, can easily be arranged in the Lords. Again, the political balance has become more evenly weighted save on highly contentious party occasions. Thus, among those peers who in 1968 were more or less regular attenders, ninety-five took the Labour whip, 125 the Conservative whip, twenty the Liberal whip and fifty were crossbenchers;[21] nevertheless, the Labour Government was faced by a clear anti-Labour majority which could at any time be swollen into an active obstructive

19. For a protest by a senior Labour peer against this attitude, see Lord Chorley, 'Bringing the legislative process into contempt' [1968] *Public Law* 52.

20. This can also be partly explained by reference to a change of attitude among the bishops and to some extent among the Law Lords. See the debates on the bill which became the Murder (Abolition of Death Penalty) Act 1965. In December 1969 a Government motion to give the measure permanent effect was passed on a free vote by the Lords as well as the Commons.

21. Cmnd 3799 (1968), p. 4.

force, and a new Conservative Government could reinforce its strength in the Lords by political appointments.

The House of Lords as at present constituted is a useful legislative chamber. As has been mentioned, many of the less controversial Government bills are introduced there; the debates will often be well informed; helpful amendments to law reform bills may be moved by Law Lords at committee stage. A recent example of a major piece of legislation thus introduced was the Courts Act 1971. The Government's legislative output is thereby enlarged and its efficiency improved. The utility of the Lords as a forum for the consideration of private bills is well recognized. Not so generally appreciated is its value as a chamber for the introduction of private members' bills which may be crowded out in the Commons; in the 1970–71 session three such bills, all dealing with not particularly controversial law reforms, became law.[22] A controversial backbench bill originating in the Lords is unlikely to pass into law that session, but by attracting publicity it can lead to the implementation of a reform soon afterwards; the Sexual Offences Act 1967 is an illustration. The function of the Lords in revising Commons' bills is potentially more important, but is not very satisfactory in practice, mainly because the Lords are apprehensive about the consequences of using their delaying powers by insisting on amendments to a Labour Government's bills, and partly because of the amateurish lack of organization within the House. The latter failing, coupled with large-scale absenteeism, is also responsible for the failure of the House to perform properly what could be its most important function, scrutiny of central administration.

Occasionally the revising powers of the Lords are used with significant effect. A mildly controversial Government bill to distribute a small sum received from the Soviet Government by way of compensation for the seizure of British-owned assets in Eastern Europe was introduced into the Commons late in 1968; the sum was to be distributed to claimants by the Foreign Compensation Commission, a statutory tribunal constituted in 1950. With the bill before the House, the House of Lords in its appellate capacity held that a provisional determination made by the Commission in 1963 was a nullity because the Commission had exceeded its jurisdiction.[23] The Government thereupon tacked on to the bill at report stage amendments designed unequivocally to exclude the supervisory jurisdiction of the courts in relation to purported determinations by the

22. Ivor F. Burton and Gavin Drewry (1972) 25 *Parliamentary Affairs* 123.
23. *Anisminic Ltd* v. *Foreign Compensation Commission* [1969] 2 A.C. 147; cf. Foreign Compensation Act 1950, s. 4(4), purporting to exclude all judicial review of the Commission's determination; and see Tribunals and Inquiries Act 1958, s. 11(3) (now replaced by Tribunals and Inquiries Act 1971, s. 14(3)) and pp. 571–2.

Commission. The bill as amended was duly passed by the Commons. But a body of informed legal opinion had been aroused. There were letters to *The Times*, and adverse comments by Law Lords and other peers at the second reading debate on the bill in the Lords; a former Lord Chancellor moved an amendment to provide for a limited right of appeal to the Court of Appeal from the Commission's determinations on jurisdictional issues, and the amendment was carried against the Government; the Government then abandoned its position, introduced alternative amendments which were accepted, and the Foreign Compensation Act 1969 became law with a novel code for judicial review of the Commission's determinations. Certainly it was relevant that the matter was of no political importance to the Government. But this episode shows the potential value of a well-informed second chamber. It also illustrates, incidentally, how a second chamber may be used by the Government to interpolate into a bill its afterthoughts instead of having to introduce an amending bill later.

This last point was illustrated still more aptly in 1972, when 610 Lords' amendments were made to the controversial and complex Local Government Bill after it had been passed by the Commons. The vast majority of those amendments were introduced by the Government.

Disagreements between the two Houses

Till 1911 the Lords and the Commons had coordinate legislative authority except in money matters.[24] By convention, and according to the privileges claimed by the Commons, bills dealing wholly or mainly with taxation or public expenditure had to be introduced in the Commons, and their money clauses could not be amended by the Lords, though the Lords retained at least a formal right to reject them. Nor could the Lords amend the financial clauses of non-money bills, save where the Commons decided not to insist on but instead to waive their privilege of having exclusive cognizance of such matters. This is broadly the constitutional position in relation to financial matters today (though see p. 232), but superimposed is the drastic rule introduced by the Parliament Act 1911.

In 1909 the House of Lords rejected the Finance Bill; they passed it in 1910 after the Liberal Government had been returned to office at a General Election. Following the second General Election of 1910, at which the Liberals retained power, the Lords were induced to pass the Parliament Bill under the threat of being swamped by a massive influx of new Liberal peers.[25] The Parliament Act 1911 was amended by the Parlia-

24. See Erskine May, op. cit., ch. 31.
25. For a readable account of the crisis, see Roy Jenkins, *Mr Balfour's Poodle*.

ment Act 1949, but not so as to affect its provisions relating to money bills.

Money bills. For the purpose of section 1 of the Parliament Act 1911, a money bill is one which in the opinion of the Speaker contains provisions *exclusively* relating to central government taxation, expenditure or loans. If before a bill leaves the Commons the Speaker certifies it as a money bill, then it may be presented for the royal assent notwithstanding that the Lords have failed to pass it without amendment after it has been before them for one month. The Speaker's certificate is to be indorsed on the bill; once given, it is conclusive for all purposes;[26] before giving it, he must, if practicable, consult two members of the chairmen's panel. It will be noted that the statutory definition of a money bill is narrow; not every Finance Bill has been so certified. But the combination of strict law and convention has deprived the Lords of all effective authority over raising and spending money.

Other bills. Other public bills (including private members' bills) passed by the Commons may also be passed into law against the opposition of the Lords. (The Commons may kill a Lords' bill simply by not passing it.) Under section 2 of the Parliament Act 1911, a bill could be presented for the royal assent if (1) it had been passed by the Commons in three consecutive sessions (whether of the same Parliament or not) in the same form or subject only to such amendments as were certified by the Speaker as being necessary through the effluxion of time or to Lords' amendments agreed to in the preceding session by the Commons; (2) the Lords had failed to pass it in each of the three sessions; (3) two years had elapsed between the second reading of the bill in the Commons in the first session and its third reading in the Commons in the third session; (4) the bill had been sent up to the Lords at least one month before the end of each session; and (5) the Speaker had certified that the requirements of the Parliament Act had been complied with. By the Parliament Act 1949 the number of sessions was reduced from three to two and the interval of time from two years to one. Hence the suspensory veto of the Lords has been reduced to one year and one month.[27]

These provisions do not, however, apply to bills to prolong the maximum duration of a Parliament beyond five years, or to provisional order confirmation bills;[28] nor do they apply to private bills. Only by resorting

26. Though cf. pp. 51, 87–8.

27. If the Lords neither reject the bill nor amend it in a manner unacceptable to the Commons but merely adjourn proceedings on the bill, the Speaker is likely to certify that the requirements of the Parliament Acts have been complied with immediately before the end of the session so that the bill can be presented for the royal assent. See Eric Taylor, *The House of Commons at Work* (8th edn), pp. 158–9. In practice the suspensory veto is unlikely to exceed a year.

28. cf. pp. 278–9.

to the unlikely, and probably self-defeating, expedient of requesting the monarch to create a sufficient number of new peers for the purpose,[29] could a Government secure the passage of such a bill against the adamant opposition of the Lords.

Only three Acts have been passed over the heads of the Lords under the Parliament Act procedure: the Welsh Church Act 1914 (disestablishing the Church of Wales); the Government of Ireland Act 1914 (providing for home rule for Ireland; the outbreak of the First World War followed at once, and this Act was never brought into operation; self-government was introduced after the war, along with partition); and the Parliament Act 1949. The 1949 Act was ostensibly designed to forestall prospective Conservative opposition to a measure for the nationalization of the iron and steel industry. A Parliament Bill was introduced late in 1947 and was passed by the Commons; the second reading in the Lords was adjourned while a conference of party leaders discussed schemes for the future composition and powers of the Lords; the conference broke down on the question of the period of delaying power over legislation; the Lords then rejected the bill on second reading by a large majority, and after the bill had again been passed and rejected in the next two sessions it was submitted for the royal assent.[30] The Government nevertheless found it expedient to accept a Lords' amendment to the Iron and Steel Bill, postponing its operation; the Government lost office soon afterwards and that measure[31] did not come fully into effect.

Under the Government's 1968 proposals for Lords' reform, the period of delay would have been reduced to sixty parliamentary days from the date of disagreement between the two Houses. Provision would also have been made for enabling the Commons to override by a simple resolution the Lords' disapproval of such delegated legislation as was subject to parliamentary proceedings;[32] the Parliament Acts do not apply to subordinate legislation.

In practice full-scale collisions between the two Houses have been infrequent. The Lords have not rejected any of the nationalization bills

29. See pp. 107–8.

30. Professor Hood Phillips has argued (*Reform of the Constitution*, pp. 18–19, 91–2) that the Parliament Act of 1949 may be a nullity, because it was enacted by a 'delegate' with limited powers (i.e. the Queen and Commons under the Parliament Act 1911 procedure) and a delegate cannot enlarge its own powers. But even if one accepts the view (rejected at p. 88) that legislation passed under the 1911 Act procedure is 'delegated' and subordinate, it is questionable whether the 1949 Act was *ultra vires* according to the canons of statutory interpretation.

31. Iron and Steel Act 1949. The industry was denationalized in 1953 and renationalized in 1967.

32. Cmnd 3799 (1968), pp. 21–23. See ch. 15.

passed by the Commons under Labour Governments; they have inserted many amendments, but most have been withdrawn after the Commons have insisted on their unacceptability, or a compromise has been reached after discussions between party leaders in the two Houses; some Lords' amendments to Government bills have been accepted on their merits or for reasons of prudence.[33] The boldest Lords' amendments to a Government bill in recent years were those inserted in the House of Commons (Redistribution of Seats) Bill 1969. The Government, unwilling either to accept the amendments or have recourse to the Parliament Acts procedure – it was under heavy pressure for seeking to escape from its obligations to implement the recommendations of independent boundary commissions – decided to opt for the least of evils, withdrew the bill and temporarily stifled the recommendations by other means.[34]

The suggestion that the Lords would carry greater weight in the legislative process if they had longer delaying powers is unconvincing. In the last analysis the most important reason why a non-Conservative Government has seldom run into serious trouble with the Lords as at present constituted is a fear of the consequences of self-assertion which the Conservative leadership in the Lords rightly entertains. The Prime Minister might, for example, obtain a dissolution of Parliament in an endeavour to distract public attention from more embarrassing and relevant problems, and the Government might then contrive to win a sufficient measure of support to be returned to power, pledged to end the Lords (under the Parliament Acts procedure, if necessary) and perhaps even the hereditary peerage itself.

Judicial duties of the Lords

The Lords have functions of a judicial nature incidental to their capacity as a legislative body, though inasmuch as the House is a superior court of record, their determinations may be reported in the law reports. Claims to peerages[35] and to a right to sit in the House by virtue of the grant of a

33. In 1947–8 the Commons, on a free vote, inserted in the Criminal Justice Bill a clause moved by a backbencher which would have abolished the death penalty; the backwoodsmen emerged, and the Lords passed an amendment by a large majority to delete the clause; the Government dropped the clause from the bill. It is unlikely that the Parliament Act procedure would be invoked to secure the passage of any private member's bill.

34. See further, pp. 247–8 and 345. Recourse to the Parliament Acts would have entailed not only the protraction of bad publicity for the Government but also a strong possibility that the period of delay would have prevented the Government's own proposals from being brought into effect before the next General Election.

35. Disputes as to the validity of the creation of a new peerage are decided by the

peerage are referred to the Committee of Privileges of the House; the House traditionally adopts the Committee's report. This procedure is also adopted when allegations of breach of the privileges of the House are made.

Magna Carta had laid it down that a free man was entitled to trial by his peers. This principle survived in the House of Lords till 1948; a peer (or his wife) charged with treason or felony was tried by the whole House of Lords; this expensive anachronism was abolished by the Criminal Justice Act 1948 and peers are now tried in the ordinary courts.

The process of impeachment[36] is obsolete but has never been abolished. If a person were to be impeached today he would be tried by the whole House of Lords, with the House of Commons as his accusers.

Another function of a judicial nature, harking back to the days when the High Court of Parliament was a judicial as well as a legislative body, was the enactment of a bill of attainder, not by the Lords alone but by the Queen in Parliament. An act of attainder is a legislative judgment declaring a person to have been guilty of treason or other high crimes. Over 250 years have passed since this ugly manifestation of 'parliamentary judicature' was last expressed. The offences of which a man was attainted were not necessarily crimes at the time when the acts complained of were committed. Modern constitutional bills of rights will usually debar the Legislature from enacting *ex post facto* penal laws,[37] and the constitution may also, either expressly[38] or by implication,[39] invalidate bills of attainder.[40]

The House of Lords is also a court of appeal, at the apex of the ordinary hierarchy of courts in the United Kingdom.[41] In this capacity it exercises the ancient jurisdiction of the High Court of Parliament. It ceased to exercise original jurisdiction in the seventeenth century. The exercise of its appellate jurisdiction gave rise to some awkward problems; the quorum

House of its own motion. Disputes as to who (if anyone) is entitled to an old peerage are determinable by the Attorney-General on behalf of the Crown but are normally referred, in practice, to the House.

36. See pp. 169, 230–31 and p. 314, note 6.

37. For example, Constitution of India, art. 20(1).

38. For example, Constitution of the United States, art. 1, s. 9.

39. For example, where the constitution vests the judicial power exclusively in the Judiciary. And before Ceylon became the Republic of Sri Lanka under a new constitution in 1972, the power of the Ceylon Parliament to make laws for the peace, order, and good government of Ceylon did not import a power to pass an Act for the condemnation of a particular individual: *Liyanage* v. *R.* [1967] 1 A.C. 259; though cf. *Kariapper* v. *Wijesinha* [1968] A.C. 717.

40. Express references to 'bills of attainder' in modern constitutions are uncommon because of the ambiguity of the phrase – an ambiguity emphasized by trends of interpretation in the United States Supreme Court.

41. For a full study, see Louis Blom-Cooper and Gavin Drewry, *Final Appeal* (1972).

of the House in its judicial as in its legislative capacity is three, and there were not always three hereditary peers with judicial experience available to sit; the judges of the common law courts could, however, be called in to offer advice.[42]

An attempt was made to strengthen the judicial element in the Lords in the mid-nineteenth century by conferring a life peerage on a judge of the Court of Exchequer, Sir James Parke; the Committee of Privileges reported that a life peer was unable to take his seat,[43] and Parke had to be given a hereditary peerage. The idea of diluting the hereditary peerage with lawyers and their progeny was unattractive to the Lords; and the need for a second and not very distinguished appellate court was not readily apparent to laymen or indeed the bar. Under the Judicature Act of 1873 the appellate jurisdiction of the Lords was to be abolished; but after the Conservatives had ousted the Liberals at the General Election of 1874 a determined and successful campaign to restore that jurisdiction was mounted.[44] The Appellate Jurisdiction Act 1876 provided for the appointment of two (there may now be eleven) Lords of Appeal in Ordinary, life peers who had held high judicial office for two years or were barristers of fifteen years' standing; they were given a *statutory* right to sit in the Lords. They retire at seventy-five (if appointed after 1959) but may still be asked by the Lord Chancellor to sit. By convention, at least two must be Scots lawyers. The Lord Chancellor, ex-Lords Chancellor and other peers who hold or have held high judicial office may also make up the necessary judicial quorum; in practice five Law Lords normally sit to hear an appeal. Lay peers are not precluded by statute from sitting uninvited with the Law Lords to hear an appeal, but by convention they abstain from doing so; the last time when such a peer sat was in 1883 and his participation in the proceedings (including his vote on the appeal) was simply ignored.

In its capacity as a court of appeal the House sits as an appellate committee; it adjourns to the chamber of the House for the formal delivery of opinions, which have been handed out in writing shortly beforehand and are not now read out by their Lordships. It may sit during a prorogation or dissolution of Parliament.

The House entertains civil and criminal appeals, with leave of itself or the court below, from the Court of Appeal. It also hears appeals from the Courts-Martial Appeal Court and in certain cases direct from the

42. The last case in which such advice was sought was *Allen* v. *Flood* [1898] A.C. 1. The advice given by the judges in that case was not accepted.
43. *Wensleydale Peerage Case* (1856); note 9. Sir James Parke was a Baron of the Exchequer, but not the holder of a title of baronage.
44. See Robert B. Stevens (1964) 80 *L.Q.R.* 343.

Divisional Court of the Queen's Bench Division, and individual High Court judges, under restrictive conditions. It exercises civil but not criminal appellate jurisdiction in respect of the Scottish courts, and hears both civil and criminal appeals from Northern Ireland.

Approaches to reform

The preamble to the Parliament Act 1911 recited the intention 'to substitute for the House of Lords as it at present exists a second chamber constituted on a popular instead of a hereditary basis . . .'. In 1917 the Bryce conference proposed[45] that three-quarters of the members of the second chamber should be indirectly elected on a regional basis by the House of Commons; this scheme, unpropitious in its timing and, like all other schemes for reform of the Lords, inconveniently controversial, was placed in a pigeon-hole, and there it remains. The inter-party conference convened after the second Parliament Bill had been passed by the Commons reached a substantial measure of agreement on an outline plan for a reconstituted upper House; the principle of indirect election, and inheritance as an automatic qualification for membership, were alike rejected; it was accepted that the House ought to be complementary to rather than a rival of the Commons, and that as far as possible matters should be so contrived that no party had a permanent majority in it.[46] Nothing was done to implement these proposals. Subsequent reforms have not undermined the hereditary principle, but the Life Peerages Act 1958 has led to an improvement in the quality of debate, an increase in the number of regular attenders and a modification in the political complexion of the more conscientious body of participants;[47] and standing orders providing for leave of absence have also helped. But a vote strictly along party lines on a matter attracting a large attendance will almost invariably give the Conservatives a majority.[48]

Discussions about the reform of the Lords have cut across party divisions without bringing about the impetus or sense of urgency needed to carry a scheme through the Commons. Agreement in principle amongst the sophisticated tends to be less than whole-hearted and to beget new disagreements when principle is translated into detail. Real enthusiasm

45. Cd 9038 (1917).

46. Cmd 7380 (1948).

47. This was also influenced, of course, by life peerages granted on the advice of Mr Wilson during his term of office from 1964 to 1970.

48. In the 1967–8 session, 115 members of the Lords took the Labour whip, 350 the Conservative whip, forty the Liberal whip and about 170 were 'crossbenchers' (independents). Among fairly *regular* attenders, the Conservative peers were the largest single group but were not in an overall majority: see p. 302.

for Lords' reform is too often to be found among the eccentric and the naïve, who may have little idea of the mediocre performance of second chambers in so many other countries or of the limited expectations that can reasonably be reposed in a reconstituted British second chamber. Party political considerations also inhibit a determined approach to reform. Conservatives would, on the whole, like to see a less unrepresentative upper House brought into existence, but preferably by agreement and under a Labour Government; for a stronger upper House would be readier to exercise its authority, and if this were used to the detriment of a Labour Government (for example, by delaying bills) the Conservatives would not have to incur the unpopularity that would be attached to the reformed House's progenitor. Radicals have tended either to favour abolition of the Lords or to let sleeping dogs lie; an unrepresentative second chamber is now unlikely to do more than growl, and occasionally bark, at a Government of the Left, whereas a renovated and more self-assured body might bite hard.

In this context the Government's abortive scheme of 1968[49] was an imaginative effort to grapple with an elusive set of problems. Briefly, it envisaged a House stronger in its composition (though with reduced delaying powers), so constituted that no party would have a permanent overall majority; but the Government of the day would have a 10 per cent majority over the combined opposition parties, with crossbench peers (including the Law Lords) and bishops holding the balance. The House would, in effect, have two tiers – those members with voting rights and those who would be entitled to sit and speak but not vote. The voting House would have 200 to 250 members apart from bishops and serving Law Lords; the members would be those hereditary peers of first creation and life peers who were prepared to attend regularly; about eighty new Labour life peers would have had to be created if the bill had become law in 1969, in order to bring the Government side up to strength. There would be a retiring age for voting members and they would be paid a salary. Non-voting members would be those peers of first creation who were unable or unwilling to meet the attendance requirements, and all existing peers by inheritance; subsequently, however, inheritance of a peerage would no longer of itself qualify for membership of the House at all.

Objections could be and were raised to the amount of discretionary patronage to be vested in the Prime Minister and indirectly in the Opposition party leaders, both at the inauguration of the scheme and upon a change of Government (inasmuch as new voting members of the House would then have to be nominated to correct the party balance), and to

49. Cmnd 3799.

the measure of importance attached to the role of the crossbenchers. But these problems were not insurmountable and the scheme was the best yet to have been devised. If it could have found its way through the Commons, its passage facilitated by a slice of the guillotine, one could have expected a less timid and more professional second chamber to emerge, better equipped for the introduction of controversial bills, for committee debate on bills in general, and for the scrutiny of executive action by new select committees or possibly joint select committees with the Commons.[50] For the first time this century (and perhaps the last) the debate on the role of a second chamber was elevated from tedious and unrealistic irrelevancy to the status of propositions to be weighed seriously. But if we ever seriously contemplate a system of government entailing a very substantial measure of regional devolution, then the idea of a new type of second chamber at Westminster will need to be reconsidered. For the most obvious basis of representation in a second chamber is a blend of the political and the regional. To reconcile the constitution of such a body with the necessity of averting recurrent and abrasive conflict with the House of Commons will be a task demanding subtle ingenuity.

50. ibid., Appendix 2.

Chapter 14
Parliamentary Privilege

General

Parliamentary privilege[1] is part of the *lex et consuetudo parliamenti*, the law and custom of Parliament. It consists of special rules evolved by the two Houses in order to protect themselves collectively, and their members acting in their public capacities, against outside interference, so as to enable them to carry out their constitutional functions effectively. Most of these special rules are non-statutory; they have been laid down by resolutions of the two Houses or by Speakers' rulings. Some are statutory. They are part of the common law in so far as their existence and validity are recognized by the courts, but they are, in general, enforced not by the courts but by each House. The two Houses justify the special rights, powers and immunities conferred by parliamentary privilege as being necessary for the welfare of the nation. Citizens denied legal redress against M.P.s, or adjudged by the House of Commons to have committed a high contempt and a breach of its privileges, tend to be less impressed by these claims. The connotation of the word 'privilege', is, moreover, unattractive. A select committee of the House of Commons, appointed to review the law of parliamentary privilege, recommended in 1967 that the expression 'parliamentary privilege' should be sent to the lumber room, and that the House should instead speak of its 'rights and immunities';[2] but the committee's recommendations for the relinquishment of particular rights and immunities were extremely cautious.

In early days the undivided Parliament was not slow to assert against the Crown a claim that its members be free from arrest while performing their duties or journeying to and from Westminster. Claims to immunity of members from punishment for words spoken or resolutions passed in Parliament soon followed. When Parliament divided into two Houses,

1. For an authoritative study, see Erskine May's *Parliamentary Practice* (18th edn), chs. 5–11. For a modern critique, see *Report from the Select Committee on Parliamentary Privilege*, H.C. 34 (1967–68). There is a useful synopsis of cases on breach of privilege in Geoffrey Wilson's *Cases and Materials on Constitutional and Administrative Law*, ch. 10.
2. H.C. 34 (1967–68), vii–viii, xlix.

the Commons, at first the weaker House, had to vindicate their rights against both the Crown and the Lords; and the privileges claimed by the Commons in respect of financial legislation were to become a fertile source of constitutional conflict. Jurisdictional conflicts also arose between the Commons on the one hand and the courts (including the House of Lords in its capacity as a court of record) on the other; these conflicts were not conclusively resolved, and, as we shall see, a tacit agreement to differ emerged from the controversies. However, most of the modern law of parliamentary privilege had taken shape before 1841.

The privileges of the Lords closely resemble those of the Commons,[3] and will not be considered separately.

Privileges of the Commons

At the commencement of a Parliament the newly elected Speaker claims from the Crown 'all the ancient and undoubted privileges' of the House, and in particular freedom of speech in debate, freedom from arrest and freedom of access to the monarch through the Speaker; and he requests that a favourable construction be placed on the Commons' proceedings.[4] The most important privileges not specifically claimed are the right of the House to regulate its own composition, its right to have exclusive cognizance of matters arising within its precincts, the right to punish for contempt and breach of privilege, its privileges in relation to the Lords in financial matters,[5] and its claim to be the sole judge of the extent of its own privileges.[6] The difference between the privileges expressly claimed and those not expressly claimed is one of form, not of substance.

Freedom of speech

This is the most crucial and controversial parliamentary privilege. In 1397 Richard II had one Haxey (who was not a member of Parliament) condemned for treason for petitioning the Commons to reduce the King's household expenses. The Commons remonstrated; they were joined by the Lords, and two years later the decision was reversed. In 1512 Strode,

3. See O. Hood Phillips, *Constitutional and Administrative Law* (4th edn), pp. 186–8. For the powers of the Lords to punish for contempt, see p. 325.

4. These last two privileges (or claims) relate back to the days when the attitude of the monarch towards petitions by the Commons and its spokesman was apt to be tempestuous.

5. See ch. 13.

6. Among the less important privileges are immunity from attendance in court as jurors or (with certain exceptions) as witnesses; and the right of impeachment. The Select Committee (note 1 above) recommended that the right of impeachment be abolished by statute.

an M.P., was imprisoned by a local court for introducing bills to regulate the Devon tin mines. He was released by the order of a superior court, and Parliament passed an Act in general terms, declaring that judicial proceedings against any person for any bill or speech in Parliament were void. Elizabeth I nevertheless punished members for words spoken in debate; and in 1629, under Charles I, Sir John Eliot and other members were convicted in the courts for seditious words spoken in the House.[7] The reversal of this conviction by the Lords on a writ of error, thirty-nine years later, was an unequivocal judicial recognition of the principle of free speech in Parliament. In James II's reign, however, Williams, Speaker of the House, was convicted of a criminal libel in that he had ordered a document defamatory of James to be published when James had been Duke of York. This case[8] was the direct historical antecedent of Article 9 of the Bill of Rights, which provided

That the freedom of speech, and debates or proceedings in Parliament ought not to be impeached or questioned in any court or place out of Parliament.

This is the basis of the modern law. Its interpretation and implications are of primary importance.

1. No action or prosecution can be brought against a member for any words used in the course of parliamentary proceedings. This rule is absolute. Thus, a member cannot be prosecuted or threatened with prosecution for sedition[9] or a breach of the Official Secrets Acts[10] for such words; a prosecution or threat to prosecute would probably be treated by the House as a breach of its own privileges.[11] If a member were to be sued for libel or slander in respect of words used in Parliament (other than in casual conversation not connected with parliamentary business) the writ should be struck out as disclosing no cause of action; if the case were to come to trial the court would hold that the member was protected by absolute privilege in the law of defamation[12] – i.e. that no action would

7. 3 St. Tr. 294.

8. For the facts, see *R.* v. *Dangerfield* (1688) 3 Mod. 68. Dangerfield, the author of the defamatory tract, was rightly convicted; Williams was wrongly convicted. Dangerfield was whipped from Newgate to Tyburn; on his return journey he was murdered by a barrister, Frances, who was hanged for the crime.

9. *Eliot*'s case (see above).

10. *Case of Duncan Sandys* (1938). See Wilson, *Cases and Materials*, pp. 272–8; H.C. 101 (1938–39). Sandys had complained that he had been threatened with prosecution for refusing to divulge his sources of information in connection with a parliamentary question he had put down about a shortage of anti-aircraft equipment.

11. This is to be inferred from the report of the Select Committee on the *Sandys* case and its adoption by the House. Members can be prosecuted for these offences in respect of disclosures or utterances which are not part of proceedings in Parliament.

12. *Dillon* v. *Balfour* (1887) 20 Ir.L.R. 600; *Goffin* v. *Donnelly* (1881) 6 Q.B.D. 307.

lie against him even if his remarks were shown to be defamatory, untrue and unfair. The defence of absolute privilege (which has no necessary connection with parliamentary privilege) also extends to judges acting in their official capacities; the risk that the immunity from suit may be abused is considered less than the risk that the absence of absolute privilege might deter M.P.s and judges from speaking bluntly, even harshly, when it is their duty to do so.

2. Parliamentary privilege (and absolute privilege in the law of defamation) also attaches to statements in official reports of the proceedings of the two Houses and their committees, and to other papers published by order of the House. This rule was laid down by the Parliamentary Papers Act 1840, passed in consequence of a judicial decision (*Stockdale* v. *Hansard* (1839)[13]) that parliamentary papers were protected not by parliamentary privilege but only by qualified privilege in the law of defamation – i.e. that untrue and libellous statements made in such documents were actionable if shown to have been actuated by malice.

3. What is the meaning of 'proceedings in Parliament'? Contributions to debate and committee discussions, oral questions, answers to parliamentary questions and voting are clearly within the definition; so are the execution of the orders of the House and the tabling of parliamentary questions. Acts done and words spoken within the precincts of Parliament which have nothing whatsoever to do with parliamentary proceedings[14] are clearly not protected. In between lie many transactions and situations that do not lend themselves easily to classification.[15] If a member tables a question and a Minister invites him to discuss it with him, the correspondence or conversations appear to be covered by parliamentary privilege.[16] It is arguable that unsolicited communications with a Minister are also covered if they are immediately related to a question or motion already tabled or a matter currently being debated in the House. If the issue has ceased to be before the House, such communications are probably no longer to be regarded as part of a proceeding *in* Parliament.

Communications with Ministers in respect of matters which may never arise in the House will not normally be covered by parliamentary privilege. Not every act done by a member in his capacity as a member is so

13. (1839) 9 A. & E. 1; see p. 327.

14. See, for example, *Rivlin* v. *Bilainkin* [1953] 1 Q.B. 485 (member of the public posting a defamatory letter within the House, not protected).

15. See, for example, *Ex p. Wason* (1869) L.R. 4 Q.B. 573 (no private prosecution for alleged conspiracy to deceive the House of Lords by false statements in the House; the matter lay within scope of parliamentary privilege). See also *Att.-Gen. of Ceylon* v. *Livera* [1963] A.C. 103 at 120–22 for judicial comment on marginal situations.

16. Speaker's Ruling, 591 H.C.Deb. 809–813 (14 July 1958).

protected.[17] A member's letter to or interview with a Minister, raising an issue of concern to an individual member of the public or a group of his constituents or any other section of the community, *may* lead to the putting down of a parliamentary question if no satisfactory informal answer is forthcoming; the issue thus raised may be a substitute for a *formal* parliamentary question (which would be privileged); but where is the line to be drawn between proceedings *in* Parliament and matters merely antecedent to possible proceedings in Parliament?

The leading modern case is that of *G. R. Strauss* (1957–8). Mr Strauss, Labour M.P. and formerly Minister of Supply, wrote to a Minister complaining about certain activities of an area board of a nationalized industry. The Minister disclaimed responsibility on the ground that the matter was one of day-to-day administration, and passed the letter on to the board. The board threatened to sue Mr Strauss for libel. Mr Strauss then raised this threat in the House as a question of privilege. The question was referred to the Committee of Privileges, which reported[18] that in writing his letter Mr Strauss was engaged in a proceeding in Parliament, and that the members of the board and their solicitors, by threatening legal proceedings against him in respect of his allegations, were in breach of parliamentary privilege. They recommended (somewhat inconsistently) that the question whether Article 9 of the Bill of Rights, restating the privilege of freedom of speech, had been impliedly repealed by an obscure eighteenth-century statute should be referred to the Judicial Committee of the Privy Council for an advisory opinion. The question was so referred; the Judicial Committee advised that the Bill of Rights (whatever it might mean) stood intact.[19] The House accepted this advice and then debated the Report of the Committee of Privileges. On a free vote it rejected by 218 to 213 the Committee's finding that in writing his letter Mr Strauss had been engaged in a proceeding in Parliament.[20]

This decision is not binding on the House when future cases arise. And the Select Committee on Parliamentary Privilege in 1967 was 'strongly of the opinion' that the decision of the House in the *Strauss* case should be reversed by legislation.[21] At present the probability is that a court would

17. See generally de Smith, 'Parliamentary privilege and the Bill of Rights' (1958) 21 *Mod. L. Rev.* at 477–82.

18. H.C. 305 (1956–57).

19. *Re Parliamentary Privilege Act 1770* [1958] A.C. 331.

20. 591 H.C.Deb. 207–346 (8 July 1958).

21. H.C. 34 (1967–68), xxvii. This view was supported by several members who spoke in the debate on the Report: see 786 H.C. Deb. 825–913 (4 July 1969). The Report had been published *nineteen months* before it was debated in the House. Its main recommendations had not been implemented by the end of 1972.

hold a letter written by an M.P. to a Minister on a matter lying within the Minister's general area of responsibility[22] to be protected only by qualified privilege in the law of defamation, unless the letter was ancillary, or an immediate preliminary, to proceedings within Parliament itself. Public policy considerations can be canvassed on either side. Letters from members of the public to M.P.s (and presumably from M.P.s to members of the public) on matters of public concern[23] enjoy only qualified privilege.[24] So do fair and accurate newspaper reports of parliamentary proceedings.[25] A statutory extension of the scope of parliamentary privilege to ease the minds of M.P.s potentially threatened with libel actions (and heavy bills of costs) would be widely interpreted as a self-endowed licence to make maliciously defamatory comments with impunity.[26] On the other hand, in 1967 communications between M.P.s and the Parliamentary Commissioner for Administration were accorded absolute privilege by statute.[27] If the law is left as it stands (or appears to stand), anomalies will remain; if the law is changed in the direction generally favoured at present by M.P.s, there will be dissatisfaction among members of the public.

4. Matters arising in the course of parliamentary proceedings cannot be challenged or relied on for the purpose of supporting legal proceedings based on events that occurred outside Parliament; for example, if an M.P. is sued for libel in connection with his remarks in a television interview, and he pleads qualified privilege or fair comment, the plaintiff is not allowed to use the defendant's comments in the House to show that the latter was actuated by malice.[28]

5. A member of the Commons who abuses his privilege of freedom of

22. e.g. a letter by an M.P. to the Lord Chancellor complaining of solicitors' conduct, even though the Lord Chancellor has no direct disciplinary authority over them: *Beach* v. *Freeson* [1972] 1 Q.B. 14.

23. Unless the M.P. is communicating to a complainant a report from the Parliamentary Commissioner for Administration (Parliamentary Commissioner Act 1967 s. 10(5)); in which case he will enjoy absolute privilege.

24. *R.* v. *Rule* [1937] 2 K.B. 375 (complaint by constituent to M.P. about public officers); see also *Beach* v. *Freeson* (above; complaint by M.P. to Lord Chancellor and Law Society).

25. *Wason* v. *Walter* (1868) L.R. 4 Q.B. 73.

26. It would seem that in an action for defamation, an M.P. who passes on a letter from a member of the public will not lose his qualified privilege by becoming automatically infected with the malice of his informant: *Meekins* v. *Henson* [1964] 1 Q.B. 472; *Egger* v. *Chelmsford* [1965] 1 Q.B. 248.

27. Parliamentary Commissioner Act 1967, s. 10(5).

28. *Church of Scientology of California* v. *Johnson-Smith* [1972] 1 Q.B. 522. See also *Dingle* v. *Associated Newspapers Ltd* [1960] 2 Q.B. 405 (action for libel against newspaper; plaintiff not entitled to contend that proceedings of select committee of House, on which offending comments were based, were void for procedural irregularity).

speech may be subjected to disciplinary sanctions by the House;[29] it is only outside Parliament that his parliamentary freedom of speech cannot be impeached.

6. The House still reserves to itself the right to treat the institution of legal proceedings against a member in respect of a matter covered, in its opinion, by parliamentary privilege, as a breach of its own privileges; but the Select Committee on Parliamentary Privilege recommended in 1967 that save in exceptional circumstances (for example, where a member is being improperly obstructed in the performance of his parliamentary functions) such matters should be left to the ordinary processes of the courts.[30]

7. Substantial interference with the exercise of a member's freedom of speech and action in his parliamentary capacity, by threats, molestation, bribes or other improper inducements may be treated by the House as a contempt or breach of privilege. What if a member agrees to act as the parliamentary spokesman of an outside pressure group? The inconclusive case of *W. J. Brown* (1947)[31] neatly stated the problems. Brown, who had been general secretary of the Civil Service Clerical Association, was elected as an Independent M.P. He entered into an agreement with the Association whereby he became their salaried 'parliamentary general secretary' but would retain full freedom to engage in his own political activities. The executive committee of the Association later became dissatisfied with his political attitudes and proposed to recommend the termination of the agreement. Brown claimed that this proposal was a breach of parliamentary privilege in that it was calculated to influence him in his conduct as an M.P. by threatening him with a financial penalty. The Committee of Privileges, dividing (unusually) along party lines, reported[32] that on the facts no breach of privilege had been committed, but it recognized that the exertion of outside financial pressure on a member for the purpose of influencing his conduct as a member could well be a breach of privilege. The House, adopting the report, resolved that it was inconsistent with the maintenance of the privilege of freedom of speech for a member to *enter into* a contractual agreement with an outside body fettering his freedom of action or stipulating that he was to act as that body's parliamentary representative.[33] In any event a court would almost

29. H.C. 34 (1967–68), xxii, xxiii.

30. H.C. 34 (1967–68), xvi–xvii. See generally de Smith, 21 *Mod.L.Rev.* 465.

31. Wilson, *Cases and Materials*, pp. 283–7.

32. H.C. 118 (1946–47).

33. The duty of a member being to his constituents and to the country as a whole, rather than to any particular section thereof (440 H.C. Deb. 365 (15 July 1947)).

certainly refuse to enforce such a contract on grounds of public policy.[34]

No similar case has arisen since 1947. But it is impossible to believe that financial aid tendered to members by sectional interest groups has always been granted on the understanding that the member is under no kind of obligation whatsoever to promote the interests of that group. The Select Committee on Parliamentary Privilege accepted as a fact the existence of such relationships and pointed out that a member speaking on a topic in which he had a financial interest might be guilty of a contempt of the House if he failed to disclose his interest. The Select Committee on Members' Interests, reporting in 1969,[35] expressed itself still more guardedly, emphasizing the distinction between improper inducements held out to or accepted by members for the promotion of *specific* matters in their parliamentary capacities, and *regular* financial assistance offered to members by outside organizations; the latter type of relationship was regarded (subject to the formal qualification interposed by the resolution of the House in *Brown*'s case) as being quite proper.

Threats of disciplinary action against members by party whips have been ruled not to constitute infringements of the privilege of freedom of speech because they are part of the conventionally established machinery of political organization within the House. Nevertheless, pressure exerted on a member by the whips may influence his conduct far more significantly than any connection he may have with an outside interest group.

8. In order to protect its freedom of speech, the House asserts ancillary privileges. It may resolve to clear the visitors' gallery by excluding strangers; in wartime it has often gone into secret session. Leave of the House must generally be obtained for evidence to be given in court of anything that occurred in the course of parliamentary proceedings. The House used to treat publication of its debates as a breach of privilege; assertion of this privilege has been discontinued.

Freedom from arrest

This immunity has lost most of its early importance, and in 1967 the Committee on Parliamentary Privilege recommended its abolition.[36] It does not protect members from arrest on criminal charges, or from preventive detention as security suspects in wartime;[37] though their arrest or detention must not be based on anything they have said in the course

34. See *Amalgamated Society of Railway Servants* v. *Osborne* [1910] A.C. 87 at 110–15 for the rationale of such a judicial attitude.

35. H.C. 57 (1969–70), viii–x. See also p. 273, note 29.

36. H.C. 34 (1967–68), xxix.

37. *Ramsay's* case (1940). See Wilson, *Cases and Materials*, p. 278.

of parliamentary proceedings. The privilege[38] protects members from arrest in civil matters for wilful disobedience to a court order – for example, refusal to comply with the terms of a maintenance order.[39] It extends for the period of a session and forty days before and after. Imprisonment of defendants in civil proceedings, and in particular of debtors who were unavoidably prevented from discharging their obligations, was a commonplace matter till the latter part of the nineteenth century; nowadays arrest in civil cases is confined to a narrow range of situations where the defendant is as a rule seriously at fault.

Right of the House of Commons to provide for its own composition

This privilege is now partly regulated by statute. For example, the trial of disputed election returns has been committed to an election court; the question whether a member is subject to a legal disqualification may be determinable by an election court or the Judicial Committee of the Privy Council. Within its narrowed field, the privilege is nevertheless important. The House has the exclusive right, while it is sitting, to determine by resolution when a writ for the holding of a by-election shall be issued. It can declare a member's seat vacant on the ground that he has incurred a legal disqualification or for any other reason it thinks fit and the courts cannot interfere; this is why it would be lawful for the Government to use its majority in the House to expel all Opposition members.[40] Self-restraint, influenced by fair-mindedness and expediency, alone prevents abuse of its privilege. The inexpediency of abuse was illustrated by the case of *John Wilkes*, the rake, wit and radical demagogue, who was elected to the House of Commons; the corrupt House decided that he was unfit to share their company, and expelled him. But the House has no privilege

38. In the eighteenth century the privilege, accompanied by the now obsolete privilege against being impleaded, had come to be invoked to protect not only members but their servants from arrest and suit, and was frequently abused to enable members to escape from their contractual obligations and to have their creditors arraigned for contempt of the House. The privilege against being impleaded was abrogated in 1770. cf. *Re Parliamentary Privilege Act 1770* [1958] A.C. 331; de Smith, loc. cit., pp. 475–6.

39. *Stourton* v. *Stourton* [1963] P. 302 (where privilege from arrest was successfully claimed by a peer). Members are privileged from arrest for civil but not criminal contempt of court: Erskine May, *Parliamentary Practice* (18th edn), pp. 104–6; *Wellesley* v. *Earl of Beaufort* (1831) 2 Russ. & M. 639. There are difficult marginal cases (see Enid Campbell, *Parliamentary Privilege in Australia*, 59–63; G. Sawer (1971) 7 *U. of Queensland L.J.* 226), but broadly it seems that members are immune from detention imposed by a court if the purpose of the detention is coercive as distinct from punitive.

40. Under a written constitution, the grounds for expulsion could be judicially reviewable. cf. *Powell* v. *McCormack* 395 U.S. 486 (1970) (the case of Adam Clayton Powell, the former Congressman for Harlem).

to prevent any person from standing as a candidate at a by-election. Wilkes was duly re-elected, and his seat was again declared vacant by the House; after this absurd process had been repeated, the House resolved in 1770 that his election was void and that the seat be awarded to the runner-up. Wilkes was again elected in 1774; the House took no step to unseat him, and in 1782 the House resolved to expunge the resolution of 1770 from its Journals.

The only modern examples of expulsion for reasons other than legal disqualification are of members who had been convicted of criminal offences involving moral turpitude or who have committed gross contempts of the House.[41]

Right to have exclusive cognizance of matters arising within the House

This right is closely linked with the rule that proceedings in Parliament cannot be called in question in any court. The leading case is *Bradlaugh* v. *Gossett* (1884).[42] Bradlaugh, a militant atheist, was elected to the House. After some vacillation, the House decided to allow him to make an affirmation of allegiance in lieu of taking an oath. A common informer then sued Bradlaugh for penalties on the ground that he was not qualified to sit and vote because he did not come within the classes of persons permitted by statute to affirm instead of taking an oath; and the courts held that Bradlaugh was not entitled to affirm.[43] Bradlaugh's seat became vacant; he was re-elected, and then sought to take the oath rather than be excluded from sitting. The House refused to allow him to do so, although on a proper construction of the Parliamentary Oaths Act 1866 he appeared entitled to take the oath if he chose, despite his position as a non-believer. Subsequently it resolved to exclude him from the House until he undertook not to disturb its proceedings. Bradlaugh brought an action, claiming a declaration that the resolution was void, and an injunction to restrain the Serjeant-at-Arms (Gossett) from excluding him. The court held that it had no jurisdiction to interfere. Assuming that the House had mis-

41. In 1947 Garry Allighan M.P. was expelled for contempt. He had made unsubstantiated allegations that M.P.s had given particulars of parliamentary party meetings, held within the precincts of the Palace of Westminster, to journalists for money or while under the influence of drink. He was himself receiving payments from a newspaper for disclosing such information and had given false answers to questions put to him in the Committee of Privileges: Wilson, *Cases and Materials*, pp. 290–95.

42. 12 Q.B.D. 271. The background is summarized in Wilson's *Cases and Materials*, pp. 265–6.

43. *Clarke* v. *Bradlaugh* (1881) 7 Q.B.D. 38. It was later held, however, that only the Crown could recover the penalties prescribed by statute: *Bradlaugh* v. *Clarke* (1883) 8 App. Cas. 354.

interpreted the Act, the matter would still fall within the exclusive privilege of the House to regulate its own proceedings. Similarly, if the House had resolved to allow Bradlaugh to take the oath, the courts would have had no power to pronounce upon that decision. But if proceedings were brought to recover a penalty from him as a disqualified person, it would be incumbent on the court to interpret the Act. In such a case the jurisdiction of the courts could not be excluded even by a resolution of the House purporting to protect Bradlaugh against an action for penalties, for the privileges of Parliament did not extend to such a matter arising outside the House.[44]

The House has not asserted a general jurisdiction over matters arising within the walls of the House if they have no direct connection with its proceedings. Theft, rape or murder are issues to be left to the criminal courts; in any event, the penal powers of the House are inadequate to deal with ordinary crimes.[45] If two members came to blows in the House, the courts and the House would have a *concurrent* jurisdiction; a magistrate could properly issue a summons for assault and try the case,[46] and the House might also decide that the fracas amounted to a contempt of the House. But when in doubt, a court may elect to tread warily for fear of encroaching on what the House may deem to be its own exclusive preserves. When A. P. Herbert, then an Independent M.P. campaigning to liberalize the liquor licensing laws, decided to embarrass members of the Kitchen Committee of the House by applying for summonses against them for selling drinks in the members' bar without a justices' licence, the chief metropolitan magistrate refused to issue summonses; and the Divisional Court of the King's Bench Division, taking a remarkably generous view of the scope of the internal affairs of the House of Commons, held that he had been right to decline jurisdiction because of parliamentary privilege.[47]

Right to punish for breach of privilege and contempt

The House can vindicate its own privileges by taking disciplinary action against members and others whom it adjudges to have broken them. All

44. (1884) 12 Q.B.D. at 281–2, *per* Stephen J. See also *Papworth* v. *Coventry* [1967] 1 W.L.R. 663 at 669–70.

45. See p. 325. In 1970, CS gas was projected into the chamber by a member of the public as a gesture of protest. The House left the matter to be dealt with by the police and the courts.

46. In *Eliot*'s case (note 7 above) where the conviction for *sedition* was ultimately quashed on a writ of error, the defendants' conviction for assaulting the Speaker in the House still stood. See also *Bradlaugh* v. *Gossett* (above) at 283–4.

47. *R.* v. *Graham-Campbell, ex p. Herbert* [1935] 1 K.B. 594.

breaches of privilege are contempts of the House. But there is also a wide range of contempts that do not fall within the scope of any nominate privilege. The following are examples of contempts:[48] offering bribes to members; molesting or otherwise obstructing members or officers of the House in the performance of their duties; casting imputations reflecting on the dignity of the House by, for example, insulting the House or its members; attempting to disrupt the proceedings of the House; tampering with witnesses before select committees of the House; refusing to give evidence, or giving false evidence, before a committee of the House. These contempts are often called breaches of privilege; this usage is misleading, for the House has accepted that it cannot by resolution enlarge the scope of its own privileges, but has not closed the categories of contempt; and – to take but one example – if revolutionary students shouted down witnesses giving evidence at a university before an itinerant select committee, they would be guilty of a contempt of the House. No matter whether the offence is styled a breach of privilege or a contempt or both, the penal powers of the House are the same.

A complaint of 'breach of privilege' must be raised by a member at the earliest opportunity. If the Speaker rules that a *prima facie* case has been made out, the matter is referred to the Committee of Privileges, a select committee appointed sessionally and in proportion to party strengths. In investigating the complaint, the Committee can require the attendance of witnesses and the production of documents; refusal to comply with its commands or to answer questions is a contempt. It does not, in practice, afford the persons against whom the complaints have been made any opportunity of being legally represented, and has sometimes reported that a complaint has been established although the 'defendant' has not been given any hearing at all. In the *Strauss* case[49] the Committee condemned the members of the area board without hearing them. Since, moreover, the members of the Committee are in a sense judges in their own cause, this disregard of the elements of natural justice is open to severe criticism. In 1967 the Select Committee on Parliamentary Privilege recommended a number of procedural reforms, which would give all persons directly concerned a right to attend its hearings, make submissions, and call, examine and cross-examine witnesses; and rights to seek the Committee's leave to be legally represented and to ask for legal aid.[50] These necessary reforms had yet to be brought into effect in 1972. There is also a case (which the Select Committee did not accept) for codifying contempts so as to introduce certainty at the expense of flexibility. In some Commonwealth

48. See Erskine May, *Parliamentary Practice* (18th edn), ch. 10.
49. See p. 317.
50. H.C. 34 (1967–68), xiv–xlvii.

countries, not only are breaches of privilege and contempts codified by statute but allegations of breach of privilege and contempt are triable by the courts.

The Committee of Privileges may find that a complaint has been established but recommend that no further action be taken. It may recommend that the House resolve that the person guilty of contempt be admonished or reprimanded by the Speaker at the bar of the House; or that a member found guilty of contempt be suspended[51] or expelled from the House; or that a member, or a member of the public, be committed to prison for contempt. The recommendations of the Committee are nearly always, but not invariably, adopted by the House. The power of the House to impose fines for contempt was last exercised three hundred years ago and is now obsolete; the Select Committee in 1967 recommended that this power be revived by statute. No person has been committed to prison for contempt since 1880 (and then only for one night). Imprisonment terminates on prorogation though it can be renewed in the next session. The House of Lords, as a court of record, may impose fines and may commit for a fixed term extending beyond prorogation. Offenders may be taken into the custody of the Serjeant at Arms (or Black Rod) and thence committed to prison if the House has so directed. Provided that the order of the House or Speaker's warrant is duly made out, the Serjeant at Arms may forcibly enter private property to carry out an arrest,[52] and is entitled to call upon the police or even the armed forces for any necessary assistance in executing the orders of the House.[53]

The Select Committee of 1967 confirmed what was already apparent – that some members had been too ready to invoke the jurisdiction of the House to deal with personal affronts as questions of privilege. It recommended that recourse to this jurisdiction should be confined to those cases where the exercise of the functions of the House was liable to be seriously impeded; that where members considered themselves to have been defamed by newspaper comments or statements by individuals, they should normally be content to pursue their remedies in the ordinary courts; and that where proceedings were brought in the House for

51. The Speaker may also order a member to withdraw from a day's sitting for grossly disorderly conduct (S.O. No. 23); and if he names a member for persistent disregard of the authority of the chair or other serious misconduct in the House, that member may be suspended forthwith upon a resolution of the House, the period of suspension for a first offender being five days (S.O. No. 24). These provisions do not affect the general inherent power of the House to suspend a member for contempt.

52. *Burdett* v. *Abbot* (1811) 14 East 1.

53. ibid. See further H.C. 34 (1967–68), pp. 115–65, 206–9 for details of the procedure adopted.

contempt, justification or reasonable belief in the allegations complained of should be admissible as defences.

Since 1967 the number of trivial complaints of breach of privilege has diminished. But it is incongruous, to say the least, that members of the House of Commons should be more sensitive than judges to hostile criticism.[54] It is also noteworthy that whereas an appeal lies from a conviction for contempt of court, no such appeal lies from a finding of contempt of the House; this rule would be left unchanged by the Select Committee's proposals. Fortunately the House has on the whole dealt sensibly with contemnors; where the Committee of Privileges has found a complaint proved, it has usually recommended that no disciplinary action be taken and the House has regularly accepted such a recommendation.

Parliamentary privilege and the courts

There are points of similarity between the royal prerogative and parliamentary privilege. Both are recognized as part of the law of the land; both embody special rules evolved for public purposes. Acts done within the recognized area of prerogative are unreviewable by the courts; acts done by either House within its acknowledged field of privilege are similarly unreviewable.[55] The Crown cannot enlarge its own prerogatives within the realm; the two Houses have recognized that they cannot extend their privileges, though their attitude towards 'contempts' not falling within the scope of a nominate privilege is ambiguous. But there are material differences between prerogative and privilege. The prerogative is essentially a residuum of ancient common-law attributes, attenuated by judicial decisions and legislation. The growth of parliamentary privilege can be traced in resolutions and rulings recorded in the Journals of the two Houses; and privilege has been and can still be expanded, as well as abrogated, by statute. The Crown cannot commit persons to prison for infringing its prerogatives; the two Houses can commit for breach of privilege, or enforce obedience to privilege by milder forms of direct action. The most interesting difference between the two bodies of law is that whereas the Crown has long since ceased to claim to be the sole judge of the limits of its prerogative, the two Houses (and the House of Commons in particular) still assert that they are the sole judges of the *extent* of their own privileges – a claim to which the courts do not accede. For example, a decision by the House of Commons that Mr Strauss's

54. For a modern (and tolerant) judicial attitude towards the concept of contempt of court, see *R.* v. *Metropolitan Police Commissioner, ex p. Blackburn (No. 2)* [1968] 2 Q.B. 150.

55. See *Bradlaugh* v. *Gossett* (1884) 12 Q.B.D. 271.

letter to the Minister *was* a 'proceeding in Parliament' would not have been treated as binding by the courts if the board had sued Mr Strauss;[56] the House, on the other hand, might have not only rejected the courts' interpretation but also treated it as an encroachment on its own privileges, and therefore a contempt, on the part of the plaintiffs, their legal advisers and the judges.

The claim of the House to be the sole interpreter of its own privileges has given rise to two major constitutional conflicts. In the first of them, the House of Lords (as an appellate court) held (*Ashby* v. *White*)[57] that a voter at Aylesbury, whose vote the returning officer had maliciously refused to accept, was entitled to damages. The House of Commons protested that this decision violated their exclusive privileges relating to parliamentary elections. Other Aylesbury voters brought similar actions against the returning officer; the House ordered them to be committed to prison. An application was made for writs of habeas corpus to secure their release from unlawful detention. In *Paty*'s case (1704) the court refused the writ;[58] counsel for the applicants, who intended to bring the case before the House of Lords, was promptly committed by the Commons to join his clients. The deadlock was broken only by a prorogation of Parliament.

The central issue revived, in a more spectacular form, at the beginning of Victoria's reign. One Stockdale published an illustrated treatise on the reproductive system. The book was found circulating among prison inmates. Stockdale considered himself to have been defamed by comments on his work made in a report by prison inspectors, published by order of the House of Commons, and sued Hansards, the parliamentary printers (then a commercial firm) for libel. The defendants were ordered by the Commons to plead that the publication was covered by parliamentary privilege. The Court of Queen's Bench rejected this plea, holding that as a matter of law such a publication was not comprised within the area of parliamentary privilege and awarded damages to Stockdale (*Stockdale* v. *Hansard*);[59] no resolution of the House could deprive the courts of their authority to interpret and apply the law of the land in a matter affecting the rights of subjects. Stockdale brought another action against Hansards; the defendants, on the instructions of the House,

56. The situation in *Bradlaugh* v. *Gossett* was different in as much as the resolution of the House in that case, ill-founded or well-founded, undoubtedly fell within the scope of the privilege of the House to regulate its own internal affairs.

57. See 2 Ld. Raym. 938, 3 Ld. Raym. 320; 14 St. Tr. 695.

58. Ld. Raym. 1105, Holt C.J. (rightly) dissenting on the ground that the cause of commitment stated in the return to the writ was insufficient in law; the facts alleged to constitute the contempt of the House had been explicitly averred.

59. (1839) 9 A. & E. 1.

entered no plea, and the plaintiff was again awarded damages. There were two sequels:[60]

(i) Execution had been levied by the Sheriff of Middlesex on Hansard's property to recover the damages. The House resolved to commit the Sheriff for breach of privilege and contempt. He applied for habeas corpus on the ground that he was being unlawfully detained (*Sheriff of Middlesex*'s case (1840)).[61] The Speaker's warrant was 'general', in that it had not recited the facts allegedly constituting the contempt. The court dismissed the application, on the ground that it would be unseemly to inquire further. Even if the House of Commons were not a superior court of record, it was entitled to as much respect as if it were; and on a habeas corpus application one superior court would not investigate the truth of the facts stated by another as a cause of commitment for contempt.[62] If, however, the facts constituting the alleged contempt had been set out by the respondent to the application, and they could not reasonably be construed as amounting to a contempt of the House, the court would be at liberty to intervene.[63]

(ii) Parliament passed the Parliamentary Papers Act 1840, conferring absolute privilege on statements in parliamentary papers, and thus achieving what could not be attained by a mere resolution.

The refusal on the part of the courts to award habeas corpus to release the Sheriff from arbitrary detention is obviously open to criticism.[64] It was supported by precedent and was defended on grounds of principle; but the court had chosen to blind itself to notorious reality, and to countenance

60. Four, if one includes the commitments of Stockdale and his solicitor for contempt of the House (cf. *Howard* v. *Gossett* (1845) 10 Q.B. 359, 411).

61. 11 A. & E. 273. In fact the two Sheriffs of Middlesex were committed by the House.

62. The precedents were the *Earl of Shaftesbury*'s case (1677) 1 Mod. 144; *Murray*'s case (1751) 1 Wils. 299; and a considered dictum in *Burdett* v. *Abbot* (1811) 14 East at 150. In *Paty*'s case (above) a majority of the court had held their jurisdiction to be excluded even though the facts constituting the alleged contempt were specified in the return to the writ. The *Sheriff of Middlesex*'s case was followed by the High Court of Australia in *R*. v. *Richards*, *ex p. Fitzpatrick and Browne* (1955) 92 C.L.R. 157 (held, also, that a House of Parliament in the Commonwealth of Australia could commit for a fixed term). See Enid Campbell, *Parliamentary Privilege in Australia*, ch. 7.

63. Adopting Holt C.J.'s view in *Paty*'s case (above) and Lord Ellenborough's dictum in *Burdett* v. *Abbot* 14 East at 150.

Ultimately the Sheriff of Middlesex declined to execute any further orders of the court against Hansards and was thereupon committed to prison for contempt of court.

64. Contrast the decisions of the Supreme Court of India in *Special Reference No. 1 of 1964* A.I.R. 1965 S.C. 746, where a general warrant of commitment for breach of privilege was held not to exclude the court's jurisdiction to inquire into the legality of the commitment. See *Annual Survey of Commonwealth Law for 1965*, pp. 41–4.

injustice. Although 'the old dualism remains unresolved',[65] in the sense that the courts still do not accept the conclusiveness of the House's pronouncements as to the scope of its own privileges and the House denies that the courts have jurisdiction to determine such a matter at all, it is not unfair to say that the courts have 'yielded the key of the fortress'[66] by accepting that the House can enforce its own view by first committing an innocent offender to prison and then refusing to give particulars of his alleged breach of privilege. Fortunately the House of Commons has not acted in such an overbearing manner since Stockdale's time; it has, moreover, acquiesced in the assumption of jurisdiction by the courts in several marginal cases, and the courts have shown circumspection when called upon to exercise jurisdiction.

Nevertheless, the House has, more than once, reiterated its own position in recent years, and only by a narrow margin was the prospect of a similar conflict averted in 1958.[67] Judges are not always better equipped than other persons to decide questions of law set in political contexts. But the unhappy combination of uncodified contempts, an unsatisfactory procedure for investigating allegations of contempt, and the insistence of the House that it must have the first and last word in matters touching the interests of its members as members, irrespective of the impact of its decisions on the interests of members of the public, suggests that the House ought to relinquish its jurisdiction over breaches of privilege and contempts to the courts, as it has in effect relinquished its privilege to determine disputed election returns.

65. *Re Parliamentary Privilege Act 1770* [1958] A.C. 331 at 354 (quoting Erskine May).

66. Keir and Lawson, *Cases in Constitutional Law* (5th edn), p. 267.

67. If the House had endorsed the report of the Committee of Privileges in the *Strauss* case, it is not at all certain that this would have deterred the board from proceeding with an action against Mr Strauss.

Chapter 15
Subordinate Legislation

General

Parliament is not the sole source of new law. The superior courts make new law by laying down rules in decided cases which form binding precedents – binding till they are overruled (by statute or in a later case), or distinguished, or otherwise explained away. Judicial law-making is almost surreptitious; a new departure is usually rationalized as a rediscovery of a long-lost principle, or as an application of an established rule to a novel set of material facts, or as the ascertainment of an unexpressed parliamentary intent. Although the idea that the courts merely declare and apply pre-existing norms may be a polite fiction, the supposed need for this verbal camouflage rests on a widely held assumption that it is for Parliament, not for the Judiciary, to bring the law up to date. The room for judicial manoeuvre is restricted by the framework of constitutional thought within which the courts operate.

As we have already noted,[1] such Community legislation as has direct effect in Britain is really *primary*, not *subordinate*, legislation, because the Community organs are not subordinate to Parliament in the eyes of Community law and their legislative output does not derive its legal force from any delegation of authority by Parliament. Community legislation is indeed normally 'secondary' in the sense that it consists of regulations made by the Council or the Commission in pursuance of powers conferred by the Community treaties, and it is therefore subordinate *within the Community legal order*, but not within our legal order.

There are other legislative institutions, forming part of the executive branch of government. The Crown, Ministers, some Departments of State, public corporations and local authorities have law-making powers. When we speak of subordinate legislation, we mean primarily the rules and regulations made by these executive bodies. We also include rules of court made by independent statutory committees composed mainly of judges. Such legislation is *subordinate* in that it is made by bodies endowed with limited powers (usually conferred by Parliament), and is always

1. See pp. 45–6, 79–82.

subject to abrogation or alteration by Act of Parliament. Unlike legislation by the Queen in Parliament, it may, moreover, be held by a court to be *ultra vires*.

The only significant source of subordinate legislation made otherwise than in pursuance of powers delegated by Parliament is the royal prerogative. But the Crown has no general inherent power to alter the law of the land.[2] It has limited prerogative powers to make new constitutions and to legislate for a slowly dwindling number of colonies acquired by conquest or cession, to regulate the affairs of the civil service and the armed services, and to determine the extent of British territorial waters.

The great bulk of subordinate legislation is made by virtue of parliamentary authority. Parliament delegates powers to legislate; the end-product is *delegated legislation*. The average annual output of delegated legislation easily exceeds the amount of parliamentary legislation. In 1971 the Public General Acts covered 2107 pages and published *Statutory Instruments* totalled 6327 pages. (*Statutory Instruments*[3] do not include by-laws made by local authorities or public corporations.) Roughly 2000 sets of rules and regulations are made by Ministers or the Crown in Council or other central rule-making authorities in the course of a year; the total number of public and private Acts of Parliament will be about 150.

Some have depicted this state of affairs as an abdication by Parliament from its principal constitutional role in favour of the Executive.[4] Acts of Parliament, sponsored by government Departments and passed into law with the acquiescence of a docile parliamentary majority, give the Executive sweeping legislative powers; and safeguards against the abuse of those powers are inadequate. The most celebrated denunciation of delegation to the Executive came in 1929 from Lord Hewart, the then Lord Chief Justice of England. In his book, *The New Despotism*, he attributed over-generous delegations of legislative power to a deep-laid bureaucratic conspiracy. The Committee on Ministers' Powers, hastily appointed in anticipation of the furore that Hewart's book would arouse, reported in 1932 that the conspiratorial allegations were unsupported by 'the smallest shred of evidence'.[5] Nevertheless, the idea still persists in some quarters that delegation of legislative power to the Executive is at best a necessary

2. *Case of Proclamations* (1611) 12 Co. Rep. 74.

3. For the meaning of this term, see p. 339. There were also thirty-seven pages of prerogative instruments in 1971.

4. See especially Lord Hewart of Bury, *The New Despotism*; C. K. Allen, *Bureaucracy Triumphant; Law and Orders* (though the 3rd edn of this work was more restrained than the first); G. W. Keeton, *The Passing of Parliament*. For more detached appraisals, see C. T. Carr, *Delegated Legislation; Concerning English Administrative Law*; John Willis, *The Parliamentary Powers of English Government Departments*.

5. Cmd 4060 (1932), p. 59.

evil, a constitutional impropriety to be half-heartedly condoned on grounds of expediency, but a potentially serious threat to the liberties of the subject. Doubtless this bogey will stubbornly refuse to be laid to rest, but a few elementary points can be made.

1. Executive initiative is the dominant feature of parliamentary legislation. It is a still more dominant feature of delegated legislation. The difference is one of degree. Differences of degree can indeed be extremely important. Delegated legislation, unlike parliamentary legislation, has no committee stage at which amendments can be put down;[6] seldom is it debated in Parliament at all. None the less, prior consultation with advisory bodies and organized interest groups is a more conspicuous characteristic of delegated legislation than of parliamentary legislation.[7]

2. Most of the doom-laden prophecies were based on the experience of war and its immediate aftermath. In both the world wars of this century, vast law-making powers were delegated to the Executive. The Defence of the Realm Acts 1914–15 conferred a general power to make Orders in Council for securing the public safety and the defence of the realm. The Emergency Powers (Defence) Acts 1939–40 were more explicit but equally permissive, and the 1940 Act specified that Defence Regulations could make provisions 'requiring persons to place themselves, their services, and their property at the disposal of His Majesty'. These enormous powers were not always exercised reasonably. Some Defence Regulations remained in force too long after the war was over; and new regulations and orders, sometimes unpopular or ill-conceived, were made under post-war emergency legislation.[8] However, most of them were revoked or lapsed long ago. This fact does not, of course, imply that contemporary criticism was groundless or had no effect.

3. Open a recent volume of *Statutory Instruments* and read the first hundred pages. The tedium of wading through a mass of abstruse technicalities, barely comprehensible to anyone lacking expert knowledge of the subject-matter, is at least an instructive experience; and if one has the

6. With the exception of special procedure orders; see p. 339.
7. See generally S. A. Walkland, *The Legislative Process in Great Britain*, ch. 5.
8. See Supplies and Services (Transitional Powers) Act 1945; Supplies and Services (Extended Purposes) Act 1947; Supplies and Services (Defence Purposes) Act 1951. Food rationing regulations were naturally among the least popular. According to a well-authenticated story, Churchill, on his return to office as Prime Minister in 1951, gave instructions that the food ration be constructed in the form of a model so that he could assess the quantity better. When the model was laid before him, he remarked 'Not a bad meal!' On being told that the model represented a week's rations he exploded: '. . . the people are starving . . .' (Harold Macmillan, *Tides of Fortune* (1969), pp. 490–91).

moral stamina, one can plough on through another six thousand pages. With such dull subject-matter, delegated legislation is in fact a dull subject for many of us.

4. Parliamentary scrutiny of delegated legislation admittedly tends to be perfunctory. But a select committee of the House of Commons has examined statutory instruments which may be open to objection on constitutional grounds.[9] During a recent five-year period, this committee reported adversely on only 1 per cent of the instruments scrutinized.[10] Before launching into a general denunciation of the content of delegated legislation, it is best to equip oneself with a sense of proportion.

5. Root and branch attacks on delegated legislation have often been prompted by a hearty dislike of public encroachments on freedom of property and contract. The assailants would have found the regulatory provisions no less objectionable if they had been embodied in Acts of Parliament rather than in rules and regulations.

There is one further preliminary point. Delegated legislation is sometimes confused with the establishment and work of administrative tribunals. Their only common feature is that both are substitutes: delegated legislation may be resorted to instead of Acts of Parliament, and administrative tribunals instead of courts. If substitutes are always a poor second best, if Parliament and the ordinary courts are the only acceptable media for legislation and adjudication, and if administrative law means delegated legislation plus administrative adjudication and is a negation of the rule of law, then it is right to place the two phenomena side by side in the same rogues' gallery. If one disagrees with these propositions, there is little point in discussing delegated legislation in conjunction with special tribunals. Such a discussion also generates confusion. The line between legislation and adjudication may often be thin, but legislation is basically the making of new rules of general application[11] for the future, and adjudication is the determination of individual claims and controversies. If new general rules emerge from adjudication, this is incidental to the main purpose of the process. Obviously, statutory regulations laying down a new procedure for determining claims to social security benefits are different in kind from a decision by a national insurance tribunal that X is or is not entitled to a benefit he has claimed in reliance on the existing

9. See pp. 345–7. For the new committee arrangements, see Addendum.

10. See H.C. 455 (1971–72), para. 54, for details.

11. The difference between 'general' legislation and 'particular' executive action or judicial decisions is one of degree and sometimes imperceptible. See Walkland, op. cit., pp. 9–10; de Smith, *Judicial Review of Administrative Action* (3rd edn), ch. 2.

rules.[12] Moreover, new tribunals are almost invariably constituted by Acts of Parliament; the normal role of delegated legislation in relation to tribunals will be to lay down detailed rules of procedure and to express in more precise terms the general functions confided in the tribunals by the enabling Act.

Delegated legislation: functions and fears
Historical note[13]

Before 1832 Parliament delegated rule-making powers to the Executlve spasmodically and, on the whole, sparingly. The plenitude of legislative authority devolved on Henry VIII by the Statute of Proclamations 1539 was not to be rivalled till 1914; the functions of central government were not wide enough to justify delegation on the grand scale. The Poor Law Amendment Act 1934, empowering the Poor Law Commissioners generally to make regulations for the management of the poor, marked the beginning of a new epoch. As the trend towards collectivism gathered momentum after 1870, so did delegations of legislative authority to the central government rapidly increase. But if this development threatened to undermine the fabric of the constitution, the dangers were hardly perceived. Dicey, among constitutional lawyers the most articulate exponent of Whiggish individualism, thought that Parliament was far too conservative in its attempts to unburden itself of detail; and, uncharacteristically, he commended the example of France, where executive decrees amplifying the general principles of legislation ranged over large areas of the law.[14] The phase of vehement denunciation began in the 1920s. Temperatures were lowered by the Report of the Committee on Ministers' Powers in 1932[15] and have never reached the same height again. The Report provided an entirely convincing account of the reasons why the delegation of legislative powers to Ministers was indispensable, as well as indicating some real or potential dangers in the practice and suggesting safeguards against abuses. Amid the torrent of regulations descending from Whitehall between 1939 and 1950, few voices were raised to question the constitutional propriety of

12. Some special tribunals have the duty of deciding in their discretion whether to *vary* existing rights (for example, by fixing fair rents) or to grant new rights and privileges (for example, licences).

13. See also Cmd 4060 (1932), pp. 10–15.

14. *Introduction to the Study of the Law of the Constitution* (10th edn), pp. 52–3.

15. Cmd 4060. The Committee is often called the Donoughmore Committee, after the name of its first chairman. See also the *Report of the Select Committee on Delegated Legislation* 1953 (H.C. 310–11 (1952–53)); *The Process of Legislation* (Second Report of the Select Committee on Procedure 1971 (H.C. 538 (1970–71)); *Report of the Joint Select Committee on Delegated Legislation* 1972 (H.C. 475 (1971–72)).

delegation. The main constitutional issues were: Where should the lines be drawn between parliamentary and delegated legislation? And how could safeguards against the misuse of delegated powers be improved? These issues became less important as other horses emerged to be flogged.

Purposes of delegation

The reasons for delegating legislative powers to the Executive can be summed up in one phrase: the promotion of efficiency.

1. It is inefficient and unnecessary to incorporate a mass of complex detail in a parliamentary bill, or indeed in the schedules to such a bill, unless such provisions are designed to make really important changes in the law (for example, imposing substantial criminal liabilities or altering taxes), in which case they ought to be exposed to full parliamentary scrutiny. Few members of any Parliament will have the expert knowledge required to table and debate amendments to highly technical legislation; but a dogged group of the initiated can consume parliamentary time in this way, often for the ulterior purpose of impeding a Government's general legislative programme. Delegation saves parliamentary time.

2. The enactment of tortuous and cumbersome legislation, bulging with minutiae, disfigures the statute book and tends to detract from the prestige of Parliament. One can admire the diligence of the draftsmen of the Land Commission Act 1967[16] without being entranced by their product; some of the provisions of this convoluted statute should have been left to subordinate legislation.

3. It may be impossible to bring a major Act (for example, on town planning, social security, nationalization of an industry, or reform of local government structure) into operation the day it receives the royal assent. Postponement may be necessary in order to undertake administrative reorganization or to conduct detailed consultations with various bodies with a view to modifying the general principles of the Act in their application to particular areas or sections of the community. Sometimes this can be effected by fixing the operative date when the bill is passed.[17] Sometimes this is impracticable, and the Act will therefore provide that it will come into force on such day as Her Majesty by Order in Council (or a Minister by statutory instrument) shall appoint. In any event, powers to make supplementary regulations on aspects of the new design will almost certainly be needed in the interest of flexibility, fairness and efficiency.

16. Now repealed: Land Commission (Dissolution) Act 1971.
17. Different dates may be fixed for bringing into operation different parts of an Act. See, for example, Local Government Act 1972, s. 273.

4. When an Act is passed, it is often reasonable to suppose that new contingencies (such as cases of special hardship, or technological developments) will arise although their exact form cannot be predicted at the date of enactment. It will be more sensible to give the responsible Minister powers to make regulations to amplify the Act should such contingencies arise than to compel him to rely on the chance of finding a place for amending legislation in an already long legislative queue.

5. Swift emergency action may have to be taken during a parliamentary recess or at a time when serious damage may be done if the normal processes of parliamentary legislation have to be followed. Sudden outbreaks of epidemics, natural disasters, the discovery and introduction of new dangerous drugs or poisons, paralysis of the economy by industrial stoppages or a threat to the stability of the pound resulting from an international financial crisis, may call for the immediate exercise of rule-making powers. Sometimes, of course, it is feasible to rush a bill through all its stages in both Houses within a few hours; the Emergency Powers (Defence) Act 1939 and the Southern Rhodesia Act 1965 (consequential on UDI) fell into this exceptional category. Sometimes a possible need for urgent action can be provided for by the enabling Act in the form of a grant of *executive* powers if *general* emergency regulations are unlikely to be required. However, when in March 1972 the United Kingdom Government decided that it was imperative to impose direct rule on Northern Ireland and suspend the institutions of Stormont, the Northern Ireland (Temporary Provisions) Act 1972 not only vested *executive* authority in respect of Northern Ireland in the Secretary of State, but also provided that Orders in Council could be made on any matter within the competence of the Northern Ireland Parliament. A series of important legislative changes were made under this wide-ranging delegated power.[18]

6. Changes in the constitutions of dependent territories, and constitutions adopted immediately before independence, are better embodied in Orders in Council than in Acts of Parliament. This is not because they are unimportant but because they are almost invariably the outcome of an intergovernmental negotiation, and if it were open to Parliament to delete or modify individual provisions of the constitution a delicate balance might be upset and the political consequences could then be very serious. American experience supports this comment. The constitutions of two dependent territories of the United States, the Virgin Islands and Guam, are contained in organic Acts alterable only by Congress. Constitutional changes agreed between the United States Administration and the Virgin Islanders were held up for several years before 1968 because of minor

18. See further ch. 30.

objections by the relevant congressional committees or pressure on the congressional timetable. This caused deep resentment locally. The United States is fortunate in having only a handful of dependent territories. The United Kingdom could not afford this leisurely and pernickety procedure.

Where delegation is open to criticism

1. It is a primary function of Parliament to determine the guidelines of legislative policy.[19] Parliament should not, therefore, delegate to Ministers power to make regulations on matters of general principle unless it lays down in the enabling Act standards delimiting the boundaries of the delegate's discretion. Skeleton legislation is justifiable only in order to deal with a state of dire emergency (such as the Northern Ireland situation in 1972) or a quite exceptional situation, such as has been created by Britain's accession to the European Communities. In countries with written constitutions, a blanket delegation of legislative power to the Executive may be held to be unconstitutional.[20]

2. Grants of delegated power ought not to be so expressed that it becomes impossible in practice for the courts to review the limits of the powers exercised. Statutory formulae purporting to oust the jurisdiction of the courts by express language[21] are now uncommon. Less uncommon are statutory provisions endowing Ministers with powers which in their opinion are requisite or expedient for a broadly framed statutory purpose. When the validity of regulations made in pursuance of such powers is challenged, very strong grounds will have to be adduced before a court will be persuaded to intervene.[22] Moreover, Ministers and their advisers endowed with so large a discretion may be unable to resist temptations to stretch their powers beyond reasonable limits. Such delegations may thus offend against proposition (1).

3. Criticism has been levelled against the so-called 'Henry VIII clause', under which Parliament delegates authority to make regulations amending Acts of Parliament.[23] This formulation is not widely used, and it is normally innocuous if the grant of power is confined to a limited period for

19. See generally J. A. G. Griffith (1951) 14 *Mod. L. Rev.* 279, 425.

20. See, for example, *Kent* v. *Dulles* 357 U.S. 116 (1958) (United States); *Re Delhi Laws Act* (1951) S.C.R. 747 (India), though see H. M. Seervai, *Constitutional Law of India*, pp. 874–86.

21. See pp. 351–2.

22. The point is well made by Lord Diplock *obiter* in *McEldowney* v. *Forde* [1971] A.C. 632 at 659–61, though see *Utah Construction and Engineering Co.* v. *Pataky* [1966] A.C. 629; *Customs and Excise Commissioners* v. *Cure and Deeley Ltd* [1962] 1 Q.B. 340. See also pp. 349–50.

23. cf. Cmd 4060 (1932), pp. 36–8, 59–61, 65.

the purpose of enabling draftsmen to make consequential adaptations to miscellaneous enactments that may have been overlooked when the principal Act was passed.[24]

4. Seldom if ever will a grant of power to make regulations imposing liabilities with retroactive effect be justified.[25]

5. The power to impose or vary taxation is, in general, too important to be delegated by Parliament. But a flexible power to make regulations modifying, for example, rates of indirect taxation or customs duties may be a valuable ancillary instrument for the management of the economy.[26]

6. In the interests of certainty, Parliament ought to identify the recipient of its delegated powers, and when delegating legislative authority it should not authorize sub-delegation of those powers to unnamed persons. In and immediately after the Second World War, when sub-delegation was expressly authorized by the Emergency Powers (Defence) Acts and their successors, instances of five-tier delegation arose.[27]

The European Communities Act 1972

Quite apart from Community regulations which will be directly applicable of their own force (section 2(1)), further regulations will have to be made in this country under powers delegated by the Act (section 2(2)) to give effect to Community directives and decisions and also to implement in fuller detail some Community regulations. Orders in Council and departmental regulations made under these delegated powers are *to have the effect of Acts of Parliament* and can include any provision that might be made in an Act of Parliament (section 2(4))[28] except that they are not to impose or increase taxation[29] or have retroactive effect or sub-delegate

24. See, for example, Kenya Independence Act 1963, s. 5(4). An unusual power to amend the parent Act itself was conferred by section 16(2) of the Race Relations Act 1968.

25. Such legislation is likely to be held to be *ultra vires* unless retroactive operation has been expressly authorized by the enabling Act. cf. authorities cited in *The Abadesa* [1968] P. 656 at 659. See also *Master Ladies Tailors Organisation* v. *Minister of Labour and National Service* [1950] 2 All E.R. 525 at 528. See, however, *Sabally & N'Jie* v. *Att.-Gen.* [1965] 1 Q.B. 273.

26. cf. Finance Act 1961, s. 9.

27. J. A. G. Griffith and H. Street, *Principles of Administrative Law* (4th edn), pp. 60–68.

28. For section 2(4), see pp. 80–82. Clearly such regulations can repeal or amend Acts of Parliament in force at the time when they are made. But it is arguable that the regulations will be *ultra vires* unless related to Community affairs.

29. But taxation can be imposed by directly applicable Community instruments (s. 2(1)).

legislative powers (other than power to make procedural rules for courts and tribunals) or create a new criminal offence punishable with more than two years' imprisonment or a fine more than £400. This is probably the most sweeping grant of delegated legislative powers to the Executive in modern times except under emergency conditions.

Statutory instruments

Subordinate legislation may be designated as rules, regulations, orders, by-laws, schemes, measures, or by a variety of other appellations. The most important generic description is 'statutory instrument'. The definition of this term is complex and raises difficult points of interpretation.[30] Broadly, the term covers delegated legislation made under (1) powers conferred by statutes after 1947 on Her Majesty in Council, or on Ministers or Departments, to make, confirm or approve subordinate legislation where the enabling Act says that the power shall be exercisable by statutory instrument and (2) powers conferred by statutes before 1948 on these authorities or other rule-making authorities (such as the Rule Committee of the Supreme Court) to make subordinate legislation, and on Ministers to confirm or approve instruments of a legislative (but not of an executive) character which also have to be laid before Parliament. A statutory instrument comes into effect when made unless (as is nearly always the case) the instrument specifies a later date on which it is to come into operation.

By-laws of local authorities and public corporations are not statutory instruments. Nor are measures of the General Synod of the Church of England.[31] Nor are provisional orders, which do not have legal effect till confirmed by Act of Parliament and are therefore not a form of delegated legislation at all. For most legal purposes, 'special procedure orders', which have replaced provisional orders under a number of Acts of Parliament, are statutory instruments; they will normally have legal effect without a confirmation Act.[32] Compulsory purchase orders, being of an

30. For a full analysis, see Griffith and Street, op. cit., pp. 44–57, considering the meaning of the Statutory Instruments Act 1946 and regulations and an Order in Council made thereunder in 1947.

31. Made in pursuance of the Synodical Government Measure 1969; these measures are submitted for the royal assent if approved by both Houses of Parliament; see Wade and Phillips, *Constitutional Law* (8th edn), ch. 34.

32. See Statutory Orders (Special Procedure) Acts 1945 and 1965; the procedure on such orders (which is attracted where an Act prescribes that an order authorized to be made shall be 'subject to special parliamentary procedure') involves opportunities to object to the order at a local inquiry and also by petition to Parliament; the order may be amended in pursuance of a report by a joint committee of the two Houses. See also Griffith and Street, op. cit., pp. 35–6.

executive rather than a legislative character, are not usually classified as statutory instruments. Nor, in general, are instruments made in pursuance of sub-delegated powers, but it is possible for them to fall within the definition of statutory instruments.[33] Nor, of course, are resolutions of the House of Commons statutory instruments; normally their legal effect is confined to matters arising within the House; but under some modern Acts of constitutional importance such resolutions have been accorded legislative effect.[34]

Statutory instruments must be printed, numbered, published and sold. They are also published in annual volumes in chronological sequence. However, local or temporary instruments, instruments made available in a separate series to persons directly concerned, and very bulky schedules, may be exempted from the requirement of publication. The annual volumes were called *Statutory Rules and Orders* before 1948;[35] since 1948 they have been entitled *Statutory Instruments*. Prerogative legislative instruments are unnumbered but are published and appear in an appendix to each volume.

Government statements of policy and intent, departmental circulars giving instructions to local authorities, and procedural rules issued by certain other public bodies, may be legislative in effect and will usually be published; but they will not be published as statutory instruments even if made in pursuance of statutory powers.[36] The extra-statutory concessions offered by the Inland Revenue in favour of taxpayers are clearly legislative in substance[37] but, just as clearly, are not within the definition of statutory instruments. The Immigration Rules are not classified as statutory instruments, perhaps because it is not clear that the power to make them is directly conferred by statute. Nor are the Code of Industrial Relations Practice and the Highway Code, which do not have quite the same legal force.

33. Regulations made by designated Ministers under the European Communities Act 1972 (see European Communities (Designation) Order 1972 (S.I. 1972, No. 1811)) are statutory instruments (s. 2(2); Sched. 2, para. 2(1)).

34. See Provisional Collection of Taxes Acts 1913 and 1968 (temporary authority to collect income tax and other annual taxes); Exchequer and Audit Departments Act 1957, s. 1(3) (increase in salary of Comptroller and Auditor-General); Parliamentary Commissioner Act 1967, s. 2(2) (increase in salary of Parliamentary Commissioner for Administration). See also House of Commons Disqualification Act 1957, s.6(2) (relieving M.P. from effect of disqualification); Murder (Abolition of Death Penalty) Act 1965, s. 1.

35. There is also a consolidation entitled *Statutory Rules and Orders and Statutory Instruments Revised*, comprising subordinate legislation in force at the end of 1948.

36. cf. *Blackpool Corporation* v. *Locker* [1948] 1 K.B. 349.

37. cf. *R.* v. *Customs and Excise Commissioners, ex p. Cook* [1970] 1 W.L.R. 450 at 454–5 (where attention was drawn to their lack of any legal basis).

Safeguards
Contraceptive and ante-natal

The most effective safeguard against the abuse of delegated powers is not to delegate them in such terms as to invite abuse. When a bill is first drafted by parliamentary counsel on instructions given by the sponsoring Department, it will go to that Department, to the Legislation Committee of the Cabinet (of which the Lord Chancellor and the Law Officers of the Crown are members) and may go to a specialized Cabinet committee or an inter-departmental committee.

A number of policy and technical decisions have to be taken: where the lines should be drawn between matters explicitly to be set out in the bill and matters to be left for amplification by the exercise of delegated powers; how precisely the limits of delegated power are to be worded; whether the Act should require subordinate legislation to be laid before Parliament at all, and if so, whether it should also be subject to annulment by resolution of either House, or should require approval by affirmative resolution of one or both Houses; and so on. To what extent general criteria have been formulated as guides to making these decisions is far from clear, though it can be assumed that the parliamentary draftsmen have regard to precedents and do not accede automatically to every eccentric departmental request. If the draftsmen consider an aspect of a draft bill to be objectionable on grounds of constitutional principle, they may succeed in carrying the sponsoring Department's legal advisers with them. If this is not enough and they wish to press their point, they will have a further opportunity when the final draft of the bill is examined by the Law Officers.

The Legislation Committee of the Cabinet also reviews departmental drafts of statutory instruments which are of exceptional importance or special interest to other Departments or may give rise to criticism on the grounds that they are unusual in their content or of doubtful constitutional propriety. The departmental legal advisers may obtain the aid of parliamentary counsel in preparing the draft of a particularly important instrument.[38]

Before regulations are made by a Department, prior consultation with advisory bodies and organized interest groups is the general practice.[39] Statutes often require that named bodies, or organizations identified by description (for example, representative of local authorities) be consulted in advance. Procedural regulations for tribunals and inquiries have to be

38. S. A. Walkland, *The Legislative Process in Great Britain*, pp. 63–5.
39. Griffith and Street, op. cit., pp. 124–41; J. F. Garner, 'Consultation in subordinate legislation' [1964] *Public Law* 105.

submitted in draft to the Council on Tribunals.[40] Drafts of social security regulations have to be submitted to the National Insurance Advisory Committee, a statutory body; the Committee must notify persons and bodies likely to be affected and give an opportunity for objections to be lodged; the Committee submits its report to the Secretary of State who, when he makes the regulations, must also lay the report before Parliament and state how far he has given effect to the Committee's recommendations and why he has not accepted them. In practice he has almost invariably accepted them.[41] Before the Secretary of State for Northern Ireland could initiate subordinate legislation under the 1972 Act he was to refer it in draft, where practicable, to the advisory Northern Ireland Commission.[42] Possibly special arrangements will be needed for institutionalized consultation before certain legislative instruments are made under the European Communities Act to implement Community rules and decisions. Far more important, however, will be the creation of effective means of bringing parliamentary influence to bear on Community decision-makers before the crucial Community decisions are taken and promulgated by *Community* organs.

Under a few statutes, the initiative in preparing draft rules and regulations (for example, for agricultural marketing schemes) is given to bodies representing persons engaged in the occupation, and occasionally to individuals so engaged; such schemes cannot normally be given legislative effect without the responsible Minister's approval.

By-laws made by local authorities are subject to confirmation by the appropriate Minister, who is in most cases the Secretary of State for the Environment. Sets of model by-laws are available, and local by-laws deviating widely from these without special reasons are unlikely to be confirmed.

Publicity

'Does any human being read through this mass of departmental legislation?' asked Lord Hewart.[43] Perhaps not; but since ignorance of the law is, in general, no excuse for breaking it, regulations ought to be readily available to members of the public and their legal advisers as soon as they come into force. The principles governing publication have already been noted.[44] An instrument may nevertheless have legal effect before it

40. Tribunals and Inquiries Act 1971, ss. 10, 11.
41. Griffith and Street, op. cit., pp. 132–8; National Insurance Act 1965, ss. 88, 108; Sched. 8.
42. Northern Ireland (Temporary Provisions) Act 1972, Sched. 1, para 1 (1).
43. *The New Despotism*, pp. 96–7.
44. p. 340.

is published and available for sale at a government bookshop.[45] This is unusual; indeed, Departments now try to follow a general rule that an instrument shall not come into operation for twenty-one days after being laid before Parliament.[46] But to mitigate the hardship that may still arise, section 3(2) of the Statutory Instruments Act 1946 provides that it shall be a defence to criminal proceedings for contravening an instrument to prove that the instrument has not been issued at the date of the contravention unless the prosecution proves that reasonable steps have previously been taken to bring its purport to the notice of the public or persons likely to be affected or the person charged.

In the best of all possible worlds, statutory instruments would be not only available but also intelligible. This desideratum may be unattainable, but the opaque has become translucent by the modern practice of appending brief explanatory notes at the end of statutory instruments, indicating their general purport and effect.

Parliamentary proceedings[47]

The parent Act may or may not require the instrument to be laid before Parliament. If there is no requirement as to laying,[48] a member of Parliament who gets to know of the instrument may still put down a question about it to the responsible Minister or seek to raise the matter in debate. If the instrument has merely to be laid, or laid in draft, before Parliament, it will be delivered to the Votes and Proceedings Office of the House of Commons.[49] No opportunity is provided by parliamentary procedure for the instrument to be discussed, but its existence will at least be brought to the notice of members and the Minister is more likely to be questioned about it than if it is not laid before Parliament at all. Moreover, any instrument required to be laid before Parliament does not become operative until so laid, unless it is essential for it to become operative at once, in which case the reason must be notified to the Lord Chancellor and the Speaker forthwith.[50]

45. See *R.* v. *Sheer Metalcraft Ltd* [1954] 1 Q.B. 586. Contrast *Johnson* v. *Sargant & Sons* [1918] 1 K.B. 101 (statutory order held not to have effect till it became known; the authority of this decision is now doubtful).

46. H.C. 475 (1971–72), para. 62. But not all instruments have to be laid before Parliament: see below.

47. See John E. Kersell, *Parliamentary Supervision of Delegated Legislation*; Report of the Joint Select Committee on Delegated Legislation (H.C. 475 (1971–2)).

48. The large majority of statutory instruments in this category are instruments of a local nature.

49. S.O. No. 120; Laying of Documents before Parliament (Interpretation) Act 1948, s. 1.

50. Statutory Instruments Act 1946, s. 4(1). See also above, and S.O. No. 121.

It is more common for the enabling Act to provide that an instrument shall be laid, or laid in draft, subject to the negative resolution procedure. This means that it is open to any member to move a prayer to annul the instrument (or, if it has been laid in draft, to move that it not be made) within forty days of being laid.[51] Such motions are put at the end of the day's business; debate on such a motion must be terminated or adjourned not later than 11.30 p.m. in the Commons.[52] When the Labour Government was in office in 1950–51 with a tiny majority, Conservatives put down a series of motions far into the night to annul statutory instruments, and it became the practice to talk of 'government by stretcher'; an amendment to standing orders eliminated this opportunity for a war of attrition.

A minority of instruments are required to be laid, or laid in draft, subject to an affirmative resolution of one or both Houses; unless a resolution approving the instrument is passed within the period (if any) prescribed by the enabling Act, the instrument ceases to have effect or cannot be made.[53] Instruments made subject to that procedure are normally those regarded as being of special constitutional importance (for example, varying constituency boundaries) or imposing taxation (in which case an affirmative resolution of the Commons alone will be needed). A statutory instrument made under the European Communities Act *may* be laid in draft subject to the affirmative resolution procedure; if not so laid in draft, it shall be subject to the negative resolution procedure.[54]

The value of the negative resolution procedure is not easily assessed. Motions to annul statutory instruments are infrequent; rarely are they successful,[55] and it is open to the Minister to present the instrument afresh; but from time to time a Minister withdraws an instrument in the face of hostile criticism and may perhaps submit it in a revised form. One substantial criticism of this procedure is that because of pressure on parlia-

51. ibid., s. 5(1).
52. S.O. No. 4. See also Addendum.
53. Passing a negative resolution or failing to pass an affirmative resolution does not have the effect of invalidating anything already done in pursuance of the instrument.
54. 1972 Act, Sched. 2, para. 2(2). See also Northern Ireland (Temporary Provisions) Act 1972, Sched. 1, para. 4(2), (5).
55. A spectacular exception to the general rule was the rejection of the revised Immigration Rules (not technically a statutory instrument, but the distinction is immaterial) made under section 3(2) of the Immigration Act 1971. The prayer to annul was carried because some Conservative backbenchers objected to giving preference to Community nationals over citizens of 'old Commonwealth' countries. See 846 H.C. Deb. 1343–459 (22 November 1972). Revised Immigration Rules had to be introduced. The House of Lords has *never* carried a negative resolution (H.C. 475 (1971–72), para. 13), although (or because) their opposition cannot be overridden under the Parliament Acts procedure.

mentary time it is not always possible to debate a prayer to annul an instrument.[56] Hardly ever does an Act make provision for the amendment of a statutory instrument. But the possibility that damaging parliamentary publicity may result from a debate on an ill-drafted or otherwise objectionable instrument is of some utility as a safeguard against the misuse of delegated power.

The affirmative resolution procedure is more important, in that the Government must find time to explain why the instrument should be approved and thus lays itself open to critical comment. In November 1969 the Home Secretary laid himself open to acrimonious criticism by moving (successfully) that four draft Orders in Council purporting to give effect to Boundary Commission recommendations be not approved by the Commons.[57] But if all statutory instruments were made subject to this procedure, a primary object of delegating legislative powers to the Executive – to make for economical use of parliamentary time – would be frustrated.

Parliamentary scrutinizing committees[57a]

Subordinate legislation subject to the affirmative resolution procedure goes before a Special Orders Committee of the House of Lords;[58] the Committee reports whether the House should examine it more fully. This Committee has blushed almost unseen, although it is not an inactive body; its unimportance is directly attributable to the subordinate role of the Lords.

In 1944 a Select Committee of the House of Commons on Statutory Rules and Orders was appointed to examine and report on certain aspects of regulations laid before the House. That the Executive should commend the subjection of its legislative output to a new form of detailed parliamentary scrutiny in time of war is remarkably interesting. The Committee has been re-appointed each session; it is now[57a] styled the Select Committee on Statutory Instruments. Its terms of reference in 1972 were to consider every statutory instrument of a general character, various other instruments which, under the parent Act, were laid or laid in draft before the House subject to the negative or affirmative resolution procedure, and also special procedure orders,[59] with a view to deciding

56. H.C. 538 (1970–71), paras. 41–6; H.C. 475 (1971–72), paras. 95–128, for proposals for enlargement of the opportunities. In 1970–71 only eleven out of forty-seven prayers were debated within the forty-day period.

57. See pp. 247–8, 307.

57a. See Addendum for changes in 1973.

58. H.C. 475 (1971–72), paras. 32–46, 58. The Committee considers certain sets of rules that are not statutory instruments (see pp. 339–40) and also 'hybrid' instruments against which persons whose interests are directly affected may petition.

59. See p. 339.

whether the special attention of the House should be drawn to the instrument on any of these grounds: that (i) it imposes charges on the subject or the public revenue; (ii) it is ostensibly immunized by the parent Act against challenge in the courts; (iii) it appears to make an unusual or unexpected use of the powers conferred by the parent Act; (iv) it purports to have retrospective effect in the absence of express authority given by the parent Act; (v) there appears to have been unjustifiable delay in publication or laying before Parliament; (vi) where it is essential for an instrument to come into effect before being laid, there has been unjustifiable delay in notifying the Speaker of this fact and the reasons; (vii) for any special reason it requires elucidation; or (viii) the draftsmanship appears to be defective; or any ground 'which does not impinge on its merits or on the policy behind it; and to report their decision with the reason thereof in any particular case'.[60]

Before deciding to draw the attention of the House to an instrument on any of these grounds, the Committee must give the Department concerned an opportunity of putting its case.

The Committee consists of eleven members and is assisted by Counsel to Mr Speaker. That its function is strictly technical and non-partisan is emphasized by the convention that the chairman shall be a member of the Opposition. Its concern is with efficiency and constitutional propriety, extending beyond (but including) consideration of the strict legality of the powers exercised by the prescribed authority. It can comment, and has commented, on inconsistencies in legislative practice (for example, in providing for parliamentary proceedings on some instruments but not on others of a similar character) and on unsatisfactory features of sub-delegation of powers. In its early years many of its adverse reports were based on undue delay in publication or laying before Parliament; departmental procrastination suddenly became very rare. The fact that regulations are on the whole less obscurely drafted than they were twenty-five years ago can be partly attributed to its influence. Perhaps the patient drudgery of the Committee has had a highly salutary effect on overweening bureaucrats; perhaps the dangers of abuse of delegated legislative powers were greatly exaggerated by some critics; but the fact is that out of 1515 instruments examined by the Committee in the 1970–71 session, exactly three were brought to the attention of the House. That a few instruments made an unusual use of the powers granted, and that others were obscurely worded – these had become the main grounds for adverse reports by the 1960s – was hardly surprising. What was surprising was the small size of this problem viewed by an experienced scrutinizing committee.

No special opportunity has been provided by parliamentary procedure

60. H.C. 475 (1971–72), para. 50. The words in quotation marks were added in 1971.

for debating the Committee's reports; this must have detracted from its efficiency. But an adverse report delivered swiftly enough may lead to a prayer for annulment, or opposition to an affirmative resolution; or such a report may persuade a Department to amend or revoke an instrument.

In August 1972 a joint select committee proposed that the existing scrutiny committees of the two Houses should be replaced by a new Joint Scrutiny Committee, combining the terms of reference of each. It also proposed that the new committee should report on an instrument requiring affirmative resolutions before the resolutions could be moved.[61] In December 1972 the Government accepted in principle that a new joint select committee should be constituted to replace the existing Lords' and Commons' committees described above and that there should be a separate Commons' committee to consider the 'merits' of delegated legislation. (For the action taken in 1973, see Addendum to this book.)

Judicial review

The courts may hold a subordinate legislative instrument to be invalid if it is *ultra vires*, i.e. in excess of powers. This jurisdiction extends to prerogative instruments as well as statutory rules, regulations and by-laws. The validity of such instruments may be impugned directly or indirectly. Direct frontal challenges are unusual and are seldom successful; a plaintiff may find it impossible to establish that his personal interests are sufficiently affected by a general legislative instrument to give him title to sue.[62] Collateral, or indirect, attack is more common; a person is prosecuted for breach of a regulation or by-law, or is sued for breach of a contract the binding force of which is dependent on the validity of a regulation or by-law, and his defence is that the regulation or by-law is invalid. Under Community law this appears to be the only method by which *Community* instruments can be impeached before national courts as being *ultra vires* the treaties.

An instrument may be invalid because of a formal or procedural defect, or because it goes beyond the limited scope of delegated authority on a matter of substance. Challenges based on defects of form or procedure present difficulties in that not every such defect is a source of invalidity. Formal or procedural requirements are classifiable as either mandatory

61. H.C. 475 (1971–72). The new committee would consider instruments made under the European Communities Act; these instruments, though potentially very important, are not likely to exceed a hundred a year.

62. But see *Hotel and Catering Industry Training Board* v. *Automobile Proprietary Co*. [1969] 1 W.L.R. 697, where the House of Lords granted a declaration that a statutory instrument was *ultra vires* in so far as it purported to impose an industrial training levy on a members' club (who had been defendants in the proceedings at first instance).

or directory. Non-compliance with a mandatory requirement is a potentially vitiating defect; if, however, the requirement is construed as being merely directory, the courts may take the view that substantial compliance is enough or even that total non-compliance is a mere error that does not affect the validity of what has been done. Prediction of how a court will regard non-compliance is difficult; precedents afford little guidance, and although the practical importance of non-compliance with the duty is the main criterion, a court will sometimes take a stringent view of failure to observe a minor formality.[63] Non-observance of duties to consult with a specified body[64] or consider objections or give an opportunity to be heard[65] are likely to be held to render regulations invalid. Rather surprisingly, it appears that mere failure to publish an instrument does not render it invalid if other prescribed preliminaries have been observed;[66] the effect of breach of a duty to lay a statutory instrument before Parliament is doubtful, but this may well be held to render the instrument inoperative.[67]

If power is delegated only to do X, the delegate cannot do Y, unless Y is necessarily implicit in or incidental to the power to do X. Power granted for purpose A cannot be used instead for purpose B. These ostensibly straightforward questions of statutory interpretation may give rise to considerable problems in practice – for example, where the statutory purpose is not clearly defined,[68] or where the existence of a link between the subject-matter of the delegated power and the statutory purpose is expressed by the parent Act to be determinable by the delegate himself.[69] Again, a strictly literal interpretation of the enabling section may frustrate the general object of the Act or wreak injustice; a court will not necessarily shut its eyes to this possibility. Nor will a court disregard the context in which regulations have been made; regulations made in a state of grave emergency may be construed more benevolently in favour of the Executive than regulations made under the same powers when the seriousness of the emergency has diminished.

Forecasts of how a court may construe the validity of regulations are

63. See, for example, *Patchett* v. *Leathem* (1949) 65 T.L.R. 69.

64. *Agricultural etc. Training Board* v. *Aylesbury Mushrooms Ltd* [1972] 1 W.L.R. 190.

65. *R*. v. *Housing Appeal Tribunal* [1920] 3 K.B. 334 at 342, 343, 346.

66. See pp. 342–3; but note the mitigating effect of s. 3(2) of the Statutory Instruments Act 1946.

67. *R*. v. *Sheer Metalcraft Ltd* [1954] 1 Q.B. 586 at 590. It is still open to the courts to resolve these difficult issues.

68. cf. the 3:2 division of opinion in the House of Lords in *McEldowney* v. *Forde* [1971] A.C. 632, a case arising under the Northern Ireland Civil Authorities (Special Powers) Act 1922.

69. See pp. 337, 350, 568.

further complicated by other factors. Thus, ordinary literal interpretation may be modified in the light of common-law presumptions of legislative intent. For instance, there is a presumption that express statutory authority is needed to validate the exercise of delegated powers interfering with the liberty of the person, or excluding the citizen from access to the ordinary courts for the determination of his legal rights and liabilities,[70] or imposing taxation,[71] or taking away property rights without compensation.[72] The circumstances in which these presumptions will carry decisive weight are not easy to predict.[73] In the First World War, power to make regulations for securing the public safety and the defence of the realm was held to justify the making of a regulation for the preventive detention of British subjects on security grounds without trial,[74] notwithstanding the strong common-law presumption in favour of individual liberty. Three years later a court held that the same statutory power was not wide enough to validate a wartime regulation prohibiting landlords from taking legal proceedings for possession orders, against tenants who were munition workers, without the prior consent of a Minister.[75] In the Second World War, an undoubtedly valid defence regulation, providing that a Secretary of State could make orders for the detention of persons whom he had 'reasonable cause' to believe to be of hostile origin or associations and in need of subjection to preventive control, was not construed by the courts as importing an objectively determinable test of reasonableness. To establish the invalidity of a detention order, a detainee would have to discharge the impossible burden of proving that the Secretary of State did not genuinely believe he had 'reasonable cause'.[76] In a number of cases in which the validity of subordinate legislation and executive acts affecting property rights was challenged during and immediately after the Second World War, the courts adopted a strictly

70. *Chester* v. *Bateson* [1920] 1 K.B. 829; *Customs and Excise Commissioners* v. *Cure & Deeley Ltd* [1962] 1 Q.B. 340.

71. *Cure & Deeley*'s case (above); see also *Att.-Gen.* v. *Wilts United Dairies Ltd* (1921) 37 T.L.R. 884 (C.A.), but see p. 284, above.

72. For example, *Newcastle Breweries Ltd* v. *R.* [1920] 1 K.B. 854.

73. Contrast, for example, in the field of town planning decisions (executive acts), the case of *Hall & Co.* v. *Shoreham-by-Sea U.D.C.* [1964] 1 W.L.R. 240 (presumption against deprivation of property rights without compensation applied) with *Westminster Bank Ltd* v. *Beverley B.C.* [1971] A.C. 508 (presumption not applied).

74. *R.* v. *Halliday, ex p. Zadig* [1917] A.C. 260.

75. *Chester* v. *Bateson* [1920] 1 K.B. 829.

76. *Liversidge* v. *Anderson* [1942] A.C. 206. Contrast, on the meaning of 'reasonable cause' or 'reasonable grounds', *Nakkuda Ali* v. *Jayaratne* [1951] A.C. 66 at 76–7. The only other ground on which a detention order could be challenged was that it had been improperly made out: *R.* v. *Secretary of State for Home Affairs, ex p. Budd* [1942] 2 K.B. 14 at 22. See ch. 23.

literal interpretation of the enabling legislation in favour of the Executive. The enabling Act was typically expressed in the form: 'If it appears to' or 'if in the opinion of' the Minister, or 'if the Minister is satisfied that' a given state of affairs existed, he could make such orders as appeared to him necessary or expedient for a generally worded purpose.[77] By the early 1950s this self-denying ordinance had been slightly modified. The Judicial Committee of the Privy Council could state that a power so exercised had to be 'capable of being related to one of the prescribed purposes'.[78]

In 1961 the pendulum had swung far enough for a High Court judge (invoking common-law presumptions of legislative intent) to hold that a statutory power authorizing the Commissioners of Customs and Excise to make regulations 'for any matter for which provision appears to them necessary for the purpose of giving effect to the Act' was too narrow to validate a regulation by which they gave themselves power to determine conclusively what amount of purchase tax was payable in individual cases.[79] This is perhaps an extreme case of judicial activism. Nowadays the courts are unlikely to review the matter *de novo* but to ask whether the competent authority had misdirected itself and whether the regulations were reasonably capable of being related to the grant of power.[80]

Judicial tests for the validity of by-laws have generally been understood to be stricter than the tests for the validity of regulations made by Ministers or Her Majesty in Council. Although by-laws made by elected local authorities for the general welfare are to be benevolently construed,[81] they may be still held *ultra vires* and invalid if they are excessively uncertain in their terms or repugnant to the general law of the land or manifestly unreasonable. The English courts have yet to hold a statutory instrument to be *ultra vires* explicitly on these grounds alone. But a court might hold an instrument to be too vague to be capable of being related to a permitted purpose;[82] so offensive to the general principles of the law as to be

77. For example, *R.* v. *Comptroller General of Patents, ex p. Bayer Products Ltd* [1941] 2 K.B. 306; *Point of Ayr Collieries Ltd* v. *Lloyd-George* [1943] 2 All E.R. 547. In *Carltona Ltd* v. *Commissioners of Works* [1943] 2 All E.R. 560 at 564, Lord Greene M.R. said, 'All that the court can do is to see that the power ... falls within the four corners of the power given by the legislature and [is] exercised in good faith. Apart from that, the courts have no power at all to inquire into the reasonableness, the policy, the sense, or any other aspect of the transaction.'

78. *Att.-Gen. for Canada* v. *Hallet & Carey Ltd* [1952] A.C. 427 at 450.

79. *Customs and Excise Commissioners* v. *Cure & Deeley Ltd* (1962) 1 Q.B. 340 (per Sachs J.). See to like effect, *Reade* v. *Smith* [1959] N.Z.L.R. 996. cf. however, *Marsh* (*Wholesale*) *Ltd* v. *Customs and Excise Commissioners* [1970] 2 Q.B. 206.

80. See note 22 above; *Hallet and Carey*'s case (note 78); *Secretary of State for Employment* v. *ASLEF* (*No. 2*) [1972] 2 Q.B. 455.

81. *Kruse* v. *Johnson* [1898] 2 Q.B. 91 at 99–100.

82. *McEldowney* v. *Forde* [1971] A.C. 632 at 643, 645, 653, 665.

beyond the contemplation of the enabling Act;[83] or so unreasonable that it could not be ascribed to the enabling provisions.[84] Perhaps, then, the differences in the scope of judicial review of by-laws, on the one hand, and statutory instruments, on the other, are only matters of degree or even verbal distinctions.

Although no English authority directly covers the point, it is highly probable that the courts, applying the maxim *delegatus non potest delegare*, will hold that the recipient of delegated legislative power cannot validly sub-delegate any part of its rule-making power to another in the absence of express statutory authorization.[85] But a power vested in a Minister or a Department to make regulations can validly be exercised by an official authorized by his superiors to act in that behalf; this is not an example of sub-delegation, for the official is the Minister's other self, his *alter ego*.[86]

In the past a great deal of heat was generated by statutory provisions purporting to oust judicial review of the validity of regulations, orders and administrative decisions and determinations.[87] The formula providing that a regulation or order, when made, was to have effect 'as if enacted in the Act', has fallen into desuetude. Whether the courts regarded it as excluding them from determining the *vires* of a subordinate instrument was never entirely clear.[88] A provision that the making or confirmation of an order was to be 'conclusive evidence' that the requirements of the Act had been complied with was probably effective to exclude judicial review,[89] despite the traditional disfavour shown by the courts to language ostensibly depriving them of their inherent supervisory jurisdiction. Exclusionary formulae create a bad impression and are seldom used today unless finality is all-important.

The Extradition Act 1870 and the House of Commons (Redistribution of Seats) Acts still have provisions to the effect that Orders in Council made thereunder shall not be questioned in any legal proceedings; the subject-matter of such Orders (application of an extradition treaty to a foreign State, and the determination of constituency boundaries) may

83. For example, by authorizing the condemnation of a person without allowing him an opportunity of being heard on his own behalf (*R.* v. *Housing Appeal Tribunal* [1920] 3 K.B. 334) or by taking away his common-law right of access to the courts: *Chester* v. *Bateson*; *Cure & Deeley*'s case (above).

84. See note 82 above.

85. There are Commonwealth authorities directly in point. See also *Jackson, Stansfield & Sons* v. *Butterworth* [1948] 2 All E.R. 558 at 564–6, and p. 588.

86. *R.* v. *Skinner* [1968] 2 Q.B. 700.

87. See generally de Smith, *Judicial Review of Administrative Action* (3rd edn), ch. 7.

88. *Institute of Patent Agents* v. *Lockwood* [1894] A.C. 347 supported the view that such a provision barred judicial review; *Minister of Health* v. *R., ex p. Yaffe* [1931] A.C. 494 indicated that it did not. Various intermediate positions are possible.

89. *Ex p. Ringer* (1909) 73 J.P. 436.

justify the exclusion of judicial review.[90] Similar formulae purporting to protect judicial-type administrative determinations against judicial review are made nugatory (with certain exceptions) by section 14 of the Tribunals and Inquiries Act 1971, if contained in Acts passed before August 1958.[91] In the present climate of opinion, one would not expect to see delegated legislation afforded special statutory protection save in highly exceptional circumstances. As we have seen, Orders in Council and regulations made in this country under the European Communities Act 1972 for the fulfilment of Community obligations enjoy extraordinary protection inasmuch as they are assimilated for most purposes to Acts of Parliament.[92]

90. Extradition Act 1870, s. 5; House of Commons (Redistribution of Seats) Act 1949, s. 3(7). See also Parliament Act 1911, s. 3; Parliament Act 1949, s. 2(2) (Speaker's certificates); West Indies Act 1967, s. 18. Judicial review of subordinate legislation is not excluded merely because provision has been made by the parent Act for the affirmative or negative resolution procedure (*R.* v. *Electricity Commissioners* [1924] 1 K.B. 171), but judicial intervention while an instrument was still before either House might be regarded as an encroachment on parliamentary privilege.

91. See further pp. 567, 571–3.

92. See p. 338. But, as was indicated, jurisdiction to determine the *vires* of such instruments is not entirely excluded. See also p. 347.

Part Four
Justice, Police
and Local Government

In this Part we shall examine aspects of three important subjects, which shade off into one another.

First, in chapter 16 we consider some features of the administration of justice in England. For detailed accounts of the structure and working of the English legal system, readers should consult textbooks devoted to the subject; here we have presented only an outline sketch. Since the first edition was published, the Administration of Justice Act 1970, reorganizing the Divisions of the High Court, has been brought into effect. Under the Courts Act 1971 there has been a major reconstruction of the system of criminal courts, and two very ancient legal institutions, Assizes and Quarter Sessions, have been replaced by a new Crown Court, which is part of the Supreme Court of Judicature. One consequence has been a big increase in the size of the professional Judiciary.

In chapter 16 we also touch upon magistrates, juries and the legal profession; and we look in more detail at the rules of law and convention, professional traditions and political practices, that help to sustain the independence of the Judiciary. This is a convenient place for considering the law of contempt of court. We also draw attention to the roles of Ministers (including the Attorney-General) and the Director of Public Prosecutions in the administration of justice. Every one of these topics is of constitutional interest and distinguishes the English system from a great many other legal systems.

Secondly, we single out, in chapter 17, some features of the constitutional status of the police, the officers directly responsible for enforcement of the criminal law and the maintenance of the Queen's peace. We shall discuss certain of their powers and duties more fully in chapters 20–22.

The status of a police officer is anomalous: in some respects he is an instrument of the executive branch of government, in others a local officer, and in others an independent public officer, but he cannot be fitted neatly into any category. Control over the police is partly a matter for the Home Office, partly for local police authorities, but a chief constable of a local force enjoys a very substantial measure of personal autonomy and authority. Public duties are cast on him by law to secure the due enforcement of law and order within his area of command; but the means of compelling him to perform those duties are still unclear. The chapter ends with a comment on the thorny problem of investigating complaints against police officers.

'Police' is often listed among local government services, though local control over the conduct of a force may be tenuous. Chapter 18 is in the nature of an essay on local government law. Books on this specialized subject are available for consultation, and this chapter does not attempt to offer a detailed synopsis of the whole field. But the books are now having to go into new editions, for after years of informed debate far-reaching changes in the structure and functions of local government in England and Wales have been prescribed by the Local Government Act 1972. Elections to the new county and district councils have taken place in 1973, but the new system will not be in full operation till April 1974. And so this has to be a picture of a system in transition. The main emphasis in the chapter is nevertheless placed on the rules regulating the new system as far as they are known. Further legislation on such important matters as local government finance and complaints arising out of local maladministration was awaited as the book went to press.

Chapter 16
The Administration
of Justice

Courts[1]
Criminal jurisdiction

The most striking feature of the English legal system is the part played by the layman, as justice of the peace, as juror or as prosecutor. It is open to an aggrieved member of the public to lay an information before a magistrate asking him to issue a summons, or in some cases an arrest warrant, against another person for a criminal offence (for example, assault). In practice most of these members of the public are police officers,[2] but purely private prosecutions are not uncommon. For some serious offences (for example, against the Official Secrets Acts) the Attorney-General's leave must be obtained before a prosecution can be instituted. There are other offences for which only the Director of Public Prosecutions, or only a local authority, may prosecute.

Apart from the issue of summonses and warrants, the chief functions of magistrates are the trial of summary offences, and the conduct of preliminary inquiries into indictable offences which are triable by a higher court.[3] Magistrates may be either lay justices of the peace – the office originated over six hundred years ago – or professional stipendiary magistrates. There are some 19,000 active justices of the peace in England and Wales, sitting in over a thousand magistrates' courts, but barely fifty stipendiaries, of whom all but a dozen are metropolitan magistrates sitting in the London area. There are no juries in magistrates' courts; in trying

1. The leading work is R. M. Jackson's *Machinery of Justice in England* (6th edn, 1972). For recent critical surveys, see Brian Abel-Smith and Robert Stevens, *Lawyers and the Courts* (1967); *In Search of Justice* (1968); Michael Zander, *Lawyers and the Public Interest* (1968); *The Judiciary* (*A Report by a subcommittee of Justice*, 1972); *Report of the Royal Commission on Assizes and Quarter Sessions* (Cmnd 4153 (1969)) – the Beeching Report. Only a brief outline of the system in England and Wales is offered in this chapter. Some important questions, like the cost of litigation and the award of costs, are omitted.

2. For the position in Scotland, see p. 380, note 3.

3. This is an oversimplification – for example, some indictable offences (triable at the Crown Court) are triable by a magistrates' court. See Jackson, op. cit., pp. 127–30.

offences, magistrates are judges of law and fact and impose sentence. Metropolitan stipendiary magistrates always sit alone to hear summary cases; other stipendiaries usually sit unaccompanied by lay justices; the size of a lay bench will be between two and seven, under a chairman elected by the magistrates. Magistrates must normally sit in open court, but when they sit as examining justices conducting a preliminary inquiry to determine whether there is sufficient evidence to commit a defendant for trial before a higher court, the evidence given at these proceedings cannot now be reported contemporaneously except at the defendant's request, unless the magistrates discharge him.[4]

On conviction, magistrates cannot, in general, impose a sentence of more than six months' imprisonment or a fine of more than £400; they may, however, commit an offender for sentence at the Crown Court if the offence is one punishable by a heavier sentence and their own powers are inadequate to meet the case. They may also remand defendants in custody; in certain circumstances they may make recommendations for deportation upon conviction; they may bind over a defendant by requiring him to enter into recognizances, with or without sureties, to be of good behaviour or to keep the peace, and send him to prison if he refuses.[5] These are formidable powers to vest in amateurs[6] whose knowledge of legal technicalities and techniques may be rudimentary. The picture is not in fact quite as alarming as it may appear. Magistrates are advised on points of law and procedure by a legally qualified clerk of the court, who is normally a full-time officer. All newly appointed justices are obliged to undergo a course of preliminary training; they are encouraged to attend refresher courses and conferences; they are kept informed by advisory Home Office circulars about sentencing policies and problems and other developments on the treatment of offenders. They are empowered to impose suspended sentences.[7] The infirm and incompetent can be placed on a supplemental list where they will be ineligible to per-

4. Criminal Justice Act 1967, ss. 3, 6. But in certain circumstances the committal proceedings may be based on written depositions (ss. 1, 2).

5. This is really a form of preventive justice. Other alternatives after a case has been proved include absolute discharge, conditional discharge, community service orders under the Criminal Justice Act 1972, putting on probation. For young offenders, a different set of sanctions or welfare orders is prescribed; see Children and Young Persons Act 1969; J. E. Hall Williams, *The English Penal System in Transition* (1970), Parts 4–6.

6. The 'great unpaid' are now paid travelling and subsistence allowances and sums for loss of earnings: Justices of the Peace Act 1949, as amended; see Administration of Justice Act 1973, ss. 5, 20 and Schedule I, Part III.

7. Criminal Justice Act 1967, s. 39, as amended by the Criminal Justice Act 1972, s. 11. If the offender is convicted again during the period of suspension he may have to serve the original sentence.

form judicial functions. In any event, magistrates are now retired or placed on the supplemental list at seventy. Except in the City of London, the *ex officio* magistrate has almost disappeared.[8] There is no adequate means of assessing the quality of criminal justice dispensed by lay magistrates, but the asperity of criticism formerly levelled against them has been softened in the last twenty years and there is a dearth of enthusiasm for the professional magistrate sitting alone.

Young offenders and young persons in need of care and protection, are normally brought before juvenile courts, differently constituted from ordinary magistrates' courts and following a less formal procedure. They are composed predominantly of lay magistrates.[9]

Fundamental changes in the system of criminal courts were introduced by the Courts Act 1971, which came into force on 1 January 1972.[10] Till then, trials on indictment had taken place at assizes (before a judge of the Queen's Bench Division on circuit) or, for rather less serious offences, at quarter sessions – in the boroughs before a part-time Recorder sitting alone and in the counties before not more than nine magistrates, the chairman and deputy chairman nearly always being legally qualified. These courts, reaching well back into the Middle Ages, were abolished, together with the special Crown courts at Liverpool and Manchester (which, like the Central Criminal Court at the Old Bailey, became integrated with the new Crown Court) and some ancient courts of civil and criminal jurisdiction. The vestigial original criminal jurisdiction of the Queen's Bench Division was also terminated. The reforms were based on the Report of the Beeching Commission on Assizes and Quarter Sessions.[11]

The Crown Court is part of the Supreme Court of Judicature. It consists of High Court judges, Circuit judges, part-time Recorders and, in certain circumstances, justices of the peace. All county court judges have become Circuit judges; so have the full-time criminal judges at the Old Bailey and in Manchester and Liverpool, and certain other holders of full-time judicial offices. There are also some fifty new judges in this category, drawn to a considerable extent from persons with judicial experience as Recorders. In December 1972 there were 235 Circuit judges. The new-style Recorders (about 300) are required to sit for twenty days a year in the Crown Court. They must be barristers or solicitors of at least ten years' standing; a large majority are in fact barristers. But the qualification

8. See Justices of the Peace Act 1968, ss. 1, 2.

9. See J. D. McClean and J. C. Wood, *Criminal Justice and the Treatment of Offenders*, ch. 5, and note 5 above. The emphasis has recently shifted from criminal responsibility and sanctions towards civil responsibility and remedial orders.

10. Jackson, op. cit., ch. 3. See also Crown Court Rules 1971 (S.I. 1971, No. 1292); Practice Directions (Crime: Crown Court Business) [1971] 1 W.L.R. 1535, 1763.

11. Cmnd 4153 (1969).

for appointment as a Circuit judge is to be a barrister of ten years' standing or to have been a Recorder for five years; it is therefore possible for a solicitor of at least fifteen years' standing to become a Circuit judge. Magistrates must be members of the Crown Court when it hears appeals from magistrates' courts or juvenile courts or committals for sentence from those courts; and they can be asked to sit with a Circuit judge or Recorder in other cases.

The Crown Court is organized in six circuits. Each of these circuits is presided over by two judges of the Queen's Bench Division, apart from the South-Eastern Circuit where the Lord Chief Justice presides with two Queen's Bench judges. Each circuit has a senior court administrator. The Court sits in twenty-four main provincial centres, staffed by High Court judges and Circuit judges. Here the High Court judge will wear two hats. Sitting in the *High Court*, he will hear civil cases; sitting in the *Crown Court*, he will hear the most serious criminal cases. But there is flexibility: the very serious criminal cases can be assigned to a Circuit judge, and a Circuit judge can also hear certain *High Court* civil cases. There is a second tier of centres, served by High Court and Circuit judges, where only criminal cases are heard. Then there is a third tier, staffed by Circuit judges only. The first tier centres bear a very loose resemblance to the old assizes, the second and third tiers to quarter sessions, but the new system is not typified by continuity with the past. The number of major centres for the administration of criminal justice outside London has been reduced from 234 to 113.

Offences are divided into four classes. Indictable offences in the first class must be tried by a High Court judge; in the second class they must be tried by a High Court judge unless the judge presiding over a circuit releases a case to another judge; in the third class they may be tried by a High Court judge or Circuit judge or Recorder. The fourth class of offence (triable summarily or on indictment) will normally be tried by a Circuit judge or Recorder. There are detailed rules directing or guiding magistrates as to the class of centre to which a particular case should be committed. All trials on indictment are by jury, as they were at assizes and quarter sessions.

Juries are now selected more or less at random from among registered electors between the ages of eighteen and sixty-five who have resided for five years or more in the British Islands since childhood.[12] The jury is

12. See generally Juries Acts 1949 and 1954; Courts Act 1971, ss. 31–40; Criminal Justice Act 1972, ss. 25–7. Sched. 2. The 1972 Act altered the age limits, disqualifications and exemptions, and substituted voters' qualification for ratepayers'. Jurors are now paid travelling and subsistence allowances and compensation for loss of earnings. Subject to certain exceptions, service is compulsory. Grand juries (interposed between

perhaps the most venerated English legal institution, lauded as a bulwark against oppression and the common-sense voice of twelve ordinary citizens. But uneasiness about the merits of jury trial has grown of late,[13] though some of the doubts cannot be reliably substantiated. In civil cases trial by jury is now rare – hardly 30 cases a year. In criminal cases the accuracy of findings by juries and the processes by which they are reached are not infrequently questioned. Bribery and intimidation of jurors are thought to be extremely uncommon; nevertheless, because this problem arose in trials involving members of London gangs, the rule that a jury's verdict in criminal proceedings had to be unanimous was varied in 1967; a majority verdict may be now accepted by the court if ten jurors agree that the accused is guilty.[14] In civil cases majority verdicts are acceptable with the consent of the parties, and without their consent subject to safeguards similar to those laid down in criminal proceedings.[15]

The system of appeals in criminal cases is complicated:[16]

1. A person convicted by a magistrates' court can appeal to the Crown Court on a question of law, fact or sentence; the appeal is by way of rehearing without a jury; a sentence may be increased.

2. Alternatively, either the prosecutor or the defendant may appeal on a point of law by case stated[17] from a conviction by a magistrates' court, or a determination by the Crown Court *on appeal or a committal for sentence*, to a Divisional Court of the Queen's Bench Division, consisting of two or more (usually three and occasionally five) judges of that Division of the High Court. This course is followed where an authoritative legal ruling is sought.

3. From the Divisional Court, a further appeal on a point of law will lie direct to the House of Lords, but only with leave, which is not to be granted unless the Divisional Court certifies that a point of law of general

committal by examining justices and trial at assizes or quarter sessions) were abolished in 1933. Special juries (selected from persons of means in civil cases) disappeared in 1949 except for City of London commercial cases and under the Courts Act they were abolished altogether. Juries are still used in coroners' courts.

13. See Glanville Williams, *The Proof of Guilt* (3rd edn); Jackson, op. cit., pp. 389–408; W. R. Cornish, *The Jury*. cf. Sir Patrick Devlin, *Trial by Jury*.

14. Criminal Justice Act 1967, s. 13. If there are only ten jurors – the normal size of a jury is eleven or twelve – nine must concur in the finding of guilt. The court must not accept a majority verdict unless the jury has deliberated for at least two hours.

15. Courts Act 1971, s. 39.

16. It is depicted diagrammatically by Jackson, op. cit., p. 153. Part of this branch of the law was consolidated in the Criminal Appeal Act 1968. It was modified by the Courts Act 1971.

17. The clerk of the court draws up a statement of the facts found and the basis of the decision, and this is signed by the magistrates.

public importance is involved, and that court or the House of Lords is of the opinion that it should be considered by the House.

4. From convictions at quarter sessions or assizes on trials on indictment, there was no regular system of appeal till 1907, when the Court of Criminal Appeal was established. In practice this court was composed of judges of the Queen's (King's) Bench Division. In 1966 the court was abolished, and its appellate jurisdiction (including jurisdiction to hear appeals from the Central Criminal Court, Crown courts, and appeals against sentences imposed by quarter sessions on committal by magistrates' courts after conviction) was transferred to the Criminal Division of the Court of Appeal, subject to various restrictive conditions.[18] Now appeals lie from the Crown Court instead. The Criminal Division sits in at least two courts, composed partly of Lords Justices of Appeal and partly of Queen's Bench judges. If new relevant evidence is received by the court, it has a discretion to order the appellant to be retried.[19]

5. A further appeal on a point of law will lie from the Court of Appeal to the House of Lords, subject to similar conditions to those in paragraph 3 above.

Ancillary points, not directly linked with appeals, need to be mentioned. First, the Home Secretary may refer the whole of a case after a conviction on indictment to the Court of Appeal; the effect is much as if the person convicted had lodged an appeal. Secondly, he may refer any aspect of such a case to the Court of Appeal for their opinion.[20] Thirdly, he may advise the Queen to exercise the prerogative of pardon. Fourthly, a prisoner may now be released on licence on the recommendation of the Parole Board (and in certain cases merely on the recommendation of a local review committee) after serving a third of his sentence.[21] Fifthly, the Attorney-General may refer to the Court of Appeal a point of law arising out of an acquittal in a trial on indictment.[22] Sixthly, determinations by magistrates' courts and the Crown Court are subject to review by the Divisional Court of the Queen's Bench Division exercising its supervisory jurisdiction – for example, an order of certiorari to quash a conviction (other than a conviction by the Crown Court in a trial on indictment) can be obtained if the court has exceeded its jurisdiction or broken the rules

18. For example, leave of the court below is required for an appeal on a question of fact, and leave of the Court of Appeal if an appeal is to be lodged against sentence. The Court of Appeal cannot increase the total period of sentence already imposed.

19. Criminal Appeal Act 1968, ss. 7, 8, 23.

20. ibid., s. 17.

21. Criminal Justice Act 1967, ss. 59–64; Schedule 2; Hall Williams, op. cit., pp. 184–90; Criminal Justice Act 1972, s. 35.

22. Criminal Justice Act 1972, s. 36. Whatever be the opinion of the court, the acquittal will still stand.

of natural justice.[23] Seventhly, a person deprived of his liberty without lawful authority may procure his release by the award of a writ of habeas corpus.[24]

Civil jurisdiction

Many justiciable claims and controversies in non-criminal matters are determined by bodies other than the ordinary courts – by special statutory tribunals, or local authorities, or Ministers (through departmental officials), or named classes of officials, or domestic tribunals (committees of clubs, trades unions and so on). Businessmen often provide in their commercial contracts that disputes shall be submitted to arbitration. Of late there have been experiments in establishing informal small claims courts. There are also specialized courts, such as the Restrictive Practices Court and the National Industrial Relations Court, outside the mainstream of the ordinary judicial system. But in almost all cases the general superior courts preserve an appellate or a supervisory jurisdiction.

Magistrates' courts have a limited civil jurisdiction. They have power to make affiliation orders, and maintenance and separation orders and decisions as to custody of children in matrimonial cases; appeal on points of law lies to a Divisional Court of the Family Division of the High Court. They also have various functions in the general field of administrative law, particularly in respect of licensing and the hearing of appeals against local authority licensing decisions; appeal usually lies to the Crown Court, with a further (or alternative) appeal by case stated on points of law to the Divisional Court of the Queen's Bench Division.

In 1969 there were 101 county court judges, sitting in 356 county courts grouped in sixty-three circuits;[25] there is no necessary connection between a county court area and an administrative or geographical county. County court judges are full-time judges. They hear undefended divorce petitions, but their main function has been to determine small monetary claims. To an increasing extent judicial functions in minor county court cases have been devolved upon registrars, who are solicitors. In practice most of the nearly two million cases that come before county courts each year are undefended; these are mainly plaints issued in respect of debts.

Their monetary jurisdiction in contract and tort has been progressively raised; in 1970 the maximum claim they could entertain was for £750. They also exercise a miscellany of functions in the fields of equity, bankruptcy, and landlord and tenant (notably applications for possession

23. See ch. 27.
24. See pp. 465–9.
25. Cmnd 4153 (1969), p. 30. In 1970 the maximum number was 125.

orders), and a wide range of jurisdiction, mainly original but sometimes appellate, arising under modern collectivist legislation. Appeals lie, normally on points of law only, to the Court of Appeal (Civil Division).

The Courts Act 1971 made an important change in the status and functions of county court judges. In the first place, they became Circuit judges, who could be called upon to exercise criminal jurisdiction in the Crown Court. Secondly, Circuit judges were appointed 'to serve in the Crown Court and county courts'.[26] Although in practice county court judges will continue to exercise mainly civil jurisdiction and the new Circuit judges mainly criminal jurisdiction, the county courts have been effectively integrated with the Crown Court and in future persons who would have been appointed county court judges will be appointed Circuit judges.

The Supreme Court of Judicature consists of the Court of Appeal, the High Court and the Crown Court. The Court of Appeal has two divisions, civil and criminal: it is presided over by the Master of the Rolls, and has up to fourteen Lords Justices of Appeal; the Lord Chancellor, ex-Lord Chancellors, the Lords of Appeal in Ordinary, the Lord Chief Justice, the Vice-Chancellor and the President of the Family Division are *ex officio* members. It normally sits with a bench of three; the Lord Chief Justice presides in one court of the Criminal Division; other High Court Judges are often called upon to sit to hear criminal appeals, but less frequently to hear civil appeals. Appeals on the civil side lie mainly from county courts and the High Court; under a recent amendment of the law, the court may be leapfrogged and an appeal raising a point of law of exceptional difficulty or importance calling for a reconsideration of a binding precedent may, with leave of the House of Lords, lie direct from the High Court to the Lords.[27]

The High Court sits in three divisions: the Queen's Bench, the Chancery, and the Family Divisions. The Family Division replaced the Probate, Divorce and Admiralty Division ('the court of wrecks') in October 1971.[28] On appointment, a judge is assigned to one of the three divisions. The Lord Chief Justice presides in the Queen's Bench Division; the Lord Chancellor, who never sits, is nominally president of the Chancery Division and there is now a Vice-Chancellor who is a Chancery judge; there is a President of the Family Division. The maximum number of

26. Courts Act 1971, ss. 16 (1), (5), 20. See also Sched. 2, s. 1 (2).

27. Administration of Justice Act 1969, ss. 12–16. A certificate must first be given by the trial judge, and the parties must consent to the leapfrogging appeal. For an illustration, see *Ealing L.B.C.* v. *Race Relations Board* [1972] A.C.342.

28. Administration of Justice Act 1970. The Admiralty work of the dissolved Division was transferred to the Queen's Bench Division and contested probate jurisdiction to the Chancery Division. The Admiralty Court and the Commercial Court became distinct courts within the Queen's Bench Division.

other High Court judges (called puisne judges) is seventy-five.[29] In 1972 there were forty-three in the Queen's Bench, ten in the Chancery and seventeen in the Family Division. The original civil jurisdiction of the High Court is unlimited as to amount and persons but subject to territorial limitations. Distribution of work between the three divisions is governed partly by statute, partly by rules of court, partly by custom, and there is a substantial area of concurrent jurisdiction; for example, actions claiming injunctions or declarations are usually brought in the Chancery Division but can be instituted in the Queen's Bench Division or even the Family Division. The High Court also has appellate and supervisory jurisdiction in relation to inferior tribunals, a jurisdiction normally exercised by a Divisional Court of the Queen's Bench Division, and power to issue writs of habeas corpus.[30] The High Court, like the Court of Appeal, sits in the Royal Courts of Justice (the Law Courts) in London, and also (as we have seen) juxtaposed with the Crown Court at the top-tier provincial centres. There Queen's Bench judges sit as Crown Court judges for criminal cases too.[31]

The House of Lords as a 'final' appellate court has already been mentioned.[32] In 1966 it reasserted power to overrule its own decisions.[33]

Independence of the Judiciary

It is clearly of great importance that justice be dispensed even-handedly in the courts and that the general public feel confidence in the integrity and impartiality of the Judiciary. Where the Government of the day has an interest in the outcome of judicial proceedings, the court should not act merely as a mouthpiece of the Executive. The Judiciary must therefore be secure from undue influence and autonomous within its own field.

These propositions may seem platitudinous. But in many countries some of them would be rejected. Whereas all governments would agree that there should be public confidence in the administration of justice, and that judges ought not to accept bribes or decide cases on the basis of personal friendship or animosity, many would not agree that the Judiciary ought to be independent of the Executive. On the contrary, they would say that the judges have a duty not to be impartial between the people and the enemies of the people; that since the Government (or the Party) is the voice of the people, critics of the regime or bourgeois elements or

29. Maximum Number of Judges Order 1970 (S.I. 1970, No. 1115).
30. See pp. 595–8.
31. See p. 358.
32. pp. 308–10 and above. But see pp. 674–5 on the European Court of Justice.
33. Practice Statement [1966] 1 W.L.R. 1234.

other classes of persons stigmatized as anti-social must be dealt with severely by the courts, which are instruments of State policy. And judges who talk out of turn or acquit persons charged with sedition or refuse to join the Party or (as the case may be) fail to uphold and apply the edicts of the military régime may be dismissed.

In many other countries, the principles of judicial independence are acknowledged but are substantially qualified in practice. This is hardly surprising when one considers the implications that can be and have been read into the concept. Does judicial independence imply that the Executive must have no voice, or a muted voice, in the appointment or promotion of judges? Does it imply that neither the Executive nor the Legislature shall be competent to remove judges? If the principle carries these implications – and it is arguable that it should import them – it is imperfectly realized in Britain. Does it imply that judges should be entirely aloof from public sentiment and always disregard the strength of local feeling on an issue before them? If not, to what extent should judges take into account considerations of public policy, and how far can the Government or its unruly supporters or opponents be permitted to determine what is the public interest? In Britain these questions seldom arise in an acutely controversial form,[34] but judges not infrequently have to determine what is in the public interest, or whether a transaction is contrary to public policy, or whether it is necessary to impose a deterrent sentence because of the prevalence of a social evil; and in coming to such decisions they are expected to have some regard to the general sense of the community and not to rely merely on idiosyncratic opinions. Moreover, in some political contexts the courts allow the Executive[35] or the House of Commons[36] the first and last word. Here we are enmeshed in the thicket of questions of degree, where generalizations are not very helpful.

Can we not at least agree that the protection of judicial independence in a liberal democracy demands that it should be unconstitutional for the Legislature to invade the domain of the Judiciary by pronouncing judgment (as in a bill of attainder)[37] or reversing a judicial decision with

34. Though cf. the controversies which arose in 1972 out of the application of the Industrial Relations Act 1971. See, for example, John Griffith, 'Reflections on the Rule of the Law', *New Statesman*, 24 November 1972, for sharp criticism; *Churchman* v. *Joint Shop Stewards' Committee* [1972] 1 W.L.R. 1094; and see pp. 375–6, on the Official Solicitor.

35. See, for example, *Chandler* v. *D.P.P.* [1964] A.C. 763; and other cases cited above, pp. 116, 132–3.

36. See, for example, the *Sheriff of Middlesex*'s case (1840) 11 A. & E. 273; *Bradlaugh* v. *Gossett* (1884) 12 Q.B.D. 271.

37. See *Liyanage* v. *R.* [1967] 1 A.C. 259 (Ceylon); though cf. *Kariapper* v. *Wijesinha* [1968] A.C. 717; *Australian Communist Party* v. *Commonwealth of Australia* (1951) 83 C.L.R. 1.

retroactive effect,[38] or enabling the Executive to designate which judges shall sit to hear a particular case,[39] or abolishing a judicial office while it has a substantive holder,[40] or reducing judicial salaries?[41] In Britain such measures would generally be regarded, in the absence of extraordinary circumstances, as unconstitutional in the sense of being contrary to constitutional convention. But in a number of Commonwealth countries they would be not only 'unconstitutional' but also invalid. And in some Commonwealth countries it would also be unconstitutional to impair the independence of the Judiciary by endowing them with functions extraneous to the judicial,[42] or to purport to oust the jurisdiction of the courts to decide the constitutionality of legislative or executive action.[43]

In Britain the independence of the Judiciary rests not on formal constitutional guarantees and prohibitions but on an admixture of statutory and common-law rules, constitutional conventions and parliamentary practice, fortified by professional tradition and public opinion.

Appointment

Appointments of High Court and Circuit judges, Recorders, and stipendiary and lay magistrates are made either by or on the advice of the Lord Chancellor. Since the Lord Chancellor is himself a political appointee and a member of the Cabinet, there appears to be ample scope for political patronage. Appointments to the Court of Appeal and to the House of Lords, and to the offices of Lord Chief Justice and President of the Family Division, are made on the advice of the Prime Minister after consultation with the Lord Chancellor. In a number of new Commonwealth countries judicial appointments other than Chief Justice are made on the advice of a Judicial Service Commission, presided over by the Chief Justice and composed mainly of judicial members. In practice appointments in England and Wales are no longer made on political grounds, except to the lay magistracy. Justices of the peace are appointed by the Lord Chancellor on the recommendation of local advisory committees whose membership is not, in general, publicly disclosed. In a circular to advisory committees

38. cf. *Burmah Oil Co.* v. *Lord Advocate* [1965] A.C. 75; War Damage Act 1965.

39. *R.* v. *Liyanage* (1963) 64 New L.R. 313 (Ceylon); see Thomas M. Franck, *Comparative Constitutional Process*, pp. 384–98. The court held that this power was one properly reposed only in members of the Judicature.

40. See, for example, Constitution of Jamaica (S.I. 1952, No. 1550, Sched. 2), s. 97 (3).

41. For example, Constitution of India, art. 124(2), proviso.

42. *Att.-Gen. for Australia* v. *R. and the Boilermakers' Society of Australasia* [1957] A.C. 288.

43. For example, *Balewa* v. *Doherty* [1963] 1 W.L.R. 949 (P.C., Nigeria).

in 1966, the then Lord Chancellor made it clear that political affiliations ought not to be disregarded because it was important that 'justices should be drawn from all sections of the community and should represent all shades of opinion'.[44]

Before 1914 it was quite common for M.P.s belonging to the party in office to be appointed to the High Court.[45] During the past thirty years hardly any judicial appointment in England appears to have been influenced by political considerations.[46] Professional standing at the bar and personal suitability are ostensibly the sole criteria. The Lord Chancellor is likely to consult the Lord Chief Justice, the Master of the Rolls, the Vice-Chancellor and the President of the Family Division before submitting a recommendation. Not long ago the Attorney-General was understood to have the first refusal of a vacancy in the office of Lord Chief Justice. In 1922 Lord Hewart, then Attorney-General, was appointed; in 1940 he was succeeded by Lord Caldecote, formerly Attorney-General and at the time Lord Chancellor. But in 1946 Caldecote was succeeded by Lord Goddard, a Law Lord who was far from being a Labour sympathizer[47] and in 1958 Lord Parker, a Lord Justice of Appeal, assumed the office. In 1971 Lord Parker was succeeded by Lord Widgery, also a Lord Justice of Appeal. There is no reason, however, why the Law Officers of the Crown, and other barristers in politics, should not be eligible for appointment to high judicial office, provided that they possess the appropriate qualities of character, temperament and intellect. Political affiliations may nevertheless operate as a disqualification inasmuch as an active proponent of revolution may be regarded as unsuitable to occupy what is in one aspect a high office of State.

A lawyer seeking appointment as a Recorder or professional magistrate should make the fact known to the Lord Chancellor's Department; candidates for such appointments are not easily identified. As we have seen, solicitors as well as barristers are eligible for these appointments, and a solicitor may become a Circuit judge after five years' service as a Recorder. Solicitors also exercise judicial functions as Masters of the Supreme Court, county court registrars and chairmen of special tribunals.

44. Quoted Jackson, op. cit., p. 217. In the counties the chairman of the advisory committee is the Lord Lieutenant; in boroughs the chairman is appointed by the Lord Chancellor. The main political parties will be represented on the committee. See Peter G. Richards [1961] *Public Law* 134.

45. See generally, H. J. Laski, *Studies in Law and Politics*, pp. 168–80.

46. This comment does not apply to Scottish judicial appointments. See I. D. Willock (1969) 14 *Juridical Review* (N.S.) 193.

47. Viscount Jowitt, Lord Chancellor under the Attlee Governments (1945–51), went to great pains not to afford any ground for suspicion that appointments to high judicial office were politically influenced.

But at present full-time judgeships are reserved for members of the bar.[48] This exclusiveness has had certain advantages. Members of the bar alone have had the right of audience in the superior courts[49]; they rub shoulders out of court with the judges, who remain members of their Inns; the bar is an autonomous, individualistic but tightly knit profession, maintaining extraordinarily high standards of professional conduct, partly, perhaps, because the number of barristers in private practice in England and Wales is still under three thousand. Recent developments, and in particular the growth in the size of the Judiciary, portend an erosion of exclusiveness. One class of lawyer, the full-time academic lawyer, is still in practice excluded from serious consideration for appointment to a superior judgeship. On this matter there are real difficulties to overcome. It would be a risk to appoint a person with little experience of advocacy to be a judge of first instance. To appoint him to the Court of Appeal or the House of Lords might evoke serious resentment among the puisne judges.

Promotion

In Britain the Judiciary is not a career service. In many countries a young man will join the judicial service, starting at the bottom and working his way upwards through the hierarchy. Such a system may tend to inhibit forthright independent-mindedness, particularly if promotion is determined by a Minister of Justice.[50] But in Britain appointments to the High Court are made from the ranks of successful practitioners;[50a] professional magistrates are not promoted to the High Court, and promotions of county court judges have been rare[51]; advancement from the High Court to the Court of Appeal may be gratifying, but it carries with it no increase in salary; appointment to the House of Lords means a relatively small increment in salary though by some a peerage is highly valued. There is no great material inducement to encourage a member of the Judiciary to curry favour with the politicians or his judicial superiors; any attempt

48. High Court puisne judges must be barristers of at least ten years' standing and other superior judges must be barristers of at least fifteen years' standing (except that the Law Lords may alternatively have held high judicial office for two years).

49. Solicitors have a right of audience in county courts, and limited rights of audience in the Crown Court (Practice Directions [1972] 1 W.L.R. 5,307).

50. In Commonwealth countries where there is a Judicial Service Commission, promotion is a matter for the Commission. This system may induce a different kind of deference.

50a. For their social background, see Henry Cecil, *The English Judge* (1972 edn), ch. 1.

51. Promotions of Circuit judges to be High Court judges may well become more common in future. At the present time there are indications of hierarchical tendencies at the lower end of the scale – for example, a magistrates' clerk may become a professional magistrate and then a deputy Circuit judge or Circuit judge.

to procure advancement by such means would bring a judge into disfavour. Moreover, a Prime Minister or Lord Chancellor has little incentive to take political considerations into account when recommending promotion or, indeed, the initial appointment of a judge. Matters might be different if we had a written constitution with entrenched guarantees and prohibitions subject to judicial interpretation, especially if it were difficult to procure constitutional amendments overturning the effect of inconvenient decisions.

Salaries

Judicial salaries and pensions are substantial by international standards. In 1973 a puisne judge of the High Court was paid £15,750 a year,[52] charged on the Consolidated Fund. Salaries may be increased, but not reduced, by the Lord Chancellor with the consent of the Minister for the Civil Service. After fifteen years' service a judge can retire on a pension equal to half his salary.[53] Practitioners are often earning more in fees than a judicial salary when appointed to the bench, but a judgeship affords not only great dignity but financial security.[54]

The Act of Settlement 1701 had provided that judges' salaries were to be 'ascertained and established'. Till well into the eighteenth century judicial salaries were nevertheless low. Judicial incomes were supplemented by fees from suitors and other sources, sundry perquisites of office and the exercise of patronage.[55] These standing temptations to corruption – which had been all the greater so long as judicial salaries had to be met out of the King's privy purse;[56] under the Stuarts they were often in arrears – were finally removed by an Act of 1826 which raised the salaries of superior judges to £5000 and abolished their income from fees.

Rules tending to protect judicial independence

Insulation from politics. First, full-time judges are disqualified from membership of the House of Commons.[57] Secondly by convention judges

52. Judges' Remuneration Act 1965; S.I. 1972, No. 1104. So were the Lords Justices of Appeal. The salary of the Lord Chief Justice was £18,500, and the salaries of the Master of the Rolls, the Lords of Appeal in Ordinary and the President of the Family Division were £17,250.

53. Administration of Justice Act 1973, s. 11; Schedule 4.

54. In 1970 a High Court judge resigned and became a member of a firm of merchant bankers; his decision aroused some professional criticism.

55. See generally W. S. Holdsworth, *History of English Law*, vol. 1, pp. 252–5.

56. For this reason William III had refused his assent in 1692 to a bill to increase judicial salaries to £1000: K. O. Roberts-Wray, *Commonwealth and Colonial Law*, pp. 485–6.

57. House of Commons Disqualification Act 1957, ss. 1(1) (*a*), 1(2); First Schedule. The disqualification of part-time Recorders for election in those constituencies where

must refrain from politically partisan activities; and although they can criticize the wording and content of legislation and the conduct of members of the Executive, they should be careful not to take sides in matters of political controversy – a precept more easily formulated than followed,[58] for ostensibly non-political matters of public concern are apt to become party issues unexpectedly. Third, by convention members of the Executive are expected to preserve a reciprocal restraint when commenting on the words and deeds of judges, though if criticized by a judge they are not obliged to remain mute, and if a judge makes politically controversial remarks a robust answer can be offered. Fourthly, in parliamentary practice members of the House of Commons are not permitted to cast aspersions on the conduct of a judge at question time, or in the course of debate except on a motion specifically criticizing the judge or supporting an address for his removal; and in general a matter cannot be raised in Parliament if it is *sub judice*.[59] Fifthly, the courts disclaim jurisdiction to inquire into proceedings in Parliament.[60] Sixthly, the charging of judicial salaries on the Consolidated Fund means that since Parliament does not authorize them annually, there is no adequate opportunity to censure judges in the debates on the estimates.

Some hold the view that the independence of the Judiciary may be prejudiced if judges are entrusted with functions alien to the judicial; or if provision is made for courts to give advisory opinions to the Executive on questions of law. The former view does not seem to be generally accepted by the present generation of English judges; they sit in the Restrictive Practices Court and the National Industrial Relations Court, and they accept appointments as chairmen of inquiries into alleged public scandals, major industrial disputes, third London airports and other politically contentious matters; they conceive these functions to be aspects of their duty towards the State.[61] There are various objections to the advisory judicial opinion, but they have only a tenuous connection with judicial involvement in executive policy. The fact that the Stuarts used judges as advisers and brought undue pressure to bear on them in private consultation does not imply that a publicly delivered advisory opinion

---

they exercised jurisdiction was repealed by the Courts Act 1971, Sched. 11, and, it would seem (despite the general words of Schedule 8 to that Act) not replaced. For Law Lords in the upper House, see ch. 13. The last judge (other than the Lord Chancellor) to hold Cabinet office was Lord Ellenborough, Chief Justice of the King's Bench, in 1806.

58. It tends to be followed more rigorously in England than in Scotland.

59. For an exception introduced in 1972, see p. 293.

60. See pp. 315, 318, 322–3, 326–8.

61. For a helpful catalogue and critique, see Graham Zellick [1972] *Public Law* 1. See also Wade and Phillips, *Constitutional Law* (8th edn), pp. 327–8.

on a specific question of law would prejudice judicial impartiality today.[62]
Judicial immunities in legal proceedings. At common law, no action will
lie against a judge for any words spoken[63] or acts done[64] while he is
exercising his judicial functions in a matter within his jurisdiction. A like
immunity is enjoyed by magistrates[65] and members of other tribunals
closely resembling courts[66] in respect of defamatory words, but a right
of action may possibly lie against such officers for malicious *acts*,[67] and
will lie for tortious acts done outside their jurisdiction where jurisdiction
has been exceeded because of an error of law or an unreasonable mistake
of fact.[68] A magistrate who has had to pay damages or costs in respect of
proceedings instituted against him in the purported exercise of his duties
is entitled to be indemnified out of public funds provided that he has acted
reasonably and in good faith.[69]

Judicial immunities from suit are conferred not for the benefit of
judges but for the benefit of the administration of justice. The risk that a
judge may abuse his privilege by making gratuitously defamatory remarks
for reasons of personal rancour is considered to be less than the risk of
his abstaining for reasons of prudence from condemning iniquity in
appropriate language. In the public interest, absolute privilege also
attaches to words used by the parties, counsel and witnesses in the course
of judicial proceedings.[70] Nor can jurors be punished for their verdict.[71]

62. Advisory opinions may be obtained from the Judicial Committee of the Privy
Council under section 4 of the Judicial Committee Act 1833; see p. 150; see also
Criminal Justice Act 1972, s. 36 (p. 360). In Canada advisory opinions on the consti-
tutionality of legislation have frequently been delivered by the courts. The International
Court of Justice has also given several advisory opinions.

63. *Scott* v. *Stansfield* (1868) L.R. 3 Ex. 220.

64. *Anderson* v. *Gorrie* [1895] 1 Q.B. 668; *Taaffe* v. *Downes* (1813) 3 Moore 16
(Wilson, *Cases and Materials*, p. 309).

65. *Law* v. *Llewellyn* [1906] 1 K.B. 487.

66. See, for example, *Addis* v. *Crocker* [1961] 1 Q.B. 11 (Disciplinary Committee of the
Law Society). The courts have, in general, refused to hold members of administrative
tribunals to be protected by absolute privilege; they enjoy qualified privilege which is
destroyed by proof of malice.

67. See, on this difficult topic, *Everett* v. *Griffiths* [1921] 1 A.C. 631; *O'Connor* v.
Isaacs [1956] 2 Q.B. 288; Justices' Protection Act 1848, s. 1; Amnon Rubinstein,
Jurisdiction and Illegality, pp. 128–33; L. A. Sheridan (1951) 14 *Mod. L. Rev.* 267;
D. Thompson (1958) 21 *Mod. L. Rev.* 517.

68. *Houlden* v. *Smith* (1850) 14 Q.B. 841; *Palmer* v. *Crone* [1927] 1 K.B. 804.

69. Administration of Justice Act 1964, s. 27. If the last conditions are absent,
indemnification is discretionary.

70. Neither a barrister nor (it seems) a solicitor can be sued for negligence in respect
of his conduct of a client's case as an advocate: *Rondel* v. *Worsley* [1969] 1 A.C. 191.
Solicitors are liable for professional negligence in other contexts, and it may well be
that barristers are liable for negligence in respect of opinions.

71. *Bushell's* case (1670) Vaugh. 135.

There may be circumstances in which a judge wrongfully declining to hear a case within his jurisdiction will incur civil liability to a person aggrieved.[72] Under the Habeas Corpus Act 1679 a judge wrongfully (and presumably wilfully) refusing to issue a writ of habeas corpus is liable to a penalty of £500 recoverable by the prisoner.

The general rules of judicial immunity do not extend to giving a judge or magistrate an open licence to be corrupt or oppressive. Corruption would be a ground for prosecution. Oppressive conduct would result in the removal of a magistrate, and the same fate might befall an oppressive judge.[73]

Contempt of court.[74] Disobedience to a court order is a civil contempt, punishable in the discretion of the court by imprisonment. This rule has nothing to do with judicial independence. Criminal contempts fall into three main categories. First, there are contempts in the face of the court – for example, the interruption of a High Court libel action by a group of Welsh Nationalist student demonstrators,[75] or a wilful refusal by a witness to answer questions put to him.[76] Secondly, there is conduct tending to prejudice a fair trial – for example, where proceedings are pending (or, apparently, imminent), publishing newspaper comment or broadcasting a television programme tending to show that a person not yet convicted (but charged or about to be charged) is in fact guilty,[77] or disclosing a party's past convictions; or putting pressure on witnesses to alter their evidence or not to give evidence, or commenting publicly on the merits of the case in such a way as to induce a party to settle the proceedings instead of pursuing his case;[78] or otherwise potentially influencing the court or the jury by revelations or comments on the proceedings. In so far as the rule precludes 'prejudicial' comment on a civil action tried by a judge without a jury, it has been relaxed.[79] Thirdly, there is conduct scandalizing the court

72. See *Ferguson* v. *Earl Kinnoull* (1842) 2 Cl. & F. 251.

73. See pp. 373–4.

74. See G. J. Borrie and N. V. Lowe, *The Law of Contempt* (1973).

75. *Morris* v. *Crown Office* [1970] 2 Q.B. 114 (power of judges to sentence summarily). See also p. 461.

76. Including refusal in proceedings before a formal judicial tribunal of inquiry: *Att.-Gen.* v. *Clough* [1963] 1 Q.B. 773; *Att.-Gen.* v. *Mulholland* [1963] 2 Q.B. 477 (journalists refusing to disclose sources of information).

77. *R.* v. *Savundranayagan* [1968] 1 W.L.R. 1761 at 1764–5 ('Trial by television is not to be tolerated in a civilized society', *per* Salmon L.J. at 1765).

78. See, on the latter point, *Att.-Gen.* v. *Times Newspapers Ltd* [1972] 3 W.L.R. 855; cf. *Att.-Gen.* v. *London Weekend Television Ltd* [1972] 3 All E.R. 1146 (the thalidomide cases). See, however, below, and Addendum.

79. As in *Vine Products Ltd* v. *Green* [1966] Ch. 484 (article dealing with subject-matter of pending proceedings); *Att.-Gen.* v. *Times Newspapers Ltd* [1973] 2 W.L.R. 452, C.A. (revg. [1972] 3 W.L.R. 855). See p. 293, note 82.

by scurrilous criticism or imputations of partiality.[80] The limits of permissible criticism have been extended by the courts themselves in recent years. In a case reported in 1936, the Judicial Committee, allowing an appeal against a conviction and fine imposed on the author of a newspaper article criticizing sentences imposed by local judges, held that members of the public were immune provided that they refrained from imputing improper motives to the judges and were not actuated by malice. 'Justice must not be a cloistered virtue; she must be allowed to suffer the scrutiny and respectful, even the outspoken, comments of ordinary men.'[81] Today, even disrespectful comments will not necessarily be construed as contempts of court. In a case decided in 1968,[82] the Court of Appeal declined to hold that an article by a Q.C. (soon to be Lord Chancellor) in *Punch*, embodying robust, jocular and inaccurate denunciations of judgments by the court, was a contempt. Lord Denning M.R. said that the court would 'never use this jurisdiction as a means to uphold our dignity. We do not fear criticism, nor do we resent it.' Salmon L.J. said that 'no criticism of a judge, however vigorous, can amount to contempt of court, providing it keeps within the limits of courtesy and good faith'.[83] Judges may adopt differing standards, but the tendency is to show more indulgence towards outspoken criticism alleging ignorance of the law or excessive harshness or leniency in sentencing.

An appeal against conviction lies to a higher court. It is a defence that the publisher or disseminator of a contempt had taken reasonable care and had no reason to suspect that proceedings were pending or that the material was prejudicial to a fair trial as the case may be.[84]

Security of judicial tenure

Before 1689 judges generally held office during the King's pleasure. When they incurred his displeasure they were apt to be summarily dismissed. Sir Edward Coke, Chief Justice of the King's Bench, was the most spectacular casualty, dismissed by James I in 1616 for presuming to dispute the prerogative claim that the King was entitled to stay judicial proceedings and require the judges to consult with him in a matter affecting his interests.[85] Tenure was governed not by statute but by the terms of

80. *McLeod* v. *St Aubyn* [1899] A.C. 549; *R.* v. *Gray* [1900] 2 Q.B. 36; *R.* v. *Editor of the New Statesman* (1928) 44 T.L.R. 301.

81. *Ambard* v. *Att.-Gen. for Trinidad and Tobago* [1936] A.C. 322 at 335.

82. *R.* v. *Metropolitan Police Commissioner, ex p. Blackburn (No. 2)* [1968] 2 Q.B. 150.

83. At 155.

84. Administration of Justice Act 1960, ss. 11–13; Smith and Hogan, *Criminal Law* (2nd edn), pp. 600–608; the defences have been criticized as being too narrow.

85. See Taswell-Langmead, *English Constitutional History* (11th edn), pp. 350–52.

prerogative appointments, and practice was not uniform. From Henry VII's time Barons of the Exchequer were normally appointed during good behaviour; if a King wished to rid himself of an Exchequer judge he would merely suspend him.[86] Other superior judges were appointed during good behaviour in the latter part of Charles I's reign, the Interregnum and the early years of Charles II. But in 1668 Charles reverted to the practice of making appointments during pleasure.[87] As in the reigns of his father and grandfather, judges had to be good King's men, prepared to act as his confidential advisers. By the end of 1683 eleven judges had been removed during a period of eight years.[88] James II's bench was compliant and of poor quality.

After 1688 all superior judges were appointed during good behaviour. The Act of Settlement 1701 placed the terms of appointment on a statutory basis: judges' commissions were to be made *quamdiu se bene gesserint* [as long as they behave themselves], 'but upon the address of both Houses of Parliament it shall be lawful to remove them'. This has often been understood to mean that a judge is irremovable except for misbehaviour, in pursuance of an address submitted to the Crown by both Houses praying for his removal on that ground. However, the better interpretation of the Act, and of modern Acts replacing it with slightly different wording,[89] is that a judge is in strict law removable by the Crown *either* for misbehaviour *or* on any other ground in pursuance of a parliamentary address.[90] Misbehaviour would include conviction for an offence involving moral turpitude, and persistent neglect of duties; it does not appear to cover mental infirmity. Removal from an office held during good behaviour has traditionally been effected by proceedings commenced by a writ of *scire facias*. Probably this procedure still survives;[91] it would seem that alternatively the Attorney-General could move for an injunction in the High Court to restrain the judge from continuing to act in an office to which he was no longer entitled, but the judge would have

86. See W. S. Holdsworth, *History of English Law*, vol. 5, p. 351, for an illustration.
87. A. R. Havighurst (1950) 66 L.Q.R. at 65.
88. ibid., p. 247. The chequered career of Pemberton during this period (see Holdsworth, op. cit., vol. 6, p. 503) is worth recording. Appointed to the King's Bench in 1679, he was removed in 1680, appointed Chief Justice in 1681, moved to the Common Pleas in 1683 and dismissed the same year. See also George W. Keeton (1962) 7 *Journal of the Society of Public Teachers of Law* (N.S.) 56.
89. Supreme Court of Judicature (Consolidation) Act 1925, s. 12(1) (tenure 'during good behaviour, subject to' a power of removal by the Crown upon an address by both Houses); Appellate Jurisdiction Act 1876, s. 6 (Lords of Appeal in Ordinary).
90. See the discussion in Sir Kenneth Roberts-Wray, *Commonwealth and Colonial Law*, pp. 486–90.
91. Despite the wording of the First Schedule to the Crown Proceedings Act 1947, the repeal of the writ may refer only to its use for the recovery of Crown debts.

to be given prior notice and a fair opportunity to be heard before being removed.[92]

In practice no judge is likely to be removed except upon a parliamentary address based on the judge's misbehaviour. Only one judge has in fact been so removed since the Act of Settlement – Sir Jonah Barrington, an Irish judge, in 1830. A few other addresses were moved unsuccessfully in the nineteenth century; the judges were permitted to defend themselves and be represented by counsel.[93] But the strictly legal safeguards of security of tenure are weak. The dearth of parliamentary addresses is attributable to the self-restraint of politicians and the circumspection maintained by the Judiciary.[94] It would be more satisfactory to introduce a new procedure whereby a judge would be removable either for mental or physical incapacity or misbehaviour in pursuance of the report of a judicial tribunal of inquiry, and on no other ground. Such a procedure has been incorporated in a number of Commonwealth constitutions since 1957.[95] Under the Administration of Justice Act 1973 the Lord Chancellor has been empowered to declare vacant (with the concurrence of senior judges) the office of a superior judge who is subject to permanent medical incapacity and is unable to tender his resignation (section 12).

Till December 1959 tenure during good behaviour was tantamount to life tenure. Superior judges appointed since then must retire at seventy-five.[96]

Circuit judges and Recorders are removable by the Lord Chancellor for incapacity or misbehaviour;[97] they have an implied right to be heard on their own behalf.[98] The normal age for compulsory retirement of a Circuit judge is seventy-two.

92. In accordance with the rules of natural justice: see authorities quoted in *Ridge* v. *Baldwin* [1964] A.C. 40.

93. See Alpheus Todd, *Parliamentary Government in England*, vol. 2, pp. 726–44, for particulars of the nineteenth-century cases.

94. From time to time senior judges have doubtless persuaded their aberrant or infirm brethren to resign. In 1969 a superior judge was fined for being in charge of a car while under the influence of alcohol; he did not resign and no further action was taken.

95. Roberts-Wray, op. cit., pp. 490–501. In Nigeria in 1963 a constitutional change substituted removal on parliamentary addresses for the judicial tribunal of inquiry procedure, presumably in order to diminish the Judiciary's security of tenure and independence of political pressure.

96. Judicial Pensions Act 1959, s. 2.

97. Courts Act 1971, ss. 17(4), 21(6). The Lord Chancellor is directed to satisfy himself before recommending a person for appointment as a Circuit judge that that person's health is satisfactory (s. 16(4)).

A Recorder may also be removed for failure to comply with the conditions of his appointment as to requirements to officiate (s. 21(3), (6)). He will be appointed for a fixed term, which may be renewed but not beyond the age of seventy-two.

98. *Ex p. Ramshay* (1852) 18 Q.B. 173.

Magistrates have no legal security of tenure, but they may be placed on the supplemental list for infirmity or non-judicial behaviour or removed altogether from the commission of the peace. Provision has now been made for both lay and stipendiary magistrates to be placed on the supplemental list or retired at seventy.[99]

The executive and the administration of justice

There is no Minister of Justice in England. Executive responsibilities in relation to the administration of justice are distributed among several Ministers – the Lord Chancellor, the Home Secretary, and the Law Officers of the Crown (the Attorney-General and the Solicitor-General for England and Wales). The Scottish Law Officers are the Lord Advocate and the Solicitor-General for Scotland; the Secretary of State for Scotland also has responsibility for aspects of the Scottish legal system, which differs in many ways from the English.

The Lord Chancellor's duties[100] are multifarious, demanding the utmost delicacy and an extensive familiarity with lawyers and the law. As we have seen, he is head of the Judiciary, a Cabinet Minister and Speaker of the House of Lords. He seldom sits as a judge, but is responsible for arranging who shall sit to hear cases in the House of Lords and the Judicial Committee of the Privy Council. Many of his functions in relation to judicial appointments have been mentioned, but there are others; thus he appoints Chancery Masters, the senior Master of the Queen's Bench Division, judges' clerks, county court registrars and the legally qualified chairmen of certain statutory tribunals. He is chairman of the committees that make rules of procedure for the Supreme Court[101] and the Crown Court and appoints the members of the corresponding body for county courts. To an increasing extent he has assumed responsibilities for matters connected with the administration of criminal justice. It was he, not the Home Secretary, who was the progenitor of the Courts Act 1971, and it is he who appoints the officials of the Crown Court. He is also the Minister responsible for law reform on the civil side. In this context by far the most important advisory body is the Law Commission,[102] composed of a High Court judge as chairman and full-time Commissioners appointed by the Lord Chancellor. The Commission has a small but

99. Justices of the Peace Act 1968, s. 2; Administration of Justice Act 1973, s. 2.
100. They are summarized in R. F. V. Heuston, *Lives of the Lord Chancellors 1885–1940*, Introduction. See also Jackson, op. cit., p. 535.
101. cf. *Bates* v. *Lord Hailsham of St Marylebone* [1972] 1 W.L.R. 1373.
102. See Law Commissions Act 1965. There is a separate Law Commission for Scotland. The Commissions have also made reports on criminal law reforms.

highly qualified research staff, and parliamentary counsel are attached to it as draftsmen. Before the Commission issues a formal report with firm proposals, it will hold extensive consultations, perhaps produce a preliminary working paper, meet with a specialist advisory committee and invite comments from representative bodies of lawyers and individuals. In the course of seven years the Commission produced detailed schemes ranging from divorce law reform to codification of the law of contracts and statute law revision, and its reports have strengthened the position of the Lord Chancellor, jostling with his ministerial colleagues for places in the legislative queue. Several bills emanating from the Law Commission have been passed as private members' bills. Part-time bodies advisory to the Lord Chancellor include the Law Reform Committee (constituted in 1934 as the Law Revision Committee) and the Committee on Private International Law. Again, he appoints the members of the Council on Tribunals[103] which has various supervisory, consultative and advisory functions with regard to statutory tribunals and inquiries; the Council makes reports to him. He exercises a general superintendence over the legal aid and advice scheme in civil matters for persons of modest means; the scheme is administered by the Law Society, the governing body of solicitors.[104] Administrative responsibility for the legal aid scheme in criminal matters is vested mainly in the Home Secretary; decisions to grant legal aid orders are made by the criminal courts themselves.[105] If the Lord Chancellor has not enough to occupy his time, he can make speeches for the Government in the House of Lords or address his mind to his extensive ecclesiastical patronage or his responsibilities for the Land Registry, the Public Record Office and the Office of the Public Trustee.

Another function of the Lord Chancellor is to appoint the Official Solicitor to the Supreme Court and to give him general directions as to the performance of his duties. Among the multifarious duties performed by the Official Solicitor as a 'general sweeper-up of messes'[106] is representation of infants, mental patients and persons committed for contempt of court, particularly if they are unrepresented in forthcoming judicial proceedings. In 1972 he emerged from anonymity to arrange for unofficial

103. See ch. 25.
104. For a short account of the scheme, see Jackson, op. cit., pp. 435–54; see especially Legal Aid and Advice Acts 1949 and 1972.
105. Criminal Justice Act 1967, Part IV. See further Jackson, op. cit., pp. 174–90; *R* v. *Derby JJ., ex p. Kooner* [1971] 1 Q.B. 147 (implied duty of magistrates to provide counsel in committal proceedings for murder).
106. The then Official Solicitor's own description (1966) 63 *Law Society's Gazette* at 338.

dock-strike leaders to appeal against an order committing them to prison for contempt of the National Industrial Relations Court.[107]

The Home Secretary is in effect the Minister of the Interior, though he also has responsibilities for Westminster's relations with the Channel Islands and the Isle of Man.[108] Some of his responsibilities with regard to law and order have only a tenuous connection with the administration of justice – for example, implementing (or not implementing) the reports of constituency boundary commissions; superintending the machinery for the conduct of elections; immigration, deportation, extradition, naturalization and the general regulation of aliens and Commonwealth immigrants; control of firearms, poisons and dangerous drugs. The Director General of the Security Service is personally answerable to him. Other functions impinge on the administration of justice; he is the police authority for the Metropolitan Police and supervises local police forces;[109] he is generally responsible for the penal system and the treatment of offenders, and looks after prisons, other custodial establishments and the probation service; he has administrative responsibilities for magistrates' courts and the general working of the system of lay magistrates (though the Lord Chancellor and local magistrates' courts committees discharge important functions in this field) and some responsibilities for legal aid. It is he who advises the Queen on the exercise of the prerogative of mercy. He is broadly responsible for not only the administration but also the reform of the criminal law, and is advised by a Criminal Law Revision Committee.

The Attorney-General[110] is the principal legal adviser to government Departments. He appears in court on their behalf in important cases, and gives them formal and informal opinions on difficult questions of law out of court. Reference has already been made to his important role in scrutinizing drafts of bills; he is also a valuable member of committees on bills. These functions, and some of his other responsibilities,[111] are dischargeable by the Solicitor-General (who is not a solicitor). The Law Officers, though members of the Government, do not now have seats in the Cabinet.

The Attorney-General has a number of non-political functions. As guardian of the public interest, he may institute civil proceedings in the High Court for the vindication of public rights – for example, to restrain a local authority from exceeding its powers, or a private individual from

107. *Churchman* v. *Joint Shop Stewards' Committee* [1972] 1 W.L.R. 1094; note 34.
108. And for Northern Ireland affairs till 1972; see p. 640.
109. See ch. 17.
110. For the fullest account, see J. Ll. J. Edwards, *The Law Officers of the Crown*.
111. See Law Officers Act 1944.

perpetrating repeated breaches of by-laws or other minor criminal offences. He may take such proceedings on his own initiative or at the request of other persons or bodies lacking a sufficient personal interest to sue on their behalf; he has an absolute discretion whether to proceed.[112] Again, he appears as an independent officer of State before judicial tribunals of inquiry. His role in criminal proceedings is of special constitutional importance. He can select the place of trial on indictment.[113] He can enter a *nolle prosequi* to stop any trial of an indictable offence. His leave is required before certain classes of criminal proceedings (for example, for breaches of the Official Secrets Acts) can be instituted. He can institute criminal proceedings, or instruct the Director of Public Prosecutions to take over a private prosecution and offer no evidence if a *nolle prosequi* cannot be entered or if it is preferable not to go through the formality of entering a *nolle prosequi*. These discretionary powers are probably unchallengeable in any court,[114] and they could be abused to serve party political purposes. But in performing these functions he is obliged by convention to exercise an independent discretion, not dictated by his colleagues in the Government, though he is at liberty to (and sometimes should) consult them and obtain their views in a case with political implications. In 1970 the Attorney-General's decision (taken after he had consulted the Secretary of State for Foreign and Commonwealth Affairs) to prosecute journalists under section 2 of the Official Secrets Act 1911 for publication of a confidential official memorandum about the Nigerian civil war aroused a great deal of criticism, but there is no reason for supposing that he acted otherwise than according to his own independent judgment.[115] In 1924 the circumstances in which the Attorney-General was suspected of having yielded to Cabinet pressure in withdrawing a prosecution for sedition led to a successful vote of censure on the Government and its downfall.[116] He is politically answerable for, and can give directions to, the Director of Public Prosecutions,[117] an official appointed by the Home Secretary but with his own Department. The Director of Public Prosecutions himself instructs counsel and solicitors to conduct

112. See generally de Smith, *Judicial Review of Administrative Action* (3rd edn), ch. 9 and Appx 3 (on the *McWhirter* case). And see Addendum to this book.

113. He can also determine the venue in civil cases involving the Crown.

114. See *R.* v. *Allen* (1862) 1 B. & S. 850 on the prerogative power to enter a *nolle prosequi*. cf. Bernard Dickens, (1972) 35 *Mod. L. Rev.* 347, suggesting that in some contexts his discretion may not be unlimited. And see Dickens (1973) 22 *I.C.L.Q.* 1.

115. See p. 485. The Franks Committee on Section 2 of the 1911 Act recommended (Cmnd 5104 (1972)) that discretion as to the institution of prosecutions in this class of case should rest with the Attorney-General.

116. Edwards, op. cit., chs. 10 and 11; Wilson, *Cases and Materials*, pp. 323–7.

117. S.R. & O. 1946, No. 1467 (S.R. & O. and S.I. Revised to 1948, v, 329), r. 5.

prosecutions in cases referred to him by Departments and in other serious or important cases (in some of which he alone is entitled to prosecute, or proceedings cannot be undertaken except with his leave), and can take over prosecutions from private persons. He undertakes about three thousand prosecutions a year. He also advises the police at their request whether there is sufficient evidence to justify a prosecution.[118] His advice, though not binding, carries great weight.

In a number of newly self-governing Commonwealth countries with politically appointed Attorney-Generals, the Director of Public Prosecutions is given judicial security of tenure by the constitution and is vested with an exclusive independent responsibility for decisions to take over, continue or discontinue prosecutions. Where he decides to institute criminal proceedings himself, the constitution will provide that he shall not act under the direction of any other person. This constitutional device – and there are others designed to produce a similar effect[119] – emphasizes both the importance attached to the maintenance of public confidence in the process of prosecution and the precarious delicacy of the balance achieved by habits of political self-restraint in Britain. It is not too much to say that in Britain the independence of the Judiciary and the impartiality of the administration of criminal justice are maintained *in spite of* the strictly legal powers vested in Parliament and the Executive.

118. The office was set up in 1878. See further Edwards, op. cit., chs. 16 and 17.
119. cf. Roberts-Wray, op. cit., pp. 354–5.

Chapter 17
Police

Status[1] and functions

A police officer has often been likened to a citizen in uniform. In the first place, every citizen has powers to arrest without warrant and to use reasonable force in the prevention of crime;[2] the police are the specialists. Secondly, for most offences it is open to any person to institute a prosecution; it so happens that prosecutors are usually policemen.[3] Thirdly, a person unlawfully arrested by a police officer is not obliged to submit tamely to restraint; he can use reasonable force to free himself. Fourthly, police officers are not above the law, and if they exceed their powers and duties they can be sued or prosecuted in the ordinary courts according to the general principles of civil and criminal liability.

For a number of reasons this kind of analogy is not very helpful. Police officers have powers of arrest, entry, search and seizure going far beyond those of the ordinary citizen. If a police officer arrests the wrong man, even if no criminal offence has been committed at all, the arrest is not necessarily wrongful in the sense of being unlawful; special defences are available to the police.[4] Since police powers of arrest are both extensive and obscure, discreet non-resistance may be the better part of valour; the citizen can vindicate his rights (if any) after the event. Police powers to prosecute for criminal offences may not differ significantly from those of other persons; in practice, however, the exercise of police discretion

1. For a searching and unorthodox analysis, see Geoffrey Marshall, *Police and Government* (1965). See, however, the judgments in the Court of Appeal in *R.* v. *Metropolitan Police Commissioner, ex p. Blackburn* [1968] 2 Q.B. 118.

2. Criminal Law Act 1967, ss. 2(2), (3), 3. See further ch. 20.

3. The use of police officers as regular procurators was criticized by the Royal Commission on the Police (Cmnd 1782 (1962), para. 381). For detailed and cogent criticisms see *The Prosecution Process in England and Wales* (*Justice*, 1970), recommending that general responsibility for prosecutions should be vested in a Department of Public Prosecutions. In Scotland such responsibilities are vested in the Lord Advocate (a Law Officer of the Crown); most prosecutions are launched by Prosecutors-Fiscal, who are appointed by and responsible to him; the police cannot initiate a prosecution, or indeed decide whether to prosecute. See also Dickens (1973) 22 *I.C.L.Q.* 1.

4. See generally ch. 20.

whether or not to prosecute can be of great importance.[5] Again, the police have special common-law duties in connection with the maintenance of law and order,[6] and it is a statutory offence for anyone wilfully to obstruct a constable in the execution of his duties.[7] It is also a statutory offence to waste the time of the police by knowingly making false reports that require investigation.[8] It is no part of a citizen's duties to investigate alleged crimes, take statements and interrogate suspects; but these are duties of the police, partly regulated by a set of rules formulated by the judges.[9] Police officers have, but the ordinary citizen has not, coercive powers to regulate traffic, processions and the conduct of public meetings. Members of a police force cannot become M.P.s[10] or indeed 'take any active part in politics'.[11] It is an offence to incite them to 'disaffection';[12] they cannot join a trade union (though they belong to a statutory negotiating body, the Police Federation);[13] they are subject to a detailed disciplinary code.

5. See A. F. Wilcox, *The Decision to Prosecute* (1972); and note 6.

6. cf. *Blackburn*'s case (above) where the court conceded that a chief constable had discretionary powers in this field but emphasized that they were not absolute. In this case the Commissioner had decided for the time being not to prosecute gaming clubs for breaches of the Gaming Acts in the absence of special circumstances; held, that this was a breach of legal duty owed to the general public, and potentially enforceable in an appropriate form of proceedings against the Commissioner. See further *Buckoke* v. *G.L.C.* [1971] Ch. 655 (wide discretion of police not to prosecute fire engine drivers ignoring red traffic signals); *R.* v. *Metropolitan Police Commissioner, ex p. Blackburn (No. 3)* [1973] 2 W.L.R. 43 (reasonable discretion conceded to police in enforcing obscenity laws).

The police have a duty to protect persons and their property against reasonably apprehended violence. In principle, therefore, a police authority cannot impose a charge for supplying extra protection to persons in need of it. However, if 'special' protection is requested going beyond what is reasonably necessary in the circumstances, a charge can be made by the police as a condition of supplying it: Police Act 1964, s. 15 (giving statutory effect to the rule laid down in *Glasbrook Bros. Ltd* v. *Glamorgan C.C.* [1925] A.C. 270). Chief constables have a discretion in determining the ambit of their duty in any given situation, but their opinion is not conclusive and the issue of financial liability for 'special' protection is potentially justiciable. For the extra protection provided to rugby clubs and associations against demonstrators during the Springbok tour in 1969, the apportionment of financial responsibilities was negotiated and agreed with the Home Secretary.

7. Police Act 1964, s. 51(3); pp. 461–3.

8. Criminal Law Act 1967, s. 5(2), replacing to this extent the judge-made offence of public mischief: *R.* v. *Manley* [1933] 1 K.B. 529.

9. Practice Note (Judges' Rules) [1964] 1 W.L.R. 152; p. 464.

10. House of Commons Disqualification Act 1957, s. 1.

11. Police (Discipline) Regulations 1968 (S.I. 1968, No. 26), Sched. 1, para. 1, r. 4.

12. Police Act 1964, s. 53.

13. ibid., ss. 44, 47. But the Home Secretary may authorize the Police Federation to become associated with a body outside the police service: Police Act 1972, s. 1.

Constables are public officers. It is arguable that they are Crown servants.[14] On appointment, a constable must declare that he will well and truly serve the Queen. For certain purposes he is undoubtedly an officer of the Crown;[15] and the maintenance of law and order, the preservation of the 'Queen's peace', is pre-eminently a function of executive government. Yet he lacks some of the elementary characteristics of a Crown servant; and books on local government law list 'police' among the local government services. A police officer is not paid directly out of central government funds, and except in the Metropolitan area he is neither appointed nor dismissible even indirectly by the Crown. He is appointed and dismissible by the chief constable of a local police force (if he is below the rank of assistant chief constable) and paid by the local police authority. He is under the command of the chief constable, who is appointed by the local authority and can be removed by that authority on prescribed grounds. If a police officer commits a tort, such as assault or negligence, in the purported exercise of his duties, vicarious liability attaches not to the Crown[16] or the local authority[17] but to the chief constable, who is entitled to be indemnified out of local police funds.[18]

A chief constable is nobody's servant but an independent officer upon whom powers and duties are directly conferred by law for the benefit of the populace.[19] His constitutional status remains anomalous and puzzling, even after the re-organization of the police system implemented by the Police Act 1964. It is still not clear whether anyone is entitled to give him instructions as to the performance of any of his duties, or to what extent the Home Secretary is politically answerable for decisions taken by chief constables outside the Metropolis. The rank and file of a police force obviously do not enjoy a comparable degree of autonomy, but one cannot identify any single person or body as their employer (or master), and for this reason they can still be regarded as 'independent' public officers rather than servants.

14. cf. W. S. Holdsworth's discussion of the constitutional position of the judges ((1932) 48 L.Q.R. 25) in which he concluded that they were not 'servants' because of the connotation of dependence. See also, on this point, Lord Diplock's dissenting judgment in *Ranaweera* v. *Ramachandran* [1970] A.C. 962 at 973–4.

15. See the review of authority and principle in *Att.-Gen. for New South Wales* v. *Perpetual Trustee Co.* [1955] A.C. 457; and see also *Fisher* v. *Oldham Corporation* [1930] 2 K.B. 364. For the purpose of the Official Secrets Acts a police officer is a person holding office under the Crown: *Lewis* v. *Cattle* [1938] 2 K.B. 454. And see *Coomber* v. *Berks JJ.* (1883) 9 App. Cas. 61.

16. See Crown Proceedings Act 1947, s. 2(6).

17. *Fisher* v. *Oldham Corporation* (above; wrongful arrest).

18. Police Act 1964, s. 48. There is a *discretion* to indemnify police officers in other circumstances.

19. See *R.* v. *Metropolitan Police Commissioner, ex p. Blackburn* [1968] 2 Q.B. 118 at 135–6, 138, 148–9.

Organization and control

The absence of a national police force is explained partly by apprehensions of central political control but mainly by the course of historical development.[20] The medieval constable was a local officer, chosen by the representatives of the township and the hundred; service was compulsory. After the office of justice of the peace had been constituted, the local constable gradually came under the control of the magistrate. As conservators of the peace, magistrates still have special common-law duties, now largely nominal, to secure the maintenance of the Queen's peace in time of civil commotion. From the days of Charles II, constables were parochial officers, untrained, usually ignorant, often ineffectual. The organization of professional disciplined police forces began at the end of the eighteenth century. In 1829 the Metropolitan Police Force was created under the direction of the Home Secretary, Sir Robert Peel.[21] The establishment of borough police forces was made compulsory in 1835 and county forces in 1856. If the broad pattern of local organization were to be disrupted, this would be construed as yet another blow at the principle of local government. In 1962 a majority of members of the Royal Commission on the Police opposed the idea of centralization, but recommended rationalization and closer Home Office involvement in promoting coordination and efficiency.[22] Most of its recommendations were accepted.

The police authority for the Metropolitan Police District (which excludes the City of London with its unique system)[23] is the Home Secretary. He recommends the appointment of the Commissioner who commands the force, and Assistant Commissioners. He appears to have a general power, exercised in practice with great restraint, to give directions to the Commissioner as to the operational control of the Metropolitan Police, and can be asked detailed questions in Parliament about the conduct of the force; but according to views expressed by the Court of Appeal he cannot give directions to the Commissioner as to the institution of prosecutions.[24] However, the special position of a police authority was

20. The leading single-volume work is now T. A. Critchley, *A History of the Police in England and Wales, 900–1966*. See also F. W. Maitland, *Justice and Police*; C. K. Allen, *The Queen's Peace*. For a monumental and highly readable survey, see L. Radzinowicz, *A History of English Criminal Law and its Administration from 1750* (4 vols.).

21. Hence the term 'bobbies'.

22. Cmnd 1728 (1962). For comments on this Report see Jenifer Hart [1963] *Public Law* 283; and on the Police Act 1964, D. E. Regan [1966] *Public Law* 13; D. W. Pollard [1966] *Public Law* 35.

23. W. O. Hart, *Introduction to the Law of Local Government and Administration* (8th edn), pp. 691–2.

24. Or, according to the views expressed in the judgments in that case (*R. v.*

illustrated in 1972 where Mr Reginald Maudling was impelled to resign from the office of Home Secretary because the Special Branch of the Metropolitan Police would be inquiring into the activities of one of his former business associates. Over local forces the Home Secretary's power is indirect, though it was extended by the Police Act 1964.[25] Each local police authority outside London is composed in the same way; two-thirds of its members are local councillors and one-third lay magistrates. Combined authorities constituted by amalgamations have the same proportions of councillors and magistrates. (Under the reformed local government system, there will be fewer combined authorities; police will be a county responsibility, subject to amalgamation, and most of the more populous new counties will correspond to police authority areas.) The police authority appoints a chief constable, a deputy chief constable and assistant chief constables, subject to the concurrence of the Home Secretary. A chief constable must have had two years' experience in another police force in the rank of inspector or above. The authority may, with the Home Secretary's approval, retire a chief, deputy or assistant chief constable compulsorily in the interests of efficiency.[26] The Home Secretary may also require an authority to retire a chief constable on this ground,[27] in which case he must appoint an independent person to conduct an inquiry into any representations made by the officer concerned; where compulsory retirement is imposed by a police authority he *may* cause such an inquiry to be held; in any event the officer must be given adequate notice coupled with a fair opportunity to be heard, according to natural justice. Senior officers are also dismissible for a breach of disciplinary regulations, after a hearing before an independent person; an appeal lies to the Home Secretary. The chief constable himself appoints and promotes other ranks and is the disciplinary authority;[28] disciplinary procedure is judicialized, and the chief constable must not sit if he is in effect a party to the proceedings or a witness; appeal again lies to the Home Secretary.[29]

Metropolitan Police Commissioner, ex p. Blackburn [1968] 2 Q.B. 118), other aspects of law enforcement; *sed quaere*. The Director General of the Security Service is directly answerable to the Home Secretary, and he also works in collaboration with the Special Branch of the Metropolitan Police.

25. The Act is amended by the Local Government Act 1972, ss. 107, 196, 272, Sched. 30.

26. Police Act 1964, ss. 5(4), 6(5). The officer must first be given an opportunity to make representations on his own behalf; cf. *Ridge* v. *Baldwin* [1964] A.C. 40, where this right was inferred from his status as the holder of a public office.

27. Police Act 1964, s. 29.

28. He is also responsible for the appointment and dismissal of special constables and police cadets.

29. See S.I. 1965, Nos. 543, 544, as amended; Police Act 1964, s. 33(3).

Operational control is vested in the chief constable. The police authority is charged with the duty of securing the maintenance of an adequate and efficient local police force.[30] Subject to Home Office regulations or approval, it is responsible for determining the size and establishment of the force and providing and maintaining buildings, vehicles and equipment. It is entitled to receive an annual report from the chief constable on the policing of the area, and to request him to give other reports from time to time, but with the Home Secretary's concurrence he may decline to supply information if its disclosure would be contrary to the public interest or unnecessary for the discharge of the authority's functions.[31] The scope of these exceptions is as obscure as the scope of those functions. It can be inferred that the authority may properly give the chief constable advice; it is doubtful whether it is competent to give him any instructions outside the administrative sphere,[32] and it cannot instruct him whether or how to comply with his duty to enforce the criminal law.[33]

The powers of the Home Office now dwarf those of local police authorities.[34] The Home Secretary's powers in relation to senior appointments and appeals have already been mentioned. In addition, he has and exercises powers to make regulations[35] on establishment, discipline, pay, pensions, allowances, training, duties, leave, housing, uniforms and equipment. He too is required to exercise his functions so as to promote police efficiency.[36] He has powers of inspection, withholding grants, inquiry and compulsory amalgamation of forces; and he may call upon chief constables to furnish him with reports on the policing of their areas.[37] There is a central inspectorate of police, with a Chief Inspector of Constabulary who makes an annual report to him; the report is published and laid before Parliament. The Home Office grant to local police forces is 50 per cent of the net expenditure of the force, the other half being raised by precepts on the local authorities within the police district. The Home Secretary has a discretion to withhold a grant if dissatisfied with the efficiency of a local force or with a proposed appointment to a senior post; this power is no formality, and has been threatened or exer-

30. Police Act 1964, s. 4(1).

31. ibid., s. 12.

32. Councillors may put questions to a designated member of a police authority as to the exercise of the authority's functions (s. 11).

33. *R.* v. *Metropolitan Police Commissioner, ex p. Blackburn* [1968] 2 Q.B. 118 (duty owed to members of the public).

34. See especially D. E. Regan [1966] *Public Law* 13.

35. See Police Regulations 1971 (S.I. 1971, No. 156) for the wide range of topics covered.

36. Police Act 1964, s. 28.

37. ibid., s. 30. An annual report must be submitted. See generally Part II of the Act.

cised several times since 1945. He can impose a compulsory scheme for amalgamation of forces by statutory instrument after holding a local inquiry, if the local police authorities concerned fail to produce an acceptable voluntary scheme; the number of separate forces was in fact substantially reduced after the Police Act 1964. He can conduct an *ad hoc* independent inquiry into the conduct of a force. The only power of importance not explicitly confided in him is to give directions to chief constables as to the conduct of their forces, but the power of suasion is reinforced by the other sanctions now available to him.

Both in strict law and in their practical operation, these go far beyond the normal range of powers exercised by central government Departments over local authorities and their officers. Moreover, the general power to call for reports from chief constables means that parliamentary accountability of the Home Secretary for local police matters is potentially wide. And it must be stressed that under section 28 of the Police Act 1964 the Secretary of State is placed under a duty so to use his enumerated powers 'in such manner and to such extent as appears to him to be best calculated to promote the efficiency of the police'. However, Home Secretaries still take a restrictive view of their obligations to answer parliamentary questions about law enforcement outside the Metropolis.

Complaints

The police in Britain have attached very great importance to the maintenance of friendly relations with the general public. For this purpose they need the backing of the Home Secretary and local police authorities. They will, moreover, go to considerable lengths to avoid the appearance of partisan bias, to be approachable and generally to be at one with the people, offering helpful advice, answering silly questions, directing passers-by to their destinations, looking after lost children and generally taking on a number of responsibilities cast on them neither by statute nor by common law. Except in parts of Northern Ireland, the police have contrived on the whole to retain the confidence of the bulk of the local community. They have been least successful in their relations with younger coloured immigrants.[38] But the self-restraint shown by the Metropolitan Police in particular in dealing with disorderly demonstrators has been at a notably higher level than that of their counterparts in many large cities abroad.

Nevertheless, complaints of unnecessary harshness and of malpractices in conducting investigations and interrogations are not uncommon and

38. See, for example, *Police–Immigrant Relations*, a Report of the House of Commons Select Committee on Race Relations and Immigration (H.C. 471—1 (1971–72)).

are sometimes substantiated. Complaints by members of the public are normally investigated not by an outside body but by the police themselves.[39] The chief constable of the local force must have every such complaint recorded. Unless the complaint is already the subject of a criminal prosecution or a disciplinary charge, an informal investigation must be held. It may, and if the Home Secretary so directs must, be conducted by an officer designated by the chief constable of another force,[40] and his report is made to the local chief constable. The local police authority and the inspectors of constabulary must be kept informed of the way in which such complaints are dealt with. If a report on an investigation indicates that a criminal offence may have been committed, the chief constable must send the report to the Director of Public Prosecutions. If a complaint results in a disciplinary hearing the complainant is entitled to attend as an observer.

It is impossible to evaluate the quality of the informal type of investigation. Nevertheless, the process is not calculated to enhance public confidence. Police resistance to fully independent investigation and review is understandable. Complaints are often instigated by miscreants or persons with political axes to grind, and many police officers naturally prefer the examination to be carried out by one who is sympathetically aware of their own problems. At present the only alternatives to an internal review are the *ad hoc* appointment of a Q.C. or another independent person to conduct a special inquiry,[41] or the sledge-hammer procedure of a judicial tribunal of inquiry.[42] The Parliamentary Commissioner for Administration has no power to investigate complaints against the individual members of police forces or against local police authorities, and his jurisdiction to consider complaints against the Home Secretary in respect of police affairs (for example, in the Metropolitan Police District) has been construed as covering administrative matters only.[43] It has been said that the introduction of new machinery for external review of com-

39. Police Act 1964, ss. 49, 50.

40. The practice of bringing in police officers from outside has increased: see 827 H.C. Deb. 652–4 (2 December 1971). A special section to deal with complaints against the Metropolitan Police was set up at Scotland Yard in 1972.

41. For example, Cmnd 2526 (1964).

42. In pursuance of a resolution of the two Houses under the Tribunals of Inquiry (Evidence) Act 1921. See Cmnd 718 (1959) – the Thurso boy case.

43. Under Schedule 2 to the Parliamentary Commissioner Act 1967 complaints against the Home Office can be entertained. Under paragraph 5 of Schedule 3 action taken by or with the authority of the Secretary of State for the purpose of investigating crime cannot be inquired into. See also section 5(2) of the Act, conditionally barring investigation of complaints about maladministration in connection with disciplinary matters. *Semble* Home Office refusal to consent to a senior local appointment could be investigated on a complaint initiated by the person aggrieved.

plaints would depress police morale and discourage recruitment; but these consequences would be likely only if more complaints were found to be justified and the reports of investigations were given wide publicity. The problem is a delicate one; local boards of review might become too friendly or too antagonistic to the police; a central investigating authority might be too remote from complainants and local problems. One answer may be to enable complainants dissatisfied with the outcome of an informal police investigation to appeal to regional complaints commissioners who would be assisted for the purpose by independent police assessors. But any new procedure would have to afford adequate safeguards for police officers also. If such safeguards could be devised without making the procedure too cumbersome, the introduction of a lay element might be favourably received by police officers who are dissatisfied with the severity often meted out to alleged offenders within the force.[44]

44. Proposals put forward by *Justice* in January 1970 included the right of a dissatisfied complainant to have the case remitted to an independent full-time investigator who would report to the chief constable. If the investigator's findings were adverse to a police officer, the matter could then go to an independent review tribunal.

In February 1973 the Home Secretary announced his intention of introducing new procedures, after full consultations, for an *ex post facto* review of complaints against the police on 'Ombudsman' lines. No police officer would be placed in double jeopardy in respect of the same offence (see 851 H.C.Deb. 993–1003 (23 February 1973)).

Chapter 18
Local Government:
A Sketch

'Radical changes in the local government of England and Wales are needed.' So proclaimed the Committee on the Management of Local Government in 1967.[1] Two years later the Royal Commission on Local Government in England, under the same chairman,[2] made recommendations for sweeping reforms in the structure and functions of local authorities.[3] The Labour Government accepted the main features of the proposed new design.[4] It lost office soon afterwards, and the incoming Conservative Government produced its own general scheme which owed a great deal to the earlier reports but departed from some of their more drastic proposals.[5] The new scheme was implemented, subject to substantial revisions during its passage through Parliament, by the Local Government Act 1972. The Act is being brought into operation by stages; it will be fully operative in April 1974, by which time new decisions about local government finance, complaints about local authorities and the internal organization of local authorities will have been taken. Local government law is therefore in a transitional state, and its main feature will be described in outline only.[6]

This chapter deals with local government in England and Wales.[7] The Scottish system is still more variegated;[8] it is to undergo a comprehensive

1. *Report,* vol. 1, *Management of Local Government,* p. ix (Ministry of Housing and Local Government, HMSO, 1967).

2. Lord Redcliffe-Maud, formerly Sir John Maud.

3. Cmnd 4040 (1969), vol. 1.

4. Cmnd 4276 (1970).

5. Cmnd 4584 (1971).

6. The main works for law students are W. O. Hart and J. F. Garner, *Introduction to the Law of Local Government and Administration* (9th edn); C. A. Cross, *Principles of Local Government Law* (4th edn); Richard Buxton, *Local Government* (2nd edn). See also R. M. Jackson, *The Machinery of Local Government* (2nd edn); J. A. G. Griffith, *Central Departments and Local Authorities* (especially ch. 1); J. F. Garner, *Administrative Law* (3rd edn), chs. 11–16.

7. Welsh local government was the subject of a separate White Paper (Cmnd 3340 (1967)). The scheme was modified after consultations and a change of government, and the revised scheme was incorporated in the Local Government Act 1972.

8. See, for an outline, J. D. B. Mitchell *Constitutional Law* (2nd edn), ch. 13. See further, Report of the Royal Commission on Local Government in Scotland (Cmnd 4150 (1969)).

reconstruction which will not have full effect until 1975.[9] In Northern Ireland, where the position is fundamentally different, the complex and controversial local government system has been simplified under Northern Ireland legislation, and major local authority functions have been or are being transferred to the central government or *ad hoc* bodies.[10]

Structure and functions: before reform

In 1969 there were forty-five administrative counties,[11] seventy-nine county boroughs, 227 non-county boroughs, 449 urban districts and 410 rural districts in England,[12] each with its own elected council. In addition, rural districts were divided into parishes; and each parish had an elected council or a general parish meeting or both. This pattern had been set by nineteenth-century legislation. Special arrangements had been provided for the London area by the London Government Act 1963 which established the Greater London Council[13] and thirty-two metropolitan boroughs.

Local government functions in the years after the Norman Conquest were a matter for the communal courts of the county and the hundred, presided over or supervised by the sheriff, a royal officer, and subject to the superintendence of the King's itinerant justices. There were also feudal manorial courts. Some towns had been granted charters of incorporation and became boroughs. During the fourteenth century the local courts in the counties were largely superseded. Local government became a matter for the justices of the peace, subject to the control of the King's Council and then the Star Chamber. From the Restoration of Charles II in 1660 till well into the nineteenth century, control over the justices was exercised predominantly by the Court of King's Bench, issuing prerogative writs of certiorari, prohibition, mandamus, quo warranto and habeas corpus, and using criminal sanctions against delinquent or seriously neglectful justices. In the boroughs, the unreformed municipal corporations had proliferated. Central control after 1660 was weak; it had never been systematic.

By the Municipal Corporations Act 1835, elected councils were con-

9. Local Government (Scotland) Bill, 1972–3, founded on Cmnd 4583 (1971). Structurally Scotland will have basically a two-tier structure, consisting of eight regions divided into districts. There will also be three unitary authorities for the outer island groups.

10. See Report of the Macrory Review Body on Local Government in Northern Ireland (Cmd 546 (N.I., 1970)); Housing Executive Act (N.I.) 1971; Local Government Act (N.I.) 1972.

11. Not necessarily coinciding with geographical counties – for example, Sussex was divided into two administrative counties.

12. Cmnd 4040 (1969), § 6.

13. The Greater London Council was the successor to the London County Council but covered a considerably larger area.

stituted in all boroughs. The Local Government Acts of 1888 and 1894 took away most of the administrative jurisdiction exercised by the magistrates at quarter sessions and substituted a new pattern of elected local authorities in the counties; but the 1888 Act, removing the larger boroughs from the jurisdiction of the county councils, and making them 'county boroughs' with powers similar to those of a county council, introduced a major source of dissension into the new system. Meanwhile, the *ad hoc* bodies set up to administer the poor law and superintend public health had been superseded and brought within the framework of a central government Department under a political head. Responsibilities for the incipient social services were shared between the Local Government Board (as it then was) and the new local authorities.

The county borough was[14] a unitary local authority. It had responsibilities for town and country planning, housing, public health, education, child care, and other personal social services,[15] consumer protection, police, civil defence, fire services, parks and recreational facilities, public libraries, roads and traffic regulation, the control of various occupational activities by licensing, inspection and registration, and a general power to make by-laws for the good rule and government of its area, as well as miscellaneous functions (for example, the conduct of trading undertakings) which it might have acquired by private or general Acts of Parliament, provisional orders or special procedure orders. The exercise of these functions was subject to varying forms of central control.

The picture in the counties was basically two-tier and the pattern more complex.[16] Responsibility for some services (for example, roads) was distributed between the county council and the county districts (non-county boroughs, urban and rural districts); and the functions of county districts were not in all respects identical. Some functions could, and in certain circumstances had to, be delegated by the county council to county districts. The county districts were housing authorities; the county council was not. For a limited range of purposes, the structure was three-tier; minor functions (for example, for allotments and footpaths) were vested in parish councils or parish meetings within the areas of rural districts. Very small non-county boroughs had had their powers reduced to those of parishes and were called rural boroughs.[17]

There were several departures from the general structural pattern. A few services could be administered by local *ad hoc* authorities (for example,

14. The past tense is used although at the time of writing (January 1973) the authorities mentioned in this section still exist.
15. Local Authority Social Services Act 1970.
16. See Cmnd 4040 (1969), Annex 3 (pp. 322–30).
17. Local Government Act 1958, s. 28 and Schedule 7.

port authorities and river boards), or by joint boards (for example, for water undertakings, education or town and country planning) covering the areas of two or more counties or county boroughs. Police authorities would normally cover an area embracing a number of local government units. Local authorities could establish joint committees (which are not bodies corporate) for a common service. The Greater London Council, with a population of eight million, exercised functions broadly similar to those of a county council but with certain exceptions; it had no responsibility for police or some welfare services and its functions as an education authority were confined to the central area, for which there was a special Inner London Education Authority, but it had concurrent responsibilities for housing and wide powers over environmental planning. The thirty-two London boroughs were roughly comparable with large county boroughs, but in respect of several services they were subordinate to the GLC. The City of London, with its common council presided over by the Lord Mayor of London, was a unique medieval survival.

The organizational structure of local government outside London was unsatisfactory. The most obvious defects were the following:

1. Authorities having the same status and responsibilities differed vastly in population and resources. For example, among the counties, Lancashire had a population of about 2,500,000 and Rutland under 30,000. Among county boroughs, Birmingham has a population of 1,000,000 and Canterbury 32,000. These were extreme cases. But even more striking was the fact that twenty county districts had populations of over 75,000 and 103 had under 5000.[18] The smaller authorities found it difficult to attract officers and members of high quality, and the central government was reluctant to entrust important responsibilities to any of the authorities of a like status.

2. There was jealousy and rivalry between counties and county boroughs. Each type of authority was represented by national associations which were often at loggerheads with one another. Moreover, the ambitions of growing urban authorities to achieve county borough status and thus liberate themselves from subordination to county hall were adamantly resisted by county councils because this would entail loss of both prestige and a main source of revenue. In fact only two county boroughs had been created since 1927.

3. The structure failed to take sufficient account of the common problems of town and country – for example, the need for coordinated physical planning, road development, and common services for city dwellers and the growing population in suburbs and new towns.

4. Within the counties, distribution of responsibilities produced a 'pock-

18. Cmnd 4040 (1969), pp. 331–3.

marked administrative pattern';[19] the county boroughs were self-contained islands, and the distribution of functions between county councils and county districts was often anomalous and engendered friction and inefficiency. There was indeed a conspicuous dearth of local interest in the work done by many county councils; more than half the candidates at county council elections were returned unopposed.[20]

Structural weaknesses in local government, the poverty of the resources at the disposal of many local authorities, and the smallness of local government areas help to explain the decline in the autonomy of local government since the Second World War. There are other reasons.[21] Governments are expected to promote minimum standards of social welfare and to reduce regional disparities in levels of employment and economic development; these tasks require central administration or direction and cannot be left primarily to local initiative or inanition. It is impracticable to organize nationalized industries on a basis of control by local authorities. Management of the national economy implies control over the amount of public expenditure; and local authorities, despite a diminution of status, have been spending 15 per cent of the gross national product and have two million employees.[22] Again, implementation of a particular policy (for example, abolition of the 'eleven plus' examination, the imposition of a prices and incomes policy, raising council rents to an economic level,[23] economizing by stopping the issue of free milk to schoolchildren,[24] or the promotion of police efficiency by the amalgamation of forces) may be attainable only by making legislative inroads on local autonomy. As physical communications have improved, the imposition of close central control over local authorities has been facilitated. Ministers regularly pay lip-service to the crucial role of local government as a means of democratic self-expression, 'grass-roots' consultation and efficient administration; but local authorities have lost their important responsibilities for hospitals, gas and electricity undertakings, and what used to be called the poor law, and have been subjected to tighter control in respect of most of the main services they still provide. At the same time, the scope of the functions vested in local authorities (notably in town and country planning, housing and traffic control) has increased. And the ordinary citizen's direct contacts with the mechanism of government still tend to be mainly with local authorities.

19. Cmnd 4040, § 72.
20. Report of the Committee on the Management of Local Government (1967), p. 193.
21. cf. William A. Robson, *Local Government in Crisis* (2nd edn).
22. Cmnd 4040, § 33.
23. See Housing Finance Act 1972.
24. See Education (Milk) Act 1971.

On the assumption that local government ought to be made more interesting and important, because it had much to contribute to the realization of the democratic idea and to administrative efficiency at all levels, the Redcliffe-Maud Commission recommended[25] that the existing structure in England should be dismantled. In its place there should be established, outside London, sixty-one new local government areas, each embracing both town and country. In fifty-eight a single elected authority would be responsible for all local government services; in three major conurbations, responsibilities should be divided between a metropolitan authority and metropolitan district authorities. The new authorities would be grouped, together with Greater London, in eight provinces; the provincial councils would be composed of indirectly elected and coopted members and would exercise regional planning functions. In addition, there would be, within the new unitary authorities, elected local councils, vested with general consultative and advisory duties and certain discretionary powers but no *duty* to supply or administer services. These councils would in fact be the existing councils other than rural district councils. The unitary authorities should have a broader range of responsibilities for local services than any existing local authority, more freedom from detailed central control, adequate financial resources, wider spending powers, fewer committees and a streamlined internal structure.

Any scheme for local government reform would have to be imposed from above, and no scheme would be free from justifiable criticism. The most cogent objections to the Redcliffe-Maud scheme were that the new unitary authorities would be geographically as remote from the rural populace as were the county councils; and that unless the local councils, reduced in status and function, were able to attract particularly able councillors, the new system would be less sensitive and responsive to the special problems of small localities, and less effective in feeding back local opinion to the central government, than the existing system.

In the event the Conservative Government rejected the Redcliffe-Maud structural pattern in favour of a two-tier system of local authorities.

Structure and functions: the new system

Under the Local Government Act 1972 England is divided into six metropolitan counties outside London (Greater Manchester, Merseyside, South Yorkshire, Tyne and Wear, West Midlands, and West Yorkshire), and thirty-nine non-metropolitan counties. The metropolitan counties have populations of between one and three million. Of the non-metropolitan counties, all but the Isle of Wight have a population of over 280,000; none

25. Cmnd 4040 (1969), ch. 1.

has more than 1,500,000. Some have familiar names but larger areas – Cambridgeshire now includes Huntingdonshire and Peterborough. Some have unfamiliar names – Avon, Cleveland, Cumbria, Humberside. The Act divides the metropolitan counties into metropolitan districts, thirty-six in all. For instance, the county borough of Manchester together with the parish of Ringway is one of twelve districts in the metropolitan county of Greater Manchester. A Local Government Boundary Commission made recommendations for the division of non-metropolitan counties into districts; there are to be 296. Each county and district will have its own council with executive powers and duties. The total number of local authorities in England is reduced by two-thirds. Only fourteen of the county districts have populations of under 40,000, and their average population is trebled to about 90,000, but there remain wide disparities; the county borough of Bristol (425,000) becomes a county district in Avon, whilst the minuscule former county of Rutland holds its ground as a separate county district in Leicestershire.

The most striking feature of the changes is the disappearance of the county borough. Like Bristol, these powerful unitary authorities become county districts, or like Liverpool, metropolitan districts; or they are merged with other authorities to form a district. However, a district council may petition for the district to be given the title of a borough, and existing cities and boroughs will retain their formal dignities. Rural districts have escaped the Redcliffe-Maud axe, but in almost every instance only by virtue of merger with other local government areas to form new county districts. Parish councils remain intact; there is also provision for urban parishes to be constituted and for parishes to be designated as towns.

In Wales the number of counties is reduced to eight; all have new names; there are thirty-seven county districts. There are to be community councils, exercising functions broadly similar to those of parish councils and meetings in England.

The distribution of functions between the Greater London Council and the London borough councils is unaffected by the Act. Elsewhere, the basic allocation (expressed in over-simplified form) is as follows. Non-metropolitan county councils will be responsible for education, personal social services, libraries, museums and art galleries, most aspects of transport (including highways, parking and lighting), structure plans and national parks in town and country planning (with concurrent powers in most other aspects), refuse disposal, consumer protection services (for example, weights and measures, food and drugs), police and fire services, residual housing powers, and certain other functions exercisable concurrently with districts. Among the more important matters for which districts will have primary or sole responsibility are housing, public health, markets, refuse collection, and local plans and development control in the field of town and country planning. But the loss by a large former county borough of its exclusive responsibilities for education and social services is a heavy blow. In the metropolitan counties, the *district* councils will be the authorities responsible for education, personal social services and libraries.

The demarcation of functions is in some respects complex and awkward, but one class of authority may agree that its functions shall be discharged by another as its agent (s. 101), and authorities may still appoint joint committees (s. 102). Parish councils will have much the same functions as heretofore – for instance, responsibilities for footpaths, cemeteries, swimming baths, parks, open spaces and allotments, with some new ones – for instance, car parks and entertainments – and wider spending powers.

Local Government Boundary Commissions for England and Wales will make recommendations to the Secretary of State about alterations in the status of counties and districts, the alteration of local government areas and the construction of new areas, and changes in electoral arrangements (Part 4); the Commission for England will have a limited jurisdiction in relation to London boroughs. No local authority can promote a private bill for altering the status, area or electoral arrangements for any local government unit or for forming or abolishing such a unit (s. 70).[26]

Members, meetings, committees and officials

In English local government authorities there is no clearly identifiable executive branch of government. Detailed administrative decisions are made by resolutions of the council itself or its committees and sub-committees, or by officials acting under specially delegated powers.[27] The council chairman is elected to hold office for one year, and if precedents set in the past are followed, he will seldom be re-elected; in any event, he is far from being a first Minister. There is no Ministry though there may be a committee with primary responsibilities for the coordination of policy; nor does a doctrine of collective responsibility (in the sense of an obligation to show or maintain unanimity) apply to committee decisions except in so far as this is required by party decisions. The council's permanent officials, unlike senior civil servants, serve the council and its committees as a whole, not merely the dominant group in those bodies.

The system of government by committee resembles the ancient institutions of government in the Channel Islands. Attempts have recently been

26. It is thought that the Attorney-General could obtain an injunction to restrain the introduction of such a bill before it was submitted to Parliament. See p. 87.

27. On delegation, see pp. 400, 402.

made (on the whole unsuccessfully) to adapt it so as to fit the needs of government in a few of Britain's minuscule dependent territories.

Members

Under the new system, county councillors will be elected for a period of four years to represent electoral divisions; all will retire together. District councillors will represent wards; in metropolitan districts, one third will retire in each year other than an election year for the county council; in others, councillors may either retire together every fourth year or follow the metropolitan district pattern. In London terms of office are for three years: councillors retire together. There is no provision for a dissolution between fixed dates of elections. There are to be no aldermen on the new councils, but they may elect honorary aldermen; the aldermanic institution in London is to be phased out. The first elections to the new councils were held in 1973.

The basic rules governing the conduct of local elections are similar to those for parliamentary elections. The qualifications of voters are almost identical;[28] qualification to vote can no longer be founded exclusively on the occupation of property.[29] To be qualified for election as a councillor, however, a person must either be on the local register of electors or have been resident or have occupied property or have had his principal place of work within the area of the local authority for the twelve months preceding nomination day and the date of the election.[30] There are also differences in the list of disqualifications.[31] The main disqualification is tenure of an office of profit at the disposal of the local authority or any of its committees; this disqualifies not only council officials but also local schoolteachers.[32] Bankruptcy, surcharge by a district auditor,[33] conviction for corrupt or illegal practices, and incurring a sentence of three months' imprisonment within five years of an election, also disqualify. Qualification to sit may be challenged either by an election petition or by moving for an injunction and a declaration that the seat is vacant. A council cannot expel one of its members, but a member's seat becomes vacant if he absents himself from meetings for six consecutive months without leave.

The chairmen and vice-chairmen of county and district councils may be paid such expense allowances as the council thinks reasonable. Other

28. For parliamentary elections, see pp. 242–3. Peers may, however, vote in local government elections.
29. Representation of the People Act 1969, s. 15.
30. Local Government Act 1972, s. 79.
31. ss. 80, 81.
32. Subject to certain exceptions (ss. 80(2), (3), 81(4)).
33. See p. 409, especially note 94, for the new position.

members of the council will receive travelling and subsistence allowances, and a new flat-rate taxable attendance allowance or (for non-elected committee members) a small reimbursement for loss of earnings while on council business.[34] The burden of committee work can be substantial,[35] and the services of council members are almost gratuitous.

We have noted that no comprehensive body of rules as yet regulates conflicts of private and public interest among M.P.s.[36] For members of local authorities there are statutory rules.[37] Their general effect is as follows. A member who has a direct or indirect financial interest in a matter arising before the council or any of its committees must disclose that interest as soon as practicable, and he is disqualified from speaking or voting on that matter save where his interest is so remote or insignificant that it cannot reasonably be regarded as likely to influence him. Non-compliance with these requirements is a criminal offence, and if a disqualified member takes part in a proceeding analogous to that of a judicial tribunal (for example, where the council is exercising licensing functions), the decision can be quashed at the instance of a person aggrieved.[38] But on grounds of necessity or in the interests of the inhabitants of the area the Secretary of State for the Environment may remove a statutory disability imposed on a member. This dispensing power has been liberally exercised where exemption is requested from disqualification for speaking on a matter, less liberally where exemption from disqualification for voting is sought.

The incidence of corrupt practices in local government is believed to be very low. Allegations of nepotism and undue influence in the making of appointments and the exercise of discretionary allocative functions (for example, in grants of council tenancies or planning permission, or in placing contracts) are more familiar but very hard to substantiate or disprove.[39] The Government has accepted in principle that there should be a Commission for Local Administration, drawing upon the experience of the Parliamentary Commissioner for Administration but distinct from his office, to investigate complaints of maladministration by local authori-

34. ss. 3(5), 5(4), 173, 174.

35. County borough councillors spent an average of two and a half hours a day on council business (Cmnd 4040 (1969), § 506).

36. See pp. 319–20.

37. See 1972 Act, ss. 94–8 (consolidating pre-existing law with minor modifications), for details.

38. *R.* v. *Hendon R.D.C., ex p. Chorley* [1933] 2 K.B. 696 (grant of opposed planning permission). cf. *Murray* v. *Epsom Local Board* [1897] 1 Ch. 35 (decision to remove obstructions to passage of vehicles; interest of member had no effect on validity of decision).

39. See the interesting article by D. E. Regan and A. J. A. Morris, 'Local Government Corruption and Public Confidence' [1969] *Public Law* 132.

ties.[40] But no system of independent investigation can be expected to reveal the extent to which local businessmen benefit from the inside information they obtain about council policies in their public capacities.[41] In fairness, one must also emphasize the accessibility of councillors to their constituents, and the zeal with which many of them seek to obtain redress for legitimate grievances. In a sense they are themselves local Ombudsmen.

Meetings

Meetings of councils are largely concerned with consideration and ratification of reports and recommendations by committees and officers. Discussions tend to become more animated when politically contentious issues arise. The growth of party politics in local government is a modern phenomenon; Labour groups in particular will cleave to a party line and may enforce discipline by the sanction of expulsion from the party group. There has been a concomitant growth in Conservative, Liberal and Scottish and Welsh Nationalist councillors. A dwindling proportion of local councillors, particularly in rural areas, stand as Independents or as members of Ratepayers' Associations; often they are crypto-Conservatives. Nowadays local elections give a rough indication of trends of national political opinion, but turn-outs at the polls are low; moreover, the personal standing of candidates at local elections matters far more than the qualities of individual candidates at parliamentary elections.

Council meetings are presided over by the chairman. Procedure is regulated by standing orders, which may give the council power to exclude a member for disorderly conduct. Under the Public Bodies (Admission to Meetings) Act 1960, members of the public and the press are entitled to be present at meetings of the council, committees of the whole council and local education committees, unless the authority resolves that publicity would be contrary to the public interest by reason of the confidential nature of the business to be transacted or for any other special reason. This principle of publicity did not extend to meetings of other council committees, even committees to which executive decision-making powers had been delegated by the council; but the principle was thus extended by section 100 of the 1972 Act.[42] Members of the public and the local press are entitled to inspect council minutes[43] but not the minutes of council committees.[44]

40. See, for example, Department of Environment Circular 121/72, § 33. Proposals for the creation of Commissioners for Local Administration had been made in *The Citizen and his Council* (Justice, 1969) – the 'Garner Report'.

41. cf. the Management Report (above), § 547.

42. Meetings of sub-committees still appear to be excluded.

43. Local Government Act 1972, s. 228(1).

44. *Wilson* v. *Evans* [1962] 2 Q.B. 283.

Committees

Committee structure depends partly on the functions vested in a local authority. Under the 1972 Act the number of committees that a local authority is *required* to appoint is reduced, but the relevant authority must appoint an education committee, a police committee and a social services committee. There are also likely to be a finance committee, committees dealing with the various services administered by the authority (for example, housing, planning, parks), probably a general purposes committee and an establishment (staff) committee , and *ad hoc* committees constituted for special purposes. There may be joint committees of two or more authorities. All committees of the council other than the finance committee and statutory committees whose composition is prescribed by law may co-opt outside members provided that two-thirds of the committee consists of members of the council. This numerical limitation does not apply to sub-committees.[45]

The powers vested in a committee may be to make recommendations to the council, or to make decisions which are merely reported to the council, or a combination of both types. A council is entitled to delegate to a committee or sub-committee (except in the case of statutory committees) any power to make decisions on behalf of the council other than power to raise money. Such a committee may also delegate powers to sub-committees.[46] These express grants of power overcome the common-law rule against sub-delegation (*delegatus non potest delegare*).[47] The council retains a concurrent power to make decisions within the scope of the delegated area,[48] but if the committee has already made a decision directly affecting individual interests the council cannot lawfully rescind or vary it,[49] though it may proceed to revoke the authority of the committee or any of its members.[50] Delegation relationships have brought forth a crop of technical legal problems, some of which remain unsolved.[51]

There is, of course, no legal reason why a committee or sub-committee endowed with executive powers should not empower a group of members or its chairman to recommend decisions (in consultation with senior officials) in individual cases, subject to the committee's or sub-committee's

45. 1972 Act, ss. 101, 102.
46. ibid.
47. *Cook* v. *Ward* (1877) 2 C.P.D. 255. Delegation of decision-making power to a sub-committee was generally unlawful before the 1972 Act.
48. *Huth* v. *Clarke* (1890) 25 Q.B.D. 391; 1972 Act, s. 101(4).
49. *Battelley* v. *Finsbury B.C.* (1958) 56 L.G.R. 165 (appointment of a council official by a committee).
50. *Manton* v. *Brighton B.C.* [1951] 2 K.B. 393.
51. See de Smith, *Judicial Review of Administrative Action* (3rd edn), ch. 6.

subsequent approval. This is in fact how a great number of detailed decisions are taken by local authorities.

Officials

The principal officer of a local authority is the chief executive or clerk to the council. His status has not been quite the same as that of a permanent secretary to a government Department. He has had no general authority to act in the council's name, and his hierarchical authority over other 'departmental' heads (for example, the surveyor, or the chief education officer) has been nebulous and incomplete. Clerks to the larger local authorities have almost invariably been solicitors; the lawyer plays a more prominent role in local administration than in the civil service. But under the new system a more varied set of patterns of authority is likely to be introduced, and it is to be expected that the chief executive will frequently not be a lawyer.[52]

Statutory obligations are cast on various classes of local authorities to appoint specified officers (for example, chief education officer, inspectors of weights and measures); the list has been shortened by the 1972 Act,[53] and there is no express obligation to appoint a clerk to the council or a treasurer, though clearly councils will have to appoint officers of comparable status. Of the senior officers, some are appointable or dismissible only with the consent of a Minister; but no Minister enjoys a power in respect of local government officers corresponding to the Home Secretary's power to retire a chief constable.

Superannuation is determined by statute; the Secretary of State for the Environment has appellate functions in individual cases. Pay and conditions of service are negotiated by national and provincial councils composed of representatives of the local authorities and their employees. National staff commissions to advise the Secretary of State on such matters as recruitment and transfer have been appointed under the 1972 Act. Unlike civil servants, local government officers do not hold office subject to an overriding common-law rule of dismissibility at pleasure. Many local officers have binding contracts of employment. By statute, they are to hold office on 'such reasonable terms and conditions, including conditions as to remuneration' as the appointing authority thinks fit.[54] In some instances a Secretary of State's concurrence is required before they can be removed.

52. cf. *The New Local Authorities: Management and Structure* (HMSO, 1972), a report of a study group appointed jointly by the Secretary of State for the Environment and the local authority associations. See also, on powers of officials generally, p. 402.
53. s. 112(1), (3), (4).
54. s. 112(2).

An officer who is unfairly dismissed may now be awarded compensation by an industrial tribunal, which may also recommend that he be reinstated.[55]

On the whole, the legal powers and duties of local government officers in relation to the public have been very limited. This generalization must be qualified. In the first place, special fiduciary duties have been cast on a borough or county treasurer in the interests of the ratepayers, and if he complies with an order to pay out money for a purpose unauthorized by law he may be sued for recovery of the money or restrained by injunction[56] or surcharged following adverse findings by the district auditor.[57] Under the 1972 reforms it may be that his position in these matters is no different from that of any other local government officer. Secondly, an officer having ostensible authority to bind his employers by contract may bind the local authority according to the general principles of agency although he is not in fact acting within the scope of his authorization.[58] Thirdly, since 1968, a local planning authority has been able to delegate to one of its officers power to determine in writing various classes of planning applications, and the authority will be bound by his decisions.[59] But this was a limited exception to the general rule, which denied local government officers power to bind their employees in such a way. However, when the 1972 Act is operative there will be a radical change in the law on this matter. For local authorities and their committees and sub-committees will have a general power (subject only to limited exceptions), to 'arrange' for the discharge of their functions by an official.[60]

Suppose that, under the new system, an official to whom no authorization has in fact been given purports to give a prospective builder an assurance that planning permission is not required for certain constructional work. The builder goes ahead on the faith of this assurance. The local authority then issues an enforcement notice, requiring him to discontinue the work and to demolish the buildings already put up, because he needed planning permission and did not obtain it. The builder contends that the local authority is 'estopped' (debarred) from repudiating the

55. cf. pp. 195, 548.

56. See *Att.-Gen.* v. *Wilson* (1840) Cr. & Phil. 1; *Att.-Gen.* v. *De Winton* [1906] 2 Ch. 106. For financial duties of officers and disclosure of pecuniary interest in contracts, see 1972 Act, ss. 114, 115, 117.

57. See p. 409.

58. On agency in public law, see pp. 411, 610. The agent cannot bind the local authority to act *ultra vires*.

59. Town and Country Planning Act 1971, s. 4, reproducing s. 64 of the Town and Country Planning Act 1968.

60. Local Government Act 1972, s. 101. A local authority can even arrange for its functions in relation to a statutory committee to be discharged by an official. Power to raise money cannot be delegated.

unauthorized assurance given by its officer, on which he has relied to his detriment. What then?

The problem of the unauthorized or misleading assurance has arisen quite frequently in administrative law, and not only in local government contexts. And it has been answered in different ways,[61] for there are competing principles at work and a court sometimes moulds the law in order to do justice in a particular case. The general principle is that if public bodies or their officers give assurances that lie outside their powers, such assurances are void;[62] they can go back on them, for they cannot extend their powers by their own conduct.[63] This principle is subject to a recognized qualification; it is open to a court to treat minor deviations from the prescribed *form* or *procedure* for exercising a power as being merely a non-compliance with a 'directory' requirement, not affecting the validity of what has been done.[64] But there is another, more radical principle, which has gained some ground of late. It can be expressed thus: when public bodies and their officers, in their dealings with a citizen, take it upon themselves to assert authority in a matter concerning him, the citizen is entitled to rely on their having that authority (and the public body will be estopped from denying its existence) if he cannot reasonably be expected to know its limits, and he ought not to suffer merely because they have overstepped their power.[65] So stated, the principle is too wide. But perhaps it can be accepted in a situation where an *officer* has exceeded his authority or acted without authority, *provided that* the employing body had power to do the act itself.[66] This has to be put tentatively in the existing confusion of the case-law.[67] However, we can see that there are at least two methods by which

61. For the particular situation set out above, contrast *Southend-on-Sea Corporation* v. *Hodgson (Wickford) Ltd* [1962] 1 Q.B. 416 (see also *Princes Investments Ltd* v. *Frimley and Camberley U.D.C.*, *ibid.* 681) (assurance void) with *Lever Finance Ltd* v. *Westminster (City) L.B.C.* [1971] 1 Q.B. 222 (C.A.) (assurance binding).

62. See, for example, *Howell* v. *Falmouth Boat Construction Co.* [1951] A.C. 837 at 845, 847.

63. See, for example, *Rhyl U.D.C.* v. *Rhyl Amusements Ltd* [1959] 1 W.L.R. 465 (council entitled to asserted invalidity of lease which it had granted in breach of statute).

64. As in *Wells* v. *Minister of Housing and Local Government* [1967] 1 W.L.R. 1000 (informal determination that planning permission not required).

65. *Robertson* v. *Minister of Pensions* [1949] 1 K.B. 227, per Denning J.; *Falmouth Boat Construction Co.* v. *Howell* [1950] 1 K.B. 16 at 26, per Denning L.J., disapproved in the House of Lords in *Howell*'s case.

66. A possible justification of the actual decisions in *Robertson* and *Lever* (notes 61, 65, above). But what if the officer's powers are limited by statute? cf. p. 610, below.

67. For recent discussions of the difficulties in reconciling the principles and the case law, see Turpin, *Government Contracts*, pp. 30–33; Bradley [1971] *Camb. L.J.* 3; Evans (1971) 34 *Mod. L. Rev.* 335; Gould (1971) 87 *L.Q.R.* 15; Fazal [1972] *Public Law* 43. See also, pp. 609–10, below. Other decisions, showing judicial reluctance to allow local

a court could reach an answer favourable to the builder who found himself in a plight in our last paragraph. Quite apart from that, the new regime will do away with an anomaly and may promote efficiency by giving officials more scope for initiative.

A local authority may also be vicariously liable in tort for damage caused by negligent mis-statements by its employees in circumstances where there is a duty to exercise reasonable care.[68]

Local government employees remain personally liable for torts committed by them, whether or not they were purporting to act in the course of their duties and whether or not the local authority is vicariously liable for the tort. But some of them have statutory powers to enter property, carry out inspections, surveys and tests, seize and destroy contaminated food and so on, which might be actionable trespasses or nuisances if done by private persons; and in some instances officers committing torts in the purported exercise of public functions have been exempted from liability provided that they have acted in good faith.[69]

Finance

The principles set out below are expected to be modified by forthcoming legislation about local government finance.

Income

Local authorities derive their income from three main sources: rates; rentals, transport undertakings, entertainments and other facilities and services; and central government grants. Rates account for a third of their income and general grants for a slightly higher percentage. Heavy dependence on central grants has been a long-standing source of weakness in English local government.

Rates[70] are local taxes, imposed not on income or wealth but upon the occupation of land and buildings. For each rating area a valuation officer

---

authorities to go back on apparently non-binding assurances, where it seems unfair to allow them to do so, are *Re L. (A.C.) (an Infant)* [1971] 3 All E.R. 743; *R.* v. *Liverpool Corporation* [1972] 2 Q.B. 299 (pp. 586–7, below).

68. cf. *Hedley, Byrne & Co.* v. *Heller & Partners Ltd* [1964] A.C. 465; *Ministry of Housing and Local Government* v. *Sharp* [1970] 2 Q.B. 223.

69. See, for example, Public Health Act 1936, s. 305. In general the courts will construe this immunity as extending only to situations where the officer has also exercised reasonable care.

70. The law of rating was consolidated by the General Rate Act 1967. See also Local Government Act 1972, ss. 147–9.

of the Inland Revenue compiles a valuation list, incorporating his assessment of the net annual value of each hereditament. The rating authority (a London borough or county district) decides annually how much it needs to raise by way of rates, and fixes the general rate at x or y pence in the pound accordingly. Thus, if the rateable value of its area is £1 million, and it has to raise £600,000, it will decide to levy a rate of 60p in the pound, and a householder whose property is valued at £200 per annum will have to pay £120 in rates in two instalments. The Greater London Council, county councils and *ad hoc* local statutory authorities obtain income from rates by issuing an annual precept to the rating authorities within their area; the rating authorities must have regard to the amount precepted when determining their own rates.

Appeals against individual assessments in the valuation list lie to local valuation courts and thence to the Lands Tribunal. Farm land is not liable to rates, and certain other classes of hereditaments are partly or wholly exempt. Ratepayers whose income is low may be entitled to claim a rebate from the local authority.

Although hallowed by antiquity and deficient in the excruciating complexities obfuscating some forms of central taxation, rates are not a satisfactory source of revenue. They bear most heavily on the occupier with a large family and a large house. Moreover, the product of the same percentage rate will vary enormously from one rating area to another. For example, in 1969 the total rateable value of Brighton was more than four times higher than that of Halifax and its rateable value per head nearly three times higher, yet its population was only 74 per cent larger.[71] Both were county boroughs. If Halifax were to provide services comparable in quality to those of Brighton, either its general rate would have to be a great deal higher or it would have to be heavily subsidized by the central government. And very big disparities between the services offered by authorities equal in status are not politically acceptable.

The chequered history of central grants need not be traced. At one time the percentage grant was favoured, but this tended to direct local authorities from the path of economy unless their conduct of the service in question was subject to detailed regulation and scrutiny. A 50 per cent grant is still paid to local police authorities. Miscellaneous grants and subsidies are paid for specific purposes – for example, for housing construction and improvements, for aspects of the acquisition and development of land for planning purposes, for the construction and improvement of major roads, and for the benefit of local authorities having special responsibilities be-

71. These calculations are based on Cmnd 4040 (1969), pp. 332, 338, 340. The figures for receipts from rents of council houses were not given; these were probably higher in Halifax than in Brighton.

cause of a high concentration of Commonwealth immigrants.[72] Grants are also made to meet the cost of rate rebates. The other form of grant is the block grant, not appropriated to specific services; its nomenclature has varied, but is now the 'rate support grant'. By 1972 it amounted to some 80 per cent of the total grants to local authorities. The sum to be allocated is determined by the Secretary of State in the light of the general economic situation and after consultation with local authority associations; he lays before the House of Commons an order giving effect to his decision, and it will have effect for at least two years if approved by resolution of the House.[73] The sums received by individual authorities vary considerably: they are dependent on local financial resources compared with the national average, and an assortment of factors such as population density, road mileage, and the proportions of schoolchildren and old people. Rises in the costs of local authority services are borne partly out of central government funds, and the amount of the central grant has increased. But although block grants offer local authorities greater freedom of manoeuvre than ear-marked grants, the Secretary of State is enabled to control expenditure by local authorities in general and thereby to influence expenditure on particular services,[74] and if he is dissatisfied with the standards maintained by an authority, he may reduce the grant to that authority after he has given it an opportunity to make representations to him and then obtained the approval of the House of Commons for his decision.[75]

Borrowing

Local authorities have general statutory borrowing powers for acquiring land and constructing buildings and public works: indeed nearly all major capital expenditure is financed out of loans. The exercise of borrowing powers has been subject to detailed and strict central control, which was relaxed in 1971.[76] A loan sanction must be obtained from the Secretary of

72. On the last point, see Local Government Act 1966, s. 11. And see, for a more general power to make grants to especially needy authorities, Local Government Grants (Social Need) Act 1969.

73. But a one-year rate support order has been made for 1973–4. See Local Government Act 1972, Sched. 13, § 27(2).

74. The Report of the Committee on the Management of Local Government observed (§ 262) that the purpose of the new rate support grant was to enable the central government for the first time to influence the expenditure on all local authority services.

75. Local Government Act 1966, s. 4. For a discussion of possible alternative ways of financing local authorities, see the Green Paper, *The Future Shape of Local Government Finance* (Cmnd 4741 (1971)).

76. Department of the Environment Circular 2/70, restricting the need for specific loan sanction approval to key sectors and items of large-scale expenditure from April 1971. See also Local Government Act 1972, Sched. 13, §§ 1–12.

State for the Environment and may be refused for a number of reasons, including the need for restricting the general level of public investment and spending.

Expenditure

Spending by local authorities is subject to more direct legal restraints. The general rule is that local authorities can spend money only for purposes authorized by statute. Any other expenditure will be *ultra vires* and can be restrained in proceedings instituted in the High Court by the Attorney-General (on his own initiative or at the relation of a ratepayer)[77] claiming an injunction or a declaration or both. Acts reasonably incidental to powers expressly granted will be valid. To take two familiar examples, one on each side of the line, a local authority could lawfully set up a stationery, printing and binding works to deal with council documents though not explicitly empowered to do so,[78] but an authority empowered to establish washhouses where people could come to do their own washing could not embark upon a venture in municipal enterprise by setting up a laundry where most of the work was done by council employees.[79] The 1972 Act stretches the concept of incidental powers by providing that local authorities have power to do anything calculated to facilitate, or conducive or incidental to, the discharge of any of their functions.[80]

The courts have held that local authority funds are impressed with some characteristics of a public trust,[81] and that councils owe a fiduciary duty to their ratepayers to spend money only for purposes authorized by law and in accordance with proper legal principles. For example, local authorities cannot, in the absence of express statutory authority, subsidize the rents of private tenants, irrespective of the tenants' means,[82] or make free gifts to the aged,[83] or set themselves up as model employers and pay wages far in excess of those paid by private commercial or industrial undertakings. In the immortal words of Lord Atkinson (*Roberts* v. *Hopwood* (1925)), the council must have regard to business-like considerations and the interests of their ratepayers, and not allow itself to be guided by 'eccentric principles of

77. Or even possibly a ratepayer suing on his own behalf: *Prescott* v. *Birmingham Corporation* [1955] Ch. 210 (an action for a declaration). See p. 603, note 38.

78. *Att.-Gen.* v. *Smethwick Corporation* [1932] 1 Ch. 562.

79. *Att.-Gen.* v. *Fulham Corporation* [1921] 1 Ch. 440.

80. Local Government Act 1972, s. 111(1).

81. See note 56, above.

82. *Taylor* v. *Munrow* [1960] 1 W.L.R. 151.

83. *Prescott* v. *Birmingham Corporation* (see above; free travel concessions on corporation's transport undertaking). What was there held unlawful is now authorized by statute: Travel Concessions Act 1964.

socialistic philanthropy, or by a feminist ambition to secure the equality of the sexes in the matter of wages . . .'.[84]

Since 1963 local authorities have been empowered by statute to incur a small amount of expenditure for any purpose not otherwise authorized which in their opinion is in the interests of their area or its inhabitants.[85] To this extent they have been relieved of the inhibitions imposed by the *ultra vires* doctrine. The Royal Commission on Local Government's recommendation[86] that a general spending power be conferred on main local authorities was not implemented.

On one view, some boroughs were exempt from most of these restrictions. Other local authorities, as statutory corporations, were limited to statutory functions. But boroughs created by royal charter before 1835 were common-law corporations. As such, they had all the powers of a natural person, save in so far as they were regulated by statute. In the performance of statutory powers and duties, they had to comply with the procedural and substantive requirements imposed by the Act. However, where the field was not occupied by statute, they could enter it and spend money out of the general rate fund for a purpose such as setting up a trading enterprise, provided that they did not encroach on vested legal rights. The controversy over this matter, which was never conclusively resolved,[87] has become academic in so far as the new local authorities constituted under the London Government Act 1963 and the Local Government Act 1972 are statutory corporations even though some may still be styled boroughs.[88]

Audit

Under the system in force in 1972, the accounts of all local authorities other than non-metropolitan boroughs, and also the accounts of several im-

84. [1925] A.C. 578 at 594. See, for the background and aftermath, B. Keith-Lucas, 'Poplarism' [1962] *Public Law* 52. Under the law as it then stood, the authority had an ostensibly unrestricted discretion to pay such wages as it thought fit to its employees; the district auditor and the courts imposed limitations on the exercise of this discretion. The present law empowers local authorities to pay 'reasonable remuneration'.

85. Local Government (Financial Provisions) Act 1963, s. 6, replaced by Local Government Act 1972, s. 137. The sum to be thus used must not exceed the product of a 2p rate in any given year (1972 Act).

86. Cmnd 4040 (1969), § 323.

87. See, for conflicting opinions, C. A. Cross, *Principles of Local Government Law* (4th edn), pp. 10–14, and J. F. Garner, *Administrative Law* (3rd edn), pp. 285–6. The decision in *Att.-Gen.* v. *Leicester Corporation* [1943] Ch. 86 supported the broad view of a borough corporation's spending powers; but see *Tynemouth Corporation* v. *Att.-Gen.* [1899] A.C. 293 at 302–3; *Att.-Gen.* v. *Manchester Corporation* [1906] 1 Ch. 643 at 651. The decision of the Court of Appeal in *Prescott*'s case (above) and the practice of district auditors reflected the narrow view.

88. The City of London Corporation is still a common-law corporation.

portant services administered by those boroughs, were subject to district audit. District auditors are civil servants appointed by the Secretary of State for the Environment but enjoying a substantial degree of independence. Boroughs had elected or professional auditors, unless they opted for district audit. Under the 1972 Act,[89] county and district councils can choose whether to come under the district auditor or an approved private auditor.

Public notice is given of the annual district audit and the accounts must be open to public inspection. Any local government elector may appear before the district auditor and object to an item in the accounts. Under the system in force in 1972, it was the district auditor's duty to disallow any item contrary to law[90] and surcharge the amount on the councillors or officers responsible for incurring or authorizing it, unless the Secretary of State had already sanctioned the expenditure.[91] Appeal at the instance of a person aggrieved by the district auditor's decision lay to the Secretary of State or to the High Court.[92] A person surcharged could, as well as or instead of appealing, apply for remission of the surcharge on the ground that he had acted reasonably or in the belief that his action was authorized by law. Private auditors had no power of surcharge.

Under the new system, the district auditor may certify that a loss was due to a person's misconduct; subject to that person's right of appeal to the court, the money is recoverable from him by the local authority. In other cases the district auditor cannot disallow expenditure contrary to law; he must instead apply to the court[93] for a declaration to that effect, unless the expenditure has been sanctioned by the Secretary of State.[94] An aggrieved elector may appeal to the court against an auditor's decision not to certify or not to apply for a declaration.

89. ss. 154–66. For the earlier system, see Local Government Act 1933, Part 10.

90. In *Roberts* v. *Hopwood* (p. 407 above), payment of a minimum wage of £4 a week to unskilled council employees was held to be an abuse of discretion and, therefore, contrary to law; the district auditor's disallowance of the excess over what was reasonably justifiable was upheld in the courts in the face of a challenge by surcharged councillors.

91. Even so, the legality of the payment could still be challenged in the High Court by the Attorney-General (see above).

92. Not to the Secretary of State if the sum in question exceeded £500. A special case on a point of law could be stated by the Secretary of State for the High Court. There is no appeal to the Secretary of State under the 1972 Act.

93. The High Court, *or* a county court if the sum involved is within the limits of that court's jurisdiction; otherwise the High Court (1972 Act, s. 161 (137)).

94. The court has a discretion whether or not to impose a surcharge (see s. 161 (3)). Surcharge may entail disqualifications (see p. 397) under the law before the 1972 Act; but under the 1972 Act only where a loss exceeding £2000 due to wilful misconduct is certified does the person responsible become disqualified for five years (s. 161 (7)).

If the audit is conducted by an approved private auditor, an aggrieved elector[95] *may* and the private auditor himself *must* apply to the Secretary of State, where it appears that there has been unlawful expenditure or other irregularities, for an extraordinary audit to be undertaken by a district auditor.

In the new system, all the decisions about disallowance (in the absence of misconduct) and surcharge are taken by courts.

Local authorities and the courts: in brief

Like other public corporations, local authorities can sue and be sued, prosecute and be prosecuted, in the courts. They are not Crown servants and have never enjoyed the legal immunities and privileges of the Crown;[96] thus, courts can award coercive orders, such as injunctions and orders of mandamus, against them.[97] Their civil liability is determined by rules essentially the same as those applicable to non-public bodies, subject to a number of particular exceptions.

1. The power of a local authority to institute civil proceedings in its own name for the protection of the interests of local inhabitants has, on the whole, been narrowly interpreted;[98] it appears to be wider under the 1972 Act.[99] Yet in a recent case under the 1933 Act a local authority was held entitled to bring an action for libel against a hostile critic for the protection of its 'governing reputation'.[100]

2. Aspects of the *ultra vires* doctrine have already been noted. If a local authority steps outside the limits of its public powers, the defect cannot be cured merely by the acquiescence of persons adversely affected;[101] nor, *in general*, is the local authority itself precluded from asserting the invalidity of its own acts if another person seeks to rely on their legality.[102] Nor is it estopped by its acquiescence in acts by other persons from exercising its

95. Who has a statutory right to inspect the accounts even if they are not subject to district audit.

96. The leading case, dealing with the liability of an *ad hoc* statutory authority for tort (but also governing the liability of local authorities) at a time when the Crown was exempt from tortious liability is *Mersey Docks and Harbour Board Trustees* v. *Gibbs* (1866) L.R.1 H.L.93.

97. On Crown privilege and local authorities, see *Blackpool Corporation* v. *Locker* [1948] 1 K.B. 349; but see p. 623, note 23 below.

98. Local Government Act 1933, s. 276; p. 604 below.

99. s. 222.

100. *Bognor Regis U.D.C.* v. *Campion* [1972] 2 Q.B. 169 (criticized by Tony Weir [1972A] *Camb. L. J.* 238). The defendant's bill of costs was enormous.

101. *Swallow & Pearson* v. *Middlesex C.C.* [1953] 1 W.L.R. 422.

102. *Rhyl U.D.C.* v. *Rhyl Amusements Ltd* [1959] 1 W.L.R. 465; but see p. 403.

powers or duties to assert its rights against them;[103] and in the absence of statutory authority to that effect it cannot grant a valid dispensation from compliance with a statute or by-law.[104]

3. By-laws, as we have already seen, can be impugned on various grounds, each of which can be classified under the general rubric of *vires*.[105]

4. Contracts of local authorities are governed basically by private law rules, though they may contain standard terms and the disparity of bargaining power between the parties (for example, in a contract for letting a council house or flat) may be such that a contract will be analogous to a by-law. Since 1960 local authority contracts have not had to be made under seal. The general rules of agency apply, but a local authority can neither make nor become bound by a contract which is *ultra vires*. Apart from the effects of the *ultra vires* doctrine, freedom of contract is not absolute. The appointment and tenure of certain senior local government officers are regulated by statute. And there is a general principle of law that public authorities cannot preclude themselves from exercising their more important discretionary powers or performing their public duties by incompatible contractual or other undertakings. [106] For example, a local authority cannot bind itself to grant or not to revoke a grant of planning permission[107] or not to make a particular kind of by-law.[108] If it makes a by-law rendering performance of a contractor's obligations more burdensome, the contractor cannot thereupon repudiate the contract, though the actual operation of the burden may subsequently entitle him to treat the contract as having been frustrated.[109]

French administrative law adopts a different and more flexible approach to contracts of a public nature.[110] They are governed by a special body of rules applied in administrative courts. These rules are designed to serve the primacy of the public interest but to do justice to the private contractor.

103. *Islington Vestry* v. *Hornsey U.D.C.* [1900] 1 Ch. 695 (informal agreement to receive sewage could be repudiated; local authority could not lawfully bind itself thus).

104. *Yabbicom* v. *R.* [1899] 1 Q.B. 444; *Redbridge L.B.C.* v. *Jaques* [1970] 1 W.L.R. 1604; *Cambridgeshire & Isle of Ely C.C.* v. *Rust* [1972] 2 Q.B. 426. For an example of an express dispensing power, see Greater London Council (General Powers) Act 1971, s. 4.

105. See generally *Kruse* v. *Johnson* [1898] 2 Q.B. 91; and pp. 350–51 above.

106. See, for example, *Ayr Harbour Trustees* v. *Oswald* (1883) 8 App. Cas. 623; and generally, J. D. B. Mitchell, *The Contracts of Public Authorities*; p. 589, below.

107. *Ransom & Luck Ltd* v. *Surbiton B.C.* [1949] Ch. 180.

108. *Cory (William) & Son Ltd* v. *City of London Corporation* [1951] 2 K.B. 475 (dicta).

109. *Cory's* case (above).

110. See Mitchell, op. cit.; H. Street, *Governmental Liability*, ch. 3; L. Neville Brown and J. F. Garner, *French Administrative Law*, pp. 66–8, 103–8.

For instance, the public authority will not be coerced into performing its obligations, and the other party will not normally be entitled to repudiate merely because performance has become very onerous through administrative action or supervening circumstances; but the courts have wide powers to supervise the execution of public contracts, and to vary their terms where the public interest or fairness to the individual so demands, directing the payment of indemnities and compensation to the private party where no damages would be obtainable as of right in English law.[111]

5. Local authorities are not liable in tort for doing what Parliament has authorized them to do, but the general rule[112] is that they must exercise their powers reasonably so as to avoid unnecessary encroachments on private rights; otherwise they may be liable for negligence, nuisance or trespass.[113] There is no sound reason of principle why a local authority should be immune from liability because it is acting *ultra vires* when it commits a tort,[114] though if the tort has been committed by one of its servants[115] there may be difficulty in establishing for the purpose of vicarious liability that he was acting in the general course of his employment.[116] In some contexts local authorities are subject to liability without fault and liability for breach of statutory duty on much the same basis as private persons. Highway authorities used to be exempt from civil liability for injury attributable to negligent failure to repair, but this immunity was abolished by statute.[117] There is no general principle of law that public authorities are free from liability in respect of damage caused by non-feasance (inaction).[118] The wilful misuse of statutory powers, causing economic loss, may possibly be an independent tort,[119] and some forms of misconduct in public office are common-law misdemeanours.[120] Torts com-

111. See, on Crown contracts, Colin Turpin, *Government Contracts* (showing that British central government *practice* is not so very different from French *law*); p. 612.

112. Subject to various exceptions: see, for example, *Marriage* v. *East Norfolk Rivers Catchment Board* [1950] 1 K.B. 284; *Dormer* v. *Newcastle-upon-Tyne Corporation* [1940] 2 K.B. 204 at 217–19 (applying a narrow test of the duty to act reasonably).

113. The leading monograph on this topic is still Gleeson Robinson, *Public Authorities and Legal Liability* (1925).

114. See *Campbell* v. *Paddington Corporation* [1911] 1 K.B. 869 (held liable).

115. On the question who is a servant of a local authority in attributing vicarious liability for his torts, see *Stanbury* v. *Exeter Corporation* [1905 2 K.B. 838; *Fisher* v. *Oldham Corporation* [1930] 2 K.B. 364.

116. cf. P. S. Atiyah, *Vicarious Liability in the Law of Torts*, pp. 383–7.

117. Highways (Miscellaneous Provisions) Act 1961.

118. But in some contexts the distinction between misfeasance and non-feasance is still material: see *Bradbury* v. *Enfield L.B.C.* [1967] 1 W.L.R. 1311.

119. See *David* v. *Abdul Cader* [1963] 1 W.L.R. 834, and de Smith, *Judicial Review of Administrative Action* (3rd edn), pp. 281, 296–7.

120. See, for example, *R.* v. *Llewellyn-Jones* [1968] 1 Q.B. 429.

mitted by public officers (and presumably public bodies) acting arbitrarily and oppressively may lead to an award of exemplary damages.[121]

6. The exercise of discretionary powers by local authorities is governed by the general standards applied by the courts to other public bodies. These will be considered in a later chapter.[122] The performance of certain public duties cast upon a local authority may be enforced by an order of mandamus. Normally a person cannot recover damages against a public body for failure to exercise a statutory *power* (or dilatoriness in exercising a power) which could have mitigated or averted the loss sustained,[123] but the position may be different where that body has taken it upon itself to assume control over the matter.[124]

7. Legal disputes (for example, about entitlement to money or property) between two local authorities, or between a local authority and another public corporation or a government Department, may be resolved by the award of a binding declaration by the High Court. Again, a local authority may obtain a declaration as to the scope of its rights, duties or powers, provided that a genuine disputed question of law is directly in issue.[125]

8. Special statutory remedies are available to persons aggrieved by certain local authority decisions. From decisions to refuse or revoke a licence to carry on an occupation, an appeal may lie to a magistrates' court and thence to the Crown Court; appeals against demolition and closing orders in respect of houses unfit for human habitation lie to a county court. In such cases appeals are not usually confined to questions of law or fact; the court can review the merits of the decision and change it, paying due regard to the special knowledge of the local authority making the decision.[126] Review of local authority decisions by the superior courts is normally limited to questions of legality.

Central control reviewed[127]

Central–local government relationships are sometimes described in the language of partnership. The foregoing account has implied that if this is

121. *Broome* v. *Cassell & Co.* [1972] A.C. 1027 (dicta).

122. ch. 26. See further David Williams in J. A. Andrews (ed.), *Welsh Studies in Public Law* (1970), ch. 8.

123. *East Suffolk Rivers Catchment Board* v. *Kent* [1941] A.C. 74 (flood damage increased through dilatory repairs).

124. *Dutton* v. *Bognor Regis U.D.C.* [1972] 1 Q.B. 373 (damage attributable to negligent exercise of power to inspect building operations).

125. ch. 27. See *Ealing L.B.C.* v. *Race Relations Board* [1972] A.C. 342.

126. *Sagnata Investments Ltd* v. *Norwich Corporation* [1971] 2 Q.B. 614; p. 589.

127. The most illuminating survey is J. A. G. Griffith, *Central Departments and Local Authorities* (1966), ch. 1.

partnership, it is a partnership (to use an analogy taken from a different context) between the rider and the horse. This would be an exaggeration. There is no uniform pattern, and in providing some services the local authorities still enjoy a large measure of autonomy. Moreover, the local authority associations influence the content of parliamentary and subordinate legislation. Government Departments regularly consult them on matters affecting local interests and great weight may be given to their representations. And from time to time the associations are instrumental in the initiation of legislation, including private members' bills. Again, everyday communications between the central Departments and individual local authorities are not a one-way process, and departmental officials are made aware of local experience and problems; this awareness affects the content of policy and the manner of exerting ultimate control.

Nevertheless, the array of controls is formidable. Where Ministers have statutory responsibilities for promoting the efficiency of services provided locally, or for coordinating or managing such services on a national scale, detailed central regulation of the administration of the services tends to follow. At the very least, the Department will be concerned to ensure a national minimum standard. We have noted the extensive control exercised by the Home Secretary over police matters by means of regulations, control of senior appointments, entertaining disciplinary appeals, inspection, financial grants, compulsory amalgamation and special inquiry. The control over local educational matters – and education is the most costly local service – exercised by the Secretary of State for Education and Science is also substantial. Control of town and country planning and housing matters by the Secretary of State for the Environment, and of public health by the Secretary of State for Social Services, is somewhat less detailed; but no one reading through two years' output of town and country planning regulations will doubt the reality of central control over matters of procedure and substance. And lurking not far behind the scenes lies the Treasury, with its general responsibilities for national expenditure and economic planning.

In brief, the apparatus of departmental controls[128] includes power to make or withhold grants; to control borrowing for capital projects;[129] to prescribe rules for the conduct of a local service, directly by regulations (and in some cases administrative instructions), or indirectly through the

128. District audit is a form of central control, but the auditors are substantially autonomous quasi-judicial officers, subject to judicial rather than administrative surveillance. Similarly the Attorney-General's power to take proceedings to restrain unlawful expenditure and *ultra vires* acts generally stands on a different footing from central political and administrative controls.

129. Including the very important power to attach detailed conditions when issuing loan sanctions.

introduction of parliamentary legislation; to inspect certain services (for example, police, education); to confirm or refuse to confirm by-laws, compulsory purchase orders, educational schemes, senior appointments, and so on; to entertain appeals in respect of certain local authority decisions (for example, refusals of planning permission, disputes about the placing of children in local schools); to conduct local inquiries under particular statutory powers (for example, where objections have been lodged to compulsory purchase orders, or into complaints about the conduct of a police force); and to exercise default powers, by removing responsibility for the conduct of a service from one authority to another or taking over responsibility at the centre (as by putting in a Housing Commissioner to supersede an authority refusing to implement the Housing Finance Act 1972) or by issuing a mandatory order or obtaining from courts an order of mandamus to compel the authority to carry out its statutory duties. Against that legal background, the extra-statutory powers of central Departments to issue advisory and hortatory circulars to local authorities bear no comparison with the functions of an information bureau.

How are recent statutory reforms likely to affect this situation? In the short term, very little. The metropolitan counties will become passenger transport authorities. Shortly before the 1972 Act received the royal assent, local authorities had been required by statute to increase most of their council rents.[130] A few months later the Government acquired power to restrict rent increases.[131] In 1973 a reorganization of the National Health Service would probably deprive local authorities of ancillary health responsibilities; and local government responsibilities for water resources and sewage disposal were to be transferred to regional boards (which would admittedly comprise a majority of local authority representatives). This looked like the protraction of a familiar trend. Moreover, in the context of a compulsory national prices and incomes policy, local authority expenditure and initiative would necessarily be restricted, even though the Government had increased the rate support grant.

There will be a relaxation of minor central controls over local authorities – for example, in the matter of senior appointments. The new authorities will have more freedom to determine their own internal structure. They may attain a higher average level of efficiency than the old authorities;[132] in particular, they may be in a position to recruit higher-powered senior officials. Possibly there will be some heightening of public interest in local

130. Housing Finance Act 1972.
131. Counter-Inflation (Temporary Provisions) Act 1972.
132. Despite the unfortunate perpetuation of boundaries between urban centres and suburban areas, though the central urban areas will be reduced to the coordinate status of districts.

authority proceedings; it remains to be seen what impact will be made by constituting urban parishes, by giving the public extended access to committees, and by changes in planning procedures designed to attract public participation.[133] Yet without new independent sources of revenue, local authorities will still lack significant opportunities for enterprise and experimentation.[134] And the reasons why the central government insists on maintaining supervisory controls over the main services provided by local government will militate against dramatic change in the foreseeable future.

133. See, for example, Richard Buxton, *Local Government* (2nd edn), ch. 7; J. P. W. B. McAuslan [1971] *Public Law* 247. Structure plans (to be drawn up by county councils) cannot be submitted to the Secretary of State for approval until members of the public have been given an adequate opportunity to make representations to the authority (Town and Country Planning Act 1971, ss. 7, 8). Local plans, to be drawn up by district councils, do not necessarily have to be submitted to the Secretary of State for approval (ss. 11–14). But the tendency to devalue the role of the public local inquiry in these procedures (see also Town and Country Planning (Amendment) Act 1972, ss. 1–3, S.I. 1972, No. 1154) may work the other way. For the duty to give fuller publicity to controversial planning applications, see 1971 Act, ss. 26–8. See also p. 558.

134. Some scope for initiative, however, is available through the medium of private legislation. For some original ideas, see Report of Working Party on Local Authority, Private Enterprise Partnership Schemes (HMSO, 1972).

Part Five
Civil Rights and Freedoms

This Part of the book covers topics which are both controversial and of immediate contemporary interest.

Chapter 19 begins with a discussion of the definition of a British subject and the implications of that status. The complex rules governing the immigration and deportation of Commonwealth citizens and aliens, and the distinctions now drawn between the 'patrial' and the 'non-patrial', are also outlined. Among the statutes considered are the British Nationality Act 1948 and the Immigration Act 1971, and the rules made under the latter Act (which give special rights to nationals of Community members). We go on to discuss some aspects of the concepts of allegiance and protection (already touched on in the latter part of chapter 4) and the rules about British passports. The law on the extradition of fugitive offenders, and race relations legislation, are also brought into chapter 19, because they tend to raise the same *kinds* of issues covered in the early part of the chapter.

In chapter 20 we deal with liberty of the person. The chapter begins with comments on the possible advantages and disadvantages of a constitutional bill of rights. It then examines the main features of English law on liberty of the person, with special reference to police powers of arrest, interrogation, search and seizure; the offence of wilfully obstructing a police officer in the execution of his duty; and remedies against unlawful physical restraint, including the writ of habeas corpus. The chapter includes a brief note on the law of privacy, which has been attracting increasing attention.

Chapter 21 is concerned with another basic freedom – freedom of expression. In order to ascertain the scope of this freedom we first have to consider the circumstances in which a person may be prevented from expressing himself at all (such as the operation of the Official Secrets Acts) or through particular media – for example, the cinema, the press, the broadcasting services. Then there is the miscellany of criminal or civil wrongs that may be committed by speech or written words or pictorial representations – for instance, treason, sedition, breaches of the Official Secrets Act (the most controversial of their provisions having recently been scrutinized by the second Franks Committee), blasphemy, defamation, contempt of court or of a House of Parliament, 'insulting words and behaviour', incitement to racial hatred, and, of course, offences in connection with 'obscene' publications.

In chapter 22 we deal with freedom of assembly and association, substantially omitting the big subject of trade union law. Here again, what one is allowed to do depends on whether any other person is entitled to prevent one, and what specific wrongs one is liable to commit in attempts at self-expression. The law is closely related to that stated in chapter 21 but has a number of special features. There is no general right to conduct a public meeting in a street or an open space. Processions are subject to police regulation. What exactly are the powers of the police in these matters, and in regard to unruly demonstrations or peaceful gatherings which attract aggressive opposition? At the present time these are important questions. As we shall see, the scope of police powers and duties for the maintenance of public order is by no means clear.

Part Five concludes with a chapter on states of emergency (which are clearly regulated by statute), the powers of the Crown in wartime, and the nature of a state of martial law.

Chapter 19
Citizens, Aliens and Others

Background

The concept of a British subject at common law was rooted in the idea of allegiance, the bond which linked a man with his feudal lord. In return for allegiance a man was entitled to his lord's protection. Persons born within His Majesty's dominions owed the King natural allegiance and were his subjects.[1] Aliens within those dominions owed a temporary local allegiance. No one could divest himself of his natural allegiance; and violation of the duty of allegiance might constitute treason.

The common law was modified by statute. By eighteenth-century legislation, children of natural-born fathers became British subjects if born outside His Majesty's dominions. An Act of 1870 enabled the Secretary of State (the Home Secretary) to naturalize an alien; formerly the only means of becoming naturalized was by promoting a private Act of Parliament.

The common law governing the admission and control of aliens was obscure. On occasion aliens had been refused admission to the realm and expelled; they had, it seems, no legal redress,[2] but whether this was because the power of regulation rested on the royal prerogative was never clear.[3] In 1905 legislation was passed giving statutory powers to exclude and deport certain classes of 'undesirable' aliens.[4] In 1914 the law was strengthened, and very wide discretionary powers over aliens were continued by the Aliens Restriction (Amendment) Act 1919, which was maintained in force from year to year by parliamentary resolutions under the Expiring Laws Continuance Act. Detailed executive powers in respect of aliens were set out in Orders in Council made under the 1919 Act.

A general statutory code dealing with the methods of acquiring and

1. *Calvin*'s case (1607) 7 Co. Rep. 1a (Scotsman born after the union of the Crowns was not an alien in England).

2. *Musgrove* v. *Chun Teeong Toy* [1891] A.C. 272.

3. See p. 127; and the discussion of conflicting authorities by Cedric Thornberry (1963) 12 *I.C.L.Q.* at 422–8. Section 33(5) of the Immigration Act 1971 preserves without spelling out the prerogative. The United Kingdom acts on the assumption that it has power to expel members of foreign diplomatic missions who have engaged in espionage activities.

4. For the background, see Thornberry (1962) 25 *Mod. L. Rev.* 654.

losing British nationality was laid down by the British Nationality and Status of Aliens Act 1914. For purposes other than naturalization and the status of married women its provisions extended throughout the British Empire. The common status of British subject flowed indirectly from the concept of common allegiance to a common Crown.

The term 'British subject' tended to connote subjection to Britain. This implication was hardly compatible with the principle that the Dominions, though united by a common allegiance to the Crown, were equal in status with the United Kingdom, 'in no way subordinate one to another in any aspect of their domestic or external affairs.'[5] Nationalist sentiment, moreover, demanded locally based nationality laws, giving primacy to a concept of local allegiance. In 1946 Canada therefore passed its own Citizenship Act. Under this Act, the primary status of its nationals was that of Canadian citizens. In Canadian law, all Canadian citizens remained or would automatically become British subjects; though not all British subjects were Canadian citizens. Canadian citizenship thus became the *gateway* in Canada to the secondary status of a British subject.

It was obvious that the Canadian example might be followed by other independent Commonwealth countries.[6] A conference of experts met in 1947 and it was agreed that each independent Commonwealth country (and Southern Rhodesia, which was internally self-governing) would adopt a broadly similar pattern, transplanting citizenship from imperial to local roots but including a substantial common element.

For this purpose the United Kingdom and its colonies, together with the Channel Islands and the Isle of Man, were to form a single citizenship unit. The United Kingdom Parliament's contribution to the new scheme was the British Nationality Act 1948 which, subject to certain amendments,[7] was still the basis of United Kingdom law on the matter at the end of 1972.

1. The primary status within the unit is citizenship of the United Kingdom and Colonies.

2. A citizen of the United Kingdom and Colonies is automatically a British subject and Commonwealth citizen.

3. All citizens of other independent Commonwealth countries,[8] *as defined*

5. The words used in the famous Report of the Inter-Imperial Relations Committee of the Imperial Conference 1926 (Cmd 2768) – the Balfour Report.

6. For the legislation enacted down to 1960, see Clive Parry, *Nationality and Citizenship Laws of the Commonwealth and the Republic of Ireland* (2 vols.).

7. See British Nationality Act 1958; British Nationality (Nos. 1 and 2) Acts 1964; British Nationality Act 1965; Commonwealth Immigrants Act 1962, s. 12(2), (4); Immigration Act 1971, s. 2 (5), Sched. 1, for the main changes.

8. The list has been modified and lengthened by individual independence Acts. At the end of 1972 Pakistan was still in the list and Bangladesh was not, although the former had left the Commonwealth and the latter had joined it. See Addendum.

by their own laws, are British subjects and Commonwealth citizens[9] *in the law of the United Kingdom and its dependencies.* This point is important but causes some confusion. A number of the newer members of the Commonwealth do not designate their own citizens as British subjects at all. A citizen of India or Ghana, for example, is not a British subject in Indian or Ghanaian law. Many Commonwealth countries, moreover, treat citizens of other Commonwealth countries as aliens or as if they were aliens; the ideal of full reciprocity has not been realized. But in the law of the United Kingdom, Indian and Ghanaian citizens are British subjects and they are legally entitled to exercise the franchise and hold public office in the same manner as persons born in this country.

4. Citizenship of the United Kingdom and Colonies may be acquired by birth or adoption,[10] descent,[11] naturalization (in the case of British protected persons and aliens[12]), registration (for example, of citizens of other Commonwealth countries, Irish citizens, or wives of citizens of the United Kingdom and Colonies)[13] or acquisition of territory. Citizenship can be

9. See section 1 of the 1948 Act, as amended.

10. i.e. birth within the U.K. and Colonies unless the father was a non-citizen diplomat or an enemy alien in occupation of British territory. For adoption, see Adoption Act 1958, s. 19.

11. i.e., birth outside the U.K. and Colonies, the father being a citizen. If the father was a citizen by descent only, additional requirements must be complied with (s. 5).

12. An alien applicant for naturalization must have resided in the U.K. or been in Crown service continuously for the preceding twelve months, and resided in the U.K. and Colonies or been in Crown service for four years out of the seven before that. He must also be of good character, have a sufficient knowledge of the English language and intend to remain resident or be in the public service (1948 Act, s. 10, Sched. 2). The Minister need give no reason for his decision and his discretion appears to be absolute: 1948 Act, s. 26; see also Tribunals and Inquiries Act 1971, s. 14. Under the 1948 Act the period of residence required of a British protected person was only one year; the Commonwealth Immigrants Act 1962, s. 12(2), extended it to five years.

13. Conditions for registration vary. Non-citizen women marrying citizens are entitled to registration (1948 Act, s. 6), but non-patrial British subjects without citizenship (see p. 422) and women who have been married to such persons are not (Immigration Act 1971, Sched. 1, Appx. A, s. 5A(7)); patrial citizens of Commonwealth countries (see pp. 425–9) are entitled after five years' residence *in the United Kingdom* or in prescribed employment under the U.K. Government, or alternatively in other prescribed employment, provided that they also have a close connection with the United Kingdom; *non-patrial* citizens of Commonwealth countries and British subjects without citizenship, and citizens of the Republic of Ireland, may apply for a *discretionary* grant of registration subject to conditions similar to those required of an applicant for naturalization in the U.K., but the prior residence requirement relates to the U.K. itself (see 1971 Act, Appx. A, s. 5A(1) – (5) for details). For registration in dependent territories, see 1948 Act, s. 8; 1971 Act, Sched. 1, §§ 1(*b*), 2, 4, Appx. B. Commonwealth and Irish citizens who, but for the 1971 Act, would have been *entitled* to registration, retain that entitlement subject to a five-year period of residence in the U.K. (Sched. 1, § 2) preceding or bestraddled by the coming into force of the Act provided that their residence is not subject to a time limit.

lost by deprivation (on specified grounds, and only in the case of naturalized and registered citizens)[14] or renunciation (if a citizen has dual nationality).[15]

5. British protected persons (i.e. inhabitants of protected states, or protectorates, or of a former protectorate such as Uganda if they have been allowed to retain that status instead of opting for local citizenship[16]) and citizens of the Republic of Ireland (in 1948, Eire), though not British subjects, are excluded from the definition of aliens for the purposes of the Act.[17] The former group may become naturalized, the latter may be registered as citizens.[18] Rules of law applicable to British subjects before 1948 remain applicable to Irish citizens as if they were British subjects.[19]

6. Citizens connected with the Channel Islands and the Isle of Man (which are neither part of the United Kingdom nor colonies, though they come within the citizenship unit) may be known as citizens of the United Kingdom, Islands and Colonies.[20]

7. There is a residual category of persons who are British subjects without citizenship[21] of any of the several Commonwealth 'citizenship units'.

The British Nationality Act 1948 drew no fundamental distinction between those British subjects who were citizens of the United Kingdom and Colonies and those who were not, except in the law relating to citizenship. All British subjects, irrespective of their citizenship, had freedom to migrate to the United Kingdom (though the dependent territories as well as the independent Commonwealth countries had their own immigration controls), and they were free from deportation. In these matters British protected persons[22] and citizens of the Republic of Ireland were in the same position as British subjects. The admission and deportation of aliens lay

14. Citizenship may be revoked if procured by misrepresentations or, in the case of naturalized persons, disloyalty or being sentenced to a year's imprisonment within five years. There is provision for rights to be heard and for the conduct of an inquiry by an independent Deprivation of Citizenship Committee into cases of proposed denaturalization.

15. For example, where a female citizen marries an alien and (under the laws of his country) acquires his nationality as well, or where a citizen becomes naturalized in a foreign country. The Secretary of State may withhold registration of a declaration of renunciation only if the country is at war.

16. See Uganda Independence Act 1962, s. 2(1), proviso.

17. 1948 Act, s. 32(1).

18. See notes 12 and 13 above.

19. 1948 Act, s. 3(2); Ireland Act 1949, s. 3(1).

20. 1948 Act, s. 33(2). Citizens of the six West Indian associated states are entitled to be known as citizens of the United Kingdom, Associated States and Colonies (West Indies Act 1967, s. 12(2)).

21. See, for example, 1948 Act, ss. 13, 16, Sched. 3; British Nationality Act 1965.

22. 1948 Act, s. 3(3).

within the discretion of the Home Office. In 1962, however, the imposition of immigration controls changed the implications of the status of British subjects and, in substance though not in form, disintegrated the United Kingdom and Colonies as a citizenship unit.

Commonwealth citizens: immigration restrictions 1962-73

The immediate background to the Commonwealth Immigrants Act 1962 was a rapid rise in the influx of British subjects from the West Indies, Pakistan and India, and the social ferment developing in areas of England where coloured immigrants were settling in large numbers. Over 160,000 Commonwealth immigrants came to Britain in 1961 – many of them, no doubt, because of a well-founded belief that the open door was about to close.

The 1962 Act imposed on certain classes of Commonwealth citizens, and citizens of the Republic of Ireland and British protected persons, restrictions on freedom to migrate to the United Kingdom.[23] The controls extended to all Commonwealth citizens other than persons who were (a) born in the United Kingdom; or (b) holders of United Kingdom passports,[24] provided that they were citizens of the United Kingdom and Colonies or provided alternatively that the passport was issued in the British Isles; or (c) included in a passport of a person falling within categories (a) and (b).

The controls, then, applied not only to citizens of independent Commonwealth countries but also to a large majority of those citizens of the United Kingdom and Colonies who had not been born in the United Kingdom. Neither in form nor in substance were the controls based on colour – indignant Canadians, Australians and New Zealanders were alike subjected to them – but the occasion for introducing them had been the growth of a colour problem in Britain.

The ambit of controls extended to visitors[25] and students as well as prospective settlers. However, the discretion vested by the Act in immigration officers was not absolute. In determining questions of fact they were obliged to act fairly, giving the would-be immigrant an adequate

23. And to the Channel Islands and the Isle of Man (s. 18; Sched. 3).

24. i.e. one issued by the United Kingdom Government (for example, through a United Kingdom High Commissioner's Office in an independent Commonwealth country) but not one issued by the Government of a colony: *R.* v. *Home Secretary, ex p. Bhurosah* [1968] 1 Q.B. 266; Commonwealth Immigrants Act 1962, ss. 1(2) (*b*), (3).

25. *R.* v. *Chief Immigration Officer, Lympne Airport, ex p. Amrik Singh* [1969] 1 Q.B. 333; see also *R.* v. *Home Secretary, ex p. Harnaik Singh* [1969] 1 W.L.R. 835. cf. *R.* v. *Chief Immigration Officer, Bradford Airport, ex p. Ashiq Hussain* [1970] 1 W.L.R. 9.

opportunity to explain himself and resolve doubts;[26] and they were not to take legally irrelevant factors into account.[27] There was a general power to refuse admission or to admit subject to conditions as to the duration of the stay and the occupation to be followed; but returning residents, and the wives and children under sixteen of Commonwealth citizens resident in the United Kingdom or accompanying them into the United Kingdom, were exempt from control altogether unless already subject to a deportation order,[28] and holders of employment vouchers, bona fide students and self-supporting persons could be refused admission only on medical or security grounds or because they had a criminal record or because they were subject to a deportation order.[29] In practice immigration controls were not applied to citizens of the Republic of Ireland.

After 1962 few Commonwealth immigrants were admitted[30] unless they were dependants, short-term visitors, students or holders of employment vouchers issued by the Department of Employment. In 1965 the number of employment vouchers issued each year was fixed at 8500.[31] In 1969 a general rule was laid down that incoming dependants had to have entry certificates,[32] to be issued, as far as possible, in the country of origin. The Commonwealth Immigrants Act 1968 enabled immigration officers to impose a wider range of landing conditions and, in order to prevent evasions of controls, defined more closely the circumstances in which dependants under sixteen would be admitted.[33]

The 1968 Act imposed immigration controls for the first time on holders of United Kingdom passports. When Kenya became independent in 1963, citizens of the United Kingdom and Colonies resident there were permitted to retain their citizenship if after two years they had not opted to become Kenyan citizens (or had refrained from renouncing their original citizenship).[34] A majority of the resident Asian community decided to retain their citizenship in preference to being citizens of Kenya; and many of them obtained United Kingdom passports from the British High Commission in Nairobi. They had been assured before independence that if they wanted

26. *Re H.K. (an Infant)* [1967] 2 Q.B. 617.

27. *R.* v. *Chief Immigration Officer, Lympne Airport* (see above).

28. See p. 432.

29. Commonwealth Immigrants Act 1962, s. 2.

30. For a general statement of Government policy in relation to Commonwealth immigrants, see Cmnd 2739 (1965).

31. Cmnd 3387 (1967), § 25. There was a special quota for Maltese workers.

32. Immigration Appeals Act 1969, s. 20.

33. ss. 2, 3, 4. See further, on conditions of admission, Cmnd 4298 and Cmnd 4295 (1970), §§ 1–28.

34. See Kenya Independence Act 1963, ss. 2, 3; Report of the Kenya Independence Conference (Cmnd 2156 (1963)), pp. 13–16; Kenya Independence Order in Council, 1963 (S.I. 1963, No. 1938), Sched. 2, ch. 1.

to come to Britain the United Kingdom had no intention of subjecting them to immigration control. But in 1967 the Kenya Government, pursuing a policy of Africanization, introduced discriminatory measures against resident non-citizens by withholding trading licences and work permits. Asian holders of United Kingdom passports began to emigrate to England. Parliament thereupon hastily erected a barrier by extending immigration controls to holders of United Kingdom passports issued outside the British Isles unless they or one of their parents or grandparents had been born, naturalized or adopted in the United Kingdom itself, or had been registered in the United Kingdom or a Commonwealth country already independent or self-governing in 1948.[35] This amendment of the 1962 Act affected a large number of citizens of the United Kingdom and Colonies other than Kenyan Asians.[36]

Immigration restrictions from 1973

The Immigration Act 1971[37] repealed the Act of 1968 and the Immigration Appeals Act 1969, nearly the whole of the 1962 Act, and much of the Aliens Restriction Acts, replacing them by a corpus of law for the immigration, regulation and deportation of aliens as well as Commonwealth citizens. It came fully into effect on 1 January 1973, together with statutory instruments made in pursuance of it. It was supplemented by immigration rules, temporarily operative although they had been rejected by the House of Commons on 22 November 1972. These rules were replaced by four new sets of immigration rules, two sets for Commonwealth citizens[38] and two for EEC and non-Commonwealth nationals,[39] on 25 January 1973. In the result, immigration law became the most complicated body of rules in the whole of our constitutional law.

The primary distinction drawn by the new law is between 'patrials' on the one hand, and 'non-patrials' on the other. Little special significance is attributed to the holding of a United Kingdom passport.[40]

35. Commonwealth Immigrants Act 1968, s. 1.
36. As a palliative, other East African holders of United Kingdom passports were allowed a special annual quota of 1500 heads of families within the permitted number of Commonwealth immigrants. The number was later raised to 3000, but was subject to diminution.
37. For a thorough analysis (prior to the issue of the 1973 immigration rules) see J. M. Evans (1972) 35 *Mod. L. Rev.* 508. See also I. A. Macdonald, *The New Immigration Law.*
38. H.C. 79 (Control on Entry), 80 (Control after Entry) (1972–73). The place of British protected persons in the new scheme is imperceptible.
39. H.C. 81 (Control on Entry), 82 (Control after Entry) (1972–73).
40. Except that citizens holding U.K. passports not indorsed to the effect that the holder is subject to immigration control will be admitted without proof of patriality

Those who are patrial have particularly close connections with the United Kingdom, and are free from immigration control. Only British subjects can be patrial. But various categories of citizens of the United Kingdom and Colonies are non-patrial, and some citizens of other Commonwealth countries are patrial. Citizens of the Republic of Ireland, and other E E C nationals, though non-patrial, have rights to enter and settle in the United Kingdom which non-patrial Commonwealth citizens lack. All this sounds very confusing. Unfortunately this is only an introduction to the convoluted intricacy of the new legislation. Its complexity is to be ascribed partly to the fact that a primary purpose of the legislation is to reduce long-term settlement from the new Commonwealth to a trickle; but the legislation is ostensibly colour-blind as are, indeed, the immigration rules.[41]

The immigration categories are superimposed on the categories recognized in citizenship law. The only direct effect of the 1971 Act on citizenship law is to make the acquisition of citizenship of the United Kingdom and Colonies by registration more difficult.[42] Although the 1971 Act was designed to be 'permanent' (as distinct from legislation continued in force from year to year by parliamentary resolutions), there can be no doubt that within a few years it will be followed by a new definition of 'United Kingdom' citizenship,[43] accompanied by a less artificial body of immigration law. This is one justification for not subjecting to close analysis

(H.C. 79, § 5), and should be admitted (even though their passports are so indorsed) if they hold a special voucher or entry certificate (§ 38). See also S. I 1972, No. 1613, r. 5.

However, the United Kingdom Government's responsibility under the European Convention on Human Rights for indignities caused to United Kingdom passport holders who are refused entry is not excluded merely by designating them as 'non-patrial'. See also note 49, below. Under the European Convention, the European Commission on Human Rights declared various complaints by East African Asians against the United Kingdom Government to be 'admissible' on the grounds of degrading treatment (art. 3), violation of the rights to security of the person and respect for family life (art. 5) and discrimination (art. 14). In the background lay the possibility that the European Court of Human Rights would make awards of damages against the United Kingdom Government. See p. 454, below.

41. 'Immigration Officers will carry out their duties without regard to the race, colour or religion of people seeking to enter the United Kingdom' (ibid. § 2).

42. See note 13, above.

43. A review of citizenship law is beginning: see 849 H.C. Deb. 653–64 (25 January 1973). In order to comply with the E E C rules about free movement of persons within the Communities the United Kingdom Government has already had to produce a definition of 'United Kingdom nationals' for this purpose. The definition covers persons who are 'patrial' as citizens of the U.K. and Colonies (or as British subjects without citizenship) in categories (a) and (b) below, and also Gibraltarians, but Channel Islanders and Manxmen (see p. 648) do not get the benefit of the free movement provisions. See Treaty and Instruments of Accession, Cmnd 4862–1 (1972), p. 118.

a body of rules which cannot even be satisfactorily summarized in a few pages.

(i) *Patrials*. These are persons having the 'right of abode' (section 2(6)) in the United Kingdom, in the sense of being free from all immigration controls or liability to deportation. Briefly,[44] a person is patrial (sections 1(1), 2) if he is a citizen of the U.K. and Colonies (a) born, adopted, naturalized or registered in the United Kingdom or the Islands (the Channel Islands and the Isle of Man); or (b) whose *parent* had that citizenship at the time of birth or adoption, *provided* that the parent had *either* acquired citizenship *in* the U.K. or the Islands *or* been born to or adopted by a citizen parent (i.e. our citizen's grandparent) who at that time had citizenship acquired in the U.K. or Islands; or (c) settled at any time in the U.K. and Islands and ordinarily resident there as a citizen for the last five years or more; or if (d), though not a citizen of the U.K. and Colonies, he is a *Commonwealth* citizen born to or adopted by a parent who at that time had citizenship of the U.K. and Colonies by *birth* in the U.K. or Islands. This fourth category is believed to include about five million persons who have emigrated (or whose parents had emigrated) from this country to Canada, Australia and New Zealand. The wives and former wives of these patrials will, in general, also have the right of abode if they are Commonwealth citizens not otherwise qualifying for it.[45] A person claiming to be patrial by virtue of (c) or (d) above may be required to prove his patriality by producing a certificate of patriality to establish his right of entry.[46]

Three special comments ought to be made at this point about non-patrials other than EEC nationals. First, those who were already settled in this country on 1 January 1973 (that is, being ordinarily resident here without any time limit imposed by immigration legislation: see sections 2(3)(*d*), 8(5), 33) are to be regarded as having been given indefinite leave to enter and remain here (section 1(2)); and although this does not in itself exempt them from liability to deportation, they may become exempt after five years' residence here, provided that they are Commonwealth or Irish citizens (section 7). Secondly, the immigration rules must not render a Commonwealth citizen or his wife or children any less free to come and

44. Anyone imprudent enough to rely on what follows as a full statement of the law does so at his own peril.

45. But a woman will not acquire the right of abode merely by virtue of registration as a citizen of the U.K. and Colonies through marriage unless she was so registered before the Act (s. 2(1) (2)); so too with registered children, but registration for the purposes of the Act includes registration by the U.K. High Commissioner in an independent Commonwealth country (s. 2(4)), subject to restrictions imposed by Schedule 1 to the Act.

46. Section 3(8), (9).

go than before the Act (section 1(5)). Thirdly, Commonwealth citizens with a *grandparent* born here (but not qualifying for patriality) are to be allowed under the immigration rules to enter without a work permit to seek work here, provided that they have an entry clearance,[47] though they remain liable to deportation. This concession, which will benefit several million Commonwealth citizens, placated Conservative critics who objected to the preference given by the former draft rules to EEC nationals over citizens of the old Commonwealth countries; it goes some distance to restoring the principle of 'grandpatriality' deleted from the original bill in committee.

(ii) *Non-patrials.* One of the main objects of the Act was partly frustrated in 1972 by President Amin's expulsion from Uganda of Asians who were not citizens of that country; most of them held United Kingdom passports and the United Kingdom Government accepted its moral responsibility (and what is generally thought to be its responsibility in international law[48]) to admit them.[49] In general, however, a prospective non-patrial immigrant, whether he be a citizen of the U.K. and Colonies, a non-citizen British subject or an alien, will be refused entry to take up employment unless he can produce a work permit, and permits are to be issued by the Department of Employment for a specific post for a limited period (normally not more than twelve months) with a particular employer. The maximum period for which a work permit will be extended will normally be three years.[50] This will effectively preclude the immigrant, if he is not already a citizen of the U.K. and Colonies, from qualifying by residence for registration or naturalization. Work permits are not needed for certain specialized forms of employment. There are rules for seamen, visitors, transit passengers, returning residents, students, *au pair* girls, businessmen and self-employed persons, young Commonwealth citizens coming for working holidays (who may be allowed to stay for five years[51]), fiancés, fiancées and family dependants.[52] A very wide range of entry conditions

47. Rules for Control on Entry (H.C. 79 (1972–73)), §§ 12, 27. Entry clearances are obtainable through the appropriate U.K. representative in the country concerned (§ 10).

48. See generally Richard Plender (1971) 19 *Amer. Jl. Comp. Law* 287. The Ugandan Asians were mainly British protected persons (Uganda Independence Act 1962, s. 2(1)), but British nationals in international law.

49. But in January 1973 the Home Secretary said that the United Kingdom could not accept responsibility for a similar mass expulsion in future (note 43, above).

50. Rules for Control on Entry, H.C. 79, §§ 25–6; H.C. 81, §§ 23–4; Rules for Control after Entry, H.C. 80, § 19; H.C. 82, § 17.

51. H.C. 79, § 28.

52. H.C. 79 §§ 37–46; H.C. 81 §§ 33–41. The rules are stricter for dependants of persons coming for settlement than for dependants of temporary workers, but even the latter are less generous than those for EEC workers.

may be imposed. Persons with diplomatic or similar status are exempt from control.[53]

Political asylum should be granted, under the immigration rules, to persons seeking entry if the only country to which they can be removed is one to which they are unwilling to go because of a well-founded fear of persecution. This principle (which does not impose a legally enforceable duty on the immigration authorities) applies equally to Commonwealth citizens and other non-patrials.[54] There is indeed a very close correspondence between the entry rules for the two classes of non-patrials. In respect of persons seeking to come here for *settlement*, the rules appear to apply *more* strictly to Commonwealth citizens than to aliens.[55] Some exceptions have already been indicated. Two other sets of exceptions are of major importance.

(a) *Citizens of the Republic of Ireland.* Citizens of the Republic of Ireland are not aliens in United Kingdom law.[56] Immigration controls have not been applied to them except under emergency conditions in Northern Ireland. The British Islands and the Republic of Ireland now form a Common Travel Area, and bona fide local journeys within that area by persons already resident there are not restricted by immigration requirements.[57] However, it is open to the Home Secretary to refuse entry to an Irish citizen if he deems it conducive to the public good in the interests of national security, or if that citizen has already been refused leave to enter, and it is possible under the 1971 Act for him to exclude the Republic from the Common Travel Area.[58]

(b) *EEC Nationals.* The immigration rules, purporting to implement Community obligations,[59] provide that when an EEC national (other than an Irish citizen) is given leave to enter, no condition may be imposed restricting his employment or occupation in the United Kingdom. Prospective

53. 1971 Act, s. 8 (2), (3); S.I. 1972, No. 1613.

54. See H.C. 79, § 54; H.C. 81, § 55.

55. A non-patrial Commonwealth citizen coming here for this purpose needs a special voucher or corresponding entry certificate issued to him as a citizen of the U.K. and Colonies holding a U.K. passport by a U.K. representative overseas (H.C. 79, § 38); there is no express corresponding requirement for aliens. The issue of vouchers will be rigorously controlled.

56. British Nationality Act 1948, s. 32(1); Ireland Act 1949, s. 2(1).

57. Immigration Act 1971, ss. 1(3), 9; Sched. 4; S.I. 1972, No. 1610. 'EEC national' excludes persons who are Netherlands or French nationals solely by reason of their connection with overseas territories.

58. 1971 Act, s. 9(4), (6).

59. For which see EEC Treaty, arts. 3(c), 48–58 and regulations and directives issued thereunder; K. R. Simmonds, (1972) 21 *I.C.L.Q.* 307; Mathijsen, *A Guide to European Community Law*, pp. 49–55.

workers, businessmen and self-employed persons are to be admitted without a work permit or other prior consent, and the rights of their dependants to accompany or join them are appreciably wider than those with respect to other aliens or non-patrial Commonwealth citizens.[60] In Community law, restrictions of freedom of migration of Community nationals can be imposed by member states only for reasons of public security, public health and certain facets of the public interest.[61] The EEC rules about freedom of movement of workers are not to apply in Northern Ireland before 1978.

Status of non-patrials within the United Kingdom

(a) *Commonwealth citizens* (*including citizens of the United Kingdom and Colonies*). They retain their civic rights as British subjects. But they will be liable to deportation for breach of entry conditions (for example, overstaying their period of entry or taking up a different job without leave) and on other grounds, though there is no formal restriction of movement within the country and they are not to be required to register with the police. Nevertheless, given the type of condition that is likely to be imposed on many of them, they will suffer a substantial curtailment of their civil liberties.

(b) *Citizens of the Republic of Ireland*. Although not British subjects, they are entitled to exercise the franchise and be elected to public office; and rules of law applicable to British subjects before the British Nationality Act 1948 still apply to them unless subsequently excluded.[62] They are, however, liable to deportation, and it is an offence to re-enter the United Kingdom while subject to a deportation order; though given the absence of effective immigration controls this is not exactly a rigorous sanction.

(c) *Aliens* (*other than EEC nationals*). In order to enter the country at all, an alien must normally have an acceptable national passport or travel document, and in some cases he needs a visa or other entry clearance. If he is given limited leave to enter, he may be subject to a condition requiring him to register with the police, and if he is granted an extension enabling

60. Admission of E E C nationals for employment will normally be for six months. If they establish themselves they will normally be given a residence permit for five years. See generally H.C. 81, §§ 49–54; H.C. 82, §§ 32–39.

61. This last term is apparently regarded as being equivalent to 'the public good', the words used in the Immigration Act; but the Community concept of '*ordre public*' is narrower in scope and cannot readily be translated into English legal language.

62. On the last point, see British Nationality Act 1948, s. 3(2); Ireland Act 1949, s. 3(1). See also note 56, above.

him to remain longer than six months such a condition will then normally be imposed.[63]

Aliens cannot exercise the franchise, sit in either House of Parliament or hold any office under the Crown within the United Kingdom unless the responsible Minister certifies either that suitably qualified British subjects are not available for such a post or that the alien has exceptional qualifications.[64] Nor, in general, may they hold other public office.[65] Discrimination against an alien by reason only of his nationality does not contravene the Race Relations Act 1968.[66] Aliens are subject to a limited range of other occupational, professional and proprietary disabilities. Certain classes of aliens (members of visiting forces[67] and persons enjoying diplomatic and other privileges[68]) enjoy immunities from the operation of various rules of United Kingdom law and in some instances are exempt from amenability to the jurisdiction of the courts.

An 'enemy alien', in the sense of a citizen of a country with which Her Majesty is in a state of war, is liable to internment or expulsion under the prerogative;[69] but if he is registered and allowed to remain within this country[70] he has an implied licence from the Crown to take legal proceedings for the protection of his interests. The term 'enemy alien' may alternatively refer to a person or company carrying on business in an enemy country.[71] Such a person or corporation need not be an enemy alien in the first sense of the term, or indeed an alien at all. But an alien in this second sense cannot sue in British courts, though if sued he can defend an action and lodge an appeal.[72] His property within the realm can be confiscated and handed over to a Custodian of Enemy Property.

(d) *EEC nationals*. Their rights to enter and remain in this country, surpassing those of non-patrial citizens, have already been noted. Within this country the general rule will be that they cannot be discriminated against by reason of their non-citizen status[73] except in relation to employment in

63. H.C. 81; H.C. 82, § 29.
64. On the last point, see Aliens Employment Act 1955, s. 1. By prerogative Order in Council, persons with alien parents may be refused employment under the Crown; see Bob Hepple, *Race, Jobs and the Law in Britain* (2nd edn), pp. 270–2.
65. Act of Settlement 1701, s. 3.
66. *Ealing L.B.C.* v. *Race Relations Board* [1972] A.C. 342.
67. Visiting Forces Act 1952; p. 207.
68. See p. 132.
69. See p. 136. A state of war for this purpose does not appear to cover a mere state of armed conflict in the absence of a prerogative declaration.
70. At large or as an internee, but not as a combatant.
71. See generally Lord McNair, *Legal Effects of War* (3rd edn).
72. *Porter* v. *Freudenberg* [1915] 1 K.B. 857.
73. Contrast note 66, above (allocation of council housing; *semble* such discrimination would be contrary to Community law).

the public service. But in 1972 detailed Community rules had yet to be adopted in relation to some areas of professional and economic activity.

Deportation

Before 1962 there was no power to deport British subjects except as fugitive offenders. Under Part II of the Commonwealth Immigrants Act 1962, courts were empowered to recommend a Commonwealth citizen (or a citizen of the Republic of Ireland or a British protected person) for deportation upon conviction for any offence (including breaches of landing conditions) punishable with imprisonment, unless he had close connections with the United Kingdom itself or had been continuously resident there for five years. Appeal lay against such a recommendation to a higher court and the recommendation was ineffective unless accepted by the Home Secretary. In the first phase some magistrates were animated by an excess of zeal, and about half of the recommendations were rejected by the Home Secretary. By section 16 of the Immigration Appeals Act 1969 he was empowered to deport Commonwealth immigrants (other than those who had been resident for five years) for breach of landing conditions without any prior recommendation by a court.[74] The 1969 Act, giving effect to most of the recommendations of the Wilson Committee on Immigration Appeals,[75] provided for appeals to lie to special tribunals against a wide range of discretionary immigration decisions in relation to aliens as well as Commonwealth immigrants.

Till 1969 the position of aliens was fundamentally different. The Home Secretary had (and still has) a general power to deport an alien whenever he deemed it to be 'conducive to the public good'. In practice the exercise of his discretion (like his discretion to exclude an alien or a class of aliens or to refuse leave to extend the stay of an alien within the country[76]) was virtually unreviewable.[77] The courts held that the Home Secretary was exercising an executive discretionary power; that he was under no duty to act judicially in the sense of being obliged to afford the deportee any right to be heard;[78] and that the validity of such an order could not be impugned

74. This power also extended to citizens of the Republic of Ireland and British protected persons.

75. Cmnd 3387 (1967).

76. See *Schmidt* v. *Home Secretary* [1969] 2 Ch. 149 (alien scientologists).

77. From 1956 an alien resident who wished to make representations against a recommendation for deportation by a court was allowed (by an administrative concession) to be heard by an official, and in other cases by the chief metropolitan magistrate, who would make a recommendation to the Secretary of State. See Cmnd 3387 (1967), §§ 53, 54.

78. *R.* v. *Leman Street Police Station Inspector, ex p. Venicoff* [1920] 3 K.B. 72 approved in *R.* v. *Brixton Prison Governor, ex p. Soblen* [1963] 2 Q.B. 243.

on the grounds that it was unreasonable.[79] Indeed, it appeared that the only legal recourse open to the deportee was to establish either that he was not an alien or that the order was defective in form or that the Home Secretary did not genuinely believe the order to be conducive to the public good; in such cases habeas corpus would be available.

The difficulty of impugning the exercise of power to deport for the public good was illustrated by the *Soblen* case.[80] Soblen, an American citizen convicted in the United States of espionage on behalf of the Soviet Union, had been granted bail pending an appeal. He fled to Israel, whence he was deported at the request of the United States. In transit by air to England, he inflicted wounds on himself and had to be detained in hospital; the immigration authorities had refused him leave to land, but he was physically present.[81] The Home Secretary made an order for his deportation on an aircraft bound for the United States. Soblen challenged the validity of the order on various grounds; the principal ground was that the deportation order was in substance an order for his extradition[82] to the United States as a fugitive offender. The offence of which he had been convicted in the United States was not extraditable. The Court of Appeal held that although the practical (and presumably intended) effect of the order was to return him as a fugitive offender, the order was valid because the applicant had failed to discharge the burden of proving that the order was a sham. To do this he would have had to show the Home Secretary was motivated by an ulterior purpose and did not genuinely believe that it would be conducive to the public good to deport him. The reasons for the decision are open to criticism.[83] Although an alien cannot become exempt from deportation merely by committing criminal offences in another country, and although the Home Secretary was clearly entitled to form the opinion that sending Soblen out of the country and back to the United States was conducive to the public good, the court could have asked itself, on the basis of inferences drawn from the material before it,[84] whether the Home Secretary's *dominant* purpose was to effect extradition for a non-extraditable

79. *Venicoff*'s case (see above).

80. *R.* v. *Brixton Prison Governor, ex. p. Soblen* [1963] 2 Q.B. 243.

81. In *R.* v. *Home Secretary, ex p. Soblen* [1963] 1 Q.B. 829 he contended unsuccessfully that he had implicitly been granted leave to land by being detained in hospital.

82. cf. pp. 441–4.

83. See Cedric Thornberry (1963) 12 *I.C.L.Q.* 414; Paul O'Higgins (1964) 27 *Mod. L. Rev.* 521. *Contra*, Hood Phillips, *Constitutional and Administrative Law* (4th edn), p. 422, note 60.

84. For example, the United States was known to want him back; Crown privilege was successfully claimed for correspondence between the Foreign Office and the United States Government on the matter; Soblen was willing to go to Czechoslovakia which was willing to receive him. cf. *Padfield* v. *Minister of Agriculture* [1968] A.C. 997 (p. 591 below) on the power of the courts to draw adverse inferences.

offence by using the simple procedure for deportation. Statutory powers cannot lawfully be used to implement an improper purpose; and it is immaterial whether their holder has acted in good faith or bad faith.[85]

The deportation provisions of the Immigration Act 1971 substantially extend the discretionary powers of the Secretary of State in relation to non-patrial Commonwealth citizens (including citizens of the UK and Colonies). Apart from those non-patrial citizens (and Irish citizens) who were ordinarily resident in the United Kingdom on 1 January 1973,[86] and special groups like diplomats and their households and consuls, any non-patrial is now subject to deportation if (i) the Home Secretary deems it to be 'conducive to the public good', or (ii) the person is over seventeen and recommended for deportation by a court on conviction for an offence punishable with imprisonment, and the recommendation is accepted by the Home Secretary, or (iii) he breaks entry conditions or overstays his permitted period of entry or (iv) he or she is the infant child or wife of a person against whom a deportation order is made.[87] Grounds (i) and (iv) are new for Commonwealth and Irish citizens. Deportation of the family with their head is not automatic; they may be allowed to stay on compassionate grounds.[88] A person liable to deportation as a 'family deportee', or as a result of a recommendation of a court, may be given financial assistance to leave instead of being deported.[89]

The rules about deportation apply to EEC nationals also; but the possibility of inconsistency with Community rules may arise.[90]

Appeals

The main features of the Immigration Appeals Act 1969[91] are preserved, subject to certain important changes. The appellate system is too complex to describe in detail, but some features are of constitutional interest.

85. Soblen committed suicide after his appeal had been dismissed.

In 1972 two Moroccan air force officers, involved in an unsuccessful plot to assassinate King Hassan, fled to Gibraltar. They were returned to Morocco forthwith and were subsequently executed.

86. Who, if at all times ordinarily resident here since then, cannot be deported on grounds of 'public good', and if ordinarily resident here for the last five years, cannot be deported at all (s. 7), unless (semble) they are in UK unlawfully: see R. v. Home Secretary, ex p. Azam, The Times, 4 May 1973.

87. ss. 3(5), (6), 5, 6; Sched. 3.

88. H.C. 80 (1972–73), §§ 45, 46; H.C. 82, §§ 51, 52.

89. Act, s. 5(6). Financial contributions may also be made to assist non-patrials wishing to leave this country to live permanently elsewhere (s. 29).

90. Such a conflict may arise because of the amplitude of the 'public good' ground for deportation (see notes 59, 61 above). Since the deportation rules are in the Act itself, inconsistency would raise the problems considered at pp. 79–82 above.

91. See B. A. Hepple, (1969) 32 Mod. L. Rev. 668.

The normal channel of appeal from the decision of an immigration officer is to an adjudicator, and thence to the independent Immigration Appeal Tribunal.[92] An appeal against a decision given in conformity with the immigration rules must be dismissed, except in so far as there is a disputed question of fact; but except where otherwise stated, the adjudicating body may review the exercise of a discretion by an immigration officer or the Secretary of State himself.[93]

In brief, appeals will lie[94] to an adjudicator against (a) exclusion from the United Kingdom (by refusal of entry or refusal of a certificate of patriality or an entry clearance), but not while the appellant is in the U.K. unless (in certain circumstances) he is refused leave at the port of entry; (b) variation of or refusal to vary the conditions of entry (for example, duration of stay or location or type of employment); (c) deportation orders (other than orders made in pursuance of a recommendation by a court after a conviction), and refusals to revoke a deportation order already in force (provided that the appellant is out of the country), but the appeal is to lie to the Appeal Tribunal and not to an adjudicator if the deportation order was made on grounds of 'public good' or if the appellants are 'family deportees'; (d) directions for removal, including objections to being removed to a particular country or territory. Small disbursements have been made out of public funds (section 23) to enable the Immigrants Advisory Service, a voluntary body, to assist immigrant appellants. If on an appeal it is alleged that an entry document is a forgery, and that disclosure of the method of its detection would be contrary to the public interest, the investigation of that allegation is to take place in the absence of the appellant and his representative (section 22(4)). Since 1972 selected Immigration Appeal Reports have been published.

There is to be no right of appeal at all against:

1. Refusal of entry if the Secretary of State certifies that he personally directed that the applicant be excluded because exclusion would be conducive to the public good, or if entry was refused in obedience to such a direction (section 13(5)).

2. Reduction of or refusal to increase the permitted period of entry, if (a) the Secretary of State certifies that the appellant's deportation would be conducive to the public good in the interests of national security or good international relations or for other political reasons, or (b) the Secretary of State took the decision in person (section 14(3)).

3. A decision to make a deportation order against him on 'conducive'

92. For the procedural rules, see S.I. 1972, No. 1684. Members of the tribunal are appointed by the Lord Chancellor and adjudicators by the Secretary of State.
93. 1971 Act, ss. 19, 20.
94. ss. 13–17.

grounds as in 2(a) above (section 15(3)), except that appeal lies as to the destination.

4. Refusal to revoke an existing deportation order if revocation has been refused by the Secretary of State in person or if he certifies that exclusion was conducive to the public good (section 15(4)).

It is most unusual – it may indeed be an innovation – for legislation to attribute special effects to the fact that a Minister has taken a decision in person. No less interesting is the method of dealing with the delicate situations mentioned in (2) and (3) above where the 'public good' is allegedly bound up with security or political factors. Under the 1969 Act appeals lay in such cases to a specially constituted panel of the Immigration Appeal Tribunal nominated by the Secretary of State and the Lord Chancellor, but the tribunal's decision would not be binding on the Secretary of State and if he certified that disclosure of relevant evidence would be contrary to the interests of national security the tribunal was not to disclose that material to the appellant or his advisers. In the case of Rudi Dutschke, the former German revolutionary student leader, who appealed in 1970/71 against the Home Secretary's refusal to extend his period of residence, this procedure was adopted and in the event gave rise to a good deal of criticism.[95] But although there is now no provision for *appeal* in such cases, there is to be an extra-statutory reference, at the request of the person aggrieved, to the Three Advisers who deal with civil servants' appeals against security dismissals and transfers.[96] The immigrant may state his case before them. Their advice to the Home Secretary will neither be disclosed[97] nor binding on him.

Does absence of provision for appeal imply total exclusion of judicial review? Not usually, for the courts have an inherent power to set aside administrative decisions if they are *ultra vires* or involve an abuse of discretion. But given the long-standing reluctance of the courts to read implied limitations into the exercise of executive discretion in immigration law, particularly where national policy considerations are involved,[98] it is unlikely that the courts will interfere unless the decision has been taken in disregard of an express substantive or procedural requirement of the Act or the rules made in pursuance of it.

95. See, for example, B. A. Hepple (1971) 34 *Mod. L. Rev.* 501.
96. 819 H.C. Deb. 375–7 (15 June 1971); see also p. 197, above.
97. The Home Secretary in the Dutschke case took the view that he would have had to resign if the tribunal had reported in favour of allowing the appeal and he had not felt able to accept this determination.
98. See especially the cases of *Soblen* and *Schmidt*, notes 76, 80 above. Informal deportation by handing a deserter over to the American military authorities (Visiting Forces Act 1952, s. 13) appears to be unreviewable on other grounds.

No appeal lies to the courts against determinations by the statutory appellate authorities, but their decisions can be impugned in the same way and on the same grounds as those of other inferior statutory tribunals – for example, by certiorari to quash for error of law on the face of the record. Wrongful refusal to entertain an appeal would be a ground for the award of a mandamus to the appellate authority.[99] An immigrant who is unlawfully detained may obtain his release on a habeas corpus application, and may be able to recover damages for false imprisonment.[100]

Allegiance and protection[101]

At common law, one who owes allegiance to the Crown is entitled to the Crown's protection; allegiance and protection are said to be correlative duties. The basic legal consequences of these principles at common law are as follows:

1. Violation of allegiance by levying war against the Queen within the realm or adhering to the Queen's enemies[102] is high treason, an offence still attracting the death penalty.

2. One who enjoys the protection of the Crown,
(a) is entitled to be physically protected by the Crown against armed attack within Her Majesty's dominions,[103]
(b) is entitled to be afforded diplomatic protection by the Crown,[104]
(c) may be made a ward of court, if an infant,[105] and
(d) can sue the Crown or its officers if the Crown commits or orders, authorizes or ratifies unlawful acts in relation to him, inasmuch as act of State is not generally available as a justification for *prima facie* wrongful interference with the legal rights of a person owing allegiance.[106]

99. See generally chs. 26, 27.

100. *Kuchenmeister* v. *Home Office* [1958] 1 Q.B. 496 (excessive detention of transit passenger; cf. p. 133, note 162, above; 'Kuchenmeister rides again'.)

101. See H. Lauterpacht (1947) 9 *Camb. L.J.* 330; Glanville Williams (1948) 10 *Camb L.J.* 54; J. C. Smith and Brian Hogan, *Criminal Law* (2nd edn), pp. 551–5.

102. Acquisition of enemy nationality by a British subject in wartime is treasonable: *R.* v. *Lynch* [1903] 1 K.B. 444.

103. See generally *China Navigation Co.* v. *Att.-Gen.* [1932] 2 K.B. 197. Hence the Crown cannot demand payment as a condition of granting such protection; *aliter* if such protection is granted outside Her Majesty's dominions to a person voluntarily exposing himself to a special hazard.

104. *Joyce* v. *D.P.P.* [1946] A.C. 347 (treason); but see below.

105. *Re P. (G.E.) (an Infant)* [1965] Ch. 568.

106. *Johnstone* v. *Pedlar* [1921] 2 A.C. 262; see also *Nissan* v. *Att.-Gen.* [1970] A.C. 179 and pp. 139–40 above, indicating possible exceptions to the general rule.

Allegiance is owed by:

1. British subjects wherever they may be;

2. friendly aliens within Her Majesty's dominions;

3. friendly aliens outside Her Majesty's dominions if they are
(a) ordinarily resident within them but are temporarily absent and evince an intention to return by leaving family or property there, or
(b) are in possession of a current British passport or a travel document entitling them to return;[107] and

4. enemy aliens within Her Majesty's dominions with the express or implied licence of the Crown; this appears to cover all enemy aliens except combatants[108] other than prisoners of war.

The local allegiance of an alien does not cease to be owed merely because the part of Her Majesty's dominions in which he is resident is occupied by hostile forces.[109] It is not clear what is the legal foundation for the suggestion[110] that the Crown may expressly withdraw its protection from a friendly alien within Her Majesty's dominions.

This pattern of rules, founded on conceptual reasoning, is nevertheless irregular. For example, it is impossible to believe that the Crown has any kind of legal *duty* to afford diplomatic protection to an alien outside Her Majesty's dominions, even if he has obtained a United Kingdom passport by misrepresenting his citizenship.[111] Nor, it is thought, would the Crown be incapacitated from pleading act of State in defence to an action in tort brought by him for ostensibly wrongful acts outside Her Majesty's dominions. Resident enemy aliens can commit treason, but they do not enjoy that modest degree of protection against the Crown which would render them immune from being interned or expelled under the prerogative. And the extent to which British protected persons owe allegiance and are entitled to protection (for example, from acts of State) has never been made clear. Allegiance and protection are not fully correlative duties for every purpose and the implications of protection may vary according to the context.

107. *Joyce*'s case; *Re P. (G.E.)* (see above).
108. *Joyce*'s case [1946] A.C. at 368.
109. *De Jager* v. *Att.-Gen. of Natal* [1907] A.C. 326 (treason).
110. Made *obiter* in *Johnstone* v. *Pedlar* (above).
111. Williams (1948) 10 *Camb. L.J.* 54, pointing out the flaw in the *ratio decidendi* of *Joyce*'s case. Joyce, an American citizen, had obtained a British passport in 1939; he went to Germany and, as 'Lord Haw-Haw', broadcast Nazi propaganda; held, he owed allegiance by virtue of the passport and was guilty of treason. Clearly, however, the Crown owed no *duty* to protect him by the *fact* of his having the passport. Why, then, did Joyce owe allegiance while in Germany?

One must also take into account modern developments in legislation and administrative practice when considering the present scope of the common-law rules. The following points pose problems:

1. Although under section 1 (3) of the British Nationality Act 1948 all Commonwealth citizens are British subjects in United Kingdom law, a Commonwealth citizen who is not a citizen of the United Kingdom and Colonies is not guilty of any offence in United Kingdom law in respect of any act or omission committed either in his own country or in a foreign country unless it would be an offence if committed by an alien in a foreign country (section 3(1) of the 1948 Act). This means that a citizen of Canada or India, for instance, cannot be convicted of treason in the United Kingdom for anything done in Canada or India unless his conduct would have been equally treasonable if perpetrated by a Frenchman in France (for example, because he was ordinarily resident in the United Kingdom or perhaps held a current United Kingdom passport).

2. As this is now the law in the United Kingdom, why should act of State not normally be pleadable by the Crown in respect of something done to a Canadian citizen in Canada or an Indian citizen in India? Canadian and Indian citizens, like citizens of other independent Commonwealth countries, will receive diplomatic protection from their own Governments. They will be issued with their own national passports, not with United Kingdom passports. Their allegiance is owed to the Governments of their own countries.

3. One might reply that there is a material difference between Canada and India, in that Canada is still part of Her Majesty's dominions (the Queen being Queen of Canada) whereas India is not (being a republic). Indians outside Her Majesty's dominions might justifiably be regarded as aliens for the application of common-law legal concepts, but Canadians should not be. This is a tenable view, but not one which sounds particularly convincing.[112] The practical distinction between those independent Commonwealth countries where the Queen remains head of State and those which are republics or which have their indigenous monarchs has worn thin. Possibly, then, the United Kingdom common-law rules about protection ought to be confined to citizens of the United Kingdom and Colonies and other persons resident in or closely connected with the United Kingdom and Colonies.

4. Even the United Kingdom and Colonies are not a coherent unit in the law of immigration and deportation or in relation to the issue of passports.

112. Wade and Phillips (8th edn), p. 269, argue that act of State cannot be pleaded in a United Kingdom court even in respect of an act done to an Indian citizen outside Her Majesty's dominions.

But perhaps no further legal consequences should be deduced from these facts. A citizen of the United Kingdom and Colonies may not have a United Kingdom passport, or, if he has one, may not be entitled to enter the United Kingdom as of right, but unless he has dual citizenship he will not be entitled to diplomatic protection from any other independent state. Hence he ought to have the protection of the United Kingdom Government and should be immune from arbitrary action cloaked as an act of State. The same principle should govern British protected persons, even if their homelands are not technically parts of Her Majesty's dominions.

The present content of the common law rules about allegiance and protection is therefore uncertain. Considerations of public policy and practical realities may be more relevant than general legal concepts for the decision of a particular case.

Passports: a note

United Kingdom passports are issued under the royal prerogative by the Passport Office, a sub-department of the Foreign and Commonwealth Office. They may be refused, revoked and impounded in the absolute discretion of the Crown, and there is no formal machinery for appeal or, apparently, any means by which a person aggrieved can obtain judicial review of a decision adverse to his interests.[113] In form a passport is a request in the Queen's name to afford the holder free passage and any necessary assistance; it is also a certificate of identity and citizenship. A holder (provided, at least, that he is in fact a citizen) is entitled to the diplomatic protection of the United Kingdom Government in a foreign country, though any such duty cast upon the Crown does not appear to be directly enforceable in judicial proceedings. Passports are sometimes refused, withheld or revoked because there is a risk that the applicant or holder, charged with a criminal offence, may leave the country. More frequently they are impounded because the holder owes the Government money for expenditure incurred in repatriating him from abroad.[114] Seizure or denial of a passport on grounds of disloyalty is very rare.[115]

113. *Secretary of State* v. *Lakdawalla* [1972] Imm. A.R.26. Contrast the position in the U.S.A. and India, where the highest courts have held that the Executive has not an arbitrary discretion to refuse or revoke a passport and thus derogate from a citizen's freedom of movement. See, for example, *Kent* v. *Dulles* 357 U.S. 116 (1958).

114. For statements of political and administrative practice, see 209 H.L. Deb. 860 (16 June 1958); 764 H.C. Deb., Written Answers 183 (13 May 1968).

115. Only about twenty passports had been denied by the United Kingdom Government on political grounds between 1945 and 1968 (764 H.C. Deb. 110) (14 May 1968). The passports of certain citizens of the U.K. and Colonies resident in Rhodesia were

In practice it is extremely difficult to travel outside the country without a valid passport or national identity card, because carriers will demand production of passports by passengers, and immigration authorities elsewhere will not normally accept the entry of non-holders. Since any decision not to grant, or to revoke or withhold, a passport may seriously restrict freedom of movement, there should be a statutory procedure for appeal or review, with special arrangements for politically sensitive cases.

Fugitive offenders

Special statutory rules govern the surrender from the United Kingdom of fugitives from criminal justice in other countries. These rules apply, in general, to all persons, irrespective of their citizenship. The relevant body of rules depends on the country seeking extradition. Rendition to the Republic of Ireland is effected by a simple procedure under the Backing of Warrants (Republic of Ireland) Act 1965; to Commonwealth countries under the Fugitive Offenders Act 1967; and to foreign countries under the Extradition Act 1870 (as amended). As we have noted,[116] a deportation order may, in certain circumstances, have the same practical effect as an extradition order.

Extradition to foreign countries is regulated by statute and treaty. There can be no extradition (as distinct from deportation) to a foreign State in the absence of a bilateral treaty to which effect is given in United Kingdom law by an Order in Council made in pursuance of the Extradition Acts. The terms of such an Order in Council must be compatible with the Acts – for example, it cannot provide for surrender of a person charged with an offence that is not an extradition crime scheduled to the Act – but there is scope for variation; thus, some extradition treaties exclude the rendition of nationals of one or both of the contracting states.

Extradition proceedings are commenced by a foreign government's issuing a requisition for surrender to the Foreign and Commonwealth Office, together with the evidence on which the request is based or the record of the conviction if any. This is forwarded to the Home Office and thence, if it appears to be in order, to the chief metropolitan magistrate who is directed to issue an arrest warrant. When the person whose surrender is sought has been arrested, the requisitioning State must make out a *prima facie* case before the magistrate at Bow Street that the accused is guilty of the offence. If the magistrate is so satisfied, and is also satisfied that the requirements of the Acts (see below) have been complied with, he

impounded when they travelled overseas after UDI; the holders were thought to be actively sympathetic to the Smith regime. Following protests in Parliament, the Secretary of State appointed an advisory committee to review these cases: see 764 H.C. Deb. 623–33, 1041–116; 766 H.C. Deb. 722–3.

116. *Soblen*'s case, p. 433 above.

will remand the accused in custody for surrender; but within fifteen days the accused may apply to the High Court for habeas corpus to secure his release, and thence appeal (with leave) to the House of Lords.[117] The superior courts cannot receive fresh evidence designed to show merely that the magistrate's conclusion as to the weight of evidence was erroneous,[118] but they may consider a wide range of questions: whether the magistrate had any reasonable ground for his conclusion that a *prima facie* case had been established;[119] whether the offence was one within the Act, the Order in Council and the treaty; whether the ingredients of the offence are substantially similar in the two legal systems; whether the surrender of the accused is being sought for the purpose of detaining or trying him for a different offence; and whether it is being sought for an offence of a political character or in order to try or punish him for an offence of a political character.[120] The House of Lords has, however, recently held that the courts have no jurisdiction to refuse extradition on the ground that surrender would be oppressive,[121] or even on the ground that the accused had been convicted by the foreign court without an opportunity to defend himself and hence in breach of natural justice;[122] it lies within the discretion of the Home Secretary[123] to decide whether, in all the circumstances, the extradition order should be enforced. The courts are also extremely reluctant to attribute ulterior motives to a foreign government with which the United Kingdom maintains diplomatic relations; consequently they will accept assurances that the accused will not be tried or detained for any other offence or on political grounds upon his surrender.[124] The Home Secretary may exercise a political discretion after the court proceedings have terminated.

Nevertheless, the magistrate, or the court on a habeas corpus application, will direct the release of the accused if of the opinion that the offence with which he has been charged is of a political character. Indeed, the

117. The requisitioning government may also appeal to the Lords against the award of habeas corpus.

118. *R.* v. *Brixton Prison Governor, ex p. Schtraks* [1964] A.C. 556.

119. ibid. See also *R.* v. *Brixton Prison Governor, ex p. Armah* [1968] A.C. 192 (Fugitive Offenders Act 1881).

120. Extradition Act 1870, s. 3. It would seem that for extradition to be refused on this last ground the 'political' offence must have already been committed. See *R.* v. *Brixton Prison Governor, ex p. Keane* [1972] A.C. 204 (a case decided on the similar but not identical wording of section 2(2) of the Backing of Warrants (Republic of Ireland) Act 1965).

121. *Atkinson* v. *United States Government* [1971] A.C. 197.

122. *R.* v. *Brixton Prison Governor, ex. p. Kotronis* [1971] A.C. 250.

123. Extradition Act 1870, s. 11.

124. *R.* v. *Brixton Prison Governor, ex p. Kotronis* (see above). cf. the differences in approach to this question in the judgments in *R.* v. *Brixton Prison Governor, ex p. Kolczynski* [1955] 1 Q.B. 540.

Home Secretary should refuse to proceed with a request for surrender in the first place if the offence is political. To this extent the law does recognize a right, and not merely a privilege, of political asylum.[125]

For a long time it was thought that an offence could not be political unless it was committed in pursuance of a struggle for power between contending factions within a State. The murder of a Swiss official in furtherance of an uprising was an offence of a political character;[126] a murder committed by a bomb-throwing anarchist whose destructive impulses were directed against organized society at large was not.[127] Up to a point this test is serviceable; thus, a family dispute about the religious education of children in Israel, leading to perjury, kidnapping and a national political controversy, did not fall within the concept of a political offence.[128] But no all-inclusive test is acceptable.[129] For example, a mutiny and assault on the high seas designed to enable the criminals to escape to the West from a communist régime – an offence which in Poland would have been regarded as treasonable – was held to be of a political character, although there was no element of a struggle for power.[130] The murder of Jews in a Nazi concentration camp was an act of State policy, but it was not a political offence because the offenders would not have been entitled to political asylum in Britain.[131] Genocide is now an extradition crime and is deemed not to be of a political character (Genocide Act 1969, s. 2). Hijacking aircraft is also an extradition crime, but the ordinary exception for political offences remains (Hijacking Act 1971).

In the eyes of the courts, the categories of offences of a political character have not been closed. In deciding whether an offence does fall within this general description, or within the list of extradition crimes, the courts are entitled to receive additional material and can review the determination of the magistrate *de novo*. If, of course, the offence (for example, espionage) is not one of the scheduled crimes, the question whether it is of a political character does not arise.

English law governing extradition to foreign countries has been substantially influenced by the law and practice of international society. Till 1967, the law relating to fugitive offenders within the Commonwealth was based on the archaic concept of a united Empire. The Fugitive Offenders

125. cf. p. 429. But to be 'political', the offence must be directed against the requisitioning State, not a third State: *R.* v. *Pentonville Prison Governor, ex p. Cheng* [1973] 2 W.L.R. 746.

126. *Re Castioni* [1891] 1 Q.B. 149.

127. *Re Meunier* [1894] 2 Q.B. 415.

128. *R.* v. *Brixton Prison Governor, ex p. Schtraks* (see above).

129. See generally C. F. Amerasinghe (1965) 28 *Mod. L. Rev.* 27.

130. *R.* v. *Brixton Prison Governor, ex p. Kolczynski* [1955] 1 Q.B. 540, *per* Cassels J.

131. *Re Extradition Act 1870, ex p. Treasury Solicitor* [1969] 1 W.L.R. 12.

Act 1881 did not preclude the rendition of an alleged political offender to a Commonwealth country, and there was no list of extradition offences. In the 1960s, when a number of dependent territories had become self-governing and independent, the omission of this safeguard was a source of serious embarrassment.[132] But the courts had a discretion, not available to them under the Extradition Acts, to discharge a prisoner on a habeas corpus application if his surrender would be unjust or oppressive; this power was sparingly exercised.[133]

Following discussions with Commonwealth countries, it was decided[134] to replace the Act of 1881 with one corresponding more closely to international practice. The Fugitive Offenders Act 1967 falls into two main parts. Rendition to designated independent Commonwealth countries is permissible only for offences listed in the schedule to the Act. This list is more up to date than the corresponding list in the Extradition Acts. Although the procedure for initiating rendition under the 1967 Act is simpler, procuring rendition is in fact harder; for the alleged offence must not merely fall within the scope of the general description of the offence in United Kingdom law but must actually *be* an offence (assuming that it had been committed in the United Kingdom) in the law of the United Kingdom[135] and (again on the same assumption) be within the territorial jurisdiction of a United Kingdom court.[136] Rendition must be refused if the offence is of a political character, or if the request has in fact been made for the purpose of prosecuting or punishing him on account of his race, religion or political opinions, or if the offender might[137] be prejudiced at his trial or detained on any of these grounds. References to offences of a political character do not include offences against the life or person of the Queen.[138]

132. See especially *Enahoro*'s case, one aspect of which was reported as *R*. v. *Brixton Prison Governor, ex p. Enahoro* [1963] 2 Q.B. 455. See also *R*. v. *Brixton Prison Governor, ex p. Armah* [1968] A.C. 192; *Zacharia* v. *Republic of Cyprus* [1963] A.C. 634.

133. Fugitive Offenders Act 1881, s. 10. See *Zacharia*'s case (above) where the courts refused to discharge the prisoners but the Home Secretary, in the exercise of his executive discretion, decided not to return them to Cyprus where their lives might have been in serious danger.

134. Cmnd 3008 (1966).

135. *R*. v. *Brixton Prison Governor, ex p. Gardner* [1968] 2 Q.B. 399. But it does not have to be an offence of the same *name* in United Kingdom law: see *R*. v. *Pentonville Prison Governor, ex p. Teja* [1971] 2 Q.B. 274.

136. *R*. v. *Brixton Prison Governor, ex p. Rush* [1969] 1 W.L.R. 165. cf. *Treacy* v. *D.P.P.* [1971] A.C. 537.

137. If the apprehended prejudice is grave, it is enough for the applicant for habeas corpus to show that a serious possibility of its occurrence exists; he does not have to show that the degree of possibility exceeds 50 per cent: *R*. v. *Pentonville Prison Governor, ex p. Fernandez* [1971] 1 W.L.R. 987.

138. 1967 Act, s. 4.

For dependent territories there is no list of scheduled offences and rendition is still permissible for any offence punishable with twelve months' imprisonment. Nor is the rendition of 'political' fugitives prohibited, though the Home Secretary has a discretionary power to refuse to return offenders on political grounds.[139]

In relation to requests for return of offenders by *any* Commonwealth country, the magistrate or court *may* order discharge, on committal proceedings or on an application for habeas corpus, if it would be unjust or oppressive to return an offender because of the triviality of the offence or the lapse of time since it was committed or because the accusation has not been made in good faith in the interests of justice.[140] The Home Secretary *must* refuse to surrender the prisoner to an independent Commonwealth country, and *may* refuse to surrender him to a dependent territory, if he is satisfied on these grounds that surrender would be unjust or oppressive; he *may* refuse surrender of an offender to any part of the Commonwealth where he faces the capital penalty for an offence not punishable with death in Britain. Taken as a whole, the safeguards against unfair rendition are better under the 1967 Act than under the Extradition Acts.

Race relations legislation[141]

As we have already noted,[142] the American constitution prohibits any state from denying citizens the equal protection of the laws. This implies that racial discrimination sanctioned by state action[143] is unconstitutional. For many years it was thought that the southern states could maintain segregated school systems for white and coloured children, provided that the separate facilities provided were in fact equal. But in 1954 the Supreme Court of the United States held that in that social context separateness necessarily implied discrimination and inequality; and it ordered the desegregation of publicly maintained schools with all deliberate speed.[144] The decision was implemented deliberately rather than speedily. Nevertheless,

139. s. 9(3).

140. s.8. The High Court may receive additional evidence for this purpose or when determining whether there are 'political' reasons for discharging him within the meaning of section 4. The Home Secretary is not to surrender a 'political' offender even if the courts refuse to order his discharge.

141. For the fullest study, see Anthony Lester and Geoffrey Bindman, *Race and Law* (Penguin, 1972). See also, Bob Hepple, *Race, Jobs and the Law in Britain* (2nd edn, Penguin, 1970).

142. See p. 245.

143. The concept of state action is extremely wide. cf. *Shelley* v. *Kraemer* 334 U.S. 1 (1948) (racially discriminatory restrictive covenants in private land transactions held unconstitutional and void).

144. *Brown* v. *Board of Education* 347 U.S. 483 (1954); 349 U.S. 294 (1955).

liberal opinion, not only in the United States, was fortified by this legal pronouncement.

The constitutions of the majority of Commonwealth countries prohibit unreasonable and unfair discrimination by the Legislature and administrative authorities. These prohibitions have not been markedly successful, partly because they embody too many exceptions,[145] partly because the judges do not usually enjoy a degree of prestige comparable to that of American federal judges, and partly because of the strength of tribal or communal sentiment in some countries. But no non-white Government will willingly accept discrimination by whites against non-whites, scant though its regard for other fundamental freedoms may be. As decolonization has swept scores of African and Asian states into independence, the proceedings of the United Nations and other international organizations have become dominated by this issue. International declarations, conventions and covenants purporting to outlaw all forms of racial discrimination have proliferated. And in 1962, before Rhodesia became Britain's albatross, the United Kingdom Parliament passed legislation intended to stem the flow of Commonwealth immigrants – all British subjects, many of them citizens of the United Kingdom and Colonies – mainly because too many of them were coloured.

The Race Relations Act 1965 was designed partly to improve Britain's tarnished international image but also (and primarily) to promote more harmonious race relations within the country. Before the Act, incitement to racial hatred was not a statutory offence unless perpetrated publicly and in circumstances giving rise to a likelihood of disorder.[146] Section 6 of the Act made such incitement an offence punishable with a maximum of two years' imprisonment; prosecutions could be undertaken only with leave of the Attorney-General.[147] The offence could be committed by the publication or distribution[148] of written matter or by words used in a public place or at a public meeting even though they were unlikely to cause a breach of

145. See, however, *Akar* v. *Att.-Gen. of Sierra Leone* [1970] A.C. 853 (P.C.).

146. Public Order Act 1936, s. 5. It might be held to be a public mischief or sedition even in the absence of a threat to public order, but the scope of these offences was extremely uncertain and prosecutions in such a context were rare.

147. cf. *Thorne* v. *BBC* [1967] 1 W.L.R. 1104 (civil proceedings for infringement could not be instituted by a member of the public). Contrast *Ealing L.B.C.* v. *Race Relations Board* [1972] A.C. 342 (council could sue for declaration, instead of waiting to be sued, to ascertain whether its policy in allocating council houses contravened 1968 Act).

148. cf. *R.* v. *Britton* [1967] 2 Q.B. 51 (distribution of racialist pamphlet to M.P.'s house not distribution to a 'section of the public' within the meaning of the Act). Distribution exclusively to members of an organization of which the publisher or distributor is a member does not come within the Act. For a successful prosecution, see *R.* v. *Malik* [1968] 1 W.L.R. 353.

the peace. In practice this penal sanction has been invoked only against a few members of the 'lunatic' fringe;[149] its utility is questionable, though it may possibly have diminished the dissemination of grossly offensive racial abuse.

The main emphasis of the 1965 Act[150] was placed not on punishment but on rendering certain discriminatory practices unlawful and devising machinery to reduce friction and promote conciliation. The Act made it unlawful for the proprietors, managers or other employees of certain places of public resort – hotels, restaurants, cafés, public houses, theatres, cinemas, dance halls, sports grounds, swimming pools and other places of public entertainment or recreation – and public transport undertakings to practise discrimination on the ground of colour, race or ethnic or national origins against persons seeking to use these facilities. Complaints of discrimination were to be made to local conciliation committees of the Race Relations Board, a body of three members appointed by the Home Secretary; the Board was to make annual reports to be laid before Parliament. A committee would investigate the complaint and try to reach a settlement and obtain an assurance that discrimination would cease. If it was unsuccessful it would report to the Board; the Board was to report to the Attorney-General if it considered that a course of discriminatory conduct in contravention of the Act was likely to continue, and the Attorney-General could then apply to the High Court or a county court for an injunction to restrain its continuance. Neither the committees nor the Board had any power to obtain information or subpoena witnesses, and no new civil remedy was given to a person aggrieved by discriminatory acts. Section 5 of the Act invalidated discriminatory restrictions on the disposal of tenancies other than in premises occupied by the owner or head tenant.

At common law a discriminatory refusal by an inn-keeper to accommodate a traveller or by a common carrier to convey a passenger was an actionable tort.[151] In a few other areas the law offered random disincentives to discrimination on racial or religious grounds.[152] but no attempt had been made to afford legislative redress against discriminatory conduct till the 1965 Act. Inevitably the Act was criticized as going too far and not far enough. On the one hand, it was asserted that standards of decent be-

149. See Lester and Bindman, op. cit., ch. 10 and p. 491.
150. For a good analysis see B. A. Hepple (1966) 29 *Mod. L. Rev.* 306. See further the same writer's *Race, Jobs and the Law* in Britain (2nd edn) and Lester and Bindman, op. cit., chs. 3, 4.
151. See *Constantine* v. *Imperial Hotels Ltd* [1944] K.B. 693 (nominal damages awarded against inn-keeper).
152. Lester and Bindman, op. cit., ch. 2. The record of the courts in these matters has been chequered. cf. the unhappy decision of the Judicial Committee of the Privy Council in *Commissioner for Local Government Lands* v. *Kaderbhai* [1931] A.C. 652.

haviour could not be imposed by legislation; or alternatively that the forms of behaviour proscribed by the Act were not to be reprobated at all. On the other hand, it was asserted that important areas of anti-social discriminatory conduct were untouched by the Act, that the powers of the investigating bodies were too weak, that legal remedies ought to be provided for persons aggrieved, and that experience in other countries suggested that outlawing racial discrimination had in fact reduced the incidence of discriminatory conduct because law-abiding citizens generally wanted to be respectable and respected.

In 1967 there was published a penetrating critique of the Act with suggestions for legislative reform drawing on the experience of civil rights legislation in the United States and Canada.[153] The Race Relations Act 1968 (the enactment of which was doubtless accelerated by the bad impression created by the Commonwealth Immigrants Act 1968) gave effect to a number of these suggestions. The Act defined discrimination so as to include segregation and a single act of discrimination could be unlawful. The ambit of unlawful discrimination was extended to cover the provision to the public, or to a section of the public, of goods and facilities (including trading, banking, insurance, credit, education and professional services); employment, and trade unions and business associations; the provision of housing accommodation and business premises; and advertisements and other notices. A number of exceptions to the general rule were introduced for particular employment and housing situations.[154] The provisions of the Act were made generally applicable to the Crown and the police.[155]

The Act[156] has posed some difficult problems of interpretation. Clearly it does not cover discrimination on grounds of sex.[157] Nor does it cover discrimination on grounds of religion alone.[158] Discrimination against Jews

153. Harry Street, Geoffrey Howe and Geoffrey Bindman, *Report on Anti-Discrimination Legislation* (1967). For accessible general accounts of the law and legal machinery in the United States, see also Jeffrey Jowell [1965] *Public Law* 119; Norman Dorsen [1968] *Public Law* 304. For Ontario see T. C. Hartley [1970] *Public Law* 20, 175.

154. ss. 1–9.

155. s. 27; subject to various exceptions – for example – the Crown was not placed under a duty to employ aliens on the same basis as British subjects (s. 27(9)(a)). On discrimination and the police, see p. 386 and John R. Lambert, *Crime, Police and Race Relations*.

156. For a commentary, see B. A. Hepple (1969) 32 *Mod. L. Rev.* 181. See also O. R. Marshall (1969) 22 *Current Legal Problems* 46; Hepple, op. cit.; Lester and Bindman, op. cit., note 141.

157. cf. Equal Pay Act 1970 (which is being implemented in stages). A private member's bill introduced into the Commons in 1973 for a more comprehensive prohibition of sex discrimination attracted much attention and some support in the House.

158. Nor does section 6 of the 1965 Act (p. 446) apply to incitements to religious hatred. Contrast p. 644, note 42.

as such may nevertheless be caught by the Act either because they are definable by reference to race or ethnic origins or because (even if such a classification is erroneous) the discrimination is based *on the ground* that they are thus definable as a group.[159] Discrimination on the grounds of a person's present nationality (as distinct from his 'national origins') is not contrary to the Act.[160] The House of Lords recently held that private social or political clubs with a genuinely selective membership did not discriminate unlawfully within the meaning of the Act by operating a colour or racial bar inasmuch as they were not providing facilities to 'the public or a section of the public'.[161]

The Act altered the procedure for investigation of complaints, strengthening the powers and enlarging the size of the Race Relations Board. Complaints may be made direct to the Board; the Board can also decide to undertake an inquiry into suspected discrimination of its own motion, and it can appoint assessors to assist it. But if a complaint is made to the Board, it is under an obligation to investigate the matter and to make a finding of unlawful discrimination if the case is made out, even though the matter is trivial.[162] Conciliation and investigation procedure is spelt out, but is essentially informal, and the Board and area committees still have no power to compel attendance or the production of information. Complaints about employment, unions and employers' associations are referred in the first instance to the Secretary of State for Employment; in certain circumstances the Board will carry out the investigation. The Act also provided for the establishment of a Community Relations Commission, an advisory, research, coordinating and promotional body.

Under the 1968 Act, the power to bring civil proceedings for an injunction to restrain a course of discriminatory conduct was transferred from the Attorney-General to the Race Relations Board. The Board may also be awarded a declaration that a discriminatory act is unlawful and special damages and damages for loss of opportunity (but not damages for humiliation and distress) on behalf of a person damnified by such an act (ss. 19–22). Courts, moreover, are expressly empowered (s. 23) to revise the terms of contracts in such proceedings so as to bring them into conformity with the Act. The county courts in which these proceedings are brought are specially designated by the Lord Chancellor, and the judge must be assisted by two expert assessors.

159. Lester and Bindman, op. cit., pp. 156–7.

160. *Ealing L.B.C.* v. *Race Relations Board* [1972] A.C. 342.

161. *Race Relations Board* v. *Charter* [1973] 2 W.L.R. 299 (Indian excluded on racial grounds from local Conservative club).

162. Hence the absurd case of the Scottish cook; Lester and Bindman, pp. 196–7 and below. In investigating a complaint, the Board and the local committees are doubtless under an implied duty to 'act fairly'. cf. pp. 585–7.

In 1969 it was announced that Government contracts would not be placed with firms using racially discriminatory employment practices.[163]

Evaluation of this legislation is not easy. The Race Relations Board and the Community Relations Commission have been handicapped by the climate of opinion about Commonwealth immigrants, and tough (and discriminatory) immigration legislation marches uneasily with anti-discrimination policies within the United Kingdom. Overt racial discrimination has not been practised to a widespread extent by public authorities in Britain; the legislation may have deterred prospective backsliders. The Acts may have made some impact on manifestations of private discrimination. 'No coloureds' advertisements have disappeared from newspapers, but it has also become unlawful to advertise for a Scottish cook; and no legislative prohibition against discrimination can effectively require a householder to sell to a bidder or a landlord of a block of flats to accept a tenant who happens to be coloured, provided that the refusal is based on extraneous grounds. It is easier to influence a prejudiced employer than prejudiced employees. The publicity now given to proven cases of discrimination may be more important than latent coercive sanctions.

In 1972 the Race Relations Board, in its annual report, made a number of suggestions for reform of the 1968 Act.[164] It should have power to investigate situations (for instance, in the field of employment) without the need for suspecting individual acts of unlawful discrimination. It should have powers to compel the production of information and to require witnesses to answer questions put by its officers. Where unlawful discrimination was established, the offender should be required to undertake not only to discontinue it but also not to repeat it. The various exceptions relating to employment on ships and the maintenance of 'racial balance' in employment situations[165] should be repealed. Damages for affront should be awardable.[166] The Board should be given a statutory discretion *not* to investigate frivolous or trivial complaints or complaints in respect of which the informant had no personal interest, so that the Act should not be brought into ridicule.

These are all sensible suggestions. Yet we are still groping in the dark. Communal sentiment, accompanied by feelings of resentment and hostility towards other communal groups – dramatized so vividly in Northern

163. 778 H.C. Deb. Written Answers 297 (22 October 1969). For criticism of the scope of this announcement, see Hepple, op. cit., 280–82; Lester and Bindman, p. 207; H.C. 296 (1971–72), §§ 94, 95.
164. H.C. 296 (1971–72), §§ 72–90. See also Lester and Bindman, ch. 11.
165. 1968 Act, s. 8.
166. See above.

Ireland – is a peculiarly intractable phenomenon in a great many countries of the world, and we have yet to discover how the law can best reduce its subtler manifestations, let alone its social incidence, in Britain.[167]

167. The body of literature on the subject of race relations, which in Britain is intimately linked with the question of immigration from Asian and Caribbean Commonwealth countries, is now formidable. See, for a substantial survey of public attitudes towards these problems, E. J. B. Rose, *Colour and Citizenship* (Institute of Race Relations, 1969); and see also Nicholas Deakin, *Colour, Citizenship and British Society* (1970).

Chapter 20
Personal Freedom

Fundamental rights

'Now, most foreign constitution-makers have begun with declarations of rights. For this they have often been in no wise to blame.'[1] Here Dicey seems almost as patronizing as Mr Podsnap of *Our Mutual Friend*: other countries 'do – I am sorry to be obliged to say it – *as* they do'. But he was at least more restrained than his mentor, Jeremy Bentham, to whom the French revolutionary Declaration of the Rights of Man was 'rhetorical nonsense – nonsense upon stilts'. There is indeed something peculiarly exasperating about a broad affirmation of fundamental human rights unaccompanied by any machinery for giving them effective legal protection. This is what Dicey had in mind: 'The Habeas Corpus Acts declare no principle and define no rights, but they are for practical purposes worth a hundred constitutional articles guaranteeing individual liberty.'[2] Had he been alive in 1948, he might have added 'or a thousand Universal Declarations of Human Rights'.

The traditional legal approach to civil liberties in Britain can be summed up in three propositions. First, freedoms are not to be guaranteed by statements of general principle. Secondly, they are residual. Freedom of public assembly, for example, means the liberty to gather wherever one chooses except in so far as others are legally entitled to prevent the assembly from being held or in so far as the holding or conduct of the assembly is a civil wrong or a criminal offence. To define the content of liberty one has merely to subtract from its totality the sum of the legal restraints to which it is subject. Thirdly, for every wrongful encroachment upon one's liberty there is a legal remedy awarded by an independent court of justice. *Ubi jus, ibi remedium.*

These are still the formal legal foundations of most of our civil liberties. Those foundations do not necessarily make for the best of all possible worlds, even in the United Kingdom. If the constitution of Northern

---

1. *Introduction to the Study of the Law of the Constitution* (10th edn), p. 198.
2. ibid., p. 199. See also Jennings, *The Approach to Self-Government*, p. 20. See generally de Smith, *The New Commonwealth and its Constitutions*, pp. 161–77.

Ireland had been equipped from the outset with more detailed guarantees against religious discrimination, coupled with efficacious machinery for their enforcement, it is just conceivable – one cannot put it more highly – that the worst of the recent troubles might have been averted.[3] If the American constitutional Bill of Rights had been transported to Britain along with Marshall Aid in the late 1940s, our laws relating to police powers of interrogation, search and seizure, legal aid for persons suspected or accused of crime, obscene publications, passports and the delimitation of electoral constituencies might have been more satisfactory though more uncertain. For the American Bill of Rights has reasonably effective machinery for judicial interpretation and enforcement of its provisions. Its terms would also have made it more difficult for Parliament and the Government to nationalize industries and implement town and country planning policies; it might have led to more criminals escaping justice; it would surely have struck down some of our recent immigration legislation.

Objections to effective constitutional guarantees of human rights may be still more vehement than objections to pious platitudes. Effective guarantees obstruct governments from doing what they want to do and are expected to do. They are therefore said to be undemocratic because they obstruct fulfilment of the will of the people as expressed by their elected representatives. They lead to 'government by judges', if the constitution is hard to amend. There will be political appointments to the bench, and public confidence in the impartial administration of justice may dwindle. Justiciable guarantees and prohibitions induce delay and uncertainty, because politicians will not be sure what they are entitled to do until the judges have told them; they engender a litigious spirit; they are irreconcilable with our ancient traditions; they are, moreover, unnecessary.

These objections cannot be disregarded. However, three comments can be made:

1. It is possible to have a bill of rights enacted as an ordinary statute without constitutional entrenchment. Canada adopted this course in 1960. Federal legislation was to be so construed and applied as to conform to the Canadian Bill of Rights except in an emergency or unless an Act expressly stated that it was to have effect notwithstanding the Bill of Rights. Its overt impact was not at first impressive. The courts held that it did not prevail over subsequent inconsistent Acts of the Federal Parliament. But it served as a guide to interpretation; and legislative draftsmen were at pains to conform to the standards it laid down. Its indirect effect on the content of legislation may have been considerable. In 1969 the Supreme Court of Canada gave the Bill of Rights a boost, holding that it rendered inoperative

3. For constitutional guarantees in Northern Ireland, see ch. 30.

a discriminatory provision of a pre-1960 Federal Act relating to Red Indians[4] and indicating that it would have made no difference had the Act been passed after 1960.

2. The United Kingdom Government is a party to the European Convention for the Protection of Human Rights and Fundamental Freedoms.[5] The terms of the Convention have not been enacted as part of United Kingdom law, but the United Kingdom is bound by international law to observe them. There is machinery for interpretation of the Convention but none for direct enforcement. Persons claiming to be aggrieved by a breach of the Convention may petition the European Commission of Human Rights, an international body of jurists, which investigates the complaint and publishes a report. If the complainant has made out a case against a signatory, and no friendly settlement can be reached, the matter will go to a Committee of Ministers; if necessary it may then be referred to the European Court of Human Rights which may award damages to the aggrieved party against the offending government.[6] Few changes have needed to be made in English law to bring it into conformity with the minimum standards set by the Convention;[7] but this self-imposed international obligation, coupled with the prospect of adverse publicity arising from well-founded complaints to the European Commission, means that the content of our legislation and also administrative practice is influenced[8] in much the same way as Canadian federal legislation is influenced by the existence of the Bill of Rights.

The Convention is formulated in quite precise and detailed language, specifying the conditions under which a guaranteed right can be abridged. There is no blanket guarantee of freedom of speech, which can never mean what it appears to say; nor is there any guarantee of 'due process of law' which can mean anything a judge thinks fit. Thus, freedom of expression is qualified by a number of provisos: the State may license broadcasting and cinemas; such restrictions on freedom of expression may be imposed 'as are necessary in a democratic society, in the interests of national

4. *R.* v. *Drybones* [1970] S.C.R. 282 (Can.).

5. For the main text of the Convention – it has been supplemented by Protocols – see Cmd 8969 (1953). The literature on the Convention and its interpretation is now very extensive. See J. E. S. Fawcett, *The Application of the European Convention on Human Rights*; A. H. Robertson, *Human Rights in Europe*. For an outstanding pioneering work, see H. Lauterpacht, *International Law and Human Rights*.

6. The United Kingdom Government accepted the individual right of petitioning the European Commission and the compulsory jurisdiction of the European Court in 1966.

7. cf. D. J. Harris [1966] *Crim. L. Rev.* 205, 266.

8. The introduction of immigration appeals legislation was probably expedited by petitions by would-be Commonwealth immigrants to the European Commission; and the decision to discontinue methods of interrogation in depth in Northern Ireland may also have been influenced by doubts as to their compatibility with the European Convention. cf. p. 425, note 40; Beddard, *Human Rights and Europe*.

security, territorial integrity or public safety, for the prevention of disorder or crime, for the protection of health or morals, for the protection of the reputation or rights of others, for preventing the disclosure of information received in confidence, or for maintaining the authority and impartiality of the judiciary' (art. 10). The implications of due process of law are spelt out in the form of detailed specification of the lawful grounds for deprivation of liberty, safeguards for persons detained pending trial, the basic require-ments of a fair hearing in criminal and civil proceedings, and a guarantee of freedom from unfair discrimination. Derogation from some rights and freedoms is permissible in time of grave emergency, but only 'to the extent strictly required by the exigencies of the situation' (art. 15). No derogation from certain rights (for example, freedom from torture or inhuman or degrading punishment or treatment) is permissible at all.

3. In the last decade the constitutions of a large majority of newly inde-pendent and partly self-governing Commonwealth countries have been equipped with full-scale entrenched bills of rights, based on the general pattern of the European Convention.[9] During its declining years, the Colonial Office moved from apathy or hostility towards this idea and began actively to press it on colonial politicians. The unmentionable became indispensable. What was obnoxious to the Westminster model is now the glory of Westminster's export models. Perhaps, after all, time-honoured Anglo-Saxon attitudes towards constitutional guarantees of fundamental rights have been slightly exaggerated. True, in many developing Common-wealth countries the guarantees exist – if they survive at all – only on paper. Yet nobody reading the judgments of the Judicial Committee of the Privy Council in two recent appeals (holding invalid a Maltese ministerial circular restricting freedom of the press,[10] and discriminatory citizenship legislation in Sierra Leone[11]) can doubt that there is *something* to be said in favour of restricting legislative and administrative competence by constitutional guarantees and prohibitions.

Legal restraints on the liberty of the person

A typical bill of rights in a Commonwealth country's constitution[12] will provide that no person shall be deprived of his personal liberty save as authorized by law and on specified grounds: unfitness to plead on a

9. The beginnings of the trend are explained and analysed in de Smith, op. cit., ch. 5.

10. See *Olivier* v. *Buttigieg* [1967] 1 A.C. 115.

11. *Akar* v. *Att.-Gen. of Sierra Leone* [1970] A.C. 853. With these two decisions there should be studied the remarkable judgment in *Liyanage* v. *R.* [1967] 1 A.C. 259 (Ceylon; implied prohibitions read into a constitution not containing a wide range of guarantees).

12. See, for example, Constitution of Jamaica (S.I. 1962, No. 1550; Sched.), ch. 1.

criminal charge; sentence by a court for a criminal offence; committal for contempt of court; detention in pursuance of any other court order, or to bring him before a court, or on reasonable suspicion of having committed or being about to commit a crime; custody for care and protection, in the case of an infant; detention to prevent spread of certain diseases; detention for mental illness, drug addiction, alcoholism or vagrancy; detention for illegal immigration, or to secure deportation or extradition; or detention under a reasonably justifiable order restricting his movements or place of residence. With the exception of the last, these are roughly the grounds on which deprivation of personal liberty may be based in English law.

The constitution will go on to lay down minimum safeguards for persons detained, arrested or tried on criminal charges. They must be brought before a court without undue delay. If they are not going to be tried within a reasonable time, they must be released on bail. They and their property are not to be arbitrarily searched. Persons unlawfully detained are entitled to compensation. One charged with a criminal offence must be given a fair hearing before an impartial court. He is to be presumed innocent till proved guilty. He is to be informed as soon as is reasonably practicable of the offence with which he is charged; he must be given proper defence facilities, including the free assistance of an interpreter if needed. He cannot be subjected to retroactive, inhuman or degrading punishment. He cannot be compelled to give evidence at his trial; nor in general can he be tried twice for the same offence.

This is, in effect, an outline sketch of some basic principles of English criminal law and procedure, transposed into a constitutional text. In England the most important legal inhibitions on personal liberty consist in the powers and duties vested in those entrusted with the task of investigating and detecting crime. To these we shall give special attention, though other matters will also be introduced.

Powers of arrest

Unfortunately no branch of English law is more obscure or complex than that relating to powers of arrest.[13] The general common-law principles have been partly codified by statute but hardly clarified.[14]

13. For an excellent general account of police powers, see Harry Street, *Freedom, the Individual and the Law* (3rd edn), ch. 1. For more detailed analyses of powers of arrest, see Glanville Williams [1954] *Crim. L. Rev.* 6, 408, 508; [1958] *Crim. L. Rev.* 73, 155; D. A. Thomas [1962] *Crim. L. Rev.* 520, 597; [1966] *Crim. L. Rev.* 639. See Enid Campbell and Harry Whitmore, *Freedom in Australia* (1966), for a work covering a field broadly similar to Street's.
14. Criminal Law Act 1967, s. 2.

To lay hands on another against his will and without lawful justification is an assault.[15] Unlawful detention (including arrest) is false imprisonment. Both are crimes and civil wrongs. In what circumstances, then, are the detention and arrest of suspected criminals justified by law?

The police have no general power to detain suspects for questioning,[16] or even to require suspects or witnesses to accompany them to a police station or to give their names and addresses[17] or to indeed answer any questions, or to compel anyone to attend for an identity parade.[18] Specific powers may be conferred by individual Acts, or in certain circumstances at common law. If a police officer decides to arrest a person on a criminal charge, he must normally obtain an arrest warrant from a magistrate by information supported by a sworn statement. The warrant must specify the name of the person to be arrested and general particulars of the offence. A general warrant, not naming the person to be arrested or failing to give adequate particulars of the offence, is illegal at common law.[19] Arrest warrants are hardly ever issued to persons other than police officers; and they are issued only in respect of arrestable offences[20] punishable (subject to various statutory exceptions) with a maximum of at least five years' imprisonment. If the issue of the warrant is outside the magistrate's jurisdiction but is *prima facie* valid on its face, a constable executing it is protected from civil liability.[21]

An arrest involves an element of compulsion, though not necessarily physical seizure; a mere request by a constable that a person accompany him to a police station is not an arrest.[22] In effecting an arrest, no more physical force must be used than is reasonably required; otherwise the arrest becomes an actionable assault.

Special difficulties arise in ascertaining the legal grounds on which an arrest may be effected without a warrant.

Any member of the public may arrest without warrant:

1. One who is, or whom he reasonably suspects to be, in the act of committing an arrestable offence.

15. Though cf. *Donnelly* v. *Jackman* [1970] 1 W.L.R. 562 (note 54).

16. See especially *Kenlin* v. *Gardiner* [1967] 2 Q.B. 510.

17. See Glanville Williams (1950) 66 *L.Q.R.* 465. The general rule is subject to certain exceptions. See, for example, Metropolitan Police Act 1839, s. 63.

18. Tom Sargant [1966] *Crim. L. Rev.* 485.

19. *Leach* v. *Money* (1765) 3 Burr. 1692, 1742. See also *Wilkes* v. *Wood* (1769) 19 St. Tr. 1406 (search warrant); *Entick* v. *Carrington* (1765) 19 St. Tr. 1030.

20. This expression has replaced the term 'felonies': Criminal Law Act 1967, Part I.

21. Constables' Protection Act 1750.

22. *Alderson* v. *Booth* [1969] 2 Q.B. 216. See, however, *Wheatley* v. *Lodge* [1971] 1 W.L.R. 29 (defendant lawfully arrested although he failed to realize, because of deafness unknown to the police officer, that he was being required to go to police station under arrest). cf. *R.* v. *Inwood* [1973] 1 W.L.R. 647.

2. Anyone who is, or whom he reasonably suspects to be, guilty of an arrestable offence, where such an arrestable offence *has been committed*.[23]

A *constable* may arrest without warrant anyone whom he reasonably suspects to have committed an arrestable offence, even though no such offence has in fact been committed.[24] He has a defence, in such circumstances, to an action for false imprisonment, provided that he had reasonable grounds for thinking such an offence had been committed. No such defence is available to a private person (for example, a store detective) who mistakenly but reasonably believes that an arrestable offence has taken place.[25] A constable also has power to arrest without warrant anyone whom he reasonably suspects to be *about to commit* an arrestable offence.[26] A member of the public is entitled to use reasonable force 'in the prevention of crime', or in effecting or assisting in the 'lawful arrest' of offenders or suspected offenders.[27] Given the uncertainty about the degree of force justifiable to prevent crime and the meaning of a lawful arrest – this includes arrest for specified arrestable offences (but few members of the public will carry the list in their heads) and arrest for breaches of the peace committed in one's presence (but even the term 'breach of the peace' has an uncertain meaning apart from acts of violence to the person) – it is obviously risky for the citizen to take a suspected offender into custody. To respond to the request of a police officer to help him apprehend a criminal may evince public spirit but does not confer immunity from liability if the arrest is unlawful. On the other hand, to refuse compliance with such a request without lawful excuse when two or more persons are actually committing a breach of the peace is an indictable common-law misdemeanour.[28]

If these prerequisites of a valid arrest are present, the arrest will still not be lawful unless, at the time of making the arrest, reasonable efforts are made to communicate to the person to be charged the grounds on which he is being taken into custody. He does not have to be told the technical name of the offence in question; nor is it necessary to say anything to him if he is caught red-handed or is otherwise obviously aware of the facts

23. Criminal Law Act 1967, ss. 2(2), (3). There may be reasonable suspicion justifying arrest although there is not yet *prima facie* proof of guilt: *Hussien* v. *Chong Fook Kam* [1970] A.C. 942.

24. ibid., s. 2(4). See also the consideration of common-law authority in *Barnard* v. *Gorman* [1941] A.C. 378 and *Wiltshire* v. *Barrett* [1966] 1 Q.B. 312.

25. *Walters* v. *Smith (W. H.) & Son Ltd* [1914] 1 K.B. 595.

26. Criminal Law Act 1967, s. 2(5).

27. ibid., s. 3; or of persons 'unlawfully at large': this category includes not only escaped prisoners but certified mental patients.

28. *R.* v. *Brown* (1841) Car. & M. 314.

giving rise to his arrest or if it is reasonable to think that announcing one's presence before seizing him would cause him to run away from the scene; nor does one have to shout the reasons to a person who, unknown to oneself, is deaf. The purpose of requiring communication, where practicable, is to enable the person arrested to clear himself by explanation at the first opportunity.[29]

A person who is unlawfully arrested may use reasonable force to free himself,[30] and possibly (though this is uncertain) a man may use such force to free his unlawfully arrested child.[31] But although passive submission may not be required by law, active resistance is apt to be perilous, because a court may hold that excessive force has been used, and not every mistaken arrest by the police is unlawful.

Bail[32]

A person taken into custody on a criminal charge must be brought before a magistrates' court as soon as practicable.[33] He may be remanded in custody or on bail pending further proceedings by way of summary trial, preliminary hearing, committal for trial on indictment or appeal. Release on bail may be granted by a police inspector following arrest without warrant,[34] or by magistrates or by a High Court judge. The powers of magistrates to refuse release on bail are broadly restricted to cases where the defendant is accused of an offence punishable with at least

29. See *Christie* v. *Leachinsky* [1947] A.C. 573; *John Lewis & Co.* v. *Tims* [1952] A.C. 676. For a marginal case, where a person was held to have been lawfully arrested although he was given the wrong legal ground for his arrest, see *Gelberg* v. *Miller* [1961] 1 W.L.R. 138; the facts constituting the reason for his arrest were, however, apparent to the defendant, and he could have been arrested for an offence arising out of those facts. See also *R.* v. *Kulynycz* [1971] 1 Q.B. 367 (original arrest wrongful, no proper reason having been given, but error rectified while defendant still in custody). Contrast *R.* v. *Holah* [1973] 1 W.L.R. 127 (wrong reason given for arrest; conviction quashed).
30. As in *Kenlin* v. *Gardiner* [1967] 2 Q.B. 510.
31. The point was left open in *R.* v. *Fennell* [1971] 1 Q.B. 428 (mistaken belief by father not a ground for using force when son in no danger of injury). See also *Devlin* v. *Armstrong* [1971] N.I. 13, a case of exercising force in resisting police.
32. See Michael Zander [1967] *Crim. L. Rev.* 25, 100, 128; A. K. Bottomley (1968) 31 *Mod. L. Rev.* 40; Michael King, *Bail or Custody* (Cobden Trust, 1971); R. M. Jackson *The Machinery of Justice in England* (6th edn), pp. 190–93.
33. *John Lewis & Co.* v. *Tims* (above) (whether brief detention of suspected shoplifter before delivering her to police custody was false imprisonment; held dependent on the reasonableness of the duration of the prior detention in all the circumstances). See also *Dallison* v. *Caffery* [1965] 1 Q.B. 348 (reasonable duration of police custody after arrest but before charge); Magistrates' Courts Act 1952, s. 38(4).
34. Magistrates' Courts Act 1952, s. 38. For granting of bail by police to persons under seventeen, see Children and Young Persons Act 1969, s. 29; Criminal Justice Act 1972, s. 43.

six months' imprisonment and is likely to commit further offences or to abscond or needs to be remanded in custody for his own protection.[35] Before being admitted to bail, the person arrested must enter into a recognizance whereby he undertakes to forfeit a sum of money unless he appears at the date of the next hearing. He may also be required to produce sureties for his appearance and other relevant conditions may be imposed. If he is refused bail or objects to the conditions under which it is offered, he may apply to a High Court judge, who has power to admit to bail or vary the conditions (including the sums required by a recognizance) under which it has been offered,[36] or to the Crown Court.[37] Nevertheless, there is some disquiet at the number of prisoners remanded in custody without trial but not subsequently sentenced to imprisonment. Powers to refuse bail or impose onerous conditions on an applicant are occasionally abused as a form of preventive detention.

Binding over to be of good behaviour or to keep the peace[38]

A person convicted of crime may, instead of being sent to prison, be bound over. This power is ancillary to the exercise of criminal jurisdiction (Justices of the Peace Act 1968, s. 1(7)) and does not presuppose the conviction of the person bound over. Alternatively, a bind-over order may be made by way of preventive justice. Under section 91 of the Magistrates' Courts Act 1952 the court may, on the complaint of X, bind Y over to enter into a recognizance, with or without sureties, to keep the peace or to be of good behaviour towards X. No such order may be made unless the complaint is properly proved. Magistrates also have a general power under the Justices of the Peace Act 1361 to bind persons over to be of good behaviour or to keep the peace; this power may be exercised without a formal complaint, and in the course of other proceedings, though if the order is to keep the peace, some threat to the peace must be disclosed by the evidence adduced.[39] If the person against whom an order is made refuses to give the required undertaking, or refuses or is unable to offer sureties for

35. See especially Criminal Justice Act 1967, s. 18.

36. Criminal Justice Act 1967, s. 22. The Bill of Rights 1689 provided that bail was not to be 'excessive' in amount.

37. Crown Court Rules 1971 (S.I. 1971, No. 1292), rr. 17, 18.

38. See generally Glanville Williams, 'Preventive Justice and the Rule of Law' (1953) 16 *Mod. L. Rev.* 417; David Williams, *Keeping the Peace*, ch. 4; [1970] *Camb. L.J.* at 103–6; D(avid) G. T. Williams [1963] *Public Law* 441; D. A. Thomas, *Principles of Sentencing*, pp. 215–17. The subject is unusually complex.

39. See generally *R.* v. *Aubrey-Fletcher, ex p. Thompson* [1969] 1 W.L.R. 872. The party against whom an order is made must first be given an opportunity to argue against it: *Sheldon* v. *Bromfield JJ.* [1964] 2 Q.B. 573.

his conduct, he can be sent to prison for a period of up to six months even though he has committed no crime. Because such an order is not a conviction, no appeal against the merits of the decision lay till one was provided by statute in 1956.[40] Binding-over orders have been used not only to restrain political agitators from repeating or encouraging violence or from inciting other persons to break the law[41] but also to prevent persons from behaving in a way likely (though not intended) to provoke others to commit breaches of the peace,[42] and to inhibit the activities of transvestites, prostitutes, protestors against nuclear weapons and increased car-parking charges, and gentlemen who peep into ladies' lavatories and bedrooms.

Committal for contempt of court

Attention has already been drawn to this matter, but it is worth noting that a person who commits a contempt in the face of the court may be sent to prison summarily, without preliminary proceedings, by the judge before whom the affront to the administration of justice has been perpetrated.[43]

Obstructing the police in the execution of their duty

Under section 51 (3) of the Police Act 1964 (substantially reproducing the wording of an Act of 1885) it is an offence, punishable with up to a month's imprisonment, wilfully to obstruct a constable in the execution of his duty. It will be considered further in the context of the law of public meeting,[44] but the case law tells us something, albeit in discordant language, about the duties of the police. The general duty of the police is to preserve public order and secure due observance of the criminal law; and they cannot divest themselves of these obligations.[45] They have other specified

40. Magistrates' Courts (Appeals from Binding-Over Orders) Act 1956 (appeal on the merits to quarter sessions, now the Crown Court). But a bind-over made without jurisdiction may be quashed at common law by the High Court on an application for certiorari (*R.* v. *Aubrey-Fletcher*, above) and appeal lies by case stated on a question of law to a Divisional Court of the Queen's Bench Division: see, for example, *Beattie* v. *Gillbanks* (1882) 9 Q.B.D. 308.

41. For example, *Lansbury* v. *Riley* [1914] 3 K.B. 229; Wilson, *Cases and Materials*, p. 400.

42. *Wilson* v. *Skeock* (1949) 65 T.L.R. 4128, approved in *Aubrey-Fletcher*'s case, above.

43. *Morris* v. *Crown Office* [1970] 2 Q.B. 114; p. 371. Late in 1972 a Scottish judge committed an abusive respondent in divorce proceedings to five years' imprisonment for contempt.

44. pp. 507–9.

45. See generally *R.* v. *Metropolitan Police Commissioner, ex p. Blackburn* [1968] 2 Q.B. 118; ch. 17.

statutory duties and numerous powers. The courts have attempted to strike a balance between facilitating the proper discharge of the functions of the police on the one hand and the maintenance of individual liberty on the other. Police powers and duties for securing public order have been widely interpreted; the police have a duty to break up public gatherings where serious disorders occur and to prevent reasonably apprehended breaches of the peace, and a refusal on the part of a member of the public to desist when called upon to do so is an obstruction of a constable in the execution of his duty.[46] Again, unreasonable use of the highway amounting to a public nuisance or wilful obstruction should be stopped by the police, and it will be an offence to refuse to comply with a police instruction to disperse.[47] In these circumstances the police have an implied power to arrest without warrant; but it would seem that there is no *general* power of arrest merely for wilful obstruction of the police,[48] though a summons may be issued. Obstruction of police investigations into suspected crime is not necessarily an offence although the police may be acting in the general execution of their functions. Deliberately attempting to prevent the apprehension of one guilty of an arrestable offence, or wasting the time of the police by making allegations one knows to be false, are separate statutory offences.[49] To give other offenders prior warning of the approach of the police so as to enable them to escape detection is a wilful obstruction of a constable in the execution of his duty,[50] and the same is probably true of the deliberate destruction or removal of relevant evidence,[51] or having an extra drink in order to frustrate a breathalyzer test that is about to be administered by a police officer to oneself,[52] or giving misleading statements while under police interrogation. But it has been held not to be an offence simply to refuse to answer police questions[53] or to resist with reasonable

46. *Duncan* v. *Jones* [1936] 1 K.B. 218; pp. 507–9. See also *Piddington* v. *Bates* [1961] 1 W.L.R. 162.

47. *Tynan* v. *Balmer* [1967] 1 Q.B. 91. See also *Gelberg* v. *Miller* [1961] 1 W.L.R. 153 (power to arrest for highway obstruction in the Metropolitan area, and see generally Highways Act 1959, s. 121(2)). See further p. 501, note 21.

48. *Gelberg* v. *Miller* (see above).

49. Criminal Law Act 1967, ss. 4, 5(2).

50. *Hinchliffe* v. *Sheldon* [1955] 1 W.L.R. 1207; *Betts* v. *Stevens* [1910] 1 K.B 1; contrast *Bastable* v. *Little* [1907] 1 K.B. 59 (warning of speed trap), and cf. *Valentine* v. *Jackson* [1972] 1 W.L.R. 528.

51. Though cf. *R.* v. *Waterfield and Lynn* [1964] 1 Q.B. 164 (attempt by police officers to prevent motor car suspected of involvement in serious offence from being driven off, held not part of their duties). See P. J. Fitzgerald [1965] *Crim. L. Rev.* 23; and criticisms of that decision in *Ghani* v. *Jones* [1970] 1 Q.B. 693 at 707–8.

52. *Dibble* v. *Ingleton* [1972] 1 Q.B. 480.

53. *Rice* v. *Connolly* [1966] 2 Q.B. 414, criticized by D. C. Holland (1967) 20 *Current Legal Problems* at 112–13, but approved in *Dibble* v. *Ingleton*, above, where a sharp distinction was drawn between non-cooperation and positive obstruction.

force detention for the purpose of being so questioned.[54] Nor do police officers have a general licence to enter upon private premises without the occupier's permission in order to investigate suspected crime.[55] Even if they enter with permission, they become trespassers once consent is withdrawn,[56] unless they have entered in pursuance of a valid warrant or to effect a lawful arrest[57] or for the prevention of a reasonably apprehended breach of the peace[58] or under other, ill-defined, conditions furnishing justification for entry. The general duty to investigate suspected crime imports powers[59] limited in scope; and a member of the public is not inevitably guilty of an offence by deliberately making it more difficult for the police to exercise those powers or effectively to discharge this general duty.

Police interrogation: a note

As we have noted, detention for questioning is unlawful except where it amounts to a lawful arrest; and a person interrogated by the police is not obliged to say anything. Moreover, confessions of guilt are inadmissible in evidence at a criminal trial if procured by duress or material inducements, and other admissions detrimental to an accused are sparingly admitted. The accused is not required to give evidence at his trial.

The American constitutional Bill of Rights provides that no one shall be compelled to be a witness against himself, that an accused shall have the assistance of counsel, and generally that due process of law shall be observed. In 1963, the United States Supreme Court held that constitutional guarantees had been infringed where the state had failed to furnish an indigent accused with counsel at his trial for felony.[60] It then went on to quash the conviction of a man who had not been allowed access to a lawyer while he was under police interrogation in custody.[61] Then, in the *Miranda* case, it held that a person detained for questioning had to be *informed* by the police of his right to consult a lawyer; that, if he was

54. *Kenlin* v. *Gardiner* [1967] 2 Q.B. 510 (a case of alleged assault on the police). Contrast *Donnelly* v. *Jackman* [1970] 1 W.L.R. 562 (where the police officer had merely touched his assailant on the shoulder with a view to questioning him).

55. For example, *Davis* v. *Lisle* [1936] 2 K.B. 434; p. 472 below. See also *Valentine* v. *Jackson* (note 50 above), where no offence was suspected.

56. See the general discussion of legal principle in *Robson* v. *Hallett* [1967] 2 Q.B. 393.

57. See Criminal Law Act 1967, s. 2(6).

58. *Thomas* v. *Sawkins* [1935] 2 K.B. 249; see pp. 502–3, below.

59. *R.* v. *Prebble* (1858) 1 F. & F. 325 (constable turned persons out of public house at landlord's invitation; resistance to him held to be an assault, but not an assault committed while he was executing his *duty*, because there was no nuisance or danger of a breach of the peace).

60. *Gideon* v. *Wainright* 372 U.S. 335 (1963).

61. *Escobedo* v. *Illinois* 378 U.S. 478 (1964).

indigent, he had to be told that counsel would be provided for him; that if he then asked for one, interrogation was to stop till the lawyer arrived; and that if interrogation nevertheless proceeded in the absence of counsel, a very heavy burden would lie on the prosecution to show that the constitutional right to counsel had been waived.[62] In any event the constitution indirectly imposed on the police the duty to tell a person in custody of his right to remain silent.

English law does not go so far in restricting methods of police interrogation.[63] The procedure to be followed is prescribed partly by the exclusionary rules of evidence indicated above, and partly by a set of rules laid down by the Queen's Bench judges, supplemented by administrative directions.

The Judges' Rules (and administrative directions)[64] are not rules of strict law in the ordinary sense. They are 'rules for the guidance of the police'. Non-compliance does not render statements by an accused person inadmissible in evidence, but the court has a discretion to exclude evidence thus obtained if to admit it would be oppressive or otherwise unfair.[65] The details of the rules and directions need not be examined here, but they are designed to ensure first that interrogation shall not be oppressive, secondly that statements to the police shall be voluntary, and thirdly that a person shall be notified, by formal cautions, that he is not obliged to say anything in answer to questions when (i) the police have reasonable grounds for suspecting him to be guilty of an offence and again (ii) when they charge him or tell him that he may be prosecuted. Normally questions should not be put after stage (ii).[66] At every stage of a police investigation a person must be allowed access to a solicitor, provided that this is unlikely to impede the processes of investigation or the administration of justice. The police have no positive duty to notify a person who is under interrogation but not in custody that he is entitled to consult a lawyer.[67] At least in form, the 'right to be silent' enjoys better protection under the American case law than under the Judges' Rules. A defence lawyer on the spot will tend to advise his client to say nothing to the police in the first instance.

In 1972 the Criminal Law Revision Committee, in a substantial and

62. *Miranda* v. *Arizona* 384 U.S. 436 (1966). Contrast *R.* v. *O'Connor* [1966] S.C.R. 619 (limited scope of guarantee of right to counsel under Canadian Bill of Rights).

63. There is a valuable comparative study of American and Commonwealth (including English) law on these matters by H. J. Glasbeek and D. D. Prentice in (1968) 23 *Cornell L. Rev.* 473. And see R. N. Gooderson (1970) 48 *Can. Bar Rev.* 270.

64. Practice Note (Judges' Rules) [1964] 1 W.L.R. 152.

65. See *R.* v. *Ovenall* [1969] 1 Q.B. 17; *R.* v. *Prager* [1972] 1 W.L.R. 260.

66. cf. *R.* v. *Collier* [1965] 1 W.L.R. 1470.

67. And are apparently not at all forthcoming, in general, in proffering the information or in facilitating access to a solicitor: Zander [1972] *Crim. L. Rev.* 342.

radical report,[68] proposed fundamental changes in the English law of evidence and procedure in criminal cases. One of these changes would permit a criminal court to draw adverse inferences from the defendant's failure when being interrogated by the police to mention a fact which he afterwards relied on in court and could reasonably have been expected to mention at the time. No immediate action was taken to implement any of the various recommendations.

Habeas corpus and other remedies

A person subjected to invalid or excessive physical restraint may exercise self-help, sue or prosecute for assault or false imprisonment. If he is prosecuted without reasonable or probable cause and for improper motives, he may sue for damages for malicious prosecution.

The most celebrated safeguard of the liberty of the subject is the prerogative writ[69] of habeas corpus. Traceable beyond Magna Carta, it was first used in pre-trial proceedings in the form of a command addressed to a royal official to bring before one of the King's courts the body of a person whose presence was needed as a defendant or witness. In the fourteenth century the modern function of the writ emerged: to require a person having custody of a prisoner to bring him before the court together with grounds for detention. The court could then test the legality of the detention and direct release if the imprisonment was found to be unlawful. It came to be used by private persons against executive officers; but until the Petition of Right 1628 it was not available to a subject to secure his release from detention by the King's special command.[70] The Habeas Corpus Act 1679 made the writ an efficient remedy in criminal cases by providing stringent safeguards against lengthy imprisonment without trial. Time limits were laid down for entering a return to the writ, and for producing the prisoner before a superior court if there were *prima facie* grounds for supposing the imprisonment to be unlawful; the court was empowered or required to admit to bail or provide for speedy trial if detention were founded on a criminal charge; heavy financial penalties were imposed on judges wrongfully refusing to issue the writ,[71] on gaolers evading service or

68. Cmnd 4991 (1972). Among critical comments, see L. H. Leigh [1972] *Public Law* 181; Tapper (1972) 35 *Mod. L. Rev.* 621, (1973) 36 *Mod. L. Rev.* 56, 167.

69. See de Smith, *Judicial Review of Administrative Action* (3rd edn), Appendix 1, on the term 'prerogative' writ.

70. *Darnel's* case (1627) 3 St. Tr. 1, such detention being a lawful exercise of prerogative.

71. s. 10. This section of the Act is still in force. Some of the other sections have been repealed, amended or indirectly superseded by new statutory provisions for the granting of bail and the expedition of trials. cf. *R.* v. *Campbell* [1959] 1 W.L.R. 646.

compliance with the writ (for example, by moving the prisoner from one gaol to another or overseas), and on persons recommitting a prisoner already discharged on an application for habeas corpus. An Act of 1816 extended some of these provisons to civil cases, and empowered the court to inquire into the truth of the return made to the writ.[72]

The modern law of habeas corpus[73] is governed partly by statute, partly by case law and partly by Rules of the Supreme Court.[74] An application is made to a Divisional Court of the Queen's Bench Division or, if no such court is then sitting, to a single judge of any division, even at his private house. Habeas corpus applications have priority over all other business. The application is to be made by or with the concurrence of the detainee unless he is incapable of consenting, in which case a relative, guardian or friend may apply on his behalf. It must be accompanied by an affidavit showing why his restraint is unlawful. If *prima facie* grounds are demonstrated, the person who ordered the detention or who has actual custody (for example, a prison governor, the officer in charge of a police station, an immigration officer, the Serjeant at Arms, the superintendent of a mental hospital, or a Minister) must then show cause, on a date fixed by the court, why the writ should not issue to release the detainee. Production of the record of an apparently valid conviction by a court places on the applicant the burden of proving that the court had exceeded its jurisdiction. On the other hand, in a case of private detention, or where a British subject is being detained by the Executive, allegedly on grounds specified by statute, the onus of proving that there existed facts justifying the detention rests on the custodian.[75]

In general, habeas corpus cannot be used as a device for impeaching the correctness of a determination made by a court of competent jurisdiction, the only appropriate means of redress being appeal;[76] though not all decisions on habeas corpus are reconcilable with this principle.[77] On habeas corpus applications made by persons committed by magistrates for extradition or rendition as fugitive offenders, the court will not substitute its own opinion for the magistrate's on the question whether there is a *prima facie* case, but it may award the writ if satisfied that his conclusion

72. The history of habeas corpus is traced by Holdsworth, *History of English Law*, vol. 10, pp. 108–25. See also Edward Jenks (1902) 18 *L.Q.R.* 64.

73. The only significant form of the writ now used is called *habeas corpus ad subjiciendum*.

74. Especially R.S.C. Ord. 54.

75. *R.* v. *Brixton Prison Governor, ex p. Ahsan* [1969] 2 Q.B. 222. Contrast *Greene* v. *Home Secretary* [1942] A.C. 284, a wartime preventive detention case.

76. *Ex p. Hinds* [1961] 1 W.L.R. 325. The court may admit to bail on an application on a criminal matter.

77. Amnon Rubinstein, *Jurisdiction and Illegality*, pp. 105–16, 178–86.

on the facts as found was such as no reasonable magistrate properly directing his mind to the issues could have reached[78] or if it disagrees with his finding that the offence was not of a political character.[79] The scope of review will in practice vary according to the context. The courts have given short shrift to alien deportees[80] and wartime security suspects;[81] they have closely scrutinized the legality of the detention of British subjects in peacetime conditions;[82] they have flinched from questioning the validity of a Speaker's warrant alleging contempt of the House of Commons in general terms, even though the inadequacy in law of the true grounds for commitment have been notorious.[83]

Applicants for habeas corpus in recent years have mostly been persons in detention for the purpose of extradition, deportation or implementation of a refusal to admit as an immigrant. The introduction of an immigration appeals system has stemmed[84] the flow by providing an alternative remedy. The abolition of conscription for military service and the creation of a Courts-Martial Appeal Court have almost ended applications made by persons complaining that they are not subject to military law or that courts-martial have exceeded jurisdiction.[85] A new procedure for determining child custody cases has rendered habeas corpus applications almost superfluous. Alternative remedies do not necessarily exclude the right to apply for habeas corpus, but they make recourse to the writ less frequent. Unusual cases of paramount importance may yet arise. It was on a habeas corpus application that slavery was declared illegal in England.[86]

Successive applications and appeals

It used to be thought that an unsuccessful applicant could renew his application before each superior court and judge in turn till his funds ran out or he obtained a favourable ruling.[87] No appeal lay from a decision to *grant* habeas corpus except in cases of private civil detention (for

78. See *R.* v. *Brixton Prison Governor, ex p. Armah* [1968] A.C. 192, especially at 229–35, *per* Lord Reid, conceding that the scope of review is not confined to strictly jurisdictional grounds.

79. See pp. 442–3.

80. For example, *Venicoff*'s case [1920] 3 K.B. 72.

81. For example, *Greene*'s case, note 75; and p. 519.

82. For example, *Ahsan*'s case, note 75.

83. *Sheriff of Middlesex*'s case (1840); p. 328.

84. See ch. 19.

85. cf. pp. 204–5.

86. *Somersett* v. *Stewart* (1772) 20 St. Tr. 1 (Negro slave brought to England; released though slavery still lawful in the territory from which he came).

87. See especially *Eshugbayi Eleko* v. *Government of Nigeria* [1928] A.C. 459. This view was aptly criticized by R. F. V. Heuston (1950) 66 *L.Q.R.* 79.

example, child custody), or against a *refusal* of habeas corpus in a criminal cause or matter.

In 1958 one Hastings, who had been sentenced to a term of imprisonment and had appealed unsuccessfully against his conviction, tried to take advantage of the supposed rule permitting successive applications. He sought habeas corpus on the ground that his conviction was incorrectly drawn up and therefore invalid. The Divisional Court of the Queen's Bench Division dismissed his application. He renewed his application before a differently constituted Divisional Court, and then before a Divisional Court of the Chancery Division. But it was held that all these courts were manifestations of a single High Court; if there was such a rule as the applicant had urged it only permitted renewed applications before different *courts*, not different *judges*.[88] In 1960 the law was restated by statute: no application for habeas corpus can be made on the same grounds to the same court or judge or any other court or judge unless fresh evidence is adduced.[89]

The Administration of Justice Act 1960 reformed the law relating to habeas corpus appeals. In civil matters the right of an unsuccessful applicant to appeal to the Court of Appeal and thence, with leave, to the House of Lords was retained, but the same rights were extended to the respondent where the application had been granted. In criminal matters (for example, extradition), a single judge may issue habeas corpus, but if minded to refuse he must refer the case for hearing by the Divisional Court. From a decision by the Divisional Court *to grant or refuse* an application in a criminal matter[90] an appeal lies, with leave either of that court or of the House of Lords, direct to the Lords at the instance of the applicant or respondent.[91] A curious feature of this type of appeal is that if the detainee is discharged on his original application, and the respondent's appeal is successful, the former detainee is nevertheless immune from recommittal unless the court below, having been notified of the respondent's intention to appeal, makes an order for his remand in custody or temporary release on bail.

88. *Re Hastings* (No. 1) [1958] 1 W.L.R. 372; *Re Hastings* (No. 2) [1959] 1 Q.B. 358; *Re Hastings* (No. 3) [1959] Ch. 368. Possibly successive applications to individual *judges* could be made in vacation.

89. Administration of Justice Act 1960, s. 14(2). The fresh evidence must be relevant and admissible: *Ex p. Schtraks* [1964] 1 Q.B. 191.

90. An application by a compulsorily detained mental patient is deemed to be in respect of a criminal matter.

91. Possibly this change in the law is attributable to the problems created by the decision in *R.* v. *Board of Control, ex p. Rutty* [1956] 2 Q.B. 109. See Harry Street, *Freedom, the Individual and the Law* (3rd edn), p. 39.

Territorial scope

Habeas corpus will not issue from the High Court to Scotland or Northern Ireland[92] or, in general, in respect of detention on foreign soil. It will not issue to a dependent territory where there is a court competent to award and supervise the execution of the writ,[93] but may issue to a colonial-type protectorate.[94] Scots law has developed its own procedures to secure release from wrongful imprisonment.[95]

Emergency powers

In wartime there is provision for preventive detention of enemy aliens and security suspects. These powers will be briefly considered in a later chapter.[96] Powers of detention in Northern Ireland will also be mentioned separately.[97]

Habeas corpus and damages

Unlawful detention is false imprisonment. Consequently a person released on habeas corpus will normally be entitled to recover damages in tort against the persons responsible for his detention. To the general rule there is a limited range of exceptions. For example, the custodian may have a special statutory defence to an action for damages if he acted in good faith. Moreover, a person whose initial arrest was wrongful may be entitled to nominal damages for false imprisonment although he is subsequently convicted and cannot obtain release on habeas corpus.

Privacy and search

Offensive invasion of personal privacy[98] is not yet recognized in English law as an independent tort.[99] An intrusion into one's private affairs may

92. *Re Keenan* [1972] 1 Q.B. 533. In this case the Court of Appeal assumed, it is thought erroneously, that habeas corpus was a discretionary remedy. cf. Yale [1972A] *Camb. L.J.* 4. But Northern Ireland courts have jurisdiction to award habeas corpus.

93. Habeas Corpus Act 1862; K. O. Roberts-Wray, *Commonwealth and Colonial Law*, pp. 612–15.

94. *Ex p. Mwenya* [1960] 1 Q.B. 241.

95. See J. D. B. Mitchell, *Constitutional Law* (2nd edn), pp. 339–41.

96. ch. 23.

97. ch. 24 and Addendum.

98. The primary source is now the Report of the Committee on Privacy (Cmnd 5012 (1972)). Appendixes I and J to the Report consider the law in England, Scotland and overseas countries. The text above is concerned only with English law. The Committee's terms of reference excluded invasions of privacy by the police and government officials.

99. The Committee, by a majority, took the view that the concept of breach of privacy was too amorphous to justify the creation of a new statutory tort except where damage was caused by the disclosure or other use of *unlawfully* obtained information.

indeed constitute the torts of defamation, trespass, nuisance, conspiracy, injurious falsehood, breach of copyright or passing off, depending on the circumstances; or if it tends to prejudice the outcome of pending judicial proceedings it may be a contempt of court. Some intrusions on privacy are criminal offences – for example, using an electronic eavesdropping device in breach of the Wireless Telegraphy Act 1949; sending out unsolicited advertisements for sex manuals;[100] conspiracy to commit a trespass on another's property.[101] An injunction and possibly damages can be claimed for certain forms of breach of confidence[102] – a civil wrong which has a capacity for development. But there is no legal redress available to one whose past life is mercilessly publicized, or who is accurately photographed in embarrassing circumstances, or whose conversations are deliberately recorded by mechanical or electronic devices in the absence of conspiracy, trespass or breach of the 1949 Act. The inviolability of the mails is apparently subject to a power vested in the Secretary of State to issue warrants for the interception of postal communications.[103] The Home Secretary also issues warrants to the police, and to members of the Security Service, to tap telephone conversations for the detection of crime (including, of course, breaches of the Official Secrets Acts)[104] and possibly other purposes;[105] these practices are still partly shrouded in mystery.[106] Even if such an interception has no lawful basis,[107] a person aggrieved has no legal remedy in the absence of an interference with his proprietary rights. Moreover, evidence obtained by an eavesdropping device is admissible in criminal proceedings;[108] so, indeed, is evidence procured as a result of an unlawful search which is a trespass;[109] the only safeguard against the ad-

100. Unsolicited Goods and Services Act 1971, s. 4.

101. *R.* v. *Kamara* [1972] 3 All E.R. 999. An agreement to plant an eavesdropping device may constitute this offence.

102. For example, *Argyll* v. *Argyll* [1967] Ch. 602; Cmnd 5012 (1972), pp. 295–9.

103. cf. Post Office Act 1953, s. 58(1), presupposing the existence of the power but not conferring it. See also Post Office Act 1969, s. 80.

104. For which purpose there is a statutory power to intercept overseas telegrams and cables: Official Secrets Act 1920, s. 4. Apparently such messages are regularly read by security officers before dispatch.

105. See generally Street, op. cit., pp. 40–46.

106. Only weakly penetrated by a Report of a Committee of Privy Councillors in 1957 (Cmnd 283). See further G. Marshall, Comment [1967] *Public Law* 261 and p. 477, note 19, below.

107. It is hard to believe that this is an exercise of prerogative power, cf. p. 120. But if authorized by a Secretary of State, telephone tapping could hardly constitute an offence of dishonest diversion of electricity (Theft Act 1968, s. 13).

108. *R.* v. *Maqsood Ali* [1966] 1 Q.B. 688. Contrast *Katz* v. *U.S.* 389 U.S. 347 (1967).

109. *Kuruma* v. *R.* [1955] A.C. 197; *King* v. *R.* [1969] 1 A.C. 304 (notwithstanding a constitutional guarantee of freedom from unreasonable search). Contrast the position in the United States: *Mapp* v. *Ohio* 367 U.S. 643 (1961).

mission of such evidence lies in the discretion of the court to reject it because of the objectionable manner in which it was acquired.

Given these principles, the law governing police powers of search assumes a lesser degree of importance. In practice the rules governing the permissible limits of police search are as obscure as those relating to arrests without warrant; and recent decisions have further obfuscated the issues.

Powers of search and seizure ancillary to a valid arrest are exercisable by the police. It seems that they may search the person arrested and detain property in his possession[110] and probably other property on the premises occupied by him if they have reasonable grounds for believing it to be material evidence of an offence, of a like nature to that for which he is arrested, committed by that person or another with whom he has been associated.[111] The common-law rules have never been made entirely clear. By statute, the police have power for the purpose of effecting a lawful arrest to enter (by force if need be) and search any place where the person to be arrested is or is reasonably suspected to be.[112] Police officers and immigration officers have certain exceptional powers to stop and detain persons without effecting any arrest, for the purpose of search or examination.[113]

In the celebrated case of *Entick* v. *Carrington* (1765)[114] it was held that a general warrant issued by a Secretary of State to arrest a named person for sedition, and to search for and seize his papers, was illegal and could not be justified on the ground of State necessity[115] or reasonable suspicion.

110. This was accepted *obiter* by all members of the Court of Appeal in *Chic Fashions (West Wales) Ltd* v. *Jones* [1968] 2 Q.B. 299 at 312, 316–17, 320.

111. This general proposition is put forward tentatively on the basis of the review of common-law doctrine in the *Chic Fashions* case and *Ghani* v. *Jones* [1970] 1 Q.B. 693 (see below) though in neither case was there an arrest at the relevant time. See also the often criticized decision in *Elias* v. *Pasmore* [1934] 2 K.B. 164; cf. E. C. S. Wade (1934) 50 *L.Q.R.* 354; and see generally D. A. Thomas [1967] *Crim. L. Rev.* 3; L. H. Leigh (1970) 33 *Mod. L. Rev.* 268. See also *Garfinkel* v. *Metropolitan Police Commissioner, The Times,* 4 September 1971, [1972] *Crim. L. Rev.* 44 (search warrant for explosives; police found none, but held entitled to seize other documents on the premises indicative of evidence that subversive organization was involved in criminal conspiracy). Here again there was no arrest of persons concerned.

112. Criminal Law Act 1967, s. 2(6).

113. See, for example, Misuse of Drugs Act 1971, s. 23 (police power to stop and search); Immigration Act 1971, s. 4; Sched. 1, §§ 2, 16 (detention for examination or prior to removal) See also Customs and Excise Act 1952, ss. 294–8.

114. (1765) 19 St. Tr. 1030 (described by Keir and Lawson, op. cit., p. 307, as 'perhaps the central case in English constitutional law'; see to like effect R. F. V. Heuston, *Essays in Constitutional Law* (2nd edn), p. 35. See note 19.

115. A ground accepted as one justification for retention of papers seized in circumstances of doubtful legality in *Elias* v. *Pasmore* (above) at 173 (police entered premises to arrest H under warrant for a seditious offence; they had no search

An Englishman's home was his castle. Indeed, the 'great end for which men entered into society was to secure their property. That right is preserved sacred . . . in all instances where it has not been abridged by some public law for the good of the whole.'[116] As Salmon L.J., a judge noted for robust assertions of individual rights, recently observed, these words today have 'an odd ring – both archaic and incongruous'. If the police have a common-law power to arrest on reasonable suspicion of 'felony' (now 'arrestable offence'), it is a curious state of affairs if the common law accords greater protection to property where there is reasonable suspicion that it provides evidence of serious crime.[117]

Here one moves from the theme of personal liberty to freedom of property – a topic with vast ramifications which we shall not explore. Powers of entry for the purpose of inspection, testing, survey, levying execution and distress, taking possession, destruction and demolition are vested by statute in numerous officials nowadays.[118] Police powers of entry, like administrative powers, are not unfettered: there is, as we have seen, no general licence to enter or remain on private property in the investigation of a crime.[119] The police can enter premises without permission for the purpose of preventing or stopping a reasonably apprehended or actual breach of the peace[120] or for effecting an arrest[121] or for the execution of a search warrant. Search warrants may be issued by magistrates or judges under a number of statutes, some of them of constitutional importance (for example, the Official Secrets Acts, the Public Order Act); they do not invariably have to specify the property to be searched for and seized,[122] nor must they always be ancillary to an arrest. If premises are lawfully searched in pursuance of a warrant specifying stolen property to be seized, the taking of property not included in the warrant is normally unlawful; but it appears that reasonable mistake, and reasonable suspicion that goods not specified have been stolen and

---

warrant, but impounded papers found there and used them in a successful prosecution of E for a similar offence).

116. *Per* Lord Camden at 1066. See also *Wilkes* v. *Wood* (1763) 19 St. Tr. 1153.

117. *Chic Fashions* case at 319. See also Lord Denning M.R. at 313; 'I see no reason why goods should be more sacred than persons'; and Diplock L.J. at 316.

118. cf. Donovan Waters (1958) 11 *Current Legal Problems* 132.

119. *Great Central Rly Co.* v. *Bates* [1921] 3 K.B. 578; *Davis* v. *Lisle* [1936] 2 K.B. 434; *McArdle* v. *Wallace* (No. 2) (1964) 108 S.J. 483.

120. As in *Thomas* v. *Sawkins* [1935] 2 K.B. 249.

121. Note 112.

122. Under s. 26 of the Theft Act 1968, a magistrate may issue a constable a warrant to search premises for goods reasonably suspected of being stolen; and a *police superintendent* may give a constable written authority to search for stolen goods on premises occupied by a person recently convicted of stealing or receiving.

are evidence on a charge of stealing or receiving against the person in possession or his associates, may justify seizure.[123] How far other deviations from the authority given by a search warrant are permissible is far from clear, but State necessity[124] or a general public interest in the detection of crime ought not to be among them. The police, having lawfully obtained entry, are not entitled to conduct a search of private property, without a warrant, in order to fish hopefully for evidence of a crime.[125] But in a recent case the Court of Appeal held *obiter*[126] that even in the absence of an arrest or a search warrant, the police, having obtained access to premises, could take property and detain it for a reasonable time if they reasonably believed that a very serious offence had been committed, that the property was the fruit of the crime or the means by which it had been committed or material evidence to prove its commission, and that the person in possession was involved in the crime *or* that his refusal to give up the property was 'quite unreasonable'.

There is a risk that the courts, having formerly leaned over backwards in their solicitude for private property, may now give too much weight to the public interest in crime detection and too little to the claims of personal privacy. That the apprehensions of the police must be shown to be reasonable is a safeguard against abuse of powers; but it is not a particularly impressive one, given the reluctance of magistrates[127] to reject assertions by the police as to the reasonableness of their own suspicions. And there are obvious dangers in attributing additional powers to the police when a member of the public exercises his liberty to be 'uncooperative'.[128]

123. *Chic Fashions* case (above). *Aliter* if there is no reasonable ground for suspecting that the person in possession is implicated (at 321). See also *Ghani* v. *Jones* (below); Theft Act 1968, s. 26.

124. cf. *Elias* v. *Pasmore* (above), at 173. Invocation of the principle of State necessity to justify the use of improperly seized documents in a prosecution was given qualified approval in *Butler* v. *Board of Trade* [1971] Ch. 680 at 690–91, a case decided in a different context. See also *Ghani* v. *Jones*.

125. *Ghani* v. *Jones* [1970] 1 Q.B. 693 at 706 (detention of Pakistani passports obtained in police search without warrant held unlawful in absence of reasonable grounds for believing plaintiffs to be implicated in a suspected murder or for believing the documents to be material evidence to prove the offence).

126. ibid. at 708–9; *R.* v. *Waterfield and Lynn* [1964] 1 Q.B. 164 (p. 462) doubted.

127. And often superior judges: see *Piddington* v. *Bates* [1961] 1 W.L.R. 164 at 170.

128. See L. H. Leigh (1970) 33 *Mod. L. Rev.* 268 for a critique of recent decisions on police search and seizure. New Zealand law is somewhat less indulgent towards police discretion in these matters: *McFarlane* v. *Sharp* [1972] N.Z.L.R. 838.

Chapter 21
Freedom of Expression

I

Bills of rights in modern Commonwealth constitutions include qualified guarantees of freedom of conscience and religion, freedom of speech and expression, and freedom of peaceable assembly and association. In practice these liberties are intimately related. If serious encroachments are made on any one of them, some or all will be diminished. Of all the basic freedoms in the world today the most precarious are the rights to express opinions and associate with like-minded persons for the purpose of opposing and eventually deposing the government in office. Fortunately in Britain these political rights, though not formally guaranteed, enjoy adequate protection in practice. In this chapter we shall consider in outline the law relating to freedom of expression. In the next we shall deal with aspects of the law of assembly and association. These areas of the law intersect but can be treated separately.

Freedom of conscience and religion does not call for an extensive discussion. Freedom of conscience falls partly within the scope of freedom of expression, partly under freedom of assembly and association. The law does not concern itself with individual beliefs or disbelief unless a person propagates his views in scurrilous terms or in circumstances likely to give rise to a breach of the peace or in a place to which he is denied lawful access. There is no compulsory State religion, no obligation to submit to any form of religious instruction, no religious test for the tenure of public office save in the case of the monarch[1] and possibly the Lord Chancellor.[2] Religious disqualifications for the franchise and sitting in Parliament had been abolished by the end of the nineteenth century.[3] Not since the sixteenth century have men and women been burnt at the stake as heretics and the worst horrors of the Inquisition passed England by. No one has yet to be required to make a public affirmation of his devotion to Chairman Heath or Wilson or to confess his political sins. Compassing or imagining

1. See pp. 109–10.
2. Inasmuch as he is historically the 'keeper of the King's conscience', it is arguable that he must be a Protestant.
3. See p. 240.

the monarch's death is still a statutory offence, but treasonable conduct must be manifested by overt acts for a conviction to be obtained;[4] 'the devil himself knoweth not the thought of man',[5] and though a person's state of mind may be an essential ingredient of a specific criminal or civil wrong, the law refrains from imposing sanctions in the absence of a wrongful act or omission.[6] Potentially subversive political opinions may, however, be a ground for preventive detention in wartime,[7] and for dismissal from the civil service or removal to a non-sensitive post at the present time.[8]

II

'Freedom of discussion', in Dicey's words, was 'in England little else than the right to write or say anything which a jury, consisting of twelve shopkeepers, think it expedient should be said or written.'[9] It was subject to no prior restraint. Press censorship had lapsed in 1695. Press libels, moreover, were triable according to the ordinary law of the land by the ordinary courts; the rule of law prevailed.

This simple picture, portraying the laws of defamation, sedition and blasphemy as the main restrictions on freedom of expression, needs to be modified today. The restrictions, though not oppressive, are multifarious. Trial of offenders is not always by jury. Moreover, restraints may operate before any legal wrong has been committed. These prior restraints are not neatly segregated from offences arising from dissemination. For example, one needs a licence to transmit a radio broadcast; if one broadcasts without such a licence, one incurs a criminal penalty. Obscene literature can be seized, condemned and destroyed; if such literature escapes suppression, it is still an offence to publish it. A public meeting held on private premises is a civil trespass if conducted without the occupier's permission and an injunction may be obtained to prevent it from being held.

Prior restraints are not all of the same kind. Some are strictly legal prohibitions coupled with a sanction; others are extra-legal and have to be analysed in different terms. If there is a sanction annexed to disregard of

4. Statute of Treasons 1351; *R.* v. *Thistlewood* (1820) 33 St. Tr. 681; Treason Act 1795, s. 1; Treason Felony Act 1848, s. 3.

5. *Per* Brian C.J. in 1477.

6. Misprision (concealment) of treason is still a common-law offence, but misprision of another's felony has been superseded by section 5(1) of the Criminal Law Act 1967 which makes it an offence to accept a valuable consideration for concealment of an arrestable offence.

7. See p. 519.

8. See pp. 196–8.

9. *Introduction to the Study of the Law of the Constitution* (10th edn), p. 246.

a prohibition, it may range from imprisonment to loss of a licence or of promotion prospects. Such restraints are more easily tabulated than classified.

Accessibility of media for publicity

I may be at liberty to express an opinion but unable to obtain an audience because nobody will let a hall to me for the conduct of a public meeting, or because the competent authority refuses me a permit to hold a meeting in a public place under its control, or because the police (if no prior authority is required by law) threaten to prosecute me for obstruction of the highway or a similar offence if I proceed; or the police may simply assert their power to stop me because they reasonably apprehend a breach of the peace,[10] though by participating in a mass demonstration I may at once achieve more publicity and gain a measure of safety in numbers. I cannot compel newspaper editors to publish my letters, or editors and publishers to accept my articles and books. If I have the money and persistence I can have my work printed privately and distributed by post. Provided that it does not contain offensive or obscene material and it is not prejudicial to public safety or security[11] it will be immune from interception and seizure in the mails. But booksellers and public libraries may refuse to purchase it, and indeed blacklist it.[12] I may offer to pay for or subscribe to the cost of an advertisement for the propagation of my opinions; newspapers may decline to print it and other bodies owning advertising space are not obliged to display it.[13] I cannot set up a private broadcasting station to air my opinions to the public at large within the United Kingdom unless I am awarded a programme contract by the Independent Broadcasting Authority.[14]

Censorship and suppression[15]

The Press. Executive censorship of the press ended in 1695, to be revived only in wartime. (Early in 1941, under Defence Regulation 2D, the *Daily Worker* was suppressed for persistent publication of matter calculated to foment opposition to the successful prosecution of the war – it was allowed

10. See ch. 22.
11. Post Office Act 1953, ss. 11, 58, 66.
12. See Harry Street, *Freedom, the Individual and the Law* (3rd edn), p. 92.
13. See ibid., pp. 106–9, on informal regulation of advertising.
14. See Wireless Telegraphy Act 1949; Marine etc. Broadcasting (Offences) Act 1967; Television Act 1964; Sound Broadcasting Act 1972.
15. See generally Paul O'Higgins, *Censorship in Britain* (1972) for radical criticism of present law and practice.

to resume publication some months later – and in 1942 the *Daily Mirror* received a formal warning following the publication of a cartoon to which the Government took exception.) The legal requirements as to the registration of newspapers and the printing of the names of their publishers and printers in each issue are not substantial restraints.

Offences committed by the publication of material by reason of its content will be considered separately, but we may note at this point that it is unlawful for the press to publish the evidence (otherwise than such as is disclosed by the judge's summing up or judgment) in divorce and nullity proceedings, or any indecent matter disclosed in judicial proceedings,[16] or (subject to limited exceptions) information divulging the identity of juveniles involved in court proceedings,[17] or in general except at the defendant's request, a contemporaneous report of the evidence given at committal proceedings before magistrates.[18]

Reference can also be made here to the 'D' Notice system. There exists a non-statutory Defence, Press and Broadcasting Committee, with a senior civil servant as chairman; it includes other senior officials, but representatives of the press, press agencies and broadcasting services are in the majority among its members; it has a full-time secretary, a retired senior officer from the armed services. Its main function is to approve the issue of 'D' Notices, which are confidential letters initiated by government Departments and addressed to newspaper, periodical and news bulletin editors, requesting that material not be published because it would have an adverse effect on national defence or security.[19] Non-compliance with such a request is not an offence in itself, but it may result in a prosecution for a breach of the Official Secrets Acts,[20] compliance with the request being in practice a safeguard against a prosecution, though an assurance that an item of information is not covered by a 'D' Notice is not in itself such a safeguard.[21] Even if disclosure of the information is not a breach

16. Judicial Proceedings (Regulation of Reports) Act 1926, s. 1. See also Domestic and Appellate Proceedings (Restriction of Publicity) Act 1968.

17. R. M. Jackson, *The Machinery of Justice in England* (6th edn), p. 23.

18. Criminal Justice Act 1967, s. 3. Proceedings for the offence thus constituted may be commenced only by or with the consent of the Attorney-General. The restrictions do not apply if the defendant is *not* committed for trial.

19. See generally Cmnd 1681 (1962), ch. 9; Cmnd 3309, 3312 (1967); David Williams, *Not in the Public Interest*, p. 80ff.; G. Marshall [1967] *Public Law* 261; Report of the (Franks) Committee on section 2 of the Official Secrets Act 1911 (Cmnd 5104 (1972)), § 65; Minutes of Evidence, vol. 2, pp. 241–5, vol. 3, pp. 51–68. 'D' Notices are also sent to book publishers from time to time, requesting non-publication of certain matters or the submission of manuscripts for security clearance.

20. See pp. 484–6.

21. This was the position in the *Sunday Telegraph* (or Biafra) case, 1970–71: see Jonathan Aitken, *Officially Secret* (1971).

of the Acts, the news medium concerned may be publicly censured and may find that confidential information formerly supplied to it from official sources is thereafter withheld.

Broadcasting services

The British Broadcasting Corporation, constituted by royal charter in 1926, provides all non-commercial radio and television services. Its functions are prescribed by its charter, the current licence and agreement[22] under which it operates, and any directions issued to it by the Minister of Posts and Telecommunications in pursuance of powers conferred on him by the governing instruments. Under the agreement he is empowered to require the Corporation to refrain from broadcasting any matter or class of matter at any time. If the Corporation fails to comply with a valid direction he may revoke its licence.[23]

He enjoys statutory powers of direction in relation to the Independent Broadcasting Authority,[24] which regulates commercial services provided by programme contractors. A number of positive duties (for example, to broadcast Government announcements but to maintain political impartiality) are cast on the BBC and the IBA.

In what circumstances (if any) can a breach of such duties by the broadcasting authorities give rise to judicial proceedings? This depends partly on the nature and wording of the duty. The duties of the BBC to send out broadcasts 'efficiently' and of the IBA to maintain a 'high quality' in programmes are so vague that no court would hold them to be enforceable. (It is, of course, possible for the Minister to cancel the BBC's licence, or to initiate the dismissal of the Governors of the BBC by the Crown or himself to dismiss the members of the IBA. Such drastic action, however, would hardly be conceivable unless there was direct disobedience of a specific ministerial direction; in the Republic of Ireland in November 1972 the members of RTE, the equivalent body to the BBC, were dismissed *en bloc* for refusal to comply with a direction.) Duties to broadcast Government announcements and to maintain political impartiality are potentially enforceable in judicial proceedings by an order of mandamus awarded by the High Court on the application of the Minister; there again, however, the duty has to be specific and clear-cut, and one doubts whether the duty of impartiality falls into that category. It is also arguable[25] that the Attorney General, as guardian of the public interest, might obtain an injunction

22. Cmnd 4095 (1969) sets out the present licence and agreement, operative till 1976.
23. Licence, clauses 13(4), 23.
24. Television Act 1964, s. 18(3).
25. Television Act 1964, s. 3(1)(*a*).

(coupled with a declaration) to restrain the IBA from breaking their duty to satisfy themselves as far as possible, that nothing indecent or offensive to public feeling is broadcast. It is submitted that an ordinary member of the public has no *locus standi* to maintain such proceedings.[26] For a private plaintiff to be entitled to sue for breach of one of these duties, he should be required to establish that he has a special and direct personal interest, different from the interest of the public in general, in the performance of the particular duty.

The broadcasting authorities maintain their own standards, subject to formal obligations and ministerial directives, in the presentation of films and plays.[27] As we have seen, they are also included within the ambit of the 'D' Notice system.

Theatres and plays. Till 1968, stage performances were subject to an authentic form of censorship. No play written after 1843 could be performed in public except under a licence granted by the Lord Chamberlain, who could insist on deletions and alterations to the script before giving his permission. It was a criminal offence to stage a play in an unapproved form. Power to license theatres was exercised by the Lord Chamberlain in Central London and Windsor and by local authorities elsewhere. Performance of an unlicensed play, or breach of conditions annexed to the grant of a theatre licence, could lead to revocation of the latter type of licence.

Following the report of a joint select committee of the two Houses, a private member's bill was introduced to abolish the Lord Chamberlain's powers; it became the Theatres Act 1968. Premises still require a local authority licence if they are to be used for the public performance of a play, but no condition may be imposed restricting the content of the 'plays' to be performed other than an exhibition of hypnotism.[28] The law relating to criminal offences and civil wrongs committed in the course of a stage performance has been redefined. The immediate practical effects of the Act were an increase in plays dealing with controversial topics such as homosexuality, the production of nude musicals, and the use of earthier language than the Lord Chamberlain would formerly have permitted.

Films.[29] Film censorship is a blend of statutory and non-statutory

26. For comment on *Att.-Gen., ex rel. McWhirter* v. *IBA* [1973] 2 W.L.R. 344 (C.A.), see Addendum. cf. *Thorne* v. *BBC* [1967] 1 W.L.R. 1104.

27. See generally Street, op. cit., pp. 78–89, 109–16. The BBC has established an independent Programmes Complaints Commission. See p. 225.

28. s. 1(2). Conditions may be imposed in the interests of physical safety and health. An appeal lies to a magistrates' court at the instance of a person aggrieved by a licensing decision (s. 14).

29. Street, op. cit., pp. 64–74.

regulation. Cinemas are licensed[30] by local authorities. Conditions may be attached to the grant of licences, restricting the admission of children, prohibiting the exhibition of films likely to be injurious to morality, and so on. A condition commonly imposed is that no film not approved by the British Board of Film Censors shall be exhibited without the express consent of the licensing authority. The Board is a non-statutory body constituted by the film industry; the president is appointed by a committee representing the industry after consultation with the Home Office and the local authority associations, but he is independent of the industry. The full-time secretary of the Board has, in practice, been its most dominant figure. Films are classified as 'U' (suitable for universal exhibition), 'A' (no formal restriction, but parents are warned that it may be undesirable for children under fourteen to be present), 'AA' (no child under fourteen being permitted to be present) or 'X' (no person under eighteen being permitted to be present). The Board may refuse a film a certificate altogether, or grant one only if prescribed cuts are made. A licensing authority cannot validly fetter its discretion by automatically following the Board's decisions[31] though it may elect to follow them unless exceptional circumstances are present. There is nothing, apart from the sanctions of the criminal law which may be applied to an exhibitor, to prevent a local authority from allowing a film to be exhibited to which the Board has denied a certificate or from permitting the restoration of cuts made at the insistence of the Board. Nor is an authority obliged to permit the exhibition of a film passed by the Board. It is not uncommon for different authorities to adopt variant attitudes towards a particularly controversial film.

Having regard to the higher attendance of children at cinemas than theatres, and to the regularity with which a great number of children and old people watch television programmes, there is a stronger case for broadcasting and film censorship than for theatrical censorship. There is, indeed, an arguable case for censorship of the dissemination of popular written matter, but this could be enforced only spasmodically or oppressively and on balance would almost certainly lead to the suppression of meritorious or innocuous material.

Official documents and civil servants' publications. As has been indicated, State papers (including Cabinet documents) are made available to public scrutiny only after the lapse of thirty years. Records may still be withheld after that period by the Lord Chancellor, with the approval or at the request of the relevant Minister, or if they might cause distress to living persons or their descendants, or if they embody information received under

30. Cinematograph Act 1952.
31. *Ellis* v. *Dubowski* [1921] 3 K.B. 621.

a pledge of confidence or liable to prejudice current trade promotion or national security.[32]

The former practice whereby whole classes of departmental documents relevant to judicial proceedings could be withheld from disclosure by virtue of a ministerial objection on the ground that their production would be injurious to the national interest has been substantially diminished in the last few years.[33] Moreover, departmental documents must be made available to the Parliamentary Commissioner for Administration for the purpose of his investigations.

Any student of central government administration in Britain will be aware of the difficulty experienced in persuading civil servants to divulge particulars of internal procedures or the undisclosed reasons for individual decisions if there is any likelihood of his publishing an account of his research. The ethos generated by the Official Secrets Acts is still pervasive, though the fog of obscurity is no longer as dense as in the 1950s. Serving and retired civil servants must obtain official approval of the manuscript of any book they themselves write before it is published. A civil servant who writes a controversial letter to the press or gives a broadcast interview will be well advised to seek approval in advance; otherwise he risks contravening service regulations and earning the severe disapproval of his superiors.

Contempt of court. A news medium proposing to publish material which would tend to prejudice a fair trial may be restrained by an injunction in proceedings instituted by the Attorney-General.[34]

Miscellaneous. In 1971 leading American newspapers published extracts from the 'Pentagon papers', a record of top-secret policy discussions about Vietnam. An attempt by the United States Government to obtain an injunction to restrain further publication of the information was rejected by the United States Supreme Court.[35] In this country it is thought that the Attorney-General would have succeeded in similar circumstances, either on the ground that publication was a breach of Crown copyright or possibly (though there is no authority directly in point) on the ground that this was a breach of confidence which the courts ought to restrain.

Prior censorship, and the seizure and destruction of documents under legal powers, are the most obvious means of suppressing freedom of expression. The prospect of incurring penal sanctions *ex post facto* will also

32. Public Records Acts 1958 and 1967.
33. See especially *Conway* v. *Rimmer* [1968] A.C. 910; and pp. 618–23.
34. *Att.-Gen.* v. *Times Newspapers Ltd* [1972] 3 W.L.R. 855; but see Addendum.
35. *New York Times Co.* v. *United States* 403 U.S. 713 (1971); *The Pentagon Papers* (Bantam Books, 1971).

tend to inhibit free expression. So will the foreknowledge that one's communications may be intercepted and read or overheard.

Freedom of expression is not an end in itself. Doctrinaire absolutism is an inept instrument for evaluating the competing claims of the individual and society. John Stuart Mill, himself a powerful defender of human liberty, declared: 'The sole end for which mankind are warranted, individually or collectively, in interfering with the liberty of action of any of their number, is self-protection.' This grudging concession is a starting point, not the conclusion, of any attempt to define the proper limits of freedom of expression. But the onus to be discharged by one seeking to justify the stifling of opinion should be heavier than that cast upon one asserting the propriety of penalizing its expression after the event. History bears witness to the insidious effects of the suppression of dissent and the denial of free interchange of ideas. These effects are all the more insidious when the fact of suppression is itself suppressed or so concealed as not to be identifiable.

III

The following are the principal wrongs in English law that may be committed by words or pictorial demonstrations.

Treason and treason felony

These offences overlap. Treason is still punishable with death, treason felony with life imprisonment. It is treason to conspire or incite to kill or overthrow the monarch, to levy war against her by raising an insurrection, or to adhere to her enemies[36] in time of war (for example, by broadcasting propaganda for the enemy).[37] Incitement to rebellion against the Government in the United Kingdom, or a conspiracy to deprive the Queen of her sovereignty in any part of her dominions, or an invitation to a foreigner to invade any part of them, is also treason felony.[38]

Seditious offences[39]

To publish spoken or written words with a seditious intention is a common-law misdemeanour. A seditious intention has been defined in very broad terms, including 'an intention to bring into hatred and contempt, or excite

36. Within or without Her Majesty's dominions (*R.* v. *Casement* [1917] 1 K.B. 98).
37. To be guilty of treason the accused must be a person owing allegiance; on which see *Joyce* v. *D.P.P.* [1946] A.C. 347; and see pp. 437–9. There must be overt acts of disloyalty.
38. Treason Felony Act 1848. Again, only persons owing allegiance may commit the offence.
39. For good synopses, see Smith and Hogan, *Criminal Law* (3rd edn), pp. 646–57; Ian Brownlie, *The Law Relating to Public Order*, pp. 85–90.

disaffection against . . . the government and constitution . . . either House of Parliament, or the administration of justice . . . or to raise discontent or disaffection among Her Majesty's subjects, or to promote feelings of ill-will and hostility between different classes of such subjects'.[40] This could encompass any forceful criticism of the existing structure of authority within the State.

In this century prosecutions for sedition have been so few that the ingredients of the offence cannot be stated with assurance, but it would seem that there must now be an intent to incite to violence against the institutions and laws of the State[41] or a section of the community[42] for a conviction to be obtained. Nevertheless, in a modern case the Privy Council held that under the laws of a colony sedition could be committed without any incitement to violence,[43] and some of the successor governments to the colonial régimes have used the wide concept of sedition as an instrument for browbeating their opponents.[44]

There are several statutory offences akin to sedition in its broadest meaning. It is an offence to do any act 'calculated to cause disaffection' among the police.[45] Under the Incitement to Disaffection Act 1934,[46] it is an offence maliciously and advisedly to endeavour to seduce a member of the forces from his duty or allegiance to the Crown, or to have in one's possession, with intent to commit or counsel the offence, literature the dissemination of which would be such an offence. Prosecutions have been very rare, and leave of the Director of Public Prosecutions is required. A search warrant may be issued by a High Court judge in respect of an offence under the Act. The Act could be used against persons distributing pacifist literature to members of the forces. Other anti-sedition legislation still on the statute book includes the Unlawful Oaths Act 1797 (successfully invoked against the Tolpuddle Martyrs) and 1812.[47] In this area of the law,

40. Sir James Stephen, *Digest of the Criminal Law* (3rd edn), art. 93.

41. *R.* v. *Burns* (1886) 16 Cox C.C. 355. See also *R.* v. *Aldred* (1909) 22 Cox C.C. 1, where the publication had been calculated to incite to violence but it was not made clear by the judge that an intent to provoke violence had to be established.

42. *R.* v. *Caunt* (1947) (unreported; an offensive attack on British Jewry; jury directed that an intent to excite violence had to be demonstrated). Such an attack might still be indictable as a public mischief.

43. *R.* v. *Wallace-Johnson* [1940] A.C. 231 (Gold Coast).

44. See, for example, G. Ezejiofor, *Protection of Human Rights under the Law*, pp. 194–8.

45. Police Act 1964, s. 53, reproducing earlier legislation. See also Aliens Restriction (Amendment) Act 1919, penalizing forms of disaffection instigated by aliens.

46. See also Incitement to Mutiny Act 1797; Williams, *Not in the Public Interest*, pp. 102–3, 113–14.

47. Partly repealed by the schedules to the Criminal Law Act 1967, which also repealed most of what remained of the Seditious Meetings Act 1817. See, however, p. 504, note 37.

restraint in instituting prosecutions, the prospect of a restrictive direction by a judge and an acquittal by a jury are the effective safeguards for the expression of political dissent.

Breaches of the Official Secrets Acts[48]

Till 1889 there was no legislation making it an offence to disclose official secrets to foreign powers or to other unauthorized persons. The present law is contained in the Official Secrets Acts 1911, 1920 and 1939. The ambit of the Acts is by no means confined to espionage. The marginal note to section 1 of the 1911 Act reads 'Penalties against spying', and makes it an offence punishable with fourteen years' imprisonment for any person, 'for any purpose prejudicial to the safety or interests of the State', not only to engage in specified conduct calculated to be useful to an enemy but also to approach, inspect or enter a 'prohibited place'[49] within the meaning of the Act. Nuclear disarmers who approached a military airfield with the intention of immobilizing it were convicted under this section,[50] although their purpose was not espionage but non-violent sabotage; the fact that in their opinion they were acting in the true interests of the State was held to be irrelevant, inasmuch as they were intentionally engaging in conduct prohibited by the Act and the policy behind the disposition and use of the armed forces of the Crown fell within the scope of the royal prerogative and could not be a subject of independent judicial scrutiny. It is also an offence to refuse to supply information to a senior police officer as to the commission of an offence under this section.[51] In a prosecution for the principal offence, the prejudicial purpose may be inferred from the circumstances in the absence of an overt act; and if information about a prohibited place is proved to have been obtained or communicated without lawful authority, the onus of proving that the purpose was not one prejudicial to the interests of the State is cast upon the accused.[52] For serious cases of espionage or betrayal of the activities of British agents, the maximum sentence of fourteen years may be inadequate; the maximum

48. The leading study is David Williams, *Not in the Public Interest*. See now Report of the Committee on Section 2 of the Official Secrets Act 1911 (Cmnd 5104 (1972)) and Minutes of Evidence in three volumes; these contain a mine of information, much of it previously undisclosed.

49. s. 3 (for example, defence establishments and places used by or belonging to the Crown and declared by a Secretary of State to be prohibited places).

50. *Chandler* v. *D.P.P.* [1964] A.C. 763; criticized by D. Thompson [1963] *Public Law* 201; but see Smith and Hogan, *Criminal Law* (3rd edn), p. 652. See also p. 116, note 67.

51. Official Secrets Act 1920, s. 6 (as amended by the Official Secrets Act 1939).

52. 1911 Act, s. 1(2).

has been raised not by amending legislation but by indirect means – by charging accused persons with a conspiracy to contravene section 1, for which there is no limit to the duration of a sentence upon conviction, or by sentencing convicted spies to consecutive terms of imprisonment on separate counts – and sentences as long as forty-two and twenty-five years were imposed in the 1960s.

Under section 2 of the 1911 Act it is an offence punishable with up to two years' imprisonment to retain without permission, or fail to take reasonable care of, information obtained as result of one's present or former employment under the Crown or a government contract; or to *communicate* information so obtained, or entrusted to one in confidence by a person holding office under Her Majesty,[53] or obtained in contravention of the Act, to anybody other than a person to whom one is authorized to convey it or to whom it is one's duty to impart it in the interests of the State; or to *receive* such information, knowing or having reasonable cause to believe it has been given in contravention of the Act. These are wide-ranging prohibitions. It may be an offence under section 2 for a civil servant to pass on, or for a research worker to acquire from him, information about internal departmental procedures although the material has no bearing on security and is not even classified as confidential. This section is indeed convoluted and abstruse. The Franks Committee which reported in 1972 described it as a 'catch-all' and a 'mess'.[54] Yet who could malign a section which creates 2324 separate offences?[55]

However, the section has undoubtedly many defects. For instance, it is not clear whether guilty knowledge (*mens rea*) has to be proved for unauthorized communication to be an offence.[56] When is communication authorized? What of 'leaks' by Ministers? According to official doctrine, Ministers 'authorize themselves' to convey information about matters of government and administration; civil servants have implied authorization depending on the nature of their job and the circumstances of the case. All this is very vague. And in the absence of authorization, when is it my duty or a journalist's duty 'in the interests of the State' to publicize official information? No intelligible answer has yet been produced. What is the

53. This term includes a police officer: *Lewis* v. *Cattle* [1938] 2 K.B. 454.
54. Cmnd 5104 (1972), §§ 17, 88.
55. Minutes of Evidence, vol. 2, p. 262 (Appendix to evidence of Bar Council).
56. In the *Sunday Telegraph* case (1971, unreported; see Jonathan Aitken, *Officially Secret*), where a military officer, a journalist and a newspaper editor were prosecuted (but acquitted) in respect of publication of a confidential appreciation of the Nigerian civil war situation written by a military official at the British High Commission in Lagos, Caulfield J. directed the jury that *mens rea* on the part of all involved in the chain of communication had to be proved. This interpretation is not universally accepted.

policy in instituting prosecutions? The Attorney-General has an absolute discretion in this matter; the criteria adopted in deciding whether to bring or authorize a prosecution are nebulous, but fortunately prosecutions have averaged only about one a year since 1945 and most (but by no means all) have involved elements of obvious impropriety. But the deterrent effect of the Act on junior and middle-grade civil servants in particular may be considerable.

The Franks Committee made detailed proposals for replacing section 2 by a new Official Information Act. They would restrict criminal sanctions to defined areas of major importance: wrongful disclosures of (i) information of major national importance in the fields of defence, security, foreign relations, currency and the reserves; (ii) Cabinet documents; and (iii) information facilitating criminal activity or violating the confidentiality of information supplied to the Government by or about individuals; and the use of official information for private gain. Mere receipt of protected information would not be an offence under the Act, but communication by journalists and others would still be if the author or speaker had reasonable grounds for believing that it had been conveyed to him in breach of the Act. Only material classified as Top Secret or Secret (or Defence-Confidential) would be protected in category (i); and before a prosecution could be brought, the responsible Minister in person would have to certify that the information was properly so classified at the relevant time. Although the prosecution would have to prove that the information fell within the scope of a classified category in the first place, the Minister's certificate as to classification at the time of instituting proceedings would be binding on the court. There should be an advisory committee (similar to the 'D' Notice committee[57]) on matters relating to classification.

The proposals, outlined very briefly above, would restrict the ambit of the criminal law, but were not really radical. There would be no defence, for example, that the public interest was not in fact injured by a disclosure; the difficulties and uncertainty inherent in the concept of implied authorization would remain; over-classification of information might still occur; there was no recommendation about giving fuller publicity to official information along the lines of American or Swedish practice. But they were a careful attempt to draw lines in an area where cartography is extraordinarily difficult.

Blasphemy

Like sedition, this common-law misdemeanour has diminished in scope by judicial interpretation and prosecutions are extremely rare. Its ambit

57. See p. 477.

has never been clearly determinate; it has been held at various times to consist in the denial of the truth of Christian doctrine, or the doctrines of the Church of England, or of the existence of a Deity. Modern judicial pronouncements support the view that anti-Christian or irreligious argument is not blasphemous provided that the decencies of controversy are observed and the language used is not calculated to give rise to a breach of the peace.[58]

Defamation[59]

A defamatory statement is one which tends to expose another to hatred, ridicule or contempt or to cause him to be shunned by reasonable persons. Defamatory matter consisting of spoken words, or gestures, is slander; in permanent form it is libel. By statute,[60] words used in a broadcast or a public performance of a play are deemed to be libel. The distinction between slander and libel is of practical importance. In the first place, although both slander and libel are torts, no action will lie for slander in the absence of proof of special pecuniary damage, save in a limited range of situations. Secondly, slander is not of itself a criminal offence, but libel may be.[61] A conviction for libel may be obtained even though the statement was published only to the person defamed and was true (unless publication was for the public benefit). A libel may also be indictable, though not actionable as a tort, if it relates to a class of persons, and possibly if it relates to a dead person. But prosecutions for libel are discouraged. No such prosecution against a newspaper proprietor, publisher or editor may be brought except with leave of a judge in chambers.[62]

For a civil action to lie, the defamatory statement must have been published to a third party. It is a defence that the statement was true, or was a fair comment on a matter of public interest, or was uttered on a privileged occasion. No action will lie in respect of an absolutely privileged statement even if it is false and malicious. Absolute privilege attaches to statements made in the course of judicial proceedings, proceedings in Parliament,

58. See especially *Bowman* v. *Secular Society Ltd* [1917] A.C. 406. 'Indecent' behaviour in a place of religious worship (an offence under s. 2 of the Ecclesiastical Courts Jurisdiction Act 1860) includes interrupting a service by shouting political slogans: *Abrahams* v. *Cavey* [1968] 1 Q.B. 479.

59. For details, see the latest editions of *Gatley on Libel and Slander*, and the leading textbooks on the law of tort (*Clerk and Lindsell*, *Salmond*, *Street*, and *Winfield and Jolowicz*). Only a very brief outline of this complex branch of the law is presented here.

60. Defamation Act 1952, s. 1; Theatres Act 1968, ss. 4, 7.

61. There remains some doubt whether it is necessary to prove, in a prosecution for libel, that the statement tended to give rise to a breach of the peace.

62. Law of Libel Amendment Act 1888, s. 8; see also Newspaper Libel and Registration Act 1881, s. 4 (certain newspaper libels are triable summarily before magistrates).

parliamentary papers, and to communications between high officers of State and to fair and accurate newspaper or broadcast reports of judicial proceedings. Qualified privilege is lost by proof of malice, which is not easily established. Among the numerous situations covered by qualified privilege are fair and accurate newspaper reports of parliamentary proceedings,[63] and of the proceedings of public meetings, local councils and administrative tribunals and inquiries;[64] and communications between members of the public and M.P.s, and M.P.s and Ministers, on matters of public interest.[65] If a person is unintentionally defamed, the innocent publisher may defend himself successfully in an action by making an offer of amends (which means the publication of a correction and an apology) as soon as possible; he must also show that he had acted with reasonable care.[66]

The law of defamation still presents many hazards for the press; and juries are still apt to make heavy awards of compensatory damages to persons defamed by newspapers.[67] Many proprietors and editors of journals would doubtless welcome a judicial decision such as one delivered in 1964 by the United States Supreme Court, that false and defamatory press statements about the conduct of a holder of a public office were not actionable provided that the critic was acting in good faith.[68] Justice may have been done in the particular circumstances of that case, but it would be deplorable if English law gave a licence for character assassination of public figures. At the present time some journals achieve a mass circulation by 'shocking revelations' about the private lives of persons in the news. As was mentioned earlier,[69] there is in general no legal remedy for the improper but non-defamatory invasion of privacy. But a complaint may be made to the Press Council,[70] a non-statutory investigatory body with a judicial chairman but composed largely of representatives of the press, and this Council can do no more than administer a public rebuke. When invoked, the sanctions of the law of defamation are quite severe, but they

63. *Wason* v. *Walter* (1868) L.R. 4 Q.B. 73.

64. See generally Defamation Act 1952, ss. 7, 16, Schedule, extending the defence of qualified privilege in respect of libellous newspaper reports. In many of these situations qualified privilege will be a defence only if the newspaper has published, at the plaintiff's request, a reasonable statement by way of contradiction or explanation.

65. See p. 318.

66. ibid., s. 4.

67. Exemplary damages in tort can only be awarded in a limited range of situations: *Broome* v. *Cassell & Co.* [1972] A.C. 1027.

68. *New York Times Ltd* v. *Sullivan*, 376 U.S. 255 (1964).

69. See p. 469.

70. See H. Phillip Levy, *The Press Council*; Report of the Committee on Privacy (Cmnd 5012 (1972)), ch. 7.

are not open to persons of modest means: actions for defamation cannot be brought in county courts, High Court costs may be extremely heavy and the legal aid scheme does not extend to such proceedings.

Contempt of court and of the Houses of Parliament[71]

In some respect these legal restrictions on free expression do bear harshly on journalists and broadcasters. The *sub judice* rule is strictly interpreted. Premature disclosure of the report of a parliamentary committee is a contempt of the House in question. A journalist who refuses to divulge relevant information in his possession, or the source of that information, in response to demands by members of a select committee (for example, the Committee of Privileges) or a court or a judicial tribunal of inquiry set up in pursuance of the Tribunals of Inquiry (Evidence) Act 1921, is guilty of contempt, and may be sent to prison.[72]

Miscellaneous wrongs involving speech or writing

A great number of criminal offences can be committed by the use of spoken words or writing. For example, it is an offence to incite another to commit a crime. A criminal conspiracy can hardly be effectuated without verbal communication. Intimidating words accompanied by threatening behaviour may be an assault although there is no physical contact with the person put in fear. Perjury, blackmail, fraud and attempting to pervert the course of justice by, for example, interfering with witnesses, all involve some form of verbal communication. It is an offence to waste the time of the police by knowingly making a false report;[73] or to pester people with false or offensive telephone calls;[74] or to publish a false description of articles and goods for sale.[75] Among torts, fraudulent misrepresentation, deceit, slander of title and passing off are essentially verbal misdeeds.

Insulting words and behaviour[76]

Under a number of local Acts and by-laws it has long been an offence to use threatening, abusive or insulting words or behaviour in a public place

71. See ch. 14 and pp. 371–2, 461.
72. In the latter class of case the offence is analogous to contempt of court: *Att.-Gen.* v. *Clough* [1963] 1 Q.B. 773; *Att.-Gen.* v. *Mulholland* [1963] 2 Q.B. 477.
73. Criminal Law Act 1967, s. 5(2).
74. Post Office Act 1969, s. 78.
75. Trade Descriptions Act 1968.
76. See David Williams, *Keeping the Peace*, pp. 153–69; Ian Brownlie, *The Law Relating to Public Order*, pp. 6–8, 11–14, 160–61, 163.

with intent to provoke a breach of the peace or whereby a breach of the peace is likely to be occasioned.[77] Section 5 of the Public Order Act 1936 made this a general offence, and extended it to public meetings. For the purpose of the offence, a public place includes a highway or any premises or place to which the public have access, on payment or otherwise.[78] A public meeting is one held in a public place or one which any section of the public is permitted to attend, with or without payment;[79] in other words, it means a meeting that is not private or confined to members of a particular organization.

In 1963 the maximum penalties for the offence were increased;[80] in 1965 the offence was extended to the distribution or display of written matter and signs;[81] and in 1968 to theatrical performances to which the public was admitted.[82]

The importance of the offence is that, measured in terms of prosecutions and convictions, it is the most significant restriction on freedom of political expression by speakers and their audiences in contemporary English law. Little difficulty arises in determining the meaning of threatening or abusive conduct. Interpretation of 'insulting' leaves more room for judicial and magisterial discretion. The perpetrator of the words or conduct must have either intended to insult others or been reckless in his behaviour; and it would seem (though this is not entirely clear) that a person must actually have been insulted by it. Still, no offence is committed under the Acts unless it is likely to cause at least one reader, listener or observer to resort to violence. But if a speaker deliberately insults a hostile audience with the result that they are likely to commit a breach of the peace, it is immaterial that he may not have intended to provoke them to acts of violence or that they would not have resorted to violence had they been reasonably phlegmatic or decorous persons. When Colin Jordan, the British Nazi, insulted a hostile audience in Trafalgar Square, calling them 'red rabble' and asserting that Britain had picked on the wrong enemy in 1939, that international Jewry was the real culprit and that 'Hitler was right', it was held that he had to take the audience as he found them; the gist of the offence was public insult, likely in the circumstances to give rise to a breach

77. See, for example, *Wise* v. *Dunning* [1902] 1 K.B. 167.

78. Criminal Justice Act 1972, s. 33, extending the former definition.

79. Public Order Act 1936, s. 9.

80. Public Order Act 1963 (twelve months or a £500 fine or both on conviction on indictment). The offence is nearly always tried summarily; the maximum is three months' imprisonment.

81. Race Relations Act 1965, s. 7. This provision (restating section 5 of the 1936 Act) had no direct connection with race relations. The distribution or display must be in a public place or at a public meetings.

82. Theatres Act 1968, s. 6.

of the peace, and he was convicted.[83] The offence is not confined to political diatribes; it includes abusive language directed against a neighbour in public.[84] However, it is not enough to show that other people were annoyed or affronted. The word 'insulting' is to be understood in its ordinary sense.[85]

Incitement to racial hatred

The creation of this offence by section 6 of the Race Relations Act 1965 has already been noted.[86] Prosecutions have been few;[87] leave of the Attorney-General must be obtained before a prosecution can be instituted; the offence is triable summarily or on indictment, and if the defendant elects to be tried by jury on indictment, the possibility of acquittal or disagreement may be very real. The offence may be committed only in a public place or at a public meeting or by the publication or distribution of written matter, but it is unnecessary to prove a consequential likelihood of a breach of the peace;[88] the perpetrator may have been preaching to the converted. The gist of the offence is the opprobrious nature of the words or conduct in question and the feelings of disgust they are liable to arouse. To this extent the offence is more akin to the old common law of obscenity than to other modern limitations imposed by the criminal law on freedom of expression.

Obscenity[89]

The law of obscenity is both complex and controversial. It encompasses a range of common-law offences, statutory offences, and provisions for search, forfeiture and destruction. And it bears on the limits of free expression and the relationship between the law and ideas about morality.

In 1663 indecent exposure, coupled with the projection of urine from a balcony upon an audience at Covent Garden, was held to be a common-

83. *Jordan* v. *Burgoyne* [1963] 2 Q.B. 744.

84. *Ward* v. *Holman* [1964] 2 Q.B. 580.

85. *Cozens* v. *Brutus* [1972] 3 W.L.R. 521, H.L. (anti-apartheid demonstration on tennis court during Wimbledon championships not an offence, though spectators angered).

86. pp. 446–7. See also Theatres Act 1968, s. 5, creating a broadly similar offence for theatrical performances.

87. See Anthony Dickey [1968] *Crim. L. Rev.* 489.

88. If a breach of the peace is likely, a prosecution may be brought under section 5 of the Public Order Act 1936, as restated by section 7 of the 1965 Act, without the Attorney-General's consent.

89. The law is well reviewed by Smith and Hogan, op. cit., pp. 562–75, and Street op. cit., pp. 119–45. See also Wade and Phillips (8th edn), ch. 39.

law misdemeanour.[90] A common-law offence of obscene libel developed from this bizarre episode. The common-law crime appeared to have been largely superseded by statute, but in 1961 the House of Lords held that an obscene publication was also indictable as a common-law conspiracy to corrupt public morals[91] and in 1972 it reaffirmed this proposition in a case where a majority of their Lordships were also of the opinion that a conspiracy to outrage public decency was an offence.[92] The defences now provided by the Obscene Publications Acts do not apply to such charges.

Statutory obscenity. Under the Obscene Publications Acts 1959 and 1964 it is an offence to publish an obscene article, or to have an obscene article for gain. Authors, photographers, artists, publishers, booksellers and other distributors may find themselves prosecuted under the Acts. Similarly, it is an offence under the Theatres Act 1968 to direct or present an obscene theatrical performance.

The test of obscenity under these Acts is similar to that laid down in a mid-Victorian case, where it was held to be whether the matter in question had a tendency to deprave and corrupt those who were open to such influences and into whose hands it might fall.[93] Under the recent Acts, the prosecution must prove that the matter, *taken as a whole*, would tend to deprave and corrupt persons likely to read or see or hear it; hence a book is not now obscene merely because it contains a few obscene words or sentences. However, a magazine or other publication consisting of a number of separate items may be obscene although only one item falls within that description.[94] But it appears that a person may be convicted under the Acts even if he had no intention to deprave or corrupt; though it is a

90. *R.* v. *Sidley* (1663) 1 Siderfin 168; *sub nom. Sydlye*'s case (1663) 1 Keb. 620, stating the facts more fully. See also Vagrancy Act 1824, s. 4; Criminal Justice Act 1925, s. 42.

91. *Shaw* v. *D.P.P.* [1962] A.C. 220 (the *Ladies' Directory* case; publication of a guide to specified prostitutes for prospective clients). There could be a criminal conspiracy without publication. The assumption by the House of Lords of the role of *custos morum* has been widely criticized, particularly on the grounds that the offence was novel or, at least, obsolescent, and judicial conceptions of corruption of public morals were unpredictable. No such prosecution can be brought in respect of a theatrical performance: Theatres Act 1968, s. 2(4).

92. *Knuller* (*Publishing, Printing and Promotions*) *Ltd* v. *D.P.P.* [1972] 3 W.L.R. 143 (agreement to publish advertisements in the *International Times* by persons seeking homosexual relationships, although such conduct between consenting adult males was no longer unlawful). Held, also, that there was an insufficient element of *publicity* for the offence of conspiracy to outrage public decency to be committed; but that the latter common-law offence could also be committed publicly by an individual in the absence of conspiracy.

93. *R.* v. *Hicklin* (1868) L.R. 3 Q.B. 360 (a seizure, not a prosecution).

94. *R.* v. *Anderson* [1972] 1 Q.B. 304 (the *Oz* 'schoolkids' issue case).

defence[95] for him to prove that he had not examined the offending article and had no reasonable cause to believe that publication or possession would be an offence.

It is also a statutory defence to a prosecution under the Act of 1959 that the publication was for the public good in the interests of science, literature, art or learning or other objects of public concern.[96] If a tendency to deprave and corrupt is proved, the defendant is entitled to acquittal if he can establish this defence on a balance of probabilities.[97] Expert opinion as to the scientific, literary or artistic merits of the book or article is admissible in evidence on both sides. However, such evidence is not admissible (save in highly exceptional circumstances[98]) on the primary issue of whether the article is obscene or not.[99]

What, then, is meant by a tendency to deprave and corrupt? And deprave and corrupt whom? Judicial pronouncements on these matters have shown a conspicuous lack of uniformity. Depravity and corruption have generally been understood to imply the weakening of moral fibre. Nowadays a judge, magistrate or jury is unlikely to be persuaded that anything less than the explicit portrayal or description of sexual activity tending to evoke erotic desires and an inclination to imitate what has been described or depicted is obscene in this sense. Yet this approach raises many problems. It is almost impossible to establish a causal connection between an erotic book or film and subsequent conduct,[100] other than masturbation. (Is this a form of depravity; and if so, should persons be convicted in the criminal courts for having conduced to it?) Few would disagree with the propositions that sadism and bestiality are forms of seriously anti-social conduct, and that the authors and purveyors of works intended to persuade others to indulge in such practices are not entitled to sympathetic treatment; but the establishment of causal connection is exceedingly difficult. Between these mild and extreme aberrations there lies a wide range of sexual acts which many people would not regard as depraved. In the decisions of magistrates and juries, and the directions of judges, there have been elements of unpredictability amounting to caprice. In 1928 the *Well of Loneliness*, a discreetly written literary work dealing with a sad theme of female homosexuality, was condemned as obscene. In the 1960s *Fanny*

95. Obscene Publications Act 1959, s. 2(5); Obscene Publications Act 1964, s. 1(3)(*a*).

96. 1959 Act, s. 4. See also Theatres Act 1968, s. 3.

97. See *R.* v. *Calder & Boyars Ltd* [1969] 1 Q.B. 151.

98. As in *D.P.P.* v. *A. & B.C. Chewing Gum Ltd* [1968] 1 Q.B. 159 (expert evidence as to effect on children).

99. *R.* v. *Anderson* [1972] 1 Q.B. 304; see also *R.* v. *Stamford* [1972] 2 Q.B. 391.

100. See, for example, the Reports of the Presidential Commission in the United States (1970) and of the Working Party of the Arts Council in Britain (1969), on obscenity (*The Obscenity Report*, Olympia Press, 1971).

Hill, a well-written and amusing eighteenth-century erotic work, was condemned, and the publishers of *Last Exit to Brooklyn*, a book containing descriptions of male homosexual intercourse and brutal violence but in a manner calculated to arouse feelings of pity and disgust, were held by a jury to be guilty of obscene libel;[101] but the publishers of *Lady Chatterley's Lover* (a serious though unconsciously funny novel, liberally interspersed with four-letter words and descriptions of extra-marital intercourse) were acquitted,[102] and no proceedings had been taken in connection with a book such as *Portnoy's Complaint*. Administrative and police practice had become more indulgent as society had become more permissive; but the outcome of judicial proceedings remained a lottery.[103]

If the tendency of a book to deprave and corrupt is established, it is not refuted merely because the most likely purchasers would already be depraved; they may be capable of being further depraved by reading it.[104] If, on the other hand, the only person to whom it was shown, for example, a senior police officer, was unlikely to be depraved or corrupted, there should be no conviction unless there was an intention to publish to others.[105] It seems that only if a significant proportion of the persons into whose hands a book may fall (not merely well brought-up fourteen-year-old girls[106]) are likely to be depraved or corrupted by it is the offence committed.[107] The circumstances of publication or offer for sale are therefore material. An expensive hard-back book may not offend against the Acts, though a cheap and easily accessible paperback edition may. Erotic prints or sculpture in a shop window may offend against them though the same representations in an art gallery may not. But the matter may still be so pornographic (for example, photographs of sexually deviant conduct) that the Act will be contravened despite the fact that display and distribution have been carefully restricted. Yet if the matter is so disgusting as to cause aversion or revulsion rather than corruption or depravity, the Acts are not contravened.[108]

101. The conviction was reversed because of a misdirection by the recorder (note 97 above).

102. See C. H. Rolph, *The Trial of Lady Chatterley*.

103. The problems of the police in enforcing the law against 'hard-core pornography' are well depicted in *R.* v. *Metropolitan Police Commissioner, ex p. Blackburn (No. 3)* [1973] 2 W.L.R. 43.

104. *D.P.P.* v. *Whyte* [1972] A.C. 849.

105. *R.* v. *Clayton and Halsey* [1963] 1 Q.B. 163; see also *R.* v. *Barker* [1962] 1 W.L.R. 349; 1964 Act, s. 1(3) (*b*).

106. cf. *R.* v. *Martin Secker & Warburg Ltd* [1954] 1 W.L.R. 1138 at 1139. Read as a whole, the direction given by Stable J. to the jury in that case (a charge of obscene libel at common law) is remarkable for its eloquent common sense.

107. *R.* v. *Calder & Boyars Ltd* (note 97 above).

108. *R.* v. *Anderson* (note 94). Because the 'aversion' defence was not put properly

The Acts are not confined to matters of sexual morality. A book extolling the pleasures of drug-taking may be an 'obscene' publication.[109] So, it seems, may a publication tending to induce violent behaviour,[110] but the publication of horror comics is a separate statutory offence.[111]

General. To outrage decency in public is a common-law misdemeanour. The offence may be committed not only by conduct, but also, it is thought, by words and pictures. If the words or conduct are both insulting and likely to cause a breach of the peace, this is a separate statutory offence.[112] Under a number of local Acts and by-laws, the use of obscene language in public, the display of obscene signs and other reprehensible forms of public conduct are also offences. There is obviously a good case for extending the reach of the criminal law to words, pictures or conduct thrust upon an unwilling hearer or observer or a captive audience who are likely to be disgusted,[113] though problems of definition will remain. It ought not to be necessary, in such cases, to prove tendency to deprave and corrupt. (The test of depravity and corruption, taken in conjunction with the 'aversion' concept and the defence that publication may still be for the public good, has left the law in a sorry state.[114]) Whether the sanctions of the criminal law of obscenity ought to extend beyond such cases at all is questionable.[115]

Obscene articles reasonably suspected of being kept for publication for gain can be searched for and seized under a magistrate's warrant.[116] Forfeiture proceedings can then be brought before the magistrate; the occupier is entitled to appear and show cause why they should not be forfeited. The defence of public good is available, but there is no provision for trial by

---

to the jury, the conviction of the defendants under the Obscene Publications Acts (though not their conviction under the Post Office Act: see below) was quashed.

109. *Calder (John) Publications Ltd* v. *Powell* [1965] 1 Q.B. 509.

110. *D.P.P.* v. *A. & B.C. Chewing Gum Ltd* [1968] 1 Q.B. 159.

111. Children and Young Persons (Harmful Publications) Act 1955. No prosecution under this Act can be commenced without the consent of the Director of Public Prosecutions.

112. See pp. 489–91.

113. cf. the Street Offences Act 1959, making it an offence to solicit *in public* for prostitution.

114. See criticisms in *D.P.P.* v. *Whyte* [1972] A.C. 849 at 861–2, *per* Lord Wilberforce, and by the Court of Appeal in *Blackburn* (*No. 3*).

115. The tentative suggestion made in the text above is superficially similar to that put forward in the Longford Report (*Pornography*, 1972, ch. 22), but the Report goes a good deal farther in that the definition of obscenity there proposed would extend to publications in general and the defence of public good would be excluded.

116. Obscene Publications Act 1959, s. 3. The warrant may be obtained only on information laid by the Director of Public Prosecutions or a constable (Criminal Justice Act 1967, s. 25). A *prosecution* under the 1959 Act can be brought by a member of the general public.

jury. The quantity of articles thus seized and condemned is very large; again, there is no uniformity of police or magisterial practice.

Indecent or obscene articles dispatched through the mails may be detained and destroyed. An article (for example a photograph) may be indecent for this purpose though not 'obscene'.[117] In this context 'obscene' is given its 'usual' meaning; an article may be obscene though repulsive, and there is no need to prove a tendency to deprave and corrupt, nor is the defence of public good available.[118] The importation of indecent or obscene works is prohibited under customs legislation and customs officers may seize them.[119] They are forfeited within a month unless the importer exercises his right of objection, in which case forfeiture can be ordered only by a magistrate; no defence of 'public good' is available in such a proceeding.

117. Post Office Act 1953, s. 11; *R.* v. *Stanley* [1965] 2 Q.B. 327, where the court quoted with approval (at 333) the following dictum in a Scottish case: 'For a male bather to enter the water nude in the presence of ladies would be indecent, but it would not necessarily be obscene. But if he directed the attention of a lady to a certain member of his body his conduct would certainly be obscene. The matter might perhaps be roughly expressed thus in the ascending scale: positive – immodest; comparative – indecent; superlative – obscene. These, however, are not rigid categories.' See also Unsolicited Goods and Services Act 1971, s. 4.

118. *R.* v. *Anderson* [1972] 1 Q.B. 304; *R.* v. *Stamford* [1972] 2 Q.B. 391.

119. Customs Consolidation Act 1876, s. 42; Customs and Excise Act 1952, ss. 275–80, Sched. 7. See also Post Office Act 1953, ss. 16, 17, 26(6); Post Office Act 1969, s. 64; Street, op. cit., pp. 139–40; *Derrick* v. *Customs and Excise Commissioners* [1972] 2 Q.B. 28.

Chapter 22
Freedom of Assembly and Association

Association

Freedom of political association in Britain is subject to two main limitations, neither of which affects movements seeking to operate within the framework of the existing constitutional order. In the first place, an agreement to effect an 'unlawful' purpose is a criminal conspiracy. That purpose need not be criminal in itself,[1] nor need overt acts be perpetrated in furtherance of the purpose, but the typical example of a political movement being a criminal conspiracy would be one directed towards the overthrow of the Government by force. This would clearly be a seditious conspiracy. Secondly, there is section 2 of the Public Order Act 1936, subheaded 'Prohibition of quasi-military organizations'. The Act was passed mainly to cope with the situation created by the activities of the British Union of Fascists in the 1930s. Under section 2, it is an offence to take part in the control, management, organization or training of a body which is *either* organized or trained or equipped for the purpose of enabling it to usurp the functions of the police or the armed forces; *or* organized or trained, or organized or equipped, for the use or display of force in promoting any political object.[2] The offence is punishable, upon conviction on indictment, with a maximum two years' imprisonment and fine of £500. No prosecution can be instituted without the Attorney-General's consent, which has been very sparingly granted. In the 1960s, leaders of Spearhead, a neo-Nazi organization, and of the Free Wales Army, were convicted under section 2.

1. See *Shaw* v. *D.P.P.* [1962] A.C. 220 (conspiracy to corrupt public morals); *Knuller* v. *D.P.P.* [1972] 3 W.L.R. 143 (conspiracy to corrupt public morals and, *semble*, to outrage public decency); *R.* v. *Kamara* [1972] 3 All E.R. 999 (conspiracy to trespass). Contrast *R.* v. *Bhagwan* [1972] A.C. 60 (indictment for conspiracy to evade immigration controls held to disclose no offence, the evasion at the time not being unlawful in itself). The state of this area of the law is still uncertain.

2. For comment on this section, see Ian Brownlie, *The Law Relating to Public Order* pp. 97–9. This book and David Williams's *Keeping the Peace* are the leading works on the topics covered by this chapter. For a valuable account and critique of some recent developments in the law and administrative practice, see D. G. T. (David) Williams, 'Protest and public order' [1970] *Camb. L.J.* 96.

In 1972 mere *membership* of the IRA was a statutory offence both in Northern Ireland and in the Republic, but not in Britain.

The law regulating other voluntary associations is mainly company law or trade union law; these matters will not be dealt with in this book, but it must be noted that under the Industrial Relations Act 1971 organizing, financing or threatening a strike or lock-out may, in certain circumstances, be an unfair industrial practice, in respect of which the National Industrial Relations Court may issue prohibitory and other coercive orders, and that there are special provisions for industrial emergencies.[3] Under counter-inflationary legislation passed late in 1972 it became an offence to call or threaten strike action for the purpose of inducing an employer to contravene statutory wage restrictions. Prosecutions could be instituted only by or with leave of the Attorney-General.[4]

Meetings and processions: prior restraints and preventive measures

It is usually said that there is no 'right of public meeting', but that public processions are *prima facie* lawful.[5] These statements need to be explained and examined.[6]

Clearly there is no right to hold any kind of meeting on private premises without the consent of the owner or occupier; such conduct will be a trespass. A trespasser may be evicted by the use of such force as is reasonable in the circumstances. Police officers may render assistance, as private individuals, to the occupier, but they are not obliged to do so and will normally refuse, though they have a common-law duty to take such steps as are reasonably required to quell a breach of the peace and to prevent a reasonably apprehended breach of the peace. Trespass is a tort,[7] for which nominal damages are recoverable; if the High Court considers that the case is serious enough and that repetition is likely, it may in its discretion award an injunction against the trespasser at the instance of the occupier.[8] Disobedience to an injunction is a contempt of court. According

3. See Otto Kahn-Freund, *Labour and the Law*, ch. 7; and pp. 521–2. Under separate legislation it is an offence for members of the forces or the police to strike. Under certain conditions strikes by seamen and strikes endangering life are also unlawful.

4. Counter-Inflation (Temporary Provisions) Act 1972, ss. 2, 5. Longer-term legislation including a similar sanction was to be introduced in 1973: see Cmnd 5205, 5206 (1973). See now Counter-Inflation Act 1973, s. 17.

5. See, for example, A. L. Goodhart (1937) 6 *Camb. L.J.* 161; E. C. S. Wade (1939) 2 *Mod. L. Rev.* 177.

6. See especially Brownlie, op. cit., ch. 12, for criticism of the usual analysis of the law relating to meetings in public places.

7. Under special Acts it may be a crime (for example, a trespass on a railway line).

8. cf. *Llandudno U.D.C.* v. *Woods* [1899] 2 Ch. 705 (trespass too trivial for injunctive relief).

to a decision of the Court of Appeal in 1972, conspiracy to trespass is a crime.[9]

Does it make any difference if the premises are public buildings belonging to a local authority? Candidates at elections are entitled to have access to locally maintained schools and other public halls in order to hold campaign meetings.[10] For the rest, local authorities have an ostensibly free discretion whether to let premises to anybody wishing to hold a meeting there. Since, however, they are public bodies, the exercise of their discretionary powers is potentially subject to judicial review. A decision not to allow *any* political meeting, or a particular *class* of political meeting, to be held on any premises under their control might possibly be held to be an unlawful fetter on their own discretion. Again, the validity of a decision to refuse the promoters of a particular meeting permission to conduct it on such premises might conceivably be impugned as being based on legally irrelevant considerations or as being so arbitrary that no reasonable body of persons could have reached it.[11]

Is there a general right or liberty to hold demonstrations or meetings in public open spaces? To conduct such a meeting is not a criminal or civil wrong merely because a Minister, a local authority, a police officer or a magistrate purports to prohibit it[12] unless their prior permission is required by law. But under a number of local Acts and by-laws prior permission is needed. For example, the permission of the Secretary of State for the Environment has to be obtained before a meeting can be held in Trafalgar Square.[13] His decision not to sanction any Irish political meeting there in 1972 could probably be justified, notwithstanding the legal principles stated above, in view of the strong possibility that serious disorders would arise. The right to hold meetings at Speakers' Corner in Hyde Park is conferred only by statutory regulations.[14] The mere fact that an open space is dedicated to the public use does not apparently entitle persons to use it for holding a public meeting.[15] If, on the other hand, the

9. *R.* v. *Kamara* [1972] 3 All E.R. 999. There had to be prior agreement to commit a trespass, coupled with knowledge or recklessness as to whether the conduct would be a trespass. The decision caused some surprise in legal circles ([1973] *Camb. L.J.* 10).

10. Representation of the People Act 1949, ss. 82, 83, Sched. 7.

11. cf. *Associated Provincial Picture Houses Ltd* v. *Wednesbury Corporation* [1948] 1 K.B. 223. See also below on by-laws.

12. *Beatty* v. *Gillbanks* (1882) 9 Q.B.D. 308; *M'Ara* v. *Edinburgh Magistrates* 1913 S.C. 1059.

13. Trafalgar Square Regulations 1952 (S.I. 1952, No. 776), r. 3. cf. *Ex p. Lewis* (1888) 21 Q.B.D. 191.

14. It is not a common-law liberty: *Bailey* v. *Williamson* (1873) L.R. 8 Q.B. 118. See Royal Parks and Gardens Act 1872; Williams, op. cit., ch. 3.

15. See *De Morgan* v. *Metropolitan Board of Works* (1880) 5 Q.B.D. 155. See also *Llandudno U.D.C.* v. *Woods* (above; religious services on the foreshore).

holding of meetings in such a place is prohibited absolutely or conditionally (for example, subject to a need to obtain prior permission in certain circumstances) by by-laws purportedly made under statutory powers, the by-laws may be challenged by a person aggrieved on the ground that they are *ultra vires*. A by-law may be held to be invalid on the grounds of uncertainty or repugnancy to the general law of the land or unreasonableness, including unfair discrimination; but in practice the courts lean in favour of upholding local by-laws unless they are very seriously objectionable.[16]

The House of Commons regularly makes a sessional order instructing the police to keep the streets leading to the Houses of Parliament free from obstruction to members. This order can have no legal effect outside the precincts of the House,[17] but the Commissioner of Police has statutory power[18] to give directions for the prevention of obstruction by assemblies in that vicinity and in various other places in the police district. Not every direction given with those purposes in view for the dispersal of a public assembly is necessarily valid, but the power is a wide one.[19]

Stationary gatherings on highways are generally regarded as trespasses at common law against the person or body in whom the highway is vested, unless the consent of the owner (usually a local authority) has been obtained. This is because the primary purpose to which a highway is dedicated is passage and repassage.[20] And since a public procession involves people marching down a highway, participation is *prima facie* lawful except perhaps while the procession is assembling. But a procession may well constitute an unlawful obstruction of the highway or a public nuisance.

The general rule that meetings on highways are trespasses is derived from private law. It gives no weight to the public interest in freedom of expression, and it seems ripe for reconsideration by the courts. In any event, the principle of dedication to passage and repassage is subject to

16. See generally *Kruse* v. *Johnson* [1898] 2 Q.B. 91; pp. 350–51.

17. *Papworth* v. *Coventry* [1967] 1 W.L.R. 663 at 669–670. See also p. 323.

18. Metropolitan Police Act 1839, s. 52. It is an offence to contravene a valid direction (s. 54(9)).

19. See *Papworth* v. *Coventry* (above). See also Town Police Clauses Act 1847, s. 21. The assembly in question in *Papworth*'s case comprised only seven stationary protesters against the Vietnam War. Although they were standing at the corner of Downing Street, it is doubtful whether they were reasonably capable of causing obstruction or annoyance.

20. See, for example, *Ex p. Lewis* (1888) 21 Q.B.D. at 197; *Harrison* v. *Duke of Rutland* [1893] 1 Q.B. 142; *Hickman* v. *Maisey* [1900] 1 Q.B. 752. See also cases cited in note 15, and the Scottish cases *M'Ara* v. *Edinburgh Magistrates* 1913 S.C. 1059, and *Aldred* v. *Miller* 1924 S.C. (J.) 117. See, however, *Burden* v. *Rigler* [1911] 1 K.B. 337 where it was held that a meeting held on a highway was not necessarily unlawful.

exceptions indeterminate in scope – ancillary activities such as holding private conversations and shopping are not trespasses, nor are brief stoppages by motor cars,[21] but what of distributing leaflets or soliciting answers from passers-by to questionnaires?[22] – and it would be sensible to replace the prevailing concept by one which equates trespass with unreasonable user. Seldom would a large meeting in a public thoroughfare be a reasonable use.

Of more practical importance than the law of trespass are the miscellany of local statutory restrictions already referred to and the law of obstruction. Wilfully to obstruct the free passage along a highway without lawful authority or excuse is a criminal offence, for which the police may arrest without warrant.[23] If there has been an appreciable and unreasonable obstruction, it is no defence that a way round it could be found or that nobody was proved to have been obstructed,[24] nor is it a defence that a speaker holding a meeting did not wish to create an obstruction, or that other speakers holding meetings in the same place had not been prosecuted.[25] The prosecution must prove its case, but since the amount and duration of an obstruction that it needs to establish in order to obtain a conviction are slight, the police and the local authority have almost a *de facto* licensing power with regard to public meetings and even the distribution of leaflets in the streets. If they decide to take no action, their abstention from prosecution means that no proceedings are likely to be taken at all. As a matter of prudence, therefore, a prior assurance should be obtained.[26] If a police officer orders a speaker, distributor, vendor or audience to 'move along', non-compliance with this direction is likely to lead to a conviction for obstruction of the highway or obstruction of a constable in the execution of his duty.

Here one sees a close connection between prior restraint and the prospect of prosecution. Other legal provisions, directed more closely to the prevention of disorder, can now be noted.

21. See *Iveagh* v. *Martin* [1961] 1 Q.B. 232 at 273; *Randall* v. *Tarrant* [1955] 1 W.L.R. 255. For picketing as obstruction, see *Hunt* v. *Broome* [1973] 2 W.L.R. 773.

22. Brownlie, op. cit., pp. 140–41.

23. Highways Act 1959, s. 121; see also Town Police Clauses Act 1847, s. 28; Metropolitan Police Act 1839, s. 54.

24. See generally *Horner* v. *Cadman* (1886) 55 L.J.M. C. 110; *Nagy* v. *Weston* [1965] 1 W.L.R. 280.

25. *Arrowsmith* v. *Jenkins* [1963] 2 Q.B. 561. Or that the local authority had acquiesced in the defendant's obstruction of the highway for a long period before deciding to prosecute: *Redbridge L.B.C.* v. *Jaques* [1970] 1 W.L.R. 1604.

26. Yet such an assurance would not be binding on them in law, for they have no power to license an obstruction of the highway: *Cambridgeshire & Isle of Ely C.C.* v. *Rust* [1972] 2 Q.B. 426; *Redbridge* case, above.

First, public processions are subject to statutory powers of regulation. Under section 3 of the Public Order Act 1936[27] a chief officer of police may, where he has reasonable grounds for apprehending that a public procession may give rise to serious public disorder, impose conditions for the preservation of public order, including the route to be followed.[28] If he is of the opinion that these powers are insufficient, he may apply to the appropriate local council for an order prohibiting all public processions, or any class of public procession (for example, political processions), for a period of up to three months, and the council may make such an order with the consent of the Home Secretary. In the metropolitan police district the prohibitory order may be made by the Commissioner of Police himself with the consent of the Home Secretary. Several such orders have in fact been made over the years, temporarily banning political processions in London. Although the validity of conditions imposed on the organizers of a procession might be challenged in a court on various grounds, it would seem that a prohibitory order could be impugned only if it were perverse or singled out an individual procession. Knowingly to contravene a valid condition or a ban is an offence.[29]

Secondly, preventive justice may be (and quite frequently is) invoked by the police in bringing potentially disorderly demonstrators or other 'agitators' before local magistrates, who may bind them over to be of good behaviour or to keep the peace.[30] If they refuse to enter into a recognizance or are unable to find sureties, they may be sent to prison for up to six months. If they break the conditions set out in the recognizance they become liable to forfeiture of the sum there specified.

Thirdly, if the police reasonably apprehend that the holding of a gathering in a public place will give rise to a breach of the peace, they are under a common-law duty to take reasonable steps to prevent that gathering from taking place or to break it up. The leading authority for this proposition is the controversial case of *Duncan* v. *Jones*;[31] its ambit will be considered below.[32]

Fourthly, if a public meeting is held on private premises, and the police reasonably apprehend that, should they not be present, a breach of the peace or an incitement to violence will occur, they are entitled to attend and insist on remaining in order to prevent such an occurrence. This is the

27. Williams, op. cit., pp. 56–63.
28. In the metropolitan area the Commissioner of Police has wider powers under section 52 of the Metropolitan Police Act 1839.
29. See *Flockhart* v. *Robinson* [1950] 2 K.B. 498.
30. Williams, op. cit., ch. 4; pp. 460–61.
31. [1936] 1 K.B. 218.
32. pp. 507–9.

narrowest possible *ratio decidendi* of *Thomas* v. *Sawkins*,[33] a decision that has been widely criticized, not least because the judgments included some unacceptably sweeping propositions about the extent of police powers.[34] Nevertheless, the principle set out above is reasonable, provided that it is confined to apprehended violence and the dissemination of incitements. The presence of a policeman on the spot can have a restraining influence at both indoor and outdoor meetings. An ordinary member of the public cannot, of course, claim a right to enter a meeting or to remain there after his invitation or licence to remain has been withdrawn, even though the meeting has been advertised as being open to the public.[35] But the police have special common-law responsibilities for the maintenance of public order, and it would be unreasonable to deny them a right of entry until a breach of the peace has actually occurred. It may be asked whether the same rule applies to private gatherings on private premises. One has to balance the public interest in the prevention of disorder against (i) the public interest in the maintenance of personal privacy against unsolicited intrusion, (ii) the possibility that a power to insist on entry might be abused, and (iii) the probability that, where incitements to violence are apprehended, the presence of police officers might not serve any useful purpose because the group could quietly arrange another meeting at a different time and place. The point is not clearly covered by English authority, but it is thought that the powers of the police do extend to insistence on being

33. [1935] 2 K.B. 249.

34. See, for example, A. L. Goodhart (1936) 6 *Camb. L.J.* 22. A meeting was organized by the Communist Party to protest against the Incitement to Disaffection Bill, then before Parliament, and to demand the dismissal of the Chief Constable of Glamorgan. Uniformed police entered the meeting and refused to leave; the speaker laid hands on a police officer whom he wished to eject as a trespasser; the officer resisted; the speaker took out a summons against the police officer for assault; the magistrates dismissed the case, holding that the police officer was not a trespasser. The speaker appealed on a point of law by way of case stated to the Divisional Court. Some passages in Lord Hewart C.J.'s judgment were too loosely expressed. Avory J. held that the police were entitled to remain if they reasonably apprehended that if they were not present seditious speeches and/or breaches of the peace would occur. He observed (at 256): 'In principle I think there is no distinction between the duty of a police constable to prevent a breach of the peace and the power of a magistrate to bind a person over to prevent a breach of the peace.'

In the text above 'sedition' has been equated with an incitement to violence (see p. 483). It should be noted that the magistrates found as a fact that the police had reasonable grounds for thinking that if they were not present there would be incitements to violence and breaches of the peace.

35. Subject to limited exceptions. Whether a person who has paid for admission to a public meeting can be ejected as a trespasser whenever the promoters think fit is questionable. A member of an organization may also have a legal right to attend a private meeting of that organization.

present at such a meeting[36] where violence at or immediately after the gathering is reasonably apprehended.

Offences and police powers

We have seen how the mere holding of a public meeting or procession may be wrongful. It may be a trespass. Apparently it may be a crime if there has been a conspiracy to trespass. It will be a criminal offence if it is held without the permission required by a local Act or by-law, or in breach of regulations made or directions given by the Commissioner of Metropolitan Police.[37] Organizers of a procession commit an offence if a ban on public processions in that area is in force, or if they infringe conditions lawfully imposed by the police. A meeting held in a public place may well constitute an obstruction of the highway. So may a public procession if it causes significant obstruction.

A demonstration, mobile or stationary, may also be a public nuisance if it entails an unreasonable user of the highway, causing obstruction or excessive noise. Prosecutions for public nuisance in this context have been uncommon,[38] but in 1963 the leader of a political demonstration in Central London was sentenced to eighteen months' imprisonment for inciting other persons to commit a nuisance. The conviction was quashed on appeal because the jury had not been directed to consider whether the obstruction caused was an unreasonable user of the highway.[39] In that case there was evidence of obstruction by a large crowd. The decision of the appellate court may indicate a benign attitude towards processions (as distinct from meetings) or a difference in the degrees of obstruction needed to obtain convictions for public nuisance and for wilful obstruction under the Highways Act 1959.[40] In any event, the most remarkable feature of the case was the sentence imposed by the court of first instance.

It is an offence to enter premises by force, whether or not there is an intention to remain in occupation.[41] Squatters or other persons who occupy

36. For example, a meeting of a student body on university premises. However, the possibility that the presence of police may provoke rather than dampen inflammatory statements is not to be disregarded.

37. See especially Metropolitan Police Act 1839, s. 52 (p. 500). Large public assemblies in the area of Westminster while Parliament and the courts are sitting may also be unlawful under obsolescent statutes: see Seditious Meetings Act 1817, s. 23; Tumultuous Petitioning Act 1661, s. 1.

38. The Attorney-General, on behalf of the general public, may also sue for an injunction to restrain the continuance or repetition of a public nuisance; see p. 603.

39. *R.* v. *Clark* (No. 2) [1964] 2 Q.B. 315.

40. On the question of unreasonable obstruction, the case-law does not point unambiguously to any such difference.

41. *R.* v. *Brittain* [1972] 1 Q.B. 357; Forcible Entry Act 1381.

premises peaceably and then barricade themselves in so as to prevent eviction commit the offence of forcible detainer;[42] they may also be convicted of conspiracy to trespass.[43]

Participants in a gathering of three or more persons will be guilty of the common-law misdemeanour of *unlawful assembly* if their common purpose is *either* to commit a crime of violence *or* to achieve any other object, lawful or unlawful, in such a manner as to give reasonably courageous persons in the vicinity reasonable grounds for apprehending a breach of the peace. The unlawful assembly will normally be in a public place, though it may be on private premises.[44] It may be but is not necessarily a procession, meeting or demonstration. Prosecutions for this offence have been fairly uncommon, but they have recently been brought against unruly student demonstrators,[45] and we need to consider the ingredients of the crime more closely because they raise difficult questions of constitutional importance. It appears that a participant in the gathering cannot properly be convicted unless he is proved to have been animated by the common purpose.

If members of the gathering publicly insult opponents who are likely to be provoked into committing a breach of the peace, they can properly be convicted of unlawful assembly, but will probably be prosecuted for the more mundane offence of 'insulting words and behaviour'.[46] Pastor Wise, the Protestant zealot who specialized in offensive attacks on the Roman Catholic religion,[47] was held to have been properly bound over to keep the peace after his mass meetings in Liverpool had evoked riots among the audience (*Wise* v. *Dunning*); [48] and there can be no doubt that, if charged with unlawful assembly, he, together with his active supporters at the meetings, could have been convicted of that offence. What if those conducting a lawful meeting or procession do not offer insults or threats but encounter, or know that they are likely to encounter, violent opposition and still go ahead? The general principle is that a lawful act does not become unlawful merely because other persons decide to offer unlawful resistance to it. Indeed, the police ought to protect the meeting first in the

42. *R.* v. *Robinson* [1971] 1 Q.B. 156; *R.* v. *Mountford* [1972] 1 Q.B. 128; Forcible Entry Act 1429; see articles in [1971] *Crim. L. Rev.* 313, 337, 342; (1971) 35 *Conveyancer* 243.

43. *R.* v. *Kamara* [1972] 3 All E.R. 999.

44. *R.* v. *Kamara* (demonstration in premises of Sierra Leone High Commission in London).

45. *R.* v. *Caird* (1970) 54 Cr. App. R. 499 (the Garden House affair at Cambridge).

46. Under section 5 of the Public Order Act 1936, as restated by section 7 of the Race Relations Act 1965; see pp. 489–91.

47. For his career, see Williams, op. cit., pp. 105–10.

48. [1902] 1 K.B. 167. The proceedings were brought under a local Act couched in the same language as section 5 of the Public Order Act 1936.

field, and it is an offence to act in a disorderly manner for the purpose of preventing the transaction of the business of a lawful public meeting.[49] On the other hand, a common-law duty is cast upon magistrates and other persons to take such measures as are reasonably required to prevent breaches of the peace. The constable who plucked an orange lily from the attire of a Protestant lady who had insisted on displaying it while walking through a Catholic quarter in Ireland (causing a hostile crowd to gather) was therefore held not liable in an action for assault;[50] and on the same grounds a magistrate who attempted to disperse a meeting to be addressed by Parnell, which was likely to be forcibly broken up by Orangemen, was held not to have committed any assault.[51]

Yet according to the celebrated decision in *Beatty* v. *Gillbanks* (1882)[52] Parnell's meeting would not have been an unlawful assembly. In the streets of Weston-super-Mare the Salvation Army held musical processions. They were regularly set upon by an organized gang of hooligans, members of a body called the Skeleton Army. The collisions of the two armies led to stone-throwing, free fights and mass uproar, to the terror of the peaceful inhabitants of Weston-super-Mare. Accordingly the local magistrates purported to forbid further processions of the Salvationists.[53] The Salvationists nevertheless formed up for their procession the following Sunday. A police officer called upon their leader to desist; he refused and was arrested. Several Salvationists were brought to court on a complaint alleging that they had been guilty of unlawfully assembling; the magistrates found the case proved and ordered them to find sureties to keep the peace. The defendants appealed successfully against this order to the Divisional Court.[54] The court emphasized that the disturbances of the peace had not been the

49. Public Meeting Act 1908, s. 1. This is not an arrestable offence. Under section 6 of the Public Order Act 1936 a constable *may*, at the chairman's request, take the name and address of a person whom he reasonably suspects of an offence under the 1908 Act, and arrest him if he refuses or is reasonably suspected of giving a false name and address.

50. *Humphries* v. *Connor* (1864) 17 Ir. C.L.R. 1; Wilson, *Cases and Materials*, p. 385.

51. *O'Kelly* v. *Harvey* (1883) 15 Cox C.C. 435. In both of these cases the 'assault' was technical.

52. 9 Q.B.D. 308. In somewhat similar cases decided in the same year in Scotland and Bombay, the conduct of Salvationist marchers was held to be unlawful: *Deakin* v. *Milne* (1882) 10 R (J.) 22; *Empress* v. *Tucker* (1882) Ind. L.R. 7 Bombay 43; Thomas M. Franck, *Comparative Constitutional Process*, pp. 477–82. See Williams, op. cit., pp. 50–51, 103, on the general background.

53. Their proclamation imposing the ban was destitute of legal effect (note 12).

54. Note that the Salvationist leaders were never *convicted* of the crime of unlawful assembly; a magistrates' court has no jurisdiction to convict for that offence. However, this is not an important point, for the judgments in the Divisional Court were concerned with the question whether the offence of unlawful assembly *had been committed*.

natural consequence of the Salvationists' conduct but had been caused by their opponents.

Some fifty years later Mrs Duncan, a Communist, put down a box in the street outside a training centre for the unemployed in South-East London and was about to climb on it to deliver a speech when the chief constable told her to desist, saying that she could hold her meeting round the corner 175 yards away. Not wishing to lose her audience, she insisted on beginning her speech, whereupon she was arrested and charged with the offence of wilfully obstructing a constable in the execution of his duty.[55] She was convicted and fined £2. Her appeal was dismissed by quarter sessions, and she appealed to the Divisional Court by case stated. She had held a meeting at the same spot a year before, and a disturbance, attributed to what had taken place at the meeting, had occurred in the centre afterwards. The deputy chairman of quarter sessions found that: (i) Mrs Duncan must have known of the probable consequences of her holding the meeting at that spot and was 'not unwilling' that they should occur; (ii) the respondent police officer reasonably apprehended a breach of the peace; (iii) it thereupon became his duty to prevent the holding of the meeting; and (iv) by attempting to hold the meeting she obstructed him in the execution of his duty. The Divisional Court dismissed the appeal.[56] *Beatty* v. *Gillbanks*, described by Lord Hewart as 'a somewhat unsatisfactory case',[57] was distinguished on the ground that it was a case of unlawful assembly, which was not in issue in the case in hand. Moreover, in *Duncan* v. *Jones* there was a causal connection between the previous meeting and the subsequent disturbance which took place *because* of that meeting.

Attempts to reconcile *Beatty* v. *Gillbanks* with *Duncan* v. *Jones* are not abstract intellectual exercises; they go to the root of a vital issue of public policy. What weight should be given to two competing values: freedom of assembly and the maintenance of public order?

1. The most popular answer, which sidesteps the main issue, is that if the *Beatty* v. *Gillbanks* situation were to be repeated today the Salvationist leaders could and should be convicted not of unlawful assembly but of the lesser offence of obstructing a constable in the execution of his duty (see now Police Act 1964, s. 51(3)).[58] This still gives primacy to the public interest in preventing reasonably apprehended breaches of the peace but reconciles the two decisions.

55. Under s. 12 of the Prevention of Crimes Act 1871, as amended by s. 2 of the Prevention of Crimes Act 1885; now replaced by s. 51 of the Police Act 1964.
56. [1936] 1 K.B. 218.
57. At 222.
58. See generally pp. 461–3.

2. Another possible answer is that the material facts in the two cases were different, in that Mrs Duncan's conduct, unlike that of the Salvationist leaders, had been provocative and the effective *cause* of the reasonably apprehended breach of the peace.[59] Again the two cases are reconciled, but the argument is that it was *not* the duty of the police to prevent the Salvationists from conducting their procession. A difficulty with this argument is that the concept of 'causation' is ambiguous.[60] There would have been no disturbance in Weston-super-Mare if the Salvationists had agreed to desist; in this sense the Salvationists, *as well as* the Skeleton Army, 'caused' the breaches of the peace. In another sense, the Skeleton Army 'caused' the disturbances because of their violent and unreasonable opposition to a peaceful procession; they were blameworthy and therefore responsible. The latter analysis seems more persuasive. On the other hand, if there is a subjective element in causation, one cannot ignore the facts that the Salvationists (like Mrs Duncan) knew the probable consequences of their conduct and were nevertheless prepared to invite trouble,[61] partly, perhaps, because they thought that this would earn them favourable publicity.

3. A third line of analysis runs as follows. *Beatty* v. *Gillbanks* was rightly decided. *Duncan* v. *Jones* was wrongly decided. Mrs Duncan was not proved to have committed any independent offence (for example, obstruction of the highway[62]) or to have intended to incite others to commit a breach of the peace or any other offence. Disobedience to a policeman's command should not have been held to render lawful conduct unlawful.[63] Even assuming that the police do have a duty to prevent all reasonably apprehended breaches of the peace, howsoever arising, and that they could therefore properly call upon Mrs Duncan to desist, her refusal merely provided the policeman with a *defence* to any proceedings she might have brought against him for a technical assault. Preventive justice ought not to be transmuted into punitive justice.

59. For example D. L. Keir and F. H. Lawson, *Cases in Constitutional Law* (5th edn), pp. 194–5.

60. See H. L. A. Hart and A. M. Honoré, *Causation in the Law*, pp. 333–5.

61. cf. *Jordan* v. *Burgoyne* [1963] 2 Q.B. 744, where it was held that unreasonably hostile reactions by a speaker's audience were irrelevant once the speaker had deliberately insulted them; the speaker could still be convicted under section 5 of the Public Order Act 1936, and had to take his audience as he found them. The Salvationists, however, had not used insulting words or behaviour. See generally, on the problem of a hostile audience, with comparisons with American law, Geoffrey Marshall, *Constitutional Theory*, ch. 8, and pp. 490–91.

62. Or insulting behaviour; cf. *Wise* v. *Dunning* (above).

63. cf. T. C. Daintith [1966] *Public Law* 248 at 258–9, and Ian Brownlie, *The Law Relating to Public Order*, pp. 18–22, 40–45.

4. Finally, it has been argued[64] that the conduct of the Salvationists in *Beatty* v. *Gillbanks* had all the ingredients of the common-law misdemeanour of unlawful assembly and the case was therefore wrongly decided. Since the maintenance of public order is a primary value, *Duncan* v. *Jones* was rightly decided on the facts.

So uncertain is the state of the law that none of these alternative analyses is demonstrably wrong. The third may appear to be the most attractive, though to adopt it would not necessarily make a great deal of difference in practice.[65] The probability is that the courts will tend to follow *Duncan* v. *Jones* even in cases where those who have declined to disperse are less blameworthy than their opponents; but in such cases the police must expect to have to produce strong grounds for apprehending that the peace could be preserved only by interfering with the freedom of the innocent party. The courts may indeed hold that obstruction of the police in the execution of their duty can be committed by persons who persist in trying to conduct a public meeting on *private premises* if a breach of the peace is reasonably apprehended. But the attitude of a court to a particular situation may well be influenced by the magistrates' or judges' impression of the merits of the contending factions. In particular, the behaviour of a hostile audience may evoke divergent judicial responses. Recently Lord Reid said, in a different context, that it would be 'going much too far to prohibit all speech or conduct likely to occasion a breach of the peace because determined opponents may not shrink from organizing or at least threatening a breach of the peace in order to silence a speaker whose views they detest'.[66]

In any event, the citizen cannot be sure of his rights, and the policeman is also in an invidious position. Whether he protects an unpopular speaker against the crowd (for example, by arresting abusive interrupters and charging them with insulting or threatening words or behaviour likely to cause a breach of the peace), or tries to disperse a gathering in order to preserve the peace, he can expect to be criticized for taking sides or stifling

64. See *O'Kelly* v. *Harvey* (1883) 15 Cox C.C. 435 (dictum), and note 57; though cf. *R.* v. *Londonderry* JJ. (1891) 28 L.R. Ir. 440, another Salvationist case, where the members of the court expressed a variety of opinions as to the relevant legal principles. In the *Londonderry* case these observations were also *obiter*; no breach of the peace was reasonably apprehended, and an order that the Salvationists give sureties to keep the peace was therefore quashed.

65. *If* the police have a legal duty to restrain a speaker physically in the *Duncan* v. *Jones* type of situation so that (assuming that they have used no more force than is reasonably necessary) they have a defence to an action or prosecution for assault, any *physical* resistance on the speaker's part will then presumably constitute the offence of assaulting or obstructing a constable in the execution of his duty.

66. *Cozens* v. *Brutus* [1972] 3 W.L.R. 521 at 526 (a case on 'insulting behaviour': see p. 491).

freedom of expression. If he intervenes too precipitately, he may be sued or prosecuted for assault and will incur the displeasure of his superiors.[67]

When an unlawful assembly is proceeding to the execution of its purpose, it constitutes a rout. If it goes on to execute that purpose in a violent manner which alarms a person of reasonable courage in the neighbourhood, it constitutes a riot. A riotous assembly may also arise spontaneously. It must be proved, in order to obtain a conviction for riot, that the rioters intended to aid one another by force if necessary to overcome any opposition to the execution of their unlawful private purpose.[68] Several of the modern reported cases on riot are concerned with civil claims to compensation out of police funds, under the Riot (Damages) Act 1886, for loss suffered by property-owners as a result of what they claim to have been riots.

Akin to riot is the common-law offence of causing an affray by fighting or threats of force giving rise to alarm in the neighbourhood.[69] Convictions for affray are apt to be more easily obtained than for riotous assembly, for an affray may be committed without any common purpose on the part of the assailants, or proof indeed that anyone was in fact alarmed if the offence occurred in a public place; and it appears that a single aggressor may be convicted of affray.[70]

Citizens are empowered, and probably obliged, to use their best endeavours for the suppression of riots,[71] and may use such force as is reasonable in the circumstances for the purpose.[72] The main burden of responsibility rests upon local magistrates and the police, who must neither overreach themselves nor fail to act when the occasion arises.[73] The magistrate's task has become somewhat less onerous since the repeal in

67. There are other problems. For instance, do the police have a *duty* to go to the assistance of an occupier wishing to evict trespassers who are also conspirators?

68. See generally *Field* v. *Metropolitan Police Receiver* [1921] 3 K.B. 334; *Munday* v. *Metropolitan Police District Receiver* [1949] 1 All E.R. 337; Brownlie, op. cit., pp. 47–54.

69. See *Button* v. *D.P.P.* [1966] A.C. 591 (affray may be committed on private premises). The revival and extensive use of prosecutions for this ancient common-law misdemeanour in recent years may be compared with the revival of prosecutions for forcible entry and detainer (see pp. 504–5).

70. *R* v. *Taylor* [1972] 3 W.L.R. 961.

71. *Charge to the Bristol Grand Jury* (1832) 5 C. & P. 262n. Certainly they are under a common-law duty to go to the aid of a constable when called upon to assist: *R.* v. *Brown* (1841) Car. & M. 314.

72. See generally Criminal Law Act 1967, s. 3. For various problems connected with excessive force, excessive resistance and the duties of the citizen, see *Devlin* v. *Armstrong* [1971] N.I. 13.

73. *R.* v. *Pinney* (1832) 3 B. & Ad. 947 (culpable failure to act where need arises is a common-law misdemeanour).

1967[74] of the Riot Act 1714, under which he was required to read to the rioters a proclamation, calling upon them in the Queen's name to disperse peaceably.[75] Troops may be called in to disperse rioters in the last resort; they should normally act only under the direction of the competent civil authorities, and the degree of force they use must be proportionate to the evil to be averted.[76]

Finally, there are three points of some importance in the conduct of public meetings but not directly associated with the foregoing discussion.

1. Section 2(6) of the Public Order Act 1936 recognized the legality of employing a reasonable number of stewards to assist in the maintenance of order in public meetings on private premises. However, they are not to be so organized as to usurp the functions of the police or to display force in the promotion of a political object.

2. It is an offence under section 1 of the Act to wear a political uniform (except with the permission of the Home Secretary) in a public place or at a public meeting. Emblems, badges and armbands will not normally be understood to be uniforms, but a shirt with a colour signifying the wearer's political associations would be so regarded. In 1965 persons wearing Ku Klux Klan attire who went through a cross-burning ritual were convicted under the section.

3. Under the Prevention of Crime Act 1953 it is an arrestable offence to have, without lawful authority or reasonable excuse, an offensive weapon in a public place. For this purpose, a public place includes a public meeting on private premises. The burden of proving lawful authority or reasonable excuse will lie on the defendant. An offensive weapon is an article made or adapted for causing injury to the person, or alternatively one that is intended by the person having it with him to be used for that purpose; in the latter case the prosecution must prove intent. The 1953 Act overlaps with and largely supersedes section 4 of the Public Order Act 1936, which made it an offence to have an offensive weapon without lawful authority at a public meeting or procession; the 1953 Act also imposes heavier penalties.[77]

The range of crimes and civil wrongs that may be committed by participants in public gatherings is therefore impressive. And the miscellany

74. Criminal Law Act 1967, s. 10(2), Sched. 3, Part III.

75. This was popularly called 'reading the Riot Act', though the rest of the Act was not read.

76. See review of the authorities in *Lynch* v. *Fitzgerald* [1938] I.R. 382; Keir and Lawson, *Cases* (5th edn), p. 212. For a colourful account of the background to this case, see R. F. V. Heuston, *Essays in Constitutional Law* (2nd edn), pp. 147–9. See further, pp. 513–14 below.

77. See Brownlie, op. cit., pp. 61–73.

of crimes and torts described in the previous chapter may be committed on such occasions. The ample scope of punitive, preventive and repressive powers (which, as is to be expected, is far wider in Northern Ireland[78]) implies that considerable self-restraint must be shown by the police and magistrates if the spokesmen of unpopular or eccentric causes are to be allowed to ventilate their opinions.

78. See Claire Palley, *The Evolution, Disintegration and Possible Reconstruction of the Northern Ireland Constitution*, pp. 400–404, 412–16, 434–40; Lord MacDermott, 'Law and order in time of emergency' (1972) 17 *Juridical Review* (N.S.) 1 and ch. 30.

Chapter 23
National Emergencies

Civil disorder

Towards the end of the last chapter we referred to the role of troops in suppressing riots.[1] The relevant section of the official *Manual of Military Law*[2] is headed 'Employment of Troops in Aid of the Civil Power'. If local rioting occurs, the civil power will be the mayor, magistrates and police; though unless the emergency arises very suddenly, it can be taken for granted that any decision to call in troops will be taken with the authority of the Prime Minister, the Secretary of State for Defence and the Home Secretary, and that there will be some measure of political direction as to the circumstances in which they are to use force.[3] Nevertheless, the military officer on the spot may have to make a snap decision whether to use force, and if so, how much, to quell a riot. It may be sufficient to use batons, tear gas, rubber bullets or water cannon. If such methods are ineffective in the circumstances, he must decide whether to order his men to open fire with lethal bullets. Failure to give such an order may lead to the triumph of the rioters and perhaps the capture of arms, followed perhaps by his being court-martialled and cashiered,[4] or even indicted for common-law misdemeanour,[5] in respect of his breach of duty. If he orders deadly violence to be used when this is not justified under the conditions, he (and possibly his subordinates)[6] may be convicted of murder or manslaughter.

1. p. 511.
2. Relevant extracts are set out in Appendix I to Brownlie's *Law Relating to Public Order*; the references to 'felony' and the Riot Act 1714 are now obsolete.
3. See, for example, Randolph Churchill, *Winston S. Churchill*, vol. 2, pp. 367–86, on how decisions were made about the use of troops in the wave of strikes in 1910–11. The General Officer Commanding British troops in Northern Ireland has been subject to the political direction of the United Kingdom Government.
4. See Professor Heuston's account of the sequel to the Bristol Riots of 1831 in *Essays in Constitutional Law* (2nd edn), pp. 137–8. For a fuller account of the use of troops in aid of the civil power at that time and in the preceding years, see L. Radzinowicz, *A History of English Criminal Law and its Administration*, vol. 4, pp. 141–52.
5. cf. *R.* v. *Pinney* (p. 51, note 73, above).
6. Subject to the doubtful defence of superior orders; see pp. 205–6.

The officer's predicament is made more acute by the obscurity of the legal principles governing the scope of his duties. Judges and writers have insisted many times over that soldiers are entitled, indeed obliged at common law, to use all necessary force, including deadly violence in the last resort, to disperse rioters who are doing serious and extensive damage to property – for example, demolishing and setting fire to colliery buildings.[7] Is this still the law? Section 3 of the Criminal Law Act 1967 provides that a person may use such force as is *reasonable* in the circumstances in the prevention of crime; and it expressly replaces the common-law rules on this matter. Referring to this section,[8] the authors of a leading textbook on criminal law assert that it can rarely, if ever, be justifiable to use deadly force merely for the protection of property.[9] What if skinheads try to burn down the National Gallery, or if revolutionaries try to demolish No. 10 Downing Street as the symbol of an immoral society? In the last analysis, answers to the question whether it can be justifiable to use lethal weapons to prevent the destruction of property, in the absence of an immediate threat to human life, may depend on value judgments which may reasonably differ. Soldiers can be expected to be equipped with common sense. They can hardly be expected to make fundamental judgments about social institutions when they are under stress in the face of mob violence; and their oath of loyalty implies an obligation to do what appears necessary for the preservation of the existing order and its physical manifestations.[10]

It is possible to analyse the duties of soldiers to quell local riots as being the duties of the ordinary citizen writ large. But when riot passes into rebellion or guerrilla warfare, emphases shift and other principles intrude. Levying 'war' against the Queen in her realm is both treason and treason felony. The civil power primarily responsible for containing and suppressing an uprising must be the Government in office. The military authorities will be obliged to act in its support. The Crown, acting through its advisers, has, moreover, a prerogative power to direct the disposition

7. See, for example, *Report of the Committee on the Featherstone Riots* (C. 7734 (1893)).

8. For an interpretation of the corresponding provision in Northern Ireland law see *Devlin* v. *Armstrong* [1971] N.I. 13 (organization of petrol-bomb throwing by Miss Devlin not reasonable to prevent invasion of Bogside by constabulary and suspected Protestant mob).

9. J. C. Smith and Brian Hogan, *Criminal Law* (2nd edn), p. 262.

10. However, the potentially grave social consequences of resorting to deadly violence, even in a situation where troops are being subjected to physical assault by riotous demonstrators, were vividly illustrated by the events of 'Bloody Sunday' in Londonderry (30 January 1972). See the Report of the Widgery Tribunal of Inquiry (H.C. 220 (1971–72)), where it seems to have been assumed that instructions to the troops to fire without warning only against persons endangering or about to endanger life (see paras. 89 et seq.) were correct in law.

and use of the armed forces. The exact limits of this prerogative are far from clear;[11] but it cannot mean that troops can lawfully be ordered to do whatever the Crown thinks fit whenever it thinks fit to maintain internal security, irrespective of what necessity requires. However, it may well imply that the strict tests of legality applied to the conduct of those entrusted with the preservation of order in local disturbances[12] should be slightly relaxed in time of extensive turmoil.

If the situation moves a stage farther and the civil authorities become incapable of governing because of a large-scale insurrection, powers to do whatever may be needed to restore peace may be handed over to (or assumed by) the military authorities. This is a new situation, different both in degree and kind. A state of martial law will then exist, and the powers of the General Officer Commanding the Forces will, so it is usually thought, become non-justiciable and, for the time being, absolute, subject only to consultation (if this is feasible) with the civil power.

Martial law has been aptly described as 'a peculiar system of legal relations'[13] which arises in time of civil war or insurrection, or, it may be added, invasion. It is a state of affairs, not a settled body of rules, though rules and orders will be promulgated and enforced by the military authorities as they see fit. It must be sharply distinguished from military law, a settled body of rules applied in accordance with prescribed procedures to members of the armed forces and ancillary personnel. Military law is simply a specialized branch of United Kingdom law administered by military officers acting summarily or sitting in courts-martial, subject to the supervisory and appellate jurisdiction of the ordinary courts.[14] Courts-martial applying military law are regular courts. Courts-martial applying martial law are not: they are informal tribunals or committees of officers,[15] and appear to be no more subject to the supervisory jurisdiction of the superior courts than are 'drumhead courts' or soldiers meting out summary punishment to armed rebels, curfew-breakers or other supposed malefactors among the civil population.

Confusion of martial law with military law was far more common before

11. The common-law rules on the prerogative in emergencies falling short of war are remarkably abstruse; see the inconclusive comments in *Halsbury's Laws of England* (3rd edn), vol. 7, pp. 260–61.

12. See *Lynch* v. *Fitzgerald* [1938] I.R. 382; Keir and Lawson, *Cases* (5th edn), p. 212.

13. Keir and Lawson, *Cases* (5th edn), p. 224; also see generally pp. 224–62; Heuston, *Essays* (2nd edn), pp. 150–63; symposium in (1902) 18 *L.Q.R.* 117–58.

14. See pp. 202–5.

15. Hence the courts will not control them by issuing prerogative orders: *Re Clifford and O'Sullivan* [1921] 2 A.C. 570 (prohibition). This House of Lords decision skirted the main issue – whether the courts had any jurisdiction at all to interfere with the decisions of the military tribunals.

a regular corpus of military law was introduced in the eighteenth century. In the Middle Ages the prerogative Court of the Constable and Marshal dispensed the 'law martial' against rebellious civilians as well as undisciplined soldiers; it lost most of its jurisdiction in 1640.[16] Under the Tudors and early Stuarts special commissions were issued from time to time under the prerogative for the trial by martial law of serious offenders against public order. The issue of such commissions was forbidden by the Petition of Right 1628. But the terminological confusion lingered on.

The term 'martial law' is also sometimes used to denote military rule over enemy territory occupied by British forces. Such a situation is regulated rather by the international law of war than by British municipal law.

Finally, 'martial law' can be used to describe an entirely different kind of situation – one where military officers overthrow the legitimate government, establish a new régime and proclaim a state of martial law. The phenomenon is all too familiar in many countries. It has not arisen in Britain in modern times and our constitutional law books are silent on its legal consequences. Briefly, one can say that the judges and officials are not obliged to recognize the validity of such a proclamation, any more than they are obliged to accept any other revolutionary *coup d'état*, but that if they defy the mailed fist, they cannot expect to retain office for long. If they do recognize the supersession of the old order as valid,[17] successful revolution has begotten its own legality.[18]

Propositions about martial law situations, as viewed by the courts, are deducible from cases arising out of the Irish troubles and the Boer War. They presuppose (i) the existence of civil authorities who (ii) are unable to cope with widespread disorders or armed conflict and who therefore (iii) authorize or acquiesce in the imposition of military government upon civilians for the purpose of restoring order.

1. A state of martial law may be introduced by or without a proclamation. A proclamation purporting to introduce a state of martial law is of no legal effect in itself; martial law is justified only by paramount necessity.

16. However, the ancient Court of Chivalry retains a minor aspect of the jurisdiction: see *Manchester Corporation* v. *Manchester Palace of Varieties Ltd* [1955] P. 133 (right to use a coat of arms).
17. As they did in Pakistan in 1958 (*The State* v. *Dosso* P.L.D. 1958 S.C. 533); though the prevailing conditions did not justify the initial proclamation of martial law in that year: see Alan Gledhill, *Pakistan: The Development of its Laws and Constitution* (2nd edn), 108. Martial law was again declared in Pakistan in 1969 during a widespread breakdown of law and order, but after the collapse of the régime early in 1972 following the defeat of the Pakistan army by India, the Pakistan Supreme Court held (*Jilani* v. *Government of the Punjab* P.L.D. 1972 S.C. 139; disapproving *Dosso*'s case) that the martial-law régime was unlawful.
18. See pp. 66–9.

2. If the ordinary courts are still sitting, it seems that they have jurisdiction to determine whether 'a state of war' (not necessarily war in the international sense, but a state of affairs requiring military 'pacification' by the imposition of martial law) exists in an area where they normally have jurisdiction. In determining this question, they will give heavy weight to the opinion of the local military commander, but his opinion is not binding on them.[19]

3. If they decide that a 'state of war' does exist, then (according to the present weight of legal opinion) they should decline to review the legality of anything done by the military authorities in the purported discharge of military responsibilities till, in their independent judgment, the 'state of war' has terminated.[20]

4. The non-justiciability of acts done by the military authorities during the 'state of war' seems to embrace situations where they have exceeded emergency powers conferred on them by statute.[21]

5. When ordinary civil proceedings can be resumed, proceedings may be brought against the military authorities by persons aggrieved by acts done during the state of martial law. According to one view, soldiers will be legally liable at common law in respect of any unnecessary use of force against persons or property.[22] A more realistic view is that liability should attach only to such conduct as was manifestly unreasonable in the circumstances.[23] In practice an Act of Indemnity is almost certain to be passed (assuming that the disturbances are quelled), exonerating from liability persons who were acting in good faith for the suppression of the uprising.[24]

States of martial law have existed in British colonial dependencies. The need for imposing martial law has practically disappeared in relation to

19. See, for example, *R.* v. *Allen* [1921] 2 I.R. 241; *R.* (*Garde*) v. *Strickland* [1921] 2 I.R. 317; cf. the striking decision in *Egan* v. *Macready* (below).

20. *Ex p. Marais* [1902] A.C. 109; *Tilonko* v. *Att.-Gen. of Natal* [1907] A.C. 93; cases cited in note 19 above and note 21 below.

21. *R.* v. *Allen* (above); but see *Egan* v. *Macready* [1921] I.R. 265, where the court held that the 'prerogative' powers exercised by the military authorities had been superseded by statute. See the valuable discussion of these cases in Keir and Lawson, op. cit., pp. 233–7. And note the courageous decision of a Pakistan court in *Mir Hasan* v. *The State* P.L.D. 1969 (2) Lahore 786, interpreting a martial-law regulation and holding an order made by a martial-law authority to be invalid; see Dias [1970] *Camb. L.J.* 49. It is arguable that public policy does not require a total abdication of judicial review during a state of martial law.

22. Dicey, op. cit., pp. 289–91.

23. Keir and Lawson, op cit., p. 231.

23. For interpretation of such an Act, see *Wright* v. *Fitzgerald* (1798) 27 St. Tr. 759. But much will depend on the wording of the particular Act and a jury's view of the merits of the case: see Paul O'Higgins (1962) 25 *Mod. L. Rev.* 413, discussing unreported Irish decisions on the activities of 'Flogger Fitzgerald'.

those dependencies covered by the Emergency Powers Order in Council 1939.[25] This Order, empowering the Governor of a territory to declare a state of emergency, endows him with almost limitless powers to make regulations for the duration of the emergency,[26] and martial law ought to be superfluous, even if troops have to be used.

War

The declaration and general conduct of war, as the term is understood in international law, are matters of prerogative. Among the specific prerogatives exercisable in time of war are powers to intern and deport enemy aliens,[27] to prohibit trading with the enemy except by licence, to requisition property (including land[28] and British ships[29]) for military purposes, to requisition neutral ships and chattels (the right of angary),[30] and to destroy property in order to impede, or deny facilities to, an advancing enemy.[31] Compensation is payable at common law for requisitioning, damaging or destroying private property (except in battle);[32] but the War Damage Act 1965 abolished the duty to pay compensation for lawful *damage* to or *destruction* of property during, or in contemplation of the outbreak of, war.[33] The exact scope of the prerogative in time of war may never be exactly ascertained. Nor is it clear how far the war prerogatives extend to a state of immediately apprehended war. Again, some of the emergency powers exercisable by the Crown (for example, to enter upon private property and construct defence works to repel an invasion)[34] may be regarded as common-law powers exercisable by all citizens as a matter of necessity, and not peculiar to the Crown; hence they would not usually be classifiable as prerogatives. In practice most of the powers that the Crown is likely to exercise during war will be regulated by statute.

25. Published in S.I. 1952, Vol. 1, p. 621. There have been various amending orders.

26. K. O. Roberts-Wray, *Commonwealth and Colonial Law*, pp. 642–3. Similar legislation has been enacted in many former dependencies.

27. *R.* v. *Bottrill, ex p. Kuechenmeister* [1947] K.B. 41.

28. See discussion of the precedents in *Att.-Gen.* v. *De Keyser's Royal Hotel Ltd* [1920] A.C. 508.

29. *The Broadmayne* [1916] P. 64.

30. *Commercial & Estates Co. of Egypt* v. *Board of Trade* [1925] 1 K.B. 271.

31. *Burmah Oil Co.* v. *Lord Advocate* [1965] A.C. 75 (destruction of British-owned oil installations in Burma in 1942, on orders of military commander, acting in pursuance of Government 'scorched earth' policy, so as to prevent Japanese army from taking them intact).

32. ibid.

33. The Act was severely criticized in that it had retroactive effect, overruling the actual decision of the House of Lords in the *Burmah Oil* case.

34. *Case of the King's Prerogative in Saltpetre* (1606) 12 Co. Rep. 12.

There seems to be no justification for the view that a state of martial law may be imposed within the realm whenever the Crown is at war; if the civil authorities are capable of governing, there is no legal warrant for the introduction of military rule by prerogative.

Reference has already been made to the vast powers conferred on the Crown in Council by the Defence of the Realm Acts 1914–15 and the Emergency Powers (Defence) Acts 1939–40.[35] The general words of the Defence of the Realm Acts, authorizing the making of regulations to secure the public safety and the defence of the realm, were construed as being wide enough to validate a regulation for the preventive detention of British subjects on security grounds.[36] The emergency legislation of the Second World War was more explicitly worded. It expressly saved the royal prerogative;[37] it authorized the sub-delegation of delegated powers and the imposition of charges on the subject,[38] and the making of regulations for the detention of persons on security grounds and for the amendment of any prior Act of Parliament.[39] The Emergency Powers (Defence) (No. 2) Act 1940 authorized the making of Defence Regulations for the trial of civilians by special courts if the military situation so required. No such regulation was in fact made. The Acts expired in 1946, but some of the Defence Regulations were continued in force and others were made under post-war emergency legislation. Those which had survived were placed on a permanent footing by statute in 1964. Regulation 18 B, authorizing the internment of security suspects, had been revoked immediately after the termination of armed hostilities with Germany.

It should be noted that in neither world war was the right to apply for the writ of habeas corpus against the Executive expressly suspended. However, regulations authorizing a Secretary of State to detain persons of hostile origins or associations were so broadly interpreted by the courts as to leave a detainee hardly any room for successfully challenging an internment order by habeas corpus or any other means.[40] During the

35. p. 332.

36. *R.* v. *Halliday, ex p. Zadig* [1917] A.C. 260 (Regulation 14B).

37. Emergency Powers (Defence) Act 1939, s. 9.

38. ibid., ss. 1(3), 2; cf. *Att.-Gen.* v. *Wilts United Dairies Ltd* (1921) 37 T.L.R. 884, where it was held that the Food Controller, purporting to act under emergency powers, could not validly require a milk purchaser to pay him 2d. a gallon as a condition of being granted a licence to purchase, since he had no express statutory authority to impose a charge.

39. ibid. ss. 1(2)(*a*), 1(4).

40. *R.* v. *Halliday* (above); *Liversidge* v. *Anderson* [1942] A.C. 206; *Greene* v. *Home Secretary* [1942] A.C. 284; cf. *R.* v. *Secretary of State for Home Affairs, ex p. Budd* [1942] 2 K.B. 14 (release by habeas corpus where detention order defective in form, followed by valid detention under detention order properly made out). For a hostile critique of the implementation of a policy of preventive detention of security suspects,

Napoleonic Wars, a different and more clumsy device had been employed: Acts of Parliament were passed, depriving persons detained on suspicion of treason under a warrant of a Secretary of State of their right to be tried or admitted to bail.[41]

Disruption of essential services

Permanent legislation gives the Executive power to deal with dislocation caused by strikes in essential services and by natural catastrophes. Under the Emergency Powers Acts 1920 and 1964 Her Majesty may proclaim a state of emergency if at any time it appears to her that there have occurred, or are about to occur, events of such a nature as to be calculated to deprive the community, or any substantial part of it, of the essentials of life by interference with the supply and distribution of food, water, fuel or light, or with the means of locomotion. If Parliament is not sitting when such a proclamation is issued, it has to meet within five days. The proclamation will be in force for one month but may be revoked before the expiry of that time or renewed after it.

During the state of emergency, such regulations may be made by Order in Council as are deemed necessary for securing and regulating the supply and distribution of the necessities of life, for preserving the peace and for other essential purposes and incidental matters.

A court would probably hold the grounds for making the proclamation to be non-justiciable;[42] and the power to make regulations is so widely drawn that it would be difficult to establish that any such regulation was *ultra vires*, though it might be less difficult to show acts done ostensibly in pursuance of a regulation were unlawful. Under a number of new Commonwealth constitutions which give power to the Executive to proclaim a state of emergency, derogation from certain guarantees of fundamental rights is permitted but only to the extent 'reasonably required' or 'reasonably justifiable' for the purposes of dealing with the emergency situation.[43]

---

see C. K. Allen, *Law and Orders* (3rd edn), Appendix 1. Earlier editions were even more critical.

41. Dicey, *Introduction to the Study of the Law of the Constitution* (10th edn), pp. 228–36. These Acts did not legalize the detention of a person who was in fact innocent; they merely prevented him from obtaining habeas corpus to secure release or speedy trial at that time. Indemnity Acts had to be passed after the Annual Acts had expired, in order to protect Ministers and officials from legal liability.

42. cf. *Ningkan* v. *Government of Malaysia* [1970] A.C. 379.

43. For reviews and critiques of 'emergency' powers in Northern Ireland, see Lord MacDermott (1972) 17 *Juridical Review* (N.S.) 1; Claire Palley, *The Evolution, Disintegration and Possible Reconstruction of the Northern Ireland Constitution* (reprinted from (1972) 1 *Anglo-American L. Rev.* 368–476); Fabian Soc., *Emergency Powers: A Fresh Start* (1972). See also pp. 642–4 and Addendum..

In a state of emergency, troops may be employed on agricultural duties;[44] and there is a statutory power (not confined to formal states of emergency) vested in the Secretary of State to call out the reserve forces,[45] if required, to assist the civil power in preserving public order.[46]

Several safeguards are provided against the serious abuse of statutory emergency powers. Regulations made under Acts of 1920 and 1964 must be laid before both Houses of Parliament as soon as may be, and expire seven days after being laid unless approved by affirmative resolutions of both Houses. They may create new criminal offences triable by magistrates' courts, but the maximum penalty is to be three months' imprisonment and a £100 fine and they cannot change existing criminal procedure or authorize punishment by imprisonment or the imposition of fines without trial.[47] Nor may any such regulation make it an offence to take part in a strike or peacefully to persuade others to take part in a strike or impose compulsory military service or industrial conscription.

States of emergency were proclaimed in 1921, 1924, and again in 1926 at the time of the General Strike followed by a miners' strike. From 1945 to the end of 1972 they were proclaimed on eight occasions, four of them under the Heath Government (arising from a dock strike and 'work to rule' at electricity power stations in 1970, and a miners' strike and a dock strike in 1972). The content of the regulations has depended on the kind of emergency situation: wide powers to fix food prices, requisition property and prohibit public gatherings may be conferred, but in the periods of emergency since 1945 the action taken in pursuance of the regulations[48] has had only a mild impact on the ordinary citizen and the emergencies have not been accompanied by civil disturbances apart from some acts of mob violence and intimidation of non-strikers in 1972. Potentially, however, very extensive authority could be exercised by the police and the armed forces under the Acts,[49] quite apart from their common-law powers and duties to secure the maintenance of public order.

Under Part 8 of the Industrial Relations Act 1971, if it appears to the Secretary of State that impending or existing industrial action is likely to cause (inter alia) serious injury to the national economy, and that deferment of such action would be conducive to a settlement, he is entitled to make

44. Emergency Powers Act 1964, s. 2.
45. See now Reserve Forces Act 1966.
46. Army Reserve Act 1950, s. 10(1).
47. The late Sir Carleton Allen's suggestion (*Law and Orders* (3rd edn), p. 378) that preventive detention orders might be made under the Emergency Powers Act 1920 is sustainable only if such detention is differentiated from punishment.
48. In 1948 the strikers went back to work before any regulations had been issued. The proclamation of emergency had an immediate psychological effect.
49. For critical comment, see Ronald Kidd, *British Liberty in Danger*, pp. 48–51.

an application to the National Industrial Relations Court, specifying the persons or organizations responsible for the action in question; and the court has jurisdiction to make an order requiring those persons or bodies to desist for up to sixty days.[50] In April 1972 the court made an order against the railwaymens' unions, imposing a fourteen days' 'cooling off period' during which an official 'work-to-rule' policy (that had led to disruption of normal services) had to be discontinued.[51] A curious feature of the court's jurisdiction is that whereas certain conditions precedent to the making of such an order are determinable by reference to the opinion of the Secretary of State (whether there was industrial action within the meaning of the Act, whether discontinuance would be conducive to a settlement, subject to the court's inherent jurisdiction to reject his opinion if he has misdirected himself or has acted in bad faith or on the basis of extraneous considerations), the court itself has to make an independent determination of the question whether the industrial action in question is of such magnitude as to be gravely injurious to the national economy.[52]

Those aspects of the court's jurisdiction empowering it to proscribe strikes and 'blacking', and to commit for contempt for disobedience to its orders, have proved to be highly contentious and have brought the court into a storm-centre of political controversy.[53]

50. Industrial Relations Act 1971, ss. 33(4), 138, 139, 140.
51. *Secretary of State for Employment* v. *ASLEF* [1972] 2 Q.B. 443.
52. This follows from the manner in which ss. 138(1), (2) and 139(1) are worded. See, to like effect ss. 141(1), (2), 142(1) (jurisdiction of court to order compulsory ballot of union members where strike action is impending; *Secretary of State for Employment* v. *ASLEF* (No. 2) [1972] 2 Q.B. 455, C.A.).
53. Partly arising from the committal of unofficial dockers' leaders for contempt in the summer of 1972: see esp. *Churchman* v. *Joint Shop Stewards' Committee* [1972] 1 W.L.R. 1094. cf. Griffith, 'Reflections on the rule of law', *New Statesman*, 24 November 1972, p. 756, for criticism of the role of some judges in these difficult episodes.

Part Six
Administrative Law

In this Part we present an introduction to the most rapidly developing area of public law in this country – the law of public administration, or administrative law. The subject has vast ramifications; here we confine ourselves to those aspects which have general constitutional importance.

Chapter 24 explains what administrative law is about and why it aroused so much passionate controversy in the past. It goes on to classify the different types and forms of decisions in the law of public administration and outlines their procedural characteristics. As we shall see, the picture is untidy.

In chapter 25 we examine the part played by special tribunals and statutory inquiries in the general scheme of administrative law. We note the work of the Committee on Ministers' Powers and the Franks Committee on Administrative Tribunals and Enquiries; the effect of the Tribunals and Inquiries Act 1958; and the functions and influence of the Council on Tribunals.

Chapter 26 summarizes the rules evolved in a very large number of decided cases. It deals with the general principles governing judicial review of administrative acts, orders, decisions and omissions. The principles are illustrated by a selection of judicial decisions. In the 1960s the courts became less reticent in reviewing administrative acts and decisions, laying down more exacting standards of legality and fair procedure to be observed by the Administration. In particular, the courts widened the scope of the duty to observe the rules of natural justice in the course of arriving at administrative decisions, and emphasized the importance of a more loosely formulated 'duty to act fairly'. One consequence of judicial activism has been a big increase in the number of reported cases on administrative law.

Some of the principles applied by the courts have already been illustrated in earlier chapters, notably those on subordinate legislation (chapter 15) and local government (chapter 18).

In chapter 27 we outline the main features of the more important remedies in administrative law. This is a complex subject which tends to generate unnecessary confusion. Simplification of the law has been proposed, and perhaps will be achieved in the not too distant future.

Chapter 28 is about civil proceedings for damages and other private law remedies by and against the Crown, with sidelong glances at proceedings against other public bodies. Here again the law has controversial features, and there has been a dramatic change in the attitude of the courts towards 'Crown privilege' – claims by Ministers to withhold relevant evidence from production in legal proceedings on the ground that its disclosure would be injurious to the public interest.

The final chapter in this Part deals with redress of individual grievances outside the system of the courts, tribunals, formal inquiries, and proceedings in Parliament. In particular we are concerned with the Parliamentary Commissioner for Administration (sometimes called the Ombudsman), and we attempt a preliminary assessment of his work. This chapter links up with earlier chapters on ministerial responsibility and the functions of the House of Commons.

Chapter 24
Administrative Law: Introduction

Definition and scope[1]

In 1846 a Select Committee on Legal Education urged that administrative law was a subject fit to be taught at universities.[2] In 1888 Maitland, the great legal and constitutional historian, observed:[3]

If you take up a modern volume of the reports of the Queen's Bench Division, you will find that about half the cases reported have to do with rules of administrative law; I mean with such matters as local rating, the powers of local boards, the granting of licences for various trades and professions, the Public Health Acts, the Education Acts, and so forth.

But in 1935 Lord Hewart, then Lord Chief Justice of England (writing in the *News of the World*) dismissed the term administrative law as 'Continental jargon'.[4]

Now, it is not very profitable to juggle with definitions. Still, such a divergence of opinion is remarkable. How did it arise?

The short answer lies in the influence exerted by Dicey. Writing shortly before Maitland, he argued that the rule or supremacy of law was a fundamental characteristic of the British constitution. The rule of law implied the absence of wide discretionary powers in the Government to encroach on personal liberty, private property rights or freedom of contract, and the proposition that officials and Ministers were responsible for their unlawful acts to the ordinary courts applying the ordinary principles of law. England had nothing corresponding to the administrative law (*droit administratif*) of France, under which legal disputes involving the Government or its servants were dealt with by a special body of administrative law applied by distinct

1. The leading general works are J. A. G. Griffith and H. Street, *Principles of Administrative Law* (4th edn); H. W. R. Wade, *Administrative Law* (3rd edn); and J. F. Garner, *Administrative Law* (3rd edn).
2. Quoted in Brian Abel-Smith and Robert Stevens, *Lawyers and the Courts*, p. 69.
3. *Constitutional History of England*, p. 505; see also p. 501: 'We are becoming a much governed nation, governed by all manner of councils and boards and officers, central and local, high and low, exercising the powers which have been committed to them by modern statutes.'
4. Lord Hewart of Bury, *Not Without Prejudice*, p. 96.

administrative courts or tribunals.[5] *Droit administratif* rested on 'ideas foreign to the fundamental assumptions of our English common law, and especially what we have termed "the rule of law".'[6] It gave special privileges and immunities to the State and its officials in their legal disputes with the citizen; these disputes were determined by bodies not independent of the Executive; the ordinary courts had no jurisdiction in such matters. Administrative justice was not necessarily a form of injustice, but it was a brand of justice akin to that dispensed by the prerogative courts, such as the Star Chamber, which were swept away by the common lawyers and parliamentarians in Charles I's time. With us, matters of State (or public law) were for the ordinary courts staffed by independent judges.

To describe this picture as a caricature may be an overstatement, for Dicey went on to qualify his generalizations and to explain some of the positive merits of the French system.[7] But his main outline was bold and confident; his style was lucid and persuasive; his manner of presentation was calculated to appeal both to insular pride and prejudice and to conservative individualism. Generations of law students were encouraged to treat his works with reverence.

Clearly we had (and have) no separate system of law like the French *droit administratif*. In a sense, then, we had no 'administrative law'. And, so ran the train of thinking, we ought not to have any, because it was the antithesis of the rule of law as we understood it.[8] Consequently, modern welfare and regulatory legislation setting up special 'administrative' tribunals to determine claims and controversies was to be viewed with serious misgivings; it savoured of *droit administratif* and threatened to undermine the 'rule of law', which was identified with adjudication by the ordinary courts. Similarly, statutes and regulations giving wide discretionary powers to Ministers and officials were constitutionally offensive, especially when they purported to exclude or diminish judicial review of administrative action.[9] In short, administrative law was an un-English interloper, which

5. *Introduction to the Study of the Law of the Constitution* (10th edn), chs. 4 and 12. See also p. 38, above.

6. ibid., p. 329. cf. Dicey's own afterthoughts on the incursion of 'administrative law' into England (1915) 31 *L.Q.R.* 148, reprinted as Appendix 2 to his 10th edn, edited by E. C. S. Wade.

7. In particular, the independence achieved by the *Conseil d'Etat*, the central administrative court.

8. See, for example, Salmon L.J.'s observation in *Re Grosvenor Hotel, London* (No. 2) [1965] Ch. 1210 at 1261: 'I do not believe that the court would be . . . obliged to accept the *ipse dixit* of the Minister just because he was a member of the Executive. There is no *droit administratif* in England.' But French administrative courts have been far more reluctant than English courts to accept a Minister's decision as final and conclusive. See, for example, C. J. Hamson, *Executive Discretion and Judicial Control*.

9. For polemical attacks on these trends, see Lord Hewart, *The New Despotism*;

ought not to be acknowledged as a regular member of our legal community. If it could not be defined out of existence, it should be rigorously curbed so as to prevent it from polluting the mainstream of justice.

With attitudes such as these we need not trouble ourselves today,[10] but a modern student needs to appreciate the passions formerly aroused by these controversies, for occasionally they obtrude even now. Some people still think of administrative law as meaning delegated legislation plus administrative adjudication, because these were the most contentious issues not so long ago.[11] But it is more convenient to define administrative law in broader terms. We can take it to mean the law relating to public administration. In other words, it is the law relating to the organization, composition, functions and procedures of public authorities and special statutory tribunals, their impact on the citizen, and the legal restraints to which they are subject. It includes the whole of the law about local authorities and the services they provide, the law relating to nationalized industries, social security, and so on. Whether one includes tax law, and the law and custom of the civil service, are matters of choice. For the purposes of exposition, boundaries have to be drawn somewhere. Still, any comprehensive work on the law of public administration (or administrative law) would be of colossal dimensions.

Books on the subject therefore tend to concentrate on matters of general principle and on the more interesting or important points of detail. They cannot deal exhaustively with the law relating to public highways or transport licensing or electricity supply or social security benefits. They will emphasize what happens when administrative action impinges on private rights, and when claims and controversies arise in the course of the administrative process, and they will lay particular stress on machinery for the redress of wrongs and grievances. These matters lie at the periphery

---

C. K. Allen, *Bureaucracy Triumphant*; *Law and Orders*. Contrast W. A. Robson, *Justice and Administrative Law*; and see W. I. (Sir Ivor) Jennings, *The Law and the Constitution*, for defence and counter-attack. For the views of a more detached observer and participant, see Sir Cecil Carr, *Concerning English Administrative Law*.

10. Thus, Lord Denning M.R. observed in *Breen* v. *A.E.U.* [1971] 2 Q.B. 175 at 189: 'It may truly now be said that we have a developed system of administrative law.'

11. See p. 333. The terms of reference of the Committee on Ministers' Powers (set up in 1929) were, significantly, 'to consider the powers exercised by or under the direction of (or by persons or bodies appointed specially by) Ministers of the Crown by way of (a) delegated legislation and (b) judicial or quasi-judicial decision and to report what safeguards are necessary to secure the constitutional principles of the sovereignty of Parliament and the supremacy of the law.' Professor Robson observed (op. cit., (3rd edn), p. 423): 'The committee started life with the dead hand of Dicey lying frozen on its neck.' For the Committee's Report, see Cmd 4060 (1932): its main value lies in the review of delegated legislation.

rather than the core of public administration. They are nevertheless of constitutional importance – the line between matters of constitutional law and administrative law is indeterminate – and in a general book on constitutional law they must be singled out for special consideration.

The overwhelming bulk of administrative law is statutory; it is to be found in public and private Acts of Parliament and subordinate legislation. Some is embodied in internal regulations for the civil service, some in departmental circulars, some in unwritten constitutional conventions. Some can be extracted from decisions of courts and statutory tribunals. In quantitative terms the body of judge-made administrative law is relatively small;[12] qualitatively it matters a good deal.

Decisions

Decisions in public administration can be classified in various ways. For example, is the decision legislative or non-legislative, judicial or non-judicial? Does the decision involve the exercise of a power or the performance of a duty? Which type of administrative authority makes the decision? Does it have to be made after a hearing, or is it subject to a subsequent hearing before it has final effect, or can it have effect without any hearing at all? Is it subject to appeal or review, and if so, what body is vested with the appellate or supervisory jurisdiction?

Classes of function[13]

Functions may be classified as legislative, administrative, judicial, quasi-judicial and ministerial. None of these terms is unambiguous or self-explanatory and there is often scope for appending two or more labels to a specific act or decision, to the confusion of all students. Briefly, we can state the ingredients of a *typical* function belonging to the main classes:

1. A legislative function involves making rules of general application with prospective effect. Legislation is made by Acts of Parliament, statutory instruments, other regulations and by-laws.

2. An administrative (or executive) function may involve making policy or carrying out a policy or simply deciding what is the most appropriate thing to do in particular circumstances. Examples of administrative decisions are determining new standard terms of public contracts, placing

12. But only relatively. There are several thousand *reported* decisions delivered by the superior courts of this country in the field of administrative law.
13. For fuller analysis of the terminology used, see de Smith, *Judicial Review of Administrative Action* (3rd edn), ch. 2.

public contracts, making decisions on public appointments, and allocating resources such as council houses.

3. A judicial function involves the determination of a question of law or fact by reference to pre-existing rules or standards.

4. A ministerial act is not normally something done by a Minister; it is the performance of a legal duty (for example, to refund overpaid income tax) into which no element of choice or discretion enters.

We shall have to use these terms because they are in common currency. The term 'legislative' does not give rise to a great deal of difficulty in practice, for most of us can recognize legislation when we see it; but we also know that legislative rules can have retrospective as well as prospective effect, that they may simply restate (by consolidation or codification) existing law, that the boundary line between a not very 'general' legislative rule and particular administrative decisions affecting many people can become so blurred as to be imperceptible, and that judges sometimes change the law under the guise of declaring or interpreting it.

Difficulties lurk in the terms 'administrative', 'judicial' and 'quasi-judicial' when they are being contrasted with one another. 'Quasi-judicial' is, on the whole, a superfluous adjective which increases rather than diminishes confusion. Usually it means a discretionary (administrative-type) decision preceded by a judicial-type procedure (for example, confirming a compulsory purchase order after a local inquiry), but the term is also sometimes used to describe the final decision itself and sometimes to describe the preliminary procedure.

As we have seen, 'administrative' acts are what administrators *typically* do and 'judicial' acts are what judges typically do. This terminology does not preclude us from saying that officials (administrators) can perform analytically 'judicial' functions – for example, deciding (subject to appeal) that X is legally obliged to pay £100 in capital gains tax, or that publications imported by Y are obscene, or that Z is not legally entitled to unemployment benefit – or that judges, especially in the Chancery Division, have to exercise wide discretionary powers. A law student's problem (sometimes so puzzling as to seem insoluble) lies in the fact that judges in the reported cases on administrative law use the terms inconsistently. A function that is judicial in one context is labelled 'administrative' in another context. Occasionally these discrepancies are nothing more than an inelegant use of language; occasionally they are attributable to the looseness of the concept of 'administrative' functions; more frequently they can be explained by looking for the legal *consequences* of calling a function 'judicial' or 'administrative' as the case may be.

For example, T's licence to sell peanuts in the street is revoked by the local authority. No appeal is provided by statute. T applies to the Divisional Court of the Queen's Bench Division for an order of certiorari to quash the decision on the grounds that the council acted *ultra vires* and refused to give him a hearing according to natural justice. Revocation of a licence is analytically an administrative act, if a decision whether or not to revoke is discretionary. The courts have sometimes said that certiorari will issue to quash only *judicial* acts. They have also said many times that an obligation to observe the rules of natural justice arises only where there is a duty to act judicially;[14] and they have quite often held that such a duty does not arise where the competent authority's functions are analytically administrative.[15] But if a court were to conclude that the local authority had acted *ultra vires*, it would make no bones today about quashing its decision by certiorari; and if it thought that in fairness to a licensee the authority ought to have given him a proper hearing before taking away his livelihood, it would probably hold that the authority was obliged to 'act judicially' according to natural justice.[16] In the course of the judgments one might even find a dictum that taking away a licence was a 'judicial act'. Suppose, however, that an action for defamation was brought against a member of a local authority for words used by him during a licensing meeting. If he pleaded absolute privilege by way of defence, the court would find against him; the proceedings of the authority would not be 'judicial' for that purpose.[17]

Duty and discretion

The contrast between public duty and discretionary power is ostensibly clear cut. A duty is an act that *must* be performed; thus, a tribunal has a duty to entertain an application or appeal in a matter within its jurisdiction; a local authority has a duty to grant a rate rebate when prescribed conditions are satisfied. Performance of such a duty can normally be enforced in judicial proceedings.[18] Compliance with some of the statutory

14. The observation in the text is tautologous, since a duty to act judicially usually *means* a duty to observe natural justice.

15. See pp. 555, 580–81, 586. This view is on the wane.

16. Thus refusing to follow (or distinguishing) *Nakkuda Ali* v. *Jayaratne* [1951] A.C. 66 and *R.* v. *Metropolitan Police Commissioner, ex p. Parker* [1953] 1 W.L.R. 1150.

17. Hence the member would be able to claim qualified privilege only: *Royal Aquarium etc. Society* v. *Parkinson* [1892] 1 Q.B. 431.

18. See further pp. 564 and 601–3. But some public duties (for example, to provide 'a varied and comprehensive educational service') are so widely framed that no court will direct their enforcement at the suit of a member of the public; and others (for example, those imposed on certain public corporations administering nationalized industries) are expressed to be unenforceable in any court; see pp. 51 and 221. Duties unenforceable by a court obviously resemble statutory powers in this context.

duties cast on local authorities is enforceable by Ministers exercising default powers.

A discretionary power implies freedom of choice; the competent authority *may* decide whether or not to act (for example, whether to order television sets for local schools) and, if so, how to act (for example, with whom should the order be placed; how many sets should be bought?). In practice, duties and powers tend to be interwoven. Seldom does a public body have no discretion at all as to the circumstances in which it is to perform a duty. Police officers, who have a general duty to enforce the law, have a limited discretion to abstain from prosecuting for particular offences. And discretionary powers are normally accompanied by express or implied duties. For instance, a licensing authority may have a discretion to attach such conditions as it thinks fit when granting a licence; but it will be under a legal duty to exercise a genuine discretion in each individual case, and not fetter its choice by adopting rigid rules; and the conditions imposed must not be irrelevant to the purposes for which the power was conferred on it.

Decision-makers

Powers and duties to make decisions in public administration may be vested in the Crown, Ministers, government Departments, civil servants, public corporations and their officers, local authorities, local government officers, tribunals and courts. The distribution of functions among them is not predetermined by any grand design; it is a product of historical accident, tenacious tradition, experiment, and largely uncoordinated decisions about the most appropriate ways of handling individual problems. Patterns are irregular, reflecting the untidy structure of administrative authority in England. A few points should be noted; some have already been mentioned in earlier chapters:

1. Government Departments with ministerial heads did not assume an important role in the provision and regulation of social services till the late nineteenth and early twentieth centuries. Even today, the main providers of public services (for example, education, environmental planning, housing, public health) are the elected local authorities. They have been joined by semi-autonomous public corporations (for example, for broadcasting, hospitals, and the management of nationalized industries). The primary initiative in the direction of national policy, particularly in legislative change and the allocation of financial resources, rests with the central government, but the immediate impact of administrative decisions on the individual citizen generally occurs at a lower level.

2. Decisions by government Departments directly affecting individual rights are usually made by officials in the Minister's name. Powers are sometimes conferred by statute on specified classes of officials (for example, immigration officers, customs and excise officers, district auditors and inspectors conducting inquiries) to be exercised in their own official capacities.

3. Local authority decisions are usually taken by councils or committees of councils. Officials do not have a general power to act on the council's behalf, but very wide powers can be delegated to them from April 1974.[19] Some functions are vested by statute directly in specified officials (for example, medical officers of health).

4. Decision-making by tribunals in the sphere of public administration has a long history. For centuries the local government authorities in the counties were the justices of the peace, who granted licences, regulated taverns, enforced the poor law and the upkeep of highways and bridges, and so on, under judicial forms. Most of their administrative functions passed to elected local authorities in the nineteenth century, but some survive – for example, liquor licensing – and other administrative jurisdiction has been vested in magistrates' courts, notably the hearing of appeals from certain decisions by local authorities. The licensing of gaming clubs is partly a matter for the Gaming Board, an independent investigatory and regulatory body which decides whether to issue certificates of consent, and partly for committees of local magistrates who then decide whether to grant licences.[20]

5. The justices of the peace and borough corporations were subject, during the Tudor and early Stuart periods, to control by the King's Council and the Star Chamber. This was replaced after 1660 by the supervisory jurisdiction of the Court of King's Bench. The basic features of this supervisory jurisdiction survive and have been extended to other types of decision-making bodies.

6. Particularly since the Second World War, power to determine a wide range of claims and controversies in administrative law has been vested in specialized 'administrative' tribunals.[21] The jurisdiction of these tribunals may be original or appellate. The High Court has powers to review their determinations.

7. The functions of the superior courts in administrative law are varied:[22] they include appellate and supervisory review of determinations by inferior

19. See p. 402.
20. Betting, Gaming and Lotteries Act 1963; Gaming Act 1968.
21. See ch. 25.
22. See chs. 26–8.

tribunals, and affording legal redress for wrongful acts committed by other administrative bodies. Seldom do they have power to make a discretionary decision themselves in the first instance, though there are important exceptions – the Restrictive Practices Court and (for limited purposes) the National Industrial Relations Court.[23]

Decisions with or without a hearing

Obviously most decisions in the fields of government and administration have to be taken without a formal inquiry or hearing. If a Minister has to make a major policy decision, he will normally consult the main interest groups likely to be affected – and in some situations he will be under a statutory duty to do so – but government could not be carried on if every important decision had to await the outcome of a full-dress inquiry. Some policy decisions affecting a large number of private individuals in a locality – for example, a decision as to the route of a motorway, or whether to develop an area as a new town – will be preceded by a formal public inquiry. But a decision by a Minister to refuse an application for a passport, an export or import licence, an industrial grant or loan, an office development permit or an industrial development certificate can be made summarily, without any antecedent hearing, though informal representations before and after the decision may be entertained. And clearly decisions made on departmental initiative (for example, to vary rates of taxation) will not usually entail formal hearings either before or after the event.

Again, a great number of decisions made by other public bodies will be made without any formal hearing or inquiry – for example, decisions to close an uneconomic pit, or to refuse an application for the installation of a telephone or for the allocation of a council house or a place in an old people's home; or to place a contract with X rather than with Y or Z, or to promote P rather than Q or R. It does not follow that such decisions will be capricious; they may be regulated or influenced by administrative precedent or general guiding principles; they may be preceded by thorough investigations and personal interviews even though these are not required by law; in some instances they will be subject to appeal.

Nevertheless, the formal pre-decision hearing or inquiry is an important feature of the administrative process in England.[24] Thus, one who applies for a licence to operate a commercial air service or a betting shop, or who claims compensation for injuries sustained as a result of violent crime, will

23. See pp. 521–2, 545.
24. See generally R. E. Wraith and G. B. Lamb, *Public Inquiries as an Instrument of Government* (1971).

be entitled or may be required to appear before a board or tribunal which will make the decision. If there are objectors to his application, they too will, in some instances, be entitled to a hearing. Of more general importance is the statutory procedure followed where public authorities wish to take away or restrict the exercise of private rights in land. A person whose property is the subject of a compulsory purchase order is entitled to be heard at a formal local inquiry before the order can be confirmed; this safeguard is absent from the legal systems of many other developed countries. Again, a local inquiry must be held if objections are lodged against proposals to close an uneconomic railway line or to impose certain types of street restrictions.

Appeals

More common than a statutory right to a prior hearing is a right to be heard on appeal against an administrative decision. Three preliminary points need to be made:

1. A right of appeal is the creature of statute and it can only be conferred by express language. There is no such thing as an implied right of appeal to a court or any other body.

2. The absence of a right of appeal does not necessarily mean that a decision cannot be challenged at all in a court of law. The jurisdiction of the High Court in matters of administrative law is supervisory as well as appellate. This question will be examined in chapters 26 and 27.

3. There is no clear pattern of rights of appeal. This point emerges only too plainly from the following outline sketch:

Ministers and civil servants. In general, no appeal will be provided against discretionary decisions involving questions of national policy or the allocation of scarce resources. Reference was made earlier to discretionary decisions made without a prior hearing; no right of appeal is provided against any of the classes of decisions there illustrated. But there is no universal rule in this matter. The Immigration Appeals Act 1969 gave rights of appeal to adjudicators from discretionary decisions of immigration officers, and to an Immigration Appeal Tribunal from discretionary orders by the Secretary of State for the deportation of aliens. However, under the Immigration Act 1971 the more politically sensitive types of decision were removed from the scope of the appellate system.[25]

Where a decision by a Minister or a civil servant entails the determination of a question of law, appeal often lies to an independent tribunal or

25. See pp. 434–7.

the superior courts; rights of appeal to the courts are usually confined to the legal issues. From decisions on liability to income tax or surtax, an appeal lies to the Commissioners of Income Tax (a special tribunal), and thence to the Chancery Division of the High Court. If a local planning authority considers that planning restrictions have been contravened, it may issue an enforcement notice; the person aggrieved may appeal to the Secretary of State against the notice, and if dissatisfied with the Secretary of State's decision he may appeal on a point of law to the Divisional Court of the Queen's Bench Division. A person dissatisfied with a decision of an officer of the Department of Health and Social Security holding that he is not entitled to a social security benefit may appeal to a local appeal tribunal and thence to the National Insurance Commissioner.

Public corporations. Decisions made by bodies administering nationalized industries are seldom subject to appeal; they are on a similar footing to decisions by privately owned commercial and industrial undertakings. Persons aggrieved by determinations made by officers of the Supplementary Benefits Commission (formerly the National Assistance Board) may appeal to special tribunals. Air licensing decisions by the Civil Aviation Authority are appealable to the Secretary of State for Trade and Industry.[27]

Local authorities. Here again, allocative decisions – decisions on the discretionary allocation of limited resources – are not, as a rule, appealable, but there are a number of exceptions. The statutory designation of appellate bodies can only be described as bizarre. For example, a full appeal lies to magistrates' courts against the merits of various kinds of licensing decisions (for example, the licensing of theatres, street traders, massage establishments); to the Crown Court against decisions on cinema licensing; and to a county court against a decision to make an order for the demolition of an individual insanitary house. Appeals against decisions to refuse planning permission (i.e., permission to 'develop' land by making a material change of use), or to grant such permission subject to conditions to which the applicant objects, lie to the Secretary of State for the Environment or, in cases of minor development raising no big policy issue, to an inspector exercising delegated powers. These appeals have reached a level of over 10,000 in a year; they are decided either on the basis of written representations or following a local inquiry.

Special tribunals

Some administrative tribunals exercise original jurisdiction; some are appellate bodies. There is usually (but not always) an appeal on the merits

27. Civil Aviation Act 1971.

of the decision from a tribunal exercising original jurisdiction to a superior tribunal; in a few cases the appellate authority is a Minister. Appeals now lie on points of law to the superior courts from the decisions of a majority of tribunals of last instance. In most cases the appellate tribunal is the Divisional Court of the Queen's Bench Division, but even in this context there is no uniform pattern; appeals lie in income tax cases to a Chancery judge; from service pensions appeal tribunals to a Queen's Bench judge; from the Transport Tribunal, the Lands Tribunal, the Foreign Compensation Commission and the Patents Appeal Tribunal to the Court of Appeal; and from some professional disciplinary bodies to the Judicial Committee of the Privy Council.

In general

We appear to be losing ourselves in a labyrinth through which even the most expert guide could not be relied on to conduct us. Are there, then, no general principles of English administrative law? Is there but a wilderness of individual instances? An answer can be offered at two levels. In the first place, to achieve a full mastery of the subject one requires an encyclopedic range of knowledge which is hardly worth while acquiring. So much depends on the wording of particular legislation, which is influenced by a motley array of policy considerations. Development of the law has been pragmatic, empirical, even adventitious; only occasionally do broad general principles intrude into the devising of a legislative scheme, and these intrusions tend to operate in the area of the *procedure* followed in decision-making rather than in the substantive structure and interrelationship of authority. Secondly, if one concentrates on the part played by the *courts* in affording legal redress for grievances, the law is still complex and rather confusing, but it is possible to elicit general principles according to which the courts will afford remedies and redress to a person aggrieved by administrative action. These principles sometimes have to be stated at a high level of generality, but they are at least intelligible.

Chapter 25
Tribunals and Inquiries

In general[1]

A section of the Report of the Committee on Ministers' Powers in 1932[2] dealt cursorily and, on the whole, superficially, with the judicial and quasi-judicial powers of the administration. First, it touched on specialized courts, such as professional disciplinary bodies and tribunals dealing with fiscal disputes, the members of which were not appointed by Ministers. It passed on to consider special 'courts' – the defunct Railway and Canal Commission, the Railway Rates Tribunal and the board of referees, and the still surviving Special Commissioners of Income Tax and the Registrar of Friendly Societies – appointed by Ministers. There was nothing sinister about these independent judicial bodies. But then there were the 'Ministerial tribunals' – specialized courts of a more informal character, of original or appellate jurisdiction, appointed by Ministers for the purpose of determining justiciable issues arising in connection with the work of a government Department. These were unemployment assistance, war pensions and other social security tribunals. Only in exceptional circumstances should judicial functions be assigned to Ministerial tribunals. Still more open to objection was the practice of entrusting judicial functions to Ministers. The *judicial* features (the ascertainment of questions of law and fact) of a *quasi*-judicial function entrusted to a Minister (for example a decision whether or not to confirm a slum clearance order after a public local inquiry) would be better entrusted to a tribunal independent of the Minister.

This part of the Report has exercised hardly any influence on legislative policy; it was unrealistic and overweighted with a bias in favour of the ordinary courts. But perhaps its one unfortunate effect was to instil the

1. The best general review is R. M. Jackson's *Machinery of Justice in England* (6th edn), ch. 6. The Report of the Committee on Administrative Tribunals and Enquiries (the Franks Committee (Cmnd 218 (1957)), is prescribed reading. The published Minutes of Evidence of the Committee also contain a wealth of information. See also the Tribunals and Inquiries Act 1971 and any of the Annual Reports of the Council on Tribunals (HMSO).
2. Cmd 4060 (1932), s. III.

impression that what it called 'Ministerial tribunals' were organs of administration, malleable instruments for the implementation of political policy. In 1957 the Report of the Franks Committee on Administrative Tribunals and Enquiries went a long way to remove this misconception. By this time statutory tribunals appointed by Ministers had proliferated. The Committee did indeed prefer to see judicial functions vested in the courts rather than special tribunals, and in special tribunals rather than in Ministers. However, it did not label special tribunals as 'Ministerial tribunals'. It insisted that tribunals were not 'appendages of Government Departments'. It considered that tribunals 'should properly be regarded as machinery provided by Parliament for adjudication rather than as part of the machinery of administration',[3] and it made detailed proposals designed to integrate them more closely with the general judicial system of the country. It drew a sharp distinction between 'administrative' adjudication, on the one hand, and discretionary decisions reached by Ministers following a local inquiry, on the other. Its proposals for reforming procedures involving inquiries in matters affecting the regulation of land use were radical but far better informed and more realistic than those of the 1932 Committee. Its detailed recommendations were too persuasive to be ignored, and most of them have been implemented.[4] Today no reasonably well-read student has any excuse for confusing tribunals with inquiries. Whitehall's terrible twins are neither terrible nor twins.

The Franks Committee itself was an outstanding example of a particular type of public inquiry. Its members were appointed by the Lord Chancellor, not under statutory authority but in virtue of the prerogative. They were judges, former high-ranking civil servants, practising lawyers, leading academics, trade unionists, elder statesmen, active politicians. It was directed to inquire into and make recommendations on matters raising broad issues of public policy. It sat in public to receive oral evidence from officials and others; it obtained a number of written memoranda; it accumulated and published a mass of factual information, much of which had not previously been divulged to the public; it was a new clearing-house for informed opinion and original ideas. Its report stimulated public debate and refertilized official thinking. In substance it fulfilled the role of a Royal Commission (the members of which are appointed by Her Majesty on the Prime Minister's advice) and unlike so many Royal Commissions, its recommendations were not disregarded.[5]

3. Cmnd 218 (1957), § 40.
4. See pp. 28–39 of the Report of the Council on Tribunals for 1963, summarizing the extent to which the recommendations had been adopted.
5. The appointment of a Royal Commission is sometimes prompted by a Government's desire to avoid making a decision on an awkward question. The matter can be

Public inquiries are basically instruments of government[6] (using the term 'government' in the broadest sense) or Parliament. As instruments of Parliament, or a House of Parliament, their role may be to investigate an alleged public scandal, or a national disaster such as the Aberfan catastrophe. Upon a resolution of both Houses, a 'tribunal' headed by a superior judge may be appointed under the Tribunals of Inquiry (Evidence) Act 1921.[7] The practice of setting up a select committee of the House of Commons to inquire into such a matter fell into disuse after the partisan report and debate on the Marconi scandal in 1913. There are other alternatives. Disquiet about covert official telephone-tapping, security leaks, 'D' Notices and interrogation techniques in Northern Ireland has led to the appointment by the Prime Minister of *ad hoc* committees of Privy Councillors to inquire and report; the outcome has sometimes been embarrassing to the Government. Lord Denning investigated aspects of the Profumo affair.[8] Major security leaks are now referred to a Security Commission under a superior judge. Another non-statutory technique, commonly employed, is for Ministers to appoint a departmental or inter-departmental committee of inquiry into a particular issue – for example, section 2 of the Official Secrets Act 1911.[9] Again, a Minister may appoint a committee or an independent person to inquire into serious complaints about the conduct of officials. The Crichel Down inquiry, conducted by a Q.C., was such a case.[10] The publication of the Report led to the censure and transfer of

---

shelved till the Commission has reported; the Government may then spend several months formulating its own reactions to the recommendations, and may find itself supplied with new reasons why nothing of importance should or could be done. See, however, William Plowden, 'An Anatomy of Commissions', *New Society*, 15 July 1971.

6. See R. E. Wraith and G. B. Lamb, *Public Inquiries as an Instrument of Government* (1971) – the fullest study of the subject.

7. cf. George W. Keeton, *Trial by Tribunal*; and the report of the Royal Commission on Tribunals of Inquiry, Cmnd 3121 (1966) suggesting procedural reforms. For the controversial Vehicle and General Inquiry (Report, H.C. 133 (1971–72)) see p. 173. In 1972 Lord Widgery conducted a one-man judicial tribunal of inquiry into the incidents on 'Bloody Sunday' in Londonderry: see Report, H.C. 220 (1971–72). These tribunals (unlike most of the other types of inquisitorial bodies) have coercive powers. See Addendum.

8. For his report, see Cmnd 2152 (1963).

9. For the second Franks Report (Cmnd 5104) (1972), see ch. 21. The first Franks Committee was also, in a sense, a departmental committee, though the Lord Chancellor, who appointed it, occupies a kind of 'crossbench' position.

10. See Cmd 9176, 9220 (1954); Griffith (1955) 18 *Mod. L. Rev.* 557; Chester (1954) 32 *Public Administration* 389. Crichel Down had been compulsorily acquired by the Air Ministry as a bombing range. After the war it was handed back to the civil authorities. Lieut.-Commander Marten, the son-in-law of the former owner, wished to buy it or alternatively to become the tenant farmer of the area. The civil servants concerned decided to re-equip the estate, to let it to another tenant, and not to accede

some officials, to the resignation of the Minister of Agriculture on his own initiative, and indirectly to the appointment of the Franks Committee (from whose terms of reference the Crichel Down type of situation was, nevertheless, excluded).

Other types of formal inquiry may be held under statutory authority to investigate allegations or suspicions of malpractice or culpable negligence or organizational deficiencies – for example, an inquiry by a Department of Trade and Industry inspector into the affairs of a company; or an inquiry into the causes of an aircraft, shipping, railway or mine disaster or a factory accident; or a military 'court of inquiry' into an untoward incident that requires special investigation; or an inquiry into complaints against police officers.

The common features of these inquiries are (i) that the persons conducting them are expected to hold hearings and ascertain facts about specified matters of public concern and (ii) that they do not make *decisions*, though their findings and recommendations may be a foundation for decisions by others, including decisions to institute legal proceedings. Indeed, in some situations a finding of culpability, or of a *prima facie* case of culpability, may be a necessary condition for the institution or continuance of such proceedings. But the fact that the investigating body may be called a 'court' or 'tribunal' does not endow it with the characteristic power of a judicial body to make decisions. On the other hand, an inquisitorial body may exceptionally be endowed with such powers. In the Plantagenet period, the itinerant royal justices in eyre conducted inquisitions and also punished transgressors. The verdict of a coroner's inquest in a case of homicide may assert that X was legally culpable but does not amount to a conviction though it may be the foundation of criminal proceedings against X; a verdict that Y committed suicide does, however, have binding legal effect; and so does a verdict that Z, who has found ancient precious coins, is legally entitled to them because they do not come within the definition of treasure trove.[11] Inspectors conducting inquiries in town planning law are generally restricted to finding and reporting on facts, and recommending a decision to be taken by or on behalf of the Minister; in 1968, however, power to make decisions in consequence of certain types of inquiries was delegated by the Minister to the inspectors themselves.[12] In these few intermediate

to Marten's requests, but failed to keep him properly informed and created false impressions in his mind. Marten pursued his grievance through political channels. The procedure for dealing with the disposition of such land was not regulated by statutory rules.

11. Treasure trove is hidden (as distinct from abandoned) treasure, and belongs to the Crown in virtue of the prerogative.

12. See now Town and Country Planning Act 1971, Sched. 9; S.I. 1972, No. 1652.

zones the distinction between tribunals and inquiries disappears; the investigator *is* the tribunal.

The typical inquiry – one which does not culminate in a binding decision by the person who presides at the hearing – may be directed to a very wide range of public purposes. The point is well illustrated by an Order made in 1967,[13] bringing within the purview of the Council on Tribunals[14] no fewer than sixty-five different types of discretionary inquiries held in pursuance of statutory powers. They ranged from inquiries held in pursuance of section 5 of the renowned Fisheries (Oyster, Crab, and Lobster) Act 1877 (empowering the Board of Trade, after receiving local representations and holding such public inquiry as it thinks expedient, to make orders temporarily prohibiting dredging for oysters from banks in the locality) to the committee of inquiry appointed by the Home Secretary to advise him before he decides whether to deprive a naturalized or registered citizen of his citizenship.[15] And they included inquiries that may be held by a person appointed by a Secretary of State for a large number of administrative purposes in local government law – for example, before the Secretary of State confirms various statutory schemes. Add to these all the sundry types of inquiries which a Minister *must* cause to be held when a prescribed state of affairs exists (for example, when he entertains an appeal against certain administrative decisions taken at a lower level), and the indeterminate miscellany of situations in which a discretionary inquiry may be set up *without* statutory authority,[16] and one has a very mixed bag. One finds, for example, Acts providing that before certain kinds of subordinate legislation can be made or confirmed a statutory inquiry may or must be held.[17] If one can offer any useful generalizations in this variegated field of public law, they ought to be focused rather on the public local inquiry. Local inquiries are used for three main purposes:[18]

1. As a means of consulting and informing local opinion, and gleaning local information as to the likely impact of a proposed administrative decision (for example, to alter constituency or local boundaries, or to amalgamate police forces) affecting the interests of persons and bodies in that locality. This slows down the pace of decision-making but provides the decision-maker with a better fund of knowledge.

13. S.I. 1967, No. 451.
14. See pp. 551–2, 554, 559, 560.
15. British Nationality Act 1948, s. 20(7).
16. In general, persons conducting inquiries in pursuance of statutory powers have authority to compel the attendance of witnesses and the production of documents, and those conducting non-statutory inquiries have not.
17. See, for example, Factories Act 1937, s. 129, Sched. 2; Griffith and Street, *Principles of Administrative Law* (4th edn), p. 129ff.
18. Neat classification is impossible. See Wraith and Lamb, op. cit., chs. 3, 4, 8.

2. As a means of giving those whose interests will be most directly affected by a proposed or provisional decision (for example, to make an order for the compulsory purchase of their land or to designate an area as the site of a new town) the legal right to put their objections orally, and through legal representatives, to a person appointed by the Minister or another competent authority before a final decision is made. Other points of view may be expressed at the inquiry, and the outcome should (as in (1)) be conducive to better decision-making. Purposes (1) and (2) are complementary. In some cases the scope of inquiry will be confined to the objections and not directed to the general merits of the proposed order.

3. As a stage in the process of determining appeals against an administrative decision that has already been taken. The best-known examples arise in planning law.

X applies to his local planning authority for permission to make a material change in the use of his land; planning permission is refused, or is granted subject to conditions that X dislikes; X is entitled to appeal to the Secretary of State for the Environment; the Secretary of State causes a local inquiry to be held through an inspector; the inspector makes a report and the Secretary of State (or a civil servant on his behalf) decides.[19] Y, without asking for planning permission, sets himself up in business in his private house; the local authority issues an enforcement notice directing him to discontinue this unauthorized change in the use of his land; Y contends that no permission was required for this particular change of use, and appeals to the Secretary of State; the latter sends down an inspector who holds a local inquiry and makes a report; again the decision on this appeal is made within the Department.[19]

In situations (1) and (2) one can speak of judicialized administration; in the third type of situation, judicialized administration merges into administrative adjudication. In 1970 nearly 7000 appeals of the kind described above were decided by the Department of the Environment.[20] Now over half of the planning appeals are decided by inspectors, and about half are decided on the basis of written representations without a local inquiry.

Special tribunals[21]

One tends to use the terms 'special tribunals', 'administrative tribunals' and 'statutory tribunals' interchangeably. Terminological inexactitude

19. Unless the power of decision has been delegated to the inspector; see note 12, above.

20. Figures are given in the Department's *Handbook of Statistics* for 1970, pp. 22–3.

does not matter much in this field, because no single term could be all-embracing; but a few preliminary points should be borne in mind.

1. Some tribunals that are commonly called 'administrative' deal with disputes between private landlords and tenants. These tribunals are the rent tribunals, rent assessment committees[22] and agricultural land tribunals.[23] Curiously enough, to many people rent tribunals are the stereotype of 'administrative' tribunals, partly because they used to evoke a good deal of controversy in the immediate post-war years and partly because they are still not at all like ordinary courts.

2. A small number of tribunals which can well be described as 'administrative' (in the sense that they deal with claims and controversies involving public authorities) are non-statutory. The most important is the Criminal Injuries Compensation Board which makes discretionary awards out of funds provided by Parliament to claimants who are victims of criminal violence.

3. Not all 'special' tribunals are in any conceivable sense 'administrative'. Commercial and industrial arbitrators, the disciplinary committees of trades unions and clubs, the stewards of the Jockey Club and the Greyhound Racing Association are obviously not 'administrative'; the disciplinary committees of private organizations are called *domestic* tribunals. Professional statutory disciplinary bodies are occasionally called 'administrative' tribunals, but they too are domestic.

4. Tribunals exercising functions in administrative law may be designated as tribunals, courts, boards, committees, commissioners, referees, umpires; the name is unimportant. The Lands Tribunal is more court-like than the local valuation courts from which it entertains appeals.

5. Tribunals dispensing 'administrative justice' may in substance be doing exactly the same kind of work, in a specialized field, as an ordinary court of law, and doing it with the same degree of freedom from political pressure and influence.

21. The body of literature on this subject is now extensive. W. A. Robson, *Justice and Administrative Law* (3rd edn) is the classic pioneering work. Apart from the sources referred to in note 1 above, the following recent monographs can be consulted: Harry Street, *Justice in the Welfare State*; H. W. R. Wade, *Towards Administrative Justice*; H. J. Elcock, *Administrative Justice*; Kathleen Bell, *Tribunals in the Social Services*; N. D. Vandyk, *Tribunals and Inquiries*. See also the textbooks on administrative law; and, for less recent studies, R. S. W. Pollard (ed.), *Administrative Tribunals at Work*; C. K. Allen, *Administrative Jurisdiction*.

22. On which see D. C. M. Yardley [1968] *Public Law* 135.

23. The Lands Tribunal (see below) also has a private law jurisdiction to vary restrictive covenants.

Specialized courts reach far back into English legal history. Some of them – for example, the courts of the stannaries (the tin mines), the courts of piepowder (for travelling merchants at fairs), and their successors, the royal courts of the staple – live on only in our history books. The ancient Court of Chivalry was rescued from quiescent oblivion for a fleeting moment in the 1950s.[24] The coroners' courts are still with us. These special courts, though standing outside the regular legal system, posed no real threat to the paramountcy of the common law courts. The more serious competitors – the ecclesiastical courts, the Court of Chancery, the Court of Admiralty, the Court of Requests and the Court of Star Chamber – all excited the jealous resentment of the common lawyers, a resentment naturally expressed in the language of high constitutional principle. Some of these courts survived the experience; others were destroyed or shorn of significant jurisdiction, but left a legacy of creative jurisprudence to enrich English law.

Neither the creation of specialized courts nor the hostility of the legal profession need cause any surprise. And any new specialized tribunal, set up to serve a general public purpose, could be assured of an ample measure of initial hostility following the struggle against the Star Chamber, especially if it neither looked nor functioned like a court of common law. Military courts-martial, professional disciplinary bodies and commercial arbitrators could be tolerated. Tribunals adjudicating informally in disputes arising out of social welfare legislation were another matter. The rules they applied interfered with freedom of property and contract; their members were appointed and removable by Ministers; often they exercised discretionary powers which could only be reposed with safety in the hands of Chancery or county court judges; if lawyers appeared before them at all, everyone tended to be ill at ease. To some, their very existence was a slur upon the legal profession and a constructive contempt of court. Dicey and Hewart were right: the rule of law was in jeopardy. So ran the train of thought – one that the Committee on Ministers' Powers did little to disturb. Nevertheless, the Committee grudgingly conceded[25] that 'Ministerial tribunals' might, in exceptional circumstances, be preferred to the ordinary courts on five grounds: cheapness, accessibility to the parties, freedom from technicality, speed, and expert knowledge of their particular subject-matter.

The climate of opinion has now changed. No longer must exceptional

24. See p. 516, note 16.
25. Cmd 4060 (1932), p. 97. See also the Franks Report, Cmnd 218 (1957), § 38, making the same point in less grudging terms.

circumstances be present to justify the establishment of a special tribunal to determine controversies arising under regulatory or welfare legislation. We have about fifty different *types* of these tribunals and some 2000 tribunals altogether. If, for instance, the question is how disputes about the entitlement of dismissed workers to redundancy payments from their employers ought to be decided under a new Act, there is an *expectation* that the deciding body will be a special tribunal. The alternatives would be (1) a Minister, (2) one of the ordinary courts, (3) a specially constituted court, and (4) an independent arbitrator. Giving the power of decision to a Minister means in practice that the parties may not know who takes the decision in the Minister's name and will not be entitled to be heard before that person;[26] and they will not usually feel confident that departmental adjudication is justice according to law. There is, therefore, a presumption in favour of vesting the power of decision in a person or body conducting oral hearings; this presumption may be rebutted only if considerations of national or regional policy, for which the Minister is responsible, will often condition the manner in which an individual issue ought to be determined, or if uniformity of decision is of primary importance. A possible compromise – and not a very satisfactory one – is to set up an independent tribunal with an appeal to the Minister.[27] Setting up a specialized court, rather than a tribunal, may be to make heavy weather of small issues. The outstanding modern example of a specialized court in the strict sense is the Restrictive Practices Court; this is a court because it is expressed to be a superior court of record and is presided over by a superior judge (though it includes expert laymen); its jurisdiction (to nullify restrictive trading agreements which are contrary to the public interest) *could* have been vested in a body styled as a tribunal, and when it was first constituted there are many who would have preferred to see that course adopted.[28] Committing issues to independent arbitrators – the last alternative – is most appropriate where the number of issues arising is relatively small and a high level of expertise, likely to be found only among specialists willing to act as part-time adjudicators, is required.

The grounds, already indicated, for giving jurisdiction to tribunals rather than courts are sometimes overstated. Certainly it would be absurd to make applicants for sickness benefit or supplementary benefits go before

26. They will have no such entitlement at common law; *Local Government Board* v. *Arlidge* [1915] A.C. 120 (housing appeal). But they may be entitled to be heard before a person appointed by the Minister to report to him.

27. For example, the Civil Aviation Authority, from which an appeal lies to the Secretary of State for Trade and Industry.

28. See R. B. Stevens and B. S. Yamey, *The Restrictive Practices Court*. The other leading example is the National Industrial Relations Court.

a High Court judge;[29] the cost, delay and formality would thwart the objectives of social security schemes and would clog up the general administration of justice. These considerations do not apply with anything like the same force to the county courts, which are more accessible and expeditious[30] than some special tribunals and hardly more expensive. County courts do, moreover, have jurisdiction in some matters of administrative law. Where the county courts have been by-passed and new statutory tribunals established instead, the reasons have generally been the following:

1. County court judges and registrars are generalists, not specialists. There is no reason to expect them to be experts in transport licensing or the rating of property or to be familiar with the problems of the sick and needy or to have the time and opportunity to acquire the necessary expertise or familiarity. A special statutory tribunal may include persons with the desired initial qualifications and others who will acquire them through specialization and experience.

2. Courts are formal. The kind of person who is aggrieved by refusal of a social security benefit or who wants to make a complaint arising out of the administration of the National Health Service may be overawed by the atmosphere of a judicial proceeding and reduced to incoherence or silence if he is precluded by the rules of evidence from telling his story in his own way. In some situations justice can be dispensed only in an informal environment. Special tribunals can be very informal. And none of them is obliged to follow all the strict rules of evidence and procedure of a court of law.

3. Tribunals usually take an active part in finding the facts for themselves; they may adopt 'inquisitorial' procedures, probing away with questions, not acting as detached umpires who rely almost entirely on the material as presented to them by the parties or their advocates. Some of them (for example, rent tribunals, valuation courts) regularly conduct site inspections. And though they must observe those minimum requirements of procedural fair play called the rules of natural justice, they can draw on their own expert and acquired knowledge in drawing inferences from the facts found.

29. Except in the last resort, where a claimant is dissatisfied with the determination of an inferior tribunal on a matter of law.

30. On delays in hearings before various kinds of special tribunals, see the Reports of the Council on Tribunals for 1967 (§§ 73, 74) and 1968 (§§ 19–25). The tempo of the Foreign Compensation Commission was disturbingly illustrated by the facts disclosed in *Anisminic Ltd* v. *Foreign Compensation Commission* [1969] 2 A.C. 147; this was aggravated by the further delays interposed by subsequent judicial review.

4. Courts are bound by precedent. Tribunals, though bound by judicial precedents laid down in their own field of the law, and capable of evolving a body of 'case law' themselves, can be more flexible in formulating standards (for example, what is reasonable under local conditions; whether premises are educationally suitable) and departing from them when the circumstances of a case warrant relaxation.[31] Indeed, one of the more formal special tribunals was warned by the Court of Appeal that it ought *not* to adopt a rigid body of case law.[32]

One of the most significant legal developments in the immediate post-war period was the replacement of the Workmen's Compensation Acts by the national insurance (industrial injuries) scheme.[33] Not only was private insurance replaced by public social insurance; the tribunals constituted to administer the new scheme were special tribunals before which legal representation was at first excluded. The jurisdiction of county court judges was ousted and the massive body of case law evolved in the many legal battles fought as far as the House of Lords was deprived of binding authority. This was a drastic repudiation of technical legalism in which social justice had too often been overlooked.

Types of tribunals[34]

No attempt will here be made to present a full synopsis. Only a broad outline under general headings will be offered.

Fiscal liability and claims, property and land. Appeals against administrative assessments to income tax, surtax, corporation tax and capital gains tax are heard either by special commissioners of income tax (who are civil servants) or by general commissioners (who are not). Appeals against value added tax assessments by the Customs and Excise lie to special value added tax tribunals. Persons aggrieved by rating assessments made by valuation officers (who are civil servants) may object before a local valuation court, which is composed largely of unpaid local councillors and magistrates. Appeal lies to the Lands Tribunal, a body which could easily be styled an administrative court; its members are professional lawyers and

31. A point well made by Street, *Justice in the Welfare State*, pp. 7–9.
32. *Merchandise Transport Co.* v. *British Transport Commission* [1962] 2 Q.B. 173 at 186, 192–3.
33. W. A. Robson, *Justice and Administrative Law* (3rd edn), pp. 209–22.
34. There is a good classification and synopsis in J. F. Garner's *Administrative Law* (3rd edn), chs. 7 and 8. Figures of cases heard by most of the various tribunals are supplied in an Appendix to the Annual Report of the Council on Tribunals. Not all special tribunals, however, come under the aegis of the Council. See further, D. C. M. Yardley, *A Source Book of English Administrative Law* (2nd edn), ch. 6.

surveyors appointed by the Lord Chancellor; its procedure is fairly in-formal but its judgments are often reported. The jurisdiction of the Tribunal also includes the assessment of compensation for compulsory acquisition of land where this is not agreed between the acquiring authority and the property-owner.

Appeals relating to the betting levy on bookmakers lie to a special appeal tribunal. Appeals against assessments to the industrial training levy, disputes concerning redundancy payments for workers and a range of questions under the Industrial Relations Act 1971, notably claims to compensation for unfair dismissal, are heard by industrial tribunals, which have acquired an extensive jurisdiction since they were first set up in 1965; they also hear appeals for compensation for loss of public office under statutory reorganization schemes. They are becoming the most important group of tribunals. In 1971 they were sitting in London and ninety other centres in England and Wales, and they heard over 9000 cases.[35] The figures for 1972 will be far bigger.

The Foreign Compensation Commission entertains claims to the award of compensation out of funds received by the British Government from foreign governments for the expropriation or destruction of British-owned property overseas, and allocates the money to successful claimants on a discretionary basis. The non-statutory Criminal Injuries Compensation Board makes discretionary awards to claimants who are victims of criminal violence.

The informal rent tribunals and rent assessment committees fix fair rents between landlord and tenant; the latter are appellate bodies, an initial determination having already been made by a rent officer. Fair rents for council tenancies under the Housing Finance Act 1972 are determined not by tribunals but by local authorities subject to review by rent scrutiny boards. The membership of the two types of tribunals has been partly integrated. Agricultural land tribunals deal with disputes between land-lords and tenant farmers about notices to quit.

Social welfare. Post-war legislation has substantially enlarged the number and jurisdiction of such tribunals. Most are appellate bodies hearing appeals lodged by persons aggrieved by initial administrative decisions; and in most of the cases before them the monetary sums in issue are small, though often of major importance to the poor and disabled. There are the local national insurance tribunals (dealing with claims to unemployment benefit, sickness benefit, industrial injuries benefit, retirement pensions, maternity and death grants, family allowances and so on), medical appeal tribunals on industrial injuries claims, and supplementary benefit appeal tri-

35. See Report of the Council on Tribunals for 1971–2 (H.C. 13 (1972–73)) p. 32.

bunals[36]. Appeals in respect of disability pensions claimed by ex-servicemen lie to separate pensions appeal tribunals. From the national insurance and medical appeal tribunals, appeals lie to senior full-time lawyers, the national insurance commissioners. Certain questions are reserved for determination by the Secretary of State. A complex network of tribunals (including the Secretary of State for Social Services) exists to hear complaints and allegations against practitioners in the National Health Service and to entertain appeals. Persons compulsorily committed to a mental hospital can seek their release from custody by application to a mental health review tribunal; these tribunals heard over 1000 cases in 1971.

Among other tribunals concerned with social welfare in a broad sense are the industrial tribunals, rent tribunals, rent assessment committees, agricultural land tribunals, the Criminal Injuries Compensation Board, independent schools tribunals (which determine whether a private school or its proprietor or any of its teachers ought to be struck off the official register or disqualified as the case may be) and tribunals exercising roughly similar functions with regard to voluntary children's homes; occasionally a scandalous abuse of quasi-parental authority is divulged in the course of these infrequent proceedings.

Regulatory. Regulation by licensing, normally coupled with powers of inspection, is a familar feature of public supervision of private activity. Powers to grant licences will be accompanied by powers to impose conditions, to refuse renewal of a licence, and to revoke a licence when prescribed violations of the terms of the licence are established; powers to revoke in the absolute discretion of the licensing authority are rarely conferred today. Licensing powers may be vested in government Departments, public corporations or local authorities.[37] Aspects of the regulation of transport communications have been committed, for reasons of practical convenience, to independent tribunals. For example, applications for licences to operate commercial air routes are heard by the Civil Aviation Authority; objectors have a right to be heard in opposition; an appeal lies to the Secretary of State for Trade and Industry. Regulation of carriage of goods and passengers by road follows a curious pattern. There are area licensing authorities. Appeal lies from decisions on passenger road services to the Secretary of State for the Environment, on goods carriers' licences to the Transport Tribunal. The latter is an anomalous body; till 1969 it also heard applications for variations of railway passenger charges in the London transport area. It is a court with judicial trappings and procedure;

36. Between them they heard about 77,000 appeals in 1971. For a good critique of the social security tribunals see Street, op. cit., pp. 11–32.

37. Street, op. cit., ch. 4; Glanville Williams (1967) 20 *Current Legal Problems* 81.

its rate-fixing functions (still exercisable for limited purposes) are successors to the jurisdiction exercised from 1921 by the Railway Rates Tribunal, the antecedents of which can be traced to the Railway and Canal Commission, a superior court and an arbitral body, set up in 1873.

Among other regulatory bodies are the Comptroller-General of Patents, Designs and Trade Marks (from which an appeal lies to the Patents Appeal Tribunal, composed of either one or two superior judges), the Plant Variety Rights Tribunal exercising similar functions, the Performing Right Tribunal, the tribunal appointed to consider alleged violations of the Prevention of Fraud (Investments) Act 1958 by dealers in securities, and the Wireless Telegraphy Appeal Tribunal set up to consider complaints of undue interference with radio broadcasts on the part of private operators.

Tribunals to consider complaints about the conduct of voluntary schools and children's homes are also regulatory bodies. Perhaps one should include the immigration appellate bodies (2000 cases in 1971) in this category too. The Gaming Board for Great Britain, which decides on the basis of police reports and other information whether to grant a certificate of consent to gaming-club proprietors, thus enabling them to apply for a local licence, is a regulatory body which may be regarded as a kind of informal tribunal.[38]

This is not a complete list, and some classes of tribunals defy classification. Informal adjudication within government Departments is also of practical importance. Civil servants in Britain are more accessible to informal interviews than in many foreign countries.

Franks and after

The Franks Committee found nothing fundamentally wrong with the system and working of statutory tribunals, and it did not seek to put tribunals into a strait-jacket. But its bias in favour of judicialization led it to make a number of recommendations designed to assimilate tribunals more closely to specialized courts. For example, it deprecated undue informality, and stressed the need for settled rules of procedure, reasons for decisions, rights to legal representation, proper channels of appeal and the removal of any suspicion of political dictation of or influence over decisions. The procedures of tribunals ought to be characterized by 'openness, fairness and impartiality'.[39] Openness implied not only reasoned decisions but also public hearings (except where the interests of the public –

38. It has to 'act fairly' in accordance with natural justice: *R.* v. *Gaming Board for Great Britain, ex p. Benaim and Khaida* [1970] 2 Q.B. 417.
39. Cmnd 217 (1957), § 23.

for example, in security – or the parties demanded privacy, as in potentially embarrassing 'national assistance' appeals and complaints against National Health Service practitioners), with evidence given orally. Fairness demanded that the parties knew their rights in advance, had proper notice of the case they had to meet, an adequate opportunity to put their own case in person or through their representatives, and rights to appeal against and obtain review of decisions. Impartiality required new safeguards for the appointment and tenure of members; and to preserve the appearance of impartiality, independent tribunals ought not to sit in departmental premises. To maintain some degree of coherence and surveillance over the tribunal system, there should be a standing Council on Tribunals.

The Tribunals and Inquiries Act 1958 provided for the establishment of the Council on Tribunals, to keep under review the constitution and working of specified tribunals; other tribunals have been added to the list. The current Act is the Tribunals and Inquiries Act 1971. The Council[40] consists of up to fifteen members appointed by the Lord Chancellor and the Secretary of State for Scotland, and the Parliamentary Commissioner for Administration *ex officio*. The chairman is salaried; the other appointed members receive fees; but the Council is essentially a part-time supervisory body with a minute official staff. It meets once a month. Members of the Council and its Scottish Committee attended only nine hearings by tribunals in 1966; in 1968 the figure soared to fifty-five but dropped to forty-one in 1971. More specifically, the functions of the Council in respect of tribunals – it has powers in connection with inquiries too[41] – are as follows:

1. To consider and report on the statutory tribunals under its supervision, and on such particular matters concerning these and other tribunals as may be referred to it by the Lord Chancellor and the Secretary of State.

Within the limited scope of its resources, it has attempted to conduct general reviews of specific classes of tribunals (for example, rent tribunals) and has reported on special matters such as the power to award costs and the law of defamation. It organizes conferences with tribunal chairmen.

2. To receive and investigate complaints about tribunals made by members of the public.

In its first ten years the Council received only 242 complaints relating to tribunals. This small figure probably indicates a widespread ignorance

40. See J. F. Garner [1965] *Public Law* 321; H. W. R. Wade, *Administrative Law* (3rd edn), pp. 266–76; *Towards Administrative Justice*. Professor Wade was an original member of the Council. For his more critical reflections, see Bernard Schwartz and H. W. R. Wade, *Legal Control of Government* (1972), pp. 179–80.
41. See pp. 559, 560.

of the Council's very existence or whereabouts rather than a general satisfaction of consumers with the work of tribunals. The Council has no power to alter a tribunal's decision and in most cases the tribunal would have no jurisdiction to rescind its own decision even if it wished to do so. However, individual complaints may lead to further investigations and recommendations for reform. The Council can get to know where the shoe pinches.

3. To make an annual report to the Lord Chancellor and the Secretary of State. The Report is laid before Parliament and is now published as a House of Commons paper. It attracts little public comment but is a very useful source of information.

4. To be consulted by the responsible Minister before procedural rules for tribunals and inquiries are made.

This is probably its most important function – one in which the minority of lawyers on the Council plays a leading role. It has helped to promote a higher degree of uniformity in tribunal procedures, and in particular to instil the essentials of judicial fairness into procedural regulations – for example, adequate notification of rights of appeal, proper notice of hearings and disclosure of the case to be answered; rights of cross-examination; rights to legal representation at oral hearings.

The Council is also consulted by the Department sponsoring legislation under which a new tribunal is to be constituted or an existing one abolished or reorganized. It has complained that in these matters it is sometimes consulted too late for its representations to have any effect, and has urged that more thought be given to coordinated rationalization of the tribunal system, involving the amalgamation of some types of tribunals and reallocations of jurisdiction.[42]

5. To make *general* recommendations to the appropriate Minister as to the appointment of members of tribunals.

In practice this has not been an important function of the Council. However, the Franks recommendations have had a significant effect on appointments and tenure. The chairmen of certain tribunals have to be legally qualified, and appointed either by the Lord Chancellor or by the Minister generally concerned with the area of administration in question from a panel maintained by the Lord Chancellor. Members of most tribunals cannot be removed except with the Lord Chancellor's concurrence;[43] they

42. Annual Report for 1969–70 (H.C. 72 (1970–71)), pp. 10–11, 29–32.
43. See Tribunals and Inquiries Act 1971, ss. 5, 7–9. For the Franks recommendations on these matters, see Cmnd 218, ch. 5. In 1969, 2281 members of tribunals (out of about 21,000) had been appointed or recommended by the Lord Chancellor (H.C. 72 (1970–71), p. 12).

may, however, be refused reappointment after their term of office has expired.

Tribunals are not cast in a common mould, but some general points are important:

(i) Most tribunals are not composed of officials,[44] though there are some exceptions – for example, Ministry inspectors deciding planning appeals, special commissioners of income tax, the Comptroller-General of Patents, Designs and Trade Marks; these officers nevertheless act independently.

(ii) A fairly typical tribunal is composed of a legally qualified chairman, appointed by one of the procedures indicated above, and two lay members, one of whom will perhaps be an employer and another a trade union official; or both may be independent specialists or local worthies.

(iii) They are bound by regulations made by the Minister, but only in highly exceptional circumstances defined by legislation will the Minister be legally entitled to give them specific directions for the determination of a particular case.

(iv) For a variety of reasons the position of a legally qualified chairman[45] may be of crucial importance. The legislation which a tribunal has to interpret and apply may be just as complicated as law in the courts. Although the parties will nearly always be *entitled* to legal representation,[46] they will seldom be so represented before tribunals like social security tribunals dealing with small matters. Unfortunately, the legal aid and advice scheme has not been applied to proceedings before tribunals except the Lands Tribunal and the Commons Commissioners. If one party is legally represented, the chairman will have to do his best to help the unrepresented party put his case without shedding his own impartiality as a fact-finder and adjudicator. Obviously this is a difficult task.

Before some tribunals legal representation, may, however, be a mixed blessing to a party. Clearly, such representation is important if a party is accused of culpability or if his vital interests are in serious jeopardy. But advocates appearing before tribunals can also sow confusion and protract

44. There is good survey of the composition of various tribunals, and the methods by which their members are appointed in practice and the classes of persons from whom they are drawn, by Susan McCorquodale in [1962] *Public Law* 298. See further, W. E. Cavanagh and D. Newton (1970) 48 *Public Administration* 449, (1971) 49 *Public Administration* 197.

45. Full-time chairmen were appointed for industrial tribunals following the heavy increase in their work-load after 1971.

46. The Franks Report (§ 87) recommended that the right to legal representation be curtailed only in the most exceptional circumstances. In 1958 a right to legal representation before industrial injuries tribunals was conferred by statutory instrument. There remain special cases – for example, a police officer on a disciplinary charge can be represented only by another officer.

the proceedings unnecessarily by reading documents at length, conducting long examinations and cross-examinations of witnesses, making elaborate submissions and generally frustrating the object of an informal hearing. Few practising lawyers appear regularly before the minor tribunals, and unfamiliarity with the atmosphere can be a serious disadvantage. There is a real dilemma: in certain cases it is very desirable for all interested parties to have the right kind of legal representation; that kind of representation may simply not be available, and the chairman has to do his best to supply the omission or remedy the deficiency.[47]

6. The last function of the Council on Tribunals in this context is concerned with reasons for decisions. Under section 12 of the Tribunals and Inquiries Act 1971, tribunals under the superintendence of the Council are required, when requested, to supply oral or written reasons for their decisions when giving or notifying their decision, unless exempted by order made by the Lord Chancellor after consultation with the Council. Only one class of tribunal has been accorded exemption.

The general statutory duty to give reasons[48] is, however, subject to qualifications. The tribunals in question are not obliged to volunteer reasons or to inform the parties of their right to request them. Some tribunals interpret their statutory duty literally and, in the absence of a request, simply do not give reasons.[49] Moreover, the duty to give reasons does not necessarily import a duty to summarize the evidence or state findings of fact. Reasons may properly be withheld on grounds of national security, or if they are asked for by somebody not primarily concerned with the decision and it would be contrary to the interest of any of the parties to supply them.[50]

Appeal and review

There is no common appellate structure. From most tribunals of last resort an appeal lies to the superior courts on questions of law,[51] but there is no such appeal from determinations by, for example, the national insurance commissioners or the immigration appeal tribunal. On questions of fact and discretion the pattern is irregular. Appeal may lie to a superior tribunal or to a Minister, or there may be no appeal on the merits at all; there is no such appeal, for instance, from decisions of rent tribunals,

47. See further, Harry Whitmore (1970) 33 *Mod. L. Rev.* 481.
48. Some tribunals were already under a duty to give reasons for decisions; the duty was not subject to all the qualifications mentioned in the text below.
49. See Street, op. cit., pp. 66–8.
50. 1971 Act, s. 12(2).
51. See p. 536, and Tribunals and Inquiries Act 1971, s. 13.

mental health review tribunals or the Foreign Compensation Commission.

Judicial review may be exercisable although no appeal is provided by statute or in addition to appellate review. A determination by a tribunal may be quashed if it is made without jurisdiction or in breach of the rules of natural justice, or if it exhibits an error of law on the face of the 'record'. A tribunal may be restrained from exceeding its jurisdiction or commanded to hear a case within its jurisdiction; it can also be ordered to perform a duty to give reasons for its decision. These matters will be discussed in the next chapter.

Inquiries and land use

The Franks Committee emphasized the need for openness and fairness in inquiries held on behalf of a Minister, but it recognized that a procedure culminating in a discretionary decision by a Minister responsible for national policy could not be expected to exhibit the same degree of impartiality as proceedings before an independent tribunal.[52]

The difference is best illustrated by situations where the purpose of the inquiry is to investigate, for the information of the Minister, objections to the Minister's own proposals.[53] The New Towns Act 1946 provided for the establishment of new towns to attract population and industry from the metropolis. Before the bill had been introduced, the Minister had already provisionally decided, as a matter of policy, to designate Stevenage as the site of a new town. While the bill was before Parliament, he imprudently made a speech in Stevenage, proclaiming that he intended to carry out a daring exercise in town planning there, and affirming (amid hostile interruptions . . . 'Gestapo' . . .) that the project would go forward because it had to go forward. Subsequently a draft order was made, designating Stevenage; objections were lodged; a public local inquiry into the objections was held by a Ministry inspector; the Minister, having received the report on the inquiry and considered the objections, finally made the order. In *Franklin* v. *Minister of Town and Country Planning*[54] objectors challenged the validity of the order in the courts, claiming that the Minister had failed to act judicially. He had manifested bias or a real likelihood of bias in favour of his proposal from the outset; and the fact that he had made the final order while important technical problems (water

52. Cmnd 218 (1957), § 25.

53. On the difficulty in applying judicial standards to procedures involving public inquiries held as part of a process in arriving at a discretionary decision, see *Wednesbury Corporation* v. *Ministry of Housing and Local Government* (No. 2) [1966] 2 Q.B. 275; and *Essex C.C.* v. *Ministry of Housing and Local Government* (1967) 66 L.G.R. 23.

54. [1948] A.C. 87.

supply and sewage disposal) remained unsolved showed that his bias had continued to the end. The House of Lords held that the standard of impartiality imposed on an independent tribunal was inapplicable to this type of situation; the Minister's role made it inevitable that he would incline in favour of his own scheme. The only duties cast upon him were to cause a properly conducted inquiry to be held and to consider the objections and the report fairly, with a mind not closed to argument. The Minister's functions were 'purely administrative'.

The decision in this case was sensible, though the term 'purely administrative' may have been unfortunate. A duty to act fairly may imply a duty to behave like an adjudicator *for certain purposes* – for example, in ensuring that everyone directly concerned is adequately informed of his rights, knows the case he has to meet and has a proper chance to put his case, and that reasons are given for decisions.[55]

A more typical situation in administrative law is where a Minister, X, has to decide a dispute between Y, a local authority, and Z, a property-owner.[56] This 'triangular' situation may arise where Y makes an order for the compulsory purchase of Z's property and Z objects; or where Z applies to Y for permission to make a material change in the use of his land or premises (planning permission), Y refuses, or consents subject to conditions, and Z appeals to the Minister, X, against the refusal or the conditions. In certain respects the Minister resembles an adjudicator determining a *lis inter partes*, a dispute between parties. Long before the Franks Committee had ever been thought of, the courts had recognized that certain *implied* duties ought to be cast on the Minister when deciding whether or not to confirm a compulsory purchase order initiated by a local authority in so far as his role was analogous to the judicial. They divided his functions into three stages. First, before objections were lodged, he had no duty to 'act judicially'; thus, if relevant communications were made to him by the local authority, he had no obligation to divulge them to the objectors; he was acting in an 'administrative' capacity.[57] Secondly, after objections had been lodged and up to the time of the final decision, he had to 'act judicially' in accordance with the minimum standards of natural justice; hence, the inspector conducting the public local inquiry had to behave impartially, and the Minister could not communicate with one party behind the other's back (for example, by viewing the site, through his officials, in company with representatives of the local authority, without

55. See now Compulsory Purchase by Ministers (Inquiries Procedure) Rules 1967 (S.I. 1967, No. 720).

56. Z may also be a public authority.

57. *Johnson (B.) & Co. (Builders) Ltd* v. *Minister of Health* [1947] 2 All E.R. 395. The leading judgment by Lord Greene M.R. contains the fullest review of the case law up to that time.

giving the objectors the opportunity to be present) on evidential matters raised at the inquiry.[58] Thirdly, in making his final decision the Minister re-assumed his 'administrative' capacity. All that this meant was that the expediency or reasonableness of the decision could not be canvassed in the courts.

These judge-made safeguards did not go very far. And the House of Lords had held that even while the Minister was acting 'judicially', he did not have to disclose the inspector's report.[59] The Franks Committee recommended disclosure of the fact-finding sections of inspectors' reports before they were submitted to the Minister, so as to enable the parties to propose corrections of fact; and full disclosure of the report with the Minister's reasoned letter of decision.[60] The recommendation for disclosure *prior* to the decision has not been implemented by legislation because it would lead to too much delay in decision-making, but subsequent disclosure must now be made on request. Most of the other Franks recommendations have been implemented. For instance, an acquiring authority must give advance particulars of its case; if a Department has expressed a view in support of the local authority's proposal or decision and this fact is stated in the local authority's submissions, a representative of the Department must be available at the inquiry to give evidence; there are statutory codes for the conduct of inquiries, specifying who has a right to be heard and who may be heard, embodying rules of procedure analogous to those for a judicial-type proceeding, and dealing with the procedure before and after the hearing.[61]

All this seemed eminently reasonable; and it was. But in practice judicialization tended to slow down the process of making decisions. Inspectors' reports, for example, and reasoned letters of decision setting out the inspectors' main findings had to be carefully composed; otherwise the decisions might be struck down in the courts for failure to comply with the requirements of the legislation.[62] This could be quite serious in

58. *Errington* v. *Minister of Health* [1935] 1 K.B. 249 (a slum clearance case; the same principles applied). For an acute analysis see Griffith and Street, *Principles of Administrative Law* (4th edn), pp. 172–6.

59. *Local Government Board* v. *Arlidge* [1915] A.C. 120.

60. Cmnd 218 (1957) §§ 343–5. Partial disclosure of reports prior to the decision is the practice followed in Scotland. The rules governing reasoned decisions by the tribunals named in the Tribunals and Inquiries Act were applied to decisions in pursuance of mandatory statutory inquiries (1971 Act, ss. 12(1), 19(1)) and to a number of voluntary inquiries held on behalf of a Minister.

61. See, for example, Compulsory Purchase by Local Authorities (Inquiry Procedure) Rules 1962 (S.I. 1962, No. 1424); and see S.I. 1967, No. 720 (note 55); Town and Planning (Inquiries Procedure) Rules 1969 (S.I. 1969, No. 1092); and cf. S.I. 1968, No. 1952 (procedure on planning appeals where the inspector makes the decision).

62. See *Givaudan & Co.* v. *Minister of Housing and Local Government* [1967] 1

the case of compulsory purchase orders, because judicial review meant uncertainty, and the work of building roads, schools or houses could not safely be begun while judicial proceedings were pending (though they had to be instituted within a few weeks of the confirmation of the order). For a different reason, delay was serious in the context of planning appeals; they were very numerous, and private development of property was held up while a backlog piled up in the Ministry. In 1967 it was taking an average of nine months to determine those planning appeals where the appellant had asked for an oral hearing.[63] One answer to the latter problem was decentralization of decision-making; hence power to decide minor appeals has been delegated to inspectors, who do not have to make a full-scale report but can simply issue a short letter of decision containing reasons.[64] Another device was to encourage appellants to agree to having the matter decided by written representations coupled with an unaccompanied site inspection. There have been other reforms in planning procedure.[65] Instead of having area planning policy settled by a development plan to which hundreds of objections could be entertained at a massive public inquiry, the larger planning authorities now prepare outline structure plans subject to ministerial approval. The Secretary of State can decide which aspects of the plan shall be considered at 'an examination in public' and whom to invite to be heard; and he has a free discretion whom to consult when he is considering the plan.[66]

In some respects implementation of the Franks recommendations did not go far enough. For example, the Government refused to carry out the proposals that there should be an express duty to acquaint the parties with relevant statements of policy and changes in policy prior to the decision. Again, at first nothing was done to implement recommendations about reopening the inquiry where the Minister proposed to disagree with the inspector's recommendations. The latter issue came to a head in the Saffron Walden chalkpit case.[67] A company sought permission to quarry

W.L.R. 250 (decision quashed because the reasons given in the letter of decision, read together with extracts from the inspector's report, were unintelligible).

63. Cmnd 3333 (1967), p. 7. In 1972 it was nearly twelve months.

64. See notes 12 and 61.

65. Richard Buxton, *Local Government* (2nd edn), ch. 7.

66. Town and Country Planning (Amendment) Act 1972, s. 3(1) modifying section 9 of the Town and Country Planning Act 1971. *Local* plans do not necessarily have to be confirmed by the Secretary of State at all (1971 Act, ss. 11, 14), unless the Secretary of State so directs, in which case he is free to consult with any interested party without having to go back to the others (1972 Act, s. 3(2)); cf. *Errington*'s case, note 58. See also S.I. 1972, No. 1154. The 1971 Act provides for local publicity and participation in the preparation of structure and local plans (ss. 8, 12). See also p. 416.

67. See J. A. G. Griffith and H. Street, *A Casebook of Administrative Law*, pp. 142–92.

chalk in a pit. Neighbouring farmers claimed that these operations would seriously damage their land and livestock. The local planning authority refused the application for planning permission; the company appealed, and an inspector, having conducted a local inquiry on behalf of the Minister and heard expert evidence, recommended that the appeal be dismissed. The Minister overruled the inspector and allowed the appeal, having consulted other experts. Naturally this created a bad impression in so far as an open inquiry had been followed first by closed consultations behind the back of the parties and then by a decision overruling the weight of the body of expert opinion already tested by public interrogation. A neighbouring landowner, Major Buxton, challenged the Minister's decision in the High Court; he failed on the technical ground that he was not a person aggrieved by the decision,[68] though certainly he thought he had a legitimate grievance. The Council on Tribunals took up the issue with the Lord Chancellor and the Minister. Eventually new rules were laid down to be applied in the future. Major Buxton had lost his private battle, but he triumphed in defeat. Now, if the Minister is minded to disagree with an inspector's recommendation on a planning appeal, he must normally notify the applicant, the local planning authority, and any other person with a direct interest in the land who gave evidence at the inquiry, and must give them an opportunity of making fresh representations to him.[69] If, moreover, the reason for the proposed disagreement is that the Minister has received new evidence, including expert opinion on a matter of fact, or has considered any new issue of fact (not being a new issue of government policy) which was not raised at the inquiry, he must be prepared to re-open the inquiry if requested to do so.[70] This change could, of course, slow down decision-making still further. In practice it has not been particularly important.[71] A recent White Paper stated that

68. *Buxton* v. *Minister of Housing and Local Government* [1961] 1 Q.B. 278 (B was only a 'third party' in the appeal to the Minister.)

69. If the Minister simply disagrees with the inspector's views about what planning policy *is*, or how that policy should be *applied* to the facts found at an inquiry, or on a matter of aesthetic taste, this decision is final: *Luke of Pavenham* v. *Minister of Housing and Local Government* [1968] 1 Q.B. 172; *Vale Estates (Acton) Ltd* v. *Secretary of State for the Environment* (1970) 69 L.G.R. 543. If there is disagreement between the Minister and inspector on a material *finding of fact*, an opportunity to make further written representations must be afforded.

70. See, for example, S.I. 1969, No. 1092, r. 12.

71. It has led to several unsuccessful applications to the courts to quash Ministers' decisions for refusing to re-open an inquiry; see *Luke*'s and *Vale*'s cases; *Continental Sprays Ltd* v. *Minister of Housing and Local Government* (1968) 67 L.G.R. 147, 19 P. & C.R. 774; *Boyer (William) & Sons Ltd* v. *Minister of Housing and Local Government* (1968) 67 L.G.R. 374; 20 P. & C.R. 176 (complaints of inadequate findings of fact in inspectors' reports).

the Minister agreed with thirty-nine out of forty recommendations by inspectors.[72]

Not many people had suggested that under the old procedure decisions were in fact unfair. Now they *look* fairer.

Scrutiny of inquiries

The functions of the Council on Tribunals are of some importance. It considers and reports on such matters as the Lord Chancellor or the Secretary of State may refer to it; on its own initiative it may also raise particular questions affecting inquiries; it has to be consulted before procedural rules are made for inquiries; it receives complaints from members of the public (there had been 302 by the end of 1968); it must be consulted before exemptions from the duty to give reasoned decisions are granted. It is not entrusted with the task of keeping the general working of statutory inquiries under review, nor is it empowered to make recommendations as to the kind of person who should be appointed to conduct them; in these respects its functions are narrower than its functions relating to tribunals, but the impediment is not a serious one.

Its tendency to emphasize the need for procedural safeguards, particularly after the termination of an inquiry,[73] and its criticisms of the procedure adopted in two controversial cases,[74] brought it into intermittent conflict with Ministers of Housing and Local Government; the Lord Chancellor, more sympathetic to its objectives, was at times hard pressed to maintain the principle of collective ministerial responsibility. Procedures involving inquiries held on behalf of Ministers tend to evoke stronger feelings than matters affecting tribunals, not only among local inhabitants but also in the Departments concerned. The potential conflict between the needs for affording fair play to individuals and for speedy implementation of policy decisions in compulsory purchase cases is apt to develop into a heated battle in which an independent scrutineer can hardly fail to earn obloquy as a busybody, a nonentity or a supposed partisan. Relations between the Council and the Departments are not generally hostile, and Departments voluntarily consult the Council when introducing bills providing for new inquiry procedures. But when conflicts arise the Council is handicapped by its lack of a political power-base.

The Parliamentary Commissioner for Administration[75] can also enter-

72. Cmnd 3333 (1967), §§ 33, 34.

73. It was instrumental in securing a more satisfactory final draft of the procedural rules for planning appeals and compulsory purchase order inquiries in 1962.

74. The Saffron Walden Chalkpit case (p. 558) and the Packington Estate case [1966] *Public Law* 1; Annual Report of the Council on Tribunals for 1965, §§ 77–82.

75. See ch. 29.

tain complaints about injustice caused by maladministration in connection with procedures involving inquiries held on behalf of a Minister; and because of the jurisdictional overlap he has been made an *ex officio* member of the Council. However, he cannot investigate a complaint unless it is addressed to him through a member of Parliament.[76] He has no power to investigate complaints of decisions by tribunals or by Ministers acting in a judicial capacity,[77] but may, in his discretion, investigate a complaint of departmental 'administrative' maladministration in presenting or otherwise handling the matter.[78]

76. For the procedure adopted for passing on to him complaints addressed to the Council and vice versa, see Annual Report of the Council for 1968 (H.C. 272 (1968–69)), § 2.

77. Parliamentary Commissioner Act 1967, s. 5(2). He is concerned only with the 'administrative' functions of Ministers and officials. Determination of a planning appeal or confirmation of a compulsory purchase order is to be regarded as 'administrative' for this purpose.

78. See David Foulkes (1971) 34 *Mod. L. Rev.* 377.

Chapter 26
Judicial Review of
Administrative Action:
Principles

This chapter is about the general principles applied by the superior courts in reviewing the validity or legality of the acts, decisions and omissions of administrative authorities, including statutory tribunals. In the chapters on delegated legislation and local authorities we have already been introduced to this subject.[1] In chapter 27 we shall consider some special features of judicial remedies in administrative law. In chapter 28 we shall have something to say about actions for damages for civil wrongs committed by public authorities, particularly the Crown.

Four preliminary words of warning are needed. First, this is an extremely complex subject with intricate ramifications.[2] We cannot cover every aspect, even in outline. And some matters will have to be oversimplified if they are to be explained at all. They may still seem rather mysterious. Secondly, a grasp of general principles is obviously important. But to apply these principles to concrete situations demands flexibility and subtlety. In approaching the solution to a particular case, the crucial questions will often be: What are the context and purpose of the legislation in question? What significance is to be attributed to the language in which a grant of statutory power is worded? To a large extent judicial review of administrative action is a specialized branch of statutory interpretation. Thirdly, administrative law is not very coherent. For example, the laws of town and country planning, social security and immigration have some points of contact but far more points of dissimilarity. Precedents laid down in one area of the law may be treated by a court as irrelevant if cited as authorities in another area. One needs to be an expert forecaster to be able to predict how a court will react to such citations in any given case. Fourthly, from time to time the courts shift their position, and they are apt not to be entirely consistent in their attitudes.

Hence, if one is asked what legal principles a public authority is obliged to observe when exercising a specific discretionary power, one's answer

1. Chs. 15 and 18.
2. See de Smith, *Judicial Review of Administrative Action* (3rd edn); H. W. R. Wade, *Administrative Law* (3rd edn).

may often have to be hedged about by words like 'probably' and 'perhaps'. The state of the law is elusive and fluid.

One further point must always be borne in mind – a point more obvious to the uninstructed layman than to a law student grappling with an intractable body of legal material. In deciding individual cases the courts will try to do justice by balancing the needs of administration and the public interest against the claims of the private citizen to fair treatment. Some judges are prepared to 'bend' the law by manipulating precedent and principle in order to achieve and vindicate what appears to them a just solution to the case in hand. Judges exercise more freedom of manoeuvre than in most of the other branches of English law.

Going to court

Judicial review of administrative action may be invoked for a wide range of purposes by a person claiming to be aggrieved.

1. To obtain damages or another private law remedy (for example, an injunction) for a civil wrong, such as a breach of contract or a tort.

2. To have an order, act or decision of a public body quashed or declared invalid on the ground that it is *ultra vires* or outside jurisdiction. This purpose may be achieved by means of an appeal (if one is provided by statute), or a statutory application to quash (for example, a decision to confirm a compulsory purchase order), or an application to the Divisional Court of the Queen's Bench Division for an order of certiorari to quash a decision, or an action claiming a declaration that the act, order or decision is invalid. Already one sees that substantive administrative law is interwoven with the law of remedies.

3. To procure, on appeal, the reversal or variation of an order or determination for error of law. This overlaps with (2); we shall try to explain the difference between *invalidity* and *error* shortly.

4. To restrain the performance or continuance of unlawful action. This may be achieved by an application for an order of prohibition, or proceedings for an injunction or a declaration, or a statutory application to restrain (for example) the making of an invalid compulsory purchase order.

5. To obtain release from unlawful detention. The appropriate remedy will be either appeal or an application for habeas corpus.

6. To secure an authoritative statement of the law governing a specific legal dispute by means of a binding declaration awarded by the courts. Consequential relief (for example, damages) does not have to be claimable as well.

7. To secure the performance of a public duty (for example, to make reimbursement; to exercise a discretion according to law; to hear an application or appeal within a tribunal's jurisdiction). Normally the judicial remedy for a wrongful omission will be an order of mandamus; a declaration, or even a mandatory injunction, are possible remedies. Sometimes non-performance of a public duty will give rise to an action for damages.

8. To defend oneself in proceedings which rely on the validity of an administrative act or order. If, for example, one is prosecuted for breach of a by-law, one can set up the defence that the by-law is *ultra vires*.

Finally, we should note that public authorities may appear in the courts for other reasons. For instance, many enforcement powers vested in public authorities (for example, to abate nuisances) are exercisable only with leave of a court or magistrate; and in most of these situations the prospective victim can be heard on his own behalf. Again, sometimes criminal proceedings can be brought *against* public authorities (for example, for breaches of the Public Health Acts).

Ultra vires and excess of jurisdiction
Vires

The ordinary courts have long exercised the important constitutional function of containing both the Executive and inferior tribunals within the limits of their authority. It was firmly established in the seventeenth century that the Crown could not set itself above the law by a bare assertion of prerogative.[3] Clearly, then, if the Crown exceeded *statutory* powers vested in it, the courts could pronounce its acts invalid; and similarly if Crown servants or local authorities proceeded to exceed their powers, the courts had a like authority provided that the matter was properly brought before them in a legal controversy. Nowadays we say that public authorities and officials must act *intra vires* (within their powers). They can only do what the law permits them to do;[4] they cannot do what the law forbids them to do. As we have noted, there is a view that public authorities established otherwise than under statute (for example, by royal charter) may be partly exempt from the *ultra vires* doctrine in that their powers may not be wholly confined to those bestowed on them by legislation.[5]

Subject to this limited exception, the general principle is clear. Naturally, problems – often difficult problems – arise in its application. Acts reasonably incidental to powers expressly granted may be construed as falling

3. See pp. 71, 114 and 118.
4. *M'Ara* v. *Edinburgh Magistrates* 1913 S.C. 1059 (proclamation prohibiting public meetings nugatory in absence of statutory basis).
5. Though if they are accorded statutory powers they must act within the scope of that authority. See further p. 408.

within the grant of power. The *Fulham*[6] and *Smethwick*[7] cases, one falling on each side of the line, illustrate the point. As we have seen, the scope of the incidental powers of the new local authorities has been slightly enlarged.[8]

Seldom are cases before the courts as clear-cut as these. Sometimes the question is what effect should be given to an order that is partly *ultra vires* but partly *intra vires* – for instance, where a public body issues a licence or permit to which invalid conditions are annexed, can the courts sever the bad from the good, perhaps leaving the plaintiff with an unconditional grant? This might defeat the intention of the licensing body. In this area the courts have trodden warily, but they are unlikely to sever invalid conditions unless they are clearly irrelevant to the subject-matter of the permit.[9] Then there are awkward problems connected with the idea of estoppel; nobody can be quite sure of some of the answers.[10] Special difficulties arise where the question is not whether a public authority has acted *ultra vires* in a matter of *substance* but whether it has acted *ultra vires* in a matter of *procedure* or *form*. On these matters there is a vast body of case law. Suppose that a statutory instrument which should have been laid before Parliament has not been so laid; or that a by-law has not been published before it is confirmed by the Minister; or that somebody should have been consulted or notified before an administrative order or notice was issued; or that the order or notice was issued according to the proper procedure but on the wrong date, or omitted words that it ought to have contained. Are these administrative acts valid or invalid? One simply cannot answer these questions in general terms. As we have already mentioned,[11] the courts classify procedural and formal requirements as 'mandatory' or 'directory'. If a mandatory requirement is not observed, an administrative act is either absolutely void, or voidable when it is challenged in a court. If the requirement is merely directory, substantial compliance will be enough to validate the act; and in some cases even total non-compliance will not affect the validity of the action taken.

This does not help us to predict when the courts will hold a procedural or formal requirement to be mandatory or directory. Perhaps we can make two general comments. First, if the practical consequences of holding compliance to be mandatory would be very serious, a requirement may be

6. *Att.-Gen.* v. *Fulham Corporation* [1921] 1 Ch. 440.

7. *Att.-Gen.* v. *Smethwick Corporation* [1932] 1 Ch. 562.

8. p. 407.

9. See *Hall & Co.* v. *Shoreham-by-Sea U.D.C.* [1964] 1 W.L.R. 240 (void condition not severable, and grant of planning permission held invalid). cf. *Kingsway Investments (Kent) Ltd* v. *Kent C.C.* [1971] A.C. 72 for divergent approaches by the Law Lords.

10. See pp. 402–4, 410–11, 610, note 9.

11. pp. 347–8, 403, above.

held to be merely directory. An extreme example comes from New Zealand. The Governor-General issued his warrant for the holding of a General Election at a later date than the law prescribed. Somebody contended that the ensuing General Election was, therefore, null and void. The courts (not surprisingly) held that the rules about time were only directory. If they had held otherwise, there would have been a legal vacuum which nobody within New Zealand could have filled, for no Parliament could lawfully have been summoned; the administration of the country might have ground to a halt.[12] Secondly, if the impact of the administrative act on private rights is important, an ostensibly small deviation from the statutory requirements may be held to render the act invalid. For instance, if an acquiring authority fails to carry out its statutory duty to notify specified classes of persons of a compulsory purchase order (thus impeding their opportunity to lodge objections)[13] or if the Minister fails to give proper reasons for his decision, a person aggrieved may have the order quashed on the ground that he has been substantially prejudiced by the non-compliance,[14] even though the merits of the order would otherwise be unassailable. But courts sometimes take a very strict view of procedural or formal requirements, treating minor deviations as invalidating the action although nobody appears to have suffered detriment as a result of non-compliance. They will try to deduce the unexpressed (and probably non-existent) intention of Parliament from the wording and general purport of the Act.[15]

Substantive *ultra vires* is a generic concept, a parent of other heads of invalidity. A body vested with discretionary powers acts *ultra vires* if it acts

12. *Simpson* v. *Att.-Gen.* [1955] N.Z.L.R. 271. The United Kingdom Parliament, under section 4 of the Statute of Westminster 1931, can legislate for New Zealand with New Zealand's request and consent, but under New Zealand law the request and consent can come only from the New Zealand Parliament.

13. See also *Lee* v. *Department of Education and Science* (1967) 66 L.G.R. 211 (failure to afford adequate *time* for persons aggrieved by proposed administrative order to make representations); *Agricultural etc. Training Board* v. *Kent* [1970] 2 Q.B. 18 (failure to notify address for lodging appeal).

14. As in *Givaudan & Co.* v. *Minister of Housing and Local Government* [1967] 1 W.L.R. 250. See also *Re Poyser & Mills' Arbitration* [1964] 2 Q.B. 467 and H. J. Elcock, *Administrative Justice*, pp. 87–97, on duties to give reasons. See further M. B. Akehurst (1970) 33 *Mod. L. Rev.* 154 and pp. 554, 557, above. Where there is a special statutory procedure to challenge decisions on planning appeals, compulsory purchase orders and the like, the Acts provide that a person aggrieved by non-compliance with a procedural or formal requirement must show that he has been 'substantially prejudiced' thereby. For an example of a trivial defect not giving rise, in the opinion of the Court of Appeal, to substantial prejudice, see *Gordondale Investments Ltd* v. *Secretary of State for the Environment* (1971) 70 L.G.R. 158.

15. As in *R.* v. *Pontypool Gaming Licensing Committee* [1970] 1 W.L.R. 1299 (overstepping an unimportant time limit). See de Smith, op. cit. (3rd edn), pp. 122–6.

in bad faith or for a wrong purpose, or (in some situations) with gross unreasonableness, or if it fails to have regard to relevant considerations or is materially influenced by irrelevant considerations. By-laws may be held to be *ultra vires* if they are manifestly unreasonable (for example, because they are unfairly discriminatory) or directed to an unauthorized purpose, or repugnant to the general law of the land, or so uncertain that nobody can be sure what it is that they are prohibiting. But the term *ultra vires* can also be interpreted in a narrow sense, as meaning *excess* of powers but not the various forms of *abuse* of powers. In *Smith* v. *East Elloe R.D.C.* (1956)[16] the validity of a compulsory purchase order confirmed by a Minister could be challenged by the property owner within six weeks on the ground that its authorization was 'not empowered to be granted' by the enabling Act. After the six weeks had expired, it could not be questioned 'in any legal proceedings whatsoever'. The property owner brought an action a long time after the event, claiming a declaration that the order was void because it had been fraudulently procured. The House of Lords held, by a majority, that the plain words of the Act precluded judicial review *after* the expiry of the six weeks' period; and some of their Lordships were also of the opinion that even *within* the six weeks' period the order could be challenged only for *ultra vires* in the strictest sense so that allegations of fraud or bad faith could not be raised at all under the statutory procedure. The latter view is unjustifiably narrow and would probably not be followed today.

The *East Elloe* case also raises the question how the jurisdiction of the courts to determine questions of *vires* can be excluded. Three methods may be adopted. The first method (which will be referred to in the next chapter) is to vest exclusive jurisdiction in the first instance in a body other than the superior courts. This does not, however, preclude the courts from *subsequently* determining whether that other body reached its decision on the basis of proper legal principles. The second is a generally worded exclusionary clause to the effect that the order, when made, shall be 'final', or 'conclusive', or 'shall have effect as if enacted in this Act', or shall not be questioned in any legal proceedings. On the whole the courts have viewed these formulae with disfavour and as far as possible have disregarded them.[17] Indeed, section 11(1) of the Tribunals and Inquiries Act 1958 emptied them of binding content in then existing legislation; though section 11(3) listed a few exceptions to this rule and preserved the effect of a general exclusionary formula if the parent Act allowed an order to be challenged within a specified period.[18]

16. [1956] A.C. 736.
17. de Smith, op. cit., ch. 7. For an extreme example, see *Tehrani* v. *Rostron* [1972] 1 Q.B. 182.
18. See further, pp. 571–3.

The other method of excluding the jurisdiction of the courts to determine questions of *vires* used to be, surprisingly, more efficacious in practice. Powers may be granted to a Minister or a local authority in 'objective' or 'subjective' terms. An 'objective' grant of power is expressed thus: 'If X conditions are present, the Minister may take Y action or make Z order.' In such a case the courts may decide for themselves whether X conditions did, as a matter of law or fact, exist; if they decide that the conditions precedent were absent, the order or act will be *ultra vires*. But Parliament may grant powers in 'subjective' language: if the competent authority 'is satisfied', or 'is of the opinion', or 'if it appears to' that authority, that a prescribed state of affairs exists, it may do certain things. In such cases the courts, till recently, were inclined to refuse to make an independent assessment whether the conditions precedent existed, especially if the authority entrusted with the power was a Minister responsible to Parliament. But nowadays the courts are less easily deterred.[19] They are still disinclined to make an independent determination of a question of fact on which there is a conflict of evidence; and if facts have been found by an inspector after an inquiry they will be slow to differ from his findings;[20] but they will not readily be deterred by a 'subjective' formula from deciding a question of law for themselves, and they will generally insist that findings of fact must not be based on a wrong legal approach or other irrelevant considerations or be manifestly unreasonable.[21]

Up to now we have been using the language of *vires*. There is another, associated language – the language of jurisdiction. The terms *ultra vires* and excess (or want, or lack) of jurisdiction are often used interchangeably, like breach of privilege and contempt of a House of Parliament. Nevertheless, they are not always identical in meaning; sometimes they have to be analysed in different terms and convey different implications. These ambiguities create difficulties for students.

19. See pp. 337, 348–50.

20. Even if they have been rejected by the Minister: *Coleen Properties Ltd* v. *Minister of Housing and Local Government* [1971] 1 W.L.R. 433.

21. For examples of this more recent attitude, see *R.* v. *Minister of Housing and Local Government, ex p. Chichester R.D.C.* [1960] 1 W.L.R. 587; *Webb* v. *Minister of Housing and Local Government* [1965] 1 W.L.R. 755; *Maradana Mosque Trustees* v. *Mahmud* [1967] 1 A.C. 13; *Durayappah* v. *Fernando* [1967] 2 A.C. 337; the *Coleen* case (above). See also *Estate and Trust Agencies* (1927) *Ltd* v. *Singapore Improvement Trust* [1937] A.C. 898; *Ashbridge Investments Ltd* v. *Minister of Housing and Local Government* [1965] 1 W.L.R. 1320; *Secretary of State for Employment* v. *ASLEF* (*No. 2*) [1972] 2 Q.B. 455. Contrast the analysis adopted in *R.* v. *Income Tax Special Purposes Commissioners* (1888) 21 Q.B.D. 313 at 319, *per* Lord Esher M.R. cf. *McEldowney* v. *Forde* [1971] A. C. 632; *Att.-Gen., ex rel. McWhirter* v. *IBA* (where the court showed deference to the opinion of the competent authority in the face of a subjectively worded grant of power) [1973] 2 W.L.R. 344. See also note 19 above, p. 522, and Addendum.

The vocabulary of 'jurisdiction' is normally used when one is discussing tribunals or similar bodies. Inferior tribunals (magistrates' courts, county courts, special tribunals, professional disciplinary bodies, committees of clubs and trades unions, arbitrators, Ministers deciding legal disputes) have a limited jurisdiction or area of authority. By the end of the seventeenth century it was settled law that the Court of King's Bench could issue the prerogative writ of certiorari to quash a decision by a statutory tribunal outside jurisdiction, and a writ of prohibition to restrain a tribunal from going outside or continuing to act outside its jurisdiction before it had come to a final decision. Jurisdiction might be exceeded because the tribunal was wrongly constituted, or because other essential preliminaries (for example, the time or manner of instituting the proceedings) had not been observed or because it tried a case outside its area of competence (for example, because it had no authority to deal with the persons or subject-matter or if the matter lay beyond its territorial jurisdiction); or because, although the stage was properly set in the first place, the tribunal went on to commit very serious procedural errors, or made an order outside its competence (for example, by imposing a fine when it could only award compensation). All these errors 'went to jurisdiction'. But on matters lying *within* the area of jurisdiction (or 'going to the merits') the tribunal might be entitled to err on matters of law and fact and remain immune from the supervisory jurisdiction of the courts. The superior courts could set aside determinations embodying errors within jurisdiction only if (i) the error was one of law and was apparent on the face of the 'record' of the tribunal, in which case certiorari would lie to quash, or (ii) a right of appeal was provided by statute. Jurisdiction to decide implied jurisdiction to decide wrongly as well as rightly, and a latent error of law within jurisdiction was beyond correction except on appeal. If every erroneous finding by an inferior tribunal were to be equated with an excess of jurisdiction, then members of tribunals might find themselves constantly being sued for damages on account of honest mistakes.

Questions about *vires* are not usually analysed in this way; and this classification of errors may seem very odd and artificial. If one takes a hypothetical example it looks a little less strange. Suppose that there is no right of appeal from the decision of a magistrates' court. Such a court convicts a person of wilful obstruction of the highway, giving no reason for its decision; in fact he is innocent. The decision is wrong, but it is one within the jurisdiction of the court and cannot be challenged. Take another case: the same magistrates' court convicts a man of manslaughter; he is in fact guilty, but the magistrates have no power to convict for that offence; the conviction will therefore be quashed by the High Court for want of jurisdiction on an application for certiorari.

In practice the distinction between matters going to jurisdiction (collateral and preliminary matters) and matters within jurisdiction (or going to the merits) is often almost impossible to draw.[22] Early in the nineteenth century the superior courts came close to abdicating from supervisory control over inferior tribunals, holding that if the necessary jurisdictional conditions were present at the outset of the hearing, every decision by an inferior tribunal on a point that it was obliged to determine fell within the scope of its jurisdiction. But this position was not consistently maintained, and the courts wavered from one stance to another, showing a broad tendency to hold wrong findings to be jurisdictional and therefore reviewable and right findings non-jurisdictional.

Today the distinction between jurisdictional (reviewable) error and non-jurisdictional (unreviewable) error has lost most of its importance for the following reasons:

1. From most inferior statutory tribunals, appeals now lie on questions of law to the superior courts.[23] It is therefore more important to know whether a finding is one of law or fact than whether it is jurisdictional or non-jurisdictional.

2. In the early 1950s the long-forgotten inherent power of the High Court to quash by certiorari for non-jurisdictional error of law was revived. If certiorari was to lie, the error had to be patent and visible on the written 'record' of the inferior tribunal.[24] The 'record' was the written statement of the tribunal's decision, read in conjunction with the relevant statutory provisions. It might (or might not) set out reasons for the decisions, and findings and inferences of fact, and could be interpreted as incorporating documents referred to in this written statement.[25] The importance of this supervisory power of the courts was affected in three ways by the Tribunals and Inquiries Act 1958. First, it was reduced by the extension of appeals on points of law from statutory tribunals. Secondly, it was increased, in those instances where no appeal still lay, by the extension of the duty to give reasons for decisions on request; if a decision was erroneous in law, the error would often be disclosed by the reasons given. Previously some tribunals had simply refused to give reasons for decisions and thus protected their decisions against effective review. Moreover, oral reasons

22. The leading work on this very difficult topic is Amnon Rubinstein, *Jurisdiction and Illegality*.

23. See especially Tribunals and Inquiries Act 1971, s. 13.

24. *R.* v. *Northumberland Compensation Appeal Tribunal, ex p. Shaw* [1951] 1 K.B. 711; affd. [1952] 1 K.B. 338 (C.A.) (error of law in computing statutory compensation for loss of office).

25. The record cannot be supplemented by additional evidence designed to disclose the error of law. Jurisdictional defects may, however, be proved by affidavits.

became part of the record.[26] Thirdly, statutory provisions purporting to exclude review by certiorari lost their effect.[27]

3. Decisions by the Minister on planning appeals, compulsory purchase orders and a number of other contested issues in the law of housing and town planning and other areas affecting private rights in land can be challenged in the High Court only on the grounds that the order is not within the *powers* conferred by the Act or that a procedural or formal requirement has not been complied with. Of late the courts have tended to proceed on the assumption that any decision by the Minister which they hold to be *erroneous in law* renders his determination *ultra vires* (outside his powers, or in excess of jursidiction) and therefore liable to be quashed.[28] There seems to be barely any room, in these contexts, for the concept of error of law *within* jurisdiction. Illegality is equated with invalidity.

4. In the recent *Anisminic* case, the House of Lords almost obliterated the jursidictional/non-jurisdictional distinction. The Foreign Compensation Commission was charged with the duty of determining (a) who was entitled to claim compensation under an Order in Council prescribing the circumstances under which claims would be admissible in respect of money received from the Egyptian Government for expropriation of British-owned assets in Egypt after the Suez venture and (b) what discretionary sum of money should be allocated to an approved claimant. The question who was entitled to claim was surely the core of the issue; it appeared to 'go to the merits' of a determination.

The Order in Council (made under the Foreign Compensation Act 1950) specified that British nationals and British successors in title to British nationals were entitled to claim; but the wording raised difficult legal problems. Anisminic Ltd, a British company, had been forced to sell their mining assets in Sinai to an Egyptian-owned company. Were Anisminic entitled to claim out of the fund? The Commission held that they were not. Anisminic brought an action claiming a declaration that the Commission's determination was a nullity. Browne J. found in their favour;[29] the Court

26. Tribunals and Inquiries Act 1958, s. 12.
27. ibid., s. 11 (p. 567 above). It was accepted that apart from section 11 they would have been effective to bar certiorari for error of law not going to jurisdiction.
28. See, for example, *Iveagh* v. *Minister of Housing and Local Government* [1962] 2 Q.B. 147, [1964] 1 Q.B. 395 (dicta); *Ashbridge Investments Ltd* v. *Minister of Housing and Local Government* [1965] 1 W.L.R. 1320; *Quiltotex Ltd* v. *Minister of Housing and Local Government* [1966] 1 Q.B. 704. See also the *Coleen* case [1971] 1 W.L.R. 433. But in *Brookdene Investments Ltd* v. *Minister of Housing and Local Government* (1970) 21 P. & C.R. 543, where the question of equivalence was raised, the point was left open.
29. See Note [1969] 2 A.C. 147 at 223 for extracts from this long judgment.

of Appeal reversed this decision;[30] the House of Lords, by a majority, restored the judgment of the court of first instance.[31] This may seem odd, for section 4(4) of the 1950 Act had laid down that a determination by the Commission was not to 'be called in question in any court of law', and section 11(3) of the Tribunals and Inquiries Act 1958 had expressly *preserved* the effect of this provision. But the Lords held that the Commission had exceeded its jurisdiction by misconstruing the Order in Council; it had asked itself and answered the wrong question, taking irrelevant considerations into account and interposing a new hurdle of its own making for a claimant to clear; its purported determination was therefore no determination at all, and could properly be impugned in a court. It was conceded that the exclusionary formula would bar judicial review of a determination exhibiting an error of law *within* jurisdiction; but one is left wondering what kind of error of law would have been held *not* to go to jurisdiction.[32] This particular question has now become academic. By section 3 of the Foreign Compensation Act 1969 appeals on question of law (including jurisdictional questions) will lie from the Commission to the Court of Appeal.

Does the *Anisminic* decision mean that *Smith* v. *East Elloe*[33] is no longer good law? Some of the Law Lords in *Anisminic* expressed serious doubts about *East Elloe*. But there are sensible reasons for distinguishing the two cases. First, in the *East Elloe* type of case there *is* an opportunity for obtaining judicial review, though the time limit is brief. Secondly, it might cause very serious hardship if the validity of a compulsory purchase order could be successfully impugned long after the event when houses, roads, perhaps a hospital or a school, had been built on the site and there was no longer any power to make a valid order.[34] But the courts might well

30. *Anisminic Ltd* v. *Foreign Compensation Commission* [1968] 2 Q.B. 862; the Court held that the determination of the question fell within the scope of the Commission's jurisdiction.

31. [1969] 2 A.C. 147.

32. [1969] *Camb. L.J.* 161 (de Smith) and 170 (H. W. R. Wade); (1969) 85 *L.Q.R.* 198 (Wade), [1970] *Public Law* 358 (Gould); (1971) 24 *Current Legal Problems* 1 (Lord Diplock). Possible examples of law *within* jurisdiction include errors as to the burden of proof or the admissibility of evidence (where rules of evidence have to be observed).

33. See p. 567.

34. The *East Elloe* decision has been followed since *Anisminic* in two cases: *Routh* v. *Reading Corporation* (1971) 217 *Estates Gazette* 1337 (C.A.) and *Hamilton* v. *Secretary of State for Scotland* 1972 S.L.T. 233 (neither case involved allegations of fraud). It has to be noted, however, that the courts tend to react sharply to suggestions that they have no jurisdiction to afford redress if fraud is established. See, for example, *Pickin* v. *British Railways Board* [1972] 3 W.L.R. 824 (p. 74 above).

Under s. 14 of the Tribunals and Inquiries Act 1971 (replacing s. 11 of the 1958 Act) statutory provisions enabling recourse to the courts to be had for a limited period are still excluded from the abrogation of ouster clauses.

exercise discretion in the plaintiff's favour if no public works had been undertaken or if no third party rights had accrued.

Law and fact

Although the relatively *un*important distinction between jurisdictional and non-jurisdictional matters is so hard to draw or define, perhaps we can explain the really important distinction between matters of law and matters of fact more easily. Unfortunately this is not so: the latter distinction is fiendishly difficult to define or even to illustrate at all clearly.

The superior courts will afford redress for errors of fact in two main situations: first, in those rare circumstances where rights of appeal are not restricted to questions of law; and secondly, where a factual error causes a tribunal to step outside its jurisdiction. As we have indicated, the courts will be somewhat reluctant to make an independent determination of a question of pure fact if the issue turns upon conflicting evidence and they have not heard the oral testimony themselves.

Whether X hit Y on the head is a question of fact. The state of X's mind at the time is also a question of fact (or of opinion). These questions will be left to the jury to answer. Whether X's conduct is *capable* of being construed as maliciously causing grievous bodily harm to Y[35] is a question of law on which the judge directs the jury; the words 'maliciously' and 'grievous bodily harm' have acquired technical legal meanings. We can describe the whole issue as one of mixed law and fact.

Decisions by special tribunals and public authorities are made without juries; so one convenient line of demarcation is absent. Still, administrative law controversies may sometimes be compartmentalized as questions partly of law and partly of fact for the purposes of judicial review. Other approaches to analysis may be adopted. An entire question may be characterized as one of law, or as one of fact (or fact and degree, which means 'fact'). The technical meaning of a term used in a public contract may be a pure question of law, because only a trained lawyer could be expected to understand it in the light of principle and decided authority. If a tribunal is obliged to observe the rules of evidence or specified statutory procedures, and there is no dispute as to what actually took place, a question whether the rules were duly observed is again purely one of law. But suppose that the question is whether a building is a dwelling-house, or 'of special architectural or historic interest', or is 'unfit for human habitation', or whether an industrial injury arose 'out of or in the course of employment', or whether consent to a particular act was 'unreasonably withheld', or

35. Offences against the Person Act 1861, ss. 18, 20, as amended by the Criminal Law Act 1967.

whether there was a 'material change in the use' of land for which planning permission was required. The tribunal or other deciding body finds the basic or primary facts (for example, who did which and with what and to whom?); it may draw inferences from the facts; it has to go on to decide whether the facts as found *fall within the ambit of the statutory description*. A court, on review or appeal, can choose whether to characterize the conclusion as one of fact or as one of law; either form of characterization is possible, for here we are in a 'grey zone'. Generally speaking, the following are categorized as questions of fact: questions decided by specialized expert tribunals in which the courts repose confidence; questions on which reasonable persons might arrive at divergent conclusions; questions which the courts consider to have been correctly decided; questions on which the courts would find it very difficult to form an independent judgment without hearing all the evidence.

Findings of fact may still be held to embody reviewable errors of *law* if they are made without any supporting evidence at all, or if the conclusions drawn from them are perverse (in that the facts as found point unmistakably the other way) or are based on the application of a wrong legal test or if the reasons given for the findings or conclusions are unintelligible or inadequate in law; in these cases the tribunal will be held to have misdirected itself in law. Nevertheless, the courts will be slow to interfere with erroneous findings, inferences or conclusions of fact. For instance, in one case the question was whether land had been developed without planning permission; the central issue was whether the change of use to which it had been put was 'material'. The only change was the installation of an automatic egg-vending machine in the forecourt of a petrol-filling station. The court held[36] that whether a change of use was 'material' was a question of 'fact and degree',[37] not a question of law; the local planning authority's decision that there had been a material change of use was surprising, but it was not so perverse as to justify the court's interference. If the question had been categorized as one of law, the court could have substituted its own opinion. Now, if the court had adopted a slightly different approach – if it had applied the following test: there is an error of law if the inference or conclusion drawn from the facts found could not *reasonably* have been arrived at[38] – it might possibly have set the decision aside. Sometimes the courts do apply this broader test to conclusions of fact.

36. *Bendles Motors Ltd* v. *Bristol Corporation* [1963] 1 W.L.R. 247 (enforcement notice) – an appeal on a question of law.

37. See the valuable articles by W. A. Wilson in (1963) 26 *Mod. L. Rev.* 609; (1969) 32 *Mod. L. Rev.* 361.

38. See, for example, *Ashbridge Investments Ltd* v. *Minister of Housing and Local Government* [1965] 1 W.L.R. 1320 at 1326.

Natural justice

The rules of natural justice are minimum standards of fair decision-making imposed by the common law on persons and bodies who are under a duty to 'act judicially'. There are two rules of natural justice: *nemo judex in causa sua* (nobody is to be judge in his own cause) and *audi alteram partem* (hear the other side; the parties are to be given a fair hearing). They were first applied to proceedings in courts of justice; they were extended by analogy to various administrative law situations. They are not precise rules of unchanging content; their scope will vary according to the context, and in some recent cases they appear to have been endowed with a kaleidoscopic unpredictability. There has been a recent tendency in the courts to speak of a 'duty to act fairly', which sometimes (but not always) is broader than the duty to observe natural justice.[39] Even where the rules of natural justice are *prima facie* applicable, they may be partly or wholly excluded by clear statutory language or necessary implication.

Nemo judex in causa sua[40]

The rule has two main aspects. First, an adjudicator must not have any direct financial or proprietary interest in the outcome of the proceedings. Secondly, he must not be reasonably suspected, or show a real likelihood, of bias.

In its first aspect, the rule is very strict. No matter how small the adjudicator's pecuniary interest may be, no matter how unlikely it is to affect his judgment, he is disqualified from acting and the decision in which he has participated will be set aside,[41] unless (i) the parties are made fully aware of his interest in the proceedings and clearly waive their right to object to his participation, or (ii) he is empowered to sit (or the validity of the proceedings is preserved if he does sit) by a special statutory dispensation[42] or (iii) in very exceptional circumstances, all the available adjudicators are affected by a disqualifying interest, in which case they may

39. See pp. 585–7.

40. de Smith, op. cit., ch. 5.

41. In *Dimes* v. *Grand Junction Canal Proprietors* (1852) 3 H.L.C. 759 a decree made by the Lord Chancellor was set aside because he was a shareholder in the company which was a party to the proceedings.

42. See *R.* v. *Barnsley Licensing JJ.* [1960] 2 Q.B. 167; Licensing Act 1953, s. 48(5). In that case all the licensing justices were members of the cooperative society which was applying for an off-licence to sell liquor, but legislation provided that their pecuniary interest was not to affect the validity of their decision. (See now Licensing Act 1964, s. 193(6).) This did not prevent the decision from being challenged on another ground (likelihood of bias). See also *Jeffs* v. *New Zealand etc. Marketing Board* [1967] 1 A.C. 551; p. 585.

have to sit as a matter of *necessity*. Perhaps we should classify under the same heading the rule that nobody should act as both judge and prosecutor, plaintiff or advocate in a controversy. But here we begin to move towards the second aspect of the rule.

If an adjudicator is likely to be biased he is also disqualified from acting. Likelihood of bias may arise from a number of causes: membership of an organization that is a party to the proceedings; partisanship expressed in extra-judicial pronouncements; the fact of appearing as a witness for a party to the proceedings; personal animosity or friendship towards a party; family relationship with a party; professional or commercial relationships with a party; and so on. The categories of situations potentially giving rise to a likelihood of bias are not closed.

The test of likelihood of bias must be applied realistically. If a controversy has aroused strong local passions, one cannot reasonably demand that every member of a local bench of magistrates deciding the issue must have maintained a total and lofty detachment from the controversy from the time when it first arose. When a Minister (like the Minister in the *Stevenage* case) is placed by a statute in a position where he must inevitably incline toward confirming his own provisional decision notwithstanding the force of objections subsequently expressed, he cannot be subjected to the rigorous standards of impartiality rightly imposed on a superior judge or indeed on a member of an independent statutory tribunal.[43]

How should the test of disqualification for likelihood of bias be formulated? The strict test of disqualification for personal interest is based on the principle that public confidence in the administration of justice must not be impaired by even the smallest suspicion of judicial impropriety; the rule looks to the *appearance* of the matter to an outsider. Occasionally the courts have adopted a similarly exacting approach to the 'likelihood of bias' test. A magistrates' clerk retired with the bench while they were considering their verdict in a case of dangerous driving; the defendant was convicted; he applied, successfully, for certiorari to quash the conviction, on the ground that the clerk belonged to a firm of solicitors acting in civil proceedings on behalf of the other party to the accident out of which the criminal proceedings arose. It was 'of fundamental importance that justice should not only be done, but should manifestly and undoubtedly be seen to be done'.[44] Yet in that case there was no evidence at all that the clerk had influenced or attempted to influence the decision. A more

43. *Franklin* v. *Minister of Town and Country Planning* [1948] A.C. 87 (pp. 555–6), where it was held that no duty to observe natural justice was cast on the Minister.
44. *R.* v. *Sussex JJ., ex p. McCarthy* [1924] 1 K.B. 256 at 259, *per* Lord Hewart C.J. But is justice 'seen' to be done when judges or magistrates or a jury retire? It cannot be 'seen' to be done in the case of departmental decisions.

common formulation of the test is: Would a member of the public, looking at the situation as a whole, *reasonably suspect* that a member of the adjudicating body would be biased? Another common formulation is: Is there in fact a *real likelihood* of bias?[45] There is no need, on either formulation, to prove *actual* bias; indeed, the courts may refuse to entertain submissions designed to establish the actual bias of a member of an independent tribunal, on the ground that such an inquiry would be unseemly. In practice the tests of 'reasonable suspicion' and 'real likelihood' of bias will generally lead to the same result. Seldom indeed will one find a situation in which reasonable persons adequately apprised of the facts will reasonably suspect bias but a court reviewing the facts will hold that there was no real likelihood of bias. Neither formulation is concerned wholly with appearances or wholly with objective reality. In ninety-nine cases out of a hundred it is enough for the court to ask itself whether a reasonable person viewing the facts would think that there was a substantial possibility of bias.[46]

Clearly there is scope for the exercise of judicial discretion, given these vague criteria. Take three recent cases. In one, the court reasonably decided that a police medical officer who had already formed an unfavourable opinion of a chief inspector's psychiatric condition should be prohibited from examining him again with a view to certifying him as permanently disabled which could lead to compulsory premature retirement.[47] In another, the court held that it was contrary to natural justice for school governors to sit as members of a local education authority's sub-committee which had to decide whether or not to uphold a decision of the governors (taken at a meeting at which they had not been present) to dismiss a teacher.[48] Yet in a third case, the court refused to interfere with a decision by governors of a teachers' training college to confirm the expulsion of a student (who had had a man in her room for some weeks) although they had initiated the disciplinary proceedings themselves.[49]

Subject to the qualifications already indicated, the principles apply to the conduct of all statutory tribunals, to bodies other than tribunals deciding

45. *R.* v. *Camborne JJ., ex p. Pearce* [1955] 1 Q.B. 41 at 51; *R.* v. *Barnsley Licensing JJ.* (above) at 187.
46. See *Metropolitan Properties Co.* (*F.G.C.*) *Ltd* v. *Lannon* [1969] 1 Q.B. 577 (quashing of decision of rent assessment committee because of the chairman's opposition in another capacity to the contentions of the landlords in similar controversies). See also *Hannam* v. *Bradford Corporation* [1970] 1 W.L.R. 937.
47. *R.* v. *Kent Police Authority, ex p. Godden* [1971] 2 Q.B. 662.
48. *Hannam*'s case (above).
49. *Ward* v. *Bradford Corporation* (1971) 70 L.G.R. 27 (*Hannam*'s case was not referred to). The only material distinctions between the two cases seem to have been that (i) H was losing his job and (ii) the court strongly disapproved of W's conduct.

matters analogous to the judicial (for example, local authorities deciding whether to grant a permit after objections have been lodged, or to revoke a licence) and to Ministers deciding disputes between parties. If the deciding body is a large one (for example, a local council), the pecuniary interest of a single member will disqualify[50] although it may be that likelihood of his being biased will not unless he took an active part in influencing the decision. This is still a doubtful point.

Audi alteram partem

This is the more interesting and important rule of natural justice.[51] In its crudest form, it means that nobody shall be penalized by a decision of a court or tribunal unless he has been given (a) *prior notice* of the charge or case he has to meet, and (b) a fair opportunity to answer the case against him and to put his own case. The rule extends to a number of situations in administrative law. To pinpoint those situations is a fascinating but complex task.

The rule has a venerable history. In a case decided in 1723, a judge ascribed it to the events in the Garden of Eden: God did not condemn Adam or Eve without first calling upon them to answer the allegation of disobedience to the divine command. The setting of this case was far removed from Eden or indeed from the proceedings of a court of law: a Dr Bentley had been deprived of his academic degrees in the University of Cambridge without notice or hearing, and he obtained a mandamus to secure reinstatement.[52] Deprivation of liberty or property, or of rights analogous to proprietary rights – and a freehold office, or an office from which the holder was removable only for cause stated, was of this character – was unlawful unless preceded by the rudiments of natural justice.[53] The same general principle governed the disciplining of the clergy by bishops, the conduct of arbitrators, and cases in which professional bodies and the executive committees of clubs and trades unions had decided to expel a member or deprive him of his status. In 1863 came the important decision in *Cooper* v. *Wandsworth Board of Works*, where a public authority de-

50. *R.* v. *Hendon R.D.C., ex p. Chorley* [1933] 2 K.B. 696 (unanimous decision by council on application to change use of land quashed because one councillor was an estate agent acting for an interested party).

51. de Smith, op. cit., ch. 4. The many ramifications of the rule are indicated by the fact that this chapter is over eighty pages long.

52. *R.* v. *Chancellor of the University of Cambridge* (1723) 1 Str. 557.

53. For the most colourful case on the implied duty to give prior notice and opportunity to be heard before depriving a person of an office in the nature of a freehold, see *Bagg*'s case (1615) 11 Co. Rep. 93b (disfranchisement of chief burgess of Plymouth for insulting behaviour towards the mayor).

molished a house without giving the owner prior notice or an opportunity to make representations on his own behalf; he obtained damages for trespass, for the public authority had failed to observe a rule 'of universal application and founded on the plainest principles of justice'; the court then 'invoked the justice of the common law to supply the omission of the legislature' which had not given the property-owner any express right to be heard.[54] This decision was followed in a number of cases of a similar nature. Three points need to be noted. First, the act or decision in question was not that of a court of justice, nor would it normally be characterized as a 'judicial' act. Secondly, the duty to act judicially (in accordance with natural justice) was inferred from the impact of an act or decision on individual rights; there was no pre-existing statutory duty to follow a judicial-type procedure. Thirdly, the decision-making body was not determining a 'triangular' situation; there were but two 'parties', itself and the person affected by its conduct.

The same general principle was applied to departmental adjudication. Ministers and officials were under an implied duty to 'act in good faith and fairly listen to both sides, for that is a duty lying upon everyone who decides anything'. But they were not bound to act like judges in a court. They could obtain information in any way they thought best, 'always giving a fair opportunity to those who are parties in the controversy for correcting or contradicting any relevant statement prejudicial to their view' (*Board of Education* v. *Rice* (1911)).[55] Still, this did not entitle a party to a housing appeal to see an inspector's report submitted to a Minister, or to be heard orally before the official who made the decision.[56]

Clearly, not every decision affecting individual interests has to be preceded by prior notice and an opportunity to be heard. It may be quite impracticable because of a paramount need for secrecy, or because the number of persons affected is so large, or because delay would make it impossible to take urgent remedial or preventive action; or there may be adequate substitutes (for example, inspection, tests, interviews) for a hearing. Again, it may be impossible to obtain certain information at all (for example, highly confidential reports) if it is known that disclosure to the person concerned (for example, an applicant for a licence or a company tendering for a contract) will take place.[57] Even where a duty to observe natural justice is applicable, the scope of the obligation imported may be

54. (1863) 14 C.B. (N.S.) 180 at 190, 194.
55. [1911] A.C. 179 at 182.
56. *Local Government Board* v. *Arlidge* [1915] A.C. 120.
57. cf. *Collymore* v. *Att.-Gen.* [1970] A.C. 538 at 549–51 (P.C.). In such situations there *may* still be a general duty to observe natural justice, subject to exceptions: *R.* v. *Gaming Board for Great Britain, ex p. Benaim and Khaida* [1970] 2 Q.B. 417 (note 89).

modified in the public interest or the interests of the parties – for example, where it would be harmful to an applicant for social security benefit to have a distressing medical report disclosed to him,[58] or where the interests of infants would suffer if a psychiatric report made to the court were to be publicized.[59]

However, it is one thing to state a general rule subject to exceptions; it is another thing to formulate the general rule in terms so narrow that it becomes an exception itself. In the period from 1920 to 1960 the courts almost ignored the general principles framed in *Cooper* v. *Wandsworth Board of Works*.[60] Thus, an alien subject to a discretionary deportation order had no legal right to make representations on his own behalf.[61] Wide discretionary powers were assumed to be inconsistent with a duty to act judicially, irrespective of their impact on individual interests, unless there was a 'triangular' situation, with X deciding a dispute between Y and Z, in which case a duty to observe natural justice was superimposed upon a pre-existing statutory duty to hold a hearing or inquiry.[62] In the early 1950s the rules of natural justice seemed to have been consigned to the lumber-room. The Controller of Textiles in Ceylon could cancel a textile dealer's licence if he had reasonable grounds for believing him to be unfit to hold a licence; no procedural duty was explicitly cast on him; the Privy Council rejected the contention of a dispossessed licence-holder that the Controller was under an *implied* duty to give him a fair hearing before depriving him of his licence; no judicial duty was cast upon the Controller, who was merely taking 'executive action to withdraw a privilege' (*Nakkuda Ali* v. *Jayaratne*).[63] In *Parker*'s case[64] the Divisional Court of the Queen's Bench Division held that the Commissioner of Metropolitan Police, who had a discretionary power to cancel cab-drivers' licences, was under no duty to observe natural justice in arriving at his decisions; his powers were

58. This is expressly provided by regulations. In *Godden*'s case (note 47, above), the court directed that the police medical officer's previous report be disclosed to the applicant's own doctor but not to the applicant himself.

59. As in a child custody case: *Re K (Infants)* [1965] A.C. 201. See also note 57.

60. Note 54.

61. *Ex p. Venicoff* [1920] 3 K.B. 72; followed in *Soblen*'s case [1963] 2 Q.B. 243.

62. See the comment on conceptual analysis of the Housing Act cases (pp. 556–7).

63. [1951] A.C. 66. This decision has been widely criticized by commentators and would probably not be followed by an English court today. See dicta cited at note 73 below, and *Ridge* v. *Baldwin* [1964] A.C. at 77, though cf. *Durayappah* v. *Fernando* [1967] 2 A.C. at 349.

64. *R.* v. *Metropolitan Police Commissioner, ex p. Parker* [1953] 1 W.L.R. 1150 (driver alleged to have allowed prostitutes to solicit from his cab). No duty to give an opportunity to be heard was imposed by statute. Contrast *Banks* v. *Transport Regulation Board* (1968) 119 C.L.R. 222 (a decision of the High Court of Australia).

administrative and disciplinary.[65] A slum landlord's legal rights in a tumbledown house had been accorded better legal protection than the 'privilege' of a man to earn his livelihood.

In the early 1960s the courts began to move towards a more flexible position; and in 1963 came the turning point. In *Ridge* v. *Baldwin* the House of Lords held that the Chief Constable of Brighton, the holder of a public office from which he was removable only for cause (neglect of duty or inability) could not validly be dismissed by the local police authority in the absence of notification of a charge and an opportunity to be heard in his defence.[66] This was in part a reversion to the old line of authority on deprivation of a 'freehold' office; in part a rejection of the mistaken ideas that natural justice could be imported only into a 'triangular' situation in which there was an express statutory duty to hold a hearing or inquiry, and that the duty to act judicially could exist only where the act or decision was analytically 'judicial'; and, above all, a recognition that the underlying basis of the *audi alteram partem* rule was a common-law obligation to act fairly.[67]

Since *Ridge* v. *Baldwin* the courts have widened the ambit of the duty. They have held, for example, that Ministers in Ceylon had an implied duty to observe the rule before taking over the assets of a denominational school in arrears with the payment of teachers' salaries,[68] and before dissolving a municipal council for incompetence;[69] that a local constituency party was entitled to the benefit of the rule before being suspended or disaffiliated by the national party organization;[70] that a Scottish schoolteacher dismissible at pleasure still had to be afforded an opportunity to be

65. See also *Ex p. Fry* [1954] 1 W.L.R. 730 (Divisional Court refused to review conduct of disciplinary proceeding against a truculent fireman, holding that the proceeding was non-judicial and interference would be contrary to public policy).

66. [1964] A.C. 40. The judgment of Lord Reid at 71–9 is the leading modern exposition of the rule. Whether breach of the rules of natural justice renders a decision void or merely voidable raises complex questions to which no short answer is possible and no uniform set of answers has yet been offered by the courts. See further H. W. R. Wade (1967) 83 *L.Q.R.* 526, (1968) 84 *L.Q.R.* 95; M. B. Akehurst (1968) 31 *Mod. L. Rev* 2, 138; de Smith, op. cit. (3rd edn), pp. 209–12, 241–2. It seems that *for most purposes* (but not necessarily all) such a decision will be held to be void.

67. cf. *Re H. K. (an Infant* [1967] 2 Q.B. 617 (a Commonwealth immigrant case), and p. 586.

68. *Maradana Mosque Trustees* v. *Mahmud* [1967] 1 A.C. 13.

69. *Durayappah* v. *Fernando* [1967] 2 A.C. 337 (a clearly 'administrative' act).

70. *John* v. *Rees* [1970] Ch. 345. It is doubtful whether the express rules of a club, political party, or other non-statutory body can validly authorize expulsion from membership in disregard of natural justice; though see *Gaiman* v. *National Association for Mental Health* [1971] Ch. 317 (company limited by guarantee). Trades unions are obliged by statute to observe the rule before expelling a member: Industrial Relations Act 1971, ss. 65(8), (9), 66.

heard before dismissal;[71] and that university students who failed an examination but could be allowed to resit at the discretion of the examiners had to be given a fair opportunity to put their own case against being refused permission to re-register.[72] There are dicta to the effect that the holder of a permit or licence should be given an opportunity to be heard before non-renewal or revocation if he had a legitimate expectation that he would retain his permit or licence.[73] And it can hardly be doubted that a university student cannot now be sent down summarily for misconduct; he must first be given a chance to put his own case.[74]

Today we can adopt a presumption that the rule will apply in the following situations:

1. Where the deciding body is a court or tribunal. Such a body may nevertheless be empowered or required by statute to act *ex parte* (hearing one side only) in special circumstances – for example, to order that a person suffering from a prescribed infectious disease be detained in hospital.

2. Where, although the deciding body is not a distinct tribunal, its functions involve the holding of hearings or inquiries, or the determination of disputes between parties; or where it is required to determine questions of law and fact in individual cases and its decisions will have a direct impact on the interests of the individuals concerned.[75]

3. Even if these conditions are lacking, a body vested with a discretionary power may be under an implied duty to observe natural justice before it acts or decides, if (a) its discretion is subject to legal limitations, so that it can be compared to a 'judicial discretion',[76] or (b) the impact of its act

71. *Malloch* v. *Aberdeen Corporation* [1971] 1 W.L.R. 1578, H.L. His office had a 'statutory flavour' and the Act was capable of being interpreted so as to entitle him to put his own case.

72. *R.* v. *Aston University Senate, ex p. Roffey* [1969] 2 Q.B. 538. A vital factor may have been that the examiners could and did take into account matters other than the bare examination results.

73. *Schmidt* v. *Home Secretary* [1969] 2 Ch. 149 at 170, 171, 173–4. See also *R.* v. *Gaming Board* (note 57) at 430; *Breen* v. *A.E.U.* [1971] 2 Q.B. at 191.

74. *Ceylon University* v. *Fernando* [1960] 1 W.L.R. 223 (expulsion for alleged cheating) was argued on the assumption that natural justice applied to this situation. Recent trends and the decision in the *Aston* case (above) imply that this assumption is now correct. See also *Glynn* v. *University of Keele* [1971] 1 W.L.R. 487 (disciplinary penalty).

75. Though cf. *Hounslow L.B.C.* v. *Twickenham Garden Developments Ltd* [1971] Ch. 233 (decision by architect terminating employment of building contractor; no duty to act judicially because no characteristics of a 'judicial situation').

76. Contrast *Aristides* v. *Minister of Housing and Local Government* [1970] 1 All E.R. 195 (Minister's ostensibly unfettered discretionary power to extend the period within which a local authority could make a compulsory purchase order in respect of a clearance area held not to import any implied duty to allow property-owners in the area to make representations against an extension of time). See also note 82.

or decision will be particularly severe on the legally recognized interests of the person directly affected by it (for example, because it deprives him of liberty or property or status or livelihood, or imposes a heavy penalty on him, or casts a serious slur on his reputation).[77]

In general, the rule does not apply in the following situations:

1. Where a body conducts an investigation but has no power to make a binding decision. However, the circumstances may still be such as to attract the operation of the rule[78] – for example, where there is a public expectation that the investigation or inquiry will be held in a judicial manner,[79] or where the investigation exposes a person to a legal hazard and is a necessary prelude to other proceedings which may culminate in his condemnation.[80]

2. Where an exhaustive statutory procedural code has been prescribed.[81] Since the establishment of the Council on Tribunals, such codes have proliferated. But the courts may hold that an ostensibly exhaustive code imports further duties to act fairly in accordance with natural justice.

3. Where a decision affects so many people that it is really a legislative act;[82] or where the range of public policy considerations that the deciding body can legitimately take into account is very wide.[83] This proposition has to be expressed guardedly, for the idea of procedural fairness is not necessarily thus restricted.

4. Where an employer decides to dismiss an employee. Unless contractual or statutory procedural duties are cast on the employer, the courts may confine the employee to damages for breach of contract if the dismissal is

77. cf. *Durayappah* v. *Fernando* (above) for an interesting reformulation of the approach to be adopted. See also *Breen* v. *A.E.U.* [1971] 2 Q.B. 175.

78. See *Wiseman* v. *Borneman* [1971] A.C. 297 (cf. *Pearlberg* v. *Varty* [1972] 1 W.L.R. 534); *Re Pergamon Press Ltd* [1971] Ch. 388.

79. As in the conduct of a preliminary investigation by magistrates (but not in a police investigation).

80. See especially *Re Pergamon Press Ltd* [1971] Ch. 388 (inquiry by company inspector; duty to apprise person of adverse impression and give him opportunity to reply before report submitted); *R.* v. *Kent Police Authority, ex p. Godden* [1971] 2 Q.B. 662 (p. 577 above). cf. *Furnell* v. *Whangarei High Schools Bd* [1973] 2 W.L. R. 92.

81. *Wiseman* v. *Borneman*; *Pearlberg* v. *Varty* (back tax assessment cases, see note 78); *Furnell*'s case (above).

82. See, for example, *Essex C.C.* v. *Ministry of Housing and Local Government* (1967) 66 L.G.R. 23 (designation of third London airport); *Bates* v. *Lord Hailsham* [1972] 1 W.L.R. 1373 (making statutory rules for solicitors' charges).

83. *Schmidt* v. *Home Secretary* [1962] 2 Ch. 149 (non-renewal of entry permits for alien scientology students); *Essex* and *Aristides* cases, above.

wrongful.[84] But there are now large exceptions to the general rule,[85] particularly since the concept of 'unfair dismissal' was introduced by the Industrial Relations Act 1971.[86]

5. Where a decision entails the allocation of scarce resources – for example, university places, council houses, industrial grants, certain discretionary licences – for which there are numerous competitors. But withdrawal or non-renewal of any such advantage *may*, in justice, have to be preceded by notice and an opportunity to make representations.[87]

In addition, as we have seen, factors such as urgency or an overriding need for confidentiality may negative the existence of a *prima facie* duty to observe the rule or aspects of the rule. Nor need the rule be observed in the exercise of a prerogative power (for example, withdrawal of a passport).

Content of the rule

Notice must be adequate in its terms, so that the prospective victim knows the essence of the case he has to meet and can prepare his answer properly; and sufficient time must be given for representations to be made. If an oral hearing is held, it may have to be adjourned where injustice would otherwise arise; a party must not be taken by surprise. There is no fixed rule that the right to be heard means a right to be heard orally; in some situations a case can be properly put in writing.[88] But there is a rebuttable presumption in favour of a duty to afford an oral hearing if one is requested. All relevant information, from whatever source it may come, should be disclosed to a person who may be prejudiced by its concealment, unless full disclosure would be injurious to the public interest.[89]

84. See, for example, *Vidyodaya University Council* v. *Silva* [1965] 1 W.L.R. 77; *Pillai* v. *Singapore City Council* [1968] 1 W.L.R. 1278. The decision in *Ridge* v. *Baldwin* [1964] A.C. 40 is not inconsistent with the principle; a chief constable is nobody's servant and enjoys a special legal *status*.

85. See *Malloch*'s case (note 71); *Hill* v. *Parsons* (*C.A.*) *& Co.* [1972] Ch. 305 (injunction to restrain wrongful dismissal).

86. Under sections 22–4 of the Act, read together with the Code of Industrial Relations Practice, a dismissal *may* be unreasonable and unfair, and therefore compensable, if the employee was denied an opportunity to put his case before dismissal: *Earl* v. *Slater & Wheeler* (*Airlyne*) *Ltd* [1973] 1 W.L.R. 51.

87. See note 73.

88. *Local Government Board* v. *Arlidge* [1915] A.C. 120; *R.* v. *Housing Appeal Tribunal* [1920], 3 K.B. 334; *Brighton Corporation* v. *Parry* (1972) 70 L.G.R. 576.

89. See, for example, *R.* v. *Gaming Board, ex p. Benaim and Khaida* [1970] 2 Q.B. 417 (applicant for gaming-club licence entitled to know essential elements of case against him but not identity of informants or details tending to reveal confidential sources of information). See also pp. 579–80.

At an oral hearing, the parties must be allowed to call witnesses and make submissions; the proceedings must be fairly conducted so as to enable the parties to put their own cases. Normally a party must not be *prevented* from cross-examining witnesses on the other side;[90] but there is no rigid duty imposed by the common law to *call* every witness (provided that relevant evidence tendered is in fact disclosed for comment), and a decision may be founded on hearsay evidence without contravening natural justice.[91] A party who is entitled to be heard in person is *prima facie* entitled to be legally represented, but this implied right does not appear to extend to proceedings before a private domestic tribunal except possibly where a person is threatened with deprivation of his livelihood.[92]

In some situations an oral hearing is conducted by a small committee or tribunal but the decision is made by a larger body. The general rule (which does not apply with the same degree of force to decisions by Ministers and government Departments)[93] is that he who decides must also 'hear'. This implies that those who listen to the evidence and make recommendations must deliver to the deciding body an adequate report of the evidence and submissions if that body is to discharge its obligation to 'hear' as well as determine the issue.[94]

Conclusion

The rules of natural justice are often described as 'fair play in action'. During the last few years the courts have veered away from conceptual reasoning and strict textual analysis and have come to place heavy emphasis on the duty of administrators to 'act fairly'.

90. In *Ceylon University* v. *Fernando* [1960] 1 W.L.R. 223, hostile witnesses and the 'accused' were questioned separately; he claimed that failure to enable him to confront those witnesses constituted a denial of natural justice; held, the hearing was fair, but it might have been otherwise if he had asked to interrogate those witnesses and his request had been *refused*. cf., however, *R.* v. *Gaming Board* (note 89).

91. See, for example, *Miller (T.A.) Ltd* v. *Minister of Housing and Local Government* [1968] 1 W.L.R. 992.

92. See the inconclusive litigation in *Pett* v. *Greyhound Racing Association Ltd* [1969] 1 Q.B. 125 (C.A.); ibid. (No. 2) [1970] 1 Q.B. 46 (Lyell J.); [1970] 1 Q.B. 67 (C.A.) (whether trainer threatened with loss of licence was entitled to legal representation at oral hearing). Eventually, the G.R.A. agreed to allow him to be legally represented. The Jockey Club had already made a like concession at disciplinary hearings. But in *Enderby Town F.C. Ltd* v. *Football Association Ltd* [1971] Ch. 591 the Court of Appeal held – in a case where a domestic tribunal had imposed a fine – that denial of independent legal representation was not a breach of natural justice.

93. *Arlidge*'s case (above).

94. *Jeffs* v. *New Zealand Dairy Production & Marketing Board* [1967] 1 A.C. 551. This decision has important implications for university disciplinary bodies.

In some judgments this duty is understood to mean something wider than a duty to 'act judicially' according to natural justice. Sometimes different judges use the same term to convey different ideas, or different terms to convey the same idea.[95] All this makes the law more uncertain – not least because ideas of fairness vary and the range of factual situations in administrative law is wide – and uncertainty invites lawyers to advise clients to try their luck in the courts. And some have been lucky. But why should it be necessary to use this concept of a duty to act fairly? After all, the rules of natural justice are flexible and adaptable; they impose no more than bare minimum standards of procedural fairness.[96] There are perhaps two reasons why some judges tend to prefer to talk of a duty to act fairly. The first is the old idea that a duty to 'act judicially' in accordance with natural justice arises only when the functions being performed are essentially of a 'judicial' character.[97] The second is that judges occasionally feel that natural justice is not really flexible enough to accommodate certain situations – for instance, the immigration officer who is trying to decide whether the 'immigrant' in front of him is over sixteen, or whether his avowed intention of coming only for a short holiday is genuine, or whether he has adequate means; or the magistrate who is asked to condemn food as being unfit for human consumption.[98] And take the following case. A council has power to increase the number of taxi licences. The town clerk assures bodies representing existing licence-holders that they will be consulted if any increase is contemplated. A sub-committee of the council recommends graduated increases after having heard the case put by the existing licensees through legal representatives. But an undertaking is then given in the council, and confirmed by the town clerk, that there will be no increase at all till forthcoming legislation has been passed. Soon afterwards the council is advised that this undertaking is an improper fetter on its discretion.[99] A new decision is taken to make an accelerated increase; no real opportunity is afforded to the existing licensees to argue against this change of policy. The Court of Appeal holds that in the circumstances the council has acted 'unfairly' and prohibits it from acting on its new

95. See, for example, *Re H.K. (an Infant)* [1967] 2 Q.B. 617; *Re Pergamon Press Ltd* [1971] Ch. 388.

96. Nor do they require that decisions be right or even just, or that reasons be given for decisions, or that proceedings be conducted in public, or that a record of the proceedings be maintained, or that there should be a right of appeal.

97. See, for example, *Glynn* v. *Keele University* [1971] 1 W.L.R. 487 at 493–5; *Bates* v. *Lord Hailsham* [1972] 1 W.L.R. 1373 at 1378.

98. See, for example, *Re H.K.* (above); *Re Mohamed Arif (an Infant)* [1968] Ch. 643; *R.* v. *Chief Immigration Officer, Lympne Airport, ex p. Amrik Singh* [1969] 1 Q.B. 333; *R.* v. *Birmingham City Justice, ex p. Chris Foreign Foods (Wholesalers) Ltd* [1970] 1 W.L.R. 1428.

99. See p. 589.

resolution until it has entertained representations from the parties affected.[100]

Maybe the court could have arrived at the same result by stretching the rules of natural justice and saying that the council has failed to 'act judicially'. But it was certainly easier for them to confine themselves to holding that the council had failed to observe its implied duty to act fairly in arriving at an 'administrative' policy decision.

A duty to act fairly is not restricted to procedural matters. Unfairness is a form of abuse of discretion – a matter considered in the pages that follow.

Discretionary powers[101]
General

As we have noted,[102] discretion implies power to choose between alternative courses of action. If X applies to a London borough council for a licence to open a massage establishment, the council may grant the licence unconditionally or subject to such conditions as it thinks fit to impose, or refuse the application. But its discretion is not unlimited; and it must exercise a genuine discretion in each individual case. Thus, it has an implied duty not to refuse the application on legally irrelevant grounds (for example, that X is a Jehovah's Witness) or to attach legally irrelevant conditions to the grant of a licence (for example, that X shall employ only persons resident in the borough); nor must it adopt a rigid rule not to grant any new applications for licences irrespective of the merits of the individual case. If no appeal lay from its decisions, X would be entitled to go to the High Court for an order of mandamus to compel it to perform its public duty. Mandamus would lie not to compel the council to give him a licence but to exercise its discretion according to law.

In fact mandamus is unnecessary, for an appeal against the merits of the decision lies to a magistrates' court. If the magistrate wrongfully refuses to entertain the appeal at all, he has declined jurisdiction in breach of his public duty and mandamus will issue to him. If he listens to submissions and then erroneously dismisses the appeal, the question might arise on an application for mandamus whether he had wrongfully declined jurisdiction or made an error of law on a matter within his jurisdiction; in this context the answer is unimportant, for an appeal will lie to the Divisional Court by case stated. In arriving at his decision, he can substitute his own opinion

100. *R. v. Liverpool Corporation, ex p. Liverpool Taxi Fleet Operators' Association* [1972] 2 Q.B. 299.
101. de Smith, op. cit., ch. 6.
102. p. 531 above.

for that of the local authority, giving due weight to the council's knowledge of local conditions. Indeed, he has a legally enforceable duty to exercise an independent discretion.[103]

It is fairly unusual to provide a full right of appeal to a court against the merits of a statutory discretionary decision. Judicial control of the exercise of discretion is normally limited to two questions: Has the discretion been exercised at all? If so, has it been exercised according to law?

Failure to exercise a discretion

1. The general rule is that, unless expressly authorized to do so, an authority cannot sub-delegate its powers to another person or body: *delegatus non potest delegare*. Application of this principle gives rise to a number of difficult problems – for example, what exactly is meant by 'delegation'?[104] – which we need not pursue. But it is not hard to illustrate the application of the general rule. A local authority empowered to issue cinema licences subject to conditions cannot validly impose a condition that *no* film shall be exhibited unless approved by the British Board of Film Censors;[105] it must preserve a residual discretion to override the rulings of the Board in an individual case; otherwise it will be held to have abdicated from its statutory duty to exercise its own discretion.[106] Again, in deciding an appeal, Minister X must not dispose of the matter solely on the basis of Minister Y's policy; otherwise the decision becomes Minister Y's.[107]

2. One authority cannot lawfully act under the dictation of another unless the other is a superior in the administrative hierarchy or is empowered by law to give instructions to it.[108] Secretaries of State are expressly empowered to give certain instructions to road and air transport licensing authorities although they are largely independent bodies.[109]

103. *Sagnata Investments Ltd* v. *Norwich Corporation* [1971] 2 Q.B. 614. The same principles apply to the Crown Court hearing an appeal from a magistrates' court.

104. In general, the rule against sub-delegation does not preclude powers vested in Ministers from being exercised on their behalf and in their name by departmental officials. See also pp. 186, 351.

105. *Ellis* v. *Dubowski* [1921] 3 K.B. 621.

106. *Mills* v. *L.C.C.* [1925] 1 K.B. 213.

107. *Lavender (H.) and Son Ltd* v. *Minister of Housing and Local Government* [1970] 1 W.L.R. 1231 (planning appeal dismissed because Minister of Agriculture always opposed such development). See also *Ratnagopal* v. *Att.-Gen.* [1970] A.C. 974 (Governor-General, appointing X to conduct an inquiry, in effect sub-delegated to X power to determine his own terms of reference; appointment therefore invalid).

108. cf. *Lavender*'s case (above).

109. Transport Act 1968, s. 59 (2); Civil Aviation Act 1971. s. 4(3).

3. An authority must not so fetter its own discretion by self-created rules as to preclude itself from applying its mind to the merits of an individual case before it. The borough council, in our hypothetical illustration, could, however, adopt a general policy of not granting any further massage establishment licences for the time being (because, for example, some of these establishments had been improperly conducted), provided that it was prepared to make an exception in a particular case.[110] It must keep its mind ajar. But an authority entitled to take general considerations of national policy into account may be entitled to refuse to consider any application belonging to a particular class. For example, the Home Secretary may validly instruct immigration officers not to admit any alien wishing to enter the country as a student member of a cult which he deems to be harmful to the public welfare.[111]

4. An authority cannot validly bargain away, or otherwise undertake not to exercise, powers vested in it for the purpose of fulfilling an important public purpose. As we have noted,[112] a local authority cannot disable itself from making a particular by-law or revoking a grant of planning permission; and in general public bodies cannot be estopped from exercising their powers by erroneous assurances given to members of the public.[113] In matters of national policy, the Crown cannot fetter its own freedom to act for the public good.[114] But these rules are easier to formulate than to apply in practice. Considerations of fairness to individuals who have been misled may influence a court's decision in their favour.[115]

Abuse of discretion

Some discretionary powers are absolute in that the propriety of the grounds on which they have been exercised cannot be canvassed in the courts; the only control is political. This is probably true of the exercise of prerogative powers; and of statutory powers while they are subject to proceedings in Parliament.[116] In practice it may also be true of statutory

110. See, for example, *R.* v. *Port of London Authority, ex p. Kynoch* [1919] 1 K.B. 176. See also *Lavender*'s case (above); *Stringer* v. *Minister of Housing and Local Government* [1970] 1 W.L.R. 1281; *Sagnata* case (note 103, above); *Cumings* v. *Birkenhead Corporation* [1972] Ch. 12 (allocation of pupils to denominational schools); *British Oxygen Co.* v. *Board of Trade* [1971] A.C. 610 (policy on investment grants).

111. See *Schmidt* v. *Home Secretary* [1969] 2 Ch. 149.

112. p. 411. See also *Stringer* case (above).

113. On assurances given by Crown servants, see *Howell* v. *Falmouth Boat Construction Co.* [1951] A.C. 837 at 845, 849 (contrast *Robertson* v. *Minister of Pensions* [1949] 1 K.B. 227). For local authorities, see now pp. 402–4.

114. *Rederiaktiebolaget Amphitrite* v. *R.* [1921] 3 K.B. 500; and see pp. 611–12.

115. As in the *Liverpool Corporation* case (pp. 586–7).

116. cf. the *Boundary Commission* cases; pp. 246–8.

powers where the element of national policy looms very large, or in time of war or serious emergency. Before a system of immigration appeals came into force, it was also substantially true to say that executive regulation of the admission and deportation of aliens was unreviewable.[117]

Nevertheless, all statutory powers must be exercised in good faith and to promote the objects of the enabling Act. Statutory discretions are potentially reviewable on these grounds at the instance of a person aggrieved by their exercise. Bad faith – the intentional misuse of power for extraneous motives – may be virtually impossible to establish if the repository of the power is a Minister. But misuse of powers in good faith – by using them for an unauthorized purpose or without regard to legally relevant considerations or on the basis of legally irrelevant considerations – need not be so difficult to prove. If a power explicitly granted for one purpose is in fact used for a different purpose, the courts ought to pronounce the administrative act invalid.[118] If such a power is used to achieve another, unauthorized, purpose as well,[119] the courts may apply various tests to determine the validity of the end-product – for example, what was the 'dominant purpose',[120] or the 'true' purpose? or was the exercise of power a colourable sham? or has the purpose for which the power was granted been substantially fulfilled? If the statutory purpose has not been spelt out, the courts may read implied limitations into an ostensibly unfettered grant of power.[121] As was pointed out in an earlier chapter,[122] the courts are nowadays reluctant to hold that an administrative authority is the sole judge of the legality of the purpose for which it exercises a discretionary power. They may interpret a statute restrictively, relying if necessary on common-law presumptions of legislative intent; and they may draw adverse inferences from the conduct of the administrative authority.

Perhaps the most outstanding recent example of judicial activism in this

117. As in *Ex p. Venicoff* [1920] 3 K.B. 72; *Schmidt*'s case (above); *Soblen*'s case [1963] 2 Q.B. 243.

118. See, for example, *Sydney Municipal Council* v. *Campbell* [1925] A.C. 338.

119. For example, *Westminster Corporation* v. *L. & N.W. Rly Co.* [1905] A.C. 426 (power to construct underground public lavatories validly exercised though a subway for non-stopping pedestrians was built).

120. If the courts had asked themselves *this* question in the *Soblen* case (above) the result might have been different. See pp. 433–4.

121. For example, *R.* v. *Paddington & St Marylebone Rent Tribunal, ex p. Bell London & Provincial Properties Ltd* [1949] 1 K.B. 666, as explained in *R.* v.*Barnet & Camden Rent Tribunal, ex p. Frey Investments Ltd* [1972] 2 Q.B. 342 (local council could not use its power to refer contracts of letting to a rent tribunal for the purpose of using the tribunal as a general rent-fixing agency irrespective of the circumstances of individual cases).

122. pp. 349–50.

field of the law was the decision of the House of Lords in *Padfield* v. *Minister of Agriculture* (1968).[123] Under a statutory marketing scheme, the Milk Marketing Board fixed prices to be paid to producers in each of eleven regions in England and Wales. Producers from the south-east region wanted an increase in the basic price paid to them by the Board. They could not get a majority on the Board for their view. But under the Act they could, and did, make a complaint to the Minister. The Act provided that, 'if the Minister . . . so directs', a committee was to be appointed to investigate and report on such a complaint. The Minister refused to appoint a committee. He claimed that he had a free discretion to do as he thought fit. But he was induced to give reasons for his refusal: the complaint raised issues affecting other regions; he would be expected to implement the report of such a committee, and this could lead to political difficulties. The House of Lords held that the Minister had had regard to irrelevant considerations and had failed to promote the implied purposes of the Act; and an order of mandamus was issued to direct him to consider the appellants' complaint according to law.[124]

Thus, a wide executive discretion was subject to judicial standards. The case shows unambiguously that English administrative law does recognize the principle that the French call *détournement de pouvoir*, or abuse of administrative power; and that misuse of power may be inferred from inadequate reasons or, indeed, so the Law Lords observed *obiter*, from the absence of any reason given in rebuttal when an aggrieved person has established a *prima facie* case.

Most of the cases in which the courts have held that statutory discretions were invalidly exercised have been concerned with licensing, the regulation of land use by individuals, and the spending powers of local authorities. In these contexts analogies with the 'judicial discretions' vested in judges, magistrates[125] and trustees have been invoked, and the usual

123. [1968] A.C. 997. This decision, though overshadowed by *Conway* v. *Rimmer* [1968] A.C. 910 (pp. 620–21) may have been equally important. cf., however, *Westminster Bank Ltd* v. *Beverley B.C.* [1971] A.C. 508 (local authority refused a bank planning permission to erect a building under Act X; if it had granted permission, it would have had to pay compensation later under a road-widening scheme to be undertaken in pursuance of Act Y when it demolished the building; held, avoidance of payment of compensation by using powers to refuse consent under Act X did not render its decision an unlawful abuse of power). Contrast *Hall & Co.* v. *Shoreham-by-Sea U.D.C.* (note 127).

124. The Minister then set up the committee; the committee reported in favour of the south-eastern producers; the Minister rejected the report.

125. See, for example, *R.* v. *Adamson* (1875) 1 Q.B.D. 201 where magistrates empowered to issue a summons if they thought fit refused to issue one against persons alleged to have conspired to break up a meeting held in support of the notorious Tichborne claimant. It appeared that the magistrates' reason was disapproval of the

grounds of invalidity have been taking irrelevant factors into account and disregarding relevant factors. The courts have seldom been deflected by the fact that the competent authority has a statutory power to take such action 'as it thinks fit' in relation to a particular matter. Local authorities have long been held to owe fiduciary duties to their ratepayers.[126] More recently, the courts have emphasized that conditions annexed by local planning authorities to grants of planning permission and caravan site licences must 'fairly and reasonably relate' to the permitted use.[127] In deciding what restrictive standards they will impose on the exercise of an apparently unfettered discretionary power, the courts exercise a broad and not readily predictable discretion of their own. In one recent case[128] the Court of Appeal took the view that the discretionary power of a local authority to refer private tenancies to a rent tribunal would not be invalid merely on the ground that an irrelevant matter had been considered or a relevant matter disregarded; it would be invoked only if the reference were arbitrary and capricious.

How far is unreasonableness to be regarded as an independent head of invalidity? By exercising statutory powers unreasonably in such a way as to cause undue interference with private rights, a public authority or official may commit a tort (for example, nuisance, negligence, trespass, false imprisonment). Here we are more concerned with cases where no actionable civil wrong has been committed but an administrative act or decision is challenged on the ground that it is so unreasonable as to be *ultra vires*.

If a statutory power is expressed to be exercisable only where there exist 'reasonable grounds', 'reasonable cause' or 'reasonable suspicion', the courts can properly inquire independently whether these conditions precedent were satisfied.[129] In practice they will not necessarily be willing to embark upon this exercise. They declined to interfere with the exercise of power by local authorities to fix 'reasonable' rents for council houses

---

object of the meeting. Held, mandamus should issue to them to exercise their discretion according to law.

126. For example, *Roberts* v. *Hopwood* [1925] A.C. 578, and pp. 407–8.

127. *Pyx Granite Co.* v. *Ministry of Housing and Local Government* [1958] 1 Q.B. 554 at 572, *per* Lord Denning M.R., a dictum approved in many subsequent cases; see, for example, *Fawcett Properties Ltd* v. *Buckingham C.C.* [1961] A.C. 636; *Kingsway Investments (Kent) Ltd* v. *Kent C.C.* [1971] A.C. 72. See also *Hall & Co.* v. *Shoreham-by-Sea U.D.C.* [1964] 1 W.L.R. 240 for an instructive example of planning conditions held to be invalid for inadequate relationship to the purposes of the Act.

128. *R.* v. *Barnet and Camden Rent Tribunal* (note 121).

129. *Nakkuda Ali* v. *Jayaratne* [1951] A.C. 66 at 76–77, distinguishing *Liversidge* v. *Anderson* [1942] A.C. 206. On Lord Atkin's dissenting judgment in the latter case, see R. F. V. Heuston (1970) 86 *L.Q.R.* 33. See further pp. 349, 519.

and flats unless the rents could be shown to be such as no reasonable body of persons could have imposed.[130]

If there is no express statutory obligation cast on the competent authority to act reasonably, the courts may nevertheless impose minimum standards of reasonableness. The Poplar councillors who voted to pay unskilled employees a minimum wage of £4 a week in the early 1920s were held to have exercised their discretion unlawfully by taking irrelevant considerations into account and failing to have regard to relevant considerations.[131] To say that they had acted unreasonably would come to the same thing. But suppose that an authority vested with a wide discretion is not deflected into the paths of irrelevancy; instead, it gives too much weight to one relevant factor and too little to others, and ends by coming to an unreasonable decision. In the *Wednesbury Corporation* case[132] a local authority, empowered to attach such conditions as it thought fit to the grant of a permit for Sunday cinema opening, imposed a condition that no child under fifteen should be admitted to a Sunday performance at all. The condition was attacked as being void for unreasonableness. The Court of Appeal held that it was valid; the courts should be slow to substitute their own opinion for that of the competent authority, and only if the condition were such as no reasonable body of persons could have imposed should they be prepared to pronounce it invalid. This seems to suggest that only a preposterous decision ('something overwhelming')[133] could be successfully impugned on its merits; and a preposterous decision would in any event probably be characterized as having been made in bad faith[134] or for an improper purpose. The test thus formulated appeared to be every bit as narrow as that adopted to determine the validity of by-laws alleged to be void for manifest unreasonableness.[136] However, cases on conditions annexed to grants of planning permission and caravan site licences show that the *Wednesbury* test of unreasonableness need not be a formality, and it has been invoked as well as the by-law test to strike down clearly

130. See especially *Luby* v. *Newcastle-under-Lyme Corporation* [1964] 2 Q.B. 64 at 70–72, [1965] 1 Q.B. 214 at 230–31. The law is now modified by the Housing Finance Act 1972.

131. *Roberts* v. *Hopwood* [1925] A.C. 578. See p. 407.

132. *Associated Provincial Picture Houses Ltd* v. *Wednesbury Corporation* [1948] 1 K.B. 223.

133. At 230, *per* Lord Greene M.R.

134. But gross unreasonableness is not necessarily synonymous with malice or dishonesty: *Horrocks* v. *Lowe* [1972] 1 W.L.R. 1625.

136. *Kruse* v. *Johnson* [1898] 2 Q.B. 91 at 99–100. From time to time local authority by-laws have been held invalid for manifest unreasonableness, though the test of validity may appear similar to the *Wednesbury* test. See, for example, *Parker* v. *Bournemouth Corporation* (1902) 66 J.P. 440; *Repton School Governors* v. *Repton R.D.C.* [1918] 2 K.B. 133.

unreasonable conditions.[137] In one recent case an attempt by a London borough council to avoid having to impose higher council rents under the Housing Finance Act 1972 by fixing the rateable value of one unoccupied council house at an artificially high figure was nullified.[138] But the courts are, on the whole, still chary of holding the exercise of local authority discretionary powers to be void for unreasonableness *per se*, especially if they contain a significant policy element.[139]

Again one must consider the importance of the contexts in which judicial review operates. Despite the revival of judicial activism in the 1960s, it would be hopeless to challenge the validity of a compulsory purchase order or any other executive act or decision on the grounds of unreasonableness *per se* if that decision could properly be based on broad considerations of national policy. It would be necessary to establish improper purpose, (possibly) the influence of irrelevant considerations or the disregard of relevant factors, breach of natural justice, non-compliance with procedural or formal requirements, or one of the other grounds for impugning the *vires* of a policy decision.[140]

137. For example, *Hall*'s case (note 127 above); *Mixnam's Properties Ltd* v. *Chertsey U.D.C.* [1965] A.C. 735; *Hartnell* v. *Minister of Housing and Local Government* [1965] A.C. 1134.

138. *Backhouse* v. *Lambeth L.B.C.*, *The Times*, 14 October 1972.

139. See, for example, the *Barnet and Camden* case (p. 592); *Re T. (A.J.J.) (an Infant)* [1970] Ch. 688 (child custody decision); *Re Lamplugh* (1968) 19 P. & C. R. 125 (order to remove building on planning grounds); *Manchester Corporation* v. *Connolly* [1970] Ch. 420 (possession order); *Cumings* v. *Birkenhead Corporation* [1972] Ch. 12 (allocation of pupils to secondary schools); *Dowty Boulton Paul Ltd* v. *Wolverhampton Corporation (No. 2)* [1973] 2 W.L.R. 618 (appropriation of land for planning purposes – a somewhat unsatisfactory decision, the grant of power having been conferred in 'objective' terms).

140. See, for example, *Venicoff*'s case [1920] 3 K.B. 72 (deportation of alien); *Johnson*'s case [1947] 2 All E.R. 395 (dicta) (compulsory purchase order); *Robinson* v. *Minister of Town and Country Planning* [1947] K.B. 702 (planning scheme). There is no good reason for supposing that the courts have shifted their position on such issues, and to impugn a new town designation order or an order for the development of a site as a new airport (see *Essex C.C.* v. *Ministry of Housing and Local Government* (1967) 66 L.G.R. 23) on the grounds of unreasonableness *per se* would seem to be a fruitless endeavour. *Padfield*'s case (p. 591) shows how an unreasonable executive decision can sometimes be successfully assailed by a more circuitous chain of reasoning. For judicial acceptance of unreviewable discretion in other contexts, see *Gallagher* v. *Post Office* [1970] 3 All E.R. 712; *Aristides* v. *Minister of Housing and Local Government* [1970] 1 All E.R. 195; *Re Fletcher's Application* [1970] 2 All E.R. 527.

Chapter 27
Judicial Review of Administrative Action: Remedies

I

English law relating to judicial remedies against administrative bodies is more intricate than the main body of substantive law.[1] We do not have to probe fully into these matters, but some of the references already made to particular remedies may seem puzzling, and if no further explanation is offered a student reading some of the cases may become still more puzzled.

Remedies may be statutory or non-statutory. Statutory remedies include the following:

1. Rights of appeal to the courts. As we have noted, from most statutory tribunals appeals lie to the High Court (normally the Divisional Court of the Queen's Bench Division) or the Court of Appeal on points of law.

2. Statutory applications to quash, or restrain the making of, compulsory purchase and similar orders, and decisions on planning appeals, on the ground that the order or decision is *ultra vires* or that the applicant has been substantially prejudiced by non-compliance with a procedural or formal requirement on the part of the competent authorities. Applications lie to a single judge of the High Court,[2] and must be brought within a brief period, normally six weeks. The statutory procedure excludes the non-statutory grounds for challenge.

Sometimes the classes of persons and bodies entitled to lodge an appeal or bring an application to quash are specified by the Act. Unfortunately, it is more common for the Act merely to afford these rights to a 'person aggrieved', leaving it to the courts to interpret what this expression means. The courts have tended to adopt a restrictive interpretation: a person aggrieved usually means a person or body whose existing legal rights have been interfered with or upon whom a new legal obligation has been imposed.[3] As we saw,[4] Major Buxton, who complained of a serious prospective loss of amenity as the result of a decision on a planning appeal, was

1. de Smith, *Judicial Review of Administrative Action* (3rd edn), Part III.
2. In practice in the Queen's Bench Division. See further, Order 94 of the Rules of the Supreme Court.
3. See, for example, *Ealing Corporation* v. *Jones* [1959] 1 Q.B. 384.
4. pp. 558–9.

held not to be a 'person aggrieved' for the purpose of an application to quash the decision. However, in another recent case, loss of amenity was held to render a householder a 'person aggrieved'.[5] Judicial attitudes have not been consistent; nor, as we shall see, have they been uniform where the question of entitlement to obtain non-statutory remedies has arisen. One has the impression that the courts are becoming more flexible in these matters.[6] In some statutory contexts, a 'person aggrieved' must clearly be given a wider meaning than usual: if a right of appeal lies from decisions of a licensing body, an unsuccessful applicant must obviously be a person aggrieved and entitled to appeal although he has not been deprived of existing legal rights by the adverse decision.[7]

3. In some contexts statutory default powers, exercisable by Ministers to enforce compliance with public duties, particularly duties imposed on local authorities, may involve proceedings in the courts.[8]

The main non-statutory remedies in administrative law are the prerogative writ of habeas corpus,[9] the orders of certiorari, prohibition and mandamus (still sometimes called 'prerogative' orders, because they were formerly prerogative writs[10]), the injunction, the declaration, and damages. Actions for damages will be touched on in the next chapter. Certiorari, prohibition and mandamus were evolved by the courts of common law. The injunction is an equitable remedy. The declaration is a nineteenth-century interloper, akin to an equitable remedy but not fitting into any neat category.

Applications for certiorari, prohibition and mandamus are made to a Divisional Court of the Queen's Bench Division. Actions for declarations

5. *Maurice* v. *L.C.C.* [1964] 2 Q.B. 362 (and hence entitled to lodge an appeal). See also *Att.-Gen. of The Gambia* v. *N'Jie* [1961] A.C. 617 at 634.

6. See, for example, *R.* v. *Liverpool Corporation* [1972] 2 Q.B. 299 (prohibition; standing accorded to organization representing competitors of prospective new licensees); *R.* v. *Hereford JJ., ex p. Harrower* [1970] 1 W.L.R. 1424 (mandamus; standing accorded to ratepayers complaining of breach of standing orders in tendering for contracts); *R.* v. *Lewes JJ., ex p. Home Secretary* [1972] 3 W.L.R. 279 (H.L.) (certiorari; standing accorded to Home Secretary and Gaming Board applying to quash witness summons issued to private prosecutor against police officer); *R.* v. *Blackpool JJ., ex p. Beaverbrook Newspapers Ltd* [1972] 1 W.L.R. 95 (certiorari awarded to newspaper proprietors to quash magistrates' order restricting reporting of committal proceedings). And see notes 33, 43 and 44.

7. *Stepney B.C.* v. *Joffe* [1949] 1 K.B. 509.

8. For example, for an order of mandamus or a declaration against the defaulter. But such proceedings are rare. On the effect of default powers on the rights of *individuals* to go to court, see pp. 606–7.

9. See pp. 465–9.

10. For the meaning of the term 'prerogative writ', and the history of the writs, see de Smith, op. cit., Appendix 1.

and injunctions are brought before a single High Court judge, usually in the Chancery Division. The possibilities of combining these proceedings, if one is not sure of the appropriate legal remedy, are therefore limited. A claim for damages may be combined with one for an injunction or a declaration but not with the prerogative orders. Statutory applications to quash cannot be combined with any other form of relief.

These facts alone suggest that the law of remedies needs to be rationalized. There ought not be so many different avenues to the courts. The case for reform is strengthened by closer investigation. For the avenues are tortuous; occasionally they run together, only to deviate unpredictably; sometimes they lead the litigant nowhere.

Each of the remedies has developed separately, and most of them originally had nothing to do with administrative law situations. Prohibition was one of the earliest writs known to the law; it was used by the common-law courts to prevent ecclesiastical courts from usurping their jurisdiction. Certiorari was simply a royal demand for information: the King, wishing to be made more certain (certiorari) of a matter, demanded that he be informed by production of documents. It was used in the late medieval period to bring up the record of an indictment, or of proceedings in an inferior court, for trial or, if necessary, retrial and review. Certiorari to remove for trial is now virtually obsolete. The modern form of certiorari, which emerged in the seventeenth century, is certiorari to quash a decision on the application of a party aggrieved. The writ lay to minor judicial bodies such as justices of the peace whose proceedings could not be reviewed by writ of error. Prohibition came to serve much the same purpose, except that it could issue only if there were something left to prohibit. The two writs were the principal means by which the King's Bench (following the demise of the Star Chamber and the atrophy of the Privy Council's jurisdiction) exercised an inherent supervisory jurisdiction over inferior tribunals. When they were invoked against local authorities and government Departments in new situations, the High Court tended to get into tangles because concepts relevant to superintendence over *tribunals* did not always adapt themselves easily to control over administrative bodies.

Of late the action for a declaration has encroached on the field formerly reserved for certiorari. In some contexts non-statutory remedies have been ousted by statutory applications to quash and restrain. Rights of appeal overlap with certiorari. So does mandamus. Confusion has become worse confounded by this wealth of remedies. However, a sense of proportion must be preserved. Nowadays the courts try not to send a litigant with a good case away empty-handed merely because he has not chosen the most appropriate remedy.

Mandamus, to compel the performance of a public duty, proved to be an adaptable remedy in public law, but it acquired certain peculiar characteristics in its formative years and these still stunt its development. The most flexible and interesting of the non-statutory remedies is the declaration; its capacity for growth has not yet been exhausted. Closely associated with the declaration is the injunction; but this is still pre-eminently a private law remedy, and it has not fitted easily into some administrative law contexts where it might have been of value.

All these remedies are discretionary: save in very exceptional circumstances, a person aggrieved cannot demand them as of right when he has made out a case of unlawful action or omission. But the principles governing the manner in which the courts will exercise their discretion vary from one remedy to another. Separate development here, as elsewhere, has been an evil.

II

Certiorari will issue to quash an order or decision on any of the following grounds:

1. Excess or want of jurisdiction. If part of an impugned order is quite distinct and severable from the rest of the order, the invalid part may be quashed, leaving the remainder intact.

2. Breach of the rules of natural justice.

3. Error of law on the face of the record.

4. Fraud, perjury or duress in procuring a decision.

As we have just noted, certiorari has become less important in administrative law because of the extension of alternative remedies. But within its own field it has been fortified by the revival of the concept of review for error of law on the face of the record, by the statutory enlargement of the 'record', by the extension of duties to give reasons for decisions and by the nullification of statutory formulae purporting to exclude judicial review.[11]

In the *Electricity Commissioners* case Atkin L.J. said[12] that certiorari and prohibition may issue to 'any body of persons having legal authority to determine questions affecting the rights of subjects, and having the duty to act judicially . . .'.

A 'body of persons' included one person – for example, a Minister.

11. See pp. 570–71.
12. *R.* v. *Electricity Commissioners* [1924] 1 K.B. 171 at 204–5

'Legal authority' was generally understood to mean authority derived from statute or royal charter. In 1967, however, it was held[13] that certiorari would lie to a judicial-type body (the Criminal Injuries Compensation Board) fulfilling public functions but created by purely administrative action.[14] Decisions by a *private* non-statutory tribunal (for example, the committee of a club or trade union) are challengeable not by certiorari but by injunctions and declarations.

The courts have sometimes refused to award certiorari and prohibition against bodies which have no power to make a final decision; such bodies are not 'determining questions'.[15] This is a difficult field of administrative law, but one can assume that a court will be prepared to afford redress today if satisfied that such a body (i) was obliged to observe the rules of natural justice and (ii) broke them.[16] There is nothing at all to be said for the decision of the Judicial Committee of the Privy Council in *Nakkuda Ali* v. *Jayaratne* – that an official deciding to revoke a trading licence, upon which a man's livelihood depended, was not 'determining a question' affecting 'rights'.[17]

We indicated earlier[18] that a duty to 'act judicially' in accordance with natural justice will sometimes be inferred from the impact of a decision on individual interests although the decision is analytically administrative. In such cases certiorari and prohibition will issue. It is no longer necessary to show that the body was a court or tribunal or was under an express duty to conduct a hearing or inquiry for its decisions to be amenable to review.[19] However, the absence of *any* feature of a judicial proceeding, coupled with a wide discretion, exercisable on policy grounds,[20] *may* incline a court to hold that the act or decision impugned was 'purely administrative' and not reviewable by certiorari or prohibition.[21] Even so, if the court is satisfied

13. *R.* v. *Criminal Injuries Compensation Board, ex p. Lain* [1967] 2 Q.B. 864.

14. Though the Board is financed out of moneys provided by Parliament under the Appropriation Act.

15. See, for example, *Jayawardane* v. *Silva* [1970] 1 W.L.R. 1365.

16. As in *R.* v. *Kent Police Authority, ex p. Godden* [1971] 2 Q.B. 662 (prohibition to doctor whose 'decision' was not final).

17. [1951] A.C. 66 at 78.

18. pp. 578–83.

19. See especially *Ridge* v. *Baldwin* [1964] A.C. 40, *per* Lord Reid at 71–9.

20. As distinct from a limited or 'judicial' discretion: *R.* v. *Manchester Legal Aid Committee, ex p. Brand (R.A.) & Co.* [1952] 2 Q.B. 413.

21. Certiorari was refused, ostensibly on these grounds, in *Venicoff*'s case [1920] 3 K.B. 72 (deportation of alien); *Nakkuda Ali* v. *Jayaratne* (see above) and *Parker*'s case (revocation of licences); and *Vidyodaya University Council* v. *Silva* [1965] 1 W.L.R. 77 (dismissal of university teacher). These decisions are all explicable mainly on the ground that the courts thought it inappropriate to import a duty to observe

that it ought in fairness to intervene (especially if there has been a clear excess of jurisdiction), it is unlikely today to trouble itself with the analytical question whether the respondent to the application was under any duty to act 'judicially'. It will be enough that the body in question was obliged to 'act fairly'.[22] Seldom will the supposed technical limitations on the scope of the *remedies* be the decisive factor. It is more profitable to ask oneself what the court did and why it did it than to dwell upon observations on the limits of certiorari as a remedy.

Locus standi to bring an application presents problems. It has often been stated that any member of the public can institute proceedings; rulings to this effect are to be found particularly in cases of prohibition for patent jurisdictional defects. On the other hand, the more usual view is that *locus standi* is limited to 'persons aggrieved', with all the ambiguities that this term connotes. Probably the term should be understood to include any person with a substantial personal interest to vindicate,[23] and members of a local community who have a special grievance of their own by virtue of membership of that community. Yet in *Durayappah* v. *Fernando*[24] the mayor of a municipal council in Ceylon that had been dissolved by a Minister in breach of natural justice was held not to be a person aggrieved who was entitled to bring certiorari on his own behalf. Decisions of the courts *may* still be dominated by a technicality.

The principles governing the discretion of the court to award certiorari have partly crystallized. The courts exercise discretion in practice when deciding whether the applicant had *locus standi*. An application may be refused for waiver of or acquiescence in an excess of jurisdiction or a breach of natural justice; or (exceptionally) because there is a more appropriate alternative remedy; or because the applicant had delayed unreasonably before instituting the proceedings, the normal time limit being six months. The Aston University students who had been denied natural justice lost their case on the ground of delay.[25] Certiorari may also be refused because to award it would serve no useful purpose, or because of the applicant's unreasonable behaviour.[26]

Prohibition does not call for special discussion. In administrative law

---

natural justice. See also *Aristides* v. *Minister of Housing and Local Government* [1970] 1 All E.R. 195 (statutory application to quash dismissed on the ground that the Minister had no duty to act judicially).

22. *R.* v. *Birmingham City Justice* [1970] 1 W.L.R. 1428. See p. 586.

23. See note 6.

24. [1967] 2 A.C. 337.

25. *R.* v. *Aston University Senate, ex p. Roffey* [1969] 2 Q.B. 538.

26. *Ex p. Fry* [1954] 1 W.L.R. 730 (C.A.) (behaviour of fireman subjected to minor disciplinary penalty).

it will lie to the same bodies as certiorari, and on similar grounds,[27] though a case for prohibition for error of law on the face of the record could hardly ever arise because by the time that the error had become apparent the order would nearly always be final. Occasionally certiorari and prohibition may be awarded in conjunction – certiorari to quash a decision already taken by a tribunal and prohibition to prevent the tribunal from proceeding or continuing to entertain other like cases outside its jurisdiction.[28]

Mandamus, to compel the performance of a public duty, was evolved by the King's Bench early in the seventeenth century to restore persons to public offices of which they had been unlawfully deprived.[29] For the next two hundred years or more it enjoyed vast popularity as a means of prodding inert and inept officials, magistrates and borough corporations into fulfilment of their public obligations. A synopsis of the case law, published in 1848, ran to 252 pages. But its importance was already dwindling as local government was reformed; and it shrivelled as new statutory remedies by way of appeal, complaint or objection to government Departments, tribunals or courts, were introduced. For mandamus was always an 'extraordinary' remedy, awarded only if no alternative remedy was equally convenient or effective.

However, it will still lie in quite a wide range of situations, and it is awarded a little more frequently than a few years ago.[30] It may be issued to compel a tribunal or a Minister or a local authority to entertain an appeal or application in respect of which they have wrongfully declined jurisdiction. It will lie to compel a body to carry out a duty to give reasons for a decision or to give adequate reasons; and to require a local authority to produce minutes and accounts for inspection. If an authority required to exercise a discretion in a matter fails to consider it on its merits because it has improperly sub-delegated its powers or acted under dictation or fettered its own discretion by unauthorized promises or a rigid self-imposed rule, mandamus will lie. It will also lie to order an authority which has abused its statutory discretion (for example, by rejecting an application on the basis of legally irrelevant considerations) to hear and determine the matter according to law: see *Padfield*'s case.[31] Although on an application for mandamus, the courts are not supposed to direct the competent authority *how* to exercise its jurisdiction or discretion (for example, to issue

27. See especially the *Liverpool* and *Godden* cases, notes 6 and 16.

28. As in the *Block Reference* case (*R.* v. *Paddington & St Marylebone Rent Tribunal* [1949] 1 K.B. 666; p. 590 above).

29. The leading case is *Bagg*'s case (1615) 11 Co. Rep. 93b; p. 578, note 53.

30. In the period 1964–6 only ten orders of mandamus were issued. But in 1969 eighteen orders were granted, seventy-six applications having been made for leave to apply.

31. *Padfield* v. *Minister of Agriculture* [1968] A.C. 997; p. 591.

a licence to X), they may in effect achieve this result by holding that only one avenue of approach to a particular case is legally permissible.[32]

Mandamus will not lie against the Crown, nor will it lie to a Crown servant to order the performance of a duty owed *only* to the Crown; but it will lie to a Minister to carry out a duty in the performance of which a member of the public has a substantial personal interest.

There are important limitations on its availability. It cannot be obtained (except in some instances on the application of a Minister) to compel a local authority to provide a public service or a board running a nationalized industry to discharge its primary duties. The courts might refuse to issue such an order on a number of different grounds – that enforcement could not be adequately supervised; that the matter is non-justiciable because judicial review has been expressly excluded or because the duty is merely descriptive of a general administrative function; that there are adequate alternative remedies; that no member of the public has *locus standi*. There has indeed been a marked (though somewhat erratic) tendency to take a narrow view of the requirements of *locus standi* in mandamus cases. In general, an applicant must show a direct and substantial personal interest, going beyond the interest of the public at large, in the performance of the duty.[33] Some cases say that he must have a specific legal right to its performance. And he must have demanded performance and been met with a wrongful refusal, communicated directly or by conduct evincing an intention not to comply or a failure to understand what compliance entails.

There are several discretionary bars to the award of the order. Alternative remedies, unreasonable delay in making an application, the absence of any useful purpose in issuing a judicial command, and the unacceptable motives of the applicant are among the most common. In a recent case[34] the Commissioners of Customs and Excise had allowed bookmakers to pay a new and heavy licensing duty on betting premises by monthly instalments. But the Finance Act 1969 had provided that the tax was to be paid in one sum or by two half-yearly instalments. There was no statutory authority for the concession made by the Commissioners acting

32. See *R.* v. *Derby JJ., ex p. Kooner* [1971] 1 Q.B. 147 (where 'may' was treated as meaning 'must').

33. For this reason it was doubtful whether the applicant in *R.* v. *Metropolitan Police Commissioner, ex p. Blackburn* [1968] 2 Q.B. 118 (p. 381) could have obtained a mandamus. Yet see *R.* v. *Metropolitan Police Commissioner ex p. Blackburn (No. 3)* [1973] 2 W.L.R. 43 (where these doubts were muted); and note *McWhirter*'s case (p. 248) where a local elector was treated as if he had *locus standi* to compel the Home Secretary to lay Boundary Commission reports before Parliament; see also *R.* v. *Hereford Corporation, ex p. Harrower* [1970] 1 W.L.R. 1424, note 6; and Addendum.

34. *R.* v. *Customs and Excise Commissioners, ex p. Cook* [1970] 1 W.L.R. 450.

under the responsible Minister's instructions. Two bookmakers who had paid their duties in accordance with the Act applied for mandamus to compel the Commissioners to administer the Act according to law. The court dismissed the application. Even assuming that the applicants had *prima facie* a sufficient legal interest to maintain the proceedings, their ulterior purpose was to put less affluent competitors out of business, and this was not a purpose for which mandamus should be granted for non-compliance with this statutory obligation.

Injunctions may be prohibitory (to restrain the commission or continuance of unlawful conduct) or mandatory (to compel the performance of a duty). Mandatory injunctions are granted sparingly;[35] and in administrative law they are of little practical importance.[36] An interim or interlocutory injunction may be awarded as a matter of urgency *ex parte* (on the strength of the plaintiff's representations alone) to restrain the commission or repetition of an allegedly wrongful act which is liable to do very serious harm, pending a full hearing of the case.

The injunction is essentially a discretionary private law remedy, awarded where damages would not be a sufficient form of redress. It is also obtainable against public authorities and officials, other than the Crown and Crown servants acting in that behalf,[37] not only for actionable wrongs (such as trespasses or nuisances) but also to restrain acts which are *ultra vires* but give no right of action for damages. For example, if a local authority spends money for a purpose outside its powers, it is not committing a tort, but it can still be restrained by injunction. Who may sue? The answer usually, though not uniformly,[38] given is that only the Attorney-General, acting in his sole discretion, can institute such proceedings on behalf of the public for the vindication of their rights. He may sue either on his own initiative or upon the information of a 'relator', who is generally a local ratepayer; the proceedings are conducted in the Attorney-General's name, though in relator actions he will not take an active part. The Attorney-General may also sue for an injunction to restrain repeated breaches of regulatory legislation where the sanctions of

35. cf. *Morris* v. *Redland Bricks Ltd* [1970] A.C. 652 for a review of the principles.
36. See, for example, *Att.-Gen.* v. *Colchester Corporation* [1955] 2 Q.B. 207 (no mandatory injunction to compel continued operation of ferry service); and see generally *Glossop* v. *Heston and Isleworth Local Board* (1879) 12 Ch. D. 102. See, however, *Ghani* v. *Jones* [1970] 1 Q.B. 693 (mandatory order to police to return wrongfully detained Pakistani passports).
37. See Crown Proceedings Act 1947, s. 21, for this exception; pp. 616–17 below.
38. In *Prescott* v. *Birmingham Corporation* [1955] Ch. 210 an action by a ratepayer succeeded; the question of his *locus standi* was not raised. He was awarded a declaration, but it can hardly be thought that the position would have been different had he sought an injunction.

the criminal law have proved inadequate.[39] He has also been awarded injunctions against individuals breaking or proposing to break the criminal law where the matter is very urgent, notwithstanding that the criminal courts have not yet dealt with this issue.[40] It is still not clear in what circumstances a local authority can take proceedings on behalf of the local community,[40a] but under the Local Government Act 1972 it seems that the new local authorities will be entitled to do so under their own names.[41] Broadly speaking, a private individual cannot sue to restrain a 'public wrong' unless his own legal rights have been encroached upon or he has suffered or is threatened with special damage peculiar to himself.[42] But in the *Enfield* cases an invalid school reorganization scheme was successfully challenged by parents who were ratepayers.[43] And in *McWhirter*'s case (1973) the Court of Appeal accepted that in very exceptional circumstances it could grant an interlocutory injunction to an ordinary member of the public to restrain the IBA from breaking a statutory duty to satisfy itself that offensive material was not broadcast.[44] There are numerous discretionary bars to the award of injunctions.

All the four non-statutory remedies mentioned up to this point are coercive. Disobedience is a contempt of court. This is not true of declaratory orders.

The declaratory judgment is basically a twentieth-century judicial remedy and has come to be used for a great variety of purposes in public and private law.[45] Declarations can be awarded in almost every situation where an injunction will lie – the most important exception is that interim relief cannot be granted by way of a declaration – and they extend to a number

39. *Att.-Gen.* v. *Harris* [1961] 1 Q.B. 74 (Manchester flower-sellers outside a cemetery, repeatedly breaking a local Act but preferring payment of the fines to desisting). Disobedience to an injunction can lead to committal to prison.

40. *Att.-Gen.* v. *Melville Construction Co.* (1968) 67 L.G.R. 309 (tree preservation order); *Att.-Gen.* v. *Chaudry* [1971] 1 W.L.R. 1614 (breach of fire safety law); *Att.-Gen.* v. *Times Newspapers Ltd* [1972] 3 W.L.R. 855 (where publication of article would have been criminal contempt of court).

40a. Compare *Warwickshire C.C.* v. *British Railways Board* [1969] 1 W.L.R. 1117 (broad view) with *Prestatyn U.D.C.* v. *Prestatyn Raceway Ltd* [1970] 1 W.L.R. 33 and *Hampshire C.C.* v. *Shonleigh Nominees Ltd*, ibid. 865 (declaration) (narrow view).

41. s. 222. This may dispose of a long-standing controversy.

42. *Boyce* v. *Paddington Corporation* [1903] 1 Ch. 109 at 114. This general principle was formulated in the context of public nuisance.

43. *Bradbury* v. *Enfield L.B.C.* [1967] 1 W.L.R. 1311; *Lee* v. *Enfield L.B.C.* (1967) 66 L.G.R. 195 (question of their *locus standi* left open). See also *Lee* v. *Department of Education and Science* (1967) 66 L.G.R. 211 (declaration).

44. *Att.-Gen., ex rel. McWhirter* v. *I B A* [1973] 2 W.L.R. 344; held that in the absence of such circumstances (for example, a clearly improper refusal by the Attorney-General to take proceedings), only the Attorney-General had *locus standi*. See Addendum.

45. See I. Zamir, *The Declaratory Judgment*. See also de Smith, op. cit., ch. 10.

of situations where an injunction would be inappropriate (for example, because there is nothing to prohibit) or could not be obtained for other reasons (for example, because the prospective defendant was the Crown). The rules governing *locus standi* are unclear,[46] but in practice they seem more liberal than in proceedings for injunctions. The plaintiff must assert a personal right or interest[47] of which the law takes cognizance; and there must be a genuine existing legal controversy which the courts have jurisdiction to resolve.[48] The declaration is also a discretionary remedy; thus, the courts may refuse a declaration if its award would serve no useful purpose or if there are more appropriate alternative remedies.

Subject to these cautionary reservations, there are few limits to the potential scope of declaratory relief in public law. For example, declarations can be obtained that administrative orders or notices directly affecting the plaintiff are invalid;[49] that conditions annexed to a grant of planning permission are invalid;[50] that one's products are exempt from tax;[51] that one enjoying a special statutory or public[52] status has been invalidly dismissed[53] or suspended[54] (though the courts will be very reluctant to make a declaration entitling an ordinary employee to reinstatement[55]); and that the decision of a tribunal is invalid for excess of jurisdiction[56] or breach of natural justice[57] or (possibly) that it is wrong in law, provided at least that the error is patent and the tribunal has power to rescind its determina-

46. Decisions on *locus standi* range from the illiberal (see *Gregory* v. *Camden L.B.C.* [1966] 1 W.L.R. 899) to the very permissive (for example, *Prescott* v. *Birmingham Corporation* [1955] Ch. 210).

47. See *Thorne R.D.C.* v. *Bunting* [1972] Ch. 470.

48. On exclusiveness of alternative remedies see pp. 606–7. On declarations (and injunctions) and legislative proceedings, see pp. 74, 87, 322, 396.

49. See especially *Dyson* v. *Att.-Gen.* [1911] 1 K.B. 410 (court had jurisdiction to declare that a tax form requiring submission of certain particulars under threat of a penalty was *ultra vires*). This was the effective starting-point for the rise of the declaratory judgment in administrative law.

50. For example, *Hall & Co.* v. *Shoreham-by-Sea U.D.C.* [1964] 1 W.L.R. 240.

51. For example, *Sebel Products Ltd* v. *Customs and Excise Commissioners* [1949] Ch. 409.

52. See *Ridge* v. *Baldwin* [1964] A.C. 40 (chief constable). And see now *Malloch* v. *Aberdeen Corporation* [1971] 1 W.L.R. 1578, pp. 581–2.

53. *Vine* v. *National Dock Labour Board* [1957] A.C. 488 (dock labourer); *Hanson* v. *Radcliffe U.D.C.* [1922] 2 Ch. 490 (schoolteacher).

54. *Barnard* v. *National Dock Labour Board* [1953] 2 Q.B. 18.

55. See, for example, *Pillai* v. *Singapore City Council* [1968] 1 W.L.R. 1278. For an exceptional case, see *Hill* v. *Parsons (C.A.) & Co.* [1972] Ch. 305.

56. For example, *Anisminic Ltd* v. *Foreign Compensation Commission* [1969] 2 A.C. 147. *Semble* if the tribunal has a record that needs to be quashed, certiorari (in the absence of a right of appeal) must be resorted to instead.

57. For example, *Cooper* v. *Wilson* [1937] 2 K.B. 309. Many decisions of non-statutory domestic tribunals have been declared invalid on this ground.

tion.[58] The declaration does not have to be accompanied by a claim for consequential relief (for example damages), nor is it necessary that such relief be claimable at all.[59] Indeed, it does not have to be a declaration of invalidity. A person may obtain a declaration as to his nationality or marital status. Declarations may be sought by one public authority to resolve a legal dispute with another (for example, as to financial obligations), or by a public authority wishing to obtain a judicial pronouncement as to the scope of its own powers or duties before it acts in relation to a specific matter.[60] And a declaration may be awarded as to the true construction of a statute or other legal document which is the subject of a controversy between parties.[61]

Declarations granted by the courts may be formulated in a number of different ways to meet the particular circumstances of a case. This is yet another characteristic of the flexibility of declaratory judgments. If judicial remedies in administrative law are simplified by amalgamation, this important feature of declaratory orders must not be lost.

Effect of alternative remedies

We have made several references to the exclusion of judicial remedies in the High Court by special statutory formulae[62] or the provision of alternative remedies. The latter type of exclusion is still important. Despite the presumption against excluding the right of access to the courts for the determination of civil rights and obligations,[63] there is a well-known principle that the *original* jurisdiction of the superior courts is ousted where a statute creates a *new* legal right or obligation and *that same Act* prescribes a specific method for its enforcement.[64] The method of enforcement may

58. This is a difficult question, still unresolved. See especially *Healey* v. *Minister of Health* [1955] 1 Q.B. 221. The main difficulty lies in the principle that an erroneous determination *within* jurisdiction is *not* invalid but binding till properly set aside. See also *Punton* v. *Ministry of Pensions and National Insurance* (No. 2) [1964] 1 W.L.R. 226.

59. This point is made clear by the relevant Rule of the Supreme Court (Order 15, r. 16).

60. See, for example, *Central Electricity Generating Board* v. *Jennaway* [1959] 1 W.L.R. 937, where the Board obtained a ruling on the question whether it had power (disputed by the landowner) to erect lines over private property. See also *C.E.G.B.* v. *Dunning* [1970] Ch. 643.

61. This type of question is regulated by other Rules of the Supreme Court (for example, Order 5, rr. 1, 4). Proceedings for this purpose are instituted by originating summons.

62. See pp. 351–2, 567, 571–3.

63. See pp. 349, 567, 568, 572.

64. *Barraclough* v. *Brown* [1897] A.C. 615.

be by taking proceedings in an inferior court or tribunal[65] or by complaint or appeal to an administrative authority or by the potential exercise of administrative default powers.[66] Particularly in declaratory proceedings or on applications for mandamus, persons attempting to obtain judicial declarations of their rights or the enforcement of public duties have often found the courts refusing to entertain their claims for these reasons. (In Scots law it seems that the courts are more resistant to this kind of argument.) But if it is possible to hold that the alternative remedy is only optional – for example, because *pre-existing* legal rights are in issue[67] or because the prescribed remedy is inadequate or less convenient[68] or if the interests of justice call for intervention by the High Court,[69] the result may be different. Moreover, even if the courts hold that their *original* jurisdiction to determine the issue in the first instance has been excluded, they can still exercise a *supervisory* jurisdiction after the appointed body or tribunal has acted, so as to see that the law has been duly observed. In exercising that supervisory jurisdiction the court will sometimes go on to declare what the correct decision is or should have been.[70]

65. For example, an income tax tribunal (*Inland Revenue Commissioners* v. *Pearlberg* [1953] 1 W.L.R. 331), or an industrial tribunal (*Road Transport Industry Training Board* v. *Wyatt* (*Haulage*) *Ltd* [1972] 3 All E.R. 913). See also *Department of Health and Social Security* v. *Walker Dean Walker Ltd* [1970] 2 Q.B. 74.

66. As with complaints about alleged breaches of duty by local education authorities (*Watt* v. *Kesteven C.C.* [1955] 1 Q.B. 408; *Wood* v. *Ealing L.B.C.* [1967] Ch. 364; *Cumings* v. *Birkenhead Corporation* [1972] Ch. 12 (though cf. *Bradbury* v. *Enfield L.B.C.* [1967] 1 W.L.R. 1311), or failure by housing authorities to provide accommodation for homeless (*Southwark L.B.C.* v. *Williams* [1971] Ch. 734)).

67. *Pyx Granite Co.* v. *Ministry of Housing and Local Government* [1960] A.C. 260 (property rights affected by planning legislation).

68. *Ealing L.B.C.* v. *Race Relations Board* [1972] A.C. 342 (council could test legality of its housing policies in High Court instead of waiting to be sued by Race Relations Board in county court).

69. *Enderby Town F.C. Ltd* v. *Football Association Ltd* [1971] Ch. 591 (dicta) (High Court could give ruling on difficult and important point of law).

70. As in *Cooper* v. *Wilson* [1937] 2 K.B. 309 and the *Anisminic* case [1969] 2 A.C. 147 (declarations as to plaintiff's rights consequential on declaration that decision of tribunal was void).

Chapter 28
Crown Proceedings

Aspects of civil proceedings to which the Crown is a party have been referred to earlier in this book. The Crown Proceedings Act 1947 made substantial changes in the law. Archaic forms of proceedings advantageous to the Crown were abolished;[1] various privileges and immunities of the Crown were abridged; the Crown was at last made liable in tort. But on a number of issues we have to look at the common-law and equitable principles evolved before the Act and left unaltered by it. Some of these principles are still remarkably obscure. New puzzles have been added by the wording of certain provisions of the Act; some of these are highly technical, and we shall not trouble to examine them in any detail[2] except where they are of general practical importance.

Contracts

Before the Crown Proceedings Act, claims against the Crown for breach of contract had to be brought by way of petition of right[3] in the High Court. The plaintiff was a 'suppliant'; the procedure was unsatisfactory – for example, the Home Secretary's fiat had to be granted before proceedings could be commenced – and too favourable to the Crown. The 1947 Act repealed the Petitions of Right Act 1860 and provided that claims formerly brought by petitions of right (with the exception of proceedings against Her Majesty in her private capacity)[4] were to be enforceable

1. In particular by section 13 of the Act and the First Schedule to the Act. For the old law, see G. S. Robertson, *Civil Proceedings by and against the Crown* (1908). The author of this treatise threw the discus at the first modern Olympic Games in 1896 in Athens, and also recited a Greek ode composed by himself. He died in 1967, aged ninety-four.
2. The leading works are Glanville Williams, *Crown Proceedings*, Peter W. Hogg, *Liability of the Crown*, and Harry Street, *Governmental Liability*. H. W. R. Wade, *Administrative Law* (3rd edn), ch. 8, offers a lucid review of the main features of the law.
3. Petitions of right also lay for recovery of land and chattels, for compensation due under a statute (for example, the *De Keyser* case [1920] A.C. 508) and in quasi-contract, but not for pure torts.
4. Which are maintainable only by petition of right and in respect of matters for which petitions of right could be brought. Section 39(1) and the Second Schedule

through ordinary civil proceedings against the Crown. These proceedings could be instituted in county courts; this was perhaps the most salutary innovation introduced by the Act. The substantive law of Crown liability in contract was left unchanged.

How far does Crown liability in this sphere differ from that of local authorities or private persons?

1. The Crown, as a corporation sole at common law, has a potentially unrestricted competence to enter into contracts, save in so far as it is disabled from so doing by the terms of a statute or an overriding common-law principle. Statutory corporations can contract only for purposes within the defined scope of their authority.

2. If the Crown is to be able to discharge its obligations under a contract, funds for this purpose must have been appropriated by Parliament. It is sometimes said that the Crown is under no contractual liability at all in the absence of such an appropriation.[5] This view seems to be correct only where a statute or the terms of a contract have expressly provided that the supply of parliamentary funds shall be a condition precedent to the validity of a contract with the Crown.[6] Normally there is, or course, no such provision. The proper analysis of the normal situation appears to be that if money is not made available to meet the Crown's obligations, the contract is not void but unenforceable against the Crown.[7]

3. Crown contracts are made by agents acting on its behalf. The agent

---

having repealed the Petitions of Right Act 1860, it is arguable that such petitions must now be brought under the still more archaic pre-1860 procedure. However, section 40(1) of the 1947 Act provides that *nothing* in the Act shall apply to proceedings against the Sovereign in his or her private capacity. This may well be understood to mean that the repeal of the 1860 Act does not include such proceedings. A petition of right under the pre-1860 procedure may still be brought under the Colonial Stock Act 1877 to sue for interest due from the Crown: *Franklin* v. *Att.-Gen.* [1973] 2 W.L.R. 255, 855.

5. See especially *Churchward* v. *R.* (1865) L.R. 1 Q.B. 173 at 209; cf. *Commercial Cable Co.* v. *Government of Newfoundland* [1916] 2 A.C. 610 at 617.

6. As was the position in *Churchward*'s case, where a long-term government contract for the carriage of mails was discontinued; the annual Appropriation Act indeed expressly stated that no more money was to be applied towards payments to Churchward. S.O. No. 96 of the House of Commons now expressly provides that in government contracts for the carriage of mails by sea, extending over a period of years, there shall be inserted the condition that the contract shall not be binding till approved by a resolution of the House.

7. See *New South Wales* v. *Bardolph* (1934) 52 C.L.R. 455 (Australia); Wilson, *Cases and Materials*, p. 502. For an incisive analysis, see Street, *Governmental Liability*, pp. 85–92. It is still not clear whether 'unenforceable' means unenforceable by the other party in an action or merely that judgment against the Crown could be awarded but not executed; if the latter is the correct interpretation, the position is the same as with any other contract with the Crown; see p. 616 below.

cannot be sued on the contract; only the Crown, as principal, is liable.[8] The agent's authority to bind the Crown may be express or implied. But what if the agent has no such authority? In private law the principal will still be liable if he has held the agent out as having the authority he lacks; this is called 'ostensible' authority. In certain situations a principal will also be liable if the agent was acting in the course of his 'usual' authority although that authority was neither implied nor ostensible. It is still unclear whether, and if so when, the Crown is bound in such cases. Possibly the Crown will be estopped from denying that its servant or agent has authority to bind it in these situations, provided that (i) the other party could not reasonably have been expected to know the limits of the agent's authority;[9] (ii) the limits of the agent's authority were not defined by legislation[10] and (iii) the Crown itself was not precluded from entering into the contract.[11] But nobody can be sure of the legal position at the present time. It has been held that if a Crown agent exceeds his authority and the Crown is not bound, the other party to the 'contract' cannot recover damages against the agent for breach of warranty of authority,[12] though the agent would be so liable in private law.

4. As we have seen,[13] the Crown is in a different legal position from other employers. The common-law rule is that civil servants hold office at the pleasure of the Crown and cannot sue for damages for wrongful dismissal, though they are legally entitled to be paid for the work they have done and

8. *Macbeath* v. *Haldimand* (1786) 1 T.R. 172.

9. In *Robertson* v. *Minister of Pensions* [1949] 1 K.B. 227 (not a case of contract) the Crown was held to be estopped from denying through one Department the binding force of assurances (about entitlement to a service pension) which another Department had given without authority but on which the other party had relied to its detriment. Even today the authority of this proposition is uncertain (cf. *Howell* v. *Falmouth Boat Construction Co.* [1951] A.C. 837). But it is to be noted that the Crown was entitled to give such an assurance itself. See also pp. 402–4 on estoppel.

10. *Att.-Gen. for Ceylon* v. *Silva* [1953] A.C. 461 (Crown not bound). In that case the agent had held *himself* out as having the authority he lacked; the principal would therefore not have been bound in private law according to the doctrine of ostensible authority. It has nevertheless been suggested that the Crown might have been bound if a superior officer had held the agent out as having authority; or alternatively that the Crown should have been bound according to the doctrine of 'usual' authority. See further G. H. Treitel [1957] *Public Law* 321 at 335–9; Griffith and Street, *Principles of Administrative Law* (4th edn), p. 265, note 3; Colin Turpin, *Government Contracts*, pp. 34–6; Hogg, *Liability of the Crown*, pp. 125–9. There are wide differences of opinion among commentators.

11. For example, because of a statutory restriction or the *Amphitrite* principle; see below.

12. *Dunn* v. *Macdonald* [1897] 1 Q.B. 401, 555, a much criticized decision, but applied in *The Prometheus* (1949) 82 Ll.L. Rep. 859.

13. pp. 194–6 and 200–201.

they can now obtain a statutory award of compensation for unfair dismissal. Military servants of the Crown cannot even sue for their pay.

5. In the *Amphitrite* case the rule that Crown servants are dismissible at pleasure was ascribed to a general principle of law that the Crown 'cannot by contract hamper its freedom of action in matters which concern the welfare of the State'.[14] In that case, which arose during the First World War, the Crown had assured the owners of a neutral ship that if it put into a British port with cargo, it would be given a clearance and allowed to depart. The ship was nevertheless detained and the owners brought a petition of right for breach of contract. It was held that there was no contract, first because the assurance given by the Crown was to be construed as no more than a statement of intent,[15] and secondly, because the Crown was incapacitated from binding itself in the manner contended by the suppliants, though it could have bound itself to perform an ordinary commercial contract. The decision raises a number of problems, and some critics have denied that any principle of law precluding a Government from fettering its future executive action exists. Nevertheless, there is no doubt that such a principle does exist;[16] the question is how to formulate it and determine its scope. The Crown, like other public authorities, ought not to be able to bind itself to abstain from exercising discretionary powers or performing public duties in matters of primary importance.[17] If it were to purport to bind itself in such ways, then the undertaking should be either of no legal effect at all or capable of being repudiated by the Crown when the national interest so demanded. But the courts must retain power to determine when, for example, executive necessity justifies the Crown in repudiating an ostensibly binding contract. It is not reasonable to insist that engagements with established civil servants must be subject to the *Amphitrite* principle – a point now indirectly conceded by the Industrial Relations Act 1971 – nor, on the other hand, does it follow that all commercial contracts are excluded from its scope (for example, in time of grave emergency). Where the principle does apply, the other party to the 'contract' has no right to damages

14. *Rederiaktiebolaget Amphitrite* v. *R.* [1921] 3 K.B. 500 at 503–4.

15. See also *Australian Woollen Mills Ltd* v. *Commonwealth of Australia* [1956] 1 W.L.R. 11. But in *Amphitrite* the ingredients of a contract were present.

16. It has seldom been relied on by the Crown in reported cases, and in *Robertson*'s case (see above) Denning J. held that it was applicable only where there was an implied term introducing it, but the principle was both recognized and applied in *Board of Trade* v. *Temperley Steam Shipping Co.* (1927) 27 Ll.L. R. 230 (charterparty of a ship to the Government) and *Crown Lands Commissioners* v. *Page* [1960] 2 Q.B. 274 (requisitioning of land in wartime and for some years after the end of the war); see especially Devlin L.J.'s judgment at 291–4.

17. See pp. 411, 589; and J. D. B. Mitchell, *The Contracts of Public Authorities*.

or compensation. It would be a useful law reform to give the courts juris-diction to award compensation (but not an injunction or a decree of specific performance) to a party damnified by the repudiation of a contract by the Crown on the grounds of executive necessity in cases where the Crown was initially bound by the agreement.

6. The Government is a large-scale purchaser and is often able to impose its own terms on a contractor. There is no special body of case law govern-ing the standard term contract;[18] the quasi-legislative character of such contracts should be recognized and their terms subject to a measure of judicial review.

Tort

Before the Crown Proceedings Act, the individual Crown servant was personally liable as a tortfeasor even though he was purporting to act in the execution of his official functions. But if sued he might not be able to pay the damages or indeed the costs. The Crown was immune from liability; the King could do no wrong and hence was immune from liability for the wrongful acts of his servants although in the same cir-cumstances other employers (including autonomous public authorities) would have been liable. Ministers and superior officials were not legally liable either,[19] unless they had authorized or otherwise participated in the wrongdoing, in which case they were personally liable as joint tort-feasors in their private capacities.

The Crown would often pay damages awarded against its servants for torts committed in the general course of their employment. It would sub-mit some claims to arbitration and abide by the result. If liability were disputed, it would sometimes put up a Crown servant as a nominated defendant though the real defendant should have been the Crown; and it would stand behind him. In two cases, where no legal duty towards the plaintiff had been owed by the nominated defendant, the courts disapproved of this convenient practice;[20] these strictures expedited the introduction of the Crown Proceedings Bill.

The Act preserved the personal immunity of the Sovereign. It did not state in general terms that the Crown was to be liable in tort; instead, it made the Crown liable in the same manner as a private person of full age and capacity for specified classes of torts which, subject to certain excep-

18. For an excellent study of what happens in practice, see Colin Turpin, *Government Contracts* (1972).
19. *Bainbridge* v. *Postmaster-General* [1906] 1 K.B. 178.
20. *Royster* v. *Cavey* [1947] K.B. 204; *Adams* v. *Naylor* [1946] A.C. 543.

tions, cover the general field.[21] The Crown is now liable for torts committed by its servants or agents[22] acting in the general course of their functions, and for breach of the common-law duties owed by employers and those owed by owners or occupiers of property. In cases of vicarious liability (liability for acts of a servant or agent) there must also be a right of action against the servant himself. Are public corporations administering nationalized industries servants or agents of the Crown? Almost certainly none of them is; the point is now usually made clear by statute, but even if it is not, they have the requisite degree of autonomy in relation to Ministers for them to be excluded from the category of Crown servants.[23] Certain public corporations – for example, the Supplementary Benefits Commission – providing social services may be in a more ambiguous position. So may incorporated bodies promoting or regulating economic activity as instruments of the central government. The Act providing for their constitution and functions is not always clear on this matter; a corporation may be a Crown servant or agent for certain purposes but not others. The question may assume practical importance only if the corporation is sued and claims a special Crown immunity (for example, from injunctions) or if the Crown is sued instead of the corporation because the latter lacks adequate funds. In determining whether a corporation is a Crown servant the court will scrutinize not only the constituent instrument but also the degree of ministerial control over the corporation.[24]

Section 2(6) has a curious look about it. It renders the Crown liable for the acts or omissions only of such of its officers as are (i) appointed, directly or indirectly, by the Crown and (ii) paid wholly out of central government funds. The main practical effect of this subsection was to exempt the Crown from liability for acts of the police.[25] Under the Police Act 1964, chief constables are now vicariously liable for the torts of police officers.[26] But section 2(6) leaves the Crown immune from liability for the torts of borrowed 'servants'.

The Crown is liable in tort for breaches of statutory duty in situations where breach gives rise to a right of civil action.[27] However, its position

21. Crown Proceedings Act 1947, s. 2. For commentaries, see note 2 above. Detailed analysis is not included in the text below.

22. 'Agent' was defined (s. 38(2)) as including an independent contractor (i.e. one who was doing work for the Crown otherwise than as a servant). The term 'officer' of the Crown includes a Crown servant.

23. See especially *Tamlin* v. *Hannaford* [1950] 1 K.B. 18.

24. See generally pp. 125 and 220.

25. Assuming, of course, that they were officers of the Crown. See ch. 17.

26. s. 48. They are indemnified out of local funds.

27. For those situations a student should consult a textbook on the law of tort. For a brief synopsis see de Smith, op. cit. (3rd edn), pp. 473–8.

is not quite the same as that of other public authorities on this matter. A statutory duty will not be held to bind the Crown unless it does so expressly or by a very necessary implication.[28] Moreover, the Crown will not be liable unless the statute is also binding on persons *other than* the Crown and its officers; there seems to be no good reason for this limitation. On the other hand, the Crown is liable for breaches of statutory duties imposed on its servants; this goes beyond the liability of other public bodies.

The Crown is not, of course, liable in respect of acts of State or acts done by virtue of the royal prerogative.[29] Section 11(2) of the Act provides that where, in proceedings under the Act, it is material to determine whether anything was properly done (or left undone) in the exercise of the prerogative, a certificate given by the responsible Minister that the act or omission was necessary for the defence of the realm or for training or maintaining the efficiency of the armed forces shall be conclusive. The exact effect of this provision, like so many other matters touching the prerogative, is obscure; the certificate will be conclusive of the facts stated but cannot conclusively determine, as a matter of law, whether the act or omission in question fell within the scope of the prerogative.

Under section 10 of the Act, no action in tort will lie against a member of the armed forces who, while on duty, causes death or injury to another member of the forces on duty or on land, premises or transport being used for the purposes of the forces, provided that the responsible Minister certifies that the death or injury was attributable to service for entitlement to a pension. Nor is the Crown liable in these circumstances. Similarly, no action will lie against the Crown for death or personal injury suffered by a member of the forces as a result of the condition of such land, premises or transport, or equipment or supplies (for example, through the crash of a defective transport plane or the premature explosion of a shell or food-poisoning in the cookhouse), provided that the appropriate certificate of pensionability is awarded. The right of civil action is barred even though in the end no pension is in fact awarded to the claimant.[30]

Section 9 excluded liability of the Crown and its officers in tort for any default in connection with postal, telephone or telegraphic services, apart from a limited financial liability for wrongful loss or damage to registered inland postal packets.[31] This immunity was justifiable on grounds of public policy; to introduce the principle of liability would probably encourage

28. See pp. 121–2, 124–5.
29. See ch. 4.
30. *Adams* v. *War Office* [1955] 1 W.L.R. 1116.
31. On the interpretation of this section, see *Triefus* v. *Post Office* [1957] 2 Q.B. 352; *Building & Civil Engineering Holidays Scheme Management Ltd* v. *Post Office* [1966] 1 Q.B. 247.

a great number of unmeritorious claims. Now that the Post Office has ceased to be a government Department and has become a public corporation, section 9 has been replaced by sections 29 and 30 of the Post Office Act 1969 which reproduce similar immunities.

The Crown is also exempt from liability for the acts or omissions of persons discharging or purporting to discharge responsibilities of a judicial nature or in connection with judicial process (section 2(5)). But for this subsection (which is presumably intended to emphasize the independence of the judicial function), interesting problems would arise in determining whether a person performing judicial functions was a Crown servant.[32] Individual liability is not affected, but the general rule is that judicial officers are liable (for example for false imprisonment, trespass or defamation) only in respect of matters outside their jurisdiction or, in the case of non-judicial *acts* within jurisdiction, where they have been actuated by improper motives.[33]

Subject to these exceptions, the tortious liability of the Crown is much the same as that of local authorities[34] and other public bodies. In other words, it is not set apart from the private law of tort. The doctrine of 'sovereign immunity', which in American law exempts governmental bodies from civil liability for discretionary acts, forms no part of English law. And, although in particular classes of situations liability without fault may be attributed,[35] there is as yet no *general* principle of English law that public authorities are liable without fault (as they are in France) for damage caused by an exceptional risk created by a public activity.

Reasonable care has to be exercised in the discharge of statutory powers and duties so as to prevent the occurrence of reasonably foreseeable damage to private rights or unnecessary aggravation of such damage as must inevitably be caused. But this general principle cannot be applied mechanically without reference to the context. For example, it would be futile for a farmer, whose fertile land had been compulsorily acquired under statutory powers, to claim damages for trespass against the acquiring authority on the ground that it was unreasonable to take his land. Even if the jurisdiction of the courts to entertain such a claim were not ousted by the provision of an exclusive alternative remedy (a statutory application to

32. cf. *Ranaweera* v. *Ramachandran* [1970] A.C. 962 (P.C.). Clearly officers sitting as members of a court-martial administering military law, and Crown servants such as the special commissioners of income tax, are officers of the Crown exercising judicial functions. Are judges officers of the Crown? And which (if any) licensing authorities exercise functions of a 'judicial' nature?

33. See p. 370, where references are supplied.

34. cf. pp. 404, 412–13.

35. For example, under the rule in *Rylands* v. *Fletcher* (1866) L.R. 1 Ex. 265 and in certain cases of breach of statutory duty.

quash the order within a limited period), he would still have to show that
the order was not merely unreasonable but tainted with a vitiating defect.
And there is a range of intermediate situations. Recently the House of
Lords held, on a preliminary point of law, that the Crown would be liable
for negligence in respect of damage to private property done by borstal
boys while they were making their escape after the officers responsible had
failed to carry out their duty to exercise proper supervision over them; but
it seems that their Lordships would not have held the Crown liable if the
conduct of its officers had been in the nature of a mere error of judgment
in selecting a particular method of custodial treatment or in directing the
release of a detainee.[36]

One final point should be noted. To cause direct economic loss by an act
or decision prompted by improper motives may be actionable.[37] Although
bad faith cannot be imputed to the Crown itself, it can be imputed to
officers of the Crown.

Procedure and evidence

Crown proceedings must be brought by or against an 'authorized Department' – the Department concerned with the general field of conduct
in issue; or if none of the authorized Departments is appropriate or if it
is not clear which is appropriate, proceedings must be brought against the
Attorney-General. A list of authorized Departments is published by the
Civil Service Department (section 17).

In general, the same periods of limitation apply to proceedings against
the Crown as against other persons. Damages and costs may likewise be
awarded against the Crown. However, execution of a judgment cannot be
levied against Crown property; this is not a matter of any consequence, for
the Crown does comply with judgments against it. Coercive orders – for
the specific restitution of land and property, for the specific performance
of contracts, and injunctions – cannot issue against the Crown; instead,
the court may make an order declaratory of the plaintiff's rights (section
21(1)). Moreover, the court cannot grant an injunction against an officer
of the Crown if the effect of granting it would be to give relief against the
Crown which could not have obtained in proceedings against the Crown
itself (section 21(2)). Interpretation of the latter subsection presents diffi-

36. *Dorset Yacht Co.* v. *Home Office* [1970] A.C. 1004; and see dicta at 1031, 1037,
1049, 1065–9. Nor, it appears, would the Crown have been held liable unless the
damage had been inflicted in the vicinity of the borstal and had been of a kind very
likely to be perpetrated by escapees. See further, C. J. Hamson [1969] *Camb. L.J.* 273;
G. Semar [1969] *Public Law* 269.

37. See *David* v. *Abdul Cader* [1963] 1 W.L.R. 834 (P.C.) (allegedly malicious refusal
of a licence by local officer). See also p. 412, note 119.

culties. It appears to preclude the award of an injunction against government Departments, those public corporations which are Crown servants, Ministers and other officers of the Crown for acts done in the purported exercise of their statutory functions,[38] save perhaps where the unlawful act is not merely *ultra vires* but also a tort,[39] in which case an injunction might be awarded against an offending Crown officer in his *personal* capacity if the act was far removed from his field of lawful authority. More liberal interpretations are possible. The state of the law before the Act was by no means crystal clear.[40] What is clear, unfortunately, is that where the courts have no jurisdiction to issue a final injunction, they have no jurisdiction to issue an interim injunction either; and although a declaration may be an effective substitute for a final injunction (because the Crown will comply with it) the courts do not issue interim declarations.[41] It would seem that unless the Crown consents to a specially expedited hearing of a declaratory action,[42] a person aggrieved may be unable to invoke the jurisdiction of the courts as a matter of urgency to restrain the Crown or its officers from inflicting irreparable damage on private rights by unlawful conduct.

A blanket exclusion of injunctive relief against the Crown and its servants is hard to justify. Mandamus (also a coercive remedy, disobedience to which is likewise a contempt of court) will lie against a Minister in his official capacity on the application of a person with a sufficient interest in the performance of the duty. So will an order of prohibition, and a statutory order to restrain the making or confirmation of a compulsory purchase order; these remedies are closely analogous to injunctions. The arguments against giving the courts a general jurisdiction to award injunctions seem to be (i) that injunctions cover a wider field than these classes of orders and (ii) that the Crown through its servants might find it necessary to

38. *Merricks* v. *Heathcoat-Amory* [1955] Ch. 567. See also *Harper* v. *Home Secretary* [1955] Ch. 238, where the question was not firmly decided. cf. Hogg, op. cit., pp. 25–6, putting the case for a more restrictive interpretation of section 21(2).

39. See, for example, J. R. Bickford Smith, *Crown Proceedings Act 1947*, p. 82.

40. The fullest survey is by B. L. Strayer in (1964) 42 *Can. Bar Rev.* 1. The Canadian Supreme Court held in *Conseil des Ports Nationaux* v. *Langelier* [1969] S.C.R. 60 that an injunction would lie to restrain the commission of a nuisance by a *public corporation* which was an agent of the Crown and was exceeding its powers. There was no provision corresponding to section 21(2) of the 1947 Act in Canada, and it is doubtful whether this decision could have been reached on the same facts in England, though the Supreme Court was purporting to apply general principles evolved before 1948.

41. *Underhill* v. *Ministry of Food* [1950] 1 All E.R. 591; *International General Electric Co. of New York* v. *Customs and Excise Commissioners* [1962] Ch. 784.

42. In *Marsh (Wholesale) Ltd* v. *Customs and Excise Commissioners* [1970] 2 Q.B. 206, where final declarations were claimed, the case was tried only three weeks after the issue arose. In *Lee* v. *Department of Education and Science* (1967) 66 L.G.R. 211, judgment was delivered within three *days* of the institution of proceedings.

disobey the strict letter of the law in an unpredictable emergency and ought not to be impeded or embarrassed by an adverse court order. But injunctions are discretionary and judges are not in the habit of ignoring the existence of a grave national emergency. In several other Commonwealth countries, injunctions can be awarded against governments and their officers in their public capacities.

'Crown privilege'

By section 28 of the 1947 Act the courts could make an order for discovery of documents against the Crown and require the Crown to answer interrogatories, but this new power was subject to important qualifications. It was not to affect any rule of law about the withholding of any document or refusal to answer any question on the ground that disclosures or answers would be injurious to the public interest; nor was it to affect any rules made to secure non-disclosure of the very existence of a document if in the opinion of a Minister it would be injurious to disclose its existence.[43]

The first proviso referred to the broad rule laid down in *Duncan* v. *Cammell, Laird & Co.*,[44] propounding the common-law doctrine of Crown privilege. The rule was not confined to proceedings to which the Crown was a party. In *Duncan*'s case dependants of men lost when the submarine *Thetis* sank on its trials sued the shipbuilders for negligence. The plaintiffs sought production of various documents in the possession of the defendants. Some of these would in fact have revealed unique features of the submarine which would, if openly divulged, have been of considerable advantage to the enemy; the proceedings were brought during the Second World War. The defendants, under Government instructions, objected to their production, and the First Lord of the Admiralty swore an affidavit to the effect that he had considered the documents and had formed the opinion that their disclosure to anybody would be injurious to the public interest. All the courts upheld this objection and declined even to inspect the documents. Viscount Simon L.C., speaking for a unanimous House of Lords, stated the principle at a high level of generality. Documents otherwise relevant and liable to production in judicial proceedings were not to be produced if the public interest required that they be withheld. The objection to production should be taken personally by the Minister in charge of the Department, or, if he were unavailable, by the permanent head of the Department. An objection properly taken should be accepted by the courts as conclusive. The test of injury to the public interest might

43. See now Rules of the Supreme Court, Order 77, r. 12(2).
44. [1942] A.C. 624.

be satisfied by reference either to the contents of the particular document or to the fact that the document belonged to a class which, as a class, had to be withheld from production. Examples of classes of documents which could properly be withheld were those where disclosure would be injurious to national defence, good diplomatic relations or the proper functioning of the public service. The public interest might well require 'a particular class of communications with, or within, a public department to be protected from production on the ground that the candour and completeness of such communications might be prejudiced if they were ever liable to be disclosed in subsequent litigation . . .'.[45] The same considerations applied to oral evidence of the contents of such documents,[46] but they did not necessarily apply to criminal proceedings.

It will be noted that 'Crown privilege', as thus formulated, was not confined to those proceedings to which the Crown was a party. Indeed, the principle was not so much a privilege of the Crown as an exclusionary rule of evidence based on the public interest, of which the Minister was deemed to be the sole judge if he expressed a view in the appropriate form; but if the Minister did not object, the judge himself ought to exclude evidence contrary to the national interest.

Probably no modern rule of English law has attracted so much criticism.[47] The courts had abdicated in favour of the Executive at the expense of the interests of litigants and the public interest in the due administration of justice. And privilege was claimed as a matter of principle for most classes of communications within and between central government Departments and many types of communications between Departments and outside bodies. In *Ellis* v. *Home Office* (1953), where a prisoner on remand, who had been assaulted and severely injured by a mentally disturbed patient in the prison hospital, sued the Crown for negligence, privilege was successfully claimed for prison medical reports on the assailant;[48] the action had to fail, and doubts were expressed by judges themselves whether justice had in fact been done.

In 1956, and again in 1962 and 1964, administrative concessions were announced: privilege would no longer be claimed for various classes of documents, including those in issue in *Ellis*'s case. The law was not modified, but the basis of the broad rule in *Duncan*'s case was being questioned. Critics harked back to a Privy Council decision (disapproved

45. At 635.

46. See *Gain* v. *Gain* [1962] 1 W.L.R. 1469.

47. One of the best critiques is by D. H. Clark (1967) 30 *Mod. L. Rev.* 489. See also pp. 188–9 and 481.

48. [1953] 2 Q.B. 135. Privilege was also successfully claimed for documents affecting international relations on an application for habeas corpus: *Soblen*'s case [1963] 2 Q.B. 243.

in *Duncan*'s case) where it had been held that the courts had an inherent power, exercisable in exceptional circumstances, to inspect documents for which privilege had been claimed and to disallow the claim altogether if it were clearly unreasonable.[49] The Scottish courts reasserted a somewhat similar residuary power (denied in *Duncan*'s case) to overrule a claim to privilege if the interests of the administration of justice so demanded.[50] In the mid-1960s, courts in some Commonwealth countries rejected the general rule laid down in *Duncan*'s case. And the Court of Appeal, in three cases decided in 1964,[51] began to undermine the authority of the rule in English law, declining to accept 'the proper functioning of the public service' as a sufficient reason for withholding disclosure and affirming that the court did have a reserve power, if dissatisfied with the Minister's reasons, to inspect and order disclosure. But the court refrained from overruling the Minister's claim in any of these cases.

In *Conway* v. *Rimmer* (1968) a probationary police constable had been prosecuted for theft; the charge was dismissed, but he was dismissed from his post soon afterwards. He brought an action for malicious prosecution against his former superintendent and in the course of preliminary proceedings for discovery, the Home Secretary objected to the disclosure of certain reports relevant to the case. His objection was made in proper form, particularizing the classes of documents into which they fell (confidential reports on police officers and reports concerning investigation into crime) and specifying that in his opinion the production of documents of each class would be injurious to the public interest. The House of Lords held[52] unanimously that the Minister's assertion as to the effect of disclosure was not to be accepted as conclusive; that although *Duncan*'s case was rightly decided on its own facts, the broader propositions for which that case had been regarded as an authority were wrong;[53] that the courts had a residuary power to inspect the documents in question privately in order to determine whether the public interest in suppressing them outweighed the interests of parties to proceedings and the general public in the unfettered administration of justice; and this power should be exercised

49. *Robinson* v. *South Australia* (No. 2) [1931] A.C. 704.

50. *Glasgow Corporation* v. *Central Land Board* 1956 S.C. (H.L.) 1; *Whitehall* v. *Whitehall* 1957 S.C. 30 (Wilson, *Cases and Materials*, p. 529).

51. *Re Grosvenor Hotel, London (No. 2)* [1965] Ch. 1210; *Merricks* v. *Nott-Bower* [1965] 1 Q.B. 57; *Wednesbury Corporation* v. *Ministry of Housing and Local Government* [1965] 1 W.L.R. 261.

52. [1968] A.C. 910.

53. If these propositions are to be regarded as part of the *ratio decidendi* in *Duncan*'s case, then the House of Lords was exercising its newly asserted power to overrule its own binding precedents. Some judges and commentators have regarded those propositions merely as *obiter dicta*. The present writer prefers the first of these opinions.

in the instant case. Having inspected the documents, their Lordships over-ruled the Minister's claim of Crown privilege and ordered disclosure.

This important decision[54] – the most striking example of judicial activism in administrative law since the war – left some questions unanswered. Five separate judgments seldom elicit a clear-cut *ratio decidendi*. Opinions differed on the criteria to be adopted by courts in evaluating claims to Crown privilege, but it can be inferred that judges ought not even to call for inspection of documents described as belonging to certain classes (for example Cabinet papers, and documents concerned with national security or diplomatic relations). Documents belonging to other classes (for example, concerning the formation of policy, or methods used in the investigation of crime) might be inspected but should not normally be disclosed.[55] Official documents of a more routine nature would be inspected and, if relevant, normally disclosed. It was still not clear what standards judges should apply in balancing the possible injury to the public interest caused by disclosure (or the prospect of disclosure) against the claims of the administration of justice in an individual case; or what criteria or procedure should be used if a claim for privilege were to be raised before an inferior court.[56] But there was no obvious reason for differentiating claims on a 'class' basis from claims for privilege based on the *contents* of a particular document. It had already been held[57] that a claim to exclude a subpoenaed witness from giving any *oral* evidence at all should be disallowed; objection should be taken to individual questions and answers on behalf of a Minister at the hearing.

Conway v. *Rimmer* appears to have substituted absolute judicial discretion for absolute executive discretion. There was no obvious reason why judicial wisdom and experience should be surer guides to the public interest on these matters than the judgments formed by the Executive. That Ministers and civil servants have tended to give far too much weight to the interests of secrecy and confidentiality and too little weight to the hardship caused to individual litigants can at once be conceded. On the other hand, the implementation of judicial policy is now unpredictable, whereas executive policy in relation to the withholding of relevant evidence was at least regulated by intelligible principles. Consistency is not an end in itself, but problems of such public importance ought not to be left to be dealt with merely on a case-to-case basis. A primary purpose of Crown

54. See D. H. Clark (1969) 32 *Mod. L. Rev.* 142; Hogg, op. cit., ch. 3.

55. Though disclosure of a report concerned with an investigation of a particular suspected crime was ordered in *Conway* v. *Rimmer*.

56. Clearly there ought to be a right of appeal or reference on this issue to a superior court before a decision to overrule the claim to privilege from disclosure is final.

57. *Broome* v. *Broome* [1955] P. 190.

privilege was to maintain the efficient conduct of affairs or 'the proper functioning of the public service'. Some important information cannot be obtained at all except under a pledge of secrecy. Many persons will not write completely candid appreciations if they have reason to think that their comments may be subsequently divulged.[58] To some people, including judges, who ought to know better, the latter statement is apparently incredible, at any rate when it is made with reference to civil servants. One can only reply by dogmatic assertions:

1. If, for example, a Department is to place a contract worth £10 millions, it must have the fullest possible information about the standing of potential contractors and any personal characteristics of their directors and managers which cast doubt on their suitability to be entrusted with a major project.

3. Similarly, if a Minister has to conduct personal negotiations with a group of people with whom he is unacquainted, he ought to be briefed by frank appreciations prepared by his advisers.

3. These comments will sometimes be disparaging and defamatory.[59]

4. They ought to be put in writing, not left to oral communication. Memory fades and Ministers change.

5. Senior civil servants do in fact express themselves on paper far more fully and bluntly on 'personnel' matters than, for example, local government officers or most university teachers.

6. The prospect of disclosure to the persons disparaged will tend to transfer comments from the departmental file to private conversations in the office or the club.

7. This tendency is not limited to a handful of moral cowards: many of us are afflicted with this foible.

And why do defamatory comments by judges in court, and M.P.s in parliamentary proceedings, need to be protected by absolute privilege?

Developments in the courts since *Conway* v. *Rimmer* have been surprising. In 1972 the Law Lords described the very term 'Crown privilege' as 'wrong', 'misleading', 'not accurate' and 'a misnomer'.[60] So perhaps

58. This point emerges in the selection of candidates for university places. Head teachers' confidential assessments are occasionally wrong-headed, but they are usually quite frank. Disclosure of such assessments would probably be self-defeating while we maintain a system of selective admissions, because some head teachers would 'pull their punches'. Testimonials for graduate students coming from certain countries where 'open testimonials' are the rule (and actions for libel against the authors of testimonials have not been uncommon) are seldom worth the paper they are written on.

59. There is admittedly a risk that disparaging comments will be unfair, irrelevant or founded on inadequate information.

60. *R.* v. *Lewes JJ.*, *ex p. Home Secretary* [1972] 3 W.L.R. 279 at 282, 289, 294.

we ought to banish the expression from our vocabulary. But in the case in question they were unanimously upholding a claim by the Home Secretary and the Gaming Board to set aside a witness summons obtained by a gaming club proprietor for the purpose of procuring disclosure of a confidential police report on him to the Gaming Board so as to enable him to prosecute a police officer for libel.[61] What they were trying to emphasize was that the withholding of evidence on grounds of public interest was not really a 'privilege' of the Crown at all. In two other cases in 1972 the Court of Appeal upheld claims by the Commissioners of Customs and Excise to withhold certain information supplied to them by traders in confidence for a restricted purpose.[62] There has been a belated acknowledgement that what used to be called Crown privilege can be justified in some circumstances on the grounds indicated above – that if certain communications were thought to be likely to be revealed, they would either not be made candidly or not be made at all – and that this might be a very undesirable state of affairs. Recognition of these elementary facts has also been shown in other contexts.[63]

The way ahead is uncertain. The problems of public policy involved are still fundamental and complex. It is easier to take refuge in platitudes such as these than to formulate clear-cut criteria for the regulation of judicial discretion. But sooner or later that task will have to be attempted.

61. There had been doubts whether 'Crown privilege' applied to criminal proceedings.

62. *Crompton (Alfred) Amusement Machines Ltd* v. *Customs & Excise Commissioners (No. 2)* [1972] 2 Q.B. 102 (documents inspected by court; non-disclosure upheld only on grounds of legal professional privilege); *Norwich Pharmacal Co.* v. *Customs and Excise Commissioners* [1972] 3 W.L.R. 870 (claim to 'Crown privilege' upheld). The House of Lords gave leave to appeal in both cases.

63. See *R.* v. *Gaming Board, ex p. Benaim and Khaida* [1970] 2 Q.B. 417 (p. 584, above); *Collymore* v. *Att.-Gen.* [1970] A.C. 538 at 549–51 (confidential information about industrial disputes); *Re D (Infants)* [1970] 1 W.L.R. 599 (local authority case records of children under care). See also, on natural justice, pp. 579–80 .

In *Blackpool Corporation* v. *Locker* [1948] 1 K.B. 349 it was held that Crown privilege could not be claimed by local authorities. Now it seems that a local authority may object to the production of evidence on grounds of public interest and that the material excluded does not even have to emanate from the central government (*Re D*, above).

Chapter 29
Redress of Grievances:
The Ombudsman and Others

Forms of redress against official conduct
Judicial redress

The main features of judicial review have been outlined in the last three chapters and need not be recited again. The most obvious defects are: (a) the centralization of the main forms of proceedings (other than actions for damages) in the High Court; this conduces to delay and expense; (b) the still quite wide range of unreviewable administrative action; (c) the difficulty in penetrating to the merits of an administrative decision; challenges to validity often have to be based on a technical procedural or formal flaw; it is very hard to impugn an act or decision for unreasonableness or even for an error of fact; the procedure of the courts is not well adapted to finding out the facts of a case, particularly where relevant material is in departmental files; (d) the limited scope of duties to give reasons for administrative decisions; (e) the fact that judicial remedies in administrative law are over-complicated and hedged about by restrictive rules, some of which are merely historical anomalies; (f) various gaps in the law governing the civil liability of public authorities; (g) perhaps above all, the fact that a successful challenge to an invalid order or decision may prove a pyrrhic victory; the winner may find himself back in 'square one', with a heavy bill of costs and no statutory entitlement to any form of compensation.[1]

Some defects have been eliminated or diminished since 1958 by statutory reform and changes in judicial attitudes. There is still room for much improvement. There is also strong resistance to significant change. In 1966 the Law Commission began a general inquiry into the possibilities of administrative law reform. In 1969 it published a report, recommending the establishment of a Royal Commission or a committee of similar status to carry out a detailed investigation.[2] The Government, however, was not

1. For imaginative proposals for reform, see *Administration under Law* (Justice, 1971). For the doubtful blessings of victory in the courts, see, for example, *Hall & Co.* v. *Shoreham-by-Sea U.D.C.* [1964] 1 W.L.R. 240 (plaintiff obtained declaration that conditions annexed to grant of planning permission were void; but the court refused to sever the conditions and the grant fell with them).

2. Cmnd 4059 (1969).

prepared to countenance any inquiry going beyond an examination of the judical remedies by the Law Commission with a view to evolving a simple and more effective procedure.[3] Proponents of larger changes fall into two main groups. First, there are those who think in terms of reform within the framework of the existing legal system; they may advocate amalgamation or simplification of judicial remedies, some extension of the scope of review and of administrative liability to pay damages and compensation, and the creation of a special Administrative Division of the High Court, which might include members or assessors with experience in public administration.[4] Secondly, there is a more radical school of thought, consisting mainly of admirers of the French *Conseil d'État*, who despair of piecemeal reform within the existing system and urge the creation of a separate administrative court staffed by members with specialized qualifications in law and administration and applying a separate body of administrative law. Only thus, so they claim,[5] can the law free itself from superficiality, burdensome precedent and inadequate fact-finding techniques and develop rules of administrative justice consonant with the needs of public authorities as well as the citizen. Their point of view has made little headway during the last few years, though it might be strengthened if the work of the Court of the Communities in administrative law – it relies heavily on the French system – were to make a favourable impression in this country.

Appeals to tribunals and Ministers

These have been considered in chapter 25.

Parliamentary safeguards

We have also considered the various opportunities to ventilate individual grievances in Parliament, and in particular in the House of Commons, by invoking the doctrine of individual ministerial responsibility at question time and in debate. Select scrutinizing committees concern themselves only

3. Extension of the scope of review was not within the terms of reference. In October 1971 the Law Commission issued a Working Paper, *Remedies in Administrative Law*, recommending the replacement of the non-statutory remedies by a unified 'application for review' (Law Comm. No. 40). The Scottish Law Commission issued a broadly similar paper (Memo No. 14) prepared mainly by Professor A. W. Bradley. The problem of remedies is less serious in Scots law.

4. See notes 1 and 3 above.

5. The most eloquent exponent of this point of view is Professor J. D. B. Mitchell. See his articles in [1965] *Public Law* 95, (1966) 15 *I.C.L.Q.* 95; (1967) 38 *Political Quarterly* 360; [1967] *Camb. L.J.* 46. See also *Let Right be Done* (Inns of Court Conservative and Unionist Society, 1966), pp. 16–23.

incidentally with *individual* grievances; and the Committee on Public Petitions, which might be expected to occupy itself actively with such matters, is almost a dormant body. Occasionally a parliamentary storm over an alleged scandal leads to the appointment of a special tribunal or committee of inquiry, but sledgehammers have too often been used to crack nuts.

Other safeguards

Letters to M.P.s (which may result in informal written questions to Ministers and, if satisfaction is not obtained, a question in the House), complaints to local councillors, to consumers' and consultative councils and committees linked with the work of nationalized industries, and to the Council on Tribunals; rights of objection at formal statutory inquiries to proposed administrative orders; opportunities to make informal representations against departmental decisions and proposals where no statutory machinery has been provided – these are among the media for voicing protest and, from time to time, securing redress in respect of administrative acts and omissions. The activities of national and local opposition political parties, of pressure groups agitating on behalf of their members, of the press and broadcasting media and of a body such as the National Council for Civil Liberties, and, at a different level, the work of the Citizens' Advice Bureaux, impose constraints on the exercise of public power and afford prospects of redress by a person injured by its abuse.

Nevertheless, in the early 1960s a widespread body of opinion had been converted to the view that a new institutional safeguard was needed. This development sprang from at least six sources. First, the report of the Franks Committee, and the detailed implementation of its recommendations, showed that a good deal of valuable work could be done in improving the facilities already provided in the area covered by statutory tribunals and inquiries. Secondly, it was noted that no comparable review had been undertaken of situations typified by the Crichel Down affair, where there was no machinery at all for statutory appeal against or review of discretionary decisions. Thirdly, there was a feeling in some quarters that Crichel Down was but the tip of an iceberg; horrendous things were being done to the detriment of the little man by faceless bureaucrats. To put the matter more conservatively, there had been an increase in State control and regulation of national resources and economic activity since 1939; the State had become a massive provider of social services and financial benefits; these developments seemed to be irreversible, and many cases of injustice arising from maladministration would surely occur. Fourthly, disenchantment with judicial and parliamentary methods of redress had grown. A new phase of judicial activism was about to begin, but commentators were more conscious of the long period of judicial self-restraint, particularly in relation to acts done by Ministers. Parliamentary questions and the like were of limited efficacy; it was noted that Commander Marten of Crichel Down was wealthy, well-connected and tenacious, but that even so he did not get his wrong redressed. Fifthly, the Danish Ombudsman, Professor Hurwitz, made a lecture tour in this country in 1958. Publicity was gradually built up; perhaps a cure-all would emerge from Scandinavia? Sixthly, the Labour Party was eventually persuaded to incorporate a version of the Ombudsman idea in its electoral programme.[6]

The Parliamentary Commissioner for Administration

In 1960, Justice, the British Branch of the International Commission of Jurists, commissioned a special research study of the machinery for investigating complaints against administrative acts or decisions in areas where there was no existing statutory procedure for dealing with them, and to consider possible reforms, with special reference to the Scandinavian Ombudsman. The study was undertaken by Sir John Whyatt, a former colonial law officer and chief justice. In 1961 the Whyatt Report, *The Citizen and the Administration*, was published. Its main recommendation was that a near relative of the Ombudsman be introduced into Britain. He would receive individual complaints against maladministration by central government Departments through M.P.s; he would conduct impartial and informal investigations and have access to departmental files; his status would be comparable to that of the Comptroller and Auditor-General; he might be styled the Parliamentary Commissioner. Unlike the Swedish Ombudsman, he would have no jurisdiction over such institutions as the Church and the Judiciary; he would not be primarily concerned with breaches of the law; he would have no power to prosecute public officers; his inquiries would not take place in a glare of publicity. Unlike the Danish Ombudsman, he would not receive complaints directly from members of the public and would have no power to order the institution of legal proceedings,[7] but he would have several common characteristics.

6. See further, Frank Stacey, *The British Ombudsman*.

7. There are substantial differences in the roles of the old-established Swedish and Finnish Ombudsmen, on the one hand, and the recently established Danish and Norwegian Ombudsmen, on the other. For surveys of Ombudsmen and similar institutions in various countries, see Walter Gellhorn, *Ombudsmen and Others*; Donald C. Rowat (ed.), *The Ombudsman: Citizen's Defender* (2nd edn). In 1972, such institutions were in existence in New Zealand, Guyana, Mauritius, Fiji, several Canadian provinces and one Australian state, and the idea was spreading more widely. For the Permanent Commission of Inquiry in Tanzania, see p. 26.

The Conservative Government rejected these recommendations as being irreconcilable with ministerial responsibility to Parliament and calculated to impede the efficient dispatch of public business.[8] But about this time New Zealand was taking the initiative in establishing its own Ombudsman, with power to receive complaints direct from members of the public.[9] In 1965 the British Labour Government published a White Paper proposing the appointment of a Parliamentary Commissioner for Administration.[10] The Parliamentary Commissioner Act 1967 was the outcome.

The Commissioner (hereinafter called the P.C.A.) is appointed by the Crown on the Prime Minister's advice; his salary is charged on the Consolidated Fund; he holds office during good behaviour, subject to a retiring age of sixty-five and a power of removal on addresses from both Houses of Parliament. His status is closely analogous to that of the Comptroller and Auditor-General; indeed, the first P.C.A. was the retiring Comptroller and Auditor-General, Sir Edmund Compton.[11] He has his own Office, and appoints his own staff subject to Treasury approval. By 1972 he had a staff of over sixty, drawn from the civil service: none of them, astonishingly, was a professional lawyer.

His terms of reference are to investigate complaints by individuals and bodies corporate (other than local authorities and other public corporations) who claim to have 'sustained injustice in consequence of maladministration', while they were in the United Kingdom, at the hands of scheduled central government Departments or persons or bodies acting on their behalf, performing or failing to perform administrative[12] functions (sections 4, 5(1) and Schedule 2).

He cannot act on his own initiative, nor can he be approached directly by a member of the public. He can act only in pursuance of a written complaint to an M.P. forwarded to him by an M.P. with the consent of the complainant. His investigations must be conducted in private, and the official head of the Department concerned and any other official implicated in the complaint must be notified and given the opportunity of commenting on the allegations. No set form of inquiry is prescribed, but the P.C.A. has adequate powers to investigate a complaint thoroughly. He can administer oaths and compel the attendance of witnesses and documents. Wilful obstruction of his investigations is punishable as if it were a contempt of court. His reports on investigations, and communications with M.P.s on

8. 666 H. C. Deb. 1125 (8 November 1962).

9. Parliamentary Commissioner (Ombudsman) Act 1962 (N.Z.).

10. Cmnd 2767 (1965).

11. For Sir Edmund's own account of his office and functions, see (1968) 10 *Jl. of the Society of Public Teachers of Law* (N.S.) 101. His successor, Sir Alan Marre, was formerly a senior civil servant.

12. As distinct from judicial or legislative. See pp. 333–4, 528–30.

the subject-matter of a complaint, are protected by absolute privilege in the law of defamation.[13] Irrespective of the Official Secrets Acts and the law relating to Crown privilege, he must be allowed access to any relevant document other than one relating to the proceedings of the Cabinet and its committees (section 8), though 'Crown privilege' may be asserted to prevent the P.C.A. and his officers from *disclosing* information thus obtained (sections 11(3)),[14] and the Official Secrets Acts apply to disclosures other than for the purposes of investigations and reports (sections 11(1), (2)).

The P.C.A. has no power to alter or rescind decisions. His statutory powers are confined to making reports on his investigations, or giving to the M.P. who referred the complaint his reasons for not investigating. Reports on investigations go to the M.P. who referred the complaint, and the official against whom the allegations were made and his departmental head. If it appears to the P.C.A. that an injustice has been caused by maladministration and has not been rectified, he may make a special report to both Houses; he may make other special reports, and must make an annual report, to each House. His special and annual reports are considered by a small Select Committee of the House of Commons on the Parliamentary Commissioner for Administration. Occasionally his special reports have been debated on the floor of the House. A considerable quantity of published material about his work is now available.

Jurisdictional limitations

'Injustice' and 'maladministration' were deliberately left undefined. 'Injustice' means something wider than legally redressible damage; it includes hardship and a sense of grievance which ought not to have arisen. 'Maladministration' covers a multitude of administrative sins, sins of commission and omission – corruption, bias, unfair discrimination, harshness, misleading a member of the public as to his rights, failing to notify him properly of his rights or to explain the reasons for a decision, general high-handedness, using powers for a wrong purpose, failing to consider relevant materials, taking irrelevant material into account, losing or failing to reply to correspondence, delaying unreasonably before making a tax refund or presenting a tax demand or dealing with an application for a grant or licence, and so on. The Commissioner is not allowed to question 'the merits of a decision taken without maladministration . . . in the exercise of a discretion . . .' (section 12(3)). He interpreted this limitation as

13. s. 10(5). The M.P. also enjoys absolute privilege in respect of such communications and in the communication of the P.C.A.'s report to the complainant.
14. It had been invoked only once in the first five years.

meaning that he could not consider whether a decision was manifestly unreasonable or even, apparently, based on a clear mistake of fact, if the appropriate procedures had been followed and there was no evidence of impropriety. He was persuaded by the Select Committee that in an extreme case he ought to infer maladministration from the 'thoroughly bad' *quality* of a decision;[15] but he has shown extreme circumspection in this matter. The Committee also persuaded him to consider the 'bad rule' – an internal departmental rule which caused undue hardship to individuals – and to find maladministration if hardship had arisen in a subsequent case arising under the same rule where it had not been properly reviewed by the Department. There are indications that his activities in this area have induced some Departments to re-examine their rules and give them better publicity.[16] The P.C.A. has also accepted that he can investigate the administrative procedures attendant on the making and review of statutory orders other than statutory instruments.

Among the matters excluded from his jurisdiction under the Third Schedule to the Act are matters arising in external relations and overseas territories, extradition, action taken for the investigation of crime or the protection of national security (including the withholding or impounding of passports), judicial proceedings, the prerogative of mercy, National Health Service complaints, government contractual and commercial transactions (subject to limited exceptions), personnel matters in the armed forces and the civil service, the award of honours and the granting of royal charters. Nor can he investigate complaints against local authorities, public corporations (other than instruments of the Crown) or the police. These are very big exclusions. If the subject-matter of a complaint lies within the jurisdiction of a special tribunal or a court of law, the P.C.A. has a discretion: normally he should abstain from investigating the matter, but he may waive the rule if it is unreasonable in the particular circumstances to expect the complainant to resort or to have resorted to the tribunal or court (section 5(2)).[17] We cannot all be experts in administrative law. In practice, wittingly or otherwise, he has frequently investigated complaints of procedural maladministration which would have been judicially reviewable. This makes it all the more incongruous that he should be so averse from treating manifest unreasonableness as maladministration. There is no bar to investigating matters that could be or have been raised at a statutory inquiry held on behalf of a Minister, provided that the inquiry leads to an 'administrative' type of decision.

Although most of these restrictions are uncomplicated, more than

15. H.C. 350 (1967–68), 11–14.
16. See Cmnd 4729 (1971), § 2; H.C. 72 (1972–73), §§ 19–40.
17. See David Foulkes (1971) 34 *Mod. L. Rev.* 377.

60 per cent of the cases considered by the end of 1972 had been referred back to M.P.s, because they were outside the P.C.A.'s jurisdiction.[18] In 1971 the percentage was nearly 64 – an amazing state of affairs.[19] Clearly many M.P.s were still failing to understand the basic features of the scheme, for over a half of the complaints thus rejected were concerned with matters not falling within the province of the scheduled Departments, or with personnel matters in the civil service and the armed forces.[20]

Evaluation

The Ombudsman was greeted by the sceptics as an Ombudsmouse. Following his special report on the Sachsenhausen case late in 1967,[21] when he found that Foreign Office officials had been guilty of procedural maladministration in dealing with an application by ex-prisoners-of-war for discretionary compensation for suffering caused by incarceration in a Nazi concentration camp, the ranks of Tuscany were cheering. The Foreign Secretary strenuously defended his officials and complained of an encroachment on the principle of ministerial responsibility, but still agreed to pay up.[22] Enthusiasm has become more muted since then. The volume of complaints transmitted by M.P.s to the P.C.A. dwindled from 1120 in 1968 to 548 in 1971, rising slightly to 575 in 1972 – hardly an impressive total for a large staff to deal with. Yet in 1971 he found elements of maladministration leading to injustice in sixty-seven of the 182 cases fully investigated. Most of the justified complaints concerned the Inland Revenue, a notoriously overloaded and understaffed Department. None proved to be of a really serious character.

The last sentence may give one clue to the reasons for the decline in the P.C.A.'s work. From him there have come no sensational exposures of bureaucratic turpitude or gross abuses of power. The general picture emerging from his reports is one of a high level of integrity (not to be confused with efficiency) in British central government administration.[23]

18. The figure was 2777 out of 4583. The P.C.A.'s reports and those of the Select Committee are published as House of Commons papers.

19. Not 44 per cent, the figure given in the Annual Report for 1971 (H.C. 116 (1971–72), § 5).

20. ibid., §§ 5, 6. The biggest single ground for rejection was that the complaint was against a local authority. But possibly the reasons for this absurd situation are more complex than indolence or carelessness by M.P.s. See Lionel H. Cohen [1972] Public Law 204.

21. H.C. 54 (1967–68).

22. 758 H.C. Deb. 107–70 (5 February 1968); Geoffrey K. Fry [1970] Public Law 336.

23. This is not to say that official turpitude is non-existent. Occasional prosecutions, and revelations of financial malversation in reports of the Comptroller and Auditor-General, show that it does exist; but all the available evidence suggests that it exists only on a very small scale at the central government level.

There are other factors impossible to quantify, which have contributed to the decline. The 'M.P. filter' has not worked well. The P.C.A. has placed a very high priority on cultivating good relations with heads of Departments, so as to obtain their cooperation in his investigations, but he is little known to the general public. He is a remote figure, neither seeking nor being accorded publicity.[24] His terms of reference are fairly narrow and have, on the whole, been conservatively interpreted,[25] despite the prodding by the Select Committee. Another possible reason for disillusionment or tepid enthusiasm is that a finding of maladministration does not necessarily lead to anything more than an expression of official regret or an under-taking that the Department will take another look at its procedures.

On the credit side of the balance, it is apparent that the P.C.A.'s investigations are extremely thorough.[26] Departments have often rescinded decisions, made *ex gratia* payments or refunds, waived or modified tax claims[27] in response to his adverse findings; they have been made more aware of the need for giving adequate and prompt explanations in response to requests and inquiries from members of the public. The Select Committee on the Parliamentary Commissioner, which has acquired a good deal of information about administrative procedures by considering his reports and examining senior departmental witnesses, has not been as inhibited as the P.C.A. in passing judgment on the merits of a rule or decision. It has been instrumental in securing a relaxation in the Inland Revenue rules for remission of tax arrears in cases of hardship,[28] though it has been unsuccessful in persuading the Government to sponsor legislation enlarging the Commissioner's terms of reference.[29] This is quite

24. His reports on investigations go to M.P.s; he does not give them any publicity himself, except in special reports and his Annual Report. Lack of publicity for the office probably tends to cause fewer complainants to *take the initiative in asking* M.P.s to bring their own cases before him.

25. Subject to exceptions, some of which (the 'bad rule' and the type of case where there might also be a successful invocation of judicial review) are mentioned below. There are others – cases where an action for negligent misstatements might have been brought (but the law on this matter is still developing), and cases where the complainant shows a *prima facie* case of injustice but cannot point to an act of maladministration, in which event the P.C.A. will often begin an investigation.

26. See, for example, Case No. 337/5 (Annual Report for 1971 (H.C. 116 (1971–72)), pp. 26–46.

27. For the dubious legal validity of some of these extra-statutory concessions, see *R*. v. *Customs and Excise Commissioners, ex p. Cook* [1970] 1 W.L.R. 450.

28. See Cmnd 4729 (1971); see also note 16.

29. Cmnd 4661 (1971), where the Government rejected its recommendations for an extension of the P.C.A.'s jurisdiction to include various personnel matters in the public service and the forces. For early appraisals of the Committee's work, see Geoffrey Marshall in Hanson and Crick (eds.), *The Commons in Transition*, ch. 6; Stacey, *op. cit.*, ch. 15.

undramatic stuff, but those who would write the experiment off as a failure would do well to read his Annual Reports and the Reports (with Minutes of Evidence) of the Select Committee. Some people have obtained redress which they would almost certainly have been denied had these institutions not existed.

To assess the impact of his work on civil service efficiency is impracticable. As he cannot deal with personnel matters or the most politically sensitive issues, there is no obvious reason why the knowledge that he has access to files should inhibit civil servants in expressing their opinions. There have been isolated complaints that he has made officers in some departments too non-committal. Complaints that he has heavily increased departmental workloads are unsubstantiated. Civil service morale does not appear to have suffered from his activities. He has been careful, as far as possible, to avoid identifying individual culprits in his reports, and in general he has shielded the service against sweeping and unwarranted aspersions. (This has indeed been the experience of Ombudsmen in several other countries.) Senior departmental officers, and Ministers, have been given a better idea of personal, organizational and procedural deficiencies at a lower level.

Although Departments cease to be monolithic under the P.C.A.'s scrutiny, the concept of individual ministerial responsibility to Parliament has not been undermined. The P.C.A.'s criticisms are indeed directed almost exclusively against officials, but the Minister remains politically vulnerable within the limits already explained;[30] and he is supplied with ample material for the meaningful discharge of his responsibility. There is no evidence at all that the P.C.A. has detracted from the traditional functions of M.P.s in procuring the redress of individual grievances. M.P.s have a wide discretion whether or not to pass a complaint on to him for investigation, as has unfortunately been demonstrated. He is able to obtain access to materials closed to M.P.s and has coercive powers that they lack. His criticisms of individual administrative decisions cannot be brushed aside as superficial or politically motivated. They have provided opportunities for well-informed parliamentary questions and some well-informed debates.

'After five years' experience of the P.C.A., any assessment of his importance in the scheme of central administration could still be no more than tentative.[31] That hardly anyone regarded him as a serious nuisance was indicated by the decision to make him the first Health Service Commissioner in 1973. In this capacity he will deal with complaints arising

30. See pp. 170–73.

31. See Paul Jackson [1971] *Public Law* 39; David Foulkes, *Introduction to Administrative Law* (3rd edn), pp. 253–63; Roy Gregory and Alan Alexander (1972) 50 *Public Administration* 313, (1973) 51 *Public Administration* 41; Cohen [1972] *Public Law* 204; Marshall [1973] *Public Law* 32.

under the National Health Service (other than complaints about the exercise of clinical judgment; and complaints against general practitioners, dentists, opticians and pharmacists, for which special machinery already existed) and he can be approached *directly* by or on behalf of a patient after the health authorities concerned have failed to satisfy the complainant.[32] This accession of work may at least compensate for the shrinkage of the job he was originally appointed to do.[33] And the scheme for dealing with complaints against local authorities[34] will be based partly on the experience of his office.

When a government of this country seriously addresses itself to administrative law reform, a primary source of information will be the reports of the Parliamentary Commissioner for Administration. In particular, he has exposed a number of situations in which administrative ineptitude has led to loss or hardship for which no legal redress may yet be obtainable as of right. Where it is proper to make an *ex gratia* award, it is often unjust that a remedy in the courts should be denied.

32. National Health Service Reorganization Bill 1973. See also Cmnd 5055 (1972), pp. 44–5, 55–6; National Health Service (Scotland) Act 1972.

33. Under the 1967 Act the P.C.A. has only a very limited jurisdiction in relation to Northern Ireland (s. 13). Northern Ireland legislation in 1969 set up an office of the same name with jurisdiction over matters within the competence of Stormont. Sir Edmund Compton was the first holder of that office. See Claire Palley, *The Evolution, Disintegration and Possible Reconstruction of the Northern Ireland Constitution* (1972), pp. 419–22. For the Northern Ireland Commissioner for Complaints, see p. 643, below.

34. See pp. 398–9.

Part Seven
Commonwealth Affairs

This Part has been compressed into a single chapter. It begins with some comments on the constitutional position of Wales and Scotland, and an outline of the status and problems of Northern Ireland. With England, these countries comprise the United Kingdom. There is also a constitutional entity called the 'British Islands', consisting of the United Kingdom, the Channel Islands and the Isle of Man. We shall note some of the peculiar constitutional features of the islands and their relationship with the United Kingdom.

Books and courses on constitutional law in this country used to include a lot of material on the British Commonwealth and Empire. The sun is setting on the British Empire, and although the United Kingdom still has a number of dependent territories they are mainly very small islands. We shall therefore dwell but briefly on the quite substantial body of general constitutional law relating to these territories, though we shall mention a new kind of dependent territory, the 'associated state'. Here the problem of Anguilla has posed some awkward constitutional problems.

Relations between the United Kingdom and the independent members of the Commonwealth are regulated less by strict law than by constitutional convention and political practice. Indeed, the Commonwealth, by the end of 1972, had become so loose an international association that it was doubtful whether one could reasonably speak of its 'constitutional structure'. Constitutional rules in Commonwealth relations are mainly about how membership is acquired and lost; there are few rules saying what members ought to do.

We have not tried to survey the internal constitutional laws of individual Commonwealth countries, save to the extent that they have a residual impact on United Kingdom constitutional law. Such a task could only be undertaken properly in a different and very large book; and it would have to be rewritten every few months if it were to be kept up to date.

Chapter 30
The United Kingdom and Commonwealth

The United Kingdom[1]

The United Kingdom means the United Kingdom of Great Britain and Northern Ireland and its territorial waters. It is a unitary sovereign State.

In 1284 Wales was annexed by the Crown. Effective integration with England was deferred till 1536, when Welshmen were placed in the same legal position as Englishmen, Welsh constituencies were given representation in the English Parliament and the English system of local government was extended to Wales. From 1746 till 1967 the word 'England' in an Act of Parliament was deemed to include Wales; for Acts passed since then this slur on the principality has been removed.[2] We have noted the existence of committees for Welsh affairs in the House of Commons.[3] There is an annual debate on Welsh affairs at Westminster. The Welsh Grand Committee is a deliberative body and does not consider bills at second reading; little use is in practice made of the 'Welsh standing committee' on bills, partly because few bills relate exclusively to Wales and partly because there is a permanent anti-Conservative majority in Wales, so that a Conservative Government's controversial legislation might flounder in that committee.[4] Administrative devolution is more important. In 1951 the office of Minister for Welsh Affairs was created; at first the office was combined with another departmental responsibility,[5] but in 1964 the Welsh Office became a separate Department headed by a Secretary of State with a seat in the

1. See D. G. T. Williams, 'The Constitution of the United Kingdom' [1972B] *Camb. L.J.* 266.

2. Welsh Language Act 1967, s. 4. Does Wales include Monmouthshire? There is no all-inclusive answer to this question, but under the Local Government Act 1972, s. 20(7), Sched. 4, it does geographically, though Monmouthshire ceases to exist as a local government unit.

3. p. 279; S.O. Nos. 62, 72, 73(2). See also Ivor Gowan in J. A. Andrews (ed.), *Welsh Studies in Public Law*, ch. 4.

4. The Local Government Bill (which became the 1972 Act) included provisions relating exclusively to Wales; on grounds of political expediency as well as practical convenience they were incorporated in the main bill. Only fifteen M.P.s for non-Welsh constituencies can be added to a standing committee on a Welsh bill.

5. The first Minister for Welsh Affairs was the then Home Secretary, Sir David Maxwell Fyfe. He was known in Wales as 'Dai Bananas'.

Cabinet. He has responsibility for primary and secondary education in Wales and a number of other local and regional services; most of the Office's work is done in Cardiff. There are also Welsh departments of some Whitehall ministries – for example the Ministry of Agriculture and Fisheries. Provision has been made for the use of the Welsh language in courts sitting in Wales, and for certain official purposes.[6] Welsh nationalism, nurtured on a distinctive culture, emerged as a political force of some consequence in the late 1960s. Further devolution of responsibilities for Welsh affairs is to be expected.

In 1603 James VI of Scotland became James I of England; this was a *personal* union and did not make Scotland and England one. In 1707 the Acts of Union created a United Kingdom of Great Britain, merging the Scottish and English Parliaments in pursuance of negotiated Articles of Union.[7] We have already referred to the controversy about the possible effect of the fundamental terms of the Treaty and Acts of Union on the sovereignty of the United Kingdom Parliament.[8] Scotland[9] has its own Established Church,[10] judicial system, criminal and civil law[11] (rooted in Roman concepts but now substantially influenced by the common law and United Kingdom legislation), local government and educational systems. Accordingly, a substantial measure of responsibility for Scotland's internal affairs rests in Scottish hands, though by no means enough to satisfy separatists in the Scottish National Party.[12] At Westminster a large majority of Scottish bills go to the Scottish Grand Committee and a Scottish standing committee, the part played by the House of Commons as a whole being little more than formal.[13] There has been a Secretary for Scotland since 1885 and a Secretary of State since 1926; he is always a member of a peace-time Cabinet. St Andrew's House, Edinburgh, is the home of the four sub-departments of the Scottish Office – the Department of Agriculture and Fisheries for Scotland, the Scottish Development De-

6. Welsh Courts Act 1942; Welsh Language Act 1967.

7. A. V. Dicey and R. S. Rait, *Thoughts on the Union.*

8. See pp. 28, 74.

9. Including Rockall: Island of Rockall Act 1972.

10. The Presbyterian Church of Scotland. The Church of Ireland was severed from the Church of England in 1869 and the Church of Wales was disestablished in 1914.

11. See T. B. Smith, *Scotland: The Development of its Laws and Constitution.* There is a separate Law Commission for Scotland and a Scottish Committee of the Council on Tribunals.

12. cf. Neil MacCormick (ed.), *The Scottish Debate*; H. J. Hanham, *Scottish Nationalism.*

13. See G. E. Edwards (1972) 25 *Parliamentary Affairs* 303; H.C.S.O. Nos. 62, 67–71; p. 278 f., above. The Scottish Grand Committee also considers the Scottish estimates. Peers of Scotland sit in the House of Lords. In January 1973 the limitation of the size of the standing committee on the Local Government (Scotland) Bill to thirty members led to a protest 'sit-in' by excluded Scottish M.P.s.

partment, the Scottish Education Department, the Scottish Home and Health Department. The Secretary of State also has responsibility for a number of minor Departments (for example, the General Register Office for Scotland, the Scottish Record Office), and for public corporations operating only in Scotland (such as the two electricity Boards and the Highlands and Islands Development Board). He also has joint responsibility for the Forestry Commission and the Crown Estate Commissioners. A number of United Kingdom Departments have regional organizations in Scotland with Scottish directors or controllers; the Secretary of State has a miscellany of coordinating functions. There are Scottish boards, councils or committees for some of the nationalized industries and other quasi-government bodies.[14] The Lord Advocate has a unique blend of responsibilities for the Scottish legal system, particularly on the criminal side. But there is a widespread view in Scotland that national identity should be more adequately recognized in institutional terms.

In the Plantagenet period Ireland was subjected to the overlordship of the Kings of England. Attempts to subdue its turbulent people were seldom sustained or efficacious. After the Reformation, Protestant settlement and discrimination against the Roman Catholic populace provoked insurrection followed by repression, more thoroughgoing in the times of Cromwell and William III than in earlier years. In 1783 the British Parliament purported to relinquish jurisdiction over Ireland; and for 'eighteen years Ireland was no more subject to England than was England to Ireland'.[15] In 1801 Ireland, which then had a separate Parliament, entered into union with Great Britain, and the Irish question entered into British politics. A hundred members of Parliament were elected for Irish constituencies.[16] Irish nationalism grew, and eventually Gladstone, at seventy-six, was converted to the cause of Irish home rule; but his party split on the issue – Dicey and Anson were among the more prominent Liberal Unionists – and his first Home Rule Bill was defeated in the Commons. The second was thrown out by the Lords. In August 1914 the Government of Ireland Act was passed under the Parliament Act procedure, providing for an internally self-governing, undivided Ireland, with its own Parliament subject to the overriding paramountcy of the United Kingdom Parliament. This measure, bitterly opposed by the Protestant majority in the province

14. See, for example, J. D. B. Mitchell, *Constitutional Law* (2nd edn); J. N. Wolfe (ed.), *Government and Nationalism in Scotland* (1969); Mitchell in Andrews (ed.), *Welsh Studies in Public Law*, ch. 5; J. P. Mackintosh, *The Devolution of Power*, ch. 6; Commission on the Constitution, Written Evidence 2 – the Scottish Office, the Lord Advocate's Department and the Crown Office; J. G. Kellas, *The Scottish Political System*.

15. F. W. Maitland, *Constitutional History of England*, p. 335.

16. There were also twenty-eight representative peers of Ireland in the Lords. See p. 299, note 8.

of Ulster and their sympathizers across the water, never came into effect. It was superseded by the Government of Ireland Act 1920, which provided for two separate (and subordinate) Parliaments, one for Northern Ireland and one for Southern Ireland. Because of an armed uprising in the South, only part of this Act became operative. In 1922 the Irish Free State (now the Republic of Ireland) was created and given Dominion status.[17] From then on,[18] the United Kingdom meant Great Britain and Northern Ireland.[19]

The constitution of Northern Ireland and the powers of its Government and Parliament were set out in the 1920 Act as amended by subsequent Acts of the United Kingdom Parliament.[20] In March 1972 the United Kingdom imposed direct rule on Northern Ireland; the functions of the Parliament and Government of Northern Ireland were vested in the Secretary of State for Northern Ireland.[21] There was no likelihood of a full restoration of the former machinery of government at Stormont. But on other matters the wisest prophet in 1972 would hold his tongue. Westminster had placed it on record that nothing done under the Act imposing direct rule was to derogate or authorize derogation from the status of Northern Ireland as part of the United Kingdom,[22] and a plebiscite on the border issue was arranged for 1973.[23]

Under the 1920 Act Northern Ireland had some of the trappings of an independent State – a Prime Minister, Cabinet and Privy Council, a bicameral Parliament (composed of a Senate and a House of Commons), responsible self-government, a Supreme Court with a Lord Chief Justice, and so on. The Northern Ireland Parliament had a general power to make

17. In United Kingdom law by virtue of the Irish Free State (Agreement) Act 1922 and the Irish Free State Constitution Act 1922. For the constitutional problems arising out of the legislation, see K. C. Wheare, *The Constitutional Structure of the Commonwealth*, pp. 90–94.

18. The exact date of the Free State's departure from the United Kingdom within the legal meaning of the latter term is not altogether clear. See K. O. Roberts-Wray, *Commonwealth and Colonial Law*, pp. 32–5.

19. Northern Ireland comprises six of the nine counties formerly comprised within the province of Ulster. The terms 'Northern Ireland' and 'Ulster' are, however, often used interchangeably.

20. The leading commentary, written from the standpoint of a moderate Unionist, is Harry Calvert's *Constitutional Law in Northern Ireland* (1968). No attempt will be made here to present a full synopsis. For an informative and close critique of events in recent years, see Claire Palley, *The Evolution, Disintegration and Possible Reconstruction of the Northern Ireland Constitution* (1972), reprinted from (1972) 1 *Anglo-American Law Review* 368–476.

21. Northern Ireland (Temporary Provisions) Act 1972.

22. ibid., s. 2; see also Ireland Act 1949, s. 1(2); Cmd 534 (N.I. 1969), § 56(1); Cmnd 4154 (1969), § 1.

23. Northern Ireland (Border Poll) Act 1972. See further Addendum.

laws for the peace, order and good government of the six counties. Appearances were not entirely deceptive. Various aspects of public law have been regulated differently in Northern Ireland. For instance, gas is not nationalized; there are no lay magistrates. In their own house the Northern Ireland authorities were, to a large extent, masters, till law and order broke down. But what were the dimensions of their house? Some features were clearly delineated; others were not.

Unless the United Kingdom Parliament otherwise provided, the Northern Ireland Parliament's competence was strictly confined to the territory of Northern Ireland (1920 Act, section 4) and did not include power to legislate repugnantly to United Kingdom legislation extending to Northern Ireland (section 6) or to make laws on 'excepted' or 'reserved'[24] matters – for example, the Crown, defence, international relations,[25] external trade, wireless telegraphy, air navigation, currency, copyright, the Supreme Court and the main forms of taxation. (When a Northern Ireland court held that Parliament at Stormont could not authorize the vesting of powers to disperse assemblies in members of the armed forces, Stormont was rapidly endowed with that power, with retrospective effect, by Parliament at Westminster.[26]) Nor could Stormont establish or restrict the free exercise of any religion or enact legislation discriminating on religious grounds (section 5).[27]

Financial relations were fairly complex. Income tax, customs and excise duties, corporation tax and other productive taxes were levied by the United Kingdom in Northern Ireland at the same rates as in Great Britain. The fraction of these taxes attributable to Northern Ireland was computed and returned to the Northern Ireland Government after sums had been subtracted for the cost of operating reserved services and for an imperial contribution made by Northern Ireland to the Exchequer. The United Kingdom subsidized Northern Ireland by grants paid to maintain the same level of social services as in Great Britain, and by other special grants. In practice Northern Ireland was and is heavily dependent on the United

24. There is no difference of substance between them. 'Reserved' matters were intended to be transferred to the Parliament of a united Ireland when partition ended. It has not ended.

25. cf. European Communities Act 1972, s. 4(3), empowering the Northern Ireland authorities to make provision for the implementation of certain Community obligations although the subject-matter would fall outside the scope of these powers under the 1920 Act.

26. *R.* v. *Londonderry JJ., ex p. Hume* (1972); Northern Ireland Act 1972. This preceded the imposition of direct rule by only a few weeks.

27. See also s. 8(6) on discrimination by executive action. Remarkably little use had been made of opportunities to impugn administrative action on this ground, but it was not clear whether the prohibition extended to local authorities. See *The Future of Northern Ireland* (HMSO, 1972), § 18.

Kingdom Government for economic purposes[28] – dependent, so it has been estimated, to the extent of some £200 millions in 1972.

The Governor of Northern Ireland was the Queen's representative,[29] appointed by the Crown after local consultations. By convention he acted on local ministerial advice. In strict law he could be instructed by a Secretary of State to reserve a local bill for the signification of Her Majesty's pleasure; this power was exercised only once, in 1922, and assent to the bill was in fact granted.

The United Kingdom Parliament retained plenary legislative powers in Northern Ireland (section 75 of the 1920 Act) and the powers of the United Kingdom Government were potentially unrestricted; but in relation to 'transferred matters' (i.e. matters assigned to Northern Ireland competence) the practice was for the United Kingdom to intervene only at the request or with the concurrence or acquiescence of the Northern Ireland Government. Nevertheless, even before orderly civil government began to collapse, the United Kingdom was able to exert some influence over Northern Ireland's policies within the transferred field because of Stormont's financial dependence.

During the period from October 1968, when communal disturbances broke out in Londonderry, till the suspension of Stormont in 1972, more constitutional and administrative reforms in Northern Ireland were introduced than in the preceding forty-eight years. The basic problem was simple to state, perhaps impossible to solve. Public life (and often private life) in Northern Ireland was dominated by sectarian faction and the problem of the border with the south. A million Protestants were overwhelmingly unionist; half a million Catholics were predominantly separatist and republican. Of the twelve M.P.s returned from Northern Ireland constituencies to Westminster, at least nine would be Protestant Unionists. The Unionist Party was permanently in office at Stormont; the minority had no prospect of attaining political power by constitutional means. In such circumstances the Westminster model of responsible government would not work in the manner familiar in Great Britain. By 1972 at the latest, as attitudes on both sides polarized amid mounting terrorism, repression and hatred, it had ceased to work at all.

In 1969 the main specific grievances of Catholics were found to be[30] the

28. See also Northern Ireland (Financial Provisions) Act 1972; and see Cmnd 4998 (1972).

29. On the imposition of direct rule he retained his office but none of his functions.

30. Report of the Cameron Commission on Disturbances in Northern Ireland (Cmd 532 (N.I. 1969), § 229). For a fuller study, see the Report of the Scarman Tribunal of Inquiry on Violence and Civil Disturbances in Northern Ireland in 1969 (Cmd 566 (N.I. 1972)). See also the Report of the Hunt Committee on the Police in Northern Ireland (Cmd 534 (N.I. 1969)).

allegedly discriminatory allocation of public housing; discrimination in local government appointments; distortion of local government boundaries (and restriction of the franchise to ratepayers) to perpetuate local unionist dominance; failure by the Government properly to investigate complaints of unfair discrimination; resentment of the existence and conduct of the Ulster Special Constabulary (the 'B Specials'), a para-military force; the existence and use of the Civil Authorities (Special Powers) Act (N.I.) 1922, a kind of permanent Emergency Powers Act.[31] A series of reforms followed, mainly prompted by Westminster, the United Kingdom having been obliged to send large reinforcements of troops to Northern Ireland in an attempt to restore order. Local government reforms, already under way, were expedited.[32] Universal suffrage for local electors was introduced and the 'business premises' vote for Stormont electors was abolished.[33] The 'B Specials' were stood down and the Royal Ulster Constabulary was (for the time being) disarmed; a new part-time local military force, the Ulster Defence Regiment, was formed;[34] the G.O.C. Northern Ireland was placed in control of the R.U.C. for security operations, with direct responsibility to United Kingdom Ministers. An interesting and potentially important innovation was the establishment of the office of Commissioner for Complaints,[35] who has power to investigate complaints of injustice caused by maladministration by local and other public bodies lying outside the jurisdiction of the Parliamentary Commissioner for Administration; he can receive complaints direct from members of the public, and if a complaint is upheld the person aggrieved can apply to a county court for damages and an injunction. Other reforms included the establishment of an independent Community Relations Commission[36] and the vesting of responsibility for prosecutions in an independent Director of Public Prosecutions subject only to the English Attorney-General.[37]

Reform came too late to satisfy the republicans, who had been brought increasingly under the sway of the Provisional wing of the Irish Republican Army. The situation was exacerbated by the introduction in August 1971

31. For the invocation of powers under this Act before disturbances began, see *McEldowney* v. *Forde* [1971] A.C. 632.

32. See p. 390. In 1969, moreover, the unionist-biased system of local government in Londonderry had been replaced by a Development Commission.

33. Electoral Law Acts (N.I.) 1968 and 1969.

34. Ulster Defence Regiment Act 1969; Cmnd 4188 (1969); Police Act 1969.

35. Commissioner for Complaints Act (N.I.) 1969. For description and evaluation, see K. P. Poole [1972] *Public Law* 131; J. F. Garner (1970) 21 *N.I.L.Q.* 353; H. J. Elcock (1972) 50 *Public Administration* 87; Claire Palley, op. cit., pp. 422–5. For the role of the P.C.A. in relation to Northern Ireland, see ch. 29.

36. Palley, op. cit., pp. 425–6.

37. S.I. 1972, No. 538 (agreed before direct rule was imposed).

of the large-scale internment of security suspects under the Civil Authorities (Special Powers) Act (N.I.) 1922;[38] and far-reaching proposals for internal constitutional reform in Northern Ireland[39] met with little overt response among the more moderate nationalists. Following the imposition of direct rule from Westminster, the situation eased temporarily, but the lurking threat of a Protestant backlash soon assumed a major dimension. Troops contrived to re-occupy the Catholic 'no-go' areas in Belfast and Londonderry and Her Majesty's Government governed again. Early in 1973 the Secretary of State was still walking his political tightrope. Internment by executive order, bereft of formal procedural safeguards,[40] had been phased out and replaced by detention in pursuance of a determination by judicial commissioners subject to appeal to a judicial tribunal.[41] Imaginative suggestions for the constitutional future of Northern Ireland were being canvassed; they included proportional representation in the legislative body, minority representation in the executive branch, an entrenched bill of rights, a loose consultative link with the Republic. Full integration with the United Kingdom, compulsory integration with the Republic, and independence for Ulster, were discountenanced.[42] The accession of the United Kingdom and the Republic of Ireland to membership of the European Communities, and the common interest of the two Governments in the suppression of organizations dedicated to the use of violence for the achievement of political ends, might mollify passions in the north in due course; but passions were already ablaze.

The Channel Islands and the Isle of Man

The Channel Islands and the Isle of Man are not parts of the United Kingdom, though in some legal contexts the term 'United Kingdom' is deemed to include them. With the United Kingdom they constitute the British Islands.[43] They are dependencies of the Crown, and belong to Her

38. For inquiries into complaints about the conduct of the security forces in connection with this operation, and in the shooting in Londonderry in January 1972, see Cmnd 4832 (1971) (the Compton Report), Cmnd 4901 (1971) (the Parker Report); see p. 172 above; and H.C. 220 (1971–72) (the Widgery Report).

39. See especially Cmd 560 (N.I. 1971), Cmd 568 (N.I. 1972).

40. cf. (1972) 23 *N.I.L.Q.* 331.

41. S.I. 1972, No. 1632.

42. *The Future of Northern Ireland*: a paper for discussion (Northern Ireland Office: HMSO, October 1972). See further Addendum.

The foregoing sketch omits references to a number of matters of general interest, such as the enactment of the Prevention of Incitement to Hatred Act (N.I.) 1970 which makes it an offence to incite to religious as well as racial hatred.

43. Interpretation Act 1889, s. 18(1). See also British Nationality Act 1948, s. 33(2).

Majesty's dominions. Although they fall within the definition of a 'British possession',[44] they are not colonies. Their status is unique.

The islands have other points of similarity. They have ancient institutions. Their affairs are subject to a degree of superintendence by the Privy Council, acting on the recommendation of the Committees of the Privy Council for the affairs of Jersey and Guernsey and for the Isle of Man, and petitions relating to matters arising in the islands may be directed to the Privy Council. The principal channel of communication between the islands and the United Kingdom Government is the Home Office, and the Home Secretary is the dominant figure in the Privy Council Committees, which hardly ever meet as deliberative bodies. Assent to local legislation is given by Order in Council and is not a mere formality. Modifications to measures passed by the States of Jersey and Guernsey are still sometimes made after representations by or through the Home Office. Control over Isle of Man legislation has been more freely exercised; bills have been dropped under Home Office pressure and in 1962 the royal assent was withheld from a Manx bill on wireless telegraphy. Public administration in each of the principal islands is conducted mainly through committees or boards of the legislatures; in this respect the pattern resembles that of a British local authority, and particularly in the Channel Islands there is no clear-cut separation of powers between Executive and Legislature. To a large extent local law is customary, lost in the mists of time. Appeals lie from the highest courts of the islands to the Judicial Committee of the Privy Council.[45] The United Kingdom Government is responsible for the defence and international relations of all the islands.[46]

44. Interpretation Act 1889, s. 18(2).

45. Appeals are infrequent. Between 1918 and 1972 there had been only one appeal to the Judicial Committee from the Isle of Man. From Jersey, there had been but one civil appeal since 1939. There are differences in judicial structure. In both Jersey and Guernsey there is a Royal Court, composed of the Bailiff (a lawyer and the principal insular officer) and elected jurats who are laymen. There is a separate Court of Appeal composed of barristers from the mainland. In the Isle of Man there are Deemsters who sit as judges, and a Judge of Appeal, an English barrister, who sits with a Deemster.

46. As far as practicable, the United Kingdom procures the insertion of a territorial application clause into treaties to which it becomes a party so that its obligations under the treaty shall not extend to matters lying ordinarily within the area of internal self-government of territories (including the Islands) for whose international obligations it is responsible. The treaty obligations will then only be extended to those territories with their concurrence. Today this is seldom practicable. Under international pressure and for reasons of self-interest, the United Kingdom often incurs international obligations (particularly under multilateral conventions) extending of their own force to such territories but dealing primarily with local domestic matters. The United Kingdom Government may then be impaled on the horns of a dilemma; either it becomes an international defaulter by failing to secure the *implementation* of the treaty

There are also important points of dissimilarity in status and internal constitutional structure. In particular, Jersey and Guernsey have full internal self-government and financial autonomy whereas the Isle of Man has not; the Lieutenant-Governor of the Isle of Man has active executive responsibilities as an agent of the United Kingdom Government,[47] unlike the Lieutenant-Governors of Jersey and Guernsey. In 1967 the United Kingdom Parliament and Government imposed on the Isle of Man the Marine etc. Broadcasting (Offences) Act,[48] outlawing broadcasting from 'marine structures' within the British Islands and the contiguous sea area. No similar imposition has been made upon Jersey or Guernsey in recent years.

The Channel Islands

When the Duke of Normandy became King of England in 1066, the Channel Islands were already part of the Dukedom; and when King John lost the mainland of Normandy, they remained as possessions of the Crown. These islands off the French coast now comprise the bailiwicks of Jersey and Guernsey. Within the bailiwick of Guernsey lie the only two other Channel Islands having a sizeable population, Alderney and Sark. Alderney has its own representative legislature, the States, and provides certain local services, but in 1948 responsibility for all the main services was vested in Guernsey. Sark, though nominally a dependency of Guernsey, is substantially autonomous. Owned by a feudal lord with anachronistic institutions, Sark ('where time stands still') is an anomalous survival of an age long past.[49]

The status of Guernsey in relation to the United Kingdom, and its institutions of government, closely resemble those of Jersey.

Jersey[50] has a Lieutenant-Governor appointed by the Crown, and insular

---

obligations in local law; or it infringes the canons of constitutional propriety by insisting on implementation, if necessary encroaching on the field of local autonomy. See further p. 648.

47. In the words of the Joint Evidence submitted in 1970 by the Home Office and Tynwald (the Isle of Man Parliament) to the Royal Commission on the Constitution, 'he is the head of the insular administration, his powers resemble those of an archetypal colonial governor, and he is subject only to the control of the Secretary of State' (Part B, s. 7).

48. Extended to the Isle of Man by S.I. 1967, No. 1276, in fulfilment of a multilateral international convention: see note 46 above.

49. In 1972 Sark (with a population of under 600) had no motor cars (though five of its residents were reputed to own private aircraft), no income tax, no divorce law and a prison for two. The octogenarian Dame of Sark continued to levy customary feudal dues from the populace and to exercise a formidable influence over local affairs.

50. See F. de L. Bois, *Constitutional History of Jersey* (1969) (Appx 1 to the Submission of the States of Jersey to the Royal Commission on the Constitution, 1970).

officers (the Bailiff, who occupies a position comparable to that of the Lord Chancellor or possibly the Lord Chief Justice, the Deputy Bailiff and the Law Officers) appointed by the Crown from among Jerseymen after local consultations. Administrative decisions are made by committees of the States, the unicameral Legislature. The closest approximation to an executive branch of government is an informal meeting of the insular officers and the presidents of the principal committees. The States are composed of the Bailiff, who presides – he acts as an impartial Speaker and has a power of 'dissent' – the Law Officers and the Dean of Jersey (who may speak but not vote), twelve senators elected for six years, twenty-eight deputies elected every three years, and twelve constables elected from the parishes. (Guernsey has two separate bodies, the States of Deliberation, a legislative body, and the States of Election, which deal with appointments.) There is universal suffrage. In 1969 allowances for the less affluent members were introduced. Legislation by the States falls into two main classes: Laws, which have effect only when assented to by Her Majesty in Council,[51] and regulations, of a more limited scope; the latter do not require the royal assent. The insular constitution is not contained in a single instrument, but much of it can be pieced together from Laws of the States.

The Crown used to legislate for Jersey by prerogative Order in Council; this power may well have been lost since the island acquired a Legislature with an elected majority.[52] Parliament retains, in strict law, plenary legislative authority for all those parts of Her Majesty's dominions which have not attained independence or over which Parliament has not renounced its sovereignty. Acts of Parliament extend to Jersey only by express words or necessary implication. The Act is accompanied by an Order in Council directing that it be registered in the Royal Court.[53] The insular authorities may suspend but not refuse registration; in any event, it would appear that such an Act is operative in the island of its own force. In practice, Parliament hardly ever legislates directly for the island; an Act intended to alter the law of the island will provide for its extension to the island by Order in Council made under the Act with such modifications of the Act as may be specified in the Order. Consultation with the insular authorities will then take place and an accommodation will be reached.

It would be contrary to constitutional convention for Parliament so to legislate for the island as to impose taxation or regulate matters of purely

51. The Lieutenant-Governor also has a power, no longer exercised, to veto a bill encroaching on the prerogative. Bills are called *projets de loi*. Transactions (including bills and regulations) passed by the States are also called 'Acts' of the States.

52. Under the rule in *Campbell* v. *Hall* (1774) 1 Cowp. 774, formulated in relation to colonies. See p. 652. However, an Order in Council establishing a Court of Appeal was made in reliance on the prerogative in 1949.

53. See note 45 above. A similar procedure applies in Guernsey.

domestic concern or derogate from the island's constitutional autonomy without the consent of the States.

Under ancient royal grants, the island has been given immunity from United Kingdom taxation – it has its own fiscal laws – and the right to duty-free entry of its produce into the United Kingdom.

The prospect of the United Kingdom's entry into the EEC posed a serious threat to the island's domestic autonomy. Under article 227(4) of the Rome Treaty, the terms of the Treaty are to apply to all European territories for whose external relations a member state is responsible. Unqualified accession by the United Kingdom would have entailed the economic integration of Jersey with the United Kingdom if the terms of the Treaty had been implemented in Jersey by the United Kingdom Parliament. They could not be so implemented against the will of the States without violation of constitutional conventions. In the event, a special Protocol was negotiated by the United Kingdom Government, whereby the Channel Islands and the Isle of Man were brought within the Communities for most purposes but exempted from the Treaty provisions relating to value added tax and fiscal harmonization.[54]

The Isle of Man

The island is situated in the Irish Sea. In 1969 and 1970 the islanders, like the Jerseymen, were seeking a redefinition of their constitutional position *vis-à-vis* the United Kingdom. However, the changes they sought in the existing relationship were larger; for the Isle of Man lacked a full measure of internal self-government. Apart from legislative controls exercised through Parliament and the Privy Council,[55] the Crown asserts an ultimate responsibility through the Lieutenant-Governor for the good government of the island in respect of such matters as financial proposals, the disposition of the police, the direction of the civil service and the nomination of members of public bodies. The Lieutenant-Governor is advised by an Executive Council composed mainly of chairmen of boards of Tynwald; but he is not obliged to act on the advice tendered. Tynwald, one of the most ancient legislative bodies in the world – originally it was a court – consists of two chambers, a directly elected House of Keys, and an in-

54. See Cmnd 4862–1 (1972), pp. 16, 17, 82–4. The islands had to accept the common external tariff, internal free trade and the common agricultural policy. Community rules on freedom of movement of persons and services extended to the islands but the islanders were not accorded reciprocal treatment in that sphere.

55. See Report of the Joint Working Party on the Constitutional Relationship between Isle of Man and the United Kingdom (Home Office, HMSO, 1969).

directly elected Legislative Council with a very small number of *ex officio* members. The island has its own system of internal taxation. Even before accession to the EEC the island was in customs union with the United Kingdom under the Isle of Man Act 1958 and received a share (about £4 million in 1972) of the duties thus collected for the island; it paid 5 per cent of this revenue as a contribution to the United Kingdom in respect of defence and common services (for example, overseas representation).[56] Insular produce was exported to the United Kingdom free of duty.

The constitutional history of the island is convoluted. Till 1266 it was under Norse rule; then it was ceded to the King of Scotland; early in the fourteenth century it passed, somewhat obscurely, to the King of England, who granted it to subjects, styled Lords of Man. In 1765 it was revested in the Crown by Act of Parliament.[57] The doubts still entertained by some Channel Islanders as to the legal omnicompetence of the United Kingdom Parliament over those islands are not shared by Manxmen.

In 1970, a joint standing consultative committee, to discuss matters of common concern, was established; it was composed of equal numbers of representatives of the United Kingdom and Manx Governments.

The Commonwealth
Terminology

The term 'Commonwealth' has no single fixed meaning. It is used in two main senses: first, to denote an association of independent member States; secondly, to include territories which are in various ways dependent on those independent members. The Commonwealth evolved from the British Empire, which came to be called the British Commonwealth of Nations in the 1920s; the latter designation was also ambiguous, usually (though not always) referring to the United Kingdom and the self-governing Dominions. In the late 1940s, after the independent membership of the Commonwealth had been broadened to include three Asian countries, the adjective 'British' was dropped from the semi-official name of the association; and the term 'Dominion' also passed into disuse,[58] the Secretary of State for Dominion Affairs being redesignated Secretary of State for Commonwealth Relations.[59]

56. For a synopsis of the position, see references cited in notes 47 and 55 above.
57. Isle of Man Purchase Act 1765. There is no corresponding or analogous legislation for the Channel Islands.
58. de Smith, *The Vocabulary of Commonwealth Relations* (1954).
59. In the late 1960s the Colonial Office was merged with the Commonwealth Office, and then the Commonwealth Office was merged with the Foreign Office under the Secretary of State for Foreign and Commonwealth Affairs.

Status[60]

The countries or territories of the Commonwealth (using the term in the broadest sense) fall into the following categories.[61]

Full Members. These are independent countries, equal in status with one another in Commonwealth affairs. They are the United Kingdom, Canada, the Commonwealth of Australia,[62] New Zealand, India, Sri Lanka (Ceylon), Ghana, Malaysia, Cyprus, Nigeria, Sierra Leone, Tanzania (Tanganyika and Zanzibar), Jamaica, Trinidad and Tobago, Uganda, Kenya, Malawi (formerly Nyasaland), Malta, Zambia (formerly Northern Rhodesia), Gambia, Singapore, Guyana (formerly British Guiana), Botswana (formerly Bechuanaland), Lesotho (formerly Basutoland), Barbados, Mauritius, Swaziland, Tonga, Western Samoa, Fiji, and Bangladesh. The Bahamas are to become independent in 1973.

Special Member. In 1968 Nauru, formerly a trust territory administered by Australia, became independent. Later that year it was admitted to what was called special membership of the Commonwealth, importing the same rights to participation in Commonwealth affairs as those of full members, except the right to be represented at meetings of Commonwealth heads of government.

Associated states. There are six Caribbean states in association with the United Kingdom – Antigua, Dominica, Grenada, St Kitts-Nevis-Anguilla, St Lucia and St Vincent. The Cook Islands, in the South Pacific, are in free association with New Zealand. None of these territories is a colony; none is independent; all may participate in the functional activities of the Commonwealth.

Protected states. These are not part of Her Majesty's dominions but are under British protection, which in all cases entails control over defence and external affairs and in some instances limited powers to intervene in internal affairs. The only remaining protected state in 1973 was Brunei (in Borneo).

Protectorates. Although not technically part of Her Majesty's dominions, most of the protectorates were ruled as if they were colonies; and if they had indigenous rulers (through whom the Crown exercised 'indirect rule'

60. The leading work on all legal matters concerning the Commonwealth is Sir Kenneth Roberts-Wray's *Commonwealth and Colonial Law* (1966). The Commonwealth is always in a state of flux, and a number of changes have taken place since the publication of that work.

61. The position here outlined is that obtaining in January 1973.

62. In Australia the term 'the Commonwealth' usually means the central or federal government of Australia, as opposed to the states.

over the territory) they were not given the jurisdictional immunity accorded in English law to the rulers of protected states. The only surviving British protectorate in 1973 was the British Solomon Islands Protectorate.

Condominia. The New Hebrides, analogous to a protectorate, are administered jointly by the United Kingdom and France. Sovereignty in the Canton and Enderbury Islands is shared between the United Kingdom and the United States.

Colonies. All the remaining colonies at the end of 1972 were islands or island groups, except Southern Rhodesia,[63] Gibraltar, British Honduras and the British Antarctic Territory. With the exception of Hong Kong (likely in due course to be retroceded to China) and Southern Rhodesia (which had purported unilaterally to declare its independence in November 1965) none had a population as high as 200,000.

Trust territory. Under the Covenant of the League of Nations, dependencies detached from the countries defeated in the First World War were placed under the administration of developed countries as mandated territories. The United Kingdom, Australia, New Zealand and South Africa became mandatories. After the Second World War, the mandated territories that had not yet achieved independence were brought under the United Nations trusteeship system, with the sole exception of South-West Africa which has been in substance (though not in form) annexed by South Africa. The United Kingdom's trust territories have all attained to independence in one manifestation or another; they had been administered as if they were protected states or protectorates. The only remaining trust territory in the Commonwealth in 1973 was New Guinea, administered by Australia.[64]

Miscellaneous. Australia and New Zealand have several small dependencies.[65]

Constitutional aspects of dependence

The large corpus of constitutional law relating to British dependent territories has dwindled in practical importance. Here it will be dealt with only in outline or selectively.

At several points in this book, reference has been made to protected states, protectorates and the status of British protected persons.[66] Only

63. Which was still a colony in strict law: Southern Rhodesia Act 1965; *Madzimbamuto* v. *Lardner-Burke* [1969] 1 A.C. 645; p. 667, note 120 below.

64. Conjointly with the dependent territory of Papua. It was likely that Papua New Guinea would become independent by 1975.

65. Roberts-Wray, op. cit., p. 88.

66. For example, pp. 129, 130, 138–9, 422, 438, 440.

two matters need to be emphasized. First, the legislative, executive and judicial powers of the Crown in protected states and protectorates are exercised by virtue of the royal prerogative as regulated by the Foreign Jurisdiction Acts 1890 and 1913. Secondly, since the authority claimed and exercised by the Crown in relation to *protected states* is often very restricted, a protected state may accede to independence merely by an agreement between the Crown and the local ruler that protection be removed, though consequential legislation may be needed to modify some rules of English law.

Colonies have traditionally been classified, for the purposes of both public law and private law, according to the methods by which they were acquired. Settled colonies were territories without a regular 'civilized' system of government when occupied by British settlers and annexed by the Crown; they included a number of territories in Australia, North America and the Caribbean. The prerogative powers of the Crown in a settled colony are narrowly circumscribed,[67] but legislative power over a settled colony which did not receive a representative legislature under the prerogative can be exercised under the British Settlements Acts 1887 and 1945.[68] The general rule is that the settlers carried the common law of England with them.

Conquered or ceded colonies were territories taken from another metropolitan power or an indigenous ruler and placed under the sovereignty of the Crown. The terms of a treaty of cession are not legally binding on the Crown unless incorporated in legislation. The Crown has plenary prerogative legislative powers with respect to such a colony, subject to the rule in *Campbell* v. *Hall* (1774)[69] – that if it grants a representative legislature to the colony (i.e., one in which at least half the members of one House are elected)[70] it cannot derogate from that grant and thus loses that prerogative power unless (as is usually the case) it has expressly reserved the power when granting the constitution. If the prerogative power has been lost but representative institutions are later revoked by statutory authority, the prerogative revives.[71] In conquered or ceded colonies, the basis of the pre-existing legal system usually survived; hence, for example,

67. They are usually stated as covering power to appoint a Governor, an Executive Council and officials and to provide for the establishment of courts to administer the common law (but not another system of law – for example, ecclesiastical law: *Re Lord Bishop of Natal* (1864) 3 Moo. P.C.C. (N.S.) 115) and a representative legislature.

68. See further *Sabally and N'Jie* v. *Att.-Gen.* [1965] 1 Q.B. 273 (Orders in Council made thereunder may be given retroactive effect; validation of elections in Gambia).

69. 1 Cowp. 204.

70. This is the definition adopted for the purposes of the Colonial Laws Validity Act 1865. In other contexts the meaning is not necessarily uniform.

71. *Sammut* v. *Strickland* [1938] A.C. 678.

the retention of Roman–Dutch law in Ceylon and French law in Quebec and Mauritius.

There is also a residual category of colonies which were merely annexed without settlement, conquest or cession. To this class belong the Falkland Islands and the British Antarctic Territory.

Constitutional changes in dependent territories are normally made by Orders in Council – under statutory powers in protectorates and settled colonies and under prerogative powers in conquered and ceded colonies. If a colony with a representative legislature has power to alter the composition, powers and procedure of that legislature, the amendments must be made in the manner and form required by existing law.[72] In practice, major constitutional changes are made by agreement after discussions or a conference with the United Kingdom Government.

The following is a typical sketch of constitutional evolution towards internal self-government.[73] There is no set pattern: trends of development have varied a great deal according to changing ideas at different periods of imperial history and the particular circumstances of individual territories.[74]

A colony will have a Governor, who is the Queen's representative and the instrument of the United Kingdom Government. He will not enjoy, at common law, the legal immunities of the monarch.[75] His powers will be laid down in the constituent instruments of the colony (normally a Constitution Order in Council and Royal Instructions) and in imperial and local legislation. He will have very far-reaching executive powers. He will be advised by an Executive Council, which will initially consist of British colonial officials and other members nominated by him; he will be free to reject the Council's advice. There will be a Legislative Council, in which elected members will be in a minority during the early stages of constitutional development.

The Legislative Council will then acquire a majority of elected members.[76]

72. Colonial Laws Validity Act 1865, s. 5; see *Att.-Gen. for N.S.W.* v. *Trethowan* [1932] A.C. 526, and the analysis of the scope of section 5 by Roberts-Wray, op. cit., pp. 403–5.

73. See further de Smith, *The New Commonwealth and its Constitutions*, ch. 2; Sir Ivor Jennings, *The Approach to Self-Government*; H. V. Wiseman, *The Cabinet in the Commonwealth*.

74. See, for example, the following works on individual countries: B. O. Nwabueze, *Constitutional Law of the Nigerian Republic*; H. F. Morris and J. S. Read, *Uganda: the Development of its Laws and Constitution*; Sir Ivor Jennings, *Constitution of Ceylon* (3rd edn); Claire Palley, *Constitutional History and Law of Southern Rhodesia, 1888–1965*; Y. P. Ghai and J. P. W. B. McAuslan, *Public Law and Political Change in Kenya*.

75. *Mostyn* v. *Fabrigas* (1774) 1 Cowp. 161; *Musgrave* v. *Pulido* (1879) 5 App. Cas. 102. 'Act of State' cannot be pleaded by way of defence merely because the defendant is a Governor.

76. For an authoritative and detailed comparative analysis of early constitutional

At the same time, other changes are likely to take place. A substantial element of elected non-officials will be introduced into the Executive Council, perhaps with the title of Ministers; the Governor will normally be required to consult the Executive Council in exercising his powers unless the matter is too urgent, trivial or secret, and to act on its advice unless there are strong grounds for not doing so; he will probably cease to act as Speaker of the Legislative Council; the constitution may vest in him a reserved legislative power to enact important measures which the Legislative Council refuses to pass. The next step may be to designate an elected member as Chief Minister, to eliminate nearly all official members from the Legislative Council, to place them in a minority in the Executive Council, and to remove the Governor's reserved legislative power. And then, in what is usually the last stage before independence, the Executive Council is redesignated as the Council of Ministers or Cabinet, presided over by the Premier instead of the Governor; the Governor's personal discretionary powers are confined to such matters as defence, external affairs, internal security and expatriate civil servants; for other purposes (apart from appointment and removal of a Premier and dissolution of the Legislature) the Governor will have to act on advice; control over judicial appointments and matters affecting judicial officers,[77] locally recruited members of the public service and police appointments and discipline will be vested in independent service commissions. This is a basic framework of internal self-government. Paths of constitutional development may diverge if a territory has extensive European settlement or is deeply riven by communal dissensions or is very small in population or has exceptional strategic importance or if sovereignty over it is disputed by another independent State.

Colonial legislatures have a general power to make laws for the peace, order and good government of the colony. Legislation cannot be impugned on the ground that it is manifestly unreasonable[78] or that it delegates legislative power to the Governor or another body within the colony; a colonial legislature is not itself a delegate[79] and it is 'sovereign within its own sphere'. There will, however, be a number of controls, both

---

development, see Martin Wight, *Development of the Legislative Council, 1606–1945*. See also ibid., *British Colonial Constitutions 1947*, Introduction.

77. For judicial *tenure* under modern Commonwealth constitutions, see p. 149. For the former legal position, see Roberts-Wray, op. cit., pp. 492–7, and *Terrell* v. *Secretary of State for the Colonies* [1953] 2 Q.B. 482 (terminability at pleasure).

78. *Riel* v. *R.* (1885) 10 App. Cas. 675.

79. *Hodge* v. *R.* (1883) 9 App. Cas. 117; *Powell* v. *Apollo Candle Co.* (1885) 10 App. Cas. 282; *R.* v. *Burah* (1878) 3 App. Cas. 889. Hence the maxim *delegatus non potest delegare* does not apply to its enactments.

internal and external, over the exercise of legislative power. The Governor's reserved legislative power and the influence of non-elected members in the Legislative Council will have disappeared before internal self-government is achieved; and at that stage the Governor's power to refuse the royal assent to a bill or ordinance will normally be exercisable only on ministerial advice. His exclusive initiative in recommending financial proposals will have been vested in Ministers. The following restrictions are likely to continue:

1. Provisions for the Governor to reserve certain classes of bills[80] for the signification of Her Majesty's pleasure through a Secretary of State. Before internal self-government the Governor is likely to have (a) a general power to reserve any bill and (b) an obligation to reserve certain classes of bills. Royal assent to a reserved bill can be refused.

2. Provision for the disallowance, by the Crown, of bills already assented to by the Governor. At the stage of internal self-government the power of disallowance may be restricted to a narrow range of legislation.[81]

3. Constitutional guarantees and prohibitions. These will generally include a bill of rights.

4. Absence of power to legislate repugnantly to United Kingdom legislation extending to the colony. This is a general common-law rule, restated by section 2 of the Colonial Laws Validity Act 1865. For this reason alone it was constitutionally impossible for the colony of Southern Rhodesia to proclaim independence in 1965.

5. Lack of plenary authority to make law with extraterritorial effect. This restriction has often been exaggerated.[82] The better opinion is that a colonial legislature *is* competent to make laws having effect outside the territorial limits of the colony, provided that those laws bear directly on the peace, order and good government of the colony[83] – for example, because they relate to acts and transactions within the colony or are performed by persons or bodies corporate ordinarily resident in the colony.[84]

80. For example, bills encroaching on the prerogative, amending the constitution or affecting international obligations.
81. For example, to Acts disadvantageously affecting the terms on which colonial stock is held.
82. As in the Privy Council decision in *Macleod* v. *Att.-Gen. for N.S.W.* [1891] A.C. 455 (conviction for bigamy, the second marriage having been contracted outside the colony, quashed).
83. See *Att.-Gen. for Canada* v. *Cain* [1906] A.C. 542; *Croft* v. *Dunphy* [1933] A.C. 156.
84. D. P. O'Connell (1959) 75 *L.Q.R.* 318. cf. Alex Castles [1962] *Public Law* at 196–200; F. A. Trindade (1971) 45 *Australian L.J.* 233.

In addition, local autonomy will be limited by the United Kingdom's continuing responsibilities for the external affairs and defence of the colony and by the paramount legislative authority of the United Kingdom Parliament. Moreover, under the majority of colonial constitutions conferring internal self-government, Her Majesty in Council retains full statutory or prerogative power to change the constitution and to legislate for the colony.

Dominion status and independence

The following is a description of the typical mechanism for the attainment of independence by an internally self-governing colony.

1. An independence conference is held in London, to determine the date of independence, the content of the independence constitution (which is likely to bear a close similarity to the self-government constitution) and consequential matters – for example, questions of nationality and citizenship.

2. A public officers' agreement, *inter alia*, facilitating the retirement, with special compensation, of expatriate officers serving locally who do not wish to continue under the new régime,[85] and an agreement for state succession to existing international obligations, will be negotiated after the introduction of self-government, to come into effect upon the date of independence.

3. An independence Act will be passed by the United Kingdom Parliament. This will be brought into effect on the 'appointed day' (independence day). It will include the following provisions:

(i) Termination of all authority and responsibility of the United Kingdom Government for the affairs of the territory.

(ii) Total abrogation of the power of the United Kingdom Parliament to make laws for the territory.[86]

(iii) Adaptations of United Kingdom law relating to nationality, citizenship and certain other matters.

(iv) Exclusion of the territory from the expression 'colony' used in United Kingdom legislation.

85. Roberts-Wray, op. cit., pp. 287–8. The agreement will deal with other questions and may be given legal effect under the independence constitution.

86. See p. 78. The power of the United Kingdom Parliament to alter the law of the territory at its request and with its consent does not appear in any *independence* Act since 1957. cf., however, the West Indies Act 1967, pp. 662–3 below.

(v) A schedule providing for
(a) repeal of the Colonial Laws Validity Act 1865 in relation to the territory;
(b) abolition of the doctrine of repugnancy to United Kingdom legislation, and conferment of authority on the local Legislature to make laws (subject to the constitution) inconsistent with United Kingdom legislation extending to the territory, including the Independence Act itself;
(c) conferment of full power to make laws with extraterritorial effect.

4. An independence Order, to which the independence constitution will be scheduled, will be made before independence by Her Majesty in Council. This Order will be made under existing statutory or prerogative powers, hardly ever under the Independence Act, but will likewise have effect on the date of independence. The Governor will become a Governor-General unless the territory becomes a republic or has a separate monarch. The Governor- General will be a constitutional representative of the Queen with very limited personal discretionary powers; in no sense will he now be a representative of the United Kingdom Government. It is open to the local Government to advise the appointment of the last colonial Governor or another person to the office. The constitution will include no provision for the reservation of bills and may have no provision for disallowance of legislation.

Equality of status with the United Kingdom and sovereignty in international law are thus achieved in one bound.

The development of Dominion status is a tortuous, oft-told tale.[87] By 1926 the following Commonwealth countries were called self-governing Dominions: Canada, Australia, New Zealand, South Africa (which left the Commonwealth in 1961),[88] the Irish Free State (which became known as Eire in 1937 and seceded from the Commonwealth, under the name of the Republic of Ireland, in 1949)[89] and Newfoundland (which relinquished its self-governing institutions after a financial collapse in 1933 and joined Canada as its tenth province in 1949).[90] In the Report of the Inter-Imperial Relations Committee (the Balfour Report) of the Imperial Conference held

87. See especially K. C. Wheare, *The Statute of Westminster and Dominion Status* (5th edn); R. McG. Dawson, *The Development of Dominion Status, 1900–1936*; Sir Ivor Jennings, *Constitutional Laws of the Commonwealth* (3rd edn), vol. 1, chs. 1–3; and more generally, W. K. Hancock, *Survey of British Commonwealth Affairs*, vols. 1 and 2, and P. N. S. Mansergh, *The Commonwealth Experience*.

88. See pp. 666–7.

89. Ireland Act 1949. For many years before this, Eire had regarded itself as being 'externally associated' with the Commonwealth. For the position in United Kingdom law, see *Murray* v. *Parkes* [1942] 2 K.B. 126.

90. British North America Act 1949. This followed a referendum in Newfoundland.

in 1926, it was declared that the United Kingdom and the Dominions were 'equal in status, in no way subordinate one to another in any aspect of their domestic or external affairs, though united by a common allegiance to the Crown, and freely associated as members of the British Commonwealth of Nations'.[91]

This affirmation was not quite an accurate reflection of the constitutional position of the Dominions at that time. There remained matters in which they were less than equal in status to the United Kingdom. Yet the declaration was substantially correct. The Dominions were more than internally self-governing colonies. They had acquired independent international personalities. Some of their governments had successfully asserted, in the early 1920s, the rights to conclude political treaties in their own names and to be represented separately in foreign capitals. In effect they were sovereign states in international law. But their status had evolved by constitutional convention and usage, not by virtue of statutory change; and no precise moment of time could be pinpointed as the date of their accession to independence. The term 'independence' was not as fashionable then as it is now; and appeals to the 'unity of the Empire' still evoked some response.

Some surviving elements of formal inequality with the United Kingdom were removed by the enunciation of constitutional conventions at Imperial Conferences held in 1926, 1929 and 1930. The ambiguous status of a Governor-General was resolved; he was to be the representative of the monarch, not of the United Kingdom Government; the United Kingdom Government could not properly give him any instructions in relation to a Dominion's affairs; his appointment (and by implication, his dismissal) was a matter for the Dominion Government alone, tendering direct advice to the monarch. These conventions apply to the newly independent members of the Commonwealth unless varied by agreement.

Other conventions were adopted, reducing provisions for the reservation of bills under Dominion constitutions to empty shells, and providing that it would be improper for the United Kingdom Government to advise that a Dominion Act be disallowed except for the protection of Dominion stockholders.

As was indicated in chapter 2,[92] some elements of inequality could be eliminated only by imperial legislation. It was necessary to pass the Statute of Westminster 1931 in order to remove the Dominions from the definition of 'colony' (section 11), to abolish the doctrine of legislative repugnancy and to exclude Dominion Parliaments from the restrictive operation of the

91. Cmd 2768 (1926), p. 14.
92. pp. 48–9.

Colonial Laws Validity Act 1865 (section 2),[93] to declare that Dominion Parliaments had full extraterritorial powers (section 3) and to provide that no future United Kingdom Act was to extend or be deemed to extend to a Dominion as part of its law unless the request and consent of the Dominion concerned were expressly recited in the Act in question.[94] In 1931 Australia and New Zealand, averse from legalistic formulas, were expressly excluded from the main provisions of the Statute; but these provisions were adopted by Australia in 1942 (with retroactive effect to September 1939) and by New Zealand in 1947. They were never adopted by Newfoundland.

Certain anomalies, preserved by the Statute, were still present in 1972. The Statute preserved the existing method of amending the British North America Act 1867 to 1930, the basis of the Canadian constitution.[95] Most of the provisions of these Acts can be amended only by the United Kingdom Parliament at the request of the Canadian Government. In 1949 the Canadian Parliament was accorded wider powers to amend the constitution,[96] but the really important provisions – notably the distribution of powers between the federal and provincial legislatures – are still alterable only at Westminster because Canadians have not been able to agree on a new procedure operating entirely in Canada. There is a possibility that the United Kingdom Government might receive advice from the Canadian Government which was strenuously opposed by some provinces.

The position in Australia was more complicated. There too the *status quo* was preserved.[97] But the Australian states were not even excluded from the operation of the Colonial Laws Validity Act 1865,[98] so that they were unable to legislate repugnantly to United Kingdom legislation extending to them as part of their law, and they lacked general extraterritorial powers. They could not abolish appeals on matters of state law from their own Supreme Courts to the Judicial Committee; nor could the Parliament of the Commonwealth of Australia. Moreover, they had and have had certain direct relationships with the United Kingdom Government. They can re-

93. Section 2 (possibly coupled with section 3) of the Statute of Westminster also made it possible for Dominion Parliaments to abolish all appeals from Dominion courts to the Judicial Committee of the Privy Council, including the appeal by special leave, which was a prerogative power placed on a statutory footing by United Kingdom legislation (see *British Coal Corporation* v. *R*. [1935] A.C. 500); this accession of power was, however, subject to any impediment that might be imposed by the Dominion constitution itself.

94. For the possible effect of this section, see pp. 76–7.

95. section 7.

96. British North America (No. 2) Act 1949.

97. Statute of Westminster 1931, ss. 8, 9; Wheare, *The Statute of Westminster and Dominion Status* (5th edn), ch. 8.

98. But they were excluded from the definition of 'colony' (Statute, s. 11).

quest the enactment of legislation at Westminster on matters falling within their exclusive sphere without the concurrence of the Commonwealth Government or Parliament; the appointment of a State Governor is made on the advice of the United Kingdom Government on local initiative; the state governments submit their own proposals to London for the award of honours.[99] It might be very difficult for the United Kingdom to remove some of these anomalies merely at the request of the Commonwealth Government and Parliament. However, there would be no difficulty at all in acceding to a Commonwealth request that the ordinary procedure for constitutional amendment in Australia should be extended by United Kingdom legislation to the preamble and first eight sections of the Commonwealth of Australia Constitution Act 1900, which provide that Australia shall be an indissoluble federal Commonwealth under the Queen.

We have seen that modern independence Acts include some of the 'Statute of Westminster' provisions. In what respects could Dominion status, as consummated by the Statute, be said to differ from independent membership of the Commonwealth today?

The main differences were secreted in the concept of 'common allegiance to the Crown'. In the first place, it was accepted (save in Eire) that a Dominion could not be a republic. Since 1949 republican membership of the Commonwealth has been possible.[100] Secondly, there was the theory of automatic belligerency. When the King declared war on the advice of his United Kingdom Ministers, the whole Commonwealth was at war. But Eire remained neutral in 1939; and her right to neutrality was perforce acknowledged. Canada and South Africa made their own separate declarations of war in 1939. Thirdly, the view was widely (though not universally) held that the common allegiance of the Dominions precluded unilateral secession from the Commonwealth. The right of a Dominion to secede was in fact conceded by the United Kingdom Government, when negotiating with Indian nationalist leaders, during the Second World War, and was exercised by Eire after the war. Fourthly, it was contended that the relations of Commonwealth countries *inter se* were not governed by international law, because of their common allegiance to the Crown; international law applied only between 'foreign' countries. This curious doctrine,[101] 'born a dying duckling', has perished quietly. Fifthly, common allegiance was the foundation for the common status of 'British subject'.

99. See further, Alex Castles [1962] *Public Law* 175; R. D. Lumb, *The Constitutions of the Australian States* (3rd edn). In practice the United Kingdom Parliament hardly ever legislates for the states. The United Kingdom would refuse a state request for the enactment of U.K. legislation to enable it to secede from the Commonwealth of Australia: see H.C. 88 (1934–35), the case of Western Australia.

100. See pp. 665–6.

101. J. E. S. Fawcett, *The British Commonwealth in International Law*, ch. 15.

The diversity of local citizenship laws in the modern Commonwealth has already been noted; few independent Commonwealth countries now designate their own citizens as British subjects. Sixthly, it was generally assumed that allegiance was owed to a common Crown. The King in the United Kingdom was not only the same *natural* person but the same *legal* person as the King of Canada; the law relating to the succession of the throne and the royal style and titles was necessarily uniform throughout the Commonwealth, and the assent of the Dominion Parliaments was needed for any modification to them. As we have seen,[102] the royal titles were diversified in 1953; and it is accepted that the Crown is divisible.

Associated statehood

Although smallness in size and population, and poverty of resources, are not absolute bars to the attainment of sovereign independence, it is sensible for a small dependent territory to achieve self-determination by means of federation or association with a larger country. Another possibility is for a territory to become independent and then delegate the discharge of its responsibilities in external affairs to a larger State; this was the solution adopted by New Zealand's former trust territory, Western Samoa, which concluded a Treaty of Friendship after independence in 1962, making New Zealand its agent for that purpose. Such a device presupposes a degree of reciprocal confidence that will rarely be present. Federalism is a more obvious solution; unfortunately federations are difficult to construct and more difficult to maintain as going concerns. The breakdown of the Federation of the West Indies, born in 1958 and dissolved in 1962[103] following Jamaica's insistence on seceding, created serious problems. Jamaica, and Trinidad and Tobago, became independent in 1962. Abortive attempts were made to recreate a federation of the smaller islands. After they had broken down in 1965, the British Government produced a scheme[104] under which six of them – Barbados proceeded to independence the following year – would cease to be colonies and instead would be states in association with the United Kingdom.

The scheme was inspired by the arrangements, brought into effect in 1965, whereby the Cook Islands had become a state in free association with New Zealand. The main features of the Cook Islands arrangement[105] were that the Cook Islands, formerly a dependency of New Zealand, became

102. p. 101.
103. On the date when the Federation had been due for independence.
104. Cmnd 2865 (1965).
105. *Annual Survey of Commonwealth Law 1965* (ed. Wade), pp. 30–35; Cook Islands Constitution Act 1964 (N.Z.); Cook Islands Constitution Amendment Act 1965 (N.Z.).

solely responsible for internal affairs, including constitutional amendment; New Zealand retained responsibility (not as a mere agent or delegate) for the external affairs and defence of the Cook Islands, but lacked paramount legislative power to give effect to these responsibilities in the law of the Cook Islands; and the Cook Islands were empowered to proceed unilaterally to independence by a prescribed constitutional procedure which involved special majorities, a period of delay and a referendum. The United Nations accepted this scheme as an authentic form of decolonization.

Associated statehood in the Eastern Caribbean came into existence in 1967,[106] without the blessing of the United Nations but by agreement with the territories concerned following constitutional conferences in London. In pursuance of the West Indies Act 1967, new constitutions were brought into force for Antigua, Dominica, Grenada, St. Kitts-Nevis-Anguilla and St Lucia, which became associated states; St Vincent joined them in 1969. We are concerned not with the individual constitutions but with the status of those territories under the complicated Act of 1967. Broadly, the Act excluded these territories from the definition of 'colony' and conferred on them 'Statute of Westminster powers', with certain exceptions. The Legislature of an associated state cannot make laws repugnant to the West Indies Act itself,[107] or United Kingdom legislation relating to nationality, citizenship, the royal style and titles, the succession to the throne, defence or external affairs; nor can it encroach on the United Kingdom Government's retained responsibilities for defence or external affairs.[108] Unlike New Zealand in the Cook Islands, the United Kingdom has positive powers to implement its responsibilities in the associated states. Thus, an Order in Council relating to defence or the external affairs of an associated state may be made with *or without* the consent of the Government of the associated state and may contain 'such provision as appears to Her Majesty to be appropriate' for changing the law of that state.[109] But the

106. See Margaret Broderick (1968) 17 *I.C.L.Q.* 368.

107. They can, however, amend their own constitutions in the manner there prescribed (see, for example, Antigua Constitution Order 1967 (S.I. 1967, No. 225) Sched. 2, s. 38), and they can abolish appeals from their own courts to the West Indies Associated States Supreme Court (from which appeals lie to the Judicial Committee of the Privy Council).

108. West Indies Act 1967, ss. 2–4, Sched. 1.

109. Including derogations from constitutional guarantees of fundamental rights (s. 7). The question whether legislation is in fact required for the discharge of the United Kingdom's responsibilities for defence or external affairs is non-justiciable (ss. 2(1) (a), 3(2), 7(2), 18). The Anguilla (Temporary Provision) Order 1969 (S.I. 1969, No. 371) giving Her Majesty's Commissioner in Anguilla very extensive powers in the secessionist island, was made with the consent of the Government of St Kitts-Nevis-Anguilla.

Act does not permit the merger or dismemberment of an associated state except at the request and with the consent of the state concerned. Consequently the United Kingdom could not directly sever Anguilla (an integral part of a unitary associated state) from St Kitts and Nevis without breach of an undertaking enshrined in an Act of Parliament, unless the consent of the associated state of St Kitts-Nevis-Anguilla, signified by a resolution of the House of Assembly, had been first obtained.[110] However, in 1971 Parliament passed the Anguilla Act, reciting that the measure was required for the discharge of Her Majesty's Government's responsibility for defence and external affairs,[111] and providing that a Commissioner could be appointed to exercise functions conferred on him by Order in Council in relation to Anguilla, and that if the associated state introduced an independence bill while the Order was in force, a further Order in Council could be made detaching Anguilla from the associated state.[112]

Associated states differ from colonies not only in the powers of their Legislatures and the legal limitation on United Kingdom authority but also in their legal capacity unilaterally to dissociate themselves from the United Kingdom and proceed to independence. Under the West Indies Act 1967, a bill to terminate association will have effect if ninety days elapse between introduction and second reading and the bill is passed by a two-thirds' majority in the Legislature at third reading and is then approved by a two-thirds' majority of the votes cast at a referendum before being submitted to the Governor for assent. The requirement of a referendum is dispensed with if a bill provides for union with an independent Commonwealth country in the Caribbean.

If the United Kingdom unilaterally decides to terminate association, an Order in Council can simply be made for the purpose.[113]

Powers have been delegated to the governments of associated states to conduct aspects of external relations,[114] but international responsibility rests with the United Kingdom; the associated states are not independent

110. 1967 Act, ss. 9, 19(5). Whether the United Kingdom *Parliament* has bound itself not to legislate on non-reserved matters otherwise than at the request or consent of an associated state (see s. 3(1)) is questionable, since the states are not independent and s. 3(1) is not *entrenched* against repeal.

111. West Indies Act 1967, s. 3(2).

112. Under this Act (passed without the consent of the associated state) the Anguilla (Constitution) Order 1971 (S.I. 1971, No. 1235) was made; this provided (r. 15) that no future legislation of the associated state was to apply in Anguilla unless so extended by local ordinance. Such action by the United Kingdom Government could hardly have been contemplated in 1966 or 1967. See further, K. R. Simmonds (1972) 21 *I.C.L.Q.* 151.

113. s. 10; Sched. 2. The United Kingdom Government has offered assurances to the governments of some of the associated states that it will give a period of notice before ending the status of association. See also Addendum.

114. See, for example, Cmnd 2963 (1966), Annex D.

countries. The Governors of the associated states are not, however, instruments of the United Kingdom Government; the latter has a special representative in the associated states.

Rules of the Commonwealth association today[115]

Relationships between the United Kingdom and its dependencies (including associated states) are governed by detailed rules. Relations between independent Commonwealth countries are not; the Commonwealth in this sense is almost a lawless association. It does not act as an international entity. It has no legislative, executive or judicial organ of government. Meetings of Commonwealth heads of government are in the nature of informal international conferences; they make few decisions, and members are not obliged in strict law to implement such decisions as may be made. The Commonwealth Secretariat, set up in 1965,[116] has no executive powers; it services Commonwealth conferences, acts as a clearing-house for furnishing information to Commonwealth countries, and assists in coordinating Commonwealth activities. The Judicial Committee of the Privy Council has no jurisdiction to entertain appeals from the courts of Canada, India, Sri Lanka, Bangladesh or most of the African member states. Britain has a constitution in the sense of rules regulating a coherent governmental structure; the Commonwealth has not.

The old fundamental rules of the British Commonwealth – the sovereignty of the Imperial Parliament and common allegiance to the Crown – have gone.[117] In so far as one can speak of the 'constitutional law of the Commonwealth' today, one means rules of convention, not rules of strict law; and the most hallowed convention can be changed by express agreement or by acquiescence in a course of deviation. 'Members decide what they want to do, and then bring the rules up to date.'[118] An interesting example of the flexibility of these rules was the devising of a new category of membership in November 1968 – 'special membership' – to accommodate the independent microstate of Nauru.

Most of the rules of the Commonwealth association today are about the methods of acquiring and relinquishing membership. The rules relating to the incidents of membership are few: they emphasize equality of status,

115. See K. C. Wheare, *Constitutional Structure of the Commonwealth*; de Smith, *The New Commonwealth and its Constitutions*, ch. 1.

116. Cmnd 2713 (1965). The Secretariat has its headquarters in London but is not in any sense an organ of the British Government. Its first Secretary-General was a Canadian; a Ghanian was his Deputy.

117. cf. R. T. E. Latham, *The Law and the Commonwealth*, for a brilliant jurisprudential essay on the Commonwealth shortly before the Second World War. The author was killed in action in the Royal Air Force during the war.

118. Wheare, op. cit., p. 119.

but the conventional obligations attached to membership are blurred, indeed scarcely tangible. One may assume, particularly in the light of the Singapore Declaration of Commonwealth heads of government in January 1971, that it is inconsistent with Commonwealth membership overtly to pursue a policy of racial discrimination. But interpretations of the meaning of racial discrimination are diverse. In 1972 Uganda was not the only Commonwealth country to be practising what to most people were clearly racialist policies.

Acquisition of membership

To become a full member of the Commonwealth, a country must (a) be independent, (b) be accepted by the existing full members and (c) recognize the Queen as Head of the Commonwealth. A dependent territory which is about to achieve independence may obtain approval of an application for full membership in advance of independence day; accession to full membership then takes effect on independence. It is possible for a country outside the Commonwealth to become a full member: Cyprus left the Commonwealth in 1960 when it became independent, but re-entered as a full member in 1961. Western Samoa joined the Commonwealth in August 1970. Consultations on applications with other members are now made through the Commonwealth Secretariat. The need for the concurrence of existing full members is implicit in the concept of equality of status. There is no settled rule that consent must be unanimous. When Bangladesh was admitted to membership in April 1972 it appears that no opposition was expressed, but several Commonwealth members had not recognized the independence of Bangladesh at that time. If there were to be substantial opposition to an application – for example, if the United Kingdom had been prepared to advance Southern Rhodesia, a colony with a white minority régime, to independence in (say) 1964 and to propose that country's admission to full membership – then either the application would be rejected or withdrawn, or a dissenting minority of members might choose to secede from the Commonwealth or refuse to participate in aspects of Commonwealth affairs.

The Queen's status as Head of the Commonwealth flows directly from the London Declaration of April 1949. India had achieved Dominion status and independence in 1947, and wished to adopt a republican constitution but remain within the Commonwealth. At a meeting of Commonwealth Prime Ministers, a formula was devised whereby (i) India proclaimed its desire to continue as a full member of the Commonwealth and its acceptance of the King as the symbol of the free association of its independent member nations, and, as such, Head of the Commonwealth, and (ii) the other members recorded their acceptance and recognition of India's continuing membership as a republic on this basis. India became a republic within the Commonwealth in January 1950.

At the time it was envisaged that India would be a special case. Inevitably, however, it set a precedent: what had been granted to India could hardly be denied to others. In 1957 Malaya (now Malaysia) became independent with its own monarch, the Yang di-Pertuan Agong, elected from among the hereditary Malay rulers. In 1964 Zambia became independent as a republic. In 1972 only a minority of Commonwealth countries had the Queen as their head of State.[119] In her capacity as Head of the Commonwealth she performs no constitutional function.

There is no other formal qualification (for example, size, ideology) for admission to full membership.

Incidents of membership. The governments of full members of the Commonwealth are entitled to be represented at meetings of Commonwealth Prime Ministers (or heads of government), which are held at irregular intervals – roughly every two years. Before 1971, all but one of these meetings had been held in London. These governments are also entitled to take part, on an equal footing, in other Commonwealth activities – for example, meetings of Finance Ministers, educational programmes, and so on. It can hardly be said that there is a clearly defined *obligation* to participate in any particular activity; though a country which decided not to cooperate in Commonwealth affairs at all would (unless it was making a temporary gesture of protest) probably withdraw from the Commonwealth altogether. The conventional duty to consult other Commonwealth members or to keep them informed on matters directly affecting their interests is ill-defined and loosely interpreted. Members have indeed broken off diplomatic relations with one another, even gone to war with one another (India and Pakistan) and still remained in the Commonwealth. Pakistan left the Commonwealth only when recognition of the independence of Bangladesh by the older States was imminent.

It is to be inferred that most of the conventions relating to equality of status (for example, regarding the constitutional position of a Governor-General) formulated in the era of Dominion status apply to the new members as well.

Retention of membership. If a member which has the Queen as head of State wishes to become a republic or separate monarchy and remain within the Commonwealth, it must obtain the concurrence of existing members. The rationale of this rule, adopted when severance of allegiance to the Crown was thought of as a serious step to take, has disappeared,

119. See p. 100.

but the practice has survived. It was used as a means of driving South Africa out of the Commonwealth in 1961. The Union wished, like India, to become a republic and to retain its place in the Commonwealth. Opposition developed among other Commonwealth members who objected strongly to South Africa's racial policies; and there was so much dissension at the meeting of Commonwealth Prime Ministers at which South Africa's application for continuance of membership on the new basis was discussed, that the Union Government withdrew its application, choosing the least of evils. Subsequently, in May 1961, South Africa became a republic and its membership of the Commonwealth automatically lapsed.

Termination of membership. This may occur in four ways: by loss of independence, by voluntary secession, by lapse (on failing to seek, or failing to obtain, the concurrence of the other members on becoming a republic or a separate monarchy), and (probably) by expulsion. The only instances of voluntary secession by countries already independent members of the Commonwealth were the withdrawal of Eire (the Republic of Ireland) in 1949 and of Pakistan in January 1972.[120] Lapse of membership had occurred only in the case of South Africa. There was no precedent for expulsion and there are still no accepted rules governing such a matter, but South Africa had in effect been forced out of the Commonwealth by a procedural device, and even if it had abandoned the idea of adopting a republican constitution there can be little doubt that it would have been evicted by a majority decision soon afterwards.

Commonwealth relations[121]

Over-enthusiastic descriptions of the Commonwealth – 'a family of like-minded nations, speaking the same political language and voluntarily co-

120. There have been other cases (for example, Burma in 1948) where a territory ceased to be part of the Commonwealth *on attaining independence*.

The unilateral declaration of independence by Southern Rhodesia in November 1965, followed by Rhodesia's adoption of a republican constitution in 1970, were regarded as void in constitutional law. Southern Rhodesia was still a colony, over which the United Kingdom was unable to exercise effective control. cf. *Southern Rhodesia Act 1965*; Southern Rhodesia Constitution Order 1965 (S.I. 1965, No. 1952); *Madzimbamuto* v. *Lardner-Burke* [1969] 1 A.C. 645.

121. For a very useful short survey, see Derek Ingram, *The Commonwealth at Work* (1969). See also P. N. S. Mansergh, *Survey of British Commonwealth Affairs*, vols. 3 and 4; *The Commonwealth Experience* (1969); J. D. B. Miller, *The Commonwealth in the World* (3rd edn, 1965); Ali Mazrui, *The Anglo-African Commonwealth* (1967); Patrick Gordon Walker, *The Commonwealth* (1962). A mass of factual information is digested in the *Year Book of the Commonwealth* published annually by the Foreign and Commonwealth Office in London.

operating on matters of common concern . . .' – have led to a reaction. Nowadays the Commonwealth is apt to be dismissed as a gigantic farce, as the emperor who had no clothes, as the disembodied grin on the face of the Cheshire cat. Relations between Commonwealth countries are indeed often disharmonious; conflicts of interest and differences of approach may run deep. In international affairs the Commonwealth now bears comparison with the United Nations writ small. And it is not and cannot be an independent power factor in the modern world. As an entity, it suffers from special disadvantages. For too many members, Commonwealth relations have meant relations with the United Kingdom;[122] and for too many people in the United Kingdom the Commonwealth ought to behave like a grateful Empire. Unrealistic expectations have been unfulfilled. Racial discord and restrictions on Commonwealth immigration into the United Kingdom, Britain's refusal to use force in order to quell the Rhodesian rebellion, its intention to resume arms sales to South Africa, and Britain's entry into the EEC in pursuit of its own interests have imposed severe stresses on the Commonwealth relationships. So has the contempt for democratic processes shown by rulers of some of the newer member States – an attitude often accompanied by a proclivity for vehement denunciation of the iniquities perpetrated or condoned by older members.

The Commonwealth, as at present constituted, has no prospect of developing supranational organs qualifying the sovereignty of its members. The small Commonwealth Secretariat, treading warily so as not to risk causing any affront to any member, symbolizes some of the weaknesses of the Commonwealth. The Secretariat, incarnated by the Secretary-General, is also a symbol that the Commonwealth exists and that its members want it to be a useful organization – the Secretariat is financed by agreed contributions from individual members – serving a limited range of agreed purposes. The Commonwealth is in fact a minor consultative and cooperative international body, whose members have certain special relationships with one another. These special relationships are not easy to define at all precisely. The representatives of Commonwealth governments in Commonwealth capitals are called High Commissioners, not Ambassadors or Ministers, and some have direct access to government Departments other than the Foreign Office. But if we search for a distinct body of Commonwealth law, we shall find only a miscellany of statutory provisions, lacking in uniformity, dealing with such matters as the rendition of fugitive offenders, reciprocal recognition of professional qualifications, grants of probate and so on; and differentiating, for some purposes, the status of

122. The grounds on which Pakistan withdrew from membership in January 1972 see p. 666) are significant.

citizens of other Commonwealth countries from that of aliens. The Commonwealth is not coextensive with the Sterling Area. Even before the United Kingdom joined the European Communities and thereby became obliged to replace Commonwealth preference by Community preference,[123] Commonwealth preference was not offered by all Commonwealth countries to imports from all other Commonwealth countries. The concept of the Commonwealth as an economic, political or legal unit is illusory.

Yet the Commonwealth survives and is unlikely to suffer total disintegration in the near future. Since not a single full member seceded voluntarily for over twenty years following 1949 (and four new full members joined in 1970–72), there were surely advantages, tangible or intangible, in belonging to such an organization. Or perhaps the matter should be phrased more negatively; the obligations imposed by membership are slight, and reasons offered for withdrawal are seldom, on balance, convincing. Few members, however, would give an identical set of reasons for wishing to remain. For a newly independent small country, the advantages of membership may be considerable. By the end of 1970 no fewer than twelve full members of the Commonwealth had populations of under a million; and Nauru, the special member, had a population of six thousand. Membership offers these countries new windows on the world; a large fund of factual information; an opportunity to reduce their sense of isolation and to resist the gravitational pull of intrusive and powerful neighbours; prospects of a helping hand from friendly countries in various parts of the world if they are in political, administrative or economic difficulties; and readier access to the London money market, technical assistance and special financial aid. Mauritius, a small, overpopulated sugar island in the Indian Ocean, a strategically important area, had the benefits of a defence agreement with Britain, British diplomatic protection for its citizens in countries where Mauritius had no representative of its own, a relatively high guaranteed price under the Commonwealth Sugar Agreement for much of its export crop, Commonwealth preference for most of the rest of its exports, and development and budgetary aid from Britain. This is, perhaps, an extreme example – and Mauritius was able to negotiate a reasonably advantageous association agreement with the EEC when the support for its sugar exports was jeopardized by Britain's accession – but the Commonwealth had become increasingly an organization attractive to small States. Of the large members, Canada, Australia and New Zealand still felt a certain sense of affinity with Britain and one another, and they appreciated the importance of cultivating good relations with developing countries. For some of the African and larger Asian

123. Subject to special transitional safeguards for New Zealand's exports and for the sugar-producing Commonwealth countries.

members, the benefits of membership were becoming more problematical; one of them might be the possibility of influencing the external policies of the 'western' members; another, a feeling that withdrawal would place them at a disadvantage *vis-à-vis* rivals who remained within the organization.

The attitudes struck at plenary sessions of meetings of Commonwealth heads of government are not characteristic of the general pattern of Commonwealth relations. Functional cooperation and interchange at official and unofficial levels are less conspicuous but more impressive. Commonwealth activities at the official level range over a very wide field – from occasional conferences of Finance Ministers or Law Ministers to the work of specialized operational, consultative or advisory bodies such as the Commonwealth Telecommunications Organization, the Commonwealth Agricultural Bureaux and the Commonwealth War Graves Commission. Educational cooperation, illustrated by the recruitment of university teachers through the Inter-University Council, the Association of Commonwealth Universities, the schemes for the interchange of teachers, the award of Commonwealth fellowships and scholarships and the training of Rhodesian Africans abroad, has been an asset to nearly every Commonwealth country. At the semi-official and unofficial levels, there are the numerous conferences organized by the Commonwealth Parliamentary Association; Commonwealth Legal Conferences; arrangements for professional conferences and exchanges of personnel, now promoted or subsidized by the Commonwealth Foundation (established in 1966); and the work of a host of voluntary bodies, mainly in the United Kingdom, which diffuse information[124] and good will and sometimes perform services of a more practical utility to Commonwealth countries and their citizens.

124. In January 1973 an official conference of Commonwealth Law Ministers agreed that the role of the tiny Legal Division of the Secretariat should be expanded, so as to enable it to supply information about legal developments (for example, on statutory consumer protection) in particular Commonwealth countries at the request of others. It would work in collaboration with the Commonwealth Legal Advisory Service (see H. H. Marshall (1972) 21 *I.C.L.Q.* 435) run by the British Institute of International and Comparative Law.

Appendix
European Community
Institutions: A Note[1]

The European Coal and Steel Community (ECSC) was established in 1952;[2] the European Economic Community (EEC)[3] and the European Atomic Energy Community (EURATOM)[4] were born in 1958; in 1969 the institutions of the three Communities were merged. The members of the Communities were Belgium, West Germany, France, Italy, Luxembourg and the Netherlands. On 1 January 1973 the United Kingdom, the Republic of Ireland and Denmark acceded to the Communities, and various modifications of the Treaties were adopted.[6] Here we offer an all too brief sketch of the functions of the principal Community institutions. A number of comments on the probable impact of Community membership on United Kingdom constitutional law have already been made in this book.[7]

The principal treaty is the EEC Treaty. Article 2 states that the EEC is to establish a common market and to approximate the economic policies of member States with a view, *inter alia*, to promoting closer relations within the Community. Article 3 specifies the activities of the Community in more detail. They include the elimination of customs duties and quantitative restrictions in trade between member States; the establishment of a common external tariff and a common commercial policy towards other countries; freedom of movement of persons, services and capital between

1. Two very helpful short studies are P. S. R. F. Mathijsen, *A Guide to European Community Law* (1972), and D. Lasok and J. W. Bridge, *Introduction to the Law and Institutions of the European Communities* (1973). See also Anthony Parry and Stephen Hardy, *EEC Law*. For a larger work of reference, see Alan Campbell, *Common Market Law*.

2. Cmnd 4863 (1972) (Treaty of Paris).

3. Cmnd 4864 (1972) (Rome Treaty).

4. Cmnd 4865 (1972).

5. Cmnd 4866 (1972).

6. Cmnd. 4862 (1972), Vols. 1 and 2 (Treaty of Brussels). These instruments presupposed that Norway would also join. In the event Norway did not join, the proposal having been rejected at a referendum. The instruments of accession consequently had to be modified.

7. See pp. 45–6, 79–82, 92, 130, 131–2, 225, 282–3, 284, 295, 330, 338–9, 342, 347, 352, 425–32, 434, 625, 641, 648, 669.

member States; the adoption of common policies for agriculture and transport; the creation of a system to prevent the distortion of competition, and the approximation of the laws of member States to the extent required for the function of the common market.

In October 1972, the heads of government of the nine existing and prospective member States agreed in principle that a full economic and monetary union should be established by the end of 1980.[8] No corresponding commitment to constitutional or political union was undertaken. But if supranational decisions are to be taken over an increasing range of politically contentious issues, it is hard to believe that this will be feasible without closer political integration.

The main areas hitherto covered by rules of Community law are agriculture, foodstuffs and fisheries; customs duties and aspects of indirect taxation; aspects of the law relating to companies, bankruptcy, patents and registered designs, monopolies and restrictive trade practices, and miscellaneous features of commercial law; social security; immigration; land transport regulation; industrial relations, and the supply and distribution of coal, steel and nuclear energy.

Community law comprises[9] the primary Treaties, and ancillary agreements entered into by the member States;[10] secondary legislation by Community organs;[11] administrative acts and decisions by Community organs, and decisions and other pronouncements by the Court of the Communities (the European Court of Justice). It is distinct from public international law and from the national (municipal) law of member States. But it is interwoven with municipal law; it is applied mainly by the courts of member States; certain rules of Community law (notably regulations made by the Council of Ministers or the Commission) are 'directly applicable'[12] in the sense that, of their own force, they create legal rights and duties enforceable in municipal courts. According to Community law doctrine as expounded by the European Court of Justice, Community law prevails over national law (even national constitutional law) to the extent that they are inconsistent with one another. Cases of inconsistency are not confined to conflicts between 'directly applicable' Community law and municipal law; they arise whenever rules of Community law (including provisions of the Treaties, directives issued by the Council or the Commission, or decisions

8. For the text of the communiqué, see *The Times*, 23 October 1972.

9. See also pp. 45–6, above.

10. The Communities also have treaty-making competence: EEC Treaty, articles 210 (see *Re European Road Transport Agreement* [1971] C.M.L. Rep. 335), 228, 238.

11. Forty-two volumes of Community regulations and directives then in force were published in English in 1972. Community legislation, though published in the *Official Journal* of the Communities, is not as accessible as are statutory instruments.

12. See Gerhard Behr (1970) 19 *I.C.L.Q.* 257.

of the Court) are incompatible with municipal laws, and inconsistency may exist without direct conflict if Community rules evince an intention to cover the whole field of the activity in question.[13] The European Communities Act 1972 provides that the Community Treaties shall have effect in United Kingdom law (section 1), that enactments 'passed or to be passed' shall 'be construed and have effect' subject to the preceding provisions (section 2(4)), and that the decisions of the European Court and the principles laid down by it (including, of course, the supremacy of Community law and the consequential denial of the legal doctrine of parliamentary sovereignty) shall be applied by United Kingdom courts. Attention has already been drawn to the incompatibility of some of these provisions with basic constitutional principles.[14]

The principal decision-making and legislative organ of the Communities is the Council of Ministers, each member State having one representative. There is an ancillary Committee of Permanent Representatives, composed of national officials of ambassadorial status. Under the Treaties, decisions by the Council are usually taken only following the submission of a proposal by the Commission. Depending on the subject-matter, the decision is to be taken either (i) by a simple majority; or (ii) by a 'qualified majority', special weightage being given to the larger member States; or (iii) unanimously – where the Council wishes to amend a proposal by the Commission (EEC Treaty, article 149). In practice, though not in strict law, where any vital British interest is at issue, the decision of the Council will have to be unanimous; this is to be inferred from the interpretation given to the Luxembourg Agreement of 1966.[15] And this is the main reason why United Kingdom Ministers have asserted that membership of the Communities will not entail a relinquishment of national sovereignty.

The Commission consists of thirteen members, one from each of the smaller member States and two from each of the larger. Its members are Community officials (though most of them have been involved in national politics; the two British commissioners, Sir Christopher Soames and Mr

13. On attitudes of national courts towards the doctrine of Community law supremacy, see Behr (1971) 34 *Mod. L. Rev.* 481; the Belgian '*Ski*' case [1972] C.M.L. Rep. 330; and p. 61, above.

14. At pp. 79–82. A *possible* (though not the only) position for a United Kingdom court to adopt could be that parliamentary sovereignty has been restricted by the fact of the United Kingdom's accession but that Parliament retains an ultimate overriding power to legislate so as to exclude the United Kingdom.

15. For the Agreement see Mathijsen, pp. 134–5; Lasok and Bridge, pp. 117–20. The Agreement does not record an *agreement* to this effect, but rather an agreement between France and the other member States to differ on this crucial point; the United Kingdom appears to have adopted the same view as France on matters affecting vital national interests.

George Thomson, were formerly Cabinet Ministers, one Conservative and the other Labour) and they owe their loyalty to the Communities, not to the government of their own country. The Commission is pre-eminently a supranational rather than an international body: initiating, supervising, coordinating, legislating within narrow limits, imposing penalties on enterprises breaking competition rules and conducting elaborate dialogues with the Council of Ministers.

The European Parliament consists of members chosen by national Parliaments from their own members. It is a deliberative, consultative and scrutinizing body, working largely through specialist committees. It has no legislative powers, but the Commission is answerable to it and it has the ultimate authority to remove the members of the Commission on a motion of no confidence passed by a two-thirds' majority. Proposals that it should be endowed with effective powers and become a directly elected body have as yet fallen on stony ground. The full quota of thirty-six seats allocated to the United Kingdom was not immediately taken up, the Parliamentary Labour Party having refused to nominate members for the seats offered to it.

The European Court of Justice[16] is composed of eleven judges; the British judge was chosen from the Scottish Court of Session. The Court is fashioned according to continental models; its procedure is inquisitorial, and written submissions by counsel are more important than oral argument; provisional conclusions are prepared by an Advocate-General, an officer who has no counterpart in the United Kingdom; in interpreting legal instruments the Court considers preparatory materials and not merely the bare text; its judgments are terse, replete with statements of general legal principle; no dissenting opinion is delivered or announced. Its jurisdiction is wide-ranging. For example, it is an 'administrative court' determining the validity of the acts and decisions of Community organs broadly according to French administrative law doctrine (EEC Treaty, article 173); it hears appeals against penalties imposed by the Commission, disputes between the Communities and their officials (or dismissed officials), claims in tort and contract against the Communities, and proceedings against Community organs for wrongful failure to act. In constitutional law its most important head of jurisdiction is to give preliminary rulings on the interpretation of the Treaties and the validity and interpretation of

16. See D. G. Valentine, *The Court of Justice of the European Communities*; Gerhard Behr, *Judicial Control of the European Communities*; L. J. Brinkhorst and H. G. Schermers, *Judicial Remedies in the European Communities*; A. W. Green, *Political Integration by Jurisprudence*; Edward H. Wall, *The Court of Justice of the European Communities*. Selected judgments are reported in English in *The Common Market Law Reports*, together with important decisions of national courts on matters of Community law.

acts (including regulations and directives) of Community organs (EEC Treaty, article 177). A national court or tribunal ought not to refer such a question unless its decision on the matter before it depends on the determination of that question. Courts and tribunals of last instance are obliged to refer such a question unless the correct interpretation is quite clear. Probably tribunals such as the national insurance commissioners, whose decisions are reviewable by certiorari (though not on appeal), are not tribunals of last instance for the purpose of article 177. Rules of court have been made prescribing the *procedure* for making references to the European Court from superior courts[17] but not stating the *principles* governing references. Those principles are, by implication, to be regulated by Community law doctrine. It is arguable that references ought to be made by lower courts if possible; this will reduce the costs of the parties and minimize the delay, which will in any event be of several months' duration.

The Court abstains, as far as possible, from interpreting national (municipal) law. Its rulings are binding on national courts,[18] which have then to decide how (if at all) the relevant provisions of municipal law can be reconciled with the European Court's pronouncements.[19]

The Court, like the Commission, has generally sought to extend the frontiers of Community law and to emphasize the concept of Community law supremacy. If the national authorities fail to comply with a ruling by the Court, the Commission (or another member State) may bring the matter before the Court, which may deliver a judgment declaring that the member State concerned has failed to fulfil its obligations under the Treaties (Treaty, articles 169–71).[20] No coercive sanction is provided against a defaulter, except under the ECSC Treaty (article 88) which empowers the Commission, with the concurrence of two-thirds of the Council, to withhold from that member State moneys due to it and to authorize other members to subject it to fiscal sanctions.

The Communities resemble a 'functional' federation, but the member States retain full international personality. The Communities also resemble a confederation, but they are more closely knit than a typical confederation, and their organs have authority to confer rights and impose obligations directly on the citizens of member States.

17. S.I. 1972, Nos. 1786, 1787, 1898.
18. Except where the Court can be expected to depart from its own rulings; it is not absolutely bound by its own decisions.
19. See pp. 81–2, above.
20. In one notable case (*Re European Road Transport Agreement* (note 10)) brought under another head of jurisdiction, the Commission took proceedings against the Council for alleged breach of Community obligations.

Addendum

This refers to miscellaneous points arising before 31 May 1973.

1. Section 1 (2) of the Ireland Act 1949 (see pp. 51, 60 above) will be repealed by the Northern Ireland Constitution Bill, which will substitute (clause 1) a statutory affirmation that Northern Ireland shall not cease to be part of Her Majesty's dominions and the United Kingdom without the consent of the *majority of the people* of Northern Ireland voting in a 'border poll' (Schedule 1).

2. Diplomatic premises situated in Britain (see p. 132, note 160 above), though inviolable for certain purposes, are nevertheless part of British territory (*Radwan* v. *Radwan* [1973] Fam.25).

3. Legislation is to be introduced (Cmnd 5313 (1973)) to give effect to the main recommendations of the Salmon Commission on Tribunals of Inquiry (Cmnd 3121 (1966)) and certain recommendations of a committee reporting in 1969 (Cmnd 4078 (1969)), so as to afford, *inter alia*, better procedural safeguards to persons at risk before judicial tribunals of inquiry constituted under the Tribunals of Inquiry (Evidence) Act 1921 (cf. pp. 173, 539, above).

4. When two Ministers resigned in May 1973 following revelations of their association with 'call-girls', it was decided not to set up a judicial inquiry but to refer to the Security Commission (pp. 197, 539 above) the question whether there had been any breach of national security. Previously the Commission had considered only cases where breaches of security had already been established.

5. *Community Legislation.* The First Report of the House of Commons Select Committee on European Community Secondary Legislation (H.C. 143 (1972–73)) made preliminary recommendations for giving M.P.s fuller publicity and explanations about draft Community legislative proposals and other Community transactions. Its recommendations were accepted in part by the Government (855 H.C. Deb. 550–619 (18 April 1973)). No formal proposals for new parliamentary committees on Community affairs had yet been put forward (cf. p. 295, above).

6. *Delegated legislation* (see pp. 345–7, above). In February 1973 it was resolved that a Joint Select Committee on Statutory Instruments be constituted to supersede the House of Commons Select Committee on Statutory Instruments and the House of Lords Special Orders Committee; the Special Orders Committee would, however, remain in existence for the time being for the consideration of 'hybrid' orders (see p. 345, note 58 above). The chairman of the new committee is a member of the Commons. Its terms of reference are those of the former House of Commons committee, slightly enlarged so as to include certain instruments that were considered by the Lords committee but not by the Commons committee (see 850 H.C. Deb. 1217–9 (13 February 1973)).

Provision was also made (see 853 H.C. Deb. 680–95 (22 March 1973)) for statutory instruments subject to the affirmative resolution procedure or against which a negative resolution had been moved (cf. p. 344) to be considered on their merits by new standing committees of the House of Commons for the remainder of the 1972–3 session. This was a modest, indeed curious, experiment. A question could be thus referred only upon the motion of a Minister and then only if fewer than twenty members objected. The function of such a committee would be merely to 'consider' the matter; it could not even report that an instrument should be annulled or not approved; its reports would be submitted to the House without debate. However, the Government undertook to consider making *ad hoc* arrangements for debating prayers to annul statutory instruments after 11.30 p.m. (cf. p. 344, above).

7. *Administration of Justice.* The new power vested in the Lord Chancellor by section 2 of the Administration of Justice Act 1973 to recommend the appointment of stipendiary magistrates outside London (pp. 356, 365 above) is to be used sparingly, and not more than forty can be appointed under the Act. But the power might conceivably be used if lay magistrates in a part of England or Wales were perversely refusing to convict for a particular class of offence.

8. *Contempt of Court* (p. 371). In *Att.-Gen.* v. *Times Newspapers Ltd* [1973] 2 W.L.R. 452 the Court of Appeal (overruling the Divisional Court [1972] 3 W.L.R. 855) held that although it was a contempt of court to bring unfair pressure to bear (by public comment or otherwise) on a party to pending civil proceedings in an attempt to induce him to withdraw from the proceedings or settle them disadvantageously to himself, it was not a contempt to publish a newspaper article criticizing the Distillers Co. for failing to make a satisfactory offer of compensation to the parents of 'thalidomide' children in proceedings which, though formally pending, had long been dormant and would almost certainly never come to trial. Moreover, in a

matter of national importance – and particularly a matter which had been debated by the House of Commons notwithstanding its own *sub judice* rule (p. 293) – it was necessary to weigh the public interest in freedom of comment against the interests of the parties. It was desirable that the *sub judice* rule applied in the courts should be similar to that applied by the House. The court doubted whether it was appropriate for the Attorney-General to institute proceedings for an injunction restraining an alleged contempt of court in a case where the interests of the Crown were not in issue.

In May 1973 the decision was on appeal to the House of Lords. At the same time a committee under Phillimore L.J. (a member of the Court of Appeal in this case) was considering reform of the law relating to contempt of court.

9. *Nationality and Citizenship* (p. 420, note 8). In May 1973 there were published the Bangladesh Bill, bringing citizens of Bangladesh within the ambit of section 1(3) of the British Nationality Act 1948; and the Pakistan Bill, a more controversial measure, under which citizens of Pakistan will cease to be British subjects and Commonwealth citizens in United Kingdom law other than specified classes of Pakistani citizens, who, within prescribed time limits, will be permitted to apply for registration as citizens of the United Kingdom and Colonies.

10. *The McWhirter/IBA/Warhol Case.* The basic facts and main implications of this case (*Att.-Gen. ex rel. McWhirter* v. *IBA* [1973] 2 W.L.R. 344) have been briefly noted in the main text (at p. 221, note 60, pp. 568, 604). The Court of Appeal was initially prepared to award M, a member of the general public, an interlocutory injunction as a matter of urgency to restrain the IBA from showing a film about Andy Warhol which, so it appeared, would constitute a breach of the Authority's statutory duty. Having heard further argument and having seen the film, the Court held (i) that the IBA was not in breach of its statutory duty, (ii) that since the Attorney-General could have been approached to lend his name to a relator action against the Authority, M had no *locus standi* to sue in his own name, but (iii) that in highly exceptional circumstances (for example, if the Attorney-General refused to proceed on manifestly improper grounds) a member of the public might be entitled to sue (cf. p. 602, note 33, above). This last expression of opinion may possibly lead to a broadening of the concept of *locus standi* to challenge administrative action or inaction (cf. pp. 220–21, 595–6, 600, 602, 604, above). If, moreover, the Attorney-General's discretion to refuse to proceed is no longer absolute (cf. p. 378), this means that the courts may take it upon themselves to review the adequacy of the grounds on which a *prerogative* power has been exercised (cf. p. 113,

note 73, above); for the power of the Attorney-General to proceed is not derived from statute. See further, de Smith, *Judicial Review of Administrative Action* (3rd edn), Appx 3.

11. *Commonwealth Affairs.* Early in 1973 the new Government of the Commonwealth of Australia was proposing to introduce legislation into the Commonwealth Parliament requesting and consenting to the enactment by the United Kingdom of legislation terminating appeals to the Privy Council from state courts. This proposal was being resisted by the state governments (cf. pp. 659–60).

The Government of Grenada, an associated state, requested the United Kingdom Government to procure the making of an Order in Council terminating the association. Grenada would thereby proceed to independence without complying with the special procedure prescribed by the West Indies Act 1967 for unilateral termination of the relationship by the associated state itself (cf. p. 663). The United Kingdom Government was not prepared to accede unconditionally to this request.

12. *Northern Ireland.* The train of developments down to January 1973 has already been outlined.[1] At a plebiscite held on 8 March 1973 under the Northern Ireland (Border Poll) Act 1972 (see p. 640) nearly 60 per cent of the entire electorate voted in favour of the province remaining part of the United Kingdom. Later that month the United Kingdom Government published *Northern Ireland Constitutional Proposals* (Cmnd 5259 (1973)), a sequel to the discussion paper of October 1972 (see p. 644, above). The 1973 White Paper will take its place among the major State documents of this century if the constitutional scheme there formulated comes to fruition.

In March 1973 the Northern Ireland (Temporary Provisions) Act 1972, under which direct rule had been imposed, was renewed for a further twelve months; it was hoped to abbreviate that period by bringing the new scheme into operation. The Northern Ireland Assembly Act 1973[2] provides for a unicameral Northern Ireland Assembly (to replace the Parliament of Northern Ireland), consisting of seventy-eight members elected in twelve multi-member constituencies on the basis of the single transferable vote system of proportional representation.[3] Elections were to be held in late June 1973.[4] Despite the prospective abolition of the Northern Ireland Parliament, there was to be no increase in the number of Northern Ireland M.P.s at Westminster from twelve; previously the under-representation of

1. At pp. 640, 642–4, above.
2. Assented to on 3 May 1973.
3. For which see pp. 250–51, above.
4. Local government elections were held on the basis of this system on 30 May 1973. Proscribed organizations, notably the I R A, were not allowed to put up candidates.

Northern Ireland had been justified on the ground that the province had its own self-governing institutions.

The principal features of the new scheme were incorporated in a separate measure, the Northern Ireland Constitution Bill, which was still before Parliament at the end of May 1973.

The Office of Governor of Northern Ireland will be abolished, and no further appointments to the Northern Ireland Privy Council will be made. Instead of a Prime Minister and Cabinet there will be a Northern Ireland Executive, composed of a chief executive member (who will be leader of the Assembly), the heads of Northern Ireland Departments (no longer Ministers) and, if necessary, other persons, bringing the Executive up to twelve members; all will be appointed to office by the Secretary of State for Northern Ireland, primarily from among members of the Assembly (clause 8) and appointments are to be such that the Executive is likely to be widely accepted throughout the Community (clause 2(1)). In other words, the Executive should not be exclusively Protestant or necessarily committed to the union. Transfer of responsibilities to the new Northern Ireland authorities is to take place only when there is 'a reasonable basis' for 'government by consent'. Manifestly this transition after the election to the Assembly might present acute difficulties, given the deep rifts within the Northern Ireland community and the multiplicity of political factions. The principle of power-sharing at the executive level may be encouraged but cannot be fulfilled merely by proportional representation in the Assembly. Members of the Executive will hold office during Her Majesty's pleasure; presumably they will be removable on the advice of the United Kingdom Government.

The departmental heads will also be chairmen of functional committees of the Assembly, the membership of which will reflect the party composition of the Assembly; the committees are to be consulted in the formation of policy and will consider legislative proposals before they are presented to the Assembly (White Paper, § 44; Constitutional Bill, clauses 7(4), 25).

Once this machinery is brought into operation to the satisfaction of the United Kingdom Government (White Paper, § 53), direct rule will be terminated and powers will be devolved by Order in Council to the Assembly and Executive. If this occurs before 30 March 1974, the Assembly will serve for four years after the Order has been made; the duration of subsequent Assemblies will also be four years, subject to a power of dissolution exercisable on the advice of the United Kingdom Government if it is impossible to constitute an Executive conforming to the standards laid down by the bill.

The legislative provisions, replacing those under the Government of Ireland Act 1920 (as amended), will be fairly complex. The paramount legislative sovereignty of the United Kingdom Parliament will be retained; and there will be 'no room for ambiguity' (White Paper, § 54) about the right of Parliament to legislate for Northern Ireland on devolved matters in exceptional circumstances without the request of the Northern Ireland Executive. 'Excepted matters', on which the Assembly will not be able to legislate at all, will now include forms of taxation, emergency powers, prosecutions, electoral law and certain judicial appointments in respect of which the Northern Ireland Parliament formerly had legislative powers. 'Reserved matters', on which the Assembly will be able to legislate only exceptionally and with the consent of the United Kingdom Government, will include the criminal law, prisons and the police; this withdrawal of 'law and order' powers from Northern Ireland competence is a particularly controversial issue in the province. All other matters will be 'transferred' and within local competence. But Measures passed by the Assembly will acquire the force of law only when approved by Order in Council on the recommendation of the Secretary of State. Once so approved, a Measure will have the same force in Northern Ireland as an Act of the United Kingdom Parliament, save in so far as it is unlawfully discriminatory (see below). The Crown will have a special power to refer Northern Ireland legislation to the Judicial Committee of the Privy Council for determination of the question whether it discriminates unlawfully against any person or class on grounds of religious belief or political opinion; a decision by the Judicial Committee that it is void for these reasons will be binding. There will also be provisions for obtaining the Secretary of State's consent for proposed Measures incidentally touching on 'excepted' matters or encroaching more substantially on a 'reserved' matter; if he withholds his consent, the question will be referred back to the Assembly; even if he consents, the proposed Measure must be laid before the United Kingdom Parliament, subject to a negative resolution procedure, save in cases of urgency, in which event an Order in Council approving the Measure is to be revoked if disapproved by either House.

The allocation of executive power will broadly correspond with the distribution of legislative power.[5] The Secretary of State for Northern Ireland will exercise most of the powers in the excepted and reserved fields; other United Kingdom Ministers (for example, the Secretary of State for Defence, the Chancellor of the Exchequer) will retain their powers. The Attorney-General for England and Wales will preserve his responsibilities assumed during the period of direct rule for prosecutions in Northern Ireland; the local Director of Prosecutions will be responsible to him.

Religious or political discrimination by public authorities in Northern Ireland will be unlawful except in the interests of national security, public

5. See further, Cmnd 5259 (1973), 65–77.

safety or public order. A person adversely affected by such discriminatory action may, in certain circumstances, obtain an injunction and damages in a court. Complaints of maladministration involving unlawful discrimination may be investigated by the Parliamentary Commissioners for Administration for the United Kingdom or for Northern Ireland or by the Commissioner for Complaints notwithstanding that the person aggrieved has a remedy in a court. There is also to be a Standing Advisory Commission on Human Rights. But there is not to be a full-scale constitutional bill of rights.

It appears that the allocation of financial resources to the Northern Ireland Executive will increase the economic dependence of Northern Ireland on the United Kingdom.[6]

The United Kingdom Government has expressed its support for the idea of forming a consultative 'Council of Ireland' which might embrace coordinated administrative action at the functional level.[7] This highly emotive question is approached obliquely in clause 12 of the Constitution Bill by means of enabling provisions; closer cooperation with the Republic can hardly be imposed on a Northern Ireland Executive.

A separate bill, the Northern Ireland (Emergency Provisions) Bill,[8] will repeal the much-criticized Civil Authorities (Special Powers) Act (N.I.) 1922 but will incorporate a number of provisions that would be unacceptable in Great Britain. These include the trial of several classes of very serious offences (set out in a Schedule) by a judge sitting without a jury, as well as numerous alterations in the rules of criminal procedure and evidence, designed to facilitate the arrest and conviction of terrorists. It will also be an offence to belong to a proscribed organization – the list includes the IRA and the Ulster Volunteer Force – and for any assembly of three or more persons to disobey an order to disperse when an army officer or a senior officer of the Royal Ulster Constabulary is of the opinion that the gathering may lead to public disorder or 'may make undue demands on the police or Her Majesty's forces' (clause 20). Existing emergency provisions for the preventive detention of suspected terrorists[9] are reproduced in a schedule to the bill. Detention orders will be made by a judicial commissioner after a hearing at which the 'respondent' may appear with legal representatives, but they may be excluded from part of the hearing in the interests of safety or security; appeal will lie to a judicial Detention Appeal Tribunal.

6. See ibid., §§ 83–9.
7. Ibid., §§ 106–15.
8. Substantially implementing the recommendations of the Diplock Commission on legal procedures to deal with terrorist activities (Cmnd 5185 (1972)).
9. S.I. 1972, No. 1632.

Aspects of the constitutional provisions for the devolution of legislative and executive powers may conceivably serve as a precedent for new regional authorities in other parts of the United Kingdom.

Table of Cases

Button v. *D.P.P.* (1966) 510
Buxton v. *Minister of Housing and Local Government* (1961) 559

Calder (John) Publications Ltd v. *Powell* (1965) 495
Calvin's case (1607) 419
Cambridgeshire and Isle of Ely C.C. v. *Rust* (1972) 411, 501
Campbell v. *Hall* (1774) 115, 129, 647, 652
Campbell v. *Paddington Corporation* (1911) 412
Canon Selwyn, ex p. (1872) 73
Carltona Ltd v. *Commissioners of Works* (1943) 49, 186, 350
Carl Zeiss Stiftung v. *Rayner and Keeler Ltd* (No. 2) (1967) 133
Carr v. *Fracis Times and Co.* (1902) 136
Case of Impositions (1606) see *Bate's case* (1606)
Case of Monopolies (1602) 123
Case of Proclamations (1611) 43, 71, 114, 118, 331
Case of Shipmoney (1637) see *R.* v. *Hampden* (1637)
Castioni, Re (1891) 443
C.E.G.B. v. *Dunning* (1970) 606
Central Electricity Generating Board v. *Jennaway* (1959) 606
Ceylon University v. *Fernando* (1960) 582, 585
Chandler v. *D.P.P.* (1964) 116, 200, 364, 484
Charge to the Bristol Grand Jury (1832) 510
Cheney v. *Conn* (1968) 73, 134
Chester v. *Bateson* (1920) 349, 351
Chic Fashions (West Wales) Ltd v. *Jones* (1968) 471, 472, 473
China Navigation Co. v. *Att.-Gen.* (1932) 126, 284, 437
Christie v. *Leachinsky* (1947) 459
Church of Scientology of California v. *Johnson-Smith* (1972) 318
Churchman v. *Joint Shop Stewards Committee* (1972) 364, 377, 522
Churchward v. *R.* (1865) 609
City of London v. *Wood* (1701) 72
Civilian War Claimants' Association Ltd v. *R.* (1932) 131
Clarke (1958) N. Ireland 262
Clarke v. *Bradlaugh* (1881) 322
Clayton v. *Heffron* (1961) Australia 86
Clifford and O'Sullivan, Re (1921) 515
Coleen Properties Ltd v. *Minister of Housing and Local Government* (1971) 568, 571
Collins v. *Minister of the Interior* (1957) S. Africa 90
Collymore v. *Att.-Gen.* (1970) 579, 623
Commercial and Estates Co. of Egypt v. *Board of Trade* (1925) 135, 518
Commercial Cable Co. v. *Government of Newfoundland* (1916) 50, 609
Commissioner for Local Government Lands v. *Kaderbhai* (1931) 447
Commonwealth of Australia v. *Bank of N.S.W.* (1950) 148
Conseil des Ports Nationaux v. *Langelier* (1969) Canada 617
Constantine v. *Imperial Hotels Ltd* (1944) 447

Table of Statutes

Index

Autochthony, 67

Bad faith *see* Improper purpose
Bagehot, Walter, on role of monarch, 99, 101
Bail, 459, 460, 465, 468
Ballot
  papers, 248–9, 250–51
  private members' bills, 276
  private members' motions, 288, 291
  secret, 241
Bank of England, 215, 223, 287
Betting levy appeal tribunal, 548
Bills
  amendments, 235, 238, 248, 280–82, 285–6, 303–4, 305, 306, 307
  Cabinet Legislation Committees, 167, 275–6, 341
  committee stage, 271, 278–81
  consolidation, 86, 265, 274, 280
  drafting, 275–6, 280, 376
  hybrid, 280–81
  introduction and first reading, 276–7
  Law Officers of the Crown, 276, 280, 341, 377
  Lords', 276, 281–2, 302, 303, 304
  Money, 47, 51, 58, 84, 88, 232, 236, 276, 279, 284, 285, 288, **304–5**
  money resolution stage, 232, 276, 278, 281, 304
  pressure groups, 272–4, 275, 276, 285
  prior consultation with interests, 273–4, 275, 286, 414, 560
  private, 73, 84–5, 87, 235, 239, 277, 280–81, 303, 305, 391, 396
  private members', 232, 235, 236, 238, 269, 272, 275, 276–7, 291, 376, 414
  provisional order confirmation, 279, 280–81, 305, 339, 390, 396
  public, 275–82, 285–8, 305
  report stage, 281
  royal assent, 47, 48, 56, 83, 86, 87, 88, 108, 282, 301, 305–6
  second reading, 271, 277–8
  Speaker's certificate, 51, 87–8, 264, 304

statute law revision, 84, 86, 87, 108, 232, 280, 376
ten-minute rule, 276–7
third reading, 281
see also House of Commons; House of Lords, Injunctions, Legislative process; Parliament Acts; Scotland; Wales
Bill of rights
  constitutional guarantees and, 22, 24, 26–7, 30–31, 79, 308, 364–5, 445–6, **452–6**, 463–4, 474, 520, 655
  Canadian Bill of Rights, 90, 453–4
  European Convention, 92, 426, 454–5
  Northern Ireland, 31, 452–3, 641, 644, Addendum
  United States, 18, 37, 245, 445–6, 453, 463
Binding-over orders, 460–61, 502, 505, 506
Bishops, 109, 127, 161, 229, 231, 298, 302, 311
Black Rod, 301, 325
Blackstone, William
  on parliamentary sovereignty, 72
  on prerogative, 114
Blasphemy, 475, 486–7
Boundary Commissions *see* Constituencies
Breach of confidence, 470, 481
Breach of statutory duty, liability for, 221, 412, 478–9, 613–14, Addendum
Breach of the peace, 458, 460–61, 463, 472, 489–90, 491, 502–3
British Airports Authority, 217
British Airways Board, 217
British Board of Film Censors, 480, 588
British Broadcasting Corporation *see* Broadcasting
British constitution
  characteristics, 35–7
  sources, 41–7
  unwritten, 19–20, 27–31, 35
British Council, 181, 182, 244

Finance – *continued*
government authorities;
Nationalized industries; Taxation;
Treasury
First Lord of the Treasury, 154, 155,
156, 184
Forcible detainer and entry, 504–5
Foreign Compensation Commission,
131, 303–4, 536, 548, 554–5, 571–2
Foreign relations, royal prerogative in,
128–40
Forestry Commission, 181, 212, 639
Franchise, 240–44
disqualifications, 244, 249, 253, 474
local government, 397
qualifications, 242–4
residence, 242
students, 243
Freedom of association and assembly
see Meetings; Processions; Public
order
Freedom of speech and expression,
474–96, 502–10
in Parliament, 314–20
French administrative law, 40, 411–12,
525–6, 591, 625
Frequency of Parliaments, 231–2
Fugitive offenders *see* Extradition

Gaming Board for Great Britain, 532,
550, 584, 623
General election, functions of, 104–8,
161, 164, 233, 249, 257
Government
dismissal, 103–4
formation, 136, 156–9, 178, 179–80
relations with Parliament, 36–7, 92–5,
165–6, 168–77, 232, 234–8, 253,
269–72, 288, 290–95
resignation, 105, 106, 156, 157, 164,
173, 174
Governor, colonial, 653–6
Governor-General
appointment, 48, 60, 61, 657, 658
discretionary powers, 24, 25, 51–2, 61,
101, 657

duties to act on local ministerial
advice, 51, 101, 657, 658
removal, 61, 658
Greater London Council *see* Local
government authorities
Great Seal of the Realm, 104, 114, 130,
184
Guernsey, 644–5, 646, 647

Habeas corpus, 204, 328, 360, 361, 371,
390, 433, 437, 442, 444, **465–9**,
519–20, 563, 596, 619
appeals, 468
damages and, 465, 469
emergency, 465, 467, 469, 519–20
procedure, 466
successive applications, 467–8
Health Service Commissioner, 633–4
Hewart of Bury, Lord
on administrative law, 525
on delegated legislation, 331
High Court of Parliament, 40, 71, 85,
142, 231, 308
Highlands and Islands Development
Board, 214
Highway
obstruction, 462, 476, 500, **501**, 504
non-repair, liability for, 412
nuisance, proceedings in respect of,
504, 564, 604
Home Secretary, 127, 147, 170, 179,
245–8, 360, **377**
Honours, 101–2, 108–9, 161, 630
monarch's personal discretion, 108–9
Political Honours Scrutiny
Committee, 147, 172
Horserace Totalizator Board, 223
House of Commons
access to, 500
adjournment debates, 238, 269, 290,
291
allocation of time, 269–72
Business Committee, 264, 272
chamber, 265–6
closure, 264, 271, 344
Committee of Selection, 279

United States – *continued*
Congress, 33, 37, 39–40, 280, 286, 321
  constitutional amendment, 41
  constitutional guarantees *see* Bills of rights
  criminal procedure, 463–4
  delegation, unconstitutional, 337
  dependent territories, 336–7
  due process of law, 18, 463
  equal protection of the laws, 18, 245, 445–6
  freedom of speech, 18
  Judiciary, 37, 40
  Presidential powers, 32, 33, 39–40, 165
  regulatory agencies, 216
Universities, central scrutiny of, 135, 147, 183, 290, 294
  see also Natural justice
University Grants Committee, 183
Unlawful assembly, 505–10
Unreasonableness, 349, 432–3, 499, 568, **592–4**, 615–16, 630, 654
  by-laws, void for manifest, 350, 500, 593
  statutory instruments, whether test applicable, 350–51
  tort liability and, 592, 615–16
  unfair discrimination and, 500, 567

  see also Abuse of discretion; Irrelevant considerations

Valuation courts, 405, 543, 546, 547
Value added tax, 81, 284, 285, 547, 648
Visiting forces, 207, 431, 436
Vote on account, 287

Wales
  administrative devolution, 208, 637–8
  bills, 279, 637
  church, 253, 306
  Grand Committee, 279, 637
  integration with England, 231, 637
  language, 637
  local government, 395
  parliamentary representation, 246
  Prince of, 99, 100, 111
  separatism, 30, 250, 257, 638
War
  Commonwealth and, 660
  prerogative and, 115, 116, 121, 133, 135, 136, 140, 518–19
  state of, 133, 517
  see also Aliens; Emergency; Martial law
Western Samoa, 100, 650, 661, 665
Whyatt Report, 627
Workmen's Compensation Acts, 547
Works of authority, 46–7

Law and Society

Race and Law
Anthony Lester and Geoffrey Bindman

... a complicated and controversial subject: the use of law to combat racial discrimination and prejudice, or, expressing the same idea positively, the use of law to promote equality of opportunity and treatment regardless of race. ... It is written as much for the general reader and the social scientist as for the law student or the legal practitioner.

Part One contains the background to the present law. Chapter 1 examines the historical response of the English judiciary to racial discrimination since the days of slavery. Chapter 2 analyses the role of legislation in combatting racial discrimination. It also discusses the nature of the problems which legislation is intended to tackle: the causes and the consequences of discrimination in employment, housing and elsewhere. Chapter 3 tells the remarkable story of how the legislation was won against formidable political odds.

Part Two describes the scope of the legislation. Chapter 4 explains the statutory meaning of unlawful discrimination in general terms and Chapters 5, 6 and 7 then examine the detailed provisions on employment, housing, and the provision of goods, facilities and services.

The crucial subject of the enforcement of the law is examined in Part Three. Chapter 8 describes the statutory machinery and the process of conciliation, drawing attention to some weaknesses in the legislation which may impair the work of the Race Relations Board and its conciliation committees.
Chapter 9 is concerned with the strengths and defects of legal proceedings – the ultimate deterrent, intended by Parliament to be invoked only when it is impossible to secure a settlement by conciliation.

The legal prohibition of racial incitement is discussed in Part Four.

The Conclusion sets out a summary of recommendations for the reform of the law and improvements in its application. There is always a danger that the law may become a ritual totem, worshipped in the name of liberal morality, without any marked effect on the conduct of the governors or the governed. Appendix 1 recalls a cautionary tale about legislation against discrimination in the Indian civil service. Appendix 2 sets out the full text of the Race Relations Acts.

Local Government
R. J. Buxton

Local government affects every person in the country, and sometimes in a very vital fashion, education, town planning, housing, highways and many other of the basic amenities of life being controlled by local authorities. The Maud Report, and the government's proposals for reform, have put local government at the centre of public interest and comment; yet much of the comment has been ill-informed, since it has failed to take into account the complex legal, political and administrative pressures on local government, or the gap which often appears between the theories in the books and the actual practices on the ground. In Part One of *Local Government*, the author scrutinizes each of these aspects of the problem in turn, paying particular attention to the impact of the law and of political organization on local government and on the rights of the individual. In Part Two three particular issues are discussed in detail, in order to show how the general theories dealt with earlier in the book work out in practice. The author here writes as a local authority member as well as a lawyer, and shows both the difficulties facing local democracy, and the mistaken nature of many of the claims made on local government's behalf. This sets the scene for Part Three, where proposals for local government reform are criticized in the light of the conclusions reached earlier in the book, and the possibility of more radical reform is suggested.

Local government cannot, however, be studied in isolation from other social forces, and in the course of the discussion many other questions are raised: the effectiveness of the law as a means of controlling administrators, the position of the professional officer in a democratic system, relations between local and national government, and the nature, form and practical implications of 'democracy'. This book should be read not only by those who seek to understand the present crisis in local government, but also by students of administrative law, politics and modern government, as an example of the relations between these disciplines and of their practical force in a particular social situation.

Family Security and Family Breakdown
John Eekelaar

This book looks at the problems facing modern families at a time when about eighty thousand divorces are expected to be filed in the first year of the new divorce law, and when the illegitimacy rate has risen faster in the last ten years than in any other decade. Is the family disintegrating or only changing its character? Do our laws give a square deal to the victims of family disintegration? Is it fair to illegitimate children, to deserted wives, to foster-parents?

The author assumes the difficulties of family living and evaluates firstly how successfully the law meets them and promotes family stability. He then deals with the legal response to defective families: how far can unmarried mothers, adults whose marriages have broken down, and their children be assisted by legal means.

The book is written for non-lawyers as well as lawyers. It explains the background to the existing laws and outlines the main issues around which future reforms will be centred.